Cases in **Financial Management**

Applications for Financial Analysis

World Scientific Series in Modern Finance: Advanced Topics in Finance for the Academician and Practitioner

Print ISSN: 2972-385X
Online ISSN: 2972-3868

Series Editor: Ivan E Brick (*Rutgers University, USA*)

Published:

Vol. 1 *Cases in Financial Management: Applications for Financial Analysis*
edited by Ivan E Brick & Harvey Poniachek

World Scientific Series in Modern Finance:
Advanced Topics in Finance for the Academician and Practitioner
Volume 1

Cases in **Financial Management**

Applications for Financial Analysis

Ivan E. Brick • Harvey A. Poniachek

Rutgers Business School at Newark and New Brunswick, USA

World Scientific

NEW JERSEY • LONDON • SINGAPORE • BEIJING • SHANGHAI • HONG KONG • TAIPEI • CHENNAI • TOKYO

Published by

World Scientific Publishing Co. Pte. Ltd.
5 Toh Tuck Link, Singapore 596224
USA office: 27 Warren Street, Suite 401-402, Hackensack, NJ 07601
UK office: 57 Shelton Street, Covent Garden, London WC2H 9HE

Library of Congress Cataloging-in-Publication Data
Names: Brick, Ivan E., author. | Poniachek, Harvey A., editor.
Title: Cases in financial management : applications for financial analysis / Ivan E. Brick, Harvey A. Poniachek, Rutgers Business School at Newark and New Brunswick, USA.
Description: Hackensack, NJ : World Scientific, [2024] | Series: World scientific series in modern finance: Advanced topics in finance for the academician and practitioner; Vol. 1 | Includes index.
Identifiers: LCCN 2022041381 | ISBN 9789811216732 (hardcover) | ISBN 9789811216749 (ebook) | ISBN 9789811216756 (ebook other)
Subjects: LCSH: Corporations--Finance--Case studies. | Finance--Management--Case studies.
Classification: LCC HG4026 .B66757 2024 | DDC 658.15--dc23/eng/20220829
LC record available at https://lccn.loc.gov/2022041381

British Library Cataloguing-in-Publication Data
A catalogue record for this book is available from the British Library.

For any available supplementary material, please visit
https://www.worldscientific.com/worldscibooks/10.1142/11728#t=suppl

Desk Editors: Soundararajan Raghuraman/Nicole Ong

Typeset by Stallion Press
Email: enquiries@stallionpress.com

https://doi.org/10.1142/9789811216749_fmatter

Preface

The case study method of instruction addresses a wide range of financial management concerns and promotes decision-making processes that require effective application of theory, analytical skills, and best practices. The cases could enhance the comprehension of the underlying theories and promote the application of quantitative methodologies for the solution of real-world challenges that are faced by the financial manager. Solving cases often requires making assumptions and projections, and some cases might require the use of analytical tools such as statistics, regression analysis, and linear programming. Although most cases contain the necessary data for analysis, consulting outside sources, including the Web, could sometimes expand the scope of interest and benefit.

The cases would be useful for undergraduate and graduate students, and for professional training. Cases provide a basis for discussion, stimulate effective learning, and group interaction that simulates the corporate environment under uncertainty, time constraints and the need to recommend solutions or answers that would satisfy various objectives. The cases in this book consist of corporations from various business sectors and industries that provide the necessary information to support beneficial decision-making and solutions. However, in some instances there is no single correct solution but rather several.

The case book organization generally reflects the subject structure of a standard corporate finance book, with greater emphasis on current issues, markets, and application. This book presents 34 cases that introduce the reader to a broad range of corporate financial management issues. The cases address the principal concern in corporate financial management and focus on practical problems that corporations face.

They focus on both traditional and contemporary issues in financial management. The case book provides real-world problems in areas of financial statement analysis, cost of capital, capital budgeting, capital structure, business valuation, real options, corporate hedging, corporate bankruptcy, and select corporate tax issues. The cases link managerial decisions to capital markets, corporate objectives, and shareholders' expectations for optimizing the value of their investments. The wide range of cases reflects the major issues of concern to the corporation, and each case addresses specific financial management concerns specific to the industry in which it operates.

The cases could be taught in different combinations and in conjunction with the materials that are addressed in class. Some cases might require assumptions and interpretation of the data and facts to reach a reasonable solution, but not necessarily a unique one. Cases will generally contain a brief statement or tutorial on the theoretical underpinning of the issue, provide an analytical "tool box" and suggest outside resources that might be useful in addressing the case.

The case book is organized in nine parts, as described below:

Part I provides a basic understanding of financial statements and the use of financial ratios to assess the strengths and weaknesses of the firm. Financial ratios can also be used to develop pro forma financial statements to enable the analyst to ascertain the external funds needed by the corporation or whether the firm is in jeopardy of violating the bond contract.

Part II introduces the time value of money which is an essential tool to evaluate assets and to determine the profitability of a firm's investment projects. To use the time value of money, one must estimate the appropriate interest rate. For firms, the appropriate interest rate is the firm's cost of capital. Its determination can be complex as shown by two of the cases in this section.

Part III introduces the capital budgeting methodology. The reader will be introduced to the use of Net Present Value, Internal Rate of Return, and Payback as criteria in determining the project's viability. The reader will also learn the definition of the firm's incremental cash flow and the use of sensitivity analysis to better understand the source of the project's profitability. Often, a firm has the option to either abandon or invest further in a project depending on how well it does. One of the cases in this section introduces real option methodology to evaluate such contingencies. The final case of the section introduces the use of linear programming for capital budgeting decisions. This procedure is very useful for determining the best outcome when projects are interdependently facing either resource or financial constraints.

Part IV provides a guide on how to evaluate the value of the firm based on traditional capital budgeting techniques or the use of multiples from comparable companies. For example, these techniques are used by investment bankers who provide fairness opinions regarding the terms of a merger agreement.

Part V provides the theoretical framework for determining the optimal capital structure of the firm. Often the capital structure of the firm mirrors the industry average. This section provides a set of guidelines for when and why firms may deviate from the industry norm. The section also shows how one might be able to forecast the firm's cost of capital when the firm changes the level of debt employed. The final case uses *pro forma* cash flow statements to predict if a firm can afford to initiate a dividend and examine if paying dividends on a regular basis is sustainable. The financing decision is not simply determining the optimal mix of debt and equity but also the maturity and the type of debt that is employed. This section considers alternatives available for long-term financing, such as debt with embedded options (convertible debt). An alternative to long-term borrowing is the use of leasing and one case in the section is devoted to how to evaluate a lease/buy/borrow decision. It also explains how the new accounting rule greatly diminishes the benefit of leasing as a form of off-balance sheet financing.

Part VI examines the vehicles used for short-term financing such as supply chain financing, factoring, letters of credit, and inventory financing.

Part VII illustrates the various issues regarding the process of mergers and acquisitions. It examines the conflict of interest between the target, the acquirer, and their investment banker. One case is devoted to providing a step-by-step approach in creating an equity cash flow model to evaluate the viability of a leverage buyout by a private equity firm.

Part VIII introduces the use of options and the importance of corporate risk management. The first case of the section provides an introduction to futures and option contracts and how they might be used to hedge risk. The cases that follow provide examples of the use of financial contracts to hedge against currency, commodity, and interest rate risk.

The final part, Part IX, explores other miscellaneous issues that the firm must consider, such as the formation of the firm, bankruptcy and liquidation, transfer pricing, and the determination of R&D tax credit.

As the above description indicates, financial management is complex and management has to deal with many issues such as asset valuation, corporate risk management, determination of capital structure, and the conflicts of interest that arise among management, stockholders, bondholders, customers, investment bankers, and vendors. We have detailed solutions for several cases. Full-time faculty members can obtain solutions by sending an email to FinanceCases@business.rutgers.edu. Please allow a week for a response.

This book would not be possible if we could not rely on the varied expertise of our authors. Below, we provide the background of each contributor to this book.

https://doi.org/10.1142/9789811216749_fmatter

About the Editors

Ivan E. Brick is the editor of the World Scientific Series in Modern Finance of World Scientific Publishing and is the co-editor along with Harvey Poniachek of this case book. Ivan Brick received his BA in Mathematics from Yeshiva University and received his M.Phil. and Ph.D. in Finance from Columbia University. He joined Rutgers Business School at Newark and New Brunswick in 1978. He has been the Chair of the Finance and Economics department from 1996 to 2023. Ivan Brick is the founding and current director of the David K. Whitcomb Center for Research in Financial Services at Rutgers University. Professor Brick has published numerous papers in academic journals such as the *Journal of Finance*, *Journal of Financial Quantitative Analysis*, *International Economic Review*, *Review of Economics and Statistics*, *Journal of Industrial Economics*, *Journal of Corporate Finance*, and *Financial Management*. His research interests include corporate finance, optimal security design, and corporate governance. Currently, he is an associate editor for the *Review of Quantitative Finance and Accounting*. Previously, he served as an Associate Editor of *Financial Management* and *Multinational Finance Journal*. Professor Brick has received several teaching awards at the Rutgers Business School. He received the "Outstanding Educator Award" by the 1995 Executive MBA Class. Professor Brick was awarded the "Farrokh Langdana Excellence in Teaching Award" by the 2011 MBA Class. In 2012, the Newark Undergraduate Program awarded him the Dean's Advisory Council Award for the "Most Knowledgeable Finance Professor," "The Most Caring Finance Professor," as well as "The Most Motivational Finance Professor." For his outstanding service, Professor Brick was awarded the RBS Dean's

Service Award in 2013 and 2016. In 2016, he was named the Dean's Professor of Business.

Harvey A. Poniachek, Ph.D., CVA, is a financial economist with experience in corporate consulting, banking, and financial markets, and Assistant Professor of Professional Practice of finance and economics at Rutgers Business School since 2011. Harvey was previously the Director of Valuation Services at RSM McGladrey in New York, the fifth largest accounting firm, where he was involved in valuation of financial derivatives, private equity, and intercompany pricing. He worked for the US Treasury Department as Lead Economist in transfer pricing, and was engaged in valuation of intellectual property and tangible assets; was Senior Manager and Economist at E&Y; and VP & Economist at Bank of America, where he gained extensive experience in the banking industry and capital markets, and advised multinational companies and senior management on currency and money market trends, trading strategies, and foreign country risk and opportunities. He was the Bank's liaison with Boston Consulting Group study of Bank of America's long-term strategic options, and a visiting economist at the Bank of America's European headquarters in London and worked extensively with Bank America Canada. Prof. Poniachek has previously been an adjunct and visiting professor of finance and international business at New York University, Stern School of Business, International Business Department and Finance Department, an adjunct associate professor of economics and finance at The City University of New York, Baruch College, and an adjunct professor of economics and finance at Pace University, Lubin School of Business. Harvey earned a Ph.D. and M.A. in Economics and International Finance from the State University of New York, Albany, and has done graduate work at New York University Stern School of Business in Corporate Finance; earned a B.A. Economics with minor in Mathematics from the State University of New York, College of Arts and Science, Plattsburgh; done Management Training at Bank of America and at US Treasury, and is a Certified Valuation Analyst (NACVA). Prof. Poniachek has published several books including *Mergers & Acquisition: A Practitioner's Guide to Successful Deal*, World Scientific Publishing; *International Corporate Finance*, Routledge; *Cases in International Finance*, John Wiley & Sons; and *Monetary Independence Under Flexible Exchange Rates*, Lexington Books. He has published several book chapters in the areas of transfer pricing, valuation of distressed companies, and valuation of hedge funds.

https://doi.org/10.1142/9789811216749_fmatter

About the Contributors

Eitan Blander is an attorney at Togut, Segal & Segal LLP, one of the nation's premier restructuring and bankruptcy boutiques, where he represents debtors, creditors, trustees, and other parties in interest in complex and often cross-border reorganization matters. Mr. Blander earned his undergraduate degree from McGill University and his law degree from Emory University School of Law. Prior to entering private practice, Mr. Blander served as a judicial law clerk to the Honorable Mary Kay Vyskocil, formerly of the United States Bankruptcy Court for the Southern District of New York.

Elizabeth Chorvat is an Associate Teaching Professor of Accounting at the University of Notre Dame Mendoza College of Business. She received her Ph.D. from the University of Chicago and S.J.D. from the University of Michigan.

Terrence Chorvat is a Professor of Law at the Antonin Scalia Law School at George Mason University and has been a Visiting Professor of Finance at the University of Iowa. He received his J.D. and Master of Financial Mathematics from the University of Chicago and Master of Laws in Taxation from NYU.

Peter F. De Nicola is Director of Taxes, FUJIFILM Holdings America Corporation, heading the tax function for FUJIFILM's Americas region. He has over 40 years of diverse tax experience, including 30 years at FUJIFILM. He oversees the company's transfer pricing policies, domestic and international tax compliance for North and South America and is heavily involved in mergers, acquisitions, and restructurings. He previously held tax management positions at General Signal, Emery Worldwide, and Siemens. A Certified Public Accountant, Peter earned a BS in Accounting and an MBA in Taxation from New York University. He currently serves on the Board of Directors of the Tax Executives Institute and is President of the Stamford Tax Association. In addition to authoring numerous articles on taxes and investments, he has been interviewed by the Wall Street Journal and has appeared on Bloomberg Television. He is a frequent speaker at tax conferences on the research and development tax credit and transfer pricing.

Chris Droussiotis is former Managing Director and Head of the Leverage Finance and Structured Finance Department at Sumitomo Mitsui Banking Corporation (SMBC), where he managed a portfolio of over $10 billion of large cap and middle market leveraged loans, as well as investments in SPV funds, CLOs, and BDCs that were backed by leveraged loans and high yield bonds. Since 2018, he has been Senior Managing Partner at Kinisis Ventures Limited (KV), where he conducts financial analysis and valuation of start-ups. Chris earned BSc and MBA degrees from Fairleigh Dickson University. He is Adjunct Professor of Finance at Columbia University and Fordham University. He has authored a couple of textbooks, including *The Analytical Approach to Finance, Investments and Credit* (August 2019) and *Credit Risk Management and Analysis* (December 2021) published by Cognella Publishing. Chris earned a BA and MBA from Fairleigh Dickinson University.

Robert A. Feinschreiber was Senior Consultant to CRA at Charles River Associates on the transfer pricing leadership team. He graduated from Trinity College, Columbia Business School, and Yale Law School, and earned an LLM in taxation from NYU. He practiced law for several decades with specialization in international tax law. He published extensively and is the author/editor of a series of transfer pricing handbooks consisting of six volumes. Robert passed away in October 2020 in Florida.

Todd Fries is an Accredited Senior Appraiser in Business Valuation with the American Society of Appraisers and is a Chartered Financial Analyst with the CFA Institute. Mr. Fries has conducted hundreds of valuation analyses for financial reporting, tax, M&A advisory, and other purposes in a broad variety of industries, including healthcare, energy, manufacturing, distribution, and technology. Mr. Fries is a contributing author for the International Risk Management Institute on topics relating to business valuation.

Armand Gilinsky Jr. is the F. Korbel Bros. Professor of Wine Business at Sonoma State University, where he has taught Strategy and Entrepreneurship since 1994. He is past chair of the North American Case Research Association and winner of best case published in the *Case Research Journal*, 1999 and 2019. He was educated at Stanford University and Clark University. His Ph.D. dissertation titled "Comparative Measures of Growth Factors: An Investigation into High Growth Medium-Size Companies in Britain and the United States, 1980–1984."

Roger J. Grabowski, FASA, is a Managing Director with Kroll LLC (formerly Duff & Phelps) in their Valuation Advisory practice and an Accredited Senior Appraiser and Fellow (FASA) of the American Society of Appraisers (ASA) (their highest designation), Business Valuation. In 2022, the ASA awarded Roger the Special Recognition Award in memory of Shannon Pratt and in 2023, the ASA awarded him their Life Achievement Award. He was formerly Managing Director of the Standard & Poor's Corporate Value Consulting practice, a partner of PricewaterhouseCoopers LLP and one of its predecessor firms, Price Waterhouse (where he founded its US Valuation Services practice and managed the real estate appraisal practice). He has directed valuations of businesses, interests in businesses, intellectual property, intangible assets, real property, and machinery and equipment. Roger has been recognized in various courts as an expert on matters of solvency, the value of closely held businesses and business interests, valuation and amortization of intangible assets, and other valuation issues. His testimony in the US District Court was referenced in the US Supreme Court opinion decided in his client's favor in the landmark Newark Morning Ledger case. Roger teaches courses for the American Society of Appraisers and lectures frequently at professional conferences.

Arthur S. Guarino is an Associate Professor of Professional Practice at the Rutgers Business School. Prior to joining the academia, he held positions in TIAA-CREF, Met Life, and The Bank of New York. His teaching experience as a full-time instructor has been primarily at Stevens Institute of Technology in Hoboken, New Jersey, and Rutgers University in Newark, New Jersey. He received his B.A. in Political Science from Seton Hall

University, his M.B.A. in Finance, and a graduate certificate in International Business from Seton Hall University, and he received a Master's degree in International Relations from The Maxwell School at Syracuse University. Arthur Guarino received his J.D. from Rutgers University School of Law in Newark.

Mark W. Guthner is a 30+ year veteran of the financial services industry. He has held position in fund management, investment banking, risk management, and sales and trading. He is the author of two books, *Quantitative Analysis in Debt Valuation and Management*, published by McGraw-Hill and *The Options Edge* published by John Wiley and Sons. He is currently an Associate Professor of Practice at Rutgers Business School. Mr. Guthner earned his BSE (ME) and his MBA from the University of Michigan.

Susan Hume is an Associate Professor of Finance in the Department of Finance at The College of New Jersey (TCNJ). She has teaching, research, and professional experience in corporate responsibility, international corporate finance and capital markets, banking, and derivatives securities, often during periods of market crisis. Her cornerstone is collaborative research with students. Prior to her appointment at TCNJ, she taught for Baruch College's Executive MBA Program in Taiwan and at Baruch College, Zicklin School of Business. She earned her doctorate at Baruch College, Zicklin School, and City University of New York. She has an MBA from Rutgers University and a BA in American Studies from Douglass College.

Lisa S. Kaplowitz is an assistant professor of professional practice in the finance and economics department at Rutgers Business School. She leverages 25+ years of experience as an investment banker and CFO to teach students the fundamentals of corporate finance, with a focus on applying these concepts to decisions typically encountered in corporations and investment banking. Ms. Kaplowitz is also the Co-founder and Executive Director of the Rutgers Center for Women in Business whose mission is to remove barriers, build community and empower women. Ms. Kaplowitz earned her BA from Brown University and her MBA from Kellogg School of Management, Northwestern University.

Margaret Kent of Feinschreiber & Associates and the Transfer Pricing Consortium has been an attorney for over 20 years, focusing on law and international taxation. Ms. Kent has been engaged in a number of tax areas including Latin American transfer pricing, escheatment, estate planning, and audit techniques. As a tax malpractice professional, Margaret Kent focuses on spoliation of evidence. She is a graduate of Barry University, holds an M.A. from Instituto Tecnologico de Estudios Superiores de Monterrey, Mexico and a J.D. from the University of Miami.

Raymond H. Lopez retired as a professor of Economics and Finance from the Lubin School of Business from PACE University in 2016. He earned his Bachelor of Business Administration in 1961, a Master of Arts from Brown University in 1963, and a Doctor of Philosophy from New York University in 1967. Dr. Lopez joined the Board of Directors of the Academic Federal Credit in 1984 and has been the Chairman of its board of directors since 1986. He was a member of a number of case writing and other professional organizations. Dr. Lopez authored or co-authored 24 case studies as well as 17 refereed journal articles and 39 referred proceedings. From 2003 to 2011, his cases won four first-place awards and two third-place awards from the John Molson International MBA Case Writing Competition.

Rosa Oppenheim is Rutgers Business School Dean's Professor of Business, Professor of Supply Chain Management, and Vice Chair of the Department of Supply Chain Management. She was previously Executive Vice Dean and Acting Dean at Rutgers Business School, and Interim Chair of the Department of Supply Chain Management. She received her Ph.D. degree in Operations Research from Polytechnic Institute of Brooklyn (now NYU Tandon School of Engineering). Her research interests are in statistical process control and total quality management. She is the author or co-author of many articles and monographs including, most recently, *Managing Supply Chain Operations* and *Quality Management*, and has conducted training programs for major corporations.

Frank A. Oswald graduated from Baruch College of the City University of New York with a BBA Cum Laude in 1983, earned a JD in 1986 from New York Law School, and was admitted to New York and New Jersey bar associations. Frank is a Partner at Togut, Segal & Segal LLP in New York City which is one of the premier restructuring and bankruptcy boutique law firms in the country. For more than 35 years he has represented Chapter 11 debtors, creditors committees, trustees, and other stakeholders in many complex and notable cases, including Chrysler, General Motors, American Airlines, Kodak, Enron, Dewey Lebouf, and Rockefeller Center Properties.

Anoop Rai is a Professor of Finance at the Frank G. Zarb School of Business at Hofstra University in New York. Before joining the faculty at Hofstra, Dr. Rai taught as an assistant professor at the University of Vermont and as a graduate instructor at Indiana University. He is the Director of the Center for International Financial Services and Markets. His current research interest centers on international banking and financial markets. His articles have been published in the *Journal of Banking and Finance*, *Journal of International Money and Finance*, *Journal of Economics and Business*, *Journal of Futures Markets*, *Journal of Financial Research Services*, *Journal of International Financial Markets, Institutions and Money*, *Financial Management* and *Journal of Risk and Insurance*. Professor Rai serves as an Associate Editor of the *Journal of Multinational Financial Management* and is on the Advisory Board of the SSRN's *History of Finance eJournal.*

Ronald Richter is an Assistant Professor of Professional Practice in the Finance & Economics at Rutgers Business School, and Principal Owner of his own Personal Financial Planning Practice. He has been associated with Rutgers University for over 25 years as both a student and professor. Prior to becoming a full-time Professor, Professor Richter worked in numerous corporate finance positions, working his way up to being a Chief Financial Officer at two companies. Subsequent to his corporate finance experience, Professor Richter started his own financial planning practice assist. He earned his B.S. from Rutgers University and his MBA from New York University.

Mark Rodgers is an Assistant Professor in the Supply Chain Management Department of the Rutgers Business School. His research interests include power grid expansion planning, simulation-based optimization, and supply chain analytics. He holds a Ph.D. in Industrial & Systems Engineering from Rutgers University and has published in peer-review journals such as *Energy*, *Applied Energy*, *Computers & Industrial Engineering*, *Journal of Manufacturing Systems*, *Socio-Economic Planning Sciences*, *Environmental Science & Technology*, *Vaccine*, *The Electricity Journal*, *International Journal of Environmental Research and Public Health*, *Journal of Pharmaceutical Innovation*, and *The TQM Journal.* Prior to joining the Rutgers Business School's faculty, Dr.

Rodgers worked in various roles in the telecommunications, pharmaceutical, transportation, and management consulting industries in various business process improvement and analytics roles.

Alisa Rusanoff received her BA in finance from Baruch College, City University of New York, and is a CFA Level 3 candidate. Alisa started her career in investment banking, working on M&A and raising capital before joining a public fund. She then joined the Trade Finance industry and co-founded a boutique firm focusing on alternative lending solutions, before becoming the first employee at a fintech platform providing working capital for Latin American exporters. Alisa has been a guest lecturer at NYU, the New School Venture Lab, Antler VC, and the GC4Women Certificate Program and recently received a 40Under40 Award by Secured Finance Network.

Michael Samonas is the Group CFO of SIDMA S.A., the leading steel service center in Greece with subsidiaries in Romania and Bulgaria. In addition, he teaches specialized courses in financial modeling and equity valuation at the American College of Greece–Deree and Mastering Credit Risk at University of Piraeus & ICAP. He is a Fellow member of Chartered Certified Accountants (FCCA) and a board member of the Hellenic Association of Risk Managers, a member of FERMA, the Federation of European Risk Management Associations. Michael holds an M.Sc. and a Ph.D. degree from the Electronic Engineering department of the University of Surrey, an MBA from the University of La Verne California, and a BSc degree in Applied Accounting from University of Oxford Brooks (with honors) and a Postgraduate Diploma from the Chartered Institute of Marketing (CIM). He is the author of *Financial Forecasting, Analysis and Modelling: A Framework for Long-Term Forecasting*, Wiley Finance Series, Feb. 2015.

Jay Soled is a tenured professor at Rutgers University and Director of Rutgers Masters in Taxation Program. He is admitted to practice in New Jersey, the US District Court, District of New Jersey, and New York. He is a member of the Essex County (Section of Taxation) and American Bar Associations. A magna cum laude and Phi Beta Kappa graduate of Haverford College, he holds a Juris Doctor degree from the University of Michigan School of Law, cum laude, and a Master of Laws degree in Taxation from the New York University School of Law where he was an editor of the *Tax Law Review*. He is the recipient of five teaching awards.

Aside from having written numerous law review articles, books, and op-eds, Professor Soled has been featured as a tax expert on several television shows and radio programs. Professor Soled has also been an expert witness in close to a dozen tax matter controversies.

Ingo Walter has been on the faculty at New York University since 1970. From 1971 to 1979, he was Vice Dean for Academic Affairs and subsequently served a number of terms as Chair of International Business and Chair of Finance. Subsequently, he served as Director of the New York University Salomon Center for the Study of Financial Institutions from 1990 to 2003 and Director of the Stern Global Business Institute from 2003 to 2006 and the Stern Infrastructure Finance Initiative from 2017 to 2020. He served as Dean of the Faculty of the Stern School from 2008 to 2012. His current areas of academic activity include international financial intermediation and banking and infrastructure finance. He has published papers in many of the professional journals in international economics and finance, and is the author, co-author, or editor of 28 books, most recently *Bridging the Gaps: Public Pension Funds and Infrastructure Finance* (London 2019). He has served as a consultant to various corporations, banks, government agencies, and international institutions, and has held a number of board memberships. Dr. Walter earned a BA in Economics from Lehigh University College of Business and a Ph.D. from New York University.

Susan White is a Clinical Professor at the University of Maryland, College Park, teaching corporate finance for undergraduates and MBAs. She received her undergraduate degree from Brown University, MBA from Binghamton University, and Ph.D. in finance from the University of Texas, Austin. Her primary area of research is case studies, with cases and articles published in the *Business Case Journal*, *CASE Journal*, *Case Research Journal*, *Journal of Financial Education*, *Journal of Financial Research*, *International Journal of Financial Education*, a restructuring case book and personal finance collection.

Edward Wu is an attorney located in New York. Mr. Wu is currently the the head of Bankruptcy Department at Reid & Wise LLC, where he counsels clients concerning business reorganizations and debtor and creditor rights. Mr. Wu previously practiced at Weil, Gotshal & Manges, Baker & McKenzie, and Togut, Segal & Segal LLP. Mr. Wu received his B.A. from New York University and his J.D. from Boston University School of Law.

https://doi.org/10.1142/9789811216749_fmatter

Contents

Part I

Introduction

https://doi.org/10.1142/9789811216749_0001

Case 1

Advanced Micro Devices, Inc.: Financial Statement Analysis and Risk Assessment

Ivan E. Brick and Harvey A. Poniachek

Rutgers Business School, USA

Introduction

This case addresses the financial statements of Advanced Micro Devices, Inc. ("AMD") and several of its main competitors. Financial statements analysis provides vital information for financial assessment and decision making. For instance, loan officers must evaluate the credit risk of applicants, and investors in corporate securities need to evaluate the prospects of future earnings and risk — all of which require a detailed understanding of the financial statements of the firm.

We begin by addressing three critical financial statements, including the balance sheet, the income statement, and the statement of cash flows. The balance sheet is a snapshot of the firm's assets, liabilities, and shareholders' equity. A balance sheet is prepared according to the Generally Accepted Accounting Principles (GAAP) on historic cost which is also referred to as book value.

Consider the balance sheet of Acme Corp that is described in Exhibit 1. The left-hand side of the balance sheet summarizes the assets of the firm. The right-hand side of the balance sheet summarizes the liabilities and owner's equity of the firm. Note that the book value of Acme is $770 million.

Exhibit 1. Acme Corp: An Example of a Balance Sheet

Cash and Marketable Securities	20	Accounts Payable	50
Accounts Receivable	100	Notes Payable	75
Inventory	150		
Total Current Assets	270	Total Current Liabilities	125
Gross Fixed Assets	700	Long-Term Debt	100
Less Accumulated Dep.	200	Common Stock	300
Net-Fixed Assets	500	Retained Earnings	245
Total Assets	770	Total Liabilities and Owner's Equity	770

The assets consist of current assets and fixed assets. Current assets are short-term assets with maturity of up to 1 year. Included in current assets are Cash, Marketable Securities, Accounts Receivables, and Inventory. Generally, firms keep cash to pay expected bills, much like you have money in a checking account. Extra money may be put in a savings account that provides you with a superior return to that obtained through checking. The firm acts similarly and invests the extra cash in short-term marketable securities that can be easily liquidated in case of an unexpected cash need.

To attract customers, firms grant credit so that buyers will immediately take possession of the goods or immediately have access to the services, with an understanding that the customer will pay the bill within a set time period. With accrual accounting, the firm will recognize the sale on its income statement and will book the sale on the balance sheet as an accounts receivable. To avoid stockouts, firms produce goods in anticipation of sales that are carried as inventory.

Now turn to the long-term assets of the firm. Generally, these assets are composed of property, plant, and equipment. They are classified as long-term assets since the firm generally holds these assets for periods longer than a year. Firms depreciate the fixed asset to reflect the lower market value of these assets as they age. The total depreciation over time is the estimated decrease in value of these long-term assets. Depreciation schedules are set by the U.S. Treasury Department and the IRS reflecting the asset's useful life and Congressional economic policies. Gross-Fixed Assets less the Accumulated Depreciation is the Net Fixed Assets of the firm. Total Assets equal the sum of the Current Assets and the Net Fixed Assets.

The right-hand side of the balance sheet is made up of current liabilities, long-term liabilities, and stockholders' equity. Stockholders' Equity has three components: Preferred Stock, Common Stock, and Retained Earnings.

Current Liabilities are composed of short-term obligations of the firm with maturities within 1 year. Accounts Payable are the obligations of the firm as a result of buying goods and services on credit. Notes Payable represent liabilities that the firm incurred via short-term borrowings from a bank or other commercial lenders and maturing debt that become due.

Long-term debt is the amount originally borrowed by the firm to finance its operations and it carried at original cost. For example, assume a firm issues $100 million bonds 5 years ago with a coupon rate of 5%. If interest rates rose, the market value of the debt obligation has declined, but the firm shows the liability based upon the original cost of $100 million. The relationship between interest rates and price of securities is addressed in the case entitled Time Value of Money — Concepts and Applications.

Common Stock represents the amount of money the firm received when it issued common stock shares, which includes the par value per stock plus the capital surplus above the par. This amount is simply a historical number. The firm may pay the shareholders either dividends or the proceeds when the firm buys back stock from the shareholders. Retained Earnings represent the cumulated earnings reinvested in the firm. For example, if the firm has a net income of $200 million and pays a dividend to its shareholders of $75 million, retained earnings will grow by $125 million. Preferred Stock represents the amount of money the firm received when it issued preferred stock shares. Preferred stockholders can also get dividends based on the stated coupon rate. No dividends can be given to common stockholders unless the promised dividends to shareholders are paid in full.

We will now turn to the Income Statement of Acme, Inc., which is outlined in Exhibit 2. An income statement that is prepared according to GAAP recognizes revenue at the time of sales and expenses through the matching principles. An income statement contains noncash items, with the most significant being depreciation. The income statement always begins with Sales. Cost of Goods Sold represents the direct cost of producing the sales. The difference between Sales and Cost of Goods Sold is Gross Profit. You may think of the ratio of the Gross Profit to Sales as the price markup of the product. The firm also incurs expenses that are not

Exhibit 2. Acme's Income Statement

Sales	$400
Cost of Goods Sold	250
Gross Profit	150
Overhead Expenses	75
Depreciation Expense	50
Earnings Before Interest and Taxes (EBIT)	25
Interest Expense	10
Earnings Before Tax	15
Tax @40%	6
Net Income	9

directly related to the production of goods and services. This is known as overhead expenses. For example, in the corporation, factory worker salaries should go into cost of goods sold since these workers produce the goods that are directly associated with the revenue) the firm receives from selling the finished products. However, the cost of administration (the CEO) would be part of the Selling, General and Administrative Expense (SG&A). Gross Profit less the SG&A and less the depreciation expense is the Earnings before Interest and Taxes or EBIT. Once you subtract out the interest expense, you have earnings before taxes or EBT. In our example below, we assume that Uncle Sam and Cousin Phil Murthy take 40% of EBT to run the government. What is left over is Net Income.

Now, let us consider a sources and uses statement that summarizes both the application of funds (uses) and source of financing. To derive the sources and uses statement you need the balance sheet of the firm for two consecutive years and the current income statement. Exhibit 3 represents the balance sheet for two consecutive years, 2018 and 2019.

Note that the balance sheet of 2019 increased by $60 million, and Gross Fixed Assets have increased by $50 million. How was that financed? The income statement tells us that the net income for 2019 was $9 million. Correspondingly, Retained Earnings have also increased by $9 million implying that the firm paid no dividends during the current fiscal year. We also know from the income statement that depreciation expense was $50 million. Depreciation expense is not a cash outlay, but an attempt to expense long-term capital (gross fixed assets) expenditures.

Exhibit 3. Acme's Balance Sheet

	2018	2019		2018	2019
Cash and Marketable Securities	20	20	Accounts Payable	40	50
Accounts Receivable	80	100	Notes Payable	34	75
Inventory	110	150			
Current Assets	210	270	Current Liabilities	74	125
Gross Fixed Assets	650	700	Long-Term Debt	100	100
Less Accumulated Dep.	150	200	Common Stock	300	300
Net Fixed Assets	500	500	Retained Earnings	236	245
Total Assets	710	770	Total Liabilities and Owner's Equity	710	770

Note that the accumulated depreciation has also increased by $50 million. Hence, the firm has generated $59 million from operations. As a result, the firm has more than sufficient internal funds to finance the increase in long-term assets. So what did the firm do with the extra $9 million if it is not paying dividends? It invested in net working capital which is the difference between current assets and current liabilities.

As working capital increases, the firm is pouring more money into current assets such as accounts receivables and inventory. Note that the working capital of the firm in 2018 is $136 million but $145 million in 2019. In other words, working capital has increased by $9 million. We can summarize these operations using the old-fashioned sources and uses statement (accountants now use a cash flow statement, but this is beyond the purview of this case). Exhibit 4 provides Acme's Statement of Cash Flows. In particular:

Uses		Sources	
Long-Term Assets (GFA)	50	Net Income	9
Change in Working Capital	9	Depreciation	50

The real question is how is the firm doing? The purpose of Financial Ratio analysis is to begin to answer this question.

Exhibit 4. Acme's Statement of Cash Flows

Cash, Beginning of Year	20
Operating Activity	
Net Income	9
Plus	
Depreciation	50
Increase in Accounts Payable	10
Less Increase in Accounts Receivable	–20
Increase in Inventory	–40
Net Cash Flow from Operating Activity	29
Investment Activity	
Fixed Assets Acquisition	–50
Financial Activity	
Increase in Notes Payable	41
Decrease in Long-Term Debt	0
Dividend Paid	0
Increase in Common Stock	
Net Cash from Financial Activity	0
Cash, End of Year	20

Financial Statement Analysis[1]

Financial statement analysis applies ratios for the purpose of

- assessing the financial conditions of the firm and its creditworthiness by creditors who seek to determine whether they will be repaid, and by equity investors' need to determine the soundness of their investment,

[1]For more information on Financial Statements see, for example, Stephen A. Ross, Randolph W. Westerfield, Jeffrey F. Jaffe, and Bradford D. Jordan, "Financial Statements Analysis and Financial Model," in *Corporate Finance*, 12th ed. (McGraw Hill Education, 2019), Ch. 3, 20–581; Eugene F. Brigham and Michael C. Ehrhardt, "Analysis of Financial Statements," in *Financial Management: Theory and Practice*, 12th ed. (Thomson South-Western, 2008), Ch. 4, 122–154; Richard A. Brealey, Stewart C. Myers, and Franklin Allen, "Financial Analysis," in *Principles of Corporate Finance*, 13th ed. (McGraw Hill Education, 2020), Ch. 28, 683–716; Jonathan Berk and Peter DeMarzo, *Corporate Finance*, 4th ed. (Pearson, 2017) ("BD"); K. R. Subramanyan, *Financial Statement Analysis*, 11th ed. (McGraw Hill Education, 2014).

- assessing management performance and efficiency,
- reviewing the firm's profitability performance relative to its own historic record and peers, and
- evaluating divisions and subsidiaries' performance.

Ratio analysis utilizes the company's balance sheet, income statement, and statement of cash flows in terms of the company's history and in comparison to peers. Financial ratios are grouped into several classes including operating performance, financial conditions, cash flows, liquidity and solvency, and capital structure and risk. Financial statements analysis could be affected by differences in international accounting practices, therefore, comparisons of companies across borders require adjustment for differences such as LIFO and FIFO accounting for inventory, depreciation policies, restating reserves, and charges for bad debts and product returns.

There are five common financial ratios that are grouped into the following categories and are commonly applied to yearend financial reports:

1. Short-term solvency, or liquidity, ratios
2. Long-term solvency, or financial leverage, ratios
3. Asset management, or turnover, ratios
4. Profitability ratios
5. Market value ratios

Exhibit 5 provides a definition of the above financial ratios.

As we look at Acme's financial statements, we cannot tell whether the firm is a well-run firm. We know that it is profitable, but that is a relative term. For example, what if we know that its direct competitor's net income was $14 million? Would you think its competitor is more profitable? You might be tempted to say yes since the competitor has a higher net income. Note that Acme's profit is 3.5% of sales. Assume that the competitor's sales are $1 billion. Its profit is only 1.4% of sales. Most probably, now you would think that Acme is more efficient. This simple example illustrates the importance of scaling the data (in our case, we scaled net income with total sales) in some fashion and comparing the resulting statistic with other firms in the industry. Financial analysts have come up with several key financial ratios that can be used to analyze firms relative to their direct competitors.

The Current Ratio tells you the relative level of current assets to current liabilities. Recall that current assets are assets that are expected to be

Exhibit 5. Definitions of Financial Ratios

1. Short-Term Solvency or Liquidity Ratios

- Current Ratio = Current Assets/Current Liabilities
- Quick Ratio = (Current Assets – Inventory)/Current Liabilities

2. Long-Term Solvency or Financial Leverage

- Total Debt Ratio = (Total Assets – Total Liabilities)/Total Assets
- Debt-Equity Ratio = Total Debt/Total Equity
- Time Interest Earned Ratio = EBIT/Interest
- Cash Coverage Ratio = (EBIT + Depreciation and Amortization)/Interest

3. Asset Management or Turnover Measures

- Inventory Turnover = Cost of Goods Sold/Inventory
- Days' Sales of Inventory = 365/Inventory Turnover
- Receivables Turnover = Sales/Accounts Receivable
- Days' Sales of Receivables = 365/Receivables Turnover
- Payables Turnover = Cost of Goods Sold/Accounts Payable
- Days' Payables Outstanding = 365/Payables Turnover
- Assets Turnover = Sales/Assets
- Fixed Asset Turnover = Sales/Fixed Assets
- Cash Cycle = Avg. Collection Period + Days Inventory Outstanding – Dates

4. Profitability Measures

- Profit Margin = Net Income/Sales
- Gross Operating Margin = EBIT/Sales
- Gross Profit Margin = (Sales – CGS)/Sales
- Net Operating Profit Margin = EBT/Sales
- Return on Assets = Net Income/Assets
- Return on Equity = Net Income/Equity

5. Market Value Measures

- Earnings Per Share (EPS) = Net Income/Shares Outstanding
- Price-Earnings Ratio (PE) = Price Per Share/Earnings Per Share
- Market to Book Ratio = Market Value Per Share/Book Value Per Share
- Market Capitalization = Price Per Share × Shares Outstanding
- Enterprise Value Multiple = EV/EBITDA

converted into cash within one year. Similarly, current liabilities are obligations that the firm must satisfy within one year. Hence, the higher is the current ratio, the more coverage the firm has to meet its short-term obligations. But if the number is too low, it might mean that the firm has antiquated accounts receivables or inventory. Many analysts use the Quick Ratio. This ratio assumes that all inventory is outdated and cannot be sold. For Acme, the current ratio is 2.16, and the quick ratio is 0.96.

Firms finance their activities using both debt and equity financing. If the firm only financed its activities by equity, then the firm will never go bankrupt. It can go out of business, but it will never be forced out of business because of non-payment to debtors. A more thorough discussion on why firms issue debt can be found in the case entitled Johnson & Johnson: Capitalization Structure and Corporate Funding Decisions. Leverage ratios measure how much debt financing is employed by the firm. The higher the leverage ratio, the more debt is used by the firm to finance its operations.

Interest Coverage Ratio measures whether the firm has sufficient earnings in a given fiscal year to cover its interest payments obligations. For Acme, the current Interest Coverage Ratio is 2.5 × (that is, 2.5 times the current interest expense). This ratio does not consider the principal payment that might come due in the current year. For example, assume that Acme must pay $10 million. You might be tempted to think the firm is still doing OK. After all, EBIT is $25 million and the firm must pay during the current fiscal year $10 million in interest and another $10 million in principal, for a total fixed obligation of $20 million. However, $25 million EBIT will not be sufficient to cover the total fixed obligations because the firm must pay its taxes before the principal payment is paid. Recall that the tax rate is 40%. The above income statement shows that the government will take $6 million from EBT. Hence, Acme only has $19 million of its EBIT that it can use to pay both the interest expense and the scheduled principal payment. Thus, unless the firm can raise additional funds from the external markets (like issuing new debt or equity), Acme will be forced into bankruptcy. The Fixed Coverage Ratio can be used to measure the firm's ability to pay off both the interest and principal payment obligations. Note that we divide the principal payment by (1 – Tax Rate) to take into account that principal payment is not tax deductible. If the fixed coverage ratio is greater than one, then the firm has sufficient earnings to meet all obligations. If it is less than one, then the firm needs to raise money from external sources to cover all of its current obligations. Assuming that the firm has to pay off the $75 million notes payable then for Acme, the fixed coverage ratio is ($25mm/$10mm + $75mm/.6) = .185.

Finally, to get a sense of the firm's burden to meet its long-term obligations, we can compute total long-term leverage ratio. For Acme, it is .13, implying that 13% of Acme's assets are financed by long-term debt. It appears that Acme does not have a lot of financial risk since its interest coverage ratio is 2.5, long-term leverage ratio is only .13, and total leverage ratio = ($175/770) = .227. But assuming that Notes Payable are due during the current year, the firm's fixed coverage ratio is EBIT/[Interest + (Principal/(1 – tax rate)] = ($25mm/$10mm + $75mm/.6) = .185. This means that earnings cover only 18.5% of current obligations due. Does the firm have too much financial risk?

Asset Management or Turnover Measures measure the efficiency of a firm's operations. The Average Collection Period determines the number of days it takes the firm to convert accounts receivables into cash. Note that too high of a number implies that a firm is taking too long to collect the debts of their customers. It can also mean that some of the accounts receivables will never be collected. If the number is too short, then it is possible the firm is not generous enough in granting credit. If so, it might affect the level of sales. For Acme, the Average Collection Period is 91.25 days.

Inventory Turnover measures the amount of inventory the firm uses to create sales. The higher the number, the less amount of inventory the firm has on hand. But it could also mean that the firm is in danger of stockouts and loss of sales. The higher the number, the larger amount of inventory the firm has on hand. It could also mean that the inventory is old. For Acme, Inventory Turnover is 1.667.

An important liquidity measure is the amount of time it takes the firm to convert inventory into cash. This is measured by the Cash Cycle (also known as the cash conversion cycle). The cash cycle sums the number of days it takes to convert the inventory to a sale (Days Inventory Outstanding) and the number of days to convert the accounts receivable into cash (Average Collection Period) less the number of days it takes the firm to pay its bills (Days Payable Outstanding). For Acme, the Days Inventory Outstanding equals 219 days. The number of days for Acme to pay its bills (Days Payable Outstanding) is 73 days. Recall that the Average Collection Period equals 91.25 days. Accordingly, the Cash Cycle is 91.25 + 219 – 73 = 237.25 days.

The last set of ratios measures the efficiency of the firm in using its assets to create sales. Two such ratios are Fixed Asset Turnover and Total Asset Turnover = Sales/ Total Assets. For Acme, the Fixed Asset Turnover is .8, and Total Asset Turnover Ratio is .52.

Profitability Ratios are designed to tell you the relative profitability of the firm. We begin with the following set of profit margin ratios:

The Profit Margin summarizes the overall rate of profitability of the firm. For Acme, it is 2.25%. Is this good? It depends upon what the competitors' net profit margin is. Let's say, the average rival to Acme has a net profit margin of 3.2%. Then the question is why is Acme less profitable? The other three ratios might point to the source of the problem. Consider the Gross Margin. This ratio tells you the average price mark-up of the firm. If it is too low, the firm may be gaining market share but at the expense of profits. If it is too high, then the firm may be overpricing itself out of the market. For Acme, the gross profit margin 37.5%.

Assume that the Gross Margin is similar to the Gross Margin of Acme's rivals. Next, let's look at the Gross Operating Margin. This depicts the profit rate after taking into account overhead expenses to run the firm. For Acme, the Gross Operating Margin is 6.25%. If the Gross Operating Margin is much lower than the industry average, the firm has too much administrative staff. If not, we can look at the Net Operating Profit Margin. Note that this margin looks at earnings before taxes but after the firm has paid off its interest expense. For Acme, the net operating profit margin is 3.75%. If the firm's net operating profit margin is lower than its competitors, it might mean that the firm has too much interest expense or too much leverage. You can seek confirmation of that hypothesis by comparing the leverage ratios listed above.

However, profits do not pay the bills that are outstanding. You are all taking and/or have taken accounting. As you know, accountants use the accrual basis of accounting whereby revenue and expenses are recognized at the time of the sales regardless to whether the customer actually paid cash for the final product. There are cash flow ratios we can use to depict the cash availability. They are:

1. *Funds from Operation* = Net Income + Depreciation
2. *Operating Cash Flow* = Funds from Operation – ΔWorking Capital
3. *Free Operating Cash Flow* = Operating Cash Flow – Capital Expenditures
4. *Free Cash Flow* = Operating Cash Flow – Dividends

Funds from operations consider that depreciation expense is not a cash flow expense but rather the accountant's attempt to expense capital expenditures. For Acme, funds from operations are $59 million. Operating Cash Flow is the cash flow available to pay dividends and capital expenditures. It is found by deducting the change in working capital from funds from operations. Working Capital is the difference between current assets and current liabilities. Recall current assets are assets that can be liquidated within a year. These assets grease the operations of the firm. For example, the firm sets aside cash to purchase inventory when needed. Firms sell their goods for credit, creating accounts receivable to generate firms. Firms can finance these assets using short-term financing, known as current liabilities. Hence, working capital represents the net amount of cash invested in short-term assets. The change in working capital is therefore how much more cash the firm used to finance its short-term operations. For Acme, Operating Cash Flow is $50 million.

Wall Street uses two other cash flow definitions to examine the amount of money available for the firm's stockholders. Free Operating Cash Flow determines how much money the firm has to pay dividends after capital expenditures. Recall Acme invested $50 million in gross fixed assets. Hence, for Acme, the Free Operating Cash flow is zero. Free Cash Flow is the amount of money the firm controls after payment of any dividends. Note Acme does not pay any dividends so for Acme, the Free Cash Flow is also zero.

It is generally assumed that the objective of the firm is to maximize the value of equity;[2] there is one more ratio to learn, the Return on Equity (ROE) which is Net Income/Stockholders Equity. But this ratio can also be written as:

Return on Equity = (Net Income/Sales)(Sales/Total Assets)(Assets/Equity)

Clearly, stockholders want a high return on equity. But what causes the high ROE? Is it the high net profit margin, the high asset turnover, or high leverage? Shareholders may not want a high ROE because of high leverage since leverage increases risk to the firm.

To evaluate a division or a firm, we need to choose a benchmark or a standard of comparison. One standard we could use is history. The second

[2]Alternatively, the objective is to maximize the value of the firm. It is possible that firm value maximizing and equity value maximizing are not the same. This has to do with the conflict of interests between bondholders and stockholder. For example, bondholders like a safe firm where the probability of default is near zero. Stockholders may like risk since greater risk potentially implies greater profits.

benchmark could be comparables or peers based on Standard Industrial Classification (SIC) codes that could range from one to several digits, and most commonly industry classifications are one which companies are denoted by four digits. In 1997, a new industry classification system was initiated, called the North American Industry Classification System (NAICS).

Risk Assessment[3]

AMD's financial leverage could be derived from the company's financial data. In addition, it's noted that the company sales and supply chain are highly related to relatively few customers and sources. The 10K for 2019 states that AMD has a wafer supply agreement with GF with obligations to purchase all of its microprocessor and APU product requirements, and a certain portion of our GPU product requirements manufactured at process nodes larger than 7 nanometers from GF, with limited exceptions. If GF is not able to satisfy the manufacturing requirements, AMD business could be adversely impacted. The 2019 10K document states that *AMD relies on third parties to manufacture its products, and if they are unable to do so on a timely basis in sufficient quantities and using competitive technologies, the company's business could be materially adversely affected.*

AMD's management states in its 2019 10K that the company may not be able to generate sufficient cash to service its debt obligations or meet its working capital requirements. AMD has a large amount of indebtedness which could adversely affect its financial position and prevent the firm from implementing its strategy or fulfilling its contractual obligations. The agreements governing the firm's notes and Secured Revolving Line of Credit[4] impose restrictions on the firm that may adversely affect the firm's ability to operate its business.

The company's credit agreements might be quite inhibiting in the event of additional needs for external credit. AMD's indentures include a 7.50% Senior Notes due 2022 and 7.00% Senior Notes due 2024 that

---

[3]See, for instance, Standard & Poor's, Corporate Ratings Criteria, www.standardpoors.com/ratings, 9-8-2020.

[4]A revolving line of credit allow the firm to borrow an amount from the credit up to its limit. Secured means that the line of credit is backed by collateral.

contain various covenants which limit its ability to incur additional indebtedness; pay dividends and make other restricted payments; make certain investments, including investments in unrestricted subsidiaries; create or permit certain liens.

Advanced Micro Devices, Inc. and Its Business

Advanced Micro Devices, Inc. (AMD or the Company) is a semiconductor company with worldwide operation.[5] The company operates in two segments, Computing and Graphics; and Enterprise, Embedded, and Semi-Custom. AMD provides microprocessors for desktop PCs, notebooks, and servers, and offers professional graphics products, processors for interactive digital signage, casino gaming, and medical imaging. The Company serves original equipment and design manufacturers, datacenters, original design manufacturers, system integrators, independent distributors, online retailers, and add-in-board manufacturers through its direct sales force, independent distributors, and sales representatives.

The Company was founded in 1969 and is headquartered in Santa Clara, California. Sales in 2019 reached $6.7 billion,[6] assets $6.0 billion, and 10,100 employees. Research and development were $1.4 billion or 21% of sales in 2018. International sales were 80% of sales in 2018, up from 74% in the prior year primarily driven by a higher revenue from China and Taiwan.

The company conducts product and system research and development activities for its products in the United States with additional design and development engineering teams located in Australia, China, Canada, India, Singapore, and Taiwan. AMD relies on contracts and intellectual property rights to protect its products and technologies from unauthorized third-party copying and use. Intellectual property rights include copyrights, patents, patent applications, trademarks, trade secrets, and mask work rights. The company has approximately 8,000 issued patents and 2,600 patent applications pending.

[5]https://finance.yahoo.com/quote/AMD/profile.

[6]AMD Form 10K, 2019.

The Assignment

Using Ratio Analysis, describe the strengths and weaknesses of AMD. Additionally, provide a risk assessment of AMD and its peers. Assume that the competing companies are Intel Corporation, Nvidia Corporation, Texas Instruments Incorporate, and Qualcomm, Inc. Balance Sheet and Income Statement data for the competing data could be obtained from https://www.sec.gov/edgar/searchedgar/companysearch.html.

See Exhibit 6 for the Income Statement of AMD. Exhibit 7 provides the Balance Sheet of AMD.

Exhibit 6. Advanced Micro Devices, Inc.

Consolidated Statements of Operations — USD ($)	**12 Months Ended**		
Shares in Millions ($ in Millions)	**2019**	**2018**	**2017**
Income Statement			
Net Revenue	$6,731	$6,475	$5,253
Cost of Sales	3,863	4,028	3,466
Gross Profit	2,868	2,447	1,787
Research and Development	1,547	1,434	1,196
Marketing, General, and Administrative	750	562	516
Licensing Gain	–60	0	–52
Operating Income	631	451	127
Interest Expense	–94	–121	–126
Other Expense, Net	–165	0	–9
Income (Loss) Before Income Taxes and Equity Loss	372	330	–8
Provision for (Benefit From) Income Taxes	31	–9	18
Equity Loss in Investee	0	–2	–7
Net Income (Loss)	$341	$337	($33)
Earnings (Loss) per Share			
Basic (in $ per Share)	$0.31	$0.34	($0.03)
Diluted (in $ per Share)	$0.30	$0.32	($0.03)
Shares used in per Share Calculation			
Basic (in Shares)	1,091	982	952
Diluted (in Shares)	1,120	1,064	952

Source: https://www.sec.gov/ 10 K.

Exhibit 7. Advanced Micro Devices, Inc.

Consolidated Balance Sheet ($ in Millions)	2019	Dec. 29, 2018
Current Assets		
Cash and Cash Equivalents	$1,466	$1,078
Marketable Securities	37	78
Accounts Receivable, Net	1,859	1,235
Inventories, Net	982	845
Prepayment and Receivables — Related Parties	20	34
Prepaid Expenses and Other Current Assets	233	270
Total Current Assets	4,597	3,540
Property and Equipment, Net	500	348
Operating Lease Right-of-Use Assets	205	
Goodwill	289	289
Investment: Equity Method	58	58
Other Assets	379	321
Total Assets	6,028	4,556
Current Liabilities		
Short-Term Debt, Net	0	136
Accounts Payable	988	834
Payables to Related Parties	213	207
Accrued Liabilities	1,084	783
Other Current Liabilities	74	24
Total Current Liabilities	2,359	1,984
Long-Term Debt, Net	486	1,114
Long-Term Operating Lease Liabilities	199	
Other Long-Term Liabilities	157	192
Stockholders' Equity:		
Common Stock, Paid-in Capital[a]	12	10
Additional Paid-in Capital	9,963	8,750
Treasury Stock at Cost	–53	–50
Accumulated Deficit	–7,095	–7,436
Accumulated Other Comprehensive Income	0	–8
Total Stockholders' Equity	2,827	1,266
Total Liabilities and Stockholders' Equity	$6,028	$4,556

Note: [a]Par value $0.01; 2,250 shares authorized, 1,175 shares issued, and 1,170 shares outstanding as of December 28, 2019; 2,250 shares authorized, 1,010 shares issued, and 1,005 shares outstanding as of December 29, 2018.

Source: https://www.sec.gov/ 10 K.

https://doi.org/10.1142/9789811216749_0002

Case 2

Trade Corporation SA (TradeCo)

Michael Samonas

American College of Greece, Deree, Greece

General Information about Trade Corporation SA

Trade Corporation SA (TradeCo) is a long-established company in the wholesale trade sector but has been hit severely by the economic downturn which followed the 2008 financial crisis. The wholesale sector is a capital-intensive sector, both in terms of warehouse facilities and working capital needs. The industry standard for leverage, as expressed by the total liabilities to equity ratio, is higher than 3. TradeCo planned to expand into new warehouse facilities after the onset of the crisis. The funding of the project has been done by a syndicated loan finalized in December 2012.

Bond Loan Term Sheet

The following terms and conditions were agreed on the bond loan provided:

Term	Value
Tenor (Years)	10
Spread	2.50%
Repayment Grace Period	68% at the 10th year 2 years

(*Continued*)

(*Continued*)

Term	Value
Amount (€ millions)	€45 mm
Covenants	Acceptable range
Current Assets/Current Liabilities	>1.5
Leverage (Total Liabilities/Shareholders Equity)	<3
Interest Cover (EBITDA/Interest Expense)	>2.0

The tenor of the loan represents the period for which the loan was granted and is usually expressed in years. The spread is used to calculate the amount of interest the borrower pays the bank for using the loan. The interest is calculated on a daily basis by applying the spread on the existing amount of the balance, divided by a 360-day year, and multiplied by the number of days being calculated from one due date to another. The repayment term refers to the amount of payment at the end of the term and anticipates that the loan will be refinanced to meet the payment obligation. Finally, before agreeing to a loan, lenders often require borrowers to agree to abide by restrictive covenants. Covenants are the provisions banks attach to long-term debt that trigger technical default when violated by the borrowing company. For example, TradeCo's bank required that it keeps its current ratio above 1.5, its leverage below 3, and its interest cover above 2.0. Breaking a covenant "triggers" a default and the lender's right to call the loan. Although banks pull the "trigger", they seldom call the loan. Doing so often results in bankruptcy for the company, bad publicity for the bank, and costly legal bills. However, the trigger forces the borrower to return to the bargaining table where the lender can demand a plan for corrective action, a higher interest rate, more collateral, and/or extra covenants. This is the case of TradeCo. The company succeeded a 2 years' loan extension in late 2019.

Problem Formulation

After the onset of the crisis, the consumption plummeted and TradeCo's results deteriorated. The cost of funding increased dramatically making things even worse. EBITDA cover deteriorated as TradeCo started funding its operations with debt instead of retained earnings. In the last quarter of FY 2019, the third covenant of the loan was breached.

The CEO of TradeCo wants to know if it may breach the other covenants before the end of the loan considering that the economic activity will start raising again. The Financial Planning and Analysis manager (FP&A)

of the company was assigned by the CEO the task of advising the Board of Directors about the possibility that TradeCo might breach the other covenants before the end of the loan. He would also like to know what the value of the company was as of 31/12/2019 so that he may offer company shares as a collateral to meet the requirements of the lending institutions.

In seeking to respond to the CEO's request and to be able to monitor the possible range of the loan covenants, the FP&A needs to build a complete financial model of the company, forecast its future performance, and thus calculate the values of the requested ratios. In other words, he needs to create the so-called Proforma Financial Statements. Proforma balance sheets are created by forecasting individual account balances at a future date and then aggregating them into a financial statement format. Account balances are forecast by identifying the forces that influence them and projecting how the accounts will be influenced in the future by such forces. Sales, company credit and payments policy, and cost structure are often significant forces. Proforma financial statements are a forecasting method that uses sales figures and costs from the previous 2 to 3 years to create financial statements into the future.

The FP&A needs a complete, fully operational financial model for just 3 ratios. Let us see why. Let us break down the problem. The first ratio is the quick ratio, and it is a measure of liquidity. For this ratio, the FP&A needs to forecast 2 balance sheet accounts, that is, current assets and current liabilities. For current assets, he needs to forecast trade receivables and inventory, and for the current liabilities trade payables and short-term debt, respectively. That is, in order to forecast just the first ratio, the FP&A needs to understand and model the whole operating cycle of the company. He needs to forecast the working capital needs and the funds required to support those needs. The other 2 ratios are measures of solvency. To forecast both total liabilities and equity requires a complete balance sheet plus an income statement. The equity at the year-end depends on the net income or net loss of the income statement. Total liabilities include the current liabilities as well as the long-term liabilities. Long-term liabilities normally include the portion of debt that has been used to finance long-lived assets such as heavy machinery and production machinery. So, in order to forecast long-term liabilities, the FP&A needs to understand the future strategic investment plan of the company. Moreover, the third ratio contains 2 income statement accounts, that is, EBITDA (operating profits) and interest expense. In turn, interest expense depends on the level of debt the company needs to operate. But the level of debt depends on the profits or losses of the year which, in turn, include interest expense. This is called a circular reference. Other information the FP&A needs to collect in order to complete the task includes the following:

- Projected sales growth rates for the period under analysis, that is, up to 2024.
- Projected profit margins.
- Projected operating expenses.
- The breakdown of the company's debt and the cost of this debt.
- Any investment plans.
- Depreciation information.

The time frame of the forecast is dictated by the tenor (lifetime) of the long-term loan. The loan expires in 2024, so he will need to forecast up to 2024 on a yearly basis. Operating expenses will be grouped into one category, Selling General & Administrative (SG&A) as they do not need much detail about them. The Key Performance Indicators (KPI) that will be forecast to address the problem in question are the 3 covenants: The quick ratio, the leverage ratio, and the interest coverage ratio. Neither sensitivity analysis nor a control panel was required for the time being.

To build the model, he needs:

- To collect 3 years' historical data of TradeCo.
- To select the key forecast drivers that will help him to forecast future financial statement accounts.
- To model the income statement.
- To model and balance the balance sheet.
- To model interest expense.

Please note that using historical information (2–3 years before the reference year) to estimate future performance has many pitfalls, mostly relating to the "anchoring" bias. In general, a macroeconomic analysis coupled with company's strategic plans to navigate the macro environment would be more appropriate. Nevertheless, for the scope of this case, the analysis of historical data is appropriate.

Other information about TradeCo:

- Sales: Projected sales for 2020 around €90 million.
- Prices: Stay fairly the same in the next 5 years.

- Raw material suppliers are located outside the EU.
- Cost structure: 30% variable according to sales volume variation and 70% fixed (increased by inflation).
- Investments: €400 thousand per year for the explicit forecast period.
- Consumer Price Index: 1.5% during 2020 and 1.7% constant up to 2024.
- Financing costs:

	2018 (%)	2019 (%)	2020 (%)
Deposit Rate	5.0	3.0	1.0
Financing Cost — LT	2.5	2.5	5.7
Financing Cost — ST	5.3	5.6	6.7

Particulars	**UOM**	**2017A**	**2018A**	**2019A**
Commercial Information				
Price				
Product Line 1	€/Unit	500	470	450
Product Line 2	€/Unit	450	480	500
Volume				
Product Line 1	Units	250.000	200.000	160.000
Product Line 2	Units	75.000	65.000	55.000
Total Sales	Units	325.000	265.000	215.000
Rate of Change	%		−18.5%	−18.9%

1. Last three fiscal years' financial statements of TradeCo:

TradeCo SA Historic Financial Statements 2017–2019				
Particulars	**UOM**	**2017A**	**2018A**	**2019A**
Income Statement				
Total Sales	€'000	**158.750**	**125.200**	**99.500**
COGS	€'000	144.463	112.680	90.048
Gross Margin w/o Depreciation	€'000	14.288	12.520	9.453
Other Operating Income	€'000	2.855	2.493	2.185

(*Continued*)

Operating Expenses	€'000	−9.116	−8.436	−6.352
Other Operating Expenses	€'000	−603	−485	−448
EBITDA	€'000	**7.423**	**6.092**	**4.837**
Net Interest Expenses	€'000	−2.513	−1.933	−2.808
Depreciation	€'000	−1.845	−1.867	−1.855
Profit/Loss Before Tax	€'000	**3.065**	**2.292**	**174**
Less: Income Tax Expense	€'000	−1.011	−756	−57
Profit/Loss After Tax	€'000	**2.054**	**1.536**	**117**
		1.3%	1.2%	0.1%

Balance Sheet				
Gross Fixed Assets	€'000	33.878	34.678	35.278
Accumulated Depreciation	€'000	−8.000	−9.867	−11.722
Other Non-Current Assets	€'000	3.500	3.500	3.500
Non-Current Assets	€'000	**29.378**	**28.311**	**27.056**
Account Receivables	€'000	58.969	47.666	37.918
Inventory	€'000	34.584	25.562	23.210
Cash	€'000	5.579	4.790	4.500
Other Current Assets	€'000	2.836	2.583	2.230
Total Assets	€'000	**131.345**	**108.912**	**94.914**
Share Capital	€'000	31.260	31.260	31.260
Retained Earnings	€'000	2.054	3.589	3.706
Owners Equity	€'000	**33.314**	**34.849**	**34.966**
Debt — Long Term	€'000	39.600	37.800	36.000
Debt — Short Term	€'000	34.857	21.384	12.593
Account Payables	€'000	21.129	13.542	9.646
Other Liabilities	€'000	2.446	1.336	1.710
Total Liabilities	€'000	**98.032**	**74.063**	**59.948**
Owners Equity & Liabilities	€'000	**131.345**	**108.912**	**94.914**

2. Input variables and suggested values for the scenario analysis of FY 2022:

Input Variables	**Best Case**	**Base Case**	**Worst Case**
Sales Turnover	105.000	103.000	97.500
Gross Margin	11.5%	9.5%	7.5%
DIOs	80	88	95
DSOs	107	115	123
DPOs	50	39	35

3. Prepare the following:
   - Prepare the Cash Flow Statement given that the following changes took place between FY 2016 and FY 2017 taking into consideration the following figures for 2017:

Decrease/(Increase) in Receivables	13.001
Decrease/(Increase) in Inventories	3.842
(Decrease)/Increase in Payables	–5.982
Decrease/(Increase) in Other Receivables & Payables	173
Purchase or Disposals of Assets	–1.427
New Bank Loans Raised/Repayments of Loans	–25.780
Cash and Cash Equivalents at the Beginning of the Period	17.853

   - Specify the Model.
   - Build the Model.
     - Write all the assumptions into the Assumptions Sheet.
     - Identify the Key Forecast Drivers — KFD.
     - Project them into the Explicit Forecast Period.
     - Build the Projected Financial Statements.
     - Build an Output Sheet.
   - Build a sensitivity analysis table between DSOs and GM% for FY 2021 to monitor Interest cover.

- Build three scenarios for FY 2022 by using the information provided above.
- Build a dashboard-like control panel to monitor Sales, Operating Performance, Debt Levels, and major KPIs of the explicit forecast period by changing the major KFDs using buttons (i.e., scrollers).

https://doi.org/10.1142/9789811216749_0003

Case 3

Intel Corporation: Financial Modeling and Capital Funding Decisions

Harvey A. Poniachek

Rutgers Business School, USA

Financial Planning and Funding Policy

Financial planning models use pro forma financial statements that summarize the financial outlook of the corporation.[1] The causality in the financial planning model runs from sales to assets and from assets to funding. The relationship between sales expansion and assets arises from the need to expand net working capital and fixed assets to fund higher sales. The growth of assets, liabilities, and equity determines how to fund the growth.

The financial planning model utilizes the percentage of sales approach to generate pro forma financial statements, where every item on the income statement increases at the same rate as sales, and some items of the balance sheet expand in proportion to their initial ratio to sales. We construct a financial planning model that includes the income statement and balance sheet and determine the items that change directly and autonomously with sales and those that do not. By assuming a sales forecast at a given level, we derive the balance sheet and determine the funding needed to support the sales evolution.

[1]Stephen A. Ross, Randolph W. Westerfield, Jeffrey Jaffe, and Bradford D. Jordan, in "Financial Statements Analysis and Financial Models," *Corporate Finance*, McGraw Hill Education, New York, 11th ed. (2013), Ch. 3, 61–74.

The income statement is constructed on the basis of the most recent growth performance record and by assuming, say, a 10% prospective sales growth going forward. We generate the pro forma income statement by assuming that the relation of each item of the income statement to sales remains at the same ratio that prevailed in the base year. That is, we assume, for instance, that cost/sales ratio will stay at the same level as in the base year. The pro forma income statement is shown in Exhibit 1 at the end of the case.

Next, we address the dividend payout ratio which is determined by the company's Board of Directors. The dividend payout ratio = Cash dividends/Net income, and the addition to the retained earnings = Net income – Dividend payout.

To construct a pro forma balance sheet, we begin with the most recent statement by observing that some of the items usually change directly or autonomously with sales, whereas others do not. For instance, if the ratio of assets/sales in the base year is 2, the amount of assets required to sustain a change in sales by \$1 is \$2 of assets. The ratio of assets/sales is defined as the capital intensity ratio, which is assumed to stay constant throughout the pro forma period.

On the liability side, some items vary directly with sales while others do not. For instance, accounts payable vary directly with sales, and as sales expand the company is expected to procure more inputs from its vendors. The change in accounts payable with sales is therefore assumed to be autonomous, whereas other accounts, such as long-term debt and common stock wouldn't autonomously change with sales.

Upon completion of the pro forma income statement and balance sheet (shown in Exhibit 1) we are likely to realize (depending on the assumed capacity utilization rate) that the projected assets exceed liabilities and equity, thus constituting a funding gap that is defined as External Funding Needs (EFN). The EFN could be funded through several methods, including an expansion of debt or equity or a combination of both. The specific funding approach of the EFN has significant implications on the firm's leverage that would be determined by the BOD.

Alternatively, instead of deriving pro forma financials and determining the EFN, a formulary approach is suggested instead as follows:

$$\begin{aligned}\text{EFN} = A/S \times \Delta S &- (\text{Autonomous liabilities/Sales}) \times \Delta\text{Sales}\\ &- \text{Profit margin} \times \text{Projected sales}\\ &\times (1 - \text{Dividend payout ratio})\end{aligned}$$

The variables in the above equation are as follows: A = assets, S = sales, and Δ = change.

Exhibit 1. Pro Form Financial Statements

Income Statement (Assume 10% Growth Rate)

	Base Period	Year 1, 10% Growth
Sales	1,000.0	1,100.0
Cost	775.0	852.5
Taxable Income	225.0	247.5
Taxes 21%	47.3	52.0
Net Income	177.8	195.5
Dividends 30%	53.3	58.7
Retained Earnings	124.4	136.9

Balance Sheet

	Base Period	Year 1, 10% Growth	Δ From Base Year
Current Assets			
Cash	75.0	82.5	7.5
Accounts Receivable	300.0	330.0	30.0
Inventory	500.0	550.0	50.0
Total	875.0	962.5	87.5
Fixed Assets			
Net Property & Equipment	1,125.0	1,237.5	112.5
Total Assets	2,000.0	2,200.0	200.0
Current Liabilities			
Accounts Payable	225.0	247.5	22.5
Notes Payable	75.0	N/A	
Total	300.0	N/A	22.5
Long-Term Debt	525.0	N/A	
Equity			
Common Stock and Paid-in Capital	700.0		
Retained Earnings	475.0	611.9	136.9
Total Liabilities and Equity	2,000.0	N/A	159.4
External Funding Needs (EFN)			**40.6**

EFN and growth are related so that higher growth induces greater need for funded assets and external funding granting if the company operates at full capacity utilization. With sales growth and excess capacity, the need for investment in productive assets diminishes and likewise the need for external funding. There is a nexus between internal growth and financial policy that is reflected by the dividend policy and the share of net income that is retained, or the plowback or retention ratio, and defined as b, as follows:

$$\text{Internal growth rate} = \text{ROA} \times b/(1 - \text{ROA} \times b),$$

where b = the plowback in or the retention ratio.

The growth rate above the internal growth is referred to as sustainable growth rate and the maximum rate of growth that a company can maintain without modifying its financial leverage is formulated as follows:[2]

$$\text{Sustainable growth rate} = \text{ROE} \times b/(1 - \text{ROE} \times b).$$

In addressing the EFN, the BOD was cognizant of the debt structure of major firms.

Intel's Business[3]

Intel Corporation ("Intel" or "The Company") is a world leader in the design and manufacturing of semiconductors and related products that was founded in 1968, headquartered in Santa Clara, California, and incorporated in Delaware. The Company's products and processes are used in notebooks, desktops, systems, communication infrastructure, automotive, industrial applications and original equipment manufacturers, and cloud service.

---

[2]For more information regarding estimating growth rates, see Ivan E. Brick *et al.*, "A Comparison of Alternative Models for Estimating Firm's Growth Rate," *Review of Quantitative Finance and Accounting* 47, no. 2 (2016): 369–393.

[3]Intel Corporation 2018 Annual Report.

Realizing the economics of Moore's Law[4] made possible the innovation of new high-performance products at exponential rates while balancing performance, cost, and power to meet customers' needs. Intel made significant investments and innovations in silicon manufacturing technologies, including investments in advanced manufacturing processes and packaging, architecture, interconnects, and embedded security features.

Intel is in the process of a corporate transformation that began several years ago — as the company grows beyond its traditional PC and server businesses into data-rich markets — by deploying IP and manufacturing technologies to redefine and expand the target market. The Company develops and manufactures its products in its own facilities using proprietary process technologies that enable it to optimize performance, shorten time-to-market, and control essential elements of supply chain. Sharing architectural innovation and IP enables the Company to spread investments over a large manufacturing base of products, which reduces costs and increases return on capital.

Intel is positioned to be a driving force of the AI — by striving to build the world's best AI platform and meet the needs of most innovative customers. Mobileye's family of products is already the automobile industry's leading solution for advanced driver assistance systems (ADAS). Intel's financial capital allocation strategy focuses on investing in R&D and capital spending at approximately 20% of revenue. The second priority is to acquire companies around the world that will complement its strategic objectives and stimulate growth of data-centric opportunities.

The Assignment

Ms. Lisa Chen, MBA and CPA, joined PWC in 2010 as Managing Director and Partner of corporate financial consulting. She earned an

[4]In 1965, Gordon E. Moore, co-founder of Intel, postulated that the number of transistors that can be packed into a given silicon chip will double about every two years, though the cost of computers will decrease by 50%. Eventually, Moore's insight became known as Moore's Law. Another tenet of Moore's Law asserts that this growth is exponential. Moore's Law definition, the principle of exponential growth, both observed and projected, in density of semiconductors and digital processors, describing the doubling of the number of components in an integrated circuit approximately every two years.

MBA in finance at Rutgers Business School, and previously attended NYU Stern School of Business, where she majored in finance and accounting. At PWC Ms. Chen is responsible for high-tech companies, including Intel, and managed a staff of over 30 partners, senior managers, and CPAs. She traveled on business in the U.S. and abroad approximately 30–40% of her time.

PWC was asked to assist Intel Corporation in creating a financial model designed to project their funding needs. Ms. Chen and her deputy called on the Company's CFO and his senior staff for a discussion, which lasted a couple of hours. Following the meeting, Ms. Chen reviewed Intel's Form 10K (which can be found at https://www.sec.gov/edgar/browse/?CIK=50863&owner=exclude) and internal financial documents, assigned the task to a couple of partners and asked to see their Intel's analysis in two weeks. Additionally, among Intel's comparable companies are Advanced Micro Devices, Inc (AMD), Texas Instruments Inc (TXN), and Nvidia Corporation (NVDA):

1. Assume that Intel is to expand in 2022 through 2026 at the same trend that it experienced from 2015 through 2019. Derive the income statement and balance sheet for 2022 through 2026 by utilizing the percent of sales approach.[5]
2. Derive the external funding needs[6] (EFN) for both 2022 and 2023 based on the pro forma financials in question #1 above.
3. Discuss your recommended funding strategy for the EFNs.
4. Assess the implications of your recommended EFNs funding on Intel's capitalization structure.
5. Discuss how your answer to the above question #2 will be affected if the firm operates at less than full capacity utilization.

[5]See, for instance, Stephen A. Ross, Randolph W. Westerfield, Jaffrey Jaffe, and Bradford D. Jordan, *Corporate Finance*, 12th ed. (McGraw Hill Education, New York, 2019), 61–65.

[6]*Ibid.*, 59–74.

Part II

Cost of Capital

https://doi.org/10.1142/9789811216749_0004

Case 4

Time Value of Money — Concepts and Applications. A Case Study: The General Motors Company Defined Benefit Pension Plan

Ivan E. Brick and Mark W. Guthner

Rutgers Business School, USA

Introduction

The time value of money is the most fundamental concept in the study of finance. At the same time, the idea itself is quite a simple one. The principle of the time value of money states that a dollar today is worth more than a dollar in the future. This concept arises out of the premise that money has earnings potential. That is to say; one can invest money today as a means to acquire more money in the future.

The application of time value of money is more difficult to apply than to describe. One knows the quantity and purchasing power of money today with certainty. However, the purchasing power of that same quantity of money in the future is unknown. Furthermore, to put money to work, one has to put that money in harm's way, so there is always the risk that money invested will diminish in value or at worst disappear. This risk is where complexity enters the picture. Going forward, the expected purchasing power of money under some circumstances is unknown, so investing is a process in which one has to make decisions under uncertainty.

The equilibrating factor that connects the uncertainty of the future with the certainty of the present is the expected or "hoped for" rate of return. The expected rate of return is a function of the expected change in purchasing power and the risk of losing money by investing today in the hopes of having more purchasing power in the future.

General Motors Company Defined Benefit Pension Plan

When people go to work for a company, they are compensated in several different ways, including earning a salary and possibly being compensated with a suite of additional benefits. That benefit package might include healthcare, life insurance benefits, incentive compensation, and retirement benefits. A properly designed incentive compensation plan aligns the interests of employees with the interests of shareholders by paying employees extra for doing good work and delivering value to the employer. These payments may come in the form of cash, stock, or stock options. Healthcare benefits are structured more like salary as companies typically pay some or most of the employee's healthcare insurance premiums alongside their salary.

Pension benefits are a form of **deferred compensation** as they are designed to provide a stream of cash flow to employees during their retirement years. Pension benefits are categorized into the Defined Contribution (DC) plan and the Defined Benefit (DB) plan. In a defined contribution plan, the employee puts some portion of their current salary aside today for use in their retirement years. Employers typically match those contributions to help employees build a nest egg. These types of plans are typically called "401(k) plans" as they are named after the section of the IRS tax code that applies to this type of deferred compensation plan. Public employees participate in "403(b) plans," which are similar to 401(k) plans.

An important aspect of the 401(k) plan is that money invested by the employee today is for use sometime in the future, typically after the person turns 59.5 years old. To encourage people to participate in salary deferral plans, the government offers a tax incentive to do so. Participants may deduct their contributions from their current taxable income, which lowers their income tax liability. Furthermore, income taxes on all the investment earnings (interest, dividends, and capital gains) are deferred until the day they are withdrawn from the 401(k) account. When money is withdrawn, the individual pays income taxes as if it were ordinary income. It is essential to recognize that the assets put aside in a DC plan are the property of the employee. The employer matching contribution as additional compensation to the employee is also the property of the employee. Since they own the assets, the individual is responsible for making investment decisions. To facilitate this, the employer will work with an asset manager who typically offers a series of investment choices through mutual funds.

Employee turnover is an expensive proposition for companies. When employees leave a company, knowledge, experience, and relationships go with them. Furthermore, there is a great deal of expense associated with the hiring and training of new employees. DB plans are designed to encourage people to stay with a company over the long haul. They do this by connecting the retirement benefit to years of service, and the average compensation in the last few years of service. A typical benefit formula might look like the following.

$$\text{Annual benefit} = \left(\frac{S_{-2} + S_{-1} + S_0}{3}\right) \times A \times T$$

Maximum benefit = Final salary
Benefit indexed to inflation
Minimum age of eligibility = 60

where
T = Years of service
A = Accrual rate per year of service
S_{-2} = Salary 2 years before leaving the firm
S_{-1} = Salary 1 year before leaving the firm
S_0 = Last year salary

Assume that Robert is 60 years old and has worked at General Motors for 32 years and his last 3 years' salary was \$82,000, \$84,000, and \$85,000, and is ready to retire. Under the plan, benefits accrue to the employee at a 3% rate per year of service times the average annual salary. Now that he is ready to retire, the pension benefit he can expect to receive in the first year of retirement is as follows:

$$\text{Annual benefit} = \left(\frac{\$82{,}000 + \$84{,}000 + \$86{,}000}{3}\right) \times 3\% \times 32$$

$$\text{Annual benefit} = \$80{,}640 \text{ per year}$$

$$\text{Annual benefit} = \frac{\$80{,}640}{12} = \$6{,}720 \text{ per month}$$

Robert will collect $6,720 a month for the first year of retirement from the company. If he continues to work beyond the age of 60, he will accrue more benefits, and his ending salary will presumably be a bit higher. If Robert does retire, he will start to collect benefits that will continue to rise with the rate of inflation. This process will go on for as long as he lives.

To determine how long someone will collect benefits, plan administrators employ **actuaries** who make estimates of how long someone is likely to live. They combine the longevity estimate with the annual expected pension benefit to derive an expected stream of cash flows to the beneficiary. That stream of cash flows resembles a growing annuity.

In a defined benefit plan, the employer has made a promise to an employee, solidified with a labor agreement. As a result, this pension benefit is a liability of the company that it must pay, just like a debt obligation. To help prepare for the day when the company has to make good on its promises, the company puts money aside every year to cover the expected pension liabilities by investing that cash in stocks, bonds, real estate, etc. so the assets grow over time to create the wealth necessary to fund the pension promises. The assets put aside to pay the commitment are the property of the company (and the employee does not have any property right to the underlying assets). All investment decisions are the responsibility of the plan sponsor (the company). If the investments perform exceedingly well, the company will be able to capture a benefit. If, on the other hand, the assets perform poorly, the company is still on the hook and will have to come up with additional resources to pay the benefits.

General Motors has several defined benefit pension plans which cover various groups of employees both domestically and internationally. Your **task as a manager** of the company's pension benefit plans is to advise the Board of Directors on the operations and status of the company's pension system. In this capacity, you have been asked to discuss the economics of the company's plan. In this respect, you determine the best way to approach this task is to (1) focus on accrual costs and (2) determine the funding status of the plan. As part of your analysis to address the funding status of the plan, you intend to estimate the residual value of the plan, that is, the amount of asset that remains after all employees have been paid their promised benefits.

To address this issue of accrual costs [the pension benefits an employee earns for a year's work] you decide to perform an analysis of how much money the company must put aside for 3 "typical" employees who are in different stages of their career. The first is a new employee, the second is an employee in mid-career, and the third is an employee approaching retirement.

To fully fund the liability created by the accrual of pension benefits, you need to compute the present value of the expected "incremental" stream of cash flows that accrue to the beneficiary for the work they perform for a year of service. To perform this analysis, you make the following assumptions.

- Inflation rate = 2.5%
- Cost of borrowing = 4.5%
- Retirement age = 65 years
- Longevity = 25 years (i.e., collect benefits till the age of 90)
- Accrual rate per year of service = 3%

For simplicity, assume that compensation keeps up with inflation and you ignore the potential for additional salary increases due to the potential for promotion.

Pension Benefit Accrual Formula

$$\text{Annual benefit} = \left(\frac{S_{-2} + S_{-1} + S_0}{3}\right) \times A \times T$$

Employee Status	**New**	**Mid-career**	**Near Retirement**
Age	21	40	60
Current Salary	\$50,000	\$75,000	\$100,000
Present Value of Accrued Liability for the Upcoming Year	?	?	?

First Assignment

- Compute the present value of the accrued liability for the upcoming year for the three typical employees selected. What conclusion can you draw?
- In the second part of your analysis, determine if the DP plan holds enough assets to pay the liabilities that have accrued to date. If the pension plan is fully funded, then the market value of the assets will equal the present value of the estimated liabilities. If the pension plan is in surplus, the market value of the assets will exceed the present value of the liabilities. If the market value of the assets falls short of the present value of the liabilities, the plan is said to be in deficit.

As you begin to take on this challenge, you review some of the company's disclosures found in their annual report that pertain to the company's pension plan. You find that to minimize the risk to plan surplus (or contain plan deficit) the company states:

Detailed periodic studies are conducted by our internal asset management group as well as outside actuaries and are used to determine the long-term strategic mix among asset classes, risk mitigation strategies, and the expected long-term return on asset assumptions for the US pension plans. The US study includes a review of alternative asset allocation and risk mitigation strategies, anticipated future long-term performance, and risk of the individual asset classes that comprise the plan's asset mix. Similar studies are performed for the significant non-US pension plans with the assistance of outside actuaries and asset managers. While the studies incorporate data from recent plan performance and historical returns, the expected long-term return on plan asset assumptions is determined based on long-term prospective rates of return.

We continue to pursue various options to fund and de-risk our pension plans, including continued changes to the pension asset portfolio mix to reduce funded status volatility. The strategic asset mix and risk mitigation strategies for the plans are tailored specifically for each plan. Individual plans have distinct liabilities, liquidity needs, and regulatory requirements.

In setting new strategic asset mixes, consideration is given to the likelihood that the selected asset mixes will effectively fund the projected pension plan liabilities while aligning with the risk tolerance of the plans' fiduciaries. The strategic asset mixes for US defined benefit pension plans are increasingly designed to satisfy the competing objectives of improving funded positions (market value of assets equal to or greater than the present value of the liabilities) and mitigating the possibility of a deterioration in funded status.

Derivatives may be used to provide cost-effective solutions for rebalancing investment portfolios, increasing or decreasing exposure to various asset classes and mitigating risks, primarily interest rate, equity and currency risks. Equity and fixed income managers are permitted to utilize derivatives as efficient substitutes for traditional securities. Interest rate derivatives may be used to adjust portfolio duration to align with a plan's targeted investment policy and equity derivatives may be used to protect equity positions from downside market losses. Alternative investment managers are permitted to employ leverage, including through the use of derivatives, which may alter economic exposure.[1]

You have examined the investment portfolios of the GM's DB plans and summarized the overall asset allocation along with the investment committee's expectation of returns in the table below.[2]

Asset Class	**Amount ($ Millions)**	**% of Portfolio (%)**	**Expected Return (%)**
Common & Preferred Stock	5,381	7.7	10.0
Government & Agency Securities	15,717	22.6	3.0
Corporate Debt Securities	27,235	39.1	5.0
Private Equity & Debt Investments	3,547	5.1	10.0
Hedge Funds	11,546	16.6	10.5
Real Estate	4,484	6.4	8.5
Other	1,720	2.5	8.0
	69,630	100.0	6.40

To value the DB plans liabilities, you have engaged the services of an actuary who has given you an estimate of GM's annual pension obligation

[1]General Motors Annual Report (SEC Form 10-K page 75).

[2]Based on General Motors Annual Report (SEC Form 10-K page 77).

that must be paid to current and future retirees for the life of the plan. That stream of cash flows is summarized below.

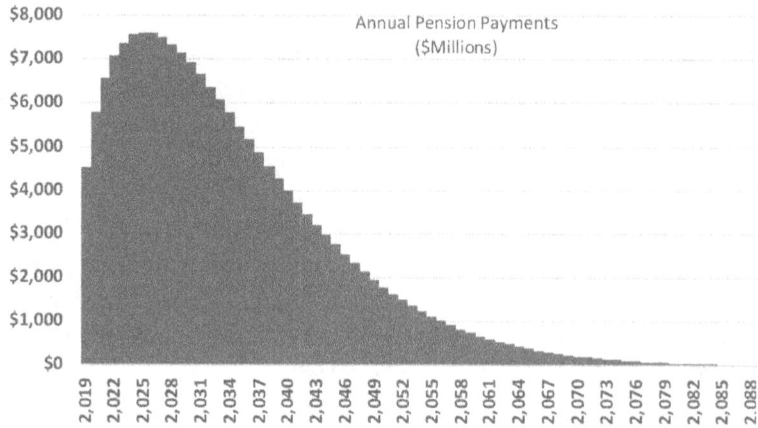

Date	Amount ($ Millions)	Date	Amount ($ Millions)	Date	Amount ($ Millions)
2019	4,530	2042	3,469	2065	399
2020	5,801	2043	3,218	2066	357
2021	6,577	2044	2,979	2067	319
2022	7,076	2045	2,751	2068	285
2023	7,385	2046	2,537	2069	254
2024	7,554	2047	2,334	2070	227
2025	7,614	2048	2,144	2071	202
2026	7,587	2049	1,966	2072	179
2027	7,490	2050	1,799	2073	159
2028	7,338	2051	1,644	2074	141
2029	7,142	2052	1,500	2075	125
2030	6,911	2053	1,366	2076	111
2031	6,654	2054	1,242	2077	98
2032	6,378	2055	1,128	2078	87
2033	6,087	2056	1,023	2079	76
2034	5,788	2057	926	2080	67
2035	5,484	2058	838	2081	59
2036	5,180	2059	756	2082	52

(Continued)

Date	Amount ($ Millions)	Date	Amount ($ Millions)	Date	Amount ($ Millions)
2037	4,877	2060	682	2083	46
2038	4,579	2061	614	2084	40
2039	4,288	2062	553	2085	35
2040	4,005	2063	496	2086	31
2041	3,732	2064	445	2087	27
				2088	24

Second Assignment

1. Compute the present value of the plan liabilities and compare it to the value of the plan assets. What can you say about the financial stability of the plan as of the end of fiscal year 2019?
2. How will the plan surplus or deficit be affected if the discount rate used to value the liability rises or falls by 1%?
3. Many DB plan sponsors, be they governments or corporations, use the expected rate of return on plan assets as the appropriate discount rate. How does this change the perception of the financial funding/stability of the plan? Does this approach have merit?
4. Assuming the plan is frozen in its current state (i.e., no new participants' will join the pension plan and the existing beneficiaries do not accrue additional benefits due to term of service). What is the expected future value of the plan assets in 2088 when the plan is expected to terminate?

Note: Pension payments are typically paid at the beginning of each month. For simplicity purposes, assume beneficiaries collect their benefits in a lump sum annually at the end of the year.

Time Value of Money

The solution to the pension problem described above is an application of the time value of money framework. The time value of money is the most fundamental concept in finance. Simply stated, it suggests that money available now is worth more than the same amount of money available in the future. Stated another way, money available in the future is worth less than the same amount of money in the present. As the availability date of a fixed amount of cash moves further into the future, the value of that cash today diminishes. Taken to an extreme, as the time to acquire cash move to infinity, the current or present value of that cash moves towards zero.

The power in this relationship resides in its ability to support financial decision making. Whether it is a person or a corporation, everyone is confronted with streams of cash flows that accrue to that economic actor. The concept of the time value of money allows these entities to put differing streams of cash flow available in the future on equal footing by placing a valuation of said cash flows with cash immediately available.

With the concept of Time Value of Money firmly established, this begs the question, "Why is a fixed amount of currency available to the user in the future worth less than that same amount of currency held today?" There are several reasons why this might be the case.

- **Time Preference:** People typically prefer to consume goods and services today rather than forestall that pleasure and consume those same goods and services sometime in the future. As a result, people must be compensated for postponing consumption today for the prospect of consuming in the future. This is another way of saying that there must be incentives for people to save.
- **Inflation:** The supply of money and credit tends to increase over time as central banks increase the money supply, and the banking industry increases the supply of credit. When the supply of money and credit grows faster than the production of goods and services, higher prices tend to result. Therefore, if people are to postpone consumption today so they can consume at least the same amount of goods and services sometime in the future, they need to accumulate more funds.
- **Risk:** When a person or business lends money, there is a risk that the borrower will fail to repay the lender. If a person invests in the equity of a business, there is a risk the business will fail. Under both circumstances, the investor ends up with less money than they started with, so they need to be compensated for this possibility.

Given these three reasons, the intuition behind the time value of money should be clear. People prefer to consume today instead of waiting for tomorrow. To induce people to save now and consume later, they must be "paid" to do so. The amount one needs to be paid is a matter of risk, inflation, and time preference. At a very minimum, one must maintain their purchasing power, so a rational saver will demand a return that is at least as large as the expected inflation rate for a risk-free investment (i.e., an investment which guarantees a return of investment and a return on that investment). If an investment has the risk of an uncertain payoff, a risk premium is appropriate.

The Mathematics of Time Value of Money

To build a mathematical relationship between the value of cash today with the value of cash in the future, it is necessary to define a few terms first. The value of a future cash flow today is known as its Present Value (PV). The value of cash sometime in the future held today is known as its Future Value (FV). The connective tissue between PV and FV is the time differential between the present and the future cash flow and a Required Rate of Return (R). The required rate of return is the compensation given to a saver who forgoes consumption today to consume in the future. While the amount of cash one hopes to acquire by saving and investing is a function of inflation, time, and risk, how that rate is determined in the marketplace is beyond the scope of this chapter. From this point forward, we will treat the interest rate as if it were explicitly known. The following relationship gives the equation that connects the present value with the future value of a single cash flow.

$$\mathrm{FV} = \mathrm{PV}(1 + r)^{t}$$

where
FV = Future value
PV = Present value
r = Return
t = Time in years

As an example, consider the following question. "What is the future value of an investment of \$100 that pays 5% at the end of each year for ten years?" Assume the periodic interest payments are reinvested at the stated rate of return.

$$\mathrm{FV} = \$100(1 + 0.05)^{10}$$

$$\mathrm{FV} = \$162.89$$

The above is an example of an investment that compounds annually. Return is paid at the end of each year and reinvested at the same rate. Many investments pay their return more often than once a year. Corporate bonds, for example, pay interest twice a year. Mortgage-backed securities pay interest 12 times a year. So, there are situations where interest payments compound many times in a year. For the sake of simplicity, we will assume annual compounding throughout this discussion.

Discounting, What It's Worth Today?

Discounting is the technique employed to calculate the present value of a single cash flow or some stream of cash flows to be received or paid over some future time horizon. To calculate the present value of a future cash flow, one simply rearranges the future value formula, solving for present value.

Single Cash Flow

$$\text{PV} = \frac{C}{(1+r)^t}$$

Stream of Differing Cash Flows Discounted at Different Rates

$$\text{PV} = \sum_{t=0}^{N} \frac{C(t)}{(1+r(t))^t}$$

where
$C(t)$ = Future cash flow received at time t
$r(t)$ = Discount rate for cash flows received at time t

Interest rates and required rates of return generally differ by time to particular cash flows. As a result, one may use a different discount rate for different holding periods.

Example #1

Assume you have the following sets of cash flows. The cumulative nominal amount of cash flows for both scenarios is the same. Further, assume that all cash flows will be discounted at a 5.00% annual rate.

	Scenario #1	Scenario #2
Year	**Cash Flows**	**Cash Flows**
1	10,000	70,000
2	20,000	60,000
3	30,000	50,000
4	40,000	40,000
5	50,000	30,000
6	60,000	20,000
7	70,000	10,000
Total	280,000	280,000

What is the present value in each scenario? The table below shows how one can use Excel to find the present value.

		Scenario #1		Scenario #2	
Year	Discount Rate	Cash Flows	Present Value	Cash Flows	Present Value
1	5.00%	10,000	9,524	70,000	66,667
2	5.00%	20,000	18,141	60,000	54,422
3	5.00%	30,000	25,915	50,000	43,192
4	5.00%	40,000	32,908	40,000	32,908
5	5.00%	50,000	39,176	30,000	23,506
6	5.00%	60,000	44,773	20,000	14,924
7	5.00%	70,000	49,748	10,000	7,107
Total		280,000	**220,185**	280,000	**242,725**

=C/(1+R)^t
=F5/(1+C5)^B5

=SUM(E4:E10)
or
=NPV(G4,H4:H10)
=NPV(rate,value1,value2,...)

The present value of the cash flows in Scenario #1 is less than the present value of the cash flows in Scenario #2. Why? On average, the cash flows in Scenario #1 come due later than the cash flows in Scenario #2. Since the present value of cash flows fall as they move further into the future, Scenario #1 will have a lower present value than the cash flows in Scenario #2.

Example #2

Is there a circumstance under which the present value of cash flows in Scenario #1 might be greater than the present value of the cash flows in

Scenario #2? Sure. If the discount rate is sufficiently higher for short-term cash flows and lower for long-term cash flows, it is possible for the present value of the cash flows in Scenario #2 to be the same or less than the present value of cash flows in Scenario #1.

		Scenario #1		Scenario #2	
Year	Discount rate	Cash Flows	Present Value	Cash Flows	Present Value
1	6.96%	10,000	9,349	70,000	65,446
2	5.96%	20,000	17,814	60,000	53,443
3	4.96%	30,000	25,947	50,000	43,244
4	3.96%	40,000	34,248	40,000	34,248
5	2.96%	50,000	43,219	30,000	25,932
6	1.96%	60,000	53,411	20,000	17,804
7	0.96%	70,000	65,482	10,000	9,355
Total		280,000	**249,471**	280,000	**249,471**

=C/(1+R)^t

=F6/(1+C6)^B6

=SUM(E5:E11)

=SUM(G5:G11)

This situation is described as an "inverted" yield curve. Under normal circumstances, the market rate on short-term investments is lower than the market rate for long-term investments. This is known as an upward-sloping or "normal" yield curve. In an environment when inflation in the short term is expected to be higher than inflation in the long term, the yield curve often inverts and slopes downward. This does not happen often, but it does happen. Note that we cannot use the Excel NPV function since that function assumes a constant interest rate.

Annuity

One of the most common and simplest of investments is the annuity. An annuity is a stream of equal cash flows that are paid at a set interval for a specific amount of time. To compute the value of an annuity one might use the long form of the present value equation.

$$\text{PV} = \sum_{t=1}^{N} \frac{C}{(1+r)^t}$$

However, this computation can be simplified if we make a few assumptions. Assume that the same cash flows are paid annually at the end of the year, and all cash flows are discounted at the same rate, then we can compute the value of an annuity with this closed-form solution.

$$PV = \frac{C}{r}\left[1 - \frac{1}{(1+r)^T}\right]$$

where
T = Time to last cash flow

Example #3

Assume one will get paid \$100 a year for the next 10 years and the payment comes at the end of the year. Further, assume that the going rate of interest is 5%. The present value of this annuity is \$772.17.

$$PV = \frac{100}{0.05}\left[1 - \frac{1}{(1+0.05)^{10}}\right] = \$772.17$$

Again, the table below explains how to use Excel time value functions to obtain the present value. Note, to find the present value of an annuity, we can use the PV instead of the NPV function.

		Scenario #1	
Year	Discount Rate	Cash Flows	Present Value
1	5.00%	100	95.24
2	5.00%	100	90.70
3	5.00%	100	86.38
4	5.00%	100	82.27
5	5.00%	100	78.35
6	5.00%	100	74.62
7	5.00%	100	71.07
8	5.00%	100	67.68
9	5.00%	100	64.46
10	5.00%	100	61.39
Total		700	**772.17**

=C/(1+R)^t
=D6/(1+C6)^B6

=SUM(E5:E11)
or
=-PV(C4,B13,D4,0,0)
=-PV(rate,nper,pmt,fv,type)
rate = discount Rate
nper = Number of Periods
pmt = Constant Payment Amount
fv = Future Value
type=> 0 if CF @ end of period, 1 if CF @ Beginning of Period

Annuity Due

An annuity is a stream of equal cash flows that are paid at a set interval for a specific amount of time. To compute the value of an annuity one might use the long form of the present value equation.

$$\mathrm{PV} = \sum_{t=1}^{N-1} \frac{C}{(1+r)^{t-1}}$$

However, this computation can be simplified if we make a few assumptions. Assume that the same cash flows are paid annually at the end of the year, and all cash flows are discounted at the same rate, then we can compute the value of an annuity with this closed-form solution.

$$\mathrm{PV} = \frac{C}{r}\left[1 - \frac{1}{(1+r)^{T}}\right](1+r)$$

$T =$ Time to last cash flow.

Example #4

Assume one will get paid \$100 a year for the next 10 years and the payment comes at the beginning of the year. Further, assume that the going rate of interest is 5%. The present value of this annuity is \$810.78.

$$\mathrm{PV} = \frac{100}{0.05}\left[1 - \frac{1}{(1+0.05)^{10}}\right](1+.05) = \$810.78$$

	Scenario #1		
Year	Discount Rate	Cash Flows	Present Value
0	5.00%	100	100.00
1	5.00%	100	95.24
2	5.00%	100	90.70
3	5.00%	100	86.38
4	5.00%	100	82.27
5	5.00%	100	78.35
6	5.00%	100	74.62
7	5.00%	100	71.07
8	5.00%	100	67.68
9	5.00%	100	64.46
Total		700	**810.78**

=C/(1+R)^t
=D6/(1+C6)^B6

=SUM(E5:E11)
or
=-PV(C4,B13+1,D4,0,1)
=-PV(rate,nper,pmt,fv,type)
rate = discount Rate
nper = Number of Periods
pmt = Constant Payment Amount
fv = Future Value
type=> 0 if CF @ end of period, 1 if CF @ Beginning of Period

Annuity Growth

Now, let's say the investor is worried about inflation, so they would like to buy a stream of growing cash flows so that each cash flow maintains its purchasing power. To calculate the value of such a stream of cash flows, one can modify the generalized PV equation above to incorporate a steady growth rate.

$$\mathrm{PV} = \sum_{t=0}^{N} \frac{C(1+g)^{t-1}}{(1+r)^{t}}$$

This busy equation can also be simplified. If we assume a constant growth rate, with annual payments made at the end of the year, discounted at the same rate, we get the following formula.

$$PV = \frac{C}{r-g}\left[1-\left(\frac{1+g}{1+r}\right)^{T}\right]$$

Example #5

Now let's modify the example above. Assume one will get paid \$100 the first year and that payment will grow by 3% every year. As before, the investor would get ten payments. Finally, the going rate of interest will remain the same at 5%. The present value of this growing annuity is \$874.86.

$$PV = \frac{100}{0.05-0.03}\left[1-\left(\frac{1+0.03}{1+0.05}\right)^{10}\right] = \$874.86$$

Most present value problems involve variable cash flows that rise and fall over time. In such cases, one must use the long form of the present value equation. But when cash flows are fixed or growing at a fixed rate, the annuity formulas simplify the computational process.

Scenario				
Year	Discount Rate	Growth Rate	Cash Flows	Present Value
1	5.00%	3.00%	100	95.24
2	5.00%	3.00%	103	93.42
3	5.00%	3.00%	106	91.64
4	5.00%	3.00%	109	89.90
5	5.00%	3.00%	113	88.19
6	5.00%	3.00%	116	86.51
7	5.00%	3.00%	119	84.86
8	5.00%	3.00%	123	83.24
9	5.00%	3.00%	127	81.66
10	5.00%	3.00%	130	80.10
Total			766	**874.76**

=Cx(1+g)^(t-1)/(1+R)^t
=E9/(1+C9)^B9

=SUM(E5:E11)
=C/(r-g))x(1-((1+g)/(1+r))^T)
=E4/(C4-D4)*(1-((1+D4)/(1+C4))^B13)

https://doi.org/10.1142/9789811216749_0005

Case 5

Investors Bank and the Capital Asset Pricing Model

Ivan E. Brick

Rutgers Business School, USA

Primer on the CAPM

Getting a mathematical representation of equilibrium requires some fancy math. Let's avoid that and use the simplifying assumption that all investors will invest in Treasury security and the S&P market portfolio. This implies that all securities will be compared to two benchmarks, the rate of the return of the Treasury security and the market risk premium. The Capital Asset Pricing Model (henceforth, "CAPM") of Lintner[1], Sharpe[2], and Mossin[3] is a mathematical representation of the market equilibrium. According to this model

$$E(R_I) = R_F + \beta_I[E(R_M) - R_F], \tag{1}$$

[1]John Lintner, "The Valuation of Risk Assets and the Selection of Risky Investments in Stock Portfolios and Capital Budgets," *Review of Economics and Statistics* 47, no. 1 (1965): 13–37.

[2]W. F. Sharpe, "Capital Asset Prices: A Theory of Market Equilibrium under Conditions of Risk," *The Journal of Finance* 19, no. 3 (1964): 425–442.

[3]J. Mossin, "Equilibrium in a Capital Asset Market," *Econometrica* 34, no. 4 (1966): 768–783.

where β_I is the beta of security i, it represents the systematic risk of security i. Note that the expected return of security i is a linear combination of the expected return of the market portfolio, $E(R_M)$, and the risk-free rate. Note that $[E(R_M) - R_F]$ is the average market risk premium. By definition a risk premium is the expected return on an asset or portfolio of assets in excess of the risk-free rate. Hence if beta is equal to two, the stock is said to be twice as risky as the market portfolio, and therefore the appropriate risk premium for this stock is twice as large as the market.

What is β and what does it mean? If, whenever the market return moves up or down by 10% the individual stock's return moves, on average, by 20%, then we say that the stock is twice as volatile or risky as the market. **The stock is said to have a beta of 2.0 (20%).**

The risk-free rate can be measured by the annualized yield on monthly treasury bills, 10 years treasury notes, or 30 years treasury bonds. $[E(R_m) - R_f]$ is the average risk premium in the market. Generally, the average risk premium in the market is measured by the historical annualized excess return of the market over the return of the 1-month treasury.

The mathematical formula for beta is

$$\beta_i = \text{Cov}(R_i, R_m)/\text{Var}(R_m). \tag{2}$$

Consider the following table. The second column states the annual return of stock for a given year. The third column provides the corresponding return for the market during that year. Please verify that the average return of stock i is 2.8% while the average return of the market for that same time period is 5.6%.

Year	Stock *i* (%)	Market (%)
2001	12	18
2002	–7	–16
2003	5	12
2004	6	11
2005	–2	3

Also verify the values of the statistics below for the above table.

Average Annual Return	2.80%	5.60%
Variance	54.7%^{2}	174.3%^{2}
Standard Deviation	7.40%	13.20%

Using the covariance formula:

$$\text{Cov}(R_i, R_j) = \sum_{t=1}^{n} (R_{it} - AR_i)(R_{jt} - AR_j)/(n-1),$$

we can obtain that the covariance is equal to 92.40 (percentage squared). According to Equation (2), beta is obtained by taking the ratio of the covariance of the returns of stock *I* with that of the market and the variance of the return of the market portfolio or 92.4/174.3 = .5301.

This is one approach to find the beta of the stock. In actuality, you are using what statisticians call linear regression. Consider the following diagram. The x's in Exhibit 1 represent a paired observation of the return of the stock and market for a given period. For example, the bold upper font X represents the monthly return of stock *i* and the market in March 2008. For that month, the stock had 7% return, while the market return was 5%. Ordinarily, we use 60-month observations and imagine there are 60 of those x's. Linear regression tries to find the best line that fits those points whereby roughly half of the x's will be above the line and the other half will be below the line. The slope of the line is the beta. The equation of the line that is being estimated is given by:

$$R_{it} = \alpha + \beta_i R_m + \varepsilon_{it}. \tag{3}$$

The α is the intercept of the line and ε_{it} is the error term for stock *i* for the time period *t*. Consider the bold capital X of Exhibit 1 again. Note that

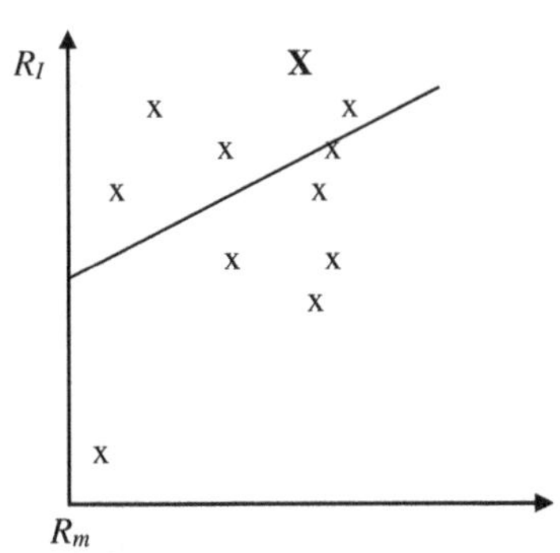

Exhibit 1. Plot of monthly returns of the stock against the monthly returns of the market

the bold X is not on the regression line but above it. The vertical distance between the **X** and the line is the value of ε_{it}.

One can calculate the cost of equity of the firm based by the **CAPM**. This model states that the risk premium of equity is related to how the stock varies from the market. This volatility is measured with beta, β, which is obtained by mathematically comparing the volatility of the return of an individual stock with the volatility of the return of the whole market. In case you don't want to do the calculation, you can obtain beta by looking it up on Yahoo Finance.

For example, if you go to http://finance.yahoo.com/ and enter XRX in the top left window that states **Enter Symbol(s)**. Go to the blue panel on the left side and click on **Key Statistics** under Company Profile. You will find the panel **Trading Information** on the right-hand side. The very first statistic is beta, which for Xerox is 1.81 as of June 15, 2021. Recall that the CAPM states that the expected return from the stock will depend on its beta, and can be calculated using the following relationship:

$$E(R) = R_f + \beta[E(R_m) - R_f].$$

$\boldsymbol{E(R)}$ is the expected return of the stock required by the market. Hence, we can interpret $E(R)$ to be the cost of equity. $\boldsymbol{R_f}$ is the risk-free rate. The risk-free rate is usually measured by the annualized yield of a 1-month Treasury bill. $\boldsymbol{[E(R_m) - R_f]}$, the average risk premium in the market, is measured by the historical annualized excess return of the market over the return of the 1-month Treasury bill. That estimate is around 9%. So, if the beta of Xerox is 1.81, and the current risk-free rate is 5%, then according to the CAPM, the cost of equity is given by $E(R) = R_f + \beta[E(R_m) - R_f] = 5\% + 1.81(9\%) = 16.30\%$.

Another approach to find the cost of equity is using the **dividend growth model**. Recall that the present value of cash flows growing at a constant rate is given by:

$$\text{Price} = (\text{Expected dividend at } t = 1)/(K - G),$$

where K is the cost of capital. We can solve for K, assuming we know the price per share of the common stock and we have an estimate of the growth rate, G. In that case:

$$R_e = (\text{Expected dividend at } t = 1)/\text{Price} + G. \tag{4}$$

For example, if firm ABC's current price is \$50 and we expect its expected dividend 1 year from now will be \$5 and it will grow at 3% per annum then Equation (4) tells us that the cost of equity for ABC is \$5/\$50 + .03 = .13 which equals 13%.

Investors Bank — Cost of Equity

On August 15, 2017, Ronnie Sevilla, Vice President, walked into Investors Bank headquarters in Short Hills, New Jersey, to attend a meeting with the Bank's CFO. At the meeting, the CFO asked Ronnie if he could help the team estimate the firm's cost of equity. He asked this of Ronnie because Ronnie recently received his Executive MBA degree from Rutgers University. Ronnie, the consummate team player, agreed to help out, even though his niche is retail lending. The CFO needs the report in 2 days.

The bank was incorporated as a New Jersey-chartered mutual savings and loan association in 1926 as the Washington Rock Building and Loan Association. Sixteen years later the bank changed its name to Investors Savings and Loan. In 1992, the charter was converted to a mutual savings bank and in 1997 the charter was converted to a New Jersey-chartered stock savings bank. It was reorganized as a two-tiered holding company whereby the bank itself became a wholly owned subsidiary of Investors Bancorp, Inc., and Investors Bancorp, Inc. became a wholly owned subsidiary of Investors Bancorp, MHC. In 2005, Investors Bancorp, Inc. became a (partially) publicly held company with the inception of its IPO, but Investors Bancorp, MHC retained 55% of the stock ownership. On May 8, 2014, Investors Bancorp became a fully public company and its ticker is ISBC.

Upon becoming public, the bank transitioned from a wholesale thrift business to a retail commercial bank. In 2005, the total assets of the bank were nearly \$5 billion. On December 31, 2016, Co. had total assets of \$23.17 billion and deposits of \$15.28 billion. The bank grew organically and through several acquisitions. Since 2008, the bank had acquired five Carteret Federal Saving Bank branches, American Bank of New Jersey, six Banco Popular branches in NJ, 17 Millennium BCP Bank branches, Brooklyn Federal Saving Bank, Marathon Bank, Roma Bank, RomAsia Bank, and GCF Bank. The bank is engaged in the business of accepting deposits from the public and borrowing funds in the wholesale markets to originate loans and to invest in securities. The Bank offers residential loans, commercial real estate loans, commercial and industrial loans, construction loans, and consumer loans.

Returning to his office in Bayonne, New Jersey, Ronnie set out to come up with the cost of equity of the bank. He knew of two approaches to come up with the cost of equity. The first approach is based upon the dividend growth model. Ronnie remembered that the present value of cash flows growing at a constant rate is given by

$$\text{Price} = (\text{Expected dividend at } t = 1)/(R_e - G),$$

where R_e is the cost of equity. We can solve for R_e, assuming we know the price per share of the common stock and we have an estimate of the growth rate, G. In that case:

$$R_e = (\text{Expected dividend at } t = 1)/\text{Price} + G.$$

The second way to calculate the cost of equity is based upon the CAPM. The CAPM states that the expected return from the stock will depend on its beta, and can be calculated using the following relationship:

$$E(R) = R_f + \beta[E(R_m) - R_f].$$

$\boldsymbol{E(R)}$ is the expected return of the stock required by the market. Hence, we can interpret $E(R)$ to be the cost of equity. $\boldsymbol{R_f}$ is the risk-free rate. The risk-free rate is usually measured by the annualized yield of a 3-month Treasury bill.[4] $\boldsymbol{[E(R_m) - R_f]}$ is the average risk premium in the market. Finally, the beta of the stock is measured by regressing the stock return of Investors Bank against the return of the market. Generally, the average

[4]Actually, many firms prefer to use T-Bonds to reflect the longer horizon of the firm. But for simplicity, the case uses the 3-month T-Bill rate since historical information on that security is readily available. Please see below.

risk premium in the market is measured by the historical annualized excess return of the market over the return of the 3-month Treasury bill. Ronnie decided to use S&P 500 Index (^GSPC) as the proxy for the market.

Upon obtaining the data, there would be no problem for Ronnie to do the regression. He would download the Data Analysis ToolPak for Excel to compute the regressions. Ronnie knew that he had to download the price and dividend history of the Investors Bancorp stock in order to use either the Dividend Growth model or the CAPM. He went to Finance.Yahoo.com to download that data and noticed something very strange. He remembered that when he bought 1,000 shares of Investors Bancorp stock on May 1, 2014, he paid $26.82 per share. Yet, Finance.Yahoo.com records the closing price of the stock on that day as only $10.52177. What is strange about that number is that the bid–ask spreads are in full pennies. Even more shocking is that he recalled dividends per share was around 4 to 5 cents per share. But Finance.Yahoo.com states that the dividend was only $0.01962. And firms do not give partial cent dividends as suggested by the website. He decided to click onto the tab of the website entitled stock splits and he saw that on May 8, 2014, Investors Bank had undergone a stock split of 2.549, or for every share a stockholder owned on the previous day, he now owns 2,549 shares on May 9th.[5] Ronnie realized that both stock prices and dividends were adjusted for the stock split. Hence, if you multiply the recorded stock price of $10.52177 by 2.549, the resulting price is $26.82. Similarly, if you multiply the recorded dividend of 1.962 cents by 2.549, the resulting dividend is 5 cents per share.

Having resolved that mystery, Ronnie needed to figure out the measurement period to calculate the beta. In the EMBA program, the instructor suggested 60-month returns. In that case, he would download pricing data from Finance.Yahoo.com from August 1, 2012 to August 1, 2017. This way, he would have 61 monthly closing prices from which he could compute 60 monthly returns. But since 2012, the bank has undergone several changes including becoming a fully publicly held company. In addition, the bank product offerings have changed. Ronnie wondered if it would not be better to calculate beta using daily returns from the past year. Therefore, he would download the price and dividend history from August

[5] The actual split was 2,549/1,000 or for each 1,000 shares held prior to the split results in 2,549 shares after the split.

1, 2016 to August 1, 2017. Ronnie decided he would do both and see if there are significant differences in beta from the two approaches.

The next issue is how to estimate the market risk premium. Again, the question is: what is the measurement period? Should it be based upon Ronnie's expectations as to how the market will do in the near future? At this point, Ronnie thought the market was overpriced and he expected the market would lose value over the next 12 months. If he placed his expectations of the market return as $E(R_m)$ in the risk premium component of the CAPM, the risk premium will be negative, implying that Investors Bank's cost of equity would be lower than the current T-Bill rate as long as the estimated beta was positive. That did not make any sense. Ronnie resolved that he should look at the historical average of how much better he would have done by investing in the market compared to buying a T-Bill. Ronnie would estimate the average difference in the performance of the market compared to the 3-month T-Bill on a monthly basis and then take the average of that difference to use as his risk premium. But that brings up other questions. Should we look at the past 12 months, 10 years, or even longer?

Ronnie knows that he can download historical monthly T-Bill Data from the Federal Reserve Board. To get the data he needs, Ronnie would have to select date range for the monthly 3-month data. For his report, Ronnie will explain the methodology he uses and attach as an appendix the raw data he uses to make the calculations.

To make sure his reasoning is sound, Ronnie decided to call his former finance professor. Unfortunately, the recorded message said that the instructor would be out for the entire month. Ronnie muttered under his breath, "Do these guys actually work?"

https://doi.org/10.1142/9789811216749_0006

Case 6

Case Study on Cost of Capital

Roger J. Grabowski* **and Todd Fries†**

**Kroll, USA*

†BVA Group, USA

Introduction

The cost of capital is a key input for decision-makers for evaluating project financing decisions, capital investment decisions, as well as estimating values of businesses or business units. The following case study will discuss the alternatives and identify the inputs for methodologies used to determine the appropriate cost of capital for a given investment or valuation analysis. The time frame for our case study will be December 31, 2016.

The subject of the case study is the Odd & Rich Corp (O&R), a closely held company that manufactures a range of plastic components that are used as inputs by other manufacturers of consumer products, automobiles, aircraft, and computers.[1] O&R is classified within the standard industrial classification (SIC) Code 3089, Plastic Products not

[1]The base data comes from *Introduction to Financial Models for Management and Planning*, 2nd ed. ("FMMP2") by James R. Morris and John P. Daley (CRC Press, a Chapman and Hall Book, 2017); used with permission.

elsewhere classified.[2] O&R employs approximately 5,000 individuals at a number of facilities located in several different regions of the US. O&R sells its products worldwide with a majority of sales within the US.

The manufacturing process involves plastic injection molding and automated assembly. O&R uses its own sales force in addition to independent representatives and distributors who sell the products as independent contractors. O&R's business is somewhat cyclical, but it has been growing in recent years and its sales are expected to grow in the foreseeable future.

A summary of financial information for O&R is contained in the exhibits below: Exhibit 1 presents the historical income statement for the five most recent years. Exhibit 2 presents the historical balance sheet for the five most recent year-ends. Exhibit 3 presents historical industry average ratios for Standard Industry Classification (SIC) code 3089 (and O&R's ratios for the same 5-year period as O&R's historical income statements).[3]

Exhibit 1. Odd & Rich Historical Income Statements

						Common Size				
(in Millions of $)	**2012**	**2013**	**2014**	**2015**	**2016**	**2012**	**2013**	**2014**	**2015**	**2016**
Sales	748.5	792.6	800.2	944.0	1,000.0	100.0%	100.0%	100.0%	100.0%	100.0%
Cost of Goods Sold	470.1	496.7	504.8	566.7	607.7	62.8%	62.7%	63.1%	60.0%	60.8%
Gross Profit	278.4	295.9	295.4	377.3	392.3	37.2%	37.3%	36.9%	40.0%	39.2%
Operating Costs	123.4	130.1	131.1	169.3	122.3	16.5%	16.4%	16.4%	17.9%	12.2%
EBITDA	155.0	165.8	164.3	208.0	270.0	20.7%	20.9%	20.5%	22.0%	27.0%
Depreciation	57.8	53.6	54.3	49.9	53.8	7.7%	6.8%	6.8%	5.3%	5.4%
EBIT	97.2	112.2	110.0	158.1	216.2	13.0%	14.2%	13.7%	16.7%	21.6%
Interest Expense	12.8	3.6	18.7	3.1	3.4	1.7%	0.5%	2.3%	0.3%	0.3%
EBT	84.4	108.6	91.3	155.0	212.8	11.3%	13.7%	11.4%	16.4%	21.3%
Non-Operating	(2.2)	2.7	6.8	—	—	−0.3%	0.3%	0.8%	0.0%	0.0%
Pretax Income	82.2	111.3	98.1	155.0	212.8	11.0%	14.0%	12.3%	16.4%	21.3%
Income Tax	29.7	29.8	26.4	62.0	85.0	4.0%	3.8%	3.3%	6.6%	8.5%
NI	52.7	81.5	71.7	93.0	127.8	7.0%	10.3%	9.0%	9.9%	12.8%
Dividends	21.1	32.6	43.1	55.8	76.7	2.8%	4.1%	5.4%	5.9%	7.7%
Retained Earnings	31.6	48.9	28.6	37.2	51.1	4.2%	6.2%	3.6%	3.9%	5.1%

[2] The online Kroll (formerly Duff & Phelps) Cost of Capital Navigator — US Benchmarking Module provides industry level cost of capital data; it now classifies businesses according to GICS (Global Industry Classification Standard). O&R is classified in GICS 1510.

[3] FMMP2 contains many financial analyses of O&R that will be referenced in this case study without the background for those analyses being repeated herein.

Exhibit 2. Odd & Rich Historical Balance Sheet

						Common Size				
(in Millions of $)	**2012**	**2013**	**2014**	**2015**	**2016**	**2012**	**2013**	**2014**	**2015**	**2016**
Assets										
Cash	129.1	149.8	143.1	160.4	170.0	7.9%	8.7%	8.2%	8.0%	8.0%
Inventory	127.3	132.0	128.0	142.8	148.2	7.8%	7.6%	7.3%	7.1%	6.9%
Net Receivables	169.1	189.1	166.1	177.5	208.1	10.3%	10.9%	9.5%	8.8%	9.8%
Other Current Assets	119.0	117.7	119.0	189.5	183.7	7.3%	6.8%	6.8%	9.4%	8.6%
Total Current Assets	544.5	588.6	556.2	670.2	710.0	33.3%	34.1%	31.9%	33.3%	33.3%
Gross Fixed Assets	1,142.6	1,200.6	1,238.3	1,356.7	1,517.8	69.8%	69.5%	71.1%	67.4%	71.1%
Allowance for depreciation	288.4	342.0	395.6	449.2	502.8	17.6%	19.8%	22.7%	22.3%	23.6%
Net fixed assets	854.2	858.6	842.7	907.6	1,015.0	52.2%	49.7%	48.4%	45.1%	47.6%
Other Assets	237.7	280.0	342.9	435.9	409.0	14.5%	16.2%	19.7%	21.6%	19.2%
Total Assets	1,636.4	1,727.2	1,741.8	2,013.7	2,134.0	100.0%	100.0%	100.0%	100.0%	100.0%
Liabilities										
Current Debt	8.7	30.8	47.4	6.9	7.0	0.5%	1.8%	2.7%	0.3%	0.3%
Accounts Payable	152.9	173.5	144.3	175.5	279.1					
Other Current Liabilities	135.7	148.9	144.0	384.0	313.9	8.3%	8.6%	8.3%	19.1%	14.7%
Other Liabilities	42.6	33.5	21.5	—	—	2.6%	1.9%	1.2%	0.0%	0.0%
Debt	31.4	26.7	21.8	37.7	73.3	1.9%	1.5%	1.2%	1.9%	3.4%
Common Stock	100.0	100.0	100.0	100.0	100.0	6.1%	5.8%	5.7%	5.0%	4.7%
Earned Surplus	1,165.1	1,213.8	1,262.9	1,309.6	1,360.7	71.2%	70.3%	72.5%	65.0%	63.8%
Stockholders Equity	1,265.1	1,313.8	1,362.9	1,409.6	1,460.7	77.3%	76.1%	78.2%	70.0%	68.4%
Total Liabilities and Equity	1,636.4	1,727.2	1,741.8	2,013.7	2,134.0	100.0%	100.0%	100.0%	100.0%	100.0%

Assume you are a financial analyst at a private equity firm who is considering acquiring O&R. You have received forecasts that appear to have been developed through a robust process such that they reasonably represent the expected (i.e., probability-weighted average) financial performance over the next 5 years prior to debt service costs. You have been tasked with developing the appropriate cost of capital in order to develop a discounted cash flow (DCF) analysis based on the pre-debt service forecast you have received so as to inform your firm as to a reasonable offering price for a controlling interest in O&R.

Exhibit 3. Odd & Rich and Industry Historical Five-Year Ratios (at Book Values)

	2012	2013	2014	2015	2016
Profitability (%)					
EBITDA/Sales					
Company	20.7%	20.9%	20.5%	22.0%	27.0%
Industry	13.8%	13.6%	12.6%	13.8%	13.5%
EBIT/Sales					
Company	13.0%	14.2%	13.7%	16.7%	21.6%
Industry	7.8%	7.6%	6.8%	8.0%	8.3%
Pretax Profit Margin					
Company	11.0%	14.0%	12.3%	16.4%	21.3%
Industry	5.0%	0.9%	3.4%	4.1%	5.8%
Net Profit Margin					
Company	7.0%	10.3%	9.0%	9.9%	12.8%
Industry	2.6%	(0.7%)	2.3%	3.0%	4.7%
Return on Assets					
Company	3.2%	4.7%	4.1%	4.6%	6.0%
Industry	3.3%	(2.7%)	0.7%	2.9%	5.4%
Return on Equity					
Company	4.2%	6.2%	5.3%	6.6%	8.7%
Industry	9.4%	(0.1%)	(16.4%)	8.6%	16.1%
Return on Invested Capital					
Company	2.4%	3.7%	2.1%	2.6%	3.3%
Industry	4.3%	(5.2%)	(0.9%)	3.5%	8.3%
Leverage					
Long-Term Debt/Equity					
Company	2.5%	2.0%	1.6%	2.7%	5.0%
Industry	91.8%	175.6%	456.1%	346.1%	168.0%
Total Debt/Invested Capital					
Company	3.1%	4.2%	4.8%	3.1%	5.2%
Industry	64.8%	65.9%	67.7%	60.3%	60.4%
Total Debt/Total Assets					
Company	2.5%	3.3%	4.0%	2.2%	3.8%
Industry	36.6%	42.8%	41.4%	40.5%	38.4%

Exhibit 3. (*Continued*)

	2012	2013	2014	2015	2016
Interest Coverage Before Tax					
Company	7.4x	31.9x	6.3x	51.0x	63.6x
Industry	261.8x	129.2x	36.2x	145.5x	67.0x
Interest Coverage After Tax					
Company	5.1x	23.6x	4.8x	31.0x	38.6x
Industry	231.3x	119.3x	32.6x	98.1x	58.5x
Total Assets/Common Equity					
Company	1.3x	1.3x	1.3x	1.4x	1.5x
Industry	4.4x	4.8x	8.6x	7.0x	4.3x
Activity: Operating Efficiency					
Inventory Turnover					
Company	3.7x	3.8x	3.9x	4.0x	4.1x
Industry	5.3x	5.2x	5.8x	6.2x	6.3x
Receivables Turnover					
Company	4.4x	4.2x	4.8x	5.3x	4.8x
Industry	6.6x	6.7x	6.8x	8.8x	7.9x
Total Asset Turnover					
Company	0.5x	0.5x	0.5x	0.5x	0.5x
Industry	1.1x	1.1x	1.1x	1.3x	1.3x
Average Collection Period (Days)					
Company	81.3	85.9	74.7	67.7	74.9
Industry	57.9	58.4	54.2	48.4	49.5
Days to Sell Inventory					
Company	97.5	95.7	91.3	90.7	87.8
Industry	85.0	90.8	81.5	76.2	75.6
Operating Cycle (Days)					
Company	178.8	181.6	166.0	158.4	162.7
Industry	142.9	149.1	135.7	124.6	125.1
Dividends					
Dividend Payout (%)					
Company	40.0%	40.0%	60.1%	60.0%	60.0%
Industry	9.4%	14.4%	11.4%	13.9%	9.6%

As is explained in any finance treatise, the cost of capital represents the required return for a given level of risk being borne by the investor. The appropriate cost of capital to be used is thus a function of the perspective of the investor. If the cash flows that are the subject of the financial analysis are cash flows to equity holders (i.e., after debt service), then the correct measure of the cost of capital is the cost of equity. If the subject of the financial analysis is the cash flows to all investors in the enterprise (common equity, debt, and when applicable, preferred equity), then the weighted average cost of capital (WACC) is the appropriate measure. In this instance, the forecasts received are before debt service, so the WACC would be the appropriate discount rate. The formula for the WACC is as follows.[4]

Formula 1:

$$\text{WACC} = K_e W_e + K_d(1 - T)W_d$$

where
K_e = Cost of equity
W_e = Equity weight (market value of equity/total invested capital)
K_d = Cost of debt
T = Effective income tax rate
W_d = Debt weight (market value of debt/total invested capital)

Thus, there are the following elements that must be determined: the capital structure (from which we will compute both W_e and W_d), the income tax rate, the cost of equity, and the cost of debt. We will stipulate the blended federal, state, and local tax rate to be 40%[5] so we can focus on the other inputs to the WACC formula.

---

[4]The WACC formula is also often presented with a component relating to preferred equity, but we will make the simplifying assumption for the purposes of this case study that here is no preferred equity in the capital structure.

[5]The case study is being performed prior to the passage of the Tax Cuts and Jobs Act, which was signed into law in December of 2017; thus the 40% stipulated combined tax rate is reasonable given the date of the study.

Capital Structure — Weight of Debt and Equity

There are a number of possible sources for estimates for the capital structure assumption. As the analyst for a private equity firm, the possible acquirer, you may think it reasonable to estimate the amount of leverage that your firm expects to employ should you close the transaction, perhaps by looking at the capital structure of other deals your firm has closed. Alternatively, you could simply look at the O&R's current capital structure. You might also consider capital structures observed within O&R's industry as well as the borrowing capacity of O&R.[6]

Ultimately, when valuing a controlling interest, you will work under the premise that a control buyer will normally attempt to optimize the capital structure of the enterprise. As an analyst, you will ultimately be required to exercise judgment in making this determination.

It is common practice to look to industry measures to inform the estimate of optimal capital structure; after all, the collective judgment of multiple professional management teams operating in the industry, as evidenced by a central tendency of a sample of capital structure data points, should be informative. As noted previously, as a plastic component manufacturer, O&R is classified within SIC 3089. Debt-to-equity and debt-to-capital metrics for SIC 308 (which incorporates 3089) as of December 31, 2016 are shown in Exhibit 4.[7]

Exhibit 4. Industry Leverage Ratios

	Leverage Ratios (%)			
	Debt/Market Value Equity		**Debt/Total Invested Capital**	
	Latest	5-Year Average	Latest	5-Year Average
Median	17.8	14.8	15.1	12.9
SIC/GICS Composite	22.3	19.5	18.2	16.3

[6]For a discussion of debt capacity and how it impacts the optimal capital structure, see Shannon P. Pratt and Roger J. Grabowski, *Cost of Capital: Applications and Examples*, 5th ed. ("CofC5") (Wiley, 2014): 550–556.

[7]Data for companies classified under SIC grouping 308 as of December 31, 2016 obtained from the Kroll Cost of Capital Navigator — US Benchmarking Module. The broader SIC 308 grouping was utilized as summary data was not available for the narrower SIC 3089 category.

Recognizing that industry conditions may fluctuate over time, rather than taking a snapshot as of December 31, 2016, you may want to consider using the 5-year average debt-to-capital ratio, in order to capture more of the business cycle within your analysis. In this instance, the differences between the current debt-to-capital ratio and the 5-year average are fairly modest. Additionally, there are multiple ways to think about the central tendency of a data set such as the median (the middle data point of the data set) and the composite (a value-weighted average).

In addition to looking at industry benchmarking, it may also be appropriate to look at particular guideline public companies (GPCs) operating in O&R's industry at a more granular level. In this case, using a search by SIC code you identify the following five GPCs with leverage ratios as shown in Exhibit 5.

A review of individual GPCs can provide additional insight into the selection of the appropriate capital structure for O&R. You might identify certain characteristics of a subset of the GPCs that might make their capital structures a better estimated optimal capital structure for O&R than the broader group as a whole. A financial analysis looking at the asset mix, risk profile, and growth expectations of the GPCs relative to the subject company might help you to identify such a subset.

In this instance, considering both the median and the composite of the SIC 3089 data as well as the average debt/capital of the GPCs, you

Exhibit 5. GPC Leverage Ratios

Company Name	Ticker	Market Capitalization (in Millions of $)	Total Debt (in Millions of $)	Invested Capital (in Millions of $)	Debt/ Capital
AptarGroup, Inc.	ATR	4,564.7	946.6	5,511.2	17.2%
Core Molding Technologies, Inc.	CMT	130.6	9.8	140.4	6.9%
Tupperware Brands Corporation	TUP	2,664.6	711.9	3,376.5	21.1%
Myers Industries, Inc.	MYE	429.3	189.5	618.8	30.6%
Alpha Pro Tech, Ltd.	APT	53.9	—	53.9	0.0%
Median		**429.3**	**189.5**	**618.8**	**17.2%**
Average		1,568.6	371.5	1,940.2	15.2%

estimate the optimal capital structure to be 15.0% debt-to-capital. The implied optimal equity-to-capital ratio for O&R is 1 minus the debt-to-capital ratio, or 85.0%.[8]

Having made a determination regarding the capital structure, you are now ready to develop estimates for your remaining elements in the WACC formula, the cost of equity and the cost of debt. For the purposes of this case study, we will start with the cost of equity and then later in this case return to address the cost of last checked.

Estimating the Cost of Common Equity

The methods commonly used to estimate the cost of common equity capital typically have the same basic framework:

Discount rate for equity capital = Risk-free rate + Premium for risk

The two commonly used methods used by valuation practitioners for estimating the discount rate applicable to discounting economic income to equity capital are:

- Build-up method; and
- Capital asset pricing model (CAPM).

Both of these methods start with a risk-free rate and then add incremental measures of risk in building-block fashion to account for the fact that investors demand *additional* return to induce them to invest in risky assets. The two methods are built on the same general foundation, but there are differences in the application.

Under the build-up method,[9] the cost of equity capital can be estimated as follows:

Formula 2:

$$E(R_i) = R_f + RP_m + RP_s \pm IRP_i \pm RP_c$$

[8]At market value weights.

[9]For a more detailed discussion of the build-up method, please see CofC5, Chapter 9, "Build-Up Method": 177–188.

where
$E(R_i)$ = Expected rate of return for common equity of company i
R_f = Rate of return on risk-free security
RP_m = Equity risk premium (market risk)
RP_s = Size premium for subject company i (when applicable)
IRP_i = Industry risk premium for industry of subject company i
RP_c = Company-specific risk premium for subject company i

The most frequently used alternative to the build-up method is the CAPM (a single-factor model) or a derivative thereof, the modified CAPM (MCAPM, a multi-factor model). The CAPM starts with a similar foundation as the build-up method starting with the risk-free rate and the ERP. The textbook or *pure* CAPM assumes that a security's equity risk premium (the required excess rate of return for a security over and above the risk-free rate) is a linear function of the security's beta. This linear function is described in this single independent variable linear regression formula:

Formula 3:

$$E(R_i) = R_f + B(RP_m)$$

where
$E(R_i)$ = Expected return (cost of capital) for common equity of company i
R_f = Rate of return on risk-free security
B = Beta appropriate for company i
RP_m = Equity risk premium (ERP) for the market as a whole

A fundamental assumption of the pure CAPM is that the risk premium portion of a company's expected return is a function of that company's market risk because CAPM assumes that investors hold, or have the ability to hold, common stocks in well-diversified portfolios. Under this assumption, investors will not require compensation (i.e., a higher return) for the unsystematic risk because they can easily diversify it away. Therefore, the only risk pertinent to a study of the *pure* CAPM is market or beta risk.

But other factors have been found to be priced by the market which are *systematic* and relevant to the estimation of cost of capital. This has led to expanded versions of the CAPM (i.e., the MCAPM) as well as other multi-factor models.[10] Similar to the build-up method, MCAPM contains elements that account for size and company-specific risk factors. If we modify CAPM to also reflect the size effect and company-specific risk, we can expand the cost of equity capital formula to add these two factors:

Formula 4:

$$E(R_i) = R_f + B(RP_m) + RP_s \pm RP_c$$

where
$E(R_i)$ = Expected rate of return for common equity of company i
R_f = Rate of return on risk-free security as of the valuation date
B = Beta appropriate for company i
RP_m = Market ERP
RP_s = Risk premium for small size of subject company (if applicable)
RP_c = Risk premium attributable to other company risk factors if applicable

Based on your analysis of the financial and operating characteristics of O&R you have determined that due to its relatively small size (at least in comparison to the public companies from which the equity risk premium is derived), and certain other risk factors that exist at O&R, you should utilize a model that accounts for these factors. Therefore, you determine that either the build-up method or the MCAPM will be appropriate. For the purposes of this case study, we will focus the discussion on the MCAPM.

Risk-Free Rate

The building block upon which both the CAPM and the MCAPM *start* is the risk-free rate. A "risk-free rate" is the return available, as of the valuation date, on a security that the market generally regards as free of the risk of default. In valuing "going concern" businesses such as O&R, practitioners generally use yields on long-term government bonds as the

[10] For example, the Fama-French 5-factor model. See Eugene Fama and Kenneth French, "A Five-Factor Asset Pricing Model," *Journal of Financial Economics* 116, no. 1 (April 2015): 1–22.

risk-free rate and estimate the ERP in relation to long-term government bond yields. This convention represents a realistic simplifying assumption when valuing going concern businesses.

It would seem that determining a yield on a US government security would be a rather simple exercise; however, there are decisions that must be made regarding the risk-free rate as there are a number of sources and approaches for obtaining the assumption for the risk-free rate.[11] For example, an argument can be made that the ultimate risk-free security is a short-term US Treasury bill. However, in estimating the cost of capital for equity investments, the short-term Treasury bill has an important shortcoming: its maturity does not match the expected life of most investments in businesses, which are typically assumed to be going concerns (i.e., to have an indefinite life).[12]

This brings us to an important concept. When developing cost of capital estimates, the valuation analyst should match the term of the risk-free rate used in the CAPM or MCAPM formulas with the duration of the expected net cash flows of the business, asset, or project being evaluated. Further, the term of the risk-free rate should also match the term of the risk-free rate used to develop the ERP. Specifically, the term of risk-free rate used in the CAPM or MCAPM should equal the expected duration of the net cash flows of the business, asset, or project being evaluated, and should also equal the term of the risk-free rate used to develop the ERP.

Therefore, most valuation analysts prefer to use the yield on a longer-term government bond as the risk-free component for estimating the cost of equity capital. For example, for valuations denominated in US dollars valuation analysts have traditionally used the spot yield to maturity (as of the valuation date) of a longer-maturity US government bond (e.g., the 10-year or 20-year US Treasury bond) as a proxy for the risk-free rate.[13]

---

[11]For a more in-depth discussion of the different sources for the risk-free rate assumption, please see CofC5, Chapter 7, "Risk-free Rate": 91–108.

[12]The expected life of an investment can be significantly different than a particular *investor's* expected or actual holding period of said investment.

[13]Most analysts in the US use the 20-year Treasury bond as the proxy for the risk-free security; use of a 10-year maturity is generally less common than use of the 20-year maturity.

A risk-free rate based on US government bond yields inherently builds in the expected long-term inflation expectations. Therefore, when this rate is used to estimate a discount rate to discount expected economic income, those future measures of economic income also should *also* reflect the expected effect of inflation. Therefore, it is important that you verify that the forecast that you received for O&R was created on a nominal (i.e., including inflation) rather than real (i.e., exclusive of inflation) basis. We'll assume for the purposes of this case study that this is the case.

Normalized Risk-Free Rates

It can be debated whether the spot yield on a long-term government bond is always the best measure to be employed for the risk-free rate. During times of crisis (e.g., the 2008 Financial Crisis or the COVID-19 Pandemic), the market yield on US government securities may decline dramatically over a short period of time due to a *flight-to-quality*. Government-issued bonds (i.e., *sovereign* bonds) have historically been regarded as a relatively safe haven in these times of economic uncertainty, and US government securities (alongside various others) are likely perceived as one of the safest of safe havens. Exacerbating the effect, in reaction to such crises, the US Federal Reserve Bank and other central banks often introduce programs to increase the money supply which can further depress yields on government bonds and potentially extend the duration of depressed yields if central banks are slow to unwind such programs once the crisis passes.

Using spot yields during times of crisis may distort estimates of the cost of capital because just as the risks are the greatest, the yields on this basic building block of the cost of equity capital decline — the opposite of what one would expect in times of relative economy-wide distress. Thus, a normalization adjustment may be considered appropriate by some analysts if all other factors are held the same. However, there are other analysts who will argue that regardless of the economic cycle or central bank intervention, notwithstanding any anomalies that may be observed, the spot yield should still be used. In our opinion, either position can be defensible but only if the ERP being used appropriately considers the selection of the risk-free rate, as will be discussed in more detail below.

By late 2016, O&R was operating in an economy that had largely recovered from the financial crisis that had begun some 8 years prior, so the capital markets were not in a "flight-to-quality" mode at the time. However, the Federal Reserve Bank had been very gradual in unwinding its accommodative monetary policy put in place during the financial crisis, such that Treasury yields, while well off their lows, were still historically low relative to long-term historical experience. Thus, if you were in the camp of analysts who prefer to normalize the risk-free rate, you could certainly justify your decision to do so; however, for the purposes of this case study, assume you have chosen to estimate the risk-free yield using the December 31, 2016 spot rate of 2.79%.

Equity Risk Premium

The next building block of the cost of equity is the equity risk premium. Equity holders receive returns from two potential sources: (1) receipt of available cash flow from the business in the form of dividends or distributions and (2) changes in the value of the underlying investment. Obviously, these expected returns on equities are much less certain (or are riskier) than the interest and maturity payments on US government obligations. This difference in risk is well documented by much greater standard deviations (year-to-year volatility) in returns on the stock market compared with the standard deviation of year-to-year returns on US government obligations. To accept this greater risk, investors demand higher expected returns for investing in equities than for investing in US government obligations. This differential in expected return on the broad stock market over US government obligations (sometimes referred to as the *excess return*) is called the *equity risk premium* (ERP) or, interchangeably, the *market risk premium*.

Like all estimates of cost of capital components (and the cost of capital itself) the ERP is a forward-looking concept. It is an expectation as of the valuation date for which no market quotes are directly observable. The ERP is a function of expected returns on a diversified portfolio of equities minus an expected yield on a risk-free security to which it is compared over a specified time period. There is no universally accepted methodology for estimating the ERP. A wide variety of premiums are used in practice and recommended by academics and financial advisors. These differences are often due to differences in how ERP is estimated.[14]

[14]For a more in-depth discussion of the different sources for the ERP assumption, please see CofC5, Chapter 8, "Equity Risk Premium": 117–131.

We will highlight a few of the methods for estimating the ERP below. The Cost of Capital Navigator — US Cost of Capital Module[15] provides three ERP estimates:

- Long-term, "historical" (i.e., realized) ERP
- Long-term, "supply-side" ERP
- Conditional, recommended ERP.

Historical ERP

In the realized (i.e., historical) ERP approach, the estimate of the ERP is the risk premium (realized return on stocks in excess of the risk-free rate) that investors have, on average, realized over some historical holding period. The underlying theory is that the past provides a reasonable indicator of how the market will behave in the future, and that investors' expectations are influenced by the historical performance of the market. Of course, because returns on both equity investments and US government bonds fluctuate from year to year, the estimate of the historical ERP will depend on the period of measurement. There is, however, no theoretical basis for choosing a look-back period other than to ensure that the period of review is sufficiently long to capture multiple economic cycles so as to minimize the impact of idiosyncratic returns that may have been realized during certain periods of the look-back period that would cause the historical series to become a poor estimate for the theoretical forward-looking rate.

The US Cost of Capital Module provides analysts with a historical long-horizon ERP calculated as the mean annual return of the S&P 500 *total* return[16] index minus the mean annual return of a long-term (20-year) US government bond *income* return series beginning in 1926 and running through the selected valuation date, in our case 2016.[17] The historical long-horizon ERP through December 31, 2016, was 6.94%.

---

[15]The Kroll Cost of Capital Navigator — US Cost of Capital Module is the online successor to the Duff & Phelps Valuation Handbook — US Guide to Cost of Capital.

[16]Total return consists of three components: (i) price (i.e., capital appreciation) returns, (ii) income returns (e.g., dividends), and (iii) reinvestment (e.g., of dividends) returns.

[17]Another source of historical ERP data is the Cost of Capital Professional platform which provides equity risk premia and size premia available by subscription at https://www.bvresources.com/products/cost-of-capital-professional.

Supply-Side ERP

The supply-side model decomposes historical equity returns into various "supply factors" including inflation, earnings, dividends, the price-to-earnings ratio, dividend payout ratio, book value, return on equity, and GDP per capita.[18] The model assumes that stock market returns are generated by the performance of companies in the real economy and that over the long run, equity returns should approximate the long-run supply estimate based on growth[19] or risk. For example, a portion of the returns on equity investments (generally) during the look-back period from 1926 can be attributed to expansion in price-to-earnings ratios. Since, as noted previously, the equity risk premium is a forward-looking concept, as an analyst, you must consider whether the historical observed expansion in price-to-earnings ratios would be expected to continue into the future. While further price-to-earnings ratio expansion is possible, you might take the position that the observed historical expansion is a non-recurring source of gains historically and that it is unlikely to be replicated. The supply-side risk premium is calculated in such a way as to adjust for this factor. The supply-side ERP data reported are again based on the entire series of years (1926 to the most recent year). Using the supply-side model, the US Cost of Capital Module reported an estimate of the ERP at the end of 2016 was 5.97%, approximately 1% less than that derived using the historical model (6.94%).

Conditional ERP

Typically, a discounted cash flow model estimates cash flows many years into the future (and often into perpetuity). Therefore, it is reasonable that the ERP being used should be a long-term estimate measured based on long-term data. However, these long-term measurements can sometimes yield counterintuitive results. For example, at a time of recession such as during the financial crisis that began in 2008 or in 2020 at the beginning of the COVID-19 pandemic, between the effects of the flight-to-quality on the markets, combined with massive Federal Reserve intervention, spot interest rates on US government securities declined sharply (resulting in an increase in bond prices) at the same time that equities performed poorly

---

[18]Roger G. Ibbotson and Peng Chen, "Long-Run Stock Returns: Participating in the Real Economy," *Financial Analysts Journal* 59, no. 1 (January/February 2003): 88–98. GDP = Gross Domestic Product.

[19]*Ibid.*, 91.

resulting in lower measured historical returns. This has the effect of *reducing* the measured historical ERP precisely at a time when intuitively one would expect the market to perceive *greater* risk in equity investments. In response to this effect, some practitioners employ a *conditional* ERP.

Research has shown that ERP varies through business cycles.[20] As the term *conditional ERP* is used to mean the ERP that reflects current market conditions, those market conditions reflect both the risk of investments and the collective risk aversion as viewed through the collective eyes of the marginal investors (those investors moving money into and out of investments at a particular date are the investors setting prices). For the marginal investor, the ERP should be greater when uncertainty is greater and less when uncertainty is less.[21]

When the economy is near or in recession (as reflected in relatively low returns on stocks and greater economic uncertainty, such as at the last several months of 2008 or at the end of the first quarter of 2020), the conditional ERP is likely at the higher end of the range. When the economy improves (with expectations of improvements reflected in recent increasing stock returns), the conditional ERP likely moves toward the midpoint of the range. When the economy is near its peak (and reflected in relatively high stock returns and increased economic certainty), the conditional ERP is likely at the lower end of the range.[22]

At times of flights-to-quality or massive Federal Reserve intervention in the markets, one must consider that if the ERP is estimated against the spot interest yields, the implied conditional ERP will be greater simply because spot yields could be considered abnormally low. Comparing conditional ERP estimates over time and comparing conditional ERP estimates

---

[20] See, for example, Robert D. Arnott, "Equity Risk Premium Myths," and Antti Ilmanen, "Time Variation in the Equity Risk Premium," in *Rethinking the Equity Risk Premium* (Research Foundation of CFA Institute, 2011).

[21] See, for example, Martin Lettau, Sydney Ludvigson, and Jessica Wachter, "The Declining Equity Risk Premium: What Role Does Macroeconomic Risk Play?" *Review of Financial Studies* 21, no. 4 (2008): 1675–1687. The authors linked changes in the ERP to changes in the volatility of economic variables such as employment, consumption, and growth in gross domestic product.

[22] Professor Aswath Damodaran publishes estimates of the implied ERP on his website which vary as the business cycle varies (see http://pages.stern.nyu.edu/~adamodar/New_Home_Page/datafile/histimpl.html); for details on how the calculations are made, see Aswath Damodaran, "Equity Risk Premiums (ERP): Determinants, Estimation and Implications — The 2021 Edition" (March 23, 2021). Available at SSRN: https://ssrn.com/abstract=3825823.

with realized risk premiums becomes difficult, as most prior years represented in the long-term means did not have interest rates influenced to the same extent by the Federal Reserve.

The Cost of Capital Navigator — US Cost of Capital Module provides an estimate for a conditional ERP based on multi-faceted analyses in order to take into account current economic information. After creating a reasonable range of unconditional ERPs, Kroll estimates where in that range the conditional ERP should lie by examining the current state of the economy as well as the perceived risk in the overall economy. Additionally, Kroll utilizes the following models to corroborate its recommended conditional ERP: the Damodaran Implied ERP Model, the Default Spread Model, and the Hassett Implied ERP.[23] Remember that what is important is not the individual components of this base equity discount rate (risk-free rate plus ERP). What matters is the total. As a general rule when using the conditional ERP as a reasonableness check, in times of crisis this base discount rate could be expected to be greater than it was in times just before the crisis.

Application to O&R

Circling back to how the above applies in our case study of O&R and focusing on the total between the risk-free rate and the ERP, if we use the spot risk-free yield as of December 31, 2016, of 2.79% and the supply-side ERP equal to 5.97%, the total *base* discount rate equals 8.76%. This compares to the normalized risk-free rate equal to 3.00% and the conditional ERP equal to 5.50%, for a total base discount rate equal to 8.50%. It stands to reason that these two values should be similar given that at the time of our case study, economic conditions were relatively stable. For the purposes of application in this case study, we will use the spot risk-free rate and the supply-side ERP.

Beta

Now that we have established estimates for our first two inputs into the cost of equity, it is necessary to begin to incorporate some of the specific

[23] See CofC5, Chapter 8, "Equity Risk Premium": 131–138; Professor Aswath Damodaran publishes estimates of the implied ERP on his website which vary as the business cycle varies (see http://pages.stern.nyu.edu/~adamodar/New_Home_Page/datafile/histimpl.html); for details on how the calculations are made, see Aswath Damodaran, "Equity Risk Premiums (ERP): Determinants, Estimation and Implications — The 2023 Edition" (March 23, 2023). Available at https://ssrn.com/abstract=4398884.

attributes of O&R itself into the equation. CAPM (and MCAPM) introduces *market* or *systematic risk* for a specific stock as a modifier to the general equity risk premium. Market risk for a particular stock is measured by a factor referred to as *beta.* Beta measures the sensitivity of excess total returns (total returns over the risk-free rates of return) on any individual security or portfolio of securities to the total excess returns on some measure of the market, such as the Standard & Poor's (S&P) 500 Index or the New York Stock Exchange (NYSE) Composite Index. Beta is an estimate of industry risk. In theory, beta equals:

Formula 5:

$$B_i = \frac{\text{Cov}(R_i, R_m)}{\text{Var}(R_m)}$$

where

B_i = Expected beta of the common stock of company i

R_i = Return on stock i

R_m = Return on market portfolio

$\text{Cov}(R_i, R_m)$ = Expected covariance between the excess return $(R_i - R_f)$ on stock of company i and the excess market return $(R_m - R_f)$

$\text{Var}(R_m)$ = Expected variance of excess return on the overall stock market

Covariance measures the degree to which two random variables (in this case, the return on a particular security and the overall market's return) move together. Covariance is not volatility. Covariance is a measure of the two variables' tendency to vary in the same direction and in the same relative amounts.

Like the other elements of the cost of capital, beta is a forward-looking concept as beta equals the *expected* covariance divided by the *expected* variance. However, if the probability distribution of historical returns has remained fairly stationary over time, then one would expect that historical returns and risk measured by beta can be used as estimates of expected returns. Remembering this caveat, we find that a common method of estimating *forward-looking* beta risk is to use realized returns on the stock of company i and the market portfolio, m, over a look-back period and run a regression. The regression beta is only an estimate of the expected relationships. Theoretically, the measure of beta is based on both the subject public company stock's and the market's *excess* return. As a practical matter, many data sources of beta use *total* returns. In most cases, the difference is insignificant.

Since O&R is not a publicly traded company, we do not have a means of directly observing its value on a frequent and regular basis. Therefore, it is not possible to directly measure the covariance of O&R's returns against those of the market. It is therefore necessary to develop a proxy beta, which can be estimated by:

a. Identifying the businesses in which the subject business operates;
b. Identifying guideline public companies (GPCs) and estimating their levered betas;
c. Unlevering the GPC beta estimates to get estimates of unlevered (asset) betas (discussed below);
d. Calculate a central tendency of these unlevered betas, such as a median, average, or weighted average where the weights are based on the relative values (or operating income) of the businesses in which the subject business operates; and
e. Levering the beta estimate using an appropriate debt-to-equity ratio for the subject business.

For the GPCs, which are publicly traded, the computation may be accomplished by performing an ordinary least squares (OLS) regression of the excess stock returns on the individual security against excess market returns during chosen sample (look-back) period. The resulting slope of the best-fit line is the beta estimate. Formula 6 shows the regression formula.

Formula 6:

$$(R_i - R_f) = \alpha + B(R_m - R_f) + \varepsilon$$

where
R_i = Historical return for publicly traded stock, i
R_f = Rate of return on risk-free security
α = Regression constant
B = Estimated beta based on historical data over the look-back period
R_m = Historical return on market portfolio, m
ε = Regression error term

A simpler method for many analysts is to use the built-in functions in Microsoft® Excel®. For example, the Excel *slope* function[24]:

= Slope(excess returns of Security A, excess returns of the S&P 500 Index)

Of course, the OLS regression equation to be used requires selection of a look-back period, as well as selection of the frequency of measurement. It is possible that an OLS regression based on, for example, monthly data measured over 5 years may differ materially from weekly-data measured over a 2-year period. While in general, greater statistical confidence is achieved by maximizing the number of data points, longer look-back periods could end up washing out important recent trends and higher frequency data may act to introduce noise that masks the true relationship between the company's risk and the market risk. Many practitioners will utilize a 5-year look-back using monthly data; however, the ultimate decision will come down to judgment based on facts and circumstances.

Adjustments to OLS Beta

Early on, researchers understood that betas estimated by OLS suffer from error in estimation and they would not forecast future betas correctly. Even though there is no one, widely acceptable technique, there are adjustment techniques that are discussed in the literature and often used.[25]

One possible adjustment (the Blume adjustment) is based on the observation that estimated beta coefficients have a tendency to converge towards 1.[26] Based on his research, Blume proposed multiplying the OLS beta estimate by two-thirds and adding one-third to mitigate the bias in the OLS estimate. This adjustment is expected to lower the difference between a historical beta and a future beta.

An alternative adjustment, the Vasicek shrinkage adjustment, shifts the OLS beta estimate towards a prior expectation, such as an industry

---

[24] There are multiple ways to perform regression analyses in Microsoft® Excel®. The *Slope* function is merely *one* of them.

[25] See, for example, Robert C. Klemkosky and John D. Martin, "The Adjustment of Beta Forecasts," *The Journal of Finance* 30, no. 4 (1975): 1123–1128.

[26] Marshall E. Blume, "Betas and Their Regression Tendencies," *The Journal of Finance* 30, no. 3 (1975): 785–795.

average, and the magnitude of that shift is greater when the standard error of the OLS estimate is higher. [27] That is, where the OLS beta estimate is more precise it is given more weight, and when it is less precise it is given less weight. Levi and Welsh suggested shrinking OLS betas using a Vasicek methodology twice to improve its forward-looking estimating power.[28]

In some instances. it may be appropriate to calculate a *sum beta* based on a lagged OLS regression analysis. Due to differences in analyst and press coverage, large and small companies' stocks may absorb information at different speeds with large company stock prices reacting to new fundamental or economic information nearly instantaneously while small companies with thinly traded stocks that may barely trade for days may require more time for new information to make its way into the stock price which could bias the OLS-based estimation of their betas. The sum beta consists of using the sum of the coefficients of the regression of small stocks excess returns on both current and lagged market excess returns to adjust for this bias. The sum beta,[29] which incorporates lagged market effects in the beta statistic.[30,31]

Finally, some researchers have found that OLS beta estimates are subject to misestimation due to the small fraction of exceptionally large or small returns, called outliers, that are not predictable with outliers observed more frequently for small companies.[32] In some instances, it may be appropriate to discard outliers based on their impact on residual

---

[27] Oldrich Vasicek, "A Note on Using Cross-sectional Information in Bayesian Estimation of Security Betas," *The Journal of Finance* 28, no. 5 (1973): 1233–1239.

[28] Yaron Levi and Ivo Welch, "Best Practice for Cost-of-Capital Estimates," *Journal of Financial and Quantitative Analysis* 52, no. 2 (2017): 427–463. Industry level Vasicek adjusted betas are provided in the US Benchmarking Module where company beta and the peer group (industry) beta are weighted. The greater the statistical confidence in the company beta, the greater the weight on the company beta relative to the peer group beta.

[29] Elroy Dimson, "Risk Measurement When Shares Are Subject to Infrequent Trading," *Journal of Financial Economics* 7, no. 2 (1979): 197–226.

[30] See, for example, Roger Ibbotson, Paul Kaplan, and James Peterson, "Estimates of Small Stock Betas Are Much Too Low," *Journal of Portfolio Management* 24 (1977): 104–111; Elroy Dimson, "Risk Measurement When Shares Are Subject to Infrequent Trading," *Journal of Financial Economics* 7, no. 7 (1979): 197–226.

[31] For a description of this method, see CofC5, Chapter 11, "Beta: Differing Definitions and Estimates": 212–214.

[32] R. D. Martin and T. T. Simin, "Outlier-Resistant Estimates of Beta," *Financial Analysts Journal* (September–October 2003): 56–69.

error in the fit to calculate a *true* beta, which provide a better estimate of forward-looking beta than the raw OLS calculation.

The above list is not meant to be an exhaustive list of possible adjustments to that may be considered. Ultimately the objective is to estimate the market's expectation of a forward-looking beta, which, of course, cannot be directly measured. Therefore, judgment is required when considering what, if any, adjustments are appropriate.

There may be circumstances in which computing your own OLS beta for GPCs and then applying adjustments may be impractical given the circumstances. In such cases, beta estimates can be obtained from a number of published sources. One will find significant differences among betas for the same stock published by different financial reporting services. This is due to differences in computation methods which can sometimes lead to widely divergent results. One of the implications of this is that the betas for all the GPCs used in a valuation should come from the same source. If not all the betas for the GPCs are available from a single source, the best solution is probably to use the source that provides betas for the largest number of GPCs, and to not use betas for the other GPCs. Ultimately, the decision on which betas to use involves judgment on the part of the analyst.

Many different financial reporting services publish betas for public company securities, a sampling of these services are shown in Exhibit 6.

Exhibit 6. Beta Measurement Characteristics of Financial Reporting Services

Financial Reporting Service	Market Index	Measurement Interval	Measurement Time Period	Paid/ Unpaid
Kroll Cost of Capital Navigator	S&P 500	Monthly	5 years	Paid
Bloomberg	S&P 500 and others	Daily, weekly, monthly, annually	Adjustable	Paid
Merrill Lynch	S&P 500	Monthly	5 years	Paid
S&P Compustat	S&P 500	Monthly	5 years	Paid
Value Line Investment Survey	NYSE Composite	Weekly	5 years	Paid
Yahoo Finance	S&P 500	Monthly	5 years	Unpaid
Refinitiv Eikon	S&P 500	Monthly	5 years	Paid
Capital IQ	S&P 500 and others	Monthly	5 years	Paid
Damodaran	S&P 500	Weekly	2 years and 5 years	Unpaid

Application to O&R

Since O&R is not publicly traded, in order to develop a proxy beta we will look to the set of GPCs identified previously. Exhibit 7 shows the previously-referenced capital structure as well as the relevant beta metrics for these companies.

Because three of the five GPCs above were rather small (by public company standards) and thus may not immediately absorb market information, you elected to use the sum beta as your starting point. You have no reason to believe that any particular GPC will provide a more accurate estimate for a proxy beta than any other, so you select the average of the set.[33] You then need to consider whether an adjustment, such as the Blume adjustment or Vasicek adjustment is warranted. The Vasicek adjustment would most likely utilize a GPC average or median as the reference point to which you would adjust, which in this case, is your starting point, so the Vasicek adjustment is not meaningful in this instance. The Blume adjustment, however, appears to be reasonable in this instance as a means to

Exhibit 7. Guideline Public Companies

Company Name	Ticker	Market Capitalization (in Millions of $)	Total Debt (in Millions of $)	Invested Capital (in Millions of $)	Debt/ Capital	OLS Beta	Sum Beta	Estimated Beta
AptarGroup, Inc.	ATR	4,564.7	946.6	5,511.2	17.2%	0.93	0.85	0.90
Core Molding Technologies, Inc.	CMT	130.6	9.8	140.4	6.9%	1.07	0.93	0.96
Tupperware Brands Corporation	TUP	2,664.6	711.9	3,376.5	21.1%	1.68	2.05	1.70
Myers Industries, Inc.	MYE	429.3	189.5	618.8	30.6%	1.46	1.20	1.14
Alpha Pro Tech, Ltd.	APT	53.9	—	53.9	0.0%	0.81	0.88	0.92
Median		**429.3**	**189.5**	**618.8**	**17.2%**	**1.07**	**0.93**	**0.96**
Average		1,568.6	371.5	1,940.2	15.2%	1.19	1.18	1.12

[33]Given the large differences in size within the GPC set, we utilized a straight average rather than an average weighted by market capitalization, to avoid concentrating the weighting among only the two largest GPCs.

account for the tendency of betas to revert to a mean of 1.0 over the full range of the business cycle. Applying the Blume adjustment to the average of the sum betas for the GPCs results in an estimated beta of 1.12 for O&R.

Levered and Unlevered Betas[34]

The amount of risk to which an equity investor is exposed is directly impacted by the degree of leverage employed with the investment. Published or calculated betas for public company stocks reflect the actual capital structure of each respective company. As a result, they can be referred to as *levered betas*, or betas reflecting the risks of the actual financial leverage of the company's capital structure. If the leverage of the company subject to valuation differs significantly from the leverage of the GPCs selected for analysis, it will be necessary to adjust the guideline betas for this difference before using them in estimating the required rate of return on equity for the subject company in the context of the CAPM or MCAPM.

This adjustment is performed by first computing *unlevered betas* for the guideline public companies. An unlevered beta is the beta that the company would have if it had no debt. The second step is to decide where the subject company's risk would fall on an unlevered basis relative to that of the GPCs. The third and final step is to lever the beta for O&R based on the assumed capital structure (determined to be 15% debt and 85% equity as determined previously). The result will be a market-derived beta that has been specifically adjusted for the degree of financial leverage of the subject company.[35]

The Hamada formula is one commonly used formula for computing an unlevered beta.

Formula 7:

$$B_U = \frac{B_L}{1 + \left[(1-T) \times \left(\frac{W_d}{W_e}\right)\right]}$$

[34]This section is adapted from CofC5, Chapter 12, "Unlevering and Levering Equity Betas": 243–261. Used with permission.

[35]Robert S. Hamada, "Portfolio Analysis, Market Equilibrium and Corporation Finance," *Journal of Finance* 24 (March 1969): 19–30.

where
B_U = Beta unlevered
B_L = Beta levered
T = Income tax rate for the company
W_d = Percentage of debt in the capital structure
W_e = Percentage of equity in the capital structure

Below is an example of the Hamada formula applied to sum beta for Tupperware Brands Corp., one of our GPCs.

Levered sum beta with Blume adjustment: 1.70 (from Exhibit 7)
Tax rate: 0.24
Capital structure: 21% debt, 79% equity (from Exhibit 7)

$$B_U = \frac{1.70}{1+\left[(1-0.24)\times\left(\frac{0.21}{0.79}\right)\right]}$$

$$B_U = \frac{1.70}{1+[(0.76)\times(0.268)]}$$

$$B_U = \frac{1.70}{1.20}$$

$$B_U = 1.42$$

We note that the Hamada formula may not provide reasonable unlevering of betas when certain simplifying assumptions are not met.[36] There are a number of alternative formulas that may be applied under circumstances in which the assumptions on which the Hamada formula is predicated to not

[36]The Hamada formula is predicated on the following assumptions:

1. The discount rate used to calculate the tax savings on interest expense equals the cost of debt capital (i.e., the tax savings on interest expense have the same risk as debt).
2. Tax deductions on the interest expense will be realized in the period in which the interest is paid.
3. The value of tax deductions on interest expense is proportionate to the market value of debt capital (i.e., $t \times W_d$).
4. The amount of debt capital is fixed as of the valuation date and remains constant.

Exhibit 8. Guideline Public Company Unlevered Betas

Ticker	Estimated Levered Beta	Debt/Capital	Tax Rate	Unlevered Beta
ATR	0.90	17.2%	31.4%	0.79
CMT	0.96	6.9%	32.9%	0.91
TUP	1.70	21.1%	24.3%	1.42
MYE	1.14	30.6%	32.8%	0.88
APT	0.92	0.0%	29.7%	0.92
Median	**0.96**	**17.2%**	**31.4%**	**0.91**
Average	1.12	15.2%	30.2%	0.98

hold.[37] Application of these alternative formulas is outside the scope of this case study. Making the calculations based on the Hamada formula for all the guideline public companies selected is shown in Exhibit 8.

For the purposes of this case study, assume you have assessed that the riskiness of O&R, on an unlevered basis, is about equal to the average for the GPCs. Thus, you have selected the average unlevered beta of the GPCs of 0.98. This is the proxy unlevered beta of O&R. The next step is to lever this unlevered beta based on O&Rs assumed capital structure with its assumed tax rate of 40%. The formula to adjust an unlevered beta to a levered beta is the reverse of Formula 7 as follows:

Formula 8:

$$B_L = B_U \times \left[1 + (1 - T) \times \left(\frac{W_d}{W_e}\right)\right]$$

where the definitions of the variables are the same as in the formula for computing unlevered betas except that they pertain to the subject closely held company.

Applying the formula for O&R:

Unlevered beta: 0.98
Tax rate: 0.40
Capital structure: 15% debt, 85% equity

[37]For further reading related to these alternative formulas and the conditions in which such alternative unlevering formulas should be applied, please see CofC5: 248–257.

$$B_L = 0.98 \times \left[1 + \left\{(1 - 0.40) \times \left(\frac{0.15}{0.85}\right)\right\}\right]$$

$$B_L = 0.98 \times \left[1 + \{(0.60) \times (0.18)\}\right]$$

$$B_L = 0.98 \times 1.11$$

$$B_L = 1.09$$

Size Premium

With $1 billion in sales in 2016, O&R is a fairly large closely-held company; however, relative to the companies of the S&P 500 from which the ERP is derived, O&R is a relatively small company. Thus, it is appropriate to consider how the company size might affect O&R's cost of capital. Many empirical studies performed since CAPM was originally developed have found that realized total returns on smaller companies have been substantially greater over a long period of time than pure CAPM (as given in Formula 3) would have predicted. The original size effect studies measured size based on market capitalization of equity; later studies expanded the definition of size to include accounting measures of size (e.g., net income). Although the size effect is not without its critics,[38] recent research continues to support the existence of such effect.[39]

There are currently two widely used sources of size premium data included in the US Cost of Capital Module:

---

[38] See a discussion of criticisms in CofC5, Chapter 15, "Criticisms of the Size Effect": 331–371.

[39] Clifford S. Asness, Andrea Frazzini, Ronen Israel, Tobias J. Moskowitz, and Lasse Heje Pedersen, "Size Matters, If You Control Your Junk," *Journal of Financial Economics* 129 (2018): 479–509. The authors find that a key variable in explaining the changing size effect over time is the markets pricing of firm quality (as measured by profitability, stability, growth, and safety) versus junk. This finding holds whether size is measured by market capitalization or non-market based ("fundamental") measures and holds for each of the 30 industries studied; see also Roger J. Grabowski, "The Size Effect Continues to Be Relevant When Estimating the Cost of Capital," *Business Valuation Review* 37, no. 3 (2018): 93–109. The author finds that the size effect is correlated to measures of fundamental risk and continues to be observed in recent periods among financially healthy, high-quality firms.

- The CRSP Deciles Size Study compiled by the Center for Research in Securities Prices (CRSP) at the University of Chicago.[40]
- Risk Premium Report (RPR) — Size Study.[41]

The size premia derived from these studies are sensitive to the method chosen for estimating beta. Over a given time horizon covered in its calculation, the sum beta approach tends to indicate *lower* size premia than other methods (e.g., beta estimated using ordinary least squares (OLS) regression of returns). Size premia estimates derived in the CRSP Size Study are based on OLS betas while the size premia estimates derived in the RPR are based on sum betas. Both find that size and return are negatively correlated (as size *decreases*, returns tend to *increases*, and vice versa).

CRSP Deciles Size Study

The CRSP Deciles Size Study is based on data from the Center for Research in Securities Prices at the University of Chicago. The CRSP Deciles Size Study examines the relationship between size, as measured by market capitalization, and return.

The CRSP Deciles Size Study includes risk-free rates, three choices of ERP, and size premia for (i) size groupings (Mid-Cap companies, Low-Cap companies, Micro-Cap companies) and (ii) Deciles groupings (1–10). Additionally, the CRSP deciles size premia data have been expanded to include a split of the 10th decile into *additional* size groupings — 10a (and its upper and lower halves 10w and 10x) and 10b (and its upper and lower halves 10y and 10z). These additional size premium categories

---

[40]The CRSP Deciles Size Study was first published in the Ibbotson® *Stocks, Bonds, Bills, and Inflation (SBBI) Valuation Yearbook* in 1999 and is now available in the online Kroll Cost of Capital Navigator-US Cost of Capital Module. The Kroll Cost of Capital Navigator-US Cost of Capital Module is available by subscription at www.kroll.com/costofcapital. One of the main sources of underlying data used to create the CRSP Deciles Size Study is: (i) CRSP US Stock Database and CRSP US Indices Database© (2020). CRSP® is a registered trademark and service mark of Center for Research in Security Prices, LLC and has been licensed for use by Kroll. The Kroll publications and services are not sponsored, sold, or promoted by CRSP.

[41]The Risk Premium Report has been published since 2000 and is available exclusively in the Kroll Cost of Capital Navigator — US Cost of Capital Module.

were introduced to help with the cost of capital estimation process for very small companies. The CRSP size premium data is summarized based on from 1926 through 2016 in Exhibit 9.[42]

To apply the CRSP Deciles Size Study to O&R, we must recognize that determining the proper size category requires knowledge of the value of O&R, which, of course, you need an estimate for the cost of capital in order to calculate. This creates a bit of an issue of a circular calculation. However, you could reasonably estimate that O&R falls near the top of the sixth decile category for the purposes of calculating an initial estimate of value based on the fact that O&R's 2016 EBITDA was $270 million and the median of the

Exhibit 9. Size Premium Data (1926–2016)

Decile	Range ($'000)		Size Premium
Mid-Cap (3 – 5)	2,392,689	10,711,194	1.02%
Low-Cap (6 – 8)	569,279	2,390,899	1.75%
Micro-Cap (9 – 10)	2,516	567,843	3.67%
1	24,361,659	609,163,498	–0.35%
2	10,784,101	24,233,747	0.61%
3	5,683,991	10,711,194	0.89%
4	3,520,566	5,676,716	0.98%
5	2,392,689	3,512,913	1.51%
6	1,571,193	2,390,899	1.66%
7	1,033,341	1,569,984	1.72%
8	569,279	1,030,426	2.08%
9	263,715	567,843	2.68%
10	2,516	262,891	5.59%
10a	127,296	262,891	4.09%
10w	190,553	262,891	3.10%
10x	127,296	190,383	5.33%
10b	2,516	127,279	8.64%
10y	73,561	127,279	7.21%
10z	2,516	73,504	11.63%

[42]The CRSP Deciles Size Study is available in the Cost of Capital Navigator — US Cost of Capital Module.

GPCs trailing EBITDA multiples as of 12/31/16 of approximately 9.0*x*, suggesting an equity value of approximately $2.35 billion.[43] To the extent that upon completing the valuation exercise, you discover that the company, in fact, falls into a different size category, say, the fifth decile category, with the greater information regarding the value of O&R, you may elect to run an additional iteration to adjust the size premium now that more precise information is available. For the purposes of this case study, however, we will simply rely on the sixth decile category for the size premium based on the estimated value of equity falling somewhere in the range of $1.6 billion and $2.4 billion, which is calculated to be 1.66%.

It is noteworthy that the size premium is *in addition* to the basic equity risk premium already modified by the effect of the beta, and betas for smaller stocks, if accurately measured, tend to be greater than those for larger stocks. This may be a factor worth considering when turning your attention to the company-specific risk factor discussed in a later section.

Risk Premium Report — Size Study[44]

Measuring size solely based on market value of equity has drawbacks. The market value of equity is a measure of market perception of the value of a company that may represent factors such as financial distress or other idiosyncratic factors that may make value a poor proxy for size. As an alternative that considers multiple other measures of size, a series of size premia studies are updated and published annually in the RPR — Size Study.[45] The RPR — Size Study quantifies the relationship between rates of return and accounting risk measures. The RPR study uses eight different measures of size:

---

[43] Calculated $270 million × 9.0 – $80.3 of current and long-term debt.

[44] The Risk Premium Report also contains the Risk Study which evaluates three fundamental risk measures of operating margin, the coefficient of variation of operating margin, and the coefficient of variation of return on book value of equity, and their correlation coefficients with observed equity risk premiums. This data can be used to further refine your cost of capital estimate based on analysis of these measures of risk. For further reading on the Risk Study contained in the RPR, please see CofC5, 508–509.

[45] "New Evidence of Size Effect and Equity Returns," *Business Valuation Review* (June 1994): 69–74 (covering the period 1963–1994); "Size Effect and Equity Returns: An Update," *Business Valuation Review* (March 1997): 22–26 (covering data through 1995 and 1996).

Measures of Equity Size:
Size premia are measured based on the size of the *equity* as measured by:

- *Market value of common equity* (common stock price times number of common shares outstanding)
- *Book value of common equity* (does not add back the deferred tax balance)
- *Five-year average net income* (net income before extraordinary items)

Measures of Company Size:
Size premia are measured based on the size of the company as measured by:

- *Market value of invested capital* [market value of common equity plus carrying value of preferred stock, long-term debt (including current portion) and notes payable]
- *Total assets* (as reported on the balance sheet)
- *Five-year average EBITDA* (operating income before depreciation plus nonoperating income)
- *Sales* (net)
- *Number of employees* (number of employees, either at year-end or yearly average, including part-time and seasonal workers and employees of consolidated subsidiaries; excludes contract workers and unconsolidated subsidiaries)

The data used in the RPR studies consist of a cross-section of company data drawn from the database of the CRSP and the S&P's *Compustat* database. The starting point for the studies is 1963 because the *Compustat* database covers public companies beginning in 1963. Excluded from the analysis are nonoperating companies and financial companies (i.e., companies in SIC code beginning with 6) and start-up and junk companies (i.e., companies lacking 5 years of history or with sales of less than $1 million or with a negative 5-year average EBITDA).[46,47]

---

[46]Because companies in SIC code beginning with 6 are excluded from the set of companies used to perform the analyses presented in the Risk Premium Report Study, the data should not be used by an analyst estimating the cost of equity capital for a financial services company or other company in SIC code beginning with 6.

[47]In addition to the 25 size-ranked portfolios, portfolios are created to include high-leverage and financially distressed companies — the high-financial-risk portfolio.

The data displayed from the RPR – Size Study in Exhibit 10 shows greater returns to portfolios with greater standard deviations of returns. Exhibit 10 includes summary statistics for portfolios 1–25 from the RPR – Size Study (data through December 31, 2016). In Exhibit 10, as size (as measured by 5-year average EBITDA in this case) *decreases*, average return tends to *increase*, from 12.49% for portfolio 1 (comprised of the largest companies), to 21.13%.[48]

Exhibit 10. Risk Premium Report Data for 2016 Based on Average EBITDA

Portfolio Rank by Size	Average EBITDA (in $millions)	Log of Average EBITDA	Beta (Sum Beta) Since '63	Arithmetic Average Return	Arithmetic Average Risk Premium	Indicated CAPM Premium	Premium over CAPM	*Smoothed Premium over CAPM*
1	22,452	4.35	0.79	12.49%	6.03%	3.99%	2.05%	*0.87%*
2	6,905	3.84	0.84	13.10%	6.65%	4.23%	2.42%	*1.65%*
3	4,343	3.64	0.88	13.07%	6.62%	4.44%	2.18%	*1.96%*
4	3,136	3.50	0.90	13.36%	6.90%	4.54%	2.35%	*2.17%*
5	2,192	3.34	0.98	13.63%	7.17%	4.94%	2.23%	*2.41%*
6	1,632	3.21	0.93	14.25%	7.79%	4.65%	3.14%	*2.60%*
7	1,338	3.13	1.03	13.85%	7.39%	5.18%	2.21%	*2.74%*
8	1,133	3.05	1.06	13.88%	7.42%	5.32%	2.10%	*2.85%*
9	934	2.97	1.11	13.04%	6.58%	5.59%	0.99%	*2.97%*
10	799	2.90	1.08	13.92%	7.46%	5.43%	2.03%	*3.08%*
11	667	2.82	1.02	15.56%	9.10%	5.13%	3.98%	*3.20%*
12	578	2.76	1.09	16.11%	9.66%	5.47%	4.19%	*3.29%*
13	478	2.68	1.07	15.80%	9.34%	5.36%	3.97%	*3.42%*
14	411	2.61	1.16	16.63%	10.18%	5.81%	4.36%	*3.52%*
15	371	2.57	1.14	14.38%	7.92%	5.73%	2.19%	*3.59%*
16	327	2.51	1.18	15.81%	9.36%	5.91%	3.45%	*3.67%*
17	287	2.46	1.19	16.05%	9.59%	5.98%	3.61%	*3.76%*
18	253	2.40	1.20	16.51%	10.05%	6.02%	4.03%	*3.84%*
19	211	2.32	1.23	16.07%	9.62%	6.16%	3.46%	*3.96%*
20	164	2.22	1.23	14.93%	8.47%	6.20%	2.27%	*4.13%*
21	125	2.10	1.20	16.86%	10.40%	6.04%	4.36%	*4.31%*
22	94	1.97	1.22	17.45%	11.00%	6.15%	4.84%	*4.49%*
23	74	1.87	1.23	17.60%	11.14%	6.15%	4.99%	*4.66%*
24	51	1.71	1.25	16.87%	10.41%	6.27%	4.14%	*4.90%*
25	17	1.23	1.30	21.13%	14.67%	6.55%	8.12%	*5.63%*

[48] The Risk Premium Report — Size Study uses return data beginning in 1963; other studies with return data from other periods show similar results.

Exhibit 11. Select Size Premia Data for O&R

Metric	Market Value of Equity	Book Value of Equity	5-year Average of NI	Market Value of Inv. Cap.	Book Value of Assets	5-year Average EBITDA	Sales	Number of Employees	Avg.
Measure	$2,349.7	$1,460.7	$85.4	$2,764.4	$2,134.0	$192.7	$1,000.0	5,000	
Portfolio Rank	16	14	18	17	18	19	21	17	
Premium* Over CAPM	3.62%	3.34%	3.97%	3.40%	3.93%	3.96%	4.49%	3.98%	**3.84%**

Note: *Represents smoothed averages.

For O&R, you can identify where it would fall in each of the size categories in Exhibit 10. As was an issue with the CRSP Decile Studies, some of the measures require knowledge of the value of O&R. A similar iterative approach, using a reasonable guess for the value of O&R can be used here as well. You have a general idea that the value of the invested capital of O&R is somewhere in the range of $2.4 billion putting O&R closest to the 18th portfolio grouping, and the value of the total equity of O&R is in the range of $2.3 billion placing O&R closest to the 14th portfolio grouping. The estimated equity returns for the relevant size portfolios for O&R are shown in Exhibit 11.

The RPR — Size Study provides two sets of size premia data (1) for use in the build-up method (risk premia over the risk-free rate) and (2) for use in the MCAPM. As an analyst, you deem each of the eight categories above to be an equally valid measure of size. Since you are applying the MCAPM, you select the average of the Premia over CAPM of 3.84% to be applied in your model.

Company-Specific Risk Premium

The notion that the only component of risk that investors care about, in the pure CAPM, is market risk (or systematic risk is) based on the assumption that all unique or unsystematic risk can be eliminated by holding a perfectly diversified portfolio of risky assets that will, by definition, have a beta of 1.0. But in practice we find that the term company-specific risk has various uses. At a basic level, the concept that returns *increase* with the standard deviation of returns (i.e., uncertainty) and not just beta is especially important for the valuation of closely held stocks. Most owners of closely held businesses or interests in closely held businesses are not in a position to diversify their investment portfolios nearly to the extent to which investors diversify their holdings of publicly traded stocks. Thus, since the unsystematic portion of total risk is unlikely to be diversified away to the same extent as for a portfolio of publicly traded securities, it is worth considering reflecting at least some part of unsystematic risk — as well as systematic risk — in estimating an appropriate expected rate of return. Thus, to the extent that the subject company's risk characteristics are greater or less than the typical risk characteristics of the GPCs from which the other components of the cost of equity were derived, a further adjustment may be necessary.

Quantification of the company-specific risk factor, under either the build-up method or MCAPM requires considerable judgment. Unlike the other building blocks of the cost of equity capital, there is not a broad set of actual or proxy market data on which to rely because company-specific risk factors are by their very nature, unique to the subject company.

Such an adjustment may be based on analysis of a number of factors. One such factor may be company size. Although presumably already captured in the size premium, if the subject company is significantly smaller than even the smallest size groupings, it may be appropriate to further adjust for size. This might be quantifiable by extrapolating based on the size premium data available to even smaller sizes.

It may also be appropriate to make an additional adjustment to account for industry risk. To the extent that the industry as a whole is sensitive to market movements, a portion of the industry's risk would be captured in beta or the IRP, measures of market risk that will capture at least some industry risk; but other industry risk factors may be systematic. If, after evaluating the GPCs, you determine that O&R has unique exposure to industry conditions such that a development within the industry could have an outsized impact on O&R, then an adjustment would be justified. For example, were you to discover that O&R is choosing to not to hedge the pricing on its feedstock while most industry competitors, including the GPCs, do choose to actively hedge their feedstock costs, then an adjustment may be justified.[49]

The effect of leverage may also warrant an adjustment for company-specific risk. Although in the MCAPM analysis, beta is modified to

[49]This example is for illustrative purposes only. In this subject case study, since your objective is to value O&R on a control basis, you will likely reason that upon acquiring control of O&R, you would likely modify the hedging strategy to be consistent with other industry participants.

account for the effect of leverage on the systematic risk, to the extent that there are unsystematic risk factors, the presence of above-average leverage will act to exacerbate them.

Finally, fundamental company-specific risk factors should be considered. These can include a variety of issues facing a company. Examples of these factors could include key-person risk, customer concentration, geographic or market segment concentration, or unique exposure to the regulatory environment, to name a few. Let's suppose as you were conducting due diligence on O&R, you discover that a key member of the sales staff holds the relationships with O&Rs three largest customers, which make up almost half of its revenue. While the salesperson is subject to a covenant-not-to-compete, recent case law in the state in which the salesperson lives and works suggests that the covenant's enforceability is limited. Certainly, all else equal, a company without such key person exposure is less risky than O&R. Even if you are able to estimate the cash-flow impact in the discounted cash flow model such that your cash flows truly represent the expected (i.e., probability-weighted average) cash flows, the standard deviation of returns will still be greater for O&R than for an otherwise identical company without the key person risk.

Of course, there could be circumstances where the company-specific risk premium could be negative if you concluded that O&R was less risky than the average of the other companies from which the proxy estimates for the other elements of the cost of equity capital were drawn. For example, perhaps in your due diligence of O&R you discover that it has a well-protected, above-average price for its products as a result of a strong trademark, resulting in less earnings volatility than that of its competitors.

For the purposes of this case study, assume that in your final analysis you determine that the risk arising from customer concentration and key person risk at O&R is only partially offset by its strong brand. Ultimately, you elect to include a 1% company-specific risk factor in your cost of equity calculation.

Concluded Cost of Equity

At this point, you have two different potential size premium applications. Reasonable analysts may diverge in terms of which of the above are utilized to determine the cost of equity. For the purposes of this case study, you decide that you elect to use the RPR size premium study given that it includes consideration for eight different dimensions of size. Thus, recapping the components of the cost of equity:

R_f = 2.79% — the spot yield on 20-year US government bonds as of December 31, 2016;

ERP = 5.97% — the supply-side equity risk premium measured from 1926 to 2016;

Beta = 1.09 — unlevered and levered for O&R's capital structure based on GPCs;

Size premium = 3.84% — based on the RPR average of the eight size measures;

Company-specific risk factor = 1.00% — key person and customer concentration partially offset by O&Rs strong trademark.

Taking these inputs and applying them into the MCAPM formula (Formula 4) below:

$$E(R_i) = R_f + B(RP_m) + RP_s \pm RP_c$$
$$E(R_{O\&R}) = 2.79\% + 1.09(5.97\%) + 3.84\% + 1.00\% = 14.14\%$$

Estimating the Cost of Debt

Now that you have completed the determination of the cost of equity, it is necessary to develop an estimate for the cost of debt. The cost of debt is a function of a number of factors, most important of which is the credit quality of the subject company. Additionally, borrowing costs will vary depending on the duration of the debt. Under most (but importantly, not all) circumstances, as the term of the debt increases, the cost of borrowing increases. Because the discounted cash flow model represents a long-term cash flow series, it is important that we develop a cost of debt assuming a long-term duration. In the case of O&R, you developed our cost of equity using an ERP that was measured based on returns of stocks relative to a 20-year maturity bond so it would be reasonable to target a cost of borrowing based on a similar assumed maturity.

There are a number of sources you might want to look to in developing an estimate for the cost of debt. Of course, information regarding

O&R's actual cost of debt can be readily determined by simply reviewing its audited financial statements. However, because you are valuing a controlling interest in O&R, to the extent that the actual capital structure has not been optimized by current management, a control level buyer would anticipate restructuring the capital structure to optimize the capital structure. This would likely result in a different borrowing cost than is currently in place. That said, you will still want to be aware of the rates that O&R's is paying for its existing debt, even if simply for a reasonableness check of your concluded cost of debt. You will also want to look at the rates that the GPCs are paying, especially if there are one or more GPCs whose capital structure closely matches your assumed capital structure. Finally, in many instances, it will be necessary to conduct a credit quality analysis and use publicly available information on borrowing costs for different credit ratings in order to develop your estimate.

Subject Company Borrowing Rates

Many companies have multiple sources of debt. Examples include lines of credit, term loans, leases, corporate bonds, subordinated or mezzanine debt, and convertible debt. Debt can be floating, fixed, or a hybrid where the rate floats subject to caps and/or floors. This debt may or may not be collateralized with specific assets of the Company, and in some cases, may be backed by third-party or personal guarantees (this is particularly common for smaller family-owned businesses). Thus, the question of what the subject companies' borrowing rate is, may not be simple. Furthermore, the majority of the subject company's borrowings may be short term, while, as noted previously, when developing an estimate of the WACC, a long-term estimate is needed. In short, there is a lot to consider when estimating a company's actual cost of debt. Depending on how much reliance will be placed on the actual cost of debt, a significant amount of analysis may be needed.

For O&R, we note that as of the end of 2016, the Company had approximately \$80 million in current and long-term debt compared to approximately \$45 million at the beginning of the year, suggesting average debt over the course of the year of approximately \$62 million. Interest expense during 2016 was \$3.4 million suggesting a cost of debt over the course of the year of 5.44%. This exercise provides perhaps a bit of an imprecise estimate of the actual cost of debt, but as noted previously, since we will need to consider that the assumed capital structure is not matching the actual capital structure for O&R, you will want to look to other indications to determine the cost of debt, so this imprecise calculation will only be used as a reasonableness test.

Guideline Public Companies

After analyzing the capital structures of the GPCs, AptarGroup, Inc., with a debt to capital ratio of 17.1% held the closest capital structure to the assumed capital structure for O&R of 15.0% debt and 85.0% equity. A review of AptarGroup's public filings shows that AptarGroup's borrowings include senior unsecured notes with maturities ranging from 1 to 10 years at fixed interest rates ranging from 3.2 to 6.0% with the longest (10-year) maturity at 3.6%. These notes, however, were placed in a private placement and are not publicly traded. Thus, the rates on these notes are not necessarily reflective of a market rate of interest as of December 2016 because market rates may have changed or the company's credit quality may have changed since issuance. Had AptarGroup had publicly traded corporate bonds outstanding, the rates on such debt would have been more meaningful. In this instance, however, you will need to rely on other indications to derive a cost of debt.

Rates Based on Bond Ratings

An analysis of key measures of credit quality can be used to determine what a rating agency, such as S&P or Moody would assign to O&R if it were to issue publicly traded debt. You can then use that hypothetical credit rating, along with information from the public debt markets, to develop an estimate for the long-term cost of debt for O&R. An important note, because you are developing our cost of debt estimate based on an assumed capital structure as opposed to the actual capital structure for O&R, it may be necessary to make some pro-forma adjustments to the credit quality statistics.

Exhibit 12 reflects average ratios for the different credit ratings as of December 31, 2020.[50]

Based on this information you can compare O&Rs financial ratios to the average debt rating ratios above to assess what O&Rs credit rating would be if it were scored by the credit rating agencies. However, because

---

[50] While this data was compiled after the effective date, credit quality statistics tend to be relatively stable such that it is reasonable to utilize these credit quality statistics for an analysis effective at an earlier time period.

Exhibit 12. Average Credit Quality Ratios

	Median Fundamentals for the S&P 500 Companies					
Metric	**AAA**	**AA**	**A**	**BBB**	**BB**	**B**
Leverage & Coverage						
Total Debt/EBITDA	1.3x	1.3x	4.3x	3.8x	5.6x	4.2x
Net Debt/EBITDA	0.3x	0.8x	3.3x	3.3x	4.7x	3.2x
Total Debt to BV Invested Capital	37.9%	35.9%	46.0%	50.8%	79.8%	52.8%
EBITDA/Interest	83.5x	93.5x	20.1x	13.6x	7.0x	2.9x
Liquidity & Cash Flow						
Current Ratio	2.0x	1.8x	1.5x	1.8x	1.6x	1.2x
Cash Ratio	1.4x	1.1x	0.6x	0.6x	0.7x	0.6x

Source: Based on the average credit quality ratios as compiled from data obtained from Capital IQ.

we are assuming a capital structure that differs from the actual capital structure, it is necessary to create pro-forma financial ratios assuming that O&R had a capital structure in line with the assumed capital structure. This will require that we compute ratios using a pro-forma value for debt as well as a pro-forma estimate for interest expense. As a starting point, you can use book values for this calculation as shown in Formula 9 below:[51]

Formula 9:

$$(BV_e + BV_d) \times W_d = PFV_d$$

where
BV_e = Book value of equity;
BV_d = Book value of debt;
W_d = Assumed weight of debt in the capital structure; and
PFV_d = Pro-forma value of debt.

The calculation is thus: (\$1,460.7 million + \$80.3 million) × 15.0% = \$231.2 million.

After completing the valuation exercise, you will likely come to a concluded value for equity that differs from the book value you used as a starting point, so it may be necessary to re-run the formula above with concluded market values replacing the book values. This iterative process

[51] Alternatively, you can use any reasonable estimate for the market value as your starting point for this analysis rather than book value.

should rapidly converge so you will likely only need to run one or two iterations before your pro-forma debt value is stable.[52] Exhibit 13 reflects the pro-forma debt calculation for the historical period.

Once completing your estimate of the debt value for your pro-forma calculation, you will need to estimate a pro-forma interest expense. As a starting point, you can use the 5.44% interest rate calculated based on the historical interest expense/average debt outstanding calculation run previously. Again, this may be necessary to run an additional iteration if the concluded cost of debt no longer reasonably approximates the interest rate used as a starting point. This iterative process should also converge quickly and the likelihood of needing to run more than one extra iteration is low. Exhibit 14 reflects the pro-forma interest expense calculation as well as relevant pro-forma income statement metrics. Exhibit 15 reflects the relevant actual historical metrics at book values for O&R.

MVIC is estimated at 9.0 times EBITDA for each year (from Exhibit 1). Market value of equity equals MVIC minus pro-forma debt.

Exhibit 13. Odd & Rich Pro-Forma Debt and Equity

(in Millions of $)	2012	2013	2014	2015	2016
MVIC	1,395.0	1,492.2	1,478.7	1,872.0	2,430.0
× Debt-to-Capital Assumed	15.0%	15.0%	15.0%	15.0%	15.0%
Pro-forma Debt	209.3	223.8	221.8	280.8	364.5
Market Value of Equity	1,185.8	1,268.4	1,256.9	1,591.2	2,065.5

Exhibit 14. Odd & Rich Pro-Forma Interest Expense

(in Millions of $)	2013	2014	2015	2016
Average Pro-Forma Debt	216.5	222.8	251.3	322.7
× Interest Rate	5.44%	5.44%	5.44%	5.44%
Pro-Forma Interest Expense	11.8	12.1	13.7	17.6
Actual EBIT	112.2	110.0	158.1	216.2
Pro-Forma Interest Expense	11.8	12.1	13.7	17.6
Pro-Forma EBT	100.4	97.9	144.4	198.6
Actual Non-Operating	2.7	6.8	—	—
Pro-Forma Pretax Income	103.1	104.7	144.4	198.6
Pro-Forma Income Tax	37.3	28.0	38.9	79.5
Pro-Forma NI	65.9	76.6	105.6	119.2

[52]For simplicity, only one iteration of the calculation was performed.

Exhibit 16 reflects the relevant pro-forma financial ratios for O&R based on the analysis above with bolded figures reflecting values that changed as a result of the pro-forma adjustment.[53]

Debt-to-EBITDA for 2016 is calculated as follows:

Actual: \$80.3 million/\$270.0 million = $0.3x$[54]

Pro-forma: \$364.5 million/\$270 million = $1.4x$

Exhibit 15. Odd & Rich Historical Ratios at Book Values (BV)

	2012	2013	2014	2015	2016
Leverage & Coverage					
Total Debt/EBITDA	0.3x	0.3x	0.4x	0.2x	0.3x
Net Debt/EBITDA	–0.6x	–0.6x	–0.4x	–0.6x	–0.3x
Total Debt/BV Total Capital	3.1%	4.2%	4.8%	3.1%	5.2%
Total Debt/BV Total Equity	3.7%	5.0%	5.7%	3.8%	6.8%
EBITDA/Interest	12.1x	46.1x	8.8x	67.1x	79.4x
Liquidity & Cash Flow					
Current Ratio	1.8x	1.7x	1.7x	1.2x	1.2x
Quick Ratio	1.4x	1.3x	1.3x	0.9x	0.9x

Exhibit 16. Odd & Rich Historical and Pro-Forma 2016 Ratios

	O&R – 2016	
	Actual	Pro-Forma
Leverage & Coverage		
Total Debt/EBITDA	0.3x	**1.4x**
Net Debt/EBITDA	–0.3x	**0.7x**
Total Debt/Book Value of Invested Capital	3.3%	**23.7%**
Total Debt/Total Equity	5.0%	**17.6%**
EBITDA/Interest	79.4x	**15.4x**
Liquidity & Cash Flow		
Current Ratio	1.2x	1.2x
Cash Ratio	0.9x	0.9x

[53] Ratios shown in bold were changed based on the assumed capital structure of 15.0% debt and 85.0% equity.

[54] \$80.3 equals Current Debt plus Debt for 2016 from Exhibit 2. \$270.0 EBITDA for 2016 from Exhibit 1.

EBITDA-to-interest is calculated as follows:

Actual: \$270.0 million/\$3.4 million = 79.4x[55]

Pro-forma: \$270.0 million/\$17.6 million = 15.3x

Based on this information, you estimate the credit rating that would correspond to each financial metric as shown in Exhibit 17.

Based on this analysis you estimate that the debt of O&R would, under the assumed capital structure, be assigned a rating of say "A" or "AA" by S&P. Obviously, not all categories fall into the same credit rating. Accordingly, a subjective assessment of the various indications will be necessary in developing your estimate for O&R's hypothetical credit rating.

Exhibit 17. Credit Rating Analysis

	Median Fundamentals for the S&P 500 Companies							Rating
Metric	**AAA**	**AA**	**A**	**BBB**	**BB**	**B**	**O&R**	**Rank**
Leverage & Coverage								
Total Debt/EBITDA	1.3x	1.3x	4.3x	3.8x	5.6x	4.2x	1.4x	AA
Net Debt/EBITDA	0.3x	0.8x	3.3x	3.3x	4.7x	3.2x	0.7x	AA
Total Debt to BV Invested Capital	37.9%	35.9%	46.0%	50.8%	79.8%	52.8%	23.7%	AAA
EBITDA/Interest	83.5x	93.5x	20.1x	13.6x	7.0x	2.9x	15.4x	BBB - A
Liquidity & Cash Flow								
Current Ratio	2.0x	1.8x	1.5x	1.8x	1.6x	1.2x	1.2x	B
Cash Ratio	1.4x	1.1x	0.6x	0.6x	0.7x	0.6x	0.9x	A - AA

Exhibit 18. Interest Rates as of December 31, 2016

S&P Capital Rating	**AAA**	**AA**	**A**	**BBB**	**BB**	**B**
10–15 Year	3.60%	4.41%	4.64%	4.61%	6.10%	7.26%
15–20 Year	3.97%	4.60%	5.54%	4.98%	6.57%	7.45%
20–25 Year	N/A	N/A	N/A	5.19%	6.82%	8.06%
Selected*	3.79%	4.51%	5.09%	5.19%	6.82%	8.06%

*Based on 20–25 year when available. When not available, based on the average of the remaining categories.

[55] From Exhibit 1.

Information for the range of interest rates can be found at the Intercontinental Exchange Inc. Index Platform.[56] An example of this data is shown in Exhibit 18.

Based on this information, we are able to estimate a cost of debt of 4.51% based on the debt rating we selected of AA (for this case).

Determination of the WACC

Now that we have our input for the weight of debt and equity, the cost of equity, and cost of debt, we can apply that input into the WACC formula (Formula 1),

Cost of equity: 14.14%
Cost of debt: 4.51%
Income tax rate: 0.40
Capital structure: 15% debt, 85% equity

$$\text{WACC} = K_e \times W_e + K_d(1 - T) \times W_d$$
$$\text{WACC} = 14.14\% \times (85.00\%) + 4.51\% \times (1 - 0.40) \times 15.00\%$$
$$\text{WACC} = 12.42\%$$

The Assignment

1. Assume that when your private equity firm acquires O&R, you are planning to use 50% leverage (i.e., debt to capital) at the time of

[56]Used with permission. ICE Data Indices, LLC ("ICE DATA"), is used with permission. ICE® is a registered trademark of ICE DATA or its affiliates, and BOFA® is a registered trademark of Bank of America Corporation licensed by Bank of America Corporation or its affiliates ("BOFA") and may not be used without BOFA'S prior written approval. ICE DATA, its affiliates and their third party suppliers disclaim any and all warranties and representations, express and/or implied, including any warranties of merchantability or fitness for a particular purpose or use, including the indices, index data and any data included in, related to, or derived therefrom. Neither ICE DATA, its affiliates nor their respective third party suppliers shall be subject to any damages or liability with respect to the adequacy, accuracy, timeliness or completeness of the indices or the index data or any component thereof, and the indices and index data and all components thereof are provided on an "as is" basis and your use at your own risk. ICE DATA, its affiliates and their respective third party suppliers do not sponsor, endorse, or recommend any part of this publication.

purchase, with the leverage trending back to the industry average over time due to principal repayment. How would your analysis be different?

2. Assume instead of seeking to acquire a controlling interest in O&R, your firm instead was going to acquire a minority position in the company with existing management remaining in pace. How might your cost of capital analysis be different?
3. How might your cost of capital analysis be different if you had been computing the WACC near the beginning of the COVID-19 pandemic in March of 2020 rather than December 2016?

Part III

Capital Budgeting

https://doi.org/10.1142/9789811216749_0007

Case 7

Vitamin Shoppe Capital Budgeting Case

Ivan E. Brick

Rutgers Business School, USA

Introduction

Vitamin Shoppe is a retailer of over 17,000 nutritional supplements sold through its brick-and-mortar retail stores, e-commerce division, and manufacturing division. It was founded by Jeffrey Horowitz in 1977. The first store was located on the East Coast in New York City. There are over 775 Vitamin Shoppe stores nationwide (including in Puerto Rico) and its market share is 2.7%. Its main brick-and-mortar retail competitor, GNC, has a market share of 3.5%. Other mortar and brick competitors include Whole Foods, Natural Grocers, Sprouts Farmers Market, Vitamin World, Costco, Wal-Mart, Rite-Aid, CVS, and Walgreens. Vitamin Shoppe has launched its e-commerce store, vitaminshoppe.com, which operates as its own entity. The main competitors to vitaminshoppe.com are bodybuilding.com and vitaminworld.com. Other internet and mail order companies that directly compete with vitaminshoppe.com are Amazon.com, Puritan's Pride, Vitacost.com, Bodybuilding.com, Doctors Trust, Swanson, and iHerb. As of December 31, 2016, Vitamin Shoppe has a total of 3,887 full-time and 1,616 part-time employees. Exhibit 1 provides a summary of key income statistics based upon the SEC 10K report that company filed for fiscal year 2016.

The customer base proactively manages their health and wellness through the use of vitamins and supplements. Vitamin Shoppe's Healthy

Exhibit 1. Income Statement Summary — All Figures Are in Thousands of Dollars

Fiscal Year	2016	2015	2014	2013	2012
Net Sales	$1,289,243	$1,266,549	$1,213,046	$1,087,469	$950,902
Cost of Goods Sold	$862,887	$847,634	$808,787	$709,823	$617,920
Gross Profit	$426,356	$418,915	$404,259	$377,646	$332,982
Selling, General and Adm. Exp.	$380,779	$329,922	$301,603	$267,354	$233,610
Income from Operations	$45,577	$88,993	$102,656	$110,292	$99,372
Interest	$9,523	$1,105	$495	$495	$659
Income Before Taxes	$36,054	$87,888	$102,161	$109,797	$98,713
Income Taxes	$11,090	$34,717	$40,920	$43,251	$37,888
Net Income	$24,964	$53,171	$61,241	$66,546	$60,825

Exhibit 2. Operating Data by Fiscal Year

	2016	2015	2014	2013	2012
Number of Stores	775	758	717	659	579
Total Retail Square Feet	2,709,000	2,662,000	2,568,000	2,390,000	2,130,000
Average Store Square Footage	3,495	3,511	3,582	3,627	3,679

Awards program helps to promote brand loyalty by allowing customers to earn points redeemable for future purchase. In fiscal 2016, 86% of net sales were attributable to the company's Healthy Awards customers. Vitamin Shoppe locates its stores primarily in attractive stand-alone locations or endcap (corner) positions in retail centers. The primary advantage for Vitamin Shoppe, when compared to its main competitor GNC, is that its brick-and-mortar locations are significantly bigger than GNC locations offering more spacious and less cluttered shopping experience for its customers. Exhibit 2 provides real estate dimensions of Vitamin Shoppe's retail stores per fiscal year since 2012.

To maintain its market share, the company's management would like to expand into more retail markets. Brenda Galgano, CFO, of Vitamin Shoppe approached Marc McDonald, a financial analyst of the Financial Planning Analyst group to examine the viability of opening a new store. The Real Estate group is recommending that Vitamin Shoppe build a retail outlet in a corner lot of a shopping strip on Bowman Road in Mount Pleasant, South Carolina. Mount Pleasant is a suburb of Charleston, located across the Cooper River. The preliminary demographics favor the location. The firm prefers to locate its shops where the median age of the population is above 35 within a 5 mile radius, and that the daily traffic passing the store site is a minimum of 20,000. The Bowman Road location boasts a traffic count of 46,100 and a median age within a 5-mile radius of 40.7 years.

The closest Vitamin Shoppe store to the Bowman location is located in Charleston and is more than 13.82 miles away. The store was opened in 2004, and it occupies a space of 5,936 square feet. Its annual sales for its first year were $1,192,048. In 2014, it posted annual sales of $2,862,337 and in 2015, the annual sales were $2,764,134. Based upon his previous experience of other stores that opened within 15 miles of an existing store, Marc estimated that the Bowman Vitamin Shoppe will cannibalize an expected annual sales of $77,000 from the Charleston store. Marc also received sales and size information of equivalent sister stores from Brenda that will enable him to estimate the expected annual sales from the new store.

According to Exhibit 3, the average size of the sister stores is 3,719 square feet. They are located in well-to-do areas where the median income of the population within a 5-mile radius is almost $77,000. The average number of households in the geographical area of the store is 30,164. The average annual sales of the first year of these stores were $734,184. In contrast, the Bowman store will be somewhat smaller, occupying 2,734 square feet. The median income is somewhat higher, $80,578, and the number of households in the surrounding area is 29,594.

Marc began his analysis by making several assumptions. He assumed based upon Exhibit 3 that initial sales will be $734,000. He examined other stores that opened up recently in areas similar to Mount Pleasant and estimated that sales growth will be 30% in the second year, 15% in the third year, 8% in the fourth year, and 2% thereafter. Given the pricing

Exhibit 3. Key Data Statistics of Nearby Stores

Store Name	State	Open Date	SqFt	5mi HH	5mi HHinc	1st Yr Sales	2015 Sales
Columbia	SC	12/26/2013	2,541	32,395	$72,821	$888,000	$1,040,362
Denver	CO	7/3/2008	4,095	29,101	$81,457	$707,577	$1,373,230
Charlottesville	VA	8/21/2008	4,238	27,171	$71,606	$637,491	$1,189,471
Round Rock	TX	1/13/2005	4,000	31,990	$81,223	$703,668	$1,488,080
Average			3,719	30,164	$76,777	$734,184	$1,272,786

strategy of Vitamin Shoppe, the gross profit margin of all stores is expected to be 53%. The company will sign a 5-year lease and the annual lease payment will be \$131,232 payable at the beginning of each year. They expect to renew the 5-year lease and that the new rent will be \$144,355 per annum. The store's advertising expense is 1.2% of total store sales, credit card fees are 1.3% of total store sales, and payroll expenses are expected to be 16% of total store sales. Miscellaneous store expenses, covering purchase of bags, internet connectivity, utilities, telephone, and insurance are expected to be 8% of total store sales. Maintenance and repairs are expected to be 2% of total store sales. Note that any cannibalization of this store with the Charlotte store will not affect the total store expenses of the Mount Pleasant store. Marc also expects to spend \$170,000 on fixtures and equipment which has an expected life of 10 years. The company's tax rate is 34% and he will use straight-line depreciation to determine the store's annual tax liability. In addition to the above assumptions, headquarters charge each store an additional 6% overhead and interest expense annual tax on sales to cover headquarters operational costs.

In order to complete his analysis, he looked over the capital budgeting chapter of his textbook to help him do his analysis. Brenda Galgano told Marc that stores should be adopted if the IRR of the investment is at least 18%, even though the ATWACC of the firm is 10%. He remembered that to calculate payback, IRR, and NPV, he will need to calculate the annual cash flows generated by the new store. Marc reviewed his favorite finance textbook and found that Net Present Value is defined as the time value of the cash flows generated by a capital expenditure less the capital expenditure. More formally:

$$\mathrm{NPV} = -I + \sum_{T=1}^{N} \mathrm{CF}_T/(1+R)^T$$

where CF_T is expected cash flow of the project in period T, R is the cost of capital (funds or the interest cost of raising money from investors), and I is the capital expenditure. The NPV rule states that firms should accept projects with NPV > 0 and reject the project if NPV < 0. IRR is found by setting the NPV of the above equation to zero and solving for the interest rate. More formally:

$$0 = -I + \sum_{T=1}^{N} \mathrm{CF}_T/(1+\mathrm{IRR})^T$$

The IRR rule states that firms should accept the project if IRR > *R*, where *R* is the cost of funds of firm's required benchmark. Generally, one uses the After-Tax Weighted Average Cost of Capital. As a result, the cash flow definition used for capital budgeting purposes is:

$$\text{Cash Flow} = \text{Sales} - \text{Expenses} - \text{Long-Term Investment} \\ - \text{Change in Working Capital} - \text{Tax Rate} \\ (\text{Sales} - \text{Expenses} - \text{Depreciation})$$

Marc is planning to build an excel model to analyze the viability of the new store. Vitamin Shoppe's excel template allows the analyst to estimate the cash flow for only 10 years. Marc believes that estimating cash flow beyond 10 years may be a foolhardy adventure. But still he wonders would the profitability of the store improve if he estimated cash flows beyond 10 years. Marc also wondered how he would estimate the change in working capital. But for now, he is going to ignore that component of the cash flow since headquarters finances all merchandise equipment for each store.

Year	2017	2018	2019	2020	2021	2022	2023	2024	2025	2026	2027
Investment											
Sales											
Sales Growth			30%	15%	8%	2%	2%	2%	2%	2%	2%
Gross Profit											
Rent											
Payroll											
Other expenses											
CFBT											
Tax											
Cash Flow											
Cumulative Cash Flow											
IRR											
NPV											
Payback											

Marc understood that CFBT is cash flow before taxes and Cumulative Cash Flow is the total cash flow generated from 2017 until the estimated fiscal year. This last term will help him determine payback. Payback is the number of years it takes the firm to recover its investment. Brenda Galgano not only wants to see the template filled out but receive Marc's recommendation as well.

https://doi.org/10.1142/9789811216749_0008

Case 8

A Scenario Analysis Case Study of Clavius Electronics Components, Inc.

Ronald Richter and Arthur S. Guarino

Rutgers Business School, USA

Introduction

Clavius Electronics Components, Incorporated in California, not far from San Francisco, is a large manufacturer of electronic connectors and many other products. Not only do they manufacture electronic connectors but were also involved in the research and development of all aspects of the product. Clavius had customers in the United States and globally and saw its business growing at a respectable annual rate. While there have been some bad years, overall the company's growth in terms of sales revenue, gross, operating, and net profit was healthy, and there was talk of taking the company public if the trend continued in the next 5 years.

Clavius was purchased by three electrical engineers, Steve Rogers, Paul Westfall, and Jerry Southern, who were also close friends from college at CalTech. Clavius was a company near bankruptcy but had a good reputation in research and development in the electronics industry. Steve Rogers, Paul Westfall, and Jerry Southern met at CalTech and took the same courses through school. After completing college, they each went to work for companies that dealt in different aspects of electrical components: from designing, to manufacturing, to researching and developing new components. They each got married, had families, and kept in touch over the years about their dream of owning their very own company. They knew it would take a substantial amount of money and business acumen to have a successful business, but they were determined and willing to make the necessary sacrifices to succeed. Paul and Jerry took out second mortgages on their homes, while Steve used inheritance money he received from his parent's estate and his children's college money to pool their funds to purchase Clavius. There were plenty of sleepless nights for all three of them, but the deal went through and they became co-owners of Clavius.

Steve handled the negotiations with the creditors and suppliers and was able to get good deals for the company. Steve was able to get an extension on paying back the money the company had originally borrowed and negotiated with the banks on a new line of credit. Steve made it a top priority that all the creditors and suppliers would get paid every penny they were owed. Paul was able to land contracts with new customers. Paul liked sales and he was able to work with the new and old customers about the products they needed for their company's products. Slowly but surely sales started to grow and Clavius' cash flow situation went from negative to positive in eighteen months. It was not easy, but the three engineers turned business owners eventually did it. Once the company showed consecutive quarters of positive cash flow, the bottom line on the income statement went from red to black. This allowed Clavius to get a line of credit from a major bank in the state which was used to increase their operations and seek new markets. It also meant hiring new workers, offering new products and services, and seeing their financial statements grow healthier every year. While there were still challenges that the three engineers faced, they knew they could do it if they had the determination and fortitude to move ahead.

Current Situation

Ralph Voras was hired as a young electrical engineer straight out of college and went to graduate school for his master's degree in finance at night. After completing his first degree he later obtained a master's degree in electrical engineering also as a part time student. He put in long hours at the company and worked his way up to product manager sometimes handling six assignments at one time. As product manager at Clavius Electronics Components, Ralph was involved in a product for an existing customer of the company. Ralph was dealing with the sales price, sales quantity, cost structure, and capital cost for tooling to manufacture the product. Ralph and his team were concerned about the rate of return for the product and the price for tooling to make it. Clavius was now involved in a new product, an electronic connector, for one of its largest clients. Ralph now had to put his knowledge of finance he picked up in graduate school to good use. Clavius was looking to expand its operations in this new product, but it had to obtain a good return and take into consideration all the variables associated with manufacturing and selling this electronic connector.

A key problem with the product was that gold was a significant part in manufacturing the product. Ralph felt that given the nature of the price of gold, Clavius would need to hedge the price of gold using futures contracts but was unsure what that really meant to Clavius. Ralph decided that is essential to perform a discounted cash flow analysis incorporating sensitivity and scenario analysis. Ralph's team knew they had to lock in on a price for gold that would make the product not only profitable but also give a good rate of return. They needed to properly recognize the project variables to focus on in negotiations with the customer. It was thought that there was a chance that this product could be used more broadly in the market and other customers may wish to purchase this product form Clavius in the future. Below are the aspects of the various components of the project with an indication of the assumptions used in communicating with the client:

Price per Connector

After some initial conversation with the client, Clavius is projecting the price per electronic connector at $3.00 each. Clavius is thinking they can achieve a price inflation factor of 2.5% each year for the next 10 years if the demand in units stays at the level the customer is forecasting (see units forecast below). The key aspect of price is that the customer is asking for discounts if the quantity ordered is above the 500,000 units.

Quantity Demanded

The customer has indicated that the first-year orders will be around 1,000,000 units and the customer is also looking for price breaks at different levels of quantity commitments. As mentioned above, the customer feels that after the first 500,000 units are ordered, that a price break of

10% on all units would make sense for this transaction. The customer has also indicated that if the product works as suspected, they will order an additional 2.5% each year for the next 10 years.

Fixed Costs (Overhead)

The cost accountant at the factory where the connector is to be made was consulted to determine the fixed costs associated with making these connectors. After long discussions with the operations and people in the factory, the cost accountant determined the fixed overhead for this project would initially be $500,000 and that will hold until the unit produced exceeds 1,400,000 units. At that time, there will need to be an additional fixed cost allocation of space and overhead of $100,000 to satisfy the demand. When talking to the cost accountant about the trends in fixed costs as they are related to inflation, the cost accountant indicated that fixed costs seem to be rising at 2.5% each year.

Variable Costs per Connector

The cost accountant has been working diligently with the engineers to get firm prices on all the components to make the connectors. Since Clavius is very familiar with the manufacturing of similar types of products, they do feel very good about the variable cost estimates. Regarding the material cost, there are four different materials that are being used. Below is the chart that shows the material and cost per connector for each material.

Material Component	Cost per Connector
Plastic	$0.05
Metal	$0.15
Gold	$1.25
Wire	$0.20

These costs are projected to increase at an inflation rate of 2.5% each year for the life of the project. The one cost that management is very concerned about is the cost of gold. It is obvious that gold is the costliest component of the connector and is also the most volatile market for the inputs into making the product. Clavius knows that once it sets the price in the contract with the customer that it will not be able to adjust as the price of gold fluctuates. It is important to be certain of these costs when discussing the sales price with the customer.

The cost accountant also worked with the operations people to understand how much labor costs go into making each connector. They did a time study based upon the machinery being used, and the labor costs are projected to be $0.35 per connector. This cost considers salary, taxes, and all benefits for the factory workers making the product. As with all other costs, these labor costs are projected to increase at an inflation rate of 2.5% each year during the life of the project.

Capital Required

This is a gigantic order for Clavius, and even though they engineered a very good product for the market, there is a huge investment needed in fixed capital to produce the connectors. Clavius has estimated that they will need to invest $500,000 in plastic molds and $1,000,000 in metal stamping equipment to meet the demand. These molds and stamps will be able to be used in existing molding and stamping machines, and the overhead costs of the machines are incorporated in the fixed costs discussed above. When depreciating the molds and stamps, Clavius will use a 7-year MACRS depreciation method for tax (cash flow) purposes and use the table below:

MACRS 7-Year Table	
Half Year Convention	
Year	**Depreciation Rate (%)**
1	14.29
2	24.49
3	17.49
4	12.49
5	8.93
6	8.92
7	8.93
8	4.46

The total investment of $1,500,000 is very large for Clavius and they have had some initial discussions with the customer about having the customer help contribute to the capital costs. If the customer does contribute to the costs, that would assist Clavius with lowering its initial investment; increasing the potential return on the project. However, the customer will then ask for exclusivity on the product and Clavius will not be able to market to others. As a result, Clavius is not sure how to proceed with discussions with the customer but is very intrigued that they are willing to contribute towards the capital investment.

Net Working Capital Investment

In order to perform the discounted cash flow analysis, you are to also consider the need to invest in working capital; specifically, receivables, inventory, and accounts payable. The terms for the customer in the past have been to pay within 30 days from the invoice date. This has usually been the case with this customer but has sometimes been about 5–10 days longer than the terms dictate. As for inventory, Clavius has been able to keep its Days Inventory Outstanding to approximately 44 days. The terms associated with accounts payable have usually resulted in Accounts Payable being approximately 3% of sales. Since this project is lasting for 10 years, it is assumed that there will be a recapture of net working capital at the end of the project.

Other General Assumptions

The corporate tax rate for Clavius is 21% and the firm believes that it will remain profitable over the next 10 years. As for the required return on this connector, Clavius feels very good about the risk factors for this project. The customer is so excited about the engineering of the connector and the value it brings to its product that the 1,000,000 initial units are forecasted with great confidence. Still, this is a new product and does come with risks. Clavius' weighted average cost of capital is 8% and being that this is a new product, Clavius is thinking that the risk-adjusted discount rate should be 10%.

Ralph wrote a memo to his team working on the product addressing key concerns.

***Assignment Memo*:**
***To*:** Susan Weiss — Financial Analyst
***From*:** Ralph Voras — Product Manager
***Date*:** February 2, 2020
***Re*:** Product Cost Analysis and Recommendation

We have been given a great opportunity to work with our customers to produce a highly engineered product that will be used in the customers' product offering. We are in negotiations with the client to determine the sales price, quantity demanded, cost structure, and capital cost for tooling to manufacture the product. We are asking you as the Financial Analyst to assist the marketing team in the negotiations with the customer. Your knowledge of capital budgeting techniques and identifying the key drivers of this project are essential in allowing us to better forecast the value this project brings Clavius.

The analyses we are looking for to assist on the negotiation with the client are the following:

- Discounted cash flow analysis showing the result of all the capital budgeting metrics (Net present value, Internal rate of return, Payback period, Discounted payback period), considering all the information about the project.
- A scenario analysis that shows a Base-case, Average-case, and Worst-case scenarios and the assumptions made to arrive at these scenarios.
- A descriptive strategy for negotiating with the client regarding all facets of the project (capital investment, sales price, sales volume, etc.).

Your response to this memo is to include your answers to the above with supporting calculations. It is imperative that we fully understand the capital budgeting metrics along with risks inherent in the project if we are to move forward with the customer. I need this analysis with your recommendations in 1 week.

https://doi.org/10.1142/9789811216749_0009

Case 9

ConocoPhillips: Real Options and Capital Budgeting

Harvey A. Poniachek

Rutgers Business School, USA

Introduction

This case study addresses capital budgeting decision by application of the net present value, the decision tree, and real options for a major oil corporation. Traditional capital budgeting theory maintains that investment in a project is commercially feasible and should be made when the net present value ("NPV") of the cash flows exceeds zero or when the internal rate of return ("IRR") exceeds the cost of capital, which is commonly defined in terms of the weighted average cost of capital. For mutually exclusive projects, the firm should select the project with the higher NPV. The traditional capital budgeting theory ignores management's flexibility, or the value of real options embedded in investment, that could affect investment valuation decision.

A firm's discretionary investment opportunities could be deemed analogous to options on real assets that are conceptually similar to options on financial assets. The option is "real" because the underlying assets are physical rather than financial securities. Real option creates economic value by offering management flexibility to act upon new information[1]

[1]Richard A. Brealey, Stewart C. Myers, and Franklin Allen, *Principles of Corporate Finance*, 13th ed. (McGraw Hill Education, New York, 2020), Ch. 22, 590 pp. ("Brealey");

that can be evaluated by using the decision trees or adapting the financial option model of Black-Scholes.[2] For instance, a firm has the option to abandon a project during its life if its performance is unsatisfactory, which is equivalent to a put option on the project, or expand it if the performance is outstanding, which is equivalent to a call option. Ignoring the option-like features embodied in investment projects could lead to erroneous decisions.[3]

According to Copeland *et al.*,[4] "The main difference between NPV and real options is that the former discounts expected cash flows at a constant discount rate. NPV implicitly assumes that no decisions will be made in the future — that all expected cash flows are recommitted. Real options analysis uses decision trees and therefore models optimal actions taken in the futures in response to the resolution of uncertainty."

Surveys show that companies rely predominantly on the NPV and IRR to make investment decisions and fewer than a quarter of them use real options.[5] A survey of *Fortune* 1000 companies shows that out of 279 respondents, 40 were using real options (14.3%), and well over half of the nonusers considered the use of real options in the future.[6] A survey of 83 studies on capital budgeting practices across firms in India, South Africa, the United Kingdom, and the United States from 1966 through 2016 shows that real option valuation (ROV) is the least used capital budgeting approach due to the lack of familiarity with this methodology and its complexity.[7]

E. Brigham and M. Ehrhardt, *Financial Management: Theory and Practice*, 11th ed. (South-Western Educational Publishing, Mason, Ohio, 2001).

[2]A. M. Brach, *Real Options in Practice* (John Wiley & Sons, Inc., 2003) ("Brach").

[3]Timothy A. Luehrman, *Capital Projects and Real Options: An Introduction*, HBS, 9-295-074, March 22, 1995.

[4]Thomas E. Copeland, J. Fred Weston, and Kuldeep Shastri, *Financial Theory and Capital Policy*, 4th ed. (Pearson Addison Wesley, Boston, 2005), 310 pp.

[5]Robert L. McDonald, "The Role of Real Options in Capital Budgeting: Theory and Practice," *Journal of Applied Corporate Finance* 18, no. 2 (Spring 2006): 28–39.

[6]Stanley Block, "Are "Real Options" Actually Used in the Real World?" *The Engineering Economist* 52, no. 3 (13 September 2007): 255–267.

[7]John Henry Hall, "The Evolution of the Application of Capital Budgeting Techniques in Enterprises," https://doi.org/10.1016/j.gfj.2019.100504.

ConocoPhillips

ConocoPhillips ("Conoco", or "CP", or "The Company") was formed through a merger between Conoco Inc. and Phillips Petroleum Company on August 30, 2002.[8] The company is headquartered in Houston, Texas, and it is the world's largest independent exploration and production ("E&P") firm with operations and activities in 17 countries, $71 billion of total assets, 11,100 employees, and production of 1,350 million barrels of oil equivalent per day (MBOED). CP's capital expenditure budget for 2019 was $6.1 billion,[9] of which Alaska accounted for $1.2 billion which includes funding for ongoing conventional and unconventional drilling programs, exploration and appraisal activities, and maintenance activities.

ConocoPhillips was one of Alaska's largest owners of exploration leases in 2019 that contributed 25% of the company's worldwide production. The company's technology programs improve its ability to develop unconventional reservoirs, produce heavy oil economically with less emissions, improve the efficiency of exploration program, increase recoveries from legacy fields, and implement sustainability measures.

There are several phases of oil and gas activities, including exploration, development, and production. Petroleum-related activities include seismic operations, construction of roads and trails for transporting equipment and supplies, drilling exploration and delineation wells, drilling production and service wells, installing pipelines, and constructing oil and gas processing facilities. Oil business involves several phases with distinct functions and financial ramifications. Upstream activities include finding and production after the reserves are found. Once crude oil and gas have been extracted, the midstream production process includes storage and transportation through pipelines. The downstream process involves refining the oil into gasoline and other finished products.

---

[8] ConocoPhillips, Form 10-K, 2019.

[9] ConocoPhillips Announces 2019 Capital Budget and Operating Plan: Recent Oil Price Volatility Highlights Investment Appeal of Company's Differentiated Value Proposition, December 10, 2018. https://www.conocophillips.com/news-media/story/conocophillips-announces-2019-capital-budget-and-operating-plan-recent-oil-price-volatility-highlights-investment-appeal-of-company-s-differentiated-value-proposition/.

Oil is classified as light or heavy (based on the API gravity), and as sweet or sour (which is a measure of how much sulfur the oil contains). Light and sweet oil requires further processing, but it is relatively easier to turn it into fuel. Heavy oil requires more intensive processing and refining. For instance, oil extracted from Alberta's tar sands (heavy, sour oil) costs more to refine than light, sweet oil from Texas. Hydraulic fracturing of rock is the main driver of the resurgence in oil production in the United States, as more and more shale formations are yielding previously inaccessible deposits of oil and gas.

CP discovered in Alaska a large oil field of up to 750 million barrels of oil equivalent (MMBOE) in the Greater Willow Area during its latest exploration campaign. The company drilled six wells plus a sidetrack and all hit oil. Appraisal work is planned for both Greater Willow as well as the Narwhal trend, where 100 MMBOE and 350 MMBOE of resources have been discovered at the Putu and Stony Hill wells. The company has continued to add to its Alaskan acreage by acquiring BP's 39.2% interest in Alaska Greater Kuparuk Area and 38% interest in the Kuparuk Transportation Co.

Conoco has room to grow because 75% of its prospective acreage remains undrilled. It could cost between $2 billion and $3 billion over 4 to 5 years to develop the above resources with the first oil possible as early as 2024. Another $2 billion to $3 billion of drilling capital would also be needed over multiple years to maintain production levels. ConocoPhillips believes that it can develop some of its new Alaska discoveries at prices in the mid-$40-per-barrel range thanks to new technologies like horizontal drilling. (In the Lower 48, some of the company's projects appear to be viable at $30 per barrel.)

In April 2019, Alaska's Department of Natural Resources, Division of Oil and Gas (DOG), called for exploration license proposals.[10] The holder of an oil and gas exploration license has the exclusive right to explore an area between 10,000 acres and 500,000 acres for up to 10 years and must commit direct expenditures for exploration. The license will be terminated if the licensee has not completed at least 25% of the total work commitment by the fourth anniversary of the exploration license terms. Twenty-five percent of the licensed area would be relinquished if the licensee has completed less than 50% of the total work commitment, and an additional 10% relinquished each successive year until half of the original acreage has been relinquished. The lessee pays an annual rental to the state of

[10]https://aws.state.ak.us/OnlinePublicNotices/Notices/View.aspx?id=193127.

\$2.00 to \$2.30 per acre[11] and the royalty rate for oil and gas produced onshore has remained at 12.5% since 1920.

Traditional Capital Budgeting

The traditional capital budgeting theory holds that investments are deemed financially feasible and should be undertaken when a prospective investment's net present value exceeds zero, or when its internal rate of return exceeds the weighted average cost of capital ("WACC").[12] The traditional capital budgeting methodologies are inadequate because they do not incorporate the value of management's ability to modify and amend earlier capital investment decisions in response to market developments.[13] The traditional approach does not recognize that management could revise its investment strategies in response to unexpected circumstances and thereby capture the future value embedded in such flexibility which is the value of real options. As a result, option pricing models, including the Black–Scholes model, have been used for capital budgeting investments embedding real options.[14] Thus, the traditional capital budgeting approach underestimates the true value of a project by omitting the value embedded in the optionality of changes.

Real Options

The DCF approach to capital budgeting implicitly assumes that the investment project is passively held and the only decision that matters is the

---

[11] Alaska Department of Natural Resources, Division of Oil & Gas, August 2, 2019.

[12] Stephen A. Ross, Randolph W. Westerfield, Jeffrey F. Jaffe, and Bradford D. Jordan, *Corporate Finance*, 12th ed. (McGraw Hill Education, New York, 2019), Chapter 7, Risk Analysis, Real Options, and Capital Budgeting ("Ross"); Brealey, *op. cit.*; Jonathan Berk and Peter DeMarzo, *Corporate Finance*, 4th ed. (Pearson, Hoboken, New Jersey, 2017), Chapter 8, Fundamentals of Capital Budgeting, and Chapter 22, Real Options ("Berk"); Eugene F. Brigham and Michael C. Ehrhardt, *Financial Management: Theory and Practice*, 12th ed. (Thomson South-Western, Mason, Ohio, 2008), Chapter 13, Real Options.

[13] Lenos Trigeorgis (ed.), *Real Options in Capital Investment: Models, Strategies, and Applications* (Praeger, Westport, Connecticut, 1995), Chapter 1, Real Options: An Overview, and Chapter 5, Nalin Kulatilaka, The Value of Flexibility: A General Model of Real Options ("Trigeorgis").

[14] Michel Benaroch and Robert J. Kauffman, "A Case for Using Real Options Pricing Analysis to Evaluate Information Technology Project Investments," *Information Systems Research* 10, no. 1 (March 1999): 70–86. https://www.jstor.org/stable/23015607?seq=1.

initial one of whether to invest or not. In reality, however, investments in projects are actively managed where management could continuously make decisions and changes in response to new circumstances.

Following an investment in a project, management opportunities to respond to changing circumstances are defined as managerial options, or strategic options, or real options.[15] Brealey *et al.* identified four main types of real options[16]:

1. The option to expand if the project succeeds;
2. Timing the investment — the option to wait before investing if conditions are unfavorable or execute ahead of schedule if conditions are attractive;
3. The option to shrink or abandon a project if the investment incurred a loss or is expected to incur a loss; and
4. The option to vary the input mix or the production methods.[17]

---

[15]Eugene F. Brigham, Louis C. Gapenski, and Phillip R. Daves, *Intermediate Financial Management*, 6th ed. (The Dryden Press, Fort Worth, Texas, 1999), 295–303; Michael C. Ehrhardt and Eugene F. Brigham, *Financial Management: Theory and Practice*, 13th ed. (South-Western Cengage Learning, Mason, Arizona, 2011), Chapter 11, 449–451.

[16]Brealey, *op. cit.*, Chapter 22, Real Options; Copeland *et al.*, Copeland, *op. cit.*, 321 pp. expanded the list of real options as follows:

- Expansion options,
- Contraction options,
- Abandonment options,
- Extension options (Extend the life of a project),
- Deferral options (Defer the start of a project),
- Compound options (Options on options).

[17]According to Lenos Trigeorgis (ed.), *Real Options in Capital Investment: Models, Strategies, and Applications* (Praeger, Westport, Connecticut, 1995), Chapter 1, the common real options include the following:

- Option to defer,
- Staged investment,
- Option to alter operating scale,
- Option to abandon,
- Option to switch inputs and outputs,
- Growth options,
- Multiple interacting options.

There are different **real option valuation procedures** that can be used including the following[18]:

1. Use DCF valuation and include a recognition of any real option's value;
2. Use decision tree analysis; and
3. Use a standard model for a financial option.

Utilization of real options could affect the NPV in the following manner[19]: Expanded NPV = Passive NPV + Value of option from active investment management. That is, real options could add considerable value to a project while ignoring them could lead to undervaluation of NPV and rejection of commercially feasible investment. The valuation of real option could be defined as follows: Value of option = New NPV of the project following management's changes – Old NPV of the projects prior to changes.[20]

An investment project could be deemed as an **option** to invest in a corporation's stock — where the Black-Scholes option pricing model could be used to value a European call option as a function of five variables as follows[21]: the stock price, S; the exercise price, X; the riskiness of the project defined as the standard deviation σ of the return on the asset; the risk-free rate of r; the time to expiration, t; and dividend payout rate.

An investment project is analogous to exercising a call option with an exercise price X, and the value of the project is equivalent to the stock price S. The parametric equivalencies of the real option of an investment in a project and to that of the Black–Scholes model are listed below.[22]

---

[18]Eugene F. Brigham and Michael C. Ehrhardt, *Financial Management Theory and Practice*, 12th ed. (Thomson South-Western, Mason, Ohio), 459–478.

[19]Lenos Trigeorgis (ed.), *Real Options in Capital Investment: Models, Strategies, and Applications* (Praeger, Westport Connecticut, 1995), Chapter 1.

[20]Eugene F. Brigham, Louis C. Gapenski, and Phillip R. Daves, *Intermediate Financial Management*, 6th ed. (The Dryden Press, 1999), 300 pp.

[21]Timothy A. Luehrman, "Capital Projects as Real Options: An Introduction," HBS, 9-295-074, March 22, 1995.

[22]Sven Remer, Hwee Ang, and Charles Baden-Fuller, "Dealing with Uncertainties in the Biotechnology Industry: The Use of Real Options Reasoning," *Journal of Commercial Biotechnology* 9, no. 2 (2001): 95–105.

Variable	Financial Option	Real Option
S	Stock price	Present value of the expected cash inflows from project
X	Exercise price	Present value of the expenditures needed to accomplish project
σ	Volatility	Uncertainty of the expected cash flows from the project
r	Risk-free rate	The risk-free rate
t	Time to expiration	Period in which the investment opportunity expires

Assume that a firm has the option of expanding its operations at time t. S is the NPV of that project at the time of the option can be exercised and the investment cost is the exercise price, X. If $S > X$, the option is in the money and would be exercised, whereas if $S < X$, the NPV is negative and out of the money the firm will not make the investment.[23] The traditional capital budgeting approach is modified by incorporating optionality. That is, the value of an investment is calculated by incorporating the management flexibility via application of the Black–Sholes formula of European call for a project extension and put options for a project abandonment on non-dividend paying stock pricing model,[24] as follows:

$$\text{Call Option } C = So\text{N}(\text{d1}) - K\text{e}^{-rt}\text{N}(\text{d2})$$

$$\text{Put Option } P = K\text{e}^{-rt}\text{N}(-\text{d2}) - So\text{N}(-\text{d1})$$

The variables in the above formulas are as follows: C is the call price, So is the spot price, N(d1) and N(d2) are the cumulative probability functions for variables with standard normal distribution, K is the strike price, e is 2.71828, r is the interest rate, T is the maturity, and P is the put price.

N(d1) and N(d2) are defined as follows:

$$\text{d1} = [\ln(So/K) + (r + \sigma^2/2)]/\sigma T^{1/2}$$

$$\text{d2} = [\ln(So/K) + (r - \sigma^2/2)T]/\sigma T^{1/2}$$

[23] Brealey, *op. cit.*, Ch. 22, Real Options.

[24] John C. Hull, *Fundamentals of Futures and Options Markets*, 9th ed. (Pearson, Hoboken, New Jersey, 2017), Chapter 13, Valuating Stock Options: The Black-Sholes-Merton Model, 304–306.

The note below cites a real option involving investments in the microcomputer industry.[25]

The Assignment

Investment in oil exploration and production can be deemed as a call option to explore if the availability of oil and/or gas is validated, and prices are sufficiently high, or forego the investment by exercising a put option in case of insufficient oil and/or gas deposits and/or prices are below the breakeven point. That is, options on an oil field provide a company the right to develop the field by expanding its investment, or abandon its investment, or switch use of some equipment.

ConocoPhillips has a portfolio of oil licenses that provide it with options on half a dozen tracks in Alaska with a 5-year maturity. In recent years, the company drilled and developed blocks when NPV > 0, and where NPV < 0 the blocks were not developed and sold to other companiės. An oil consultant that Conoco hired advised it that instead of calculating what the tracks would be worth if the company started developing the assets immediately, it should value its opportunity as an option to develop. The option value derived through application of the decision tree and/or the Black-Scholes option valuation model could turn a project with a negative NPV into a positive one.

ConocoPhillips was seeking to explore and develop its 50,000 acres leased field in Great Willow, Alaska that has an expected oil reserve of 100 MBOED that could cost \$12 to \$15 per barrel and perhaps up to \$20 to develop, or an estimated \$1.2 to \$1.5 billion and could cost up to

[25]A firm considered entering into the microcomputer business through an investment in manufacturing (Project I) that yielded a negative NPV and was thus commercially unfeasible. However, the firm was adamant on making the investment for strategic reasons and deemed it as a call option on further investment projects that would be strategically necessary to enhance its competitive position in the emerging industry (through Project II and others). The valuation of the call option could be done by application of the Black–Scholes or the decision tree model. Implementing Project II 3 years later yielded negative NPV, but accepting it produced a positive adjusted present value for Project I. Although Project II call option is out of the money at $T = 0$, its relatively long maturity could generate an NPV in excess of the strike price. Richard A. Brealey, Stewart C. Myers, and Franklin Allen, *Principles of Corporate Finance*, 13th ed. (McGraw Hill Education, 2020), Ch. 22, Real Options, 591–594.

$2.0 billion. The issue before the company is whether the project is economically feasible? To assess the commercial feasibility, the company intends to apply the traditional discount cash flow analysis plus the real option model that explicitly consider management's ability to suspend operations if oil prices are below the breakeven point pr due to other adverse circumstances.

The company's head of investment in the treasury department, Vice President Nancy Northfield, is aware of the following market facts that could equally apply to ConocoPhillips:

- Crude Brent oil prices averaged $40 in June 2020, compared with $64 a year ago. According to the US Energy Information Administration[26] (EIA) worldwide crude oil prices are expected to be at $50/b in 2021, $79/b by 2025, $146/b by 2040, and $214/b by 2050.
- According to EIA, the average global exploration and development (E&D) cost of oil and gas was $16 per barrel of oil equivalent (BOE) in 2019 but the cost going forward is unclear.
- Various Web sources suggest that the average finding and development costs are between $7 and $15 a barrel (and could be as high as $20), and the wide cost spread is attributed to geographic and geological differences.
- The average cost of (on land) oil rigs ranges from $20 million to $1 billion, and drilling equipment could account for up to 90% of total investment, while offshore drilling could cost 15 to 20 times more than land drilling and deeper drilling is even more costly.
- The high cost of drilling induces companies to spend more time and resources on performing extensive seismological surveys to determine the probable availability of reserves.
- The minimum bid to lease public land for fossil fuel production has been $2 per acre and the royalty rate for oil and gas produced onshore has remained at 12.5% since 1920.

Various real options may be embedded in capital investment projects. An oil company that has a lease to start drilling on land with potential for oil needs to make several capital investments in exploratory cost, followed by construction of roads, construction of new processing facilities, then

[26]Oil Price Forecast 2020–2050, https://www.thebalance.com/oil-price-forecast-3306219.

extraction can start. Depending on the oil market conditions, management could reduce the scale of investment or resort to different operating options that were identified above.

VP Nancy Northfield and her analysts need to develop ConocoPhillps' Alaska Exploration & Development Cash Flow and financial projections under three different scenarios that include high, average, and low, with corresponding probabilities of 30%, 40%, and 30%. The initial investment is expected at $500 million that includes several phases: Exploration, including seismic operation (10% of the investment budget); development, including roads construction (20%); and drilling and production (70% of total investment). The CFO's office provided Ms. Northfield with a couple of scenarios that are referred to here as Appendices A and B that were prepared by the company's outside consultant a few years ago. The work by the consultant could assist the analysts but they're at liberty to derive their own.

The initial investment (Investment I) analysis could be assisted by application of the NPV model and utilization of the relevant data in Appendix A. Although the initial investment (under the underlying assumptions in Appendix A) yielded commercially unfeasible results, ConocoPhillips made a **strategic decision** to invest an additional $750 million in year 4 (Investment II) to develop an adjacent oil track. To determine the capital budgeting feasibility of Investments I and II, Nancy Northfield utilizes the underlying data in Appendix B and applies **Brealey's real option methodology**[27] by application of the NPV cum Black–Scholes model to Investment II. That is, first apply the NPV to Investment II, second use the Black–Scholes call formula as specified above with $750 being the exercise price, the NPV of the project is the underlying asset value, and derive the standard deviations of the firm's equity. She expects that in aggregate Investments I and II outcome would assure ConocoPhillips that their capital budgeting decisions are of acceptable merit and produce positive NPV.

They were required to submit to the CFO and the investment committee a feasibility analysis of the Great Willow project in Alaska by application of an **NPV model and the Black–Scholes formula**. The analysis is due in a couple of weeks.

---

[27]Richard A. Brealey, Stewart C. Mayer, and Franklin Alen, *Principles of Corporate Finance*, 13th ed. (McGraw Hill Education, New York, 2020), Ch. 22, Real Options, 590–593.

Appendix A. Initial Case

Conocophillips Alaska Exploration & Development Project Cash Flow

Initial Investment, Million		$500.00			
Output, Barrels Per Day		7,000			
Price Per Barrel		$70.00			
Discount Rate		20%			
Tax Rate		21%			
Standard Deviation					
CAPEX		500,000,000			
	2021	**2022**	**2023**	**2024**	**2025**
Oil Output Annual Barrels	2,555,000	2,682,750	2,816,888	2,957,732	3,105,618
Price Per Barrel	70	70	70	70	70
Revenue	178,850,000	187,792,500	197,182,125	207,041,231	217,393,293
Cost Per Barrel	20	20	20	20	20
Output Cost	51,100,000	53,655,000	56,337,750	59,154,638	62,112,369
Depreciation	100,000	100,000	100,000	100,000	100,000
Interest Expenses	4,292,400	4,507,020	4,732,371	4,968,990	5,217,439
NWC	44,712,500	46,948,125	49,295,531	51,760,308	54,348,323
Changes in NWC	60,000,000	2,235,625	2,347,406	2,464,777	2,588,015
EBIT	127,650,000	134,037,500	140,744,375	147,786,594	155,180,923
EBIT After Taxes	100,843,500	105,889,625	111,188,056	116,751,409	122,592,930
EBIT After Tax + Depreciation	100,943,500	105,989,625	111,288,056	116,851,409	122,692,930
Changes in NWC	60,000,000	2,235,625	2,347,406	2,464,777	2,588,015
Free Cash Flows	40,943,500	103,754,000	108,940,650	114,386,633	120,104,914
CAPEX	500,000,000				
FCFs	(459,056,500)	103,754,000	108,940,650	114,386,633	120,104,914
PV FCFs	(382,547,083)	72,051,389	63,044,358	55,163,307	48,267,471
Total FCF	(11,870,303)				

Notes: The project is assumed to live 5 years and produce 10,000 barrels per day.
The analysis applies the standard capital budgeting model by deriving
The free case flows and the net Present value

Operating Cash Flow = EBIT * (1 – T) + Depreciation T = Tax rate of 21%

Free Cash Flow = EBIT * (1 – T) + DEP-CH NWC-CAPEX

Appendix B. Three Years Delay

Conocophillips Alaska Exploration & Development Project Cash Flow, Investment 3 Years Later

Initial Investment, Billions		$750.00						
Output, Barrels Per Day		15,000						
Price Per Barrel		**70.00**						
Discount Rate		20%						
Tax Rate		21%						
	2021	**2022**	**2023**	**2024**	**2025**	**2026**	**2027**	**2029**
Oil Output Annual Barrels				5,475,000	5,475,000	5,475,000	5,475,000	5,475,000
Price Per Barrel				70	70	70	70	70
Revenue Per Year				383,250,000	383,250,000	383,250,000	383,250,000	383,250,000
Cost Per Barrel				20	20	20	20	20
Output Cost				109,500,000	109,500,000	109,500,000	109,500,000	109,500,000
Depreciation				150,000,000	150,000,000	150,000,000	150,000,000	150,000,000
Interest Expenses				9,198,000	9,198,000	9,198,000	9,198,000	9,198,000
NWC				76,650,000	76,650,000	76,650,000	76,650,000	76,650,000
Changes in NWC				75,000,000	75,000,000	75,000,000	75,000,000	75,000,000
EBIT				123,750,000	123,750,000	123,750,000	123,750,000	123,750,000
EBIT After Taxes				97,762,500	97,762,500	97,762,500	97,762,500	97,762,500
EBIT After Tax + Depreciation				247,762,500	247,762,500	247,762,500	247,762,500	247,762,500
Changes in NWC				75,000,000	75,000,000	75,000,000	75,000,000	75,000,000
Free Cash Flows (FCF)				172,762,500	172,762,500	172,762,500	172,762,500	172,762,500
Investment				750,000,000				
PV FCFs				(278,374,566)	69,429,374	57,857,812	48,214,843	40,179,036
Total FCF				**(62,693,501)**				

Notes: Present valued at 20% to year 2021. For instance, the PV of FCFs in 2024 was discounted at 20% and 4 years back.

Source: Harvey Poniachek

https://doi.org/10.1142/9789811216749_0010

Case 10

Rutgers University's Pathway to Complete Renewable Electricity Generation

Mark Rodgers and Rosa Oppenheim

Rutgers Business School, USA

Introduction

The electric power grid includes power generation and delivery at the instant of demand. Fossil fuels are primary sources of energy for electricity generation since they are typically cost-effective and reliable fuel sources. However, the electricity sector generates the largest share of greenhouse gas emissions, which contribute to anthropogenic climate change.[1] Furthermore, burning fossil fuels creates harmful pollutants and by-products that contribute to ground-level ozone, particulates, and acid rain. Exposure to these elements can lead to a multitude of respiratory-related illnesses, which are potentially fatal.[2] Given these negative consequences, particularly in the context of current energy and geopolitical issues, it is imperative for institutions to evaluate their energy use and

[1]Rodgers, M. D., Coit, D. W., Felder, F., and Carlton, A. G. 2019. "Assessing the Effects of Power Grid Expansion on Human Health Externalities." *Socio-Economic Planning Sciences* 66: 92–104.

[2]U.S. Environmental Protection Agency. 2013. "www.epa.gov." July 2013. http://www.epa.gov/cleanenergy/energy-and-you/affect/air-emissions.html.

lower their carbon emissions to mitigate the effects of climate change.[3] Energy companies are already increasingly investing in low-carbon technologies,[4] and recent crises in Texas and California have highlighted the need for reexamining, upgrading, and modifying our reliance on traditional and alternative energy resources.[5]

In response to these challenges, Rutgers University, a public research university in New Jersey, has taken a leadership role in protecting the well-being of New Jersey citizens, and has served, for nearly a decade, as the secretariat for the New Jersey Climate Change Alliance, a statewide network of diverse organizations that share the goal of advancing science-informed climate change strategies at the state and local levels in New Jersey. In 2017, Rutgers President Robert L. Barchi signed the "We Are Still In" pledge, in support of the Paris Climate Accord,[6] with the goal of carbon neutrality by 2050. In alignment with this pledge, dozens of Rutgers research centers and programs are collaborating with government and industry to optimize clean energy technologies and policies. Rutgers has completed several initiatives to reduce energy consumption and transition to renewable energy sources, including various building upgrades to improve energy efficiency, as well as investments in solar and cogeneration technologies and the integration of solar panels and cogeneration plants. This allowed Rutgers to generate nearly 30% of the university's total energy usage in the year 2016–2017, and to increase that to 38.8% in FY 2019.

In support of these climate change mitigation efforts, Rutgers has made a significant investment in a large solar array on its Livingston campus in Piscataway, NJ. The structure consists of 7,993 solar panels with a capacity of 1.4 MW, which supplies the Livingston campus with 10% of its energy needs and reduces annual utility costs and carbon emissions by $200,000 and over 1,300 tons, respectively.[7] In addition to these capital

---

[3]Yergin, D. 2020. *The New Map: Energy, Climate, and the Clash of Nations*. New York: Penguin Press.

[4]Lee, J. 2021. "Exxon Joins Carbon-Capture Trend." *Wall Street Journal,* 9 February 2021.

[5]Penn, I. 2021. "Texas Storms, California Heat Waves and 'Vulnerable' Utilities." *New York Times*, 19 February 2021.

[6]Nieto-Munoz, S. 2017. "N.J. colleges and universities sign pledge supporting Paris Climate Accord." http://www.nj.com.

[7]"Rutgers University: Continued Commitment to Saving Energy." http://www.njcleanenergy.com/files/file/success_stories/Rutgers%20Success%20Story%20-%20final.pdf.

investments, other energy initiatives at Rutgers include high-temperature hot water pipe replacements; solid waste and electronics recycling; reduced mowing for green landscaping; and environmentally-friendly transportation practices such as using electric, biodiesel, and natural gas vehicles, and reducing fuel usage.

The Challenge

In September 2019, Rutgers University announced the creation of the President's Task Force on Carbon Neutrality and Climate Resilience, charged with developing a comprehensive Climate Action Plan to reduce its carbon footprint.[8] As part of this plan, the University aims to identify pathways to achieving carbon neutrality and ways to reduce its vulnerability to climate impacts. An interim report issued in July 2020 provides a comprehensive analysis of greenhouse gas emissions and presents a work plan for a final report in 2021.[9] Rutgers University would like to make strategic capacity investments in non-carbon emitting technologies that will minimize total costs to the University, while ultimately generating all its electricity from its own renewable energy sources. The United States Department of Energy has faced similar challenges and has deployed a toolkit of power sector analytical models to address similar problems on a larger scale.[10]

What We Know About Rutgers University

In 2018, Rutgers University consumed a total of 569,000 MWh of electricity. Based on enrollment projections, its electricity demand is expected

---

[8]Rutgers University. 2020. "Rutgers Advances Work on Climate Action Plan." *Rutgers Today*, 24 January 2020. https://news.rutgers.edu/news/rutgers-advances-work-climate-action-plan/20200124#.XlboXWhKhPZ.

[9]Rutgers University. 2017. "Developing Pathways toward a Carbon Neutral, Climate Resilient Rutgers, Interim Report of the President's Task Force on Carbon Neutrality and Climate Resilience." 17 July 2020. https://climatetaskforce.rutgers.edu/wp-content/uploads/sites/332/2020/07/2020-07-17-Interim-Report-FINAL.pdf.

[10]Boyd, E. 2016. "Power Sector Modeling 101 | Department of Energy — Office of Energy Policy and Systems Analysis." https://www.energy.gov/sites/prod/files/2016/02/f30/EPSA_Power_Sector_Modeling_FINAL_021816_0.pdf.

Exhibit 1. Generating Technology Costs and Net Capacity Ratings

	Capital Investment Costs (2018, \$/MW of Installed Capacity)	Fixed Operating & Maintenance Costs (2018, \$/MW of Installed Capacity)	Variable Generation Costs (2018, \$/MWh of Electricity Generated)	Existing Capacity (in MW)
Combined Heat & Power (CHP)	\$1,866,975	\$19,865	\$19.50	23
Solar	\$2,728,000	\$38,483	—	9.48
Geothermal (GT)	\$2,746,000	\$119,870	—	—

to increase annually by 3%.[9] Additionally, there are four different technologies that are being considered as part of the capacity expansion portfolio.[9] Exhibit 1 details their respective costs (capital investment costs, fixed operating and maintenance costs, and variable generation costs) and the amount of existing capacity at Rutgers University for each technology under consideration.[9] We assume all investments in capacity are available instantaneously.

Currently, Rutgers University purchases its electricity from the local utility company, at a rate of ***\$0.09/kWh (or \$90 MWh)*** but cannot exceed an annual spending limit of ***\$37MM (which decreases by 10% annually)***.[9] This augments the existing generation capacity to satisfy electricity demand.

Additional Assumptions

- All electricity demand must be satisfied.
- Rutgers University's Climate Action Plan planning horizon is 32 years (2018 through 2050).
- All costs are in 2018 USD (\$) and will increase annually at an inflation rate of 2%.
- Megawatts (MW) are units of capacity for the generation technologies. This capacity is reduced based on its net capacity rating.
- Megawatt-hours (MWh) are units of generation output based on the hourly dispatch of generating technologies with available capacity.
- For a given technology available in a region, total annual generation cannot exceed its effective capacity, where effective capacity = installed capacity * 8,760 hours per year.

- For each generation technology being considered, Rutgers University can only invest in a maximum of 45 MW of capacity over the planning horizon.

The Assignment

Determine a capacity investment portfolio that allows Rutgers University to meet its demand for electricity over the planning horizon from 2018 through 2050, without exceeding its capacity investment and budget limits. All future costs must be discounted back to 2018, assuming a discount rate of 3%.[11] We recognize that based on the WACC (weighted average cost of capital) or cost of equity, the discount rate could be significantly higher, and an alternative rate used instead. In the analysis, include exhibits that describe the investment portfolio and show how electricity demand will be satisfied annually. Provide a clear justification for the final recommendation. A linear programming tutorial appears in Appendix A.

Appendix A. Linear Programming Tutorial

In this Appendix, we present a brief overview of linear programming, a methodology for formulating and solving constrained optimization problems in which a linear objective function is to be maximized or minimized subject to set of linear inequality or equality constraints. A simple portfolio selection model is introduced below, formulated as a linear programming model, and the solution is presented.

General LP Formulation

We wish to find the numerical values of a set of n decision variables which optimize the value of a linear objective function, z, subject to a set of m linear constraints, and the requirement that all decision variables take on non-negative values:

Objective Function

$$\text{Maximize (or minimize) } z = c_1x_1 + c_2x_2 + \cdots + c_nx_n$$

[11]Federal Energy Management Program | Department of Energy. 2019. "2019 Discount Rates." https://www.energy.gov/sites/prod/files/2019/05/f62/2019discountrates.pdf.

Subject to:
Constraints

$$a_{11}x_1 + a_{12}x_2 + \cdots + a_{1n}x_n \; [\leq, =, \geq] \; b_1$$

$$a_{21}x_1 + a_{22}x_2 + \cdots + a_{2n}x_n \; [\leq, =, \geq] \; b_2$$

$$\vdots$$

$$a_{m1}x_1 + a_{m2}x_2 + \cdots + a_{mn}x_n \; [\leq, =, \geq] \; b_m$$

$$x_1, x_2, \ldots, x_n \geq 0$$

where
x_i = decision variables, $i = 1, \ldots, n$
c_i = objective function coefficients of the decision variables, $i = 1, \ldots, n$
a_{ij} = technological coefficients of the decision variables, $i = 1, \ldots, n$ and $j = 1, \ldots, m$
b_j = right-hand sides of constraints, $j = 1, \ldots, m$.

An Example

Gamma Finance, Inc. has $350,000 available in cash and is seeking to invest these funds in renewable energy sources: wind, solar, geothermal, and hydropower. The following guidelines have been proposed:

- No more than $100,000 is to be allocated to investments in any one of these sources.
- The total investment in geothermal and hydropower should be no more than 70% of the total invested.
- The investment in wind should be at least as much as the investment in solar.
- At least $75,000 must be invested in geothermal.

Exhibit A1 shows the projected rate of return for each investment.

Exhibit A1. Projected Rate of Return for Each Investment

Investment	Projected Rate of Return (%)
Wind	8.2
Solar	10.1
Geothermal	5.6
Hydropower	7.4

Gamma would like to determine how much to allocate to each investment opportunity to maximize the projected return.

Problem Formulation

Let x_1 = \$ invested in wind energy resources
x_2 = \$ invested in solar energy resources
x_3 = \$ invested in geothermal energy resources
x_4 = \$ invested in hydropower energy resources

$$\text{Maximize } z = 0.082x_1 + 0.101x_2 + 0.056x_3 + 0.074x_4$$

Subject to:

$$\begin{array}{lllllllll} x_1 & + & x_2 & + & x_3 & + & x_4 & \leq & 350{,}000 \\ x_1 & & & & & & & \leq & 100{,}000 \\ & & x_2 & & & & & \leq & 100{,}000 \\ & & & & x_3 & & & \leq & 100{,}000 \\ & & & & & & x_4 & \leq & 100{,}000 \\ & & & & x_3 & + & x_4 & \leq & (0.7)(x_1 + x_2 + x_3 + x_4) \\ x_1 & & & & & & & \geq & x_2 \\ & & & & x_3 & & & \geq & 75{,}000 \end{array}$$

$x_i \geq 0\ \forall i$ (for all i)

Solution

Writing each constraint with the variables on the left side of the inequalities and constants on the right side, we have:

$$\text{Maximize } z = 0.082x_1 + 0.101x_2 + 0.056x_3 + 0.074x_4$$

Subject to:

$$\begin{array}{lllllllll} x_1 & + & x_2 & + & x_3 & + & x_4 & \leq & 350{,}000 \\ x_1 & & & & & & & \leq & 100{,}000 \\ & & x_2 & & & & & \leq & 100{,}000 \\ & & & & x_3 & & & \leq & 100{,}000 \\ & & & & & & x_4 & \leq & 100{,}000 \\ -0.7x_1 & - & 0.7x_2 & + & 0.3x_3 & + & 0.3x_4 & \leq & 0 \\ x_1 & - & x_2 & & & & & \geq & 0 \\ & & & & x_3 & & & \geq & 75{,}000 \end{array}$$

$x_i \geq 0\ \forall i$ (for all i)

Various software packages exist for solving linear programs, depending upon the particular structure of the problem and the number of decision variables and constraints; these include Microsoft Excel Solver, General Algebraic Modeling System (GAMS), and Linear, Interactive, and Discrete Optimizer (LINDO).

Using Microsoft Excel Solver, Exhibit A2 shows the input, Exhibit A3 shows the completed Solver dialog box, and Exhibit A4 shows the solution.

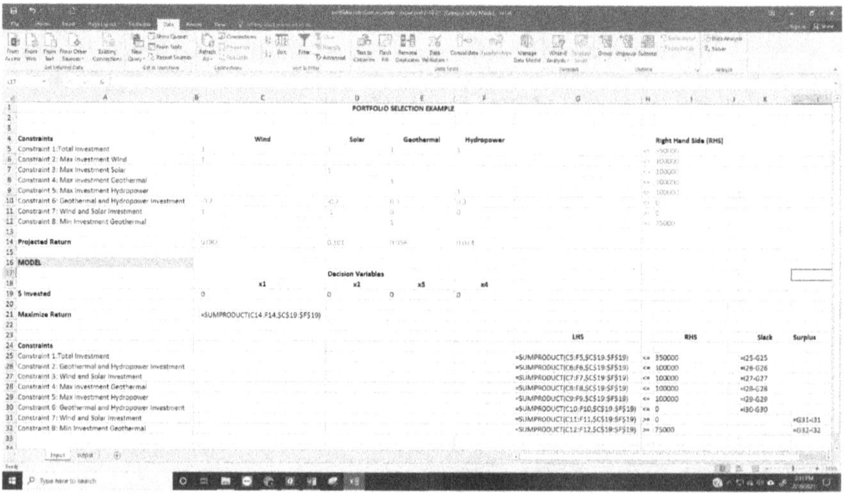

Exhibit A2. Problem Input

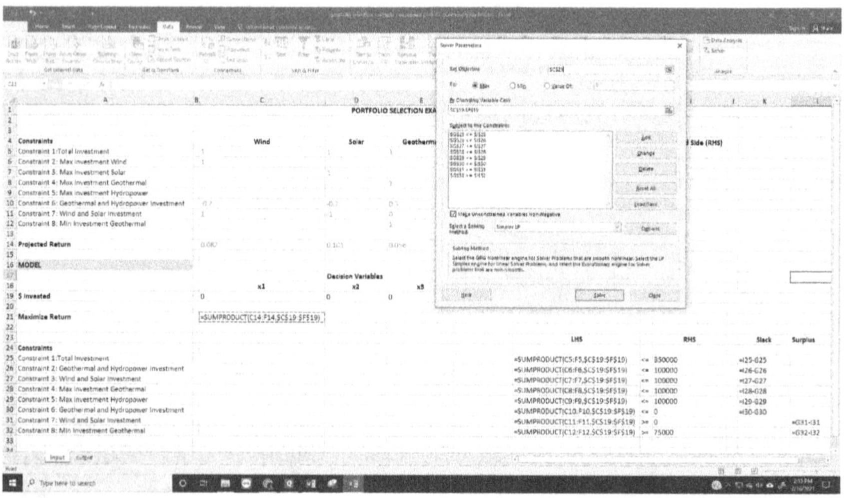

Exhibit A3. Solver Input

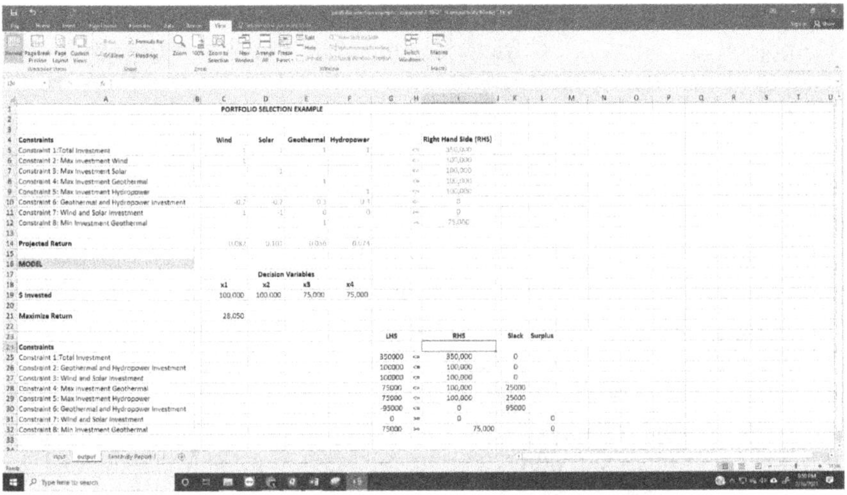

PORTFOLIO SELECTION EXAMPLE

Constraints	Wind	Solar	Geothermal	Hydropower		Right Hand Side (RHS)
Constraint 1:Total Investment	1	1	1	1	<=	350,000
Constraint 2: Max investment Wind	1				<=	100,000
Constraint 3: Max Investment Solar		1			<=	100,000
Constraint 4: Max Investment Geothermal			1		<=	100,000
Constraint 5: Max investment Hydropower				1	<=	100,000
Constraint 6: Geothermal and Hydropower Investment	-0.7	-0.7	0.3	0.3	<=	0
Constraint 7: Wind and Solar Investment	1	-1	0	0	>=	0
Constraint 8: Min Investment Geothermal			1		>=	75,000
Projected Return	0.082	0.101	0.056	0.074		

MODEL

	x1	x2	x3	x4
$ Invested	100,000	100,000	75,000	75,000
Maximize Return	28,050			

Constraints	LHS		RHS	Slack	Surplus
Constraint 1:Total Investment	350000	<=	350,000	0	
Constraint 2: Geothermal and Hydropower Investment	100000	<=	100,000	0	
Constraint 3: Wind and Solar Investment	100000	<=	100,000	0	
Constraint 4: Max investment Geothermal	75000	<=	100,000	25000	
Constraint 5: Max Investment Hydropower	75000	<=	100,000	25000	
Constraint 6: Geothermal and Hydropower Investment	-95000	<=	0	95000	
Constraint 7: Wind and Solar Investment	0	>=	0		0
Constraint 8: Min Investment Geothermal	75000	>=	75,000		0

Exhibit A4. Problem Output

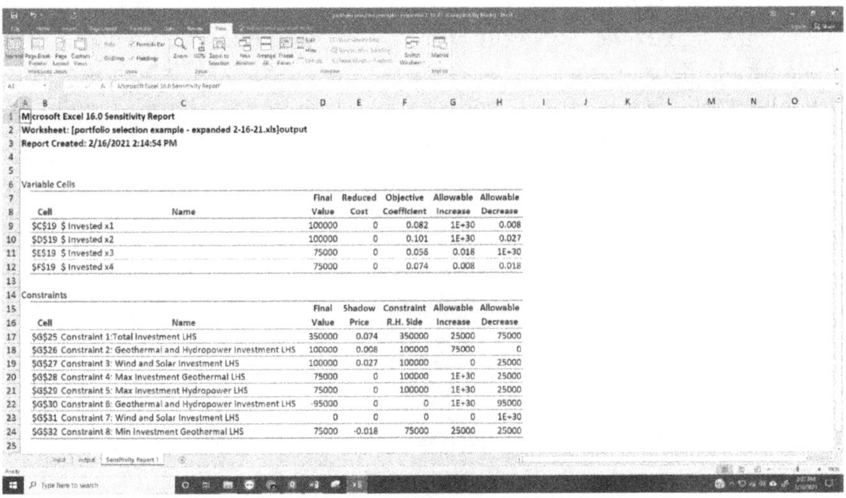

Microsoft Excel 16.0 Sensitivity Report
Worksheet: [portfolio selection example - expanded 2-16-21.xls]output
Report Created: 2/16/2021 2:14:54 PM

Variable Cells

Cell	Name	Final Value	Reduced Cost	Objective Coefficient	Allowable Increase	Allowable Decrease
C19	$ Invested x1	100000	0	0.082	1E+30	0.008
D19	$ Invested x2	100000	0	0.101	1E+30	0.027
E19	$ Invested x3	75000	0	0.056	0.018	1E+30
F19	$ Invested x4	75000	0	0.074	0.008	0.018

Constraints

Cell	Name	Final Value	Shadow Price	Constraint R.H. Side	Allowable Increase	Allowable Decrease
G25	Constraint 1:Total Investment LHS	350000	0.074	350000	25000	75000
G26	Constraint 2: Geothermal and Hydropower Investment LHS	100000	0.008	100000	75000	0
G27	Constraint 3: Wind and Solar Investment LHS	100000	0.027	100000	0	25000
G28	Constraint 4: Max Investment Geothermal LHS	75000	0	100000	1E+30	25000
G29	Constraint 5: Max Investment Hydropower LHS	75000	0	100000	1E+30	25000
G30	Constraint 6: Geothermal and Hydropower Investment LHS	-95000	0	0	1E+30	95000
G31	Constraint 7: Wind and Solar Investment LHS	0	0	0	0	1E+30
G32	Constraint 8: Min Investment Geothermal LHS	75000	-0.018	75000	25000	25000

Exhibit A5. Sensitivity Report

For this illustrative example, the optimal solution is to invest $100,000 in wind energy resources, $100,000 in solar energy resources, $75,000 in geothermal energy resources, and $75,000 in hydropower energy resources, with a maximum projected return of $28,500.

Solver also generates a Sensitivity Report, shown in Exhibit A5, which can be used to determine the impact of changes in model parameter(s) on the optimal solution. The top section refers to changes in the objective function coefficients, and the bottom section refers to changes in the right-hand sides.

As an illustration, if the rate of return for solar energy resources (the objective function coefficient of decision variable x_2) is any value in the allowable range between 0.082 – 0.008 and 0.082 + 0.008, or any value greater than 0.074, the optimal allocation (the optimal values of the decision variables) will remain the same. If the rate of return is outside this allowable range (or less than 0.074), the allocation of funds to the different energy sources will change. Similarly, if the shadow price (also called the dual value, or marginal value) for Constraint 1 is 0.074, this indicates that if the right side of the constraint, or the total amount available for investment, were changed to any value within the allowable range 350,000 – 75,000 to 350,000 + 25,000, the maximum return would change at a rate of $0.074 per unit change in the right side. So if an additional $10,000 were available (which is within the allowable increase of 25,000), the maximum return would be $28,050 + (0.074)(10,000) = $28,790. Similarly, the shadow price for Constraint 8 is –0.018; this indicates that if the right side of the constraint, or the minimum required investment in geothermal energy resources, were increased to $85,000 (which is within the allowable increase of 25,000), the maximum return would be $28,050 – (0.018)(10,000) = $27,870.

Part IV

Valuation of Financial Assets, Projects, and Firms

https://doi.org/10.1142/9789811216749_0011

Case 11

Microsoft Corporation Notes Offering Valuation

Harvey A. Poniachek

Rutgers Business School, USA

Mr. Andrew Dow has been Senior Managing Director at J. P. Morgan Securities LLC's fixed income division for the past 5 years. He earned an undergraduate degree in mathematics from Rutgers and an MBA in finance from Wharton Business School over a decade ago. Since graduation, he has worked in the financial services industry, which includes investments analysis, risk management, design, and development of fixed income trading systems. He has extensive experience interacting with senior investment and trading personnel on performance evaluation and risk attribution of fixed-income investments, and thorough working knowledge of the industry's databases and programming skills. Andrew was a senior member of the fixed-income investment team and was responsible for quantitative analysis, risk assessment, and measurement. He provided investment and market expertise to the trading desk and bank management, and quantitative analyst of fixed income, develops quantitative techniques, and supports the investment process and hedging through duration and liability matching.

In recent years, Andrew engaged in several bond underwritings that were deemed quite challenging, including the underwriting of convertible bonds, bonds with embodied options, and multicurrency bonds of which some were sold via Dutch auctions.[1] Andrew has developed a remarkable reputation among investment banking companies and corporate bond issuers that often contributed to JP Morgan Securities LLC's selection as lead bonds underwritings.

On August 1, 2016, Microsoft Corporation ("MSFT") announced the offering of $19.75 billion aggregate senior unsecured notes consisting of seven tranches and unlisted.[2] The notes are senior unsecured obligations that bear fixed interest paid semi-annually. Microsoft has the option to redeem the notes of any series, in whole or in part, at any time or from time to time prior to maturity. The note prices, underwriting discounts and proceeds are listed below.

	Price to Public (1)	Underwriting Discounts	Proceeds, Before Expenses, to Microsoft
Per 2019 Note	99.897%	0.150%	99.747%
Total	$2,497,425,000	$3,750,000	$2,493,675,000
Per 2021 Note	99.895%	0.300%	99.595%
Total	$2,747,112,500	$8,250,000	$2,738,862,500

[1] In a Dutch auction, the underwriter does not set a fixed price for the shares to be sold, but the price is determined by auction based on the submitted bids. Suppose that Z Company seeks to sell 400 shares to the public and it receives the following bids:

Bidder	Quantity	Price
A	100 shares	$16
B	100 shares	14
C	200 shares	12
D	100 shares	12
E	200 shares	10

Bidder A is willing to buy 100 shares at $16 each, Bidder B is willing to buy 100 shares at $14, and so on. The Z Company observes that the highest price that will result in all 400 shares being sold is 12. Thus, bidders A through D will receive shares at the price of $12 per share. See Stephen A. Ross *et al.*, *Fundamentals of Corporate Finance*, 12th ed. (McGraw Hill Education, New York, 2019), Chapter 15, 503 pp.

[2] Microsoft debt offerings are described by its Prospectus and applicable Prospectus Supplement. Additional information is available in its annual report on Form 10-K, a quarterly report on Form 10-Q and current Form 8-K filed with the SEC. The Prospectus and Prospectus Supplement were edited to adopt for the case study purpose.

(Continued)

	Price to Public (1)	Underwriting Discounts	Proceeds, Before Expenses, to Microsoft
Per 2023 Note	99.701%	0.350%	99.351%
Total	$1,495,515,000	$5,250,000	$1,490,265,000
Per 2026 Note	99.814%	0.400%	99.414%
Total	$3,992,560,000	$16,000,000	$3,976,560,000
Per 2036 Note	99.613%	0.750%	99.863%
Total	$2,241,292,500	$16,875,000	$2,224,417,500
Per 2046 Note	99.515%	0.750%	98.765%
Total	$4,478,175,000	$33,750,000	$4,444,425,000
Per 2056 Note	97.505%	0.750%	96.755%
Total	$2,193,862,500	$16,875,000	$2,176,987,500

The notes are new issues of securities with no established trading markets, while the underwriters intend to make a market in each series of the notes. In addition, the underwriters are permitted to engage in transactions that stabilize the market prices of the notes. Investing in the notes involves various risks, including liquidity risk. The indenture governing the notes does not contain financial covenants or restrictions from incurring additional debt or other liabilities. The market prices of the notes will depend on several factors, including the following:

- Ratings on the issuer debt securities assigned by rating agencies;
- The prevailing interest rates paid by comparable companies;
- Performance, financial condition and prospects; and
- The condition of the financial markets.

Medium-term notes (MTN) are corporate debt instruments offered continuously to investors with maturities ranging from 9 months to 30 years.[3] MTNs are registered with the SEC and are fixed- or floating-rate notes denominated in dollars or in a foreign currency. Companies issue bonds through a competitive and negotiated mechanism, where under the latter approach an underwriter may purchase bonds from an issuer for reoffering to the public. The specific method is determined by

[3]Frank J. Fabozzi, *Bond Markets, Analysis, and Strategies*, 9th ed. (Pearson, New York, 2016), 153.

several factors, including the issuer's credit, issue size, financial terms, and market conditions. Competitive bond sales assure the lowest interest rates and underwriting fees. Large issues provide underwriters opportunities to form syndicates and to reduce risk by diversifying their portfolios. A negotiated sale allows the sale date to be timed more closely in accordance with market conditions.

An unsecured note or bond is backed by a promise to pay, whereas secured notes and bonds are collateralized by corporate assets and are graded by the major credit rating agencies that assess how likely are the notes and bonds issuers to default on their obligations. For a note or bond to make investment grade, it must have a minimum rating of Baa or BBB. Bond ratings by the three major rating agencies are listed below.

Credit Ratings	**Moody's**	**S&P**	**Fitch**
Prime	Aaa	AAA	AAA
Excellent	Aa	AA	AA
Upper Medium	A	A	A
Lower Medium	Baa	BBB	BBB
Speculative	Ba	BB	BB
Very Speculative	B, Caa	B, CCC, CC, C	B, CCC, CC, C
Default	Ca, C	D	DDD, DD, D

Callable notes or bonds at a scheduled fixed premium provide the issuer the right to call back the security within a certain time period, which could pose a disadvantage for the investor in a declining interest rate market.[4] The investor loses the higher interest rate, and the issuer can reissue bonds at a lower rate. Because of this, callable notes or bonds carry a higher interest rate. Puttable notes or bonds provide investors with the right to "put" the bond back to the issuer at par value plus accrued interest at pre-determined intervals.

The notes to be issued by Microsoft Corporation were underwritten by several investment banks, including J.P. Morgan Securities LLC, Merrill Lynch, Wells Fargo Securities, LLC, Barclays Capital Inc.,

[4]The second type of call option uses an indexed price, wherein the strike price is specified as a fixed-spread over a reference risk-free rate. This feature is referred to as a make-whole call option. The call option is in-the-money only when the firm's credit spread decreases below the fixed-spread used to set the call price.

Citigroup Global Markets Inc., Goldman, Sachs & Co., and 15 additional firms. The complete list of the underwriters is available on the Prospectus that is available in Appendix A. J.P. Morgan Securities, the US investment banking arm of J. P. Morgan Chase provides debt and equity underwriting, mergers and acquisitions and corporate restructuring advisory, securities dealing and brokerage, and trade execution services for large companies and institutional investors.[5] J.P. Morgan Securities is part of its parent company's private banking operations, which also includes the private wealth management business. It operates offices in New York, Chicago, Los Angeles, Boston, Atlanta, and other cities.

The main issue before the underwriting banks was whether to acquire the issue and sell it to prospective investors or manage it on a best-effort basis. In the first instance, the banks would bear the risk, whereas in the second option the risk will be borne by Microsoft. J.P. Morgan Securities LLC's role, in addition to acting as an underwriter, was to provide analytical consulting to the issuer. This function was offered by George Smith, Managing Director, and his team, who acted separately and independently of the underwriting function of the bank. George was a senior fixed income analyst at the firm and was reporting on a dotted line to Andrew. The analytical issues raised by Microsoft Corporation for which J.P. Morgan's services were required are as follows:

1. Pricing the issue;
2. Analyze the marketing approach in terms of the best effort versus underwriters acquiring the issue, and compare the recommended marketing approach with the experience of other high-tech companies; and
3. Debt leverage aspects of Microsoft and its peers.

J.P. Morgan Securities LLC was also requested by the investment divisions to provide the following information for the purpose of sharing it with prospective investors:

---

[5]According to the 10 K for 2019, J.P. Morgan Chase & Co. is a leading global financial services firm and one of the largest banking institutions in the United States and $2.7 in assets at the end of 2019. The company's activities are organized in four major business segments, and a Corporate segment. The wholesale business segments are the Corporate & Investment Bank ("CIB"), Commercial Banking ("CB"), and Asset & Wealth Management ("AWM").

1. YTM of the issue;
2. Duration;
3. Convexity; and
4. Hedging methods against a price decline.

In addressing the issues, George provided his team with a summary of Microsoft Corporation's bond Prospectus that was filed with the SEC and is enclosed here as Appendix A. He also recommended that his staff reviews the Primer on Corporate Bonds that is enclosed as Appendix B. J.P. Morgan Securities LLC was under a tight timeline of two weeks after which the underwriting group is expected to hold a preliminary meeting at the firm's offices. George plans of having two of his top assistants participate in the meeting. He requested a draft report within a week for internal review and discussion.

Appendix A. Prospectus and Prospectus Supplement[6]

Microsoft Debt Offerings

On August 1, 2016, Microsoft Corporation announced the offering of $19.75 billion aggregate senior unsecured notes consisting of the following tranches:

- $2.50 billion of 1.100% notes due August 8, 2019
- $2.75 billion of 1.550% notes due August 8, 2021
- $1.50 billion of 2.000% notes due August 8, 2023
- $4.00 billion of 2.400% notes due August 8, 2026
- $2.25 billion of 3.450% notes due August 8, 2036
- $4.50 billion of 3.700% notes due August 8, 2046
- $2.25 billion of 3.950% notes due August 8, 2056

[6]Microsoft debt offerings are described by its Prospectus and applicable Prospectus Supplement. Additional information is available in its annual report on Form 10-K, a quarterly report on Form 10-Q or a current report on Form 8-K filed with the SEC. The Prospectus and Prospectus Supplement were edited to adopt for the case study purpose.

The notes will be senior unsecured obligations and will be ranked equally with other unsecured and unsubordinated debt. Net proceeds from the offering are to be used for general corporate purposes, which may include acquisitions, funding for working capital, capital expenditures, repurchases of its capital stock, and repayment of its existing debt. The offerings are expected to close on August 8, 2016.

Interest on the notes will accrue from August 8, 2016, and will be paid semi-annually in arrears on February 8 and August 8 of each year, beginning on February 8, 2017. Microsoft will have the option to redeem the notes of any series, in whole or in part, at any time or from time to time prior to August 8, 2019 (in the case of the 2019 Notes), July 8, 2021 (in the case of the 2021 Notes), June 8, 2023 (in the case of the 2023 Notes), May 8, 2026 (in the case of the 2026 Notes), February 8, 2036 (in the case of the 2036 Notes), February 8, 2046 (in the case of the 2046 Notes), and February 8, 2056 (in the case of the 2056 Notes) at the redemption price of 100% of the principal amount of the notes plus accrued and unpaid interest.

The note prices, underwriting discounts, and proceeds are listed below.

	Price to Public[a]	Underwriting Discounts	Proceeds, Before Expenses, to Microsoft[a]
Per 2019 Note	99.897%	0.150%	99.747%
Total	$2,497,425,000	$3,750,000	$2,493,675,000
Per 2021 Note	99.895%	0.300%	99.595%
Total	$2,747,112,500	$8,250,000	$2,738,862,500
Per 2023 Note	99.701%	0.350%	99.351%
Total	$1,495,515,000	$5,250,000	$1,490,265,000
Per 2026 Note	99.814%	0.400%	99.414%
Total	$3,992,560,000	$16,000,000	$3,976,560,000
Per 2036 Note	99.613%	0.750%	99.863%
Total	$2,241,292,500	$16,875,000	$2,224,417,500
Per 2046 Note	99.515%	0.750%	98.765%
Total	$4,478,175,000	$33,750,000	$4,444,425,000

(*Continued*)

(*Continued*)

	Price to Public[a]	Underwriting Discounts	Proceeds, Before Expenses, to Microsoft[a]
Per 2056 Note	97.505%	0.750%	96.755%
Total	$2,193,862,500	$16,875,000	$2,176,987,500

Note: [a]Plus accrued interest, if any, from August 8, 2016.

Trading

The notes are new issues of securities with no established trading markets, and the issuer does not intend to apply for listing of the notes on any securities exchange. The underwriters have advised that they currently intend to make a market in each series of the notes, but they are not obligated to do so and may, in their sole discretion, discontinue market-making at any time without notice.

Risk Factors

Investing in the notes involves risks. The indenture governing the notes does not contain financial covenants or meaningful restrictions, neither Microsoft Corporation nor any of its subsidiaries are restricted from incurring additional debt or other liabilities, including debt secured by liens, under the indenture. In addition, the issuer is not restricted from paying dividends or making distributions on capital stock or purchasing or redeeming capital stock under the indenture.

The market prices of the notes will depend on many factors, including, among others, the following:

- Ratings on the issuer debt securities assigned by rating agencies;
- The prevailing interest rates being paid by comparable companies;
- Performance, financial condition and prospects; and
- The condition of the financial markets.

The condition of the financial markets and prevailing interest rates have fluctuated in the past and are likely to fluctuate in the future, which could have an adverse effect on the market prices of the notes. Rating agencies continually review the ratings they have assigned to companies and debt securities. Negative changes in the ratings assigned to the issuer or its debt securities could have an adverse effect on the market prices of the notes.

Capitalization

The following sets forth Microsoft Corporation capitalization on a consolidated basis as of June 30, 2016, on both an actual and an as-adjusted basis to reflect the issuance and sale of the notes offered hereby, but not the application of the net proceeds from the issuance and sale of such notes.

	As of June 30, 2016	
	Actual	**As-Adjusted**
	(Unaudited) (in Millions)	
Long-Term Debt (Including Current Portion)		
0.875% Notes Due 2017	$600	$600
1.000% Notes Due 2018	450	450
1.300% Notes Due 2018	1,750	1,750
1.625% Notes Due 2018	1,250	1,250
4.200% Notes Due 2019	1,000	1,000
1.850% Notes Due 2020	1,500	1,500
3.000% Notes Due 2020	1,000	1,000
2.000% Notes Due 2020	2,250	2,250
4.000% Notes Due 2021	500	500
2.125% Notes Due 2021[a]	1,944	1,944
2.375% Notes Due 2022	1,500	1,500
2.650% Notes Due 2022	1,000	1,000
2.125% Notes Due 2022	750	750
2.375% Notes Due 2023	1,000	1,000
3.625% Notes Due 2023	1,500	1,500
2.700% Notes Due 2025	2,250	2,250
3.125% Notes Due 2025	3,000	3,000
3.125% Notes Due 2028[b]	1,944	1,944
2.625% Notes Due 2033[c]	611	611
3.500% Notes Due 2035	1,500	1,500
4.200% Notes Due 2035	1,000	1,000
5.200% Notes Due 2039	750	750
4.500% Notes Due 2040	1,000	1,000
5.300% Notes Due 2041	1,000	1,000

(Continued)

(*Continued*)

	As of June 30, 2016	
	Actual	As-Adjusted
	(Unaudited) (in Millions)	
3.500% Notes Due 2042	900	900
3.750% Notes Due 2043	500	500
4.875% Notes Due 2043	500	500
3.750% Notes Due 2045	1,750	1,750
4.450% Notes Due 2045	3,000	3,000
4.000% Notes Due 2055	2,250	2,250
4.750% Notes Due 2055	1,000	1,000
1.100% Notes Due 2019 Offered Hereby	—	2,500
1.550% Notes Due 2021 Offered Hereby	—	2,750
2.000% Notes Due 2023 Offered Hereby	—	1,500
2.400% Notes Due 2026 Offered Hereby	—	4,000
3.450% Notes Due 2036 Offered Hereby	—	2,250
3.700% Notes Due 2046 Offered Hereby	—	4,500
3.950% Notes Due 2056 Offered Hereby	—	2,250
Unamortized Debt Discount	(166)	(270)
Total Debt	40,783	60,429
Total Stockholders' Equity	71,997	71,997
Total Capitalization	$112,780	$132,426

Notes: [a]Represents €1,750 million principal amount (using the exchange rate of €1.00 = $1.11095 in effect on June 30, 2016).

[b]Represents €1,750 million principal amount (using the exchange rate of €1.00 = $1.11095 in effect on June 30, 2016).

[c]Represents €550 million principal amount (using the exchange rate of €1.00 = $1.11095 in effect on June 30, 2016).

Ratio of Earnings to Fixed Charges

For purposes of calculating the ratio of earnings to fixed charges, earnings represents earnings from continuing operations before income taxes and before income (losses) from equity method investments plus: (a) fixed charges; and (b) cash distributions from equity method investments. Fixed charges include (a) interest expense; (b) capitalized debt issuance costs; and (c) the portion of operating rental expense which management believes is representative of the interest component of rent expense. The following table sets forth the historical ratio of our earnings to fixed charges for the periods indicated.

	Year Ended June 30				
	2016	**2015**	**2014**	**2013**	**2012**
Ratio of Earnings to Fixed Charges	16×	22×	43×	57×	52×

Underwriting

Microsoft Corporation and the representatives of the underwriters named below have entered into an underwriting agreement relating to the offer and sale of the notes agreed to sell to each underwriter the principal amount of notes that appears opposite the name of that underwriter below:

Underwriter	**Principal Amount of 2019 Notes**	**Principal Amount of 2021 Notes**	**Principal Amount of 2023 Notes**
J.P. Morgan Securities LLC	$575,000,000	$632,500,000	$345,000,000
Merrill Lynch, Pierce, Fenner & Smith Incorporated	$575,000,000	$632,500,000	$345,000,000
Wells Fargo Securities, LLC	$575,000,000	$632,500,000	$345,000,000
Barclays Capital Inc.	$137,500,000	$151,250,000	$82,500,000
Citigroup Global Markets Inc.	$137,500,000	$151,250,000	$82,500,000
Goldman, Sachs & Co.	$137,500,000	$151,250,000	$82,500,000
HSBC Securities (USA) Inc.	$137,500,000	$151,250,000	$82,500,000
U.S. Bancorp Investments, Inc.	$137,500,000	$151,250,000	$82,500,000
The Williams Capital Group, L.P.	$12,500,000	$13,750,000	$7,500,000
Academy Securities, Inc.	$6,250,000	$6,875,000	$3,750,000
Blaylock Beal Van, LLC	$6,250,000	$6,875,000	$3,750,000
CastleOak Securities, L.P.	$6,250,000	$6,875,000	$3,750,000
C.L. King & Associates, Inc.	$6,250,000	$6,875,000	$3,750,000
CAVU Securities, LLC	$6,250,000	$6,875,000	$3,750,000
Drexel Hamilton, LLC	$6,250,000	$6,875,000	$3,750,000
Lebenthal & Co., LLC	$6,250,000	$6,875,000	$3,750,000
Loop Capital Markets LLC	$6,250,000	$6,875,000	$3,750,000
MFR Securities, Inc.	$6,250,000	$6,875,000	$3,750,000
Mischler Financial Group, Inc.	$6,250,000	$6,875,000	$3,750,000
Samuel A. Ramirez & Company, Inc.	$6,250,000	$6,875,000	$3,750,000
Siebert Brandford Shank & Co., L.L.C.	$6,250,000	$6,875,000	$3,750,000
Total	$2,500,000,000	$2,750,000,000	$1,500,000,000

(Continued)

(*Continued*)

Underwriter	Principal Amount of 2026 Notes	Principal Amount of 2036 Notes	Principal Amount of 2046 Notes	Principal Amount of 2056 Notes
J.P. Morgan Securities LLC	$920,000,000	$517,500,000	$1,035,000,000	$517,500,000
Merrill Lynch, Pierce, Fenner & Smith Incorporated	$920,000,000	$517,500,000	$1,035,000,000	$517,500,000
Wells Fargo Securities, LLC	$920,000,000	$517,500,000	$1,035,000,000	$517,500,000
Barclays Capital Inc.	$220,000,000	$123,750,000	$247,500,000	$123,750,000
Citigroup Global Markets Inc.	$220,000,000	$123,750,000	$247,500,000	$123,750,000
Goldman, Sachs & Co.	$220,000,000	$123,750,000	$247,500,000	$123,750,000
HSBC Securities (USA) Inc.	$220,000,000	$123,750,000	$247,500,000	$123,750,000
U.S. Bancorp Investments, Inc.	$220,000,000	$123,750,000	$247,500,000	$123,750,000
The Williams Capital Group, L.P.	$20,000,000	$11,250,000	$22,500,000	$11,250,000
Academy Securities, Inc.	$10,000,000	$5,625,000	$11,250,000	$5,625,000
Blaylock Beal Van, LLC	$10,000,000	$5,625,000	$11,250,000	$5,625,000
CastleOak Securities, L.P.	$10,000,000	$5,625,000	$11,250,000	$5,625,000
C.L. King & Associates, Inc.	$10,000,000	$5,625,000	$11,250,000	$5,625,000
CAVU Securities, LLC	$10,000,000	$5,625,000	$11,250,000	$5,625,000
Drexel Hamilton, LLC	$10,000,000	$5,625,000	$11,250,000	$5,625,000
Lebenthal & Co., LLC	$10,000,000	$5,625,000	$11,250,000	$5,625,000
Loop Capital Markets LLC	$10,000,000	$5,625,000	$11,250,000	$5,625,000
MFR Securities, Inc.	$10,000,000	$5,625,000	$11,250,000	$5,625,000
Mischler Financial Group, Inc.	$10,000,000	$5,625,000	$11,250,000	$5,625,000
Samuel A. Ramirez & Company, Inc.	$10,000,000	$5,625,000	$11,250,000	$5,625,000
Siebert Brandford Shank & Co., L.L.C.	$10,000,000	$5,625,000	$11,250,000	$5,625,000
Total	$4,000,000,000	$2,250,000,000	$4,500,000,000	$2,250,000,000

Price Stabilization and Short Positions

In connection with the offering, the underwriters are permitted to engage in transactions that stabilize the market prices of the notes. Such transactions consist of bids or purchases to peg, fix or maintain the price of the notes. If an underwriter creates a short position in the notes of a series in connection with the offering (i.e., if it sells more notes of that series than are on the cover page of this prospectus supplement), the underwriter may reduce that short position by purchasing notes of that series in the open market. Purchases of a security to stabilize the price or to reduce a short position could cause the price of the security to be higher than the price that otherwise would exist in the open market in the absence of such transactions. These transactions may be affected in the over-the-counter market or otherwise and, if commenced, may be discontinued at any time.

Neither the issuer nor any of the underwriters make any representation or prediction as to the direction or magnitude of any effect that the transactions described above may have on the prices of the notes. In addition, neither Microsoft Corporation nor any of the underwriters make any representation that any of the underwriters will engage in such transactions, or that such transactions, once begun, will not be discontinued without notice.

The Company

Founded in 1975, Microsoft Corporation (Microsoft or the Company) operates worldwide and has offices in more than 100 countries. The company develops, licenses, and supports a wide range of software products, services, and devices that deliver new opportunities, greater convenience, and enhanced value to people's lives. It offers an array of services, including cloud-based services, to consumers and businesses, and designs, manufactures, and sells devices that integrate with our cloud-based services, and we deliver relevant online advertising to a global audience.

Microsoft is incorporated under the laws of the State of Washington. Its principal executive offices are located at One Microsoft Way, Redmond, Washington 98052-6399, and its main telephone number is (425) 882-8080.

Debt securities denominated in US dollars will be issued in denominations of $2,000 and any integral multiple of $1,000 in excess thereof, unless otherwise specified in the applicable prospectus supplement. If the debt securities of a series are denominated in a foreign or composite currency, the applicable prospectus supplement will specify the denomination or denominations in which those debt securities will be issued. The issuer will repay the debt securities of each series at 100% of their principal amount, together with accrued and unpaid interest thereon at maturity.

Unless otherwise specified in the applicable prospectus supplement, the debt securities of each series will not be listed on any securities exchange.

Fixed-Rate Debt Securities

If the debt securities of a series being offered will bear interest at a fixed rate of interest, the debt securities of that series will bear interest at the annual interest rate specified on the cover page of the applicable prospectus supplement. Interest on those debt securities will be payable in arrears on the interest payment dates specified in the applicable prospectus supplement for those debt securities. If the maturity date, the redemption date, or an interest payment date is not a business day, the issuer will pay principal, premium, if any, the redemption price, if any, and interest on the next succeeding business day, and no interest will accrue from and after the relevant maturity date, redemption date or interest payment date to the date of that payment. Unless otherwise specified in the applicable prospectus supplement, interest on the fixed-rate debt securities will be computed on the basis of a 360-day year of 12 30-day months.

Floating Rate Debt Securities

If the debt securities of a series being offered will bear interest at a floating rate of interest, the debt securities of that series will bear interest during each relevant interest period at the rate determined as set forth in the applicable prospectus supplement and as otherwise set forth below. Each floating rate debt security will have an interest rate basis or formula specified in the applicable prospectus supplement.

Unless otherwise specified in the applicable prospectus supplement, Microsoft will base that formula on the London Interbank Offered Rate ("LIBOR") for the LIBOR Currency. The "LIBOR Currency" means the currency specified in the applicable prospectus supplement as to which LIBOR will be calculated or, if no such currency is specified in the applicable prospectus supplement, US dollars. The applicable prospectus supplement indicates any spread or spread multiplier to be applied in the interest rate formula to determine the interest rate applicable in any interest period. Unless otherwise specified in the applicable prospectus supplement, interest will be computed on the basis of the actual number of days elapsed during the relevant interest period and a 360-day year.

The floating rate debt securities may have a maximum or minimum rate limitation. In no event, however, will the rate of interest on the debt securities be higher than the maximum rate of interest permitted by New York law as that law may be modified by US laws of general application.

The applicable prospectus supplement will identify the calculation agent for each series of floating rate debt securities, which will compute the interest accruing on the debt securities.

If any interest payment date for the debt securities of a series bearing interest at a floating rate based on LIBOR (other than the maturity date or the redemption date, if any) would otherwise be a day that is not a business day, then the interest payment date will be postponed to the following date which is a business day, unless that business day falls in the next succeeding calendar month, in which case the interest payment date will be the immediately preceding business day. If the maturity date or the redemption date, if any, is not a business day, we will pay principal, premium, if any, the redemption price, if any, and interest on the next succeeding business day, and no interest will accrue from and after the maturity date or the redemption date, if any, to the date of that payment.

Redemption at Microsoft Option

Microsoft may elect to redeem all or part of the outstanding debt securities of a series from time to time before the maturity date of the debt securities of that series. Upon such election, the issuer will notify the trustee of the redemption date and the principal amount of debt securities of the series to be redeemed. If less than all the debt securities of the series are to be redeemed, the particular debt securities of that series to be redeemed will be selected by the trustee by such method as the trustee deems fair and appropriate. The applicable prospectus supplement will specify the redemption price for the debt securities to be redeemed (or the method of calculating such price), in each case in accordance with the terms and conditions of those debt securities.

Notice of redemption will be given to each holder of the debt securities to be redeemed not less than 30 nor more than 60 days prior to the date set for such redemption. This notice will include the following information: the redemption date; the redemption price (or the method of calculating such price); if less than all of the outstanding debt securities of such series are to be redeemed, the identification (and, in the case of partial redemption, the respective principal amounts) of the particular debt securities to be redeemed; the place or places where such debt securities are to be surrendered for payment of the redemption price; and, if applicable, the CUSIP number of the debt securities to be redeemed.

On the redemption date, the redemption price will become due and payable upon all of the debt securities to be redeemed, and interest, if any, on the debt securities to be redeemed will cease to accrue from and after that date.

Repayment at Holder's Option

If specified in the applicable prospectus supplement, the holders of the debt securities of a series will have the option to elect repayment of those debt securities by us prior to the stated maturity of the debt securities of that series at time or times and subject to the conditions specified in the applicable prospectus supplement. The optional repayment price is the price at which, together with accrued interest to the optional repayment date, the debt security may be repaid at the holder's option on each such optional repayment date.

Covenants

The indenture sets forth limited covenants, including the covenant described below, that will apply to each series of debt securities issued under the indenture unless otherwise specified in the applicable prospectus supplement.

Consolidation, Merger, and Sale of Assets

The indenture provides that Microsoft may consolidate with or merge with or into any other person, and may sell, transfer, or lease or convey all or substantially all of its properties and assets to another person; provided that the following conditions are satisfied:

- Microsoft is the continuing entity, or the resulting, surviving or transferee person (the "Successor") is a person organized and existing under the laws of the United States of America, any state thereof or the District of Columbia and the Successor (if not us) will expressly assume, by supplemental indenture, all of our obligations under the debt securities and the indenture and, for each security that by its terms provides for conversion, provide for the right to convert such security in accordance with its terms;

- Immediately after giving effect to such transaction, no default or event of default under the indenture has occurred and is continuing; and
- If requested, the trustee receives from Microsoft, an officers' certificate and an opinion of counsel that the merger, consolidation or transfer and such supplemental indenture, as the case may be, complies with the applicable provisions of the indenture.

If the issuer consolidates or merges with or into any other person or sell, transfer, lease or convey all or substantially all of its properties and assets in accordance with the indenture, the Successor will be substituted Microsoft in the indenture, with the same effect as if it had been an original party to the indenture. As a result, the Successor may exercise the issuer's rights and powers under the indenture, and we will be released from all our liabilities and obligations under the indenture and under the debt securities.

Events of Default

If an event of default relating to certain events of bankruptcy, insolvency, or reorganization of us occurs and is continuing, the principal of and premium, if any, and accrued and unpaid interest on the debt securities of that series will become and be immediately due and payable without any declaration or other act on the part of the trustee or any holders. An event of default for a particular series of debt securities does not necessarily constitute an event of default for any other series of debt securities issued under the indenture. Microsoft is required to furnish the trustee annually a statement by certain of its officers to the effect that, to the best of their knowledge, we are not in default in the fulfillment of any of their obligations under the indenture or, if there has been a default in the fulfillment of any such obligation, specifying each such default. No holder of any debt securities of any series will have any right to institute any judicial or other proceeding with respect to the indenture, or for the appointment of a receiver or trustee, or for any other remedy unless:

1. An event of default has occurred and is continuing and such holder has given the trustee prior written notice of such continuing event of default with respect to the debt securities of that series;

2. The holders of not less than 25% of the aggregate principal amount of the outstanding debt securities of that series have requested the trustee to institute proceedings in respect of such event of default;
3. The trustee has been offered indemnity reasonably satisfactory to it against its costs, expenses and liabilities in complying with such request;
4. The trustee has failed to institute proceedings 60 days after the receipt of such notice, request and offer of indemnity; and
5. No direction inconsistent with such written request has been given for 60 days by the holders of a majority in aggregate principal amount of the outstanding debt securities of that series.

The indenture provides that if an event of default occurs and is continuing, the trustee will exercise such of its rights and powers under the indenture and use the same degree of care and skill in their exercise, as a prudent person would exercise or use under the circumstances in the conduct of such person's own affairs. Subject to such provisions, the trustee will be under no obligation to exercise any of its rights or powers under the indenture at the request of any of the holders of the debt securities of a series unless they will have offered to the trustee security or indemnity satisfactory to the trustee against the costs, expenses and liabilities which might be incurred by it in compliance with such request.

Notwithstanding the foregoing, the holder of any debt security will have an absolute and unconditional right to receive payment of the principal of and premium, if any, and interest on that debt security on or after the due dates expressed in that debt security and to institute suit for the enforcement of payment.

Discharge, Defeasance, and Covenant Defeasance

The indenture provides that Microsoft may elect either (1) to defease and be discharged from any and all obligations with respect to the debt securities of a series (except for, among other things, obligations to register the transfer or exchange of the debt securities, to replace temporary or mutilated, destroyed, lost or stolen debt securities, to maintain an office or agency with respect to the debt securities and to hold money for payment in trust) ("legal defeasance") or (2) to be released from our obligations to comply with the restrictive covenants under the indenture, and any omission to comply with such obligations will not constitute a default or an event of default with respect to the debt securities of a series and clauses (4) and (7) under "—Events of Default" will no longer be applied ("covenant defeasance"). Legal defeasance or covenant defeasance, as the case may be, will be conditioned upon, among other things, the irrevocable deposit Microsoft with the trustee, in trust, of an amount in US dollars, or US government obligations, or both, applicable to the debt securities of that series which through the scheduled payment of principal and interest in accordance with their terms will provide money in an amount sufficient to pay the principal or premium, if any, and interest on the debt securities on the scheduled due dates therefore.

If Microsoft effects covenant defeasance with respect to the debt securities of any series, the amount in US dollars, or US government obligations, or both, on deposit with the trustee will be sufficient, in the opinion of a nationally recognized firm of independent accountants, to pay amounts due on the debt securities of that series at the time of the stated maturity but may not be sufficient to pay amounts due on the debt securities of that series at the time of the acceleration resulting from such event of default. However, we would remain liable to make payment of such amounts due at the time of acceleration.

Microsoft will be required to deliver to the trustee an opinion of counsel that the deposit and related defeasance will not cause the holders and beneficial owners of the debt securities of that series to recognize income, gain, or loss for federal income tax purposes. If we elect legal defeasance, that opinion of counsel must be based upon a ruling from the US Internal Revenue Service or a change in law to that effect.

Microsoft may exercise its legal defeasance option notwithstanding our prior exercise of our covenant defeasance option.

Ownership of Beneficial Interests

Upon the issuance of each global security, DTC will credit, on its book-entry registration and transfer system, the respective principal amount of the individual beneficial interests represented by the global security to the accounts of participants. Ownership of beneficial interests in each global security will be limited to participants or persons that may hold interests through participants. Ownership of beneficial interests in each global security will be shown on, and the transfer of those ownership interests will be effected only through, records maintained by DTC (with respect to participants' interests) and such participants (with respect to the owners of beneficial interests in the global security other than participants).

Interest and Interest Rates

The calculation agent will reset the rate of interest on the debt securities of a series bearing interest at a floating rate based on LIBOR on each interest payment date. If any of the interest reset dates for the debt securities is not a business day, then that interest reset date will be postponed to the next succeeding business day, unless that day is in the next succeeding calendar month, in which case, the interest reset date will be the immediately preceding business day. The interest rate set for the debt securities on a particular interest reset date will remain in effect during the interest period commencing on that interest reset date. Each interest period will be the period from and including the interest reset date to, but excluding the next interest reset date or until the maturity date or redemption date, if any, of the debt securities, as the case may be.

If the debt securities bear interest at a floating rate based on LIBOR, the calculation agent will determine LIBOR according to the following provisions:

a. With respect to any interest determination date, LIBOR will be the rate (expressed as a percentage per annum) for deposits in US dollars having a maturity of the Index Maturity commencing on the relevant interest reset date that appears on Reuters Page LIBOR01 as of 11:00 a.m. (London time) on that interest determination date. If no such rate appears, LIBOR for that interest determination date will be determined in accordance with the following clause (b).
b. With respect to an interest determination date on which no rate appears on Reuters Page LIBOR01, as specified in the preceding clause (a), the calculation agent will request the principal London offices of each of four major reference banks in the London interbank market (which may include affiliates of underwriters or the trustee), as selected by the issuer, to provide the calculation agent with its offered quotation (expressed as a percentage per annum) for deposits in US dollars for the Index Maturity, commencing on the relevant interest reset date, to prime banks in the London interbank market at approximately 11:00 a.m. (London time) on that interest determination date

and in a principal amount that is representative for a single transaction in US dollars in that market at that time. If at least two quotations are provided, then LIBOR on that interest determination date will be the arithmetic mean of those quotations. If fewer than two quotations are provided, then LIBOR on the interest determination date will be the arithmetic mean of the rates quoted at approximately 11:00 a.m. (New York City time), on the interest determination date by three major banks in New York City (which may be affiliates of underwriters) selected by the issuer for loans in US dollars to leading European banks, having an Index Maturity, commencing on the relevant interest reset date, and in a principal amount that is representative for a single transaction in US dollars in that market at that time. If at least two such rates are so provided, LIBOR on the interest determination date will be the arithmetic mean of such rates. If fewer than two such rates are so provided, LIBOR on the interest determination date will be LIBOR in effect with respect to the immediately preceding interest determination date.

"Reuters Page LIBOR01" means the display that appears on Reuters (or any successor service) on page LIBOR01 (or any page as may replace such page on such service) for the purpose of displaying London interbank offered rates of major banks for US dollars.

"Index Maturity" means the period to maturity of the debt securities with respect to which the related interest rate basis or formula will be calculated. For example, the Index Maturity may be 1 month, 3 months, 6 months, or 1 year.

All percentages resulting from any calculation will be rounded, if necessary, to the nearest one hundred-thousandth of a percentage point, with five one millionths of a percentage point rounded upwards [e.g., 4.876545% (or .04876545) would be rounded to 4.87655% (or .0487655)], and all US dollar amounts used in or resulting from such calculation will be rounded to the nearest cent (with one-half cent being rounded upward).

Appendix B. A Primer on Corporate Bonds

A bond is a contractual agreement, or indenture, between the issuer and the investors that addresses the terms and conditions of the bond issuing, and includes maturity, par value or face value, coupon rate frequency of payments, and currency denomination. A bond is a corporate or government debt obligation (subject to legal, regulatory, and tax considerations) with a face value or principal of $1,000, where the issuing company or government pays annually or semiannually interest, or coupon, on the principal and at maturity redeems the principal.[7] The bond indenture or bond agreement (as well as the bond prospectus or offering memorandum) describes how the issuer intends to service the bond by paying coupons and redeems the principal through its ability to generate cash flows primarily through its operations.

Bonds have a priority claim on the company's earnings and assets compared with the claims of common shareholders. In the event of default unsecured bonds or debentures with no collateral backing are paid after secured bonds. Bonds involve credit risk that could be mitigated through several means, including credit enhancements through collateral backing to ensure debt repayment in the event of defaults, bond covenants that include affirmative and negative covenants; sinking funds arrangements that allow bond issuers to set aside funds over a time to retire the bond. The sinking fund arrangement specifies the portion of the bond's principal that must be repaid annually throughout the life of the bond after a specified date.

Bonds constitute the most common instruments for raising capital. Companies issue bonds to fund business investment, mergers and acquisitions, buyback their shares, pay dividends or refinance debt. Investors in bonds effectively lend money to the issuing company at financial terms established in the bond offering, which include the price, face value (par value), maturity, coupon rate, and yield to maturity ("YTM"). Corporate bonds constitute the second largest segment of the bond market after government bonds.[8] After the 2008 big recession, non-financial companies have raised $6.9 trillion through corporate bond issues, with non-investment

---

[7]Lionel Martellini, Philippe Priaulet, and Stephane Priauket, *Fixed-Income Securities, Valuation, Risk Management and Portfolio Strategies* (Wiley, Hoboken, New Jersey, 2003); Frank J. Fabozzi, *Bond Market, Analysis, and Strategies*, 9th ed. (Pearson, Hoboken, New Jersey, 2016); Bruce Tuckman, *Fixed Income Securities*, 6th ed. (Wiley, Hoboken, New Jersey, 2002); James F. Adams and Donald J. Smith, *Fixed Income Analysis*, 4th ed. CFA Institute Investment Series (Wiley, 2019) ("Adams & Smith"); SEC, Investor Bulletin, "What Are Corporate Bonds?" https://www.google.com/search?client=firefox-b-1&q=SEC%2C+Investor+Bulletin%2C+What+Are+Corporate+Bonds%3F.

[8]Yener Altunbas, Alper Kara, and David Marques-Ibanez, "Large Debt Financing: Syndicated Loans Versus Corporate Bonds," European Central Bank Working Paper Series, N. 1028/March 2009.

grade bonds increasing from 4% to 18% of all corporate bonds issued.[9] The average maturity of United States investment-grade bonds issued by non-financial companies was 13.4 years in 2013 or 5.7 years longer than the same figure for other OECD.

Bonds are issued in primary markets and traded in secondary markets at par (priced at 100% or $1,000 per bond), premium (above 100% or above $1,000) or discount (below 100% or under $1,000). Bonds could trade at par when market interest rate is equivalent to the coupon rate, at premium when the market interest rate is below the coupon rate, or at discount when the market rate is above the coupon rate. The price of a bond is inversely related to the market interest rate; that is, the bond price moves in the opposite direction of the market interest rates. Bonds provide several yields, including current yield that equals to the bond's annual coupon divided by the bond's price and expressed as a percentage; Yield to maturity (YTM) which is the internal rate of return on a bond's expected cash flows, or the discount rate which equates the present value of the bond's expected cash flow to maturity with the bond's price. The YTM is an estimate of the bond's annual expected return that an investor will earn on a bond if the bond is held to maturity. There is an inverse relationship between the bond's price and YTM.

The bond par value is the amount that the issuer agrees to repay the bondholders on maturity and its price is expressed as a percent of face value. For instance, a bond price of 95% implies 95% of $1,000 or $950. The coupon rate is the interest rate on the par value that was agreed to pay annually or semi-annually until maturity. Bond prices are expressed as a percentage of the par value in terms of bid and ask, such as 99.25–99.75, where the bid price is the price that the bidder offers to pay for the bond at 0.9925 × 1,000 and the ask price is the price that the bond is offered for sale to sell the bond at 0.9975 × 1,000.

The bond par value is the amount that the issuer agrees to repay the bondholders on maturity and its price is expressed as a percent of face value. For instance, a bond price of 95% implies 95% of $1,000 or $950. The coupon rate is the interest rate on the par value that was agreed to pay annually or semi-annually until maturity.

A bond's price equals the present value of its contractual cash flows. The price is determined by the coupon rates, maturity, credit rating, and

[9] Serdar Çelik, Gül Demirtaş, and Mats Isaksson, "Corporate Bonds, Bondholders and Corporate Governance," OECD Corporate Governance Papers, No. 16, 2016.OECD

the general level of interest. Corporate bonds offer higher interest rates than government bonds of similar maturity due to the need to compensate investors for higher risk. A plain vanilla bond (fixed rate paying coupon semiannually or annually) pricing model, is as follows:

$$Bond\ Price = \frac{C}{1+i} + \frac{C}{(1+i)^2} + \cdots + \frac{C}{(1+i)^n} + \frac{M}{(1+i)^n}$$

where

C = coupon payment, and it is equal to the coupon rate in % × the face value,[10]

i = required yield, or yield to maturity,

M = par value, and

n = number of payments.

Example: Suppose that a bond is selling for $950 and has an annual coupon rate of 7%; it matures in 4 years, and the par value is $1,000. What is the YTM? Assuming annual payment, the coupon payment per annum is $70 (i.e., 7% of $1,000). We solve the following equation and obtain the following results:

$$70(1+i)^{-1} + 70(1+i)^{-2} + 70(1+i)^{-3} + 70(1+i)^{-4} + 1{,}000(1+i)^{-4} = 950$$

i or the YTM is 8.53%.

The YTM is greater than the current yield, which is $70/$950 = 7.37%, which, in turn, is greater than the coupon rate.

Bond-Equivalent Yields

If a 10-year bond paying $45 semi-annually and paying $1,000 at maturity was selling for $937.69, its 6-month yield to maturity would be 5% and its simple annualized rate, i^A, would be 10%:

$$\$937.69 = \sum_{t-1}^{20} \frac{\$45}{(1+y)^t} + \frac{\$1{,}000}{(1+y)^{20}}$$

$$y^A = Simple\ annualized\ rate = (n)(y) = (2)(.05) = .10$$

[10] US bonds typically pay interest on a semi-annual payment. However, for simplicity, I am assuming annual payments.

In this example, the simple annualized rate is determined for semi-annual coupon bond and then multiplying it by 2. Because US Treasury bonds and many corporate bonds pay coupons semiannually, the rate obtained by multiplying the semi-annual periodic rate by 2 is called the ***bond-equivalent yield***. Bonds with different payment frequencies often have their rates expressed in terms of their bond-equivalent yields so that their rates can be compared on a common basis to other bonds. Bond-equivalent yield does not consider the reinvestment of the bond's cash flows during the year. Therefore, it underestimates the actual rate of return earned. Thus, an investor earning 5% semi-annually would have $1.05 after 6 months from a $1 investment that can be reinvested for the next 6 months. If the bond is reinvested at 5%, their annual rate would be 10.25% [= $(1.05)(1.05) - 1 = (1.05)^2 - 1$], not 10%. As noted earlier, the 10.25% annual rate, which considers compounding, is known as the effective annual rate.

Fixed income securities carry inflation risk, liquidity risk, call risk, and credit and default risks for both issuers and counterparties. Any fixed-income security sold or redeemed prior to maturity may be subject to loss.

Corporate Bonds Classification by Maturity, Coupons, and Ratings

- Bonds are classified according to their **maturity** as short term (less than 3 years), medium term (between 4 and 10 years), and long term (over 10 years). An alternative classification of corporate bonds maturity is provided by PIMCO,[11] where short-term notes have maturity of up to 5 years; medium-term notes have maturity ranging between 5 and 12 years; and long-term bonds have maturities greater than 12 years.
- Medium-term notes are corporate bonds that are registered with the SEC as a Rule 415 shelf registration, which allows the corporation to register up to $1 billion worth of bonds at one time, but which are then offered in relatively small amounts as the need for funds arises over a 2-year period.
- There is a primary market for both government bonds and corporate bonds.[12] The largest Primary and Secondary Markets are for United States Treasury Securities.

---

[11] PIMCO, "What Are Corporate Bonds and What Potential Benefits Do They Offer?"

[12] https://thismatter.com/money/bonds/primary-bond-market.htm.

- Because there are many more bonds than stocks — about 800,000 bond issues compared to about 8,000 stocks traded on the New York Stock Exchange and NASDAQ — most bonds are traded over the telephone rather than on an electronic exchange. The illiquidity of most bond issues makes it difficult to list current prices. An electronic system can facilitate trading by making it easier to get multiple quotes from bond dealers for a particular issue. **MarketAxess** and **TradeWeb** are 2 electronic systems that allows prospective buyers of bonds to do just that.

Bonds are classified as fixed-rate interest that pay interest or coupons semiannually or annually and the coupon stays the same through life of the bond. Some bonds offer floating rates that are reset periodically, say semi-annually, based on a bond index or another benchmark, such as LIBOR or Treasury bond. Floating-rate notes coupon (FRN's) will fluctuate periodically during the bond's life, following the changes in the reference rate. Some bonds do not offer interest payments and are called zero-coupon bonds that are issued at steep discounts Payment-in-kind (PIK) coupon bond allows the issuer with high debt burden to pay interest in the form of additional amounts of the bond issued rather than as a cash payment. Other forms of PIK payments, such as paying the bondholders with common shares worth the amount of the coupon due, with the option being held by the issuer. Many bonds have an embedded call feature that permits the firm to call the bond prior to its final maturity. A convertible bond is a hybrid security with both debt and equity features that could be viewed as the combination of a straight bond plus an embedded equity call option. It gives bondholder the right to exchange the bond for a specified number of common shares in the issuing company. The conversion provision is valuable to the bondholder and therefore its price is higher than a similar bond without the conversion provision.

Bonds Risk

- *Credit or default risk.* The bond issuer could fail to make timely interest or principal payments and thus defaults on the bonds. The corporate bond contract (called an indenture) includes covenants designed to limit the amount of debt the company can raise or required to maintain certain financial ratios. Violation of the terms may constitute a default. The bond trustee monitors the company's compliance with the terms of the indenture and may act on behalf of the bondholders and pursue remedies.

- *Interest rate risk.* Changes in interest rate and bond prices are inversely related. A bond's maturity and coupon rate affect its sensitivity to changes in interest rates. Bonds with longer maturity are more sensitive to interest rate changes, and bonds with lower coupon rates are more sensitive to interest rate changes. Duration and convexity address the relationship between bond prices and interest rates, as discussed below.

To improve the attractiveness of its bonds and the credit rating, a corporation may purchase bond insurances to enhance its creditworthiness and the appeal of the security. Bond insurance "guarantees" an investor timely receipt of principal and interest payments in the event of the issuer's default but does not insure against fluctuation in market value.

If a company goes bankrupt and defaults on its bonds, bondholders have a priority over shareholders in claims on the company's assets and cash flows in accordance with their seniority — whether the bond is senior secured, a senior debt, or junior unsecured bond (or subordinated). In the case of secured bonds, the company pledged specific collaterals, including property and equipment as security for the bond. If the company defaults, holders of the security bond have a legal right to foreclose on the collateral to satisfy their claim. Bonds without collateral pledged are unsecured or debentures and have a general claim on the company's assets and cash flows. A summary of the capital structure of a company by collateralization and seniority in the event of bankruptcy reorganization is stated in the footnote below.[13]

Bonds are also classified according to their credit ratings that are of significant concern to bondholders. Investment in bonds involves credit

[13] PWC, "Issuing Corporate Bonds in the Nordic Capital Markets," June 2016.

Senior secured debt — lowest interest cost and collateralized

Senior debt — low interest cost

Junior/subordinated debt — Relatively higher interest cost, debt is not secured and subordinated by other debt

Hybrids — Lower interest cost than in subordinated debt, debt could be converted into equity (also referred as mezzanine debt)

Common shares — carry no interest, dividends paid out of net income.

risk that the company may fail to make timely payments of interest or principal and thus default on its bond. In general, a bond issue with a lower credit rating would need to offer a higher interest rate to compensate investors for the greater risk associated with investment in a lower-rated issue as compared with investment in a higher-rated bond issue.

The major rating agencies for corporate bonds are Standard & Poor (S&P), Moody's Investor Services, and Fitch. Ratings are based on historic and pro forma financial data and the industry in which the issuer operates as well as the macroeconomic conditions. Periodically, a rating agency may adjust an issue's rating in accord with a change within the issuing company. It is the responsibility of the issuing company to apply for a rating and pay for it.

Each credit rating agency has its own rating system that does not necessarily equate to another company's rating scale, but they are all similar. Fitch and Standard & Poor's use AAA for the highest credit quality, AA for the next best, followed by A, then BBB for good credit. Rating below BBB is considered speculative or worse, down to a D rating, which indicates default. Investment-grade bonds are considered more likely than non-investment-grade bonds to be paid on time. Non-investment-grade bonds are also called high-yield, or junk, bonds that offer higher interest rates to compensate investors for higher risk. A bond is considered investment-grade bond if its credit rating is BBB or higher by Standard & Poor's; or Baa3 or higher by Moody's, or BBB by Fitch. Ratings play a critical role in determining how much interest companies must pay on their issued debt. The difference between rates for first-class government bonds and investment-grade bonds is called investment-grade spread. The higher these investment-grade spreads (or risk premiums) are, the weaker the economy is.

Duration

Macaulay Duration measures the weighted average time to maturity of a bond, where the maturity of each cash flow is multiplied by the present value of that cash flow as a ratio of the bond price.[14] The sum of the weighted average time to maturity of each of the bond's contractual cash flows, where each flow is present valued and derived as a ratio of the bond

[14]Fabozzi, *op. cit.*, Chapter 4.

price, constitutes the Macaulay duration.[15] The equations below define the weighted average time and the duration.

The weight, Wt, is determined by the cash flows, CF, yield to maturity, i, time, t, and the bond market price, P, as follows:

- $\mathrm{Wt} = \mathrm{CF}t/(1 + i)^t/P$
- $D = \sum t \times \mathrm{Wt},\ t = 1, 2,\ldots, n$

Modified duration estimates bond price change in response to a change in interest rates, and a higher duration implies greater price sensitivity. Duration enables us to quantify the bond's price sensitivity to interest rates changes in the following manner:

- Macaulay Duration = $[\sum t * \mathrm{CF}/(1 + i)^t + n * M/(1 + i)^n]/P$, where $t = 1, 2,\ldots, n$
- M is the principal payment paid at maturity n
- Modified Duration = Macaulay Duration/$(1 + i)$
- $(\mathrm{d}P/\mathrm{d}i)(1/P) = -1/(1 + i) \times$ Macaulay Duration = Percentage Price Change
- $(\mathrm{d}P/\mathrm{d}i)(1/P) =$ –Modified Duration = Percentage Price Change
- $\mathrm{d}P/P =$ –Modified Duration $\times\ \mathrm{d}i$, measures the percentage price movement where $\mathrm{d}i$ is the change in yield
- $\mathrm{d}P/\mathrm{d}i =$ –Modified Duration $\times\ P$, measures dollar price change

For every 1% increase or decrease in interest rates, a bond's price will change approximately 1% in the opposite direction for every year of duration. For example, if a bond has a duration of 5 years and interest rate increases by 1%, the bond's price will decline by approximately 5%. Whereas the price of a bond with a duration of 2 would be expected to increase (decline) by about 2.00% for each 1.00% move down (up) in rate.

Several factors determine duration and how sensitive a bond's price is to interest rate changes[16]:

- A bond's duration increases with time to maturity. Bonds with a long duration have a higher price fluctuation than bonds with a short duration;

---

[15] Zvi Bodie, Alex Kane, and Alan J. Marcus, *Investments*, 10th ed. (McGraw Hill Education, New York, 2014), 519–632.

[16] https://www.jhinvestments.com/viewpoints/investing-basics/bond-duration-and-why-it-matters?

- A bond's duration is lower when the coupon rate is higher; the higher the coupon, the lower the volatility, and the lower the coupon, the higher the volatility;
- The duration of a coupon bond is higher when the bond's yield to maturity (YTM) is lower; Bonds with poor credit rating will have higher YTM than higher-rated bonds with low YTM and lower price volatility than bonds with excellent ratings;
- As interest rates increase, duration decreases, and the bond becomes less sensitive to future rate changes;
- The duration of a zero-coupon bond equals its time to maturity;
- The duration of a perpetuity equals $(1 + i)/i$.

Convexity[17]

The duration approximation assumes a straight-line relationship between the bond price and yield and as such it always underestimates the increase in the bond price due to a yield decline, or overestimates the decline in price in response to a yield increase. Duration is an imperfect way of measuring a bond's price change, as it indicates that this change is linear in nature when in fact it is a "convex" shape. A bond's *convexity* is a measurement of how duration changes as yields change. These two measurements can provide insight into how a bond is expected to perform should interest rates change. A bond is said to have positive convexity if it will have larger price increases due to a decline in yields than price declines due to an increase in yields. Positive convexity works in the investor's favor since the price becomes less sensitive when yields rise than when yields decline.

Convexity corrects the duration approximation by accounting for it in the following manner:

- Percentage change in price $= -D *$ (Change in yield) $+ 1/2 \times$ Convexity $\times$ (Change in yield)^2, and convexity is defined below
- Convexity $= 1/(P \times (1 + i)^2)\Sigma(t^2 + t)][\mathrm{CF}_t/(1 + i)^t]$

[17]Zvi Bodie, *op. cit.*, 519–632.

Duration and convexity are two metrics used to measure how the price of a bond will be affected by changes in interest rates. A bond's price responds to changes in interest rates is measured by its duration, and the change in a bond's duration for a given change in yields can be measured by its convexity. Bonds with shorter durations will be less sensitive to a rise in yields and will fall in price less than bonds with higher durations. If rates are to decline, bonds with higher durations will experience price increase more than bonds with lower duration.

Call risk exists when the bond issuer exercises the right to call it back before the maturity date when interest rates decline, and it is more advantageous to refund existing bonds and issue new bonds at lower cost. Such call provisions constitute a risk for the bondholder because interest rates have declined or the opportunity to obtain similar or higher coupon rates is unavailable.

Inflation risk caused by raising inflation that diminishes the coupon and principal purchasing power.

Liquidity risk is defined as the risk of selling a bond at a substantial loss of the principal or below the fair market value when the market is illiquid, that is, when there are no willing buyers. Secondary market activity impacts the cost of issuing new debt in the primary market.[18] Firms with existing illiquidity debt have higher costs when issuing new debt. An improvement in the price discovery process was brought by the introduction of the Trade Reporting and Compliance Engine (TRACE) reporting. Firms that became TRACE listed subsequently had a lower cost of debt.[19] The bulk of the trading takes place during the first few days after the issue, but after the first several months, the long-term annual average turnover is around 25%. Of all bonds traded in the US, the 50 most traded bonds in 2012 were traded on an average of only 90 times a day.

- Risk Reduction could be obtained through diversification or investment in mutual funds of ETFs that focus on bonds.

---

[18] Ryan L. Davis, David A. Masler, and Brian S. Roseman, "Secondary Market Trading and the Cost of New Debt Issuance,"
https://www.mtsu.edu/econfin/DavidMaslar.pdf.

[19] *Ibid.*

Steps in the Bond Issuing Process[20]

- The company hires an investment bank;
- Term sheet is drafted, and the underwriter starts preparing the bond prospectus;
- Launch data — pre-sounding among a few investors, main terms are finalized, and presentation is prepared;
- Launch data — deal is announced, and book is opened;
- Road show — Company's senior managers and investment bank are on road show to investors, making presentations and distributing the term sheet;
- Closing — final pricing is determined and announced;
- Settlement — distribution of prospectus, fund is transferred to bond issuers; and
- Listing — bond is listed on public exchange.

When a corporation decides that it needs to raise capital through a bond offering, it retains an investment banker to underwrite the bonds. The underwriting conducts due diligence. In the underwriting process of corporate bonds there are two models: One is where the bonds are offered on a best-efforts basis by the underwriter who ultimately sells them to investors: Second, the underwriter may purchase the bonds from the issuer and sell them to investors. While expecting to make a profit, there is also a risk of loss, particularly if bond prices decline. To reduce the risk and enhance the marketing opportunity, underwriters often invite others to form a syndicate and join in underwriting the issue. Members of the syndicate group may become part of a Selling Group[21] to resell the issue to investors.

Both the issuer and the underwriter are represented by legal counsels to assist in the offering documentation throughout the underwriting process. The issuer's counsel confirms that the issuer has met all legal and regulatory requirements necessary for issuance and advises the issuer regarding the debt indenture and prospectus. The underwriter's counsel assists the underwriter in meeting the due diligence obligations, reviews

---

[20]PWC, "Issuing Corporate Bonds in the Nordic Capital Markets," June 20, 2016.

[21]"Corporate Operational Underwriting Process, Business Practices in Plain English," 2004.

the prospectus for accuracy and disclosure, and prepares the Agreement Among Underwriters and the purchase contract.

The Trustee is usually a bank which administers the indenture provisions of a debt issue for the benefit of the bondholders. In many cases, the trustee also acts as a transfer agent, or paying agent, for the bonds. The transfer agent simply transfers the bonds from issuer to bondholder. The paying agent is responsible for transmitting payments of interest and principal from the issuer to the bondholders.

The Securities and Exchange Commission (SEC) rules place regulatory responsibility on the underwriters to ensure that the issuers whose securities are being underwritten have fully committed to provide current and ongoing disclosure of financial details and material events that may impact their ability to meet debt service requirements. SEC Regulation M regulates the activities of the issuers, underwriting syndicate members and securities purchasers during an offering.

The SEC examines the prospectus and if approved the bond issue may be sold thereafter. Rule 144A permits firms to raise capital from "Qualified Institutional Buyers" (QIB) without requiring registration of the securities and compliance with US GAAP. The 144A market is currently the principal debt market for foreign issues in the United States. Regulation S allows US companies to sell securities to persons or entities located outside of the US without registering them with the SEC. Many US companies utilize this regulation for their offshore offerings.

The SEC has a provision for shelf offerings, where an issuer may register a new debt security, but the issuer may delay making an offering (or make several offerings at various times) for up to a 2-year period. "On the shelf" registration significantly shortens the time required to underwrite a new issue. The issuer prepares a preliminary official statement known as a Red Herring or Prospectus with the help of the issuer's counsel. The Red Herring includes information about the issuer, such as what the issuing corporation does and historical financial information. After approval, the Red Herring was distributed to potentially investors.

Corporate bond issuance requires an underwriting process by investment banks that could include a firm commitment, best efforts, or an auction. Under a firm commitment, the underwriter purchases the entire issue for resale to the public, and its profit is based on the difference between its purchase price and the selling price or the underwriting spread. Under a best-efforts basis, which is the most common form of commitment, the underwriter commits to sell as much of the issue at the agreed price and has no financial or legal obligation for unsold bonds.

Auctions allow the issuer to sell directly to the investors, eliminating the underwriting fee. The US government sells Treasuries using auctions. In a competitive bidding for bonds, bidders submit the yield that they are willing to accept, or the price that they are willing to pay, and the amount of the issue that they want. The bonds are then distributed to prospective buyers depending on whether it is a multiple-price auction, a single-price, or Dutch, auction. In a **multiple-price auction**, the winning bidders pay the price that they bid for the amount that they requested. If there is an equal price bid among bidders, then each bidder will get a part of the remaining shares that is proportional to the amount that they requested. In a **single-price auction**, or a **Dutch auction**, all winning bidders will receive the highest winning yield, or in the case of a discount bond, will pay the same price. In 1997, issuers started using internet auctions to sell directly to investors as a way to save on investment banking fees. The US Security Act of 1933 requires that securities offered to the public be registered with the Security Exchange Commission (SEC). Registration consists of a prospectus which is publicly distributed and supplemental information that is available to the public on request. Following SEC's registration approval, the securities could be sold to the public. SEC Rule 144 allows private placement,[22] which is selling of unregistered securities, including stocks or bonds, to qualified institutional investors. No prospectus is required but must furnish info that the SEC in the form of a private placement memorandum to prospective investors.

[22]The cost of a private placement is much less than a public offering because the securities do not have to be registered with the SEC, the issuer does not have to comply with US generally accepted accounting principles (GAAP), and because there are usually only a few institutional investors involved, marketing costs are much less.

https://doi.org/10.1142/9789811216749_0012

Case 12

PepsiCo, Inc. Stock Valuation*

Harvey A. Poniachek

Rutgers Business School, USA

The Assignment

Ms. Jane Edwards, a research associate at East Coast Investment Management Company, Inc. of New York ("ECIM") and a recent MBA graduate from Rutgers Business School, Department of Finance & Economics, was reviewing several food and beverage companies for possible addition to the firm's stock portfolio. Her research process generally followed the recommendations of the CFA (that is addressed in Appendix A), and ECIM commonly utilizes brokerage reports on companies, the industry and the macroeconomic outlook.

She began her task by reviewing PepsiCo's annual and quarterly reports, including Form 10K, 10Q, and some dozen brokerage reports on food and beverage companies.

Following the review, Ms. Edwards was ready to address the following issues.

1. Whether PepsiCo's common stock price on 12/31/2019 was supported by the fundamentals?
2. Forecast PepsiCo's stock price in 3 and 5 years based on the Dividend Discount Model, the cash flow to the firm, and the market approach.

---

*The case was prepared for classroom discussion and should not be used for any other purpose.

3. Compare PepsiCo's stock price with The Coca-Cola Company and Constellation Brands, Inc. prices.
4. Recommend whether the East Coast Investment Management Company, Inc. of New York should rather allocate funds to high-tech companies such as Apple and Microsoft than to PepsiCo? Base the answers on the basis of which of the above stocks are correctly priced, and the outlook for the next couple of 3 and 5 years.

Financial Data

Use the following websites to obtain the necessary information on PepsiCo.:

https://pepsico.gcs-web.com/; https://www.pepsico.com/investors/financial-information/quarterly-earnings.

Appendix A. Valuation of Common Stocks

Introduction

Valuation of common stock could involve publicly traded and private companies. Stock valuation of public firms could indicate whether the market prices are supported by the fundamentals. Overvalued or undervalued stock prices could provide investors with an indication of whether to sell, buy or hold the stock. Stock valuation of private firms could be more challenging primarily due to insufficient data, and prevailing discounts for lack of marketability and control premium, as well as by abnormal management compensation.

This appendix introduces the reader to the state-of-the-art valuation of common stock and provides useful examples on the application of the various methodologies. Stock valuation models could be classified in terms of the income approach, the market approach, and the assets approach.[1]

[1]Stephen A. Ross, Randolph W. Westerfield, Jeffrey Jaffe, and Bradford D. Jordan, *Corporate Finance*, 12th ed. (McGraw-Hill Education, New York, 2019), Chapters 4, 9 ("Ross"); "2019 Curriculum CFA Program Level II Equity Investments, Equity Valuation:

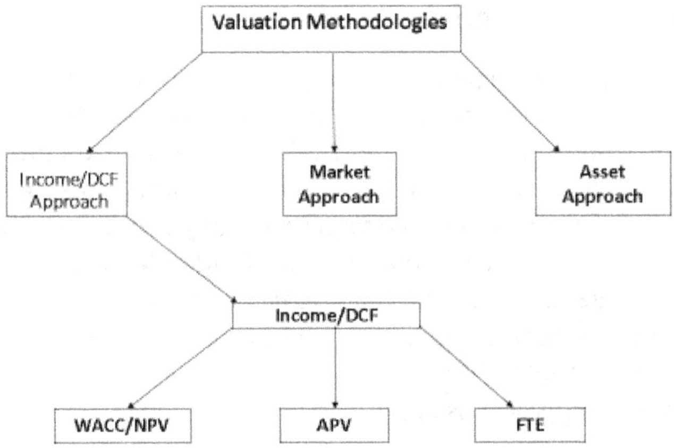

Exhibit 1. Valuation Methodologies for Stocks

Ledger
DCF = Discount Cash Flow
WACC = Weighted Average Cost of Capital
NPV = Net Present Value
APV = Adjusted Present Value
FTE = Flow to Equity

Exhibit 1 illustrates the stock valuation approaches that are further discussed below.

The stock valuation process has several steps.[2]

- Understanding the business,
- Forecasting the company's performance,
- Selecting the appropriate valuation model, and
- Converting forecasts to a valuation.

Applications and Processes," https://www.cfainstitute.org/membership/professional-development/refresher-readings/2019/equity-valuation-applications-processes.

[2]Zvi Bodie, Alex Kane, and Alan J. Marcus, *Investments*, 10th ed. (McGraw Hill Education, New York, 2014), Chapter 18, Equity Valuation Models; Aswath Damodaran, *Investment Valuation* (Wiley, Hoboken, New Jersey, 1996), Chapters 11, 13; Tim Koller, Marc Goedhardt, and David Wessels, *Valuation: Measuring and Managing the Value of Companies*, 5th ed. (Wiley, 2010).

The Income Approach

The income approach applies the discount cash flow ("DCF"), where value is defined as the present value of the expected free cash flows ("FCF") discounted at a required rate of return, or discount rate. The discount rate is based on the nature of the cash flows, the capitalization structure, and the riskiness of the target company and its cash flows. The income valuation approach applies the Fair Market Value ("FMV") or the investment value standard[3] and the premise that the company is a going concern. The valuation could determine how much is the firm worth, but the market price could differ.

The income approach is applied to several different circumstances, as follows:

1. Free Cash Flows to the Firm ("**FCFF**") discounts the free cash flows to the firm for the first 5 years and then assumes a perpetual growth rate discounted at the WACC.[4] This approach yields the enterprise value from which liabilities are subtracted to obtain the equity value, and by dividing the equity value by the number of shares the price per share is obtained. Because the WACC methodology was derived by using the after-tax cost of debt, the cash flows do not include payments to debtholders.[5]
2. The Adjusted Present Value ("**APV**") approach values the company's free cash flows to the firm by discounting it at the unlevered cost of capital; and then estimate and add the present value of the interest tax shields attributed to debt discounted at the cost of debt, as well as other financial side effects, such as subsidies.

[3]There are four standards of value, including the fair market value, fair value, intrinsic value, and investment value. The fair market value is the price, at which property would change hands between a hypothetical willing and able buyer and a hypothetical willing and able seller, acting at arm's length in an open and unrestricted market, when neither is under compulsion to buy or sell and when both have reasonable knowledge of the relevant facts. Investment value means the value of an asset or business to a specific prospective owner that reflects a unique situation. See Alfred M. King, *Executive's Guide to Fair Value* (Wiley, 2008), Ch. 1; Jay E. Fishman, Shannon P. Prat, and William J. Morrison, *Standards of Value: Theory and Applications* (Wiley, 2007), 21–26.

[4]Berk, *op. cit.*, 627.

[5]See I. E. Brick and D. G. Weaver, "A Comparison of Capital Budgeting Techniques in Identifying Profitable Investments," *Financial Management* 3, no. 4 (1984): 29–39.

3. The Free Cash Flows to Equity ("**FTE**") discounted at the cost of equity. Often, the analyst would estimate the perpetual growth rate[6] of the dividend and use the dividend growth model to estimate the stock price. Alternatively, forecast dividends for 5 years and then assume a perpetual growth rate.

Free Cash Flow to the Firm ("FCFF")

The first step in this valuation process is to prepare pro forma financial statements based on the percent of sales growth approach.[7] In the next step, the free cash flows to the firm and the discount rate or the WACC are derived. The discount rate is determined by the capital structure of the company, that is, the share of debt and equity in total capitalization, the cost of debt, the tax rate, and the cost of equity that is derived through the application of the Capital Asset Pricing Method ("CAPM"). The risk characteristics of the anticipated cash flows are implied in the cost of debt and equity.

The valuation analysis is based on a forecast period that commonly consists of 5 years, and a terminal value to perpetuity that assumes that the company will live to infinity. Based on the forecast period, free cash flows to the company are derived for each year and discounted at the WACC to determine the present value. The terminal value in year 6 is derived either through a formulary approach or assuming that the free cash flow in year 6 divided by the WACC less the expected growth rate to perpetuity. The sum of the discounted cash flows of the forecast period and the terminal value determines the enterprise value from which debt is deducted to derive the equity value. That is, the company's equity equals the enterprise value minus debt and cash. The price per common share equals to the equity value divided by the number of outstanding shares.

Usually three valuation scenarios are derived, including high or optimistic, average, and low or pessimistic, and probabilities are assigned to

---

[6]For how one might be able to estimate the growth rate of dividends, see I. E. Brick, H. Y. Chen, C. H. Hsieh, and C. F. Lee, "A Comparison of Alternative models for Estimating Firm's Growth Rate," *Review of Quantitative Finance and Accounting* 47, no. 2 (2016): 369–393.

[7]Ross, *op. cit.*, 98. See Case 3 of this book for a more thorough discussion of based on the percent of sales growth approach.

each[8] to obtain a probability-weighted average scenario. The reasonableness of the valuations could be further examined through sensitivity analysis, including an application of a Monte Carlo simulation technique.[9] Control and liquidity discounts and premiums could be applied as necessary.[10]

Free Cash Flows

The free cash flows ("FCF") from assets equals to earnings before interest and taxes ("EBIT") plus depreciation, which is a non-cash expense, minus taxes (ignoring the tax deductibility of interest), minus capital expenditures ("CAPEX") and changes in net working capital ("NWC"). Stated algebraically, FCF is defined as follows:

FCF = EBIT + Depreciation – Taxes – CAPEX – ΔNWC, or alternatively stated as

$$\text{FCF} = \text{EBIT}\,(1 - t) + \text{Depreciation} - \text{CAPEX} - \Delta\text{NWC}$$

The definitions of the variables are as follows:
FCF = Free cash flows,
EBIT = Earnings before interest and taxes,
EBIT $(1 - t)$ is EBIT after taxes,
t is the marginal tax rate,
CAPEX = Capital expenditure, which equals the change in Net fixed assets + Depreciation – Sale of long-term asset,
ΔNWC = Change in working capital, where working capital is Current assets (CA) – Current liabilities (CL).

Terminal Value

A terminal value ("TV") reflects the value from the end of the projected period to perpetuity, and it usually constitutes a significant component of the company's enterprise value, and often accounts for as much as 70% of

[8] *Ibid.*, 353, 357.

[9] Palisade, "Monte Carlo Simulation," http://www.palisade.com/risk/monte_carlo_simulation.asp.

[10] Shannon P. Pratt, *Business Valuation Discounts and Premiums* (Wiley, Hoboken, New Jersey, 2001), Chapter 1.

the enterprise total value. The terminal value could be estimated through a formulary approach based on the last forecasted FCF, the growth rate, and the discount rate, as follows:

TV = FCF $(1 + g)/(\text{WACC} - g)$, where
FCF $(1 + g)$ = The expected growth of free cash flow for the year after the last year of the forecasted cash flow, which is commonly year 6 and onward,
WACC = The weighted average cost of capital,
g = The expected constant annual growth rate of FCF in perpetuity, that is, the model assumes a sustainable growth of cash flow to perpetuity.

Alternatively, the TV could be estimated based on a multiple of EBIT or EBITDA, where the multiple is derived from comparable companies or comparable mergers and acquisitions. The differences between the two estimates of the TV could be attributed to too high or low discount rate; too high or low growth rate; and to comparable multiples of companies with different expected risk, growth, or macroeconomic conditions.

The Discount Rate

The discount rate should reflect the risk associated with the free cash flows. Based on the capital structure of the company being valued, we derive a weighted average cost of capital or WACC, which serves as the discount rate for free cash flows of the subject company.[11] The formula for WACC is as follows:

WACC = WdRd$(1 - t)$ + WeRe, where
Wd = The share of debt in the capital structure, or $D/(D + E)$,
We = The share of equity in the capital structure, or $E/(D + E)$,
Rd = Cost of debt (interest rate on debt or yield to maturity on corporate bonds),
t = Marginal tax rate,

Re is the cost of equity capital that can be derived from the Capital Asset Pricing Model or CAPM, as follows:

[11] For a more thorough discussion on how to estimate the ATWACC, see Case 7 of this book.

Re $= R_f + \beta(R_m - R_f)$, where

Re = Cost of equity or the expected rate of return on the company's equity,

R_f = Risk-free rate of return on government securities, which is the risk-free rate of return over a time horizon consistent with the investment horizon. There are various risk-free rates that could be used, but the practice is to use Treasury Bills for up to 1-year maturity, Treasury Notes for up to 10-year maturity, and Treasury Bonds for 30-year maturity.

β = The beta is a measure of the company's systematic risk or market risk or non-diversifiable risk, which reflects the company's volatility compared to the overall market index.

$(R_m - R_f)$ = Risk-adjusted rate of return or the market risk premium, or equity risk premium. It is usually estimated as the difference between the returns on the broad common stocks market index, such as the S&P500, and medium or long-term government bonds, depending on the horizon of the valuation. The market-risk premium ranges between 4.5% and 5.5%.[12]

The cost of equity provides an estimate of an investor's required rate of return for a given risk level associated with an investment that could be estimated based on the CAPM. However, application of the CAPM to divisions, business segments or private companies is hampered by lack of beta information. In such instances, we could derive the betas by using comparable companies through a process of unlevering and relevering (described in the Appendix).

Flow to Equity ("FTE")

Flow to Equity discounts the cash flow from the firm to the shareholders of the levered firm at the cost of levered equity capital, Rs, by the following approach: (1) Calculate the levered cash flows, LCFs, (2) Calculate Rs, and (3) Value the levered cash flow at Rs.

[12] William N. Goetzmann and Roger G. Ibbotson, *The Equity Risk Premium, Essays and Explorations* (Oxford University Press, New York, 2006); Pablo Fernandez, Alberto Ortiz Pizarro, and Isabel Fernandez Acín, "Market Risk Premium Used in 71 Countries in 2016: A Survey of 6,932 Respondents," IESE Business School, University of Navarra, Madrid, http://www.valuewalk.com/wp-content/uploads/2016/05/SSRN-id2776636.pdf.

The free cash flow to equity is shown in the following equation:

FCFE = FCF – (1 – *t*) * (Interest payments) + Borrowing.
FCFE = (Net income + Depreciation – ΔNet working capital) – Gross capital expenditures + (New preferred equity issues – Preferred dividends + New debt issues – Principal repayments)

1. Determine the equity cost of capital, Re; and
2. Discounting the free cash flow to equity using the equity cost of capital.

The Dividend Discount Model

The dividend discount model ("DDM"), which is also referred to as the Dividend Growth Model ("DGM") or the Gordon Model, values common stock prices as the *present value of* all *expected future dividends*. More specifically, dividend growth patterns are usually considered under three scenarios

Zero growth — where the firm pays a constant dividend, and the stock price is computed using a perpetuity formula.
Constant growth — the firm increases the dividend by a constant *percent* every period, and the stock price is computed using the growing to perpetuity model.
Supernormal growth — where dividend growth is not consistent initially, but settles down to constant growth eventually, and the stock price is computed using a multistage model.

The Adjusted Present Value ("APV")

The adjusted present value ("APV") is designed to value operations or assets in place.[13] The APV, like all DCF methodologies, involves projection of cash flows of the business in a two-tier approach by first valuing the operation, then valuing the financial side effects, and adding both values to constitute the value of the enterprise. Specifically, we can value

[13] Timothy A. Luehrman, *Using APV: A Better Tool for Valuing Operations* (Harvard Business Review, May–June 1997).

an unlevered target company's free cash flows by discounting it at the unlevered cost of capital; and then estimate and add the present value of the interest tax shield attributed to debt discounted at the cost of debt, as well as other financial side effects, such as subsidies. Because interest payments are deductible expenses for the corporation, debt financing creates an interest tax shield for the firm, that is included explicitly or implicitly in the valuation of the firm. In applying the APV, we first derive the pro forma income statement and balance sheet for the first 5 years by utilizing the percent of sales approach. On the basis of the 5th-year free cash flows, the expected growth rate to perpetuity and the discount rate, we derive the terminal value (as discussed in the prior section). The free cash and the terminal value are discounted by the cost of equity for an unlevered company and added to form the value of the operating business.

In the second step, we value the financial side effects, which include the debt shielding tax effect of interest, subsidies, cost of financial distress, cost of hedging and cost of issuing new securities.[14] For instance, the financial side effects of interest tax shields are equal to $D * r * t$, where D is the interest-bearing debt, r is the cost of debt, and t is the marginal tax rate.[15] The enterprise value of the firm is the sum of the value of operation plus the value of the financial side effects, that is, APV = NPV + NPVF, where NPV is the value of the unlevered firm and NPVF is the present value of the financial side effects.

The Market Approach

The market approach assesses the value of a common share on the basis of comparable companies' various multiples. Common multiples include the ratio of the price per share to earnings per share ("P/E"), the ratio of the price per share to sales per share ("P/S"), the ratio of the price per share to assets per share ("P/A"), the ratio of the price per share to EBIT per share ("P/EBIT"), the ratio of the price per share to EBITDA per share ("P/EBITDA") and several additional multiples. The financial multiples are selected from a sample of comparable companies or comparable M&A

---

[14] Ross, *op. cit.*, Chapter 18.

[15] This is only true if the level of Debt is constant. For more information, see Appendix B and especially the last footnote of that appendix.

transactions and are applied to the subject company to estimate its feasible range of values. Ideal comparables, also referred to as guideline companies, are in the same industry as the subject company, and are similar to the subject company in terms of markets, products, growth, profitability, and business risk. The market approach provides a popular valuation approach, but its reliability depends on the goodness of the comparables. In the application of the market approach, several adjustments of the comparables might be necessary for the following factors: geographic location, company-specific risk, marketability or liquidity, differences in the tax conditions, profitability, and company size. Because the comparables might not be exact or sufficiently close to the subject company, we analyze the results by utilization of the interquartile distribution range. There are a variety of sources for comparable or guideline companies, including the SEC Form 10-K filings on the SEC website or through EDGAR; S&P Compustat, and S&P Capital IQ, which are electronic searchable databases of US and foreign public companies.

Asset-Based Valuation

The asset-based approach to valuation is based on the financial accounting concept that the owners' equity is determined by subtracting the book value of a company's liabilities from the book value of its assets.[16] Under the generally accepted accounting principles ("GAAP"), most assets on the balance sheet are recorded at historical cost, whereas most long-term liabilities are recorded at the present value, and there is no recognition of intangible assets. Therefore, the "book value" of the owners' equity will normally be underestimated. However, the book value could be adjusted to fair market value, by deriving the fair market value of each asset and liability on the balance sheet of the subject company or entity, and then subtracting the total adjusted liabilities from the total adjusted assets to derive the adjusted book value. This approach increases the valuation cost and complexity, but still ignores intangible assets if they are not listed on the balance sheet.[17]

The FIFO method of inventory usually provides the best indicator of fair value for inventory. The value of plant, property, and equipment is

[16]NACVA, Chapter 6, Commonly Used Methods of Valuation.

[17]*Ibid.*

typically not at fair value and will need an appraisal if the amounts are significant. If the amount is not significant an adjusted depreciation using reasonable useful lives and a non-accelerated depreciation method may result in an acceptable estimate of fair value. Other assets may also need a separate appraisal, depending on their nature. Liabilities are usually at fair value. But loans from related parties may need to be adjusted to reflect their fair value using market interest rates.

Another assessment method is the liquidating value for firms in financial distress, or for firms whose operating prospects are very cloudy. This method may be appropriate if there is doubt regarding the probability of the company staying in business. Below, I provide multiples for companies in PepsiCo's industry:

Price Multiples of PepsiCo and Select Comparables December 31, 2019

	Price	Dividend	EPS	P/E	PEG	P/S	P/B
PepsiCo, Inc.	53.74	3.82	9.03	14.44	6.35	2.79	13.08
Coca-Cola Company	47.20	1.60	1.64	32.77	4.92	7.00	12.64
J&J Snack Foods Corp	185.12	1.04	4.88	37.93	5.48	2.96	4.31
Mondelez International, Inc.	54.81	3.00	2.21	24.83	3.80	3.07	3.06
Constellation Brand, Inc.	200.95		12.61	15.94	3.66	4.72	3.15

Notes: EPS = Net income per share divided by the number of shares, P/E = Price per share divided by earnings per share,
PEG = Price per share to earnings per share divided by growth rate, P/S = Price per share divided by sales per share,
P/B = Price per share divided by book value per share.
Source: https://finance.yahoo.com/quote/.

Closing Comment

The income and market approaches are most common stock valuation methodologies. Valuation is subject to errors due to data and projection shortcomings. Therefore, no valuation is "right" in any absolute sense. It is appropriate to use several scenarios and methodologies in common stock valuation.

Appendix. Unlevered and Relevered Betas

When firms are financed entirely by equity, the risk faced by investors reflects only the business risks borne by the firm's investment and the equity beta equals the asset beta.[18] When firms are funded by debt and equity, the return is split between debtholders and shareholders; however, because debtholders have the first claim on the company's cash flows, the riskiness of the residual flows to shareholders is magnified. Thus, shareholders bear both the business risk of the company's assets and the financial risk associated with the use of debt financing. Hence, the company's equity beta exceeds its asset beta.

Case 7 of this book suggested a methodology to find the ATWACC of a firm. However, in some cases, where the firm is not public, one must use comparable public firms to find the appropriate discount rate. When measuring indirectly the cost of capital by using a proxy company we need the asset beta of the comparable firm but have instead the equity beta. The asset beta could then be used to determine the ATWACC of the subject firm as a discount rate for the free cash flows. Therefore, the equity beta of the comparable firm needs to be transformed into asset beta through a process of unlevering and relevering the proxy beta. The proxy's asset beta could be stated as follows:

$$\beta_{\text{assets}} = \beta_{\text{equity}} E/(E + D) + \beta_{\text{debt}} D/(E + D)$$

However, debt is relatively risk free and thus beta debt is zero, which modifies the above equation as follows:

$$\beta_{\text{assets}} = \beta_{\text{equity}} E/(E + D) \text{ or } \beta_{\text{assets}} = \beta_{\text{equity}}/(D + E)/E = \beta_{\text{equity}}/(1 + D/E)$$

$$\beta_{\text{equity}} = \beta_{\text{assets}}(1 + D/E)$$

Upon introduction of taxes, the above betas are stated as follows:

$$\beta_{\text{assets}} = \beta_{\text{equity}}/(1 + (1 - t)D/E)$$

$$\beta_{\text{equity}} = \beta_{\text{assets}}(1 + (1 - t)D/E)$$

An alternative formulation with taxes, define leveraged and unleveraged betas as follows[19]:

---

[18] See, for instance, Alan C. Shapiro, *Modern Corporate Finance* (Macmillan, New York, 1990), 279–280.

[19] James C. Van Horn, *Financial Management and Policy*, 11th ed. (Prentice Hall, Hoboken, New Jersey, 1988), 206–217; Tim Koller, Marc Goedhart, and David Wessels, McKinsey & Company, *Valuation: Measuring and Managing the Value of Companies*, 5th ed. (Wiley, Hoboken, New Jersey, 2010), 784–785.

$$\beta_l = \beta_u(1 + (1 - t)(D/E)) \text{ and } \beta_u = \beta_l/(1 + (1 - t)(D/E))$$

where t, D, and E are the tax rate, debt and equity, respectively.[20]

To derive the beta for a subject company, select comparable publicly listed companies from the same industry, with similar size and cyclicality, then unlevered their betas by application of the following model:

$$\beta_u = \beta_l/(1 + (1 - t)(D/E))$$

The debt equity ratio is that of the comparable firm. Then reveler the betas using the (D/E) ratio of the subject private firm and marginal tax rate t^* of the subject firm whose levered beta (β_l) we seek to estimate by application of the following model:

$$\beta_l^* = \beta_u(1 + (1 - t^*)(D/E)^*)$$

β_{assets} is weighted average of the beta equity and debt. Alternatively, one can use b_u to estimate the cost of equity of the unlevered firm to be used in the APV methodology.

[20]This popular formula assumes that the firm maintains a constant level of debt. For a separate approach when the firm maintains a constant book value of leverage, see Brick and Weaver, "Calculating the Cost of Capital of an Unlevered Firm for Use in Project Evaluation," *Review of Quantitative Finance and Accounting* 9, no. 2 (1997): 111–129. If the firm's leverage policy is to maintain a constant percentage of the market value of the firm, see J. R. Ezzell and J. A. Miles, "Capital Project Analysis and the Debt Transaction Plan," *Journal of Financial Research* (Spring 1983): 6, no. 1, 25–31; and W. G. Lewellen and D. R. Emery, "Corporate Debt Management and the Value of the Firm," *Journal of Financial and Quantitative Analysis* (December 1986): 21, no. 4, 415–425.

https://doi.org/10.1142/9789811216749_0013

Case 13

Salesforce.Com Inc. Acquisition of Slack Technologies Inc.: Valuation of Firms

Harvey A. Poniachek

Rutgers Business School, USA

Salesforce to Acquire Slack for $27.7 Billion

On December 1, 2020, Salesforce and Slack Technologies, Inc. entered into an agreement under which Salesforce will acquire Slack[1] for $26.79 in cash and 0.0776 shares of Salesforce common stock for each Slack share. The acquisition is valued at approximately $27.7 billion based on the closing price of Salesforce's common stock on November 30, 2020. Salesforce expects to fund the cash portion of the transaction with a combination of new debt and cash on Salesforce's balance sheet. Salesforce has obtained a commitment from Citigroup Global Markets Inc., Bank of America, N.A., and JPMorgan Chase Bank, N.A. for a $10.0 billion senior unsecured 364-day bridge loan facility, subject to customary conditions. Upon approval of the transaction by its shareholders, Slack will become an operating unit of Salesforce and will continue to be led by CEO Stewart Butterfield. According to Marc Benioff, Chair and CEO of Salesforce "this transaction is a match made in heaven, and Salesforce and Slack will shape the future of enterprise

[1] https://investor.salesforce.com/press-releases/press-release-details/2020/Salesforce-Signs-Definitive-Agreement-to-Acquire-Slack/default.aspx.

software and transform the way everyone works in the digital environment anywhere in the world."

The board of directors of Salesforce and Slack has approved the transaction and the Slack board recommends that its stockholders approve the transaction and adopt the merger agreement. The transaction is anticipated to close in the second quarter of Salesforce's fiscal year 2022, subject to approval by the Slack stockholders, the receipt of required regulatory approvals, and other customary closing conditions. The Slack shares subject to the agreement represent approximately 55% of the current outstanding voting power of the Slack common stock. Salesforce has also entered into a voting agreement with certain stockholders of Slack common stock, under which each such stockholder has agreed to vote all their Slack shares in favor of the transaction at the special meeting of Slack stockholders to be held in connection with the transaction, subject to certain terms and conditions.

Connecting people and data across systems, apps, and devices is one of the biggest challenges companies face in today's all-digital world. Together, Salesforce and Slack will create the most extensive open ecosystem of apps and workflows for business and empower millions of developers to build the next generation of apps, with clicks not code. Slack is the leading channel-based messaging platform, used by millions to align their teams, unify their systems, and drive their businesses forward. It offers a secure, enterprise-grade environment that can scale with the largest companies in the world. It is a new layer of the business technology stack where people can work together more effectively, connect all their other software tools and services, and find the information they need to do their best work. Slack's open platform seamlessly integrates with more than 2,400 apps that people use to collaborate, communicate and get work done. With the largest enterprise app ecosystem, the Salesforce platform is the easiest way to build and deliver apps to connect with customers in a new way.

BofA Securities, Inc. is serving as the exclusive financial advisor to Salesforce, and Wachtell, Lipton, Rosen & Katz and Morrison & Foerster LLP are serving as legal counsel to Salesforce. Qatalyst Partners LP and Goldman Sachs & Co LLC are serving as financial advisors to Slack. Latham & Watkins LLP and Goodwin Procter LLP are serving as legal counsel to Slack.

The registration statement on Form S-4 and proxy statement/prospectus that will be filed with the Securities and Exchange Commission ("SEC") reflects the proposed transaction.

The Assignment

Ms. Linda Smith is CEO and Chair of Valuation Services, Inc. ("VSI") that she established with several colleagues and the backing of private equity a dozen years ago. She and three founders control 60% of the firm and the private equity company owns the balance. Obtaining engagements is vital and performing outstanding and in a timely manner assures an impeccable reputation and continuous growth. Ms. Smith graduated with an MBA in Finance from Rutgers Business School and previously earned an undergraduate degree in computer science from the State University of New York at Stony Brook. Upon graduation from Rutgers, she joined PWC valuation services where she obtained her first valuation experience and an accreditation by the American Society of Appraiser (ASA). Ms. Smith gained an outstanding reputation in valuation of high-tech companies, specifically in the software field. She published several important papers in professional journals and is a common speaker at business conferences. Her firm, VSI, was hired by Slack Technologies Board of Directors with a mandate to assess the valuation of the firm and assist the Board in determining if the price offered by Salesforce was right by application of the **Income Approach** and the **Market Approach**. VSI has a staff of two dozen professionals, including four Managing Directors that include Robert Johnson and Christine Gonzales, who were assigned to address the valuation engagement. Both Managing Directors split the task, where Robert and team engaged in the Income Approach and Christine in the Market Approach. They were asked to submit a draft report to Ms. Smith in a couple of weeks for discussion and thereafter be ready to discuss their findings with the client, Slack Technologies. The **Appendix** provides very useful data on Slack Technologies. Additional information could be obtained from SEC.gov and the complete prospectus Form S-4 was filed by Salesforce.

Valuation Methodologies

The major valuation approaches that are commonly used include the income approach, the market approach, and the asset approach, with the first two being the primary valuation methodologies. The main features of the valuation approaches[2] are as follows:

---

[2]For further discussion on valuation methodologies, see Case 12 of this book and the following references: Enrique R. Arzac, *Valuation for Mergers, Buyouts and Restructuring*, 2nd ed. (Wiley, Hoboken, New Jersey, 2008); Tim Koller, Marc Goedhart, and David

1. The income approach could be applied in three different versions, depending on the nature of the cash flows, the capital structure of the firm or entity, and the discount rate. The approach derives the enterprise value ("EV") of a subject company or project based on the present value of the expected free cash flows. The discount rate could be the Weighted Average Cost of Capital ("WACC"), or the cost of equity. The income approach requires a good measure of judgment due to the inherently uncertain business forecasts surrounding merger synergies.[3]
2. The market approach assesses the enterprise value or equity based on comparable companies or comparable transactions, by utilizing various multiples, such as the ratio of the price per share to earnings per share ("P/E"), the ratio of the enterprise value to earnings before interest and tax ("EV/EBIT"), and several other multiples.

The Income Approach

The income valuation approach applies the Fair Market Value ("FMV") or the investment value standard and premises that the subject company or entity is a going concern. The valuation determines the company's or project's worth, but the price paid for it would ultimately be negotiated between the buyer and seller that would consist of the stand-alone value of the target company plus a fraction of the expected synergies. Because different prospective parties expect different synergies from mergers and acquisitions ("M&As"), their offer prices could vary considerably. For

---

Wessels, *Valuation, Measuring and Managing the Value of Companies*, 5th ed., McKinsey & Company (Wiley, Hoboken, New Jersey, 2010); Luis E. Pereiro, *Valuation of Companies in Emerging Markets: A Practical Approach* (Wiley, Hoboken, New Jersey, 2002); Aswath Damodaran, *Damodaran on Valuation: Security Analysis for Investment and Corporate Finance*, 2nd ed. (Wiley, Hoboken, New Jersey, 2006); Aswath Damodaran, *The Dark Side of Valuation, Valuing Young, Distressed, and Complex Businesses*, 2nd ed. (FT Press, Upper Saddle River, New Jersey, 2012); Rosenbaum Joshua and Joshua Pearl, *Investment Banking, Valuation, Leveraged Buyouts, and Mergers and Acquisitions*, 2nd ed. (Wiley, Hoboken, New Jersey, 2013); Duff & Phelps, *2015 Valuation Handbook, Guide to Cost of Capital* (Wiley, Hoboken, New Jersey, 2015).

[3]W. Todd Brotherson, Kenneth M. Eades, Robert S. Harris, and Robert C. Higgins, "Company Valuation in Mergers and Acquisitions: How Is Discounted Cash Flow Applied by Leading Practitioners?" *Journal of Applied Finance* (formerly *Financial Practice and Education*) 24, no. 2 (2014): 43–51. Available at SSRN: https://ssrn.com/abstract=2681112.

instance, one prospective buyer could obtain significant synergies via reduction of cost, expansion of sales and earnings, R&D, and international expansion into new markets. However, not every prospective buyer might have the same opportunities. Therefore, different prospective buyers are likely to bid for the subject at different prices. The income approach applies the discount cash flow ("DCF") and the methodology is based on solid corporate finance theories[4] and could be applied to three different circumstances, as follows:

- The net present value ("NPV") methodology, which **often** referred to as the WACC methodology, discounts the unlevered free cash flows to the firm ("FCFF") for the first 5 years and to infinity by application of a formulary approach.[5] The value to infinity or the terminal value is derived either through a formulary approach based on the last year's free cash flow ("FCF"), the growth rate to perpetuity and the WACC, or through a multiple of EBIT or EBITDA. The sum of the discounted free cash flow of the forecast period **plus** the present value of the terminal value determines the enterprise value. Debt is deducted from the enterprise value to derive the equity value. We note that because the WACC was derived by using the after-tax interest rate, this approach incorporates the tax benefit of debt implicitly through the cost of capital.
- Alternatively, we could value an unlevered company's free cash flows to the firm by discounting it at the unlevered cost of capital; and then add the present value of the interest tax shields attributed to debt (discounted at the cost of debt), as well as other financial side effects, such as subsidies. This approach is called the adjusted present value ("APV") method.
- The third DCF method is based on free cash flows to equity ("FTE") discounted at the cost of equity for an unlevered entity, or the cost of equity for a levered company.

Usually three valuation scenarios are derived, including high or optimistic, average, and low or pessimistic, and probabilities are assigned to

[4]Jonathan Berk and Peter DeMarzo, *Corporate Finance*, 3rd ed. (Pearson, Hoboken, New Jersey, 2014), Chapter 8, 233–260; Stephen A. Ross, Randolph W. Westerfield, Jeffrey Jafee, and Bradford D. Jordan, *Corporate Finance*, 11th ed. (McGraw-Hill Education, New York, 2013), Chapters 4, 9.

[5]Berk, *op. cit.*, 627.

each[6] scenario to obtain a probability-weighted average scenario. The reasonableness of the valuations could be further examined through sensitivity analysis, including an application of a Monte Carlo simulation technique.[7] Control and liquidity discounts and premiums could be applied as necessary.[8]

The FCF from assets equals to earnings before interest and taxes ("EBIT") plus depreciation, which is a non-cash expense, minus taxes, minus capital expenditures ("CAPEX"), and minus changes in net working capital ("NWC"). Stated algebraically, FCF is defined as follows:

FCF = EBIT + Depreciation – Taxes – CAPEX – ΔNWC, or alternatively stated as

FCF = EBIT(1 – t) + Depreciation – CAPEX – ΔNWC

The definitions of the variables are as follows:

FCF = Free cash flows,
EBIT = Earnings before interest and taxes,
EBIT(1 – t) is EBIT after taxes,
t is the marginal tax rate,
CAPEX = Capital expenditure, which equals Net fixed assets t = 2 – (Net fixed assets t = 1 + Depreciation),
ΔNWC = Change in net working capital, which equals NWC2 – NWC1, and NWC equals Current assets (CA) – Current liabilities (CL).

The net working capital includes cash, receivables, inventory, and payables required for the operation of the business.

A terminal value ("TV") reflects the value of all cash flows from the end of the projected period to perpetuity, and it constitutes a significant component of the company's enterprise value that often accounts for as much as 70% of the total value. The terminal value could be estimated in two ways: First, through a formulary approach based on the last forecasted FCF, the growth rate, and the discount rate, as follows:

---

[6] *Ibid.*, 353, 357.

[7] Palisade, "Monte Carlo Simulation," http://www.palisade.com/risk/monte_carlo_simulation.asp.

[8] Shannon P. Pratt, *Business Valuation Discounts and Premiums* (Wiley, Hoboken, New Jersey, 2001), Chapter 1.

TV = FCF$(1 + g) \div (\text{WACC} - g)$, where FCF$(1 + g)$ is the expected growth of free cash flow following the last year of the forecasted period, which is commonly year 6 and onward, and WACC is the weighted average cost of capital. The growth rate is denoted as g.

Alternatively, the terminal value could be derived as a multiple of EBIT or EBITDA, where the multiple is derived from comparable companies or comparable transactions. The differences between the two estimates of the TV could be attributed to differences in the discount rate, growth rate, or the use of comparable multiples that fail to match the subject company in the terminal period.

The discount rate[9] should reflect the risk associated with the free cash flows. Based on the capital structure of the company being valued, a weighted average cost of capital or WACC is derived, which serves as the discount rate for the free cash flows of the subject company or project.

The formula for WACC is as follows:

WACC = WdRd$(1 - t)$ + WeRe, where the variables are specified below:

Wd = The % share of debt in the capital structure, or $D/(D + E)$,

We = The % share of equity in the capital structure, or $E/(D + E)$,

D = Interest bearing debt,

E = Equity, or the market capitalization of the firm, which equals Price per share × The number of outstanding shares,

Rd = Pretax cost of debt is the yield to maturity on corporate bonds with the same credit rating and maturity of the subject company or the cost of borrowing of the subject company,

T = Marginal tax rate,

Re is the cost of equity capital that can be obtained from the Capital Asset Pricing Model or CAPM, as follows:

Re = $R_f + \beta(R_m - R_f)$, where

R_f = Risk-free rate of return on government securities over a time horizon consistent with the investment horizon. The practice is to use Treasury Bills for up to 1-year maturity, Treasury Notes for up to 10-year maturity, and Treasury Bonds for 30-year maturity.

[9] See Case 6 for a more thorough discussion of how to estimate the WACC.

β = The beta is a measure of the company's stock systematic risk or market risk or non-diversifiable risk, which reflects the company's volatility compared with the overall market index.

$(R_m - R_f)$ = The market risk premium, or equity risk premium, and is usually estimated as the difference between the returns on the broad common stocks market index, such as the S&P500, and short or medium, or long-term government bonds, depending on the horizon of the valuation. The market-risk premium ranges between 4.5% and 5.5%.[10]

The cost of equity is an estimate of an investor's required rate of return on an investment that could be estimated based on the CAPM, however, application of the CAPM to divisions, business segments, or private companies is hampered by lack of beta information. In such instances, we could derive the betas by using comparable companies through a process of unlevering and relevering (described below), or by applying the Dividend Growth Model ("DGM"[11]) as an alternative to CAPM.

The Market Approach

The market approach determines the value of a company or entity by comparing it to comparable companies or comparable transactions. The method is based on the application of various multiples, with the following being the most common:

The P/E ratio of the price per share to earnings per share.
The EV/EBIT ratio of the enterprise value to operating income.
The EV/EBITDA ratio of the enterprise value to gross operating profit + depreciation and amortization.

---

[10] William N. Goetzmann and Roger G. Ibbotson, *The Equity Risk Premium, Essays and Explorations* (Oxford University Press, New York, 2006); Pablo Fernandez, Alberto Ortiz Pizarro, and Isabel Fernandez Acín, "Market Risk Premium Used in 71 Countries in 2016: A Survey of 6,932 Respondents," IESE Business School, University of Navarra, Madrid, http://www.valuewalk.com/wp-content/uploads/2016/05/SSRN-id2776636.pdf.

[11] Stephen A. Ross, Randolph W. Westerfield, Jeffrey Jafee, and Bradford D. Jordan, *Corporate Finance*, 11th ed. (McGraw-Hill Education, New York, 2013), 243, Chapters 4, 9.

EV/FCF is the ratio of the enterprise value to operating free cash flow, and EV/Sales is the ratio of the enterprise value to company sales.

The financial multiples are selected from a sample of comparable companies or transactions and are applied to the subject company to estimate its feasible range of values. Ideal comparables, also referred to as guideline companies, are in the same industry as the subject company being valued, and generally have similar markets, products, growth, profitability, and business risk. The market approach provides a popular valuation approach, but the reliability of the outcome depends on the goodness of the comparables.

If comparable companies or guideline companies are used, a decision needs to be made whether to use Market Value of Invested Capital (MVIC) or Market Value of Equity (MVE). MVIC is defined as the entire invested capital value of the firm, including equity investment and debt investment.

There are a variety of sources for comparable or guideline companies, including the SEC 10-K filings on the SEC website or through EDGAR, the vendor for the SEC; S&P Compustat and S&P Capital IQ, which are searchable databases of US and foreign public companies. Comparable transactions, or comparable deals, are commonly used alongside comparable companies. The difference between comparable companies and comparable transaction multiples is that the latter will reflect a "control premium," typically 30% to 50%, that is not present in the comparable companies. The "control premium" depends on the uniqueness of the assets sought and to what extent there are close substitutes for the technology, expertise, or capability in question, the distribution of financial resources between the bidder and target, or the possibility that the ex-ante target price was unduly inflated by market rumors. Since publicly traded stocks are minority shares, if a controlling interest is being valued, a control premium should be considered.

In the application of the market approach, several adjustments of the ratios might be necessary to reflect differences in the comparables.

Degree of marketability and/or liquidity,
Timing differences between market transactions and the valuation date,
Strategic or investment value issues, and
Size, depth of management, diversification of markets, products and services, and relative growth and risk.

The Adjusted Present Value ("APV")

The adjusted present value ("APV") is designed to value operations or assets-in-place[12] in a two-step approach by first valuing the operation, and then valuing the financial side effects and adding both values together to constitute the value of the enterprise. Specifically, we can value an unlevered company's free cash flows by discounting it at the unlevered cost of capital; and then add the present value of the interest tax shields attributed to debt discounted at the cost of debt, as well as other financial side effects, such as subsidies. Because interest payments are tax-deductible expenses, debt financing creates an interest tax shield that is included explicitly or implicitly in the valuation of the firm. The enterprise value of the firm is the sum of the value of operation plus the value of the financial side effects, that is, APV = NPV + NPVF, where NPV is the value of the unlevered firm and NPVF is the present value of the financial side effects. To find the total value of equity, we deduct the value of debt (and preferred stock) from the enterprise value.

Determine the entity's value without leverage Vu, by discounting its free cash flows at the unlevered cost of capital, Ru. Assuming a constant level of debt, Ru = ATWACO/$(1 - tL)$, where L is the percentage of debt representing the total firm value. If the level of debt is constant, the value of the debt tax shields is TD.[13]

Flow to Equity ("FTE")

Flow to Equity discounts the cash flow from the firm to the shareholders of the levered firm at the cost of levered equity capital, Rs. The free cash flow to equity is shown in the following equation:

FCFE = FCF$(1 - t)$ * (Interest payments) + Net borrowing

FCFE = (Net income + Depreciation – ΔNet working capital) – Gross capital expenditures + (New preferred equity issues – Preferred dividends + New debt issues – Principal repayments).

---

[12] Timothy A. Luehrman, "Using APV: A Better Tool for Valuing Operations," *Harvard Business Review* (May–June 1997).

[13] Please see Cases 8 and 12 for more information regarding how to find the cost of equity of the unlevered firm.

Appendix. Selected Historical Consolidated Financial Data of Slack

The following table sets forth selected historical consolidated financial data of Slack (i) as of and for each of the 4 years ended January 31, 2020, 2019, 2018, and 2017.

	Year Ended January 31			
	2020	2019	2018	2017
	(in Thousands, except per Share Data)			
Consolidated Statements of Operations Data				
Revenue	$630,422	$400,552	$220,544	$105,153
Cost of Revenue	97,191	51,301	26,364	15,517
Gross Profit	533,231	349,251	194,180	89,636
Operating Expenses:				
Research and Development	457,364	157,538	141,350	96,678
Sales and Marketing[a]	402,780	233,191	140,188	104,006
General and Administrative	261,365	112,730	56,493	37,455
Total Operating Expenses	1,121,509	503,459	338,031	238,139
Loss From Operations	(588,278)	(154,208)	(143,851)	(148,503)
Interest Income (Expense) and Other Income, Net	20,510	16,146	4,581	1,749
Loss Before Income Taxes	(567,768)	(138,062)	(139,270)	(146,754)
Benefit (Provision) for Income Taxes	(589)	(840)	(793)	(155)
Net Loss	(568,357)	(138,902)	(140,063)	(146,909)
Net Income (Loss) Attributable to Noncontrolling Interest[b]	2,701	1,781	22	(45)
Net Loss Attributable to Slack	(571,058)	(140,683)	(140,085)	(146,864)
Less: Deemed Dividends to Preferred Stockholders	—	—	40,883	—
Net Loss Attributable to Slack Common Stockholders	$(571,058)	$(140,683)	$(180,968)	$(146,864)

(Continued)

(*Continued*)

	Year Ended January 31			
	2020	2019	2018	2017
	(in Thousands, except per Share Data)			
Basic and Diluted Net Loss per Share:				
Net Loss per Share Attributable to Slack Common Stockholders, Basic and Diluted	$(1.43)	$(1.16)	$(1.47)	$(1.28)
Weighted-Average Shares Used in Computing Net Loss per Share Attributable to Slack Common Stockholders, Basic and Diluted	399,461	121,732	122,865	114,887

(1) Includes stock-based compensation as follows:

	Year Ended January 31			
	2020	2019	2018	2017
	(in Thousands)			
Cost of Revenue	$16,013	$732	$491	$630
Research and Development	226,507	9,948	35,260	34,546
Sales and Marketing	98,797	2,677	8,044	9,744
General and Administrative	85,207	9,775	4,288	5,171
Total Stock-Based Compensation	$426,524	$23,132	$48,083	$50,091

Note: Slack's consolidated financial statements include Slack's majority-owned subsidiary, Slack Fund. The ownership interest of minority investors in Slack Fund is recorded as a non-controlling interest.

(2)

	January 31		
	2020	2019	2018
	(in Thousands)		
Consolidated Balance Sheet Data			
Cash, Cash Equivalents, and Marketable Securities	$768,592	$841,071	$548,761
Working Capital	450,463	650,324	440,258
Total Assets	1,441,706	1,198,956	697,780
Total Deferred Revenue	376,714	241,873	125,453
Convertible Senior Notes, Net	—	—	—
Convertible Preferred Stock[a]	—	1,392,101	965,221
Total Stockholders' Equity	723,899	841,606	519,288

Note: [a]Prior to the completion of the direct listing in fiscal year 2020, all of the 373.4 million shares of convertible preferred stock converted into an equivalent number of shares of Class B common stock.

Projected Financial Information

Slack's senior management made unaudited prospective extrapolations based on the Updated Three-Year Plan for the fiscal years 2025 through 2031 that are referred to any of the Initial Three-Year Plan, the Updated Three-Year Plan, and related extrapolated projections for fiscal years 2025 through 2031 and the NOL Schedule as the "Management Projections."

Initial Three-Year Plan

FYE Jan ($ in Millions)	**FQ4'21E**	**2022E**	**2023E**	**2024E**
Revenue	**$245**	**$1,188**	**$1,562**	**$2,012**
% Growth	*35%*	*33%*	*31%*	*29%*
Non-GAAP Gross Profit	**$214**	**$1,045**	**$1,388**	**$1,812**
% Margin	*87%*	*88%*	*89%*	*90%*
Non-GAAP Operating Income (Loss)[a]	**%(9)**	**$10**	**$155**	**$322**
% Margin	*(4)%*	*1%*	*10%*	*16%*

Note: [a]Excludes the impact of stock-based compensation.

Updated Three-Year Plan and Related Extrapolations

FYE Jan ($ in Millions)	**FQ4'21E**	**2022E**	**2023E**	**2024E**	**2025E**	**2026E**	**2027E**	**2028E**	**2029E**	**2030E**	**2031E**
Revenue	**$245**	**$1,188**	**$1,562**	**$2,012**	**$2,516**	**$3,082**	**$3,698**	**$4,363**	**$5,105**	**$5,922**	**$6,810**
% Growth	*35%*	*32%*	*31%*	*29%*	*25%*	*23%*	*20%*	*18%*	*17%*	*16%*	*15%*
Non-GAAP Gross Profit	**$214**	**$1,045**	**$1,388**	**$1,812**	**$2,265**	**$2,775**	**$3,330**	**$3,929**	**$4,597**	**$5,333**	**$6,133**
% Margin	*87%*	*88%*	*89%*	*90%*	*90%*	*90%*	*90%*	*90%*	*90%*	*90%*	*90%*
Non-GAAP Operating Income (Loss)[a]	**$(9)**	**$10**	**$155**	**$322**	**$503**	**$740**	**$998**	**$1,294**	**$1,532**	**$1,777**	**$2,043**
% Margin	*(4)%*	*1%*	*10%*	*16%*	*20%*	*24%*	*27%*	*30%*	*30%*	*30%*	*30%*
Unlevered Free Cash Flow[a,b]	**$19**	**$71**	**$166**	**$349**	**$557**	**$843**	**$1,101**	**$1,374**	**$1,606**	**$1,843**	**$2,127**
% Margin	*8%*	*6%*	*11%*	*17%*	*22%*	*27%*	*30%*	*31%*	*31%*	*31%*	*31%*
Unlevered Free Cash Flow Less Stock-Based Compensation[c]	**$(43)**	**$(231)**	**$(235)**	**$(149)**	**$(15)**	**$205**	**$408**	**$644**	**$854**	**$1,089**	**$1,397**
% Margin	*(17%*	*(19)%*	*(15)%*	*(7)%*	*(1)%*	*7%*	*11%*	*15%*	*17%*	*18%*	*21%*

Notes: [a]Excludes the impact of stock-based compensation.

[b]Unlevered free cash flow is calculated as non-GAAP operating income (loss), subtracting the impact of cash taxes, and adding or subtracting (as applicable) the net impact of depreciation and amortization, capital expenditures, changes in net working capital, amortization of deferred costs, non-cash operating lease expense and payroll taxes related to stock-based compensation. Unlevered free cash flow excludes the impact of stock-based compensation. Unlevered free cash flow was used by Qatalyst Partners in performing its financial analysis in connection with its opinion as described in more detail in the section "*—Opinion of Qatalyst Partners LP, Slack's Financial Advisor.*"

[c]Unlevered free cash flow less stock-based compensation was used by Goldman Sachs in performing its financial analysis in connection with its opinion as described in more detail in the section "*—Opinion of Goldman Sachs & Co. LLC, Slack's Financial Advisor.*"

Selected Companies Analysis

Goldman Sachs reviewed and selected the following software companies:

- Collaboration Peers:
  - Zoom Video Communications, Inc.
  - Atlassian, Inc.
  - DocuSign, Inc.
  - Dropbox Inc.
  - Box, Inc.
- High Growth Software Peers:
  - Shopify Inc.
  - Okta, Inc.
  - Twilio Inc.
  - Coupa Software Inc.
  - Zscaler, Inc.
  - HubSpot, Inc.
  - Elastic, Inc.
  - Anaplan, Inc.
- SaaS Application Peers:
  - Salesforce
  - ServiceNow, Inc.
  - Workday, Inc.
- Large Cap Software Peers:
  - Microsoft
  - Intuit Inc. ("Intuit")
  - Autodesk Inc. ("Autodesk")
  - SAP

https://doi.org/10.1142/9789811216749_0014

Case 14

Celgene Corporation: A Pharmaceutical Case Study in Financial Planning and Analysis

Lisa S. Kaplowitz

Rutgers Business School, USA

Introduction

Alana Garcia is a 23-year-old first-generation college graduate. Her family immigrated to the US from Mexico when Alana was in middle school and while it was challenging at times, Alana persevered and graduated with honors from Rutgers Business School with a degree in finance. Currently, she is a buy-side research analyst at Capital Partners, LLC, a top investment manager with $10 billion in assets under management. Alana focuses on the pharmaceutical sector and one of the companies in her portfolio, Celgene Corporation, just announced its latest earnings and forward estimates for the next fiscal year. Alana needs to update her financial model with these latest estimates, taking into account historical trends and future expectations of growth and expense leverage in order to advise the portfolio manager to Buy, Sell, or Hold Celgene.

The Company

Celgene Corporation was formed as an independent biotech company in 1986 as a result of the spinoff from Celanese following its merger with

American Hoechst. It went public in 1987. The Company originally set out to look for "microbes that ate toxic waste" but ended up discovering that thalidomide could be used to treat leprosy and certain types of cancer. Its first commercial success came in 1998, with the FDA approval of Thalomid to treat leprosy. Its next success came with the approval of Revlimid in 2005 for certain cancer treatments. (For more information, see How Celgene leaves a legacy of chutzpah in science and drug pricing (statnews.com).) Throughout the late 1990s and 2000s, Celgene acquired a number of companies to further its expansion and leadership position in the treatment of cancer and skin disease.

Today, Celgene is an integrated global biopharmaceutical company that creates innovative therapies for the treatment of cancer and inflammatory diseases. Celgene is involved in all stages of the pharmaceutical process, including the discovery, development, manufacturing, marketing, distribution, and sale of its products. The Company's purpose is to change the course of human health through bold pursuits in science" and its current business strategy is focused on executing its business objectives, accelerating its new product pipeline, and expanding the distribution of its product portfolio. The Company generates revenue from the following main (4) products:

REVLIMID® — Used alone, or in combination with other drugs, to treat multiple myeloma, a cancer that forms in plasma cells (type of white blood cell). Multiple myeloma occurs when cancer cells accumulate in the bone marrow and push out healthy cells.

POMALYST®/IMNOVID® — Also used to treat multiple myeloma.

OTEZLA® — Used to treat psoriatic arthritis (arthritis caused by psoriasis) and plaque psoriasis (skin disease).

ABRAXANE® — Used to treat breast cancer after other chemo treatments have failed. Also treats certain lung cancer for patients that cannot have surgery or radiation treatment.

Celgene's long-term goal is to be the global leader in cellular immunotherapy. In addition, Celgene is striving to make healthcare more affordable and is limiting price increase to only once per year.

Review of Historic Performance

Alana knows that before she can reforecast the next two years of sales and expenses, she needs to analyze the historical numbers and better understand the underlying trends that drive the resulting financials. She has entered the 2015–2017 financials from Celgene's 10-Q quarterly and 10-K annual filings on an excel spreadsheet (Appendix A). She then performs the following analyses to better understand Celgene's historical financial results:

A. **Year-Over-Year Percent Change:** Calculates how much each line item increases or decreases from one year to the next. This is calculated using the following formula:
   = (CY – PY)/PY or (CY/PY) – 1 (CY = current year and PY = prior year)
B. **Common Size Income Statement:** Calculates each line item in a given fiscal year to the total revenue of that same fiscal year. It is used to determine how much each revenue from each product line contributed to the total company revenue and how much of the total company revenue was sent on each line item (category) of expense. This is calculated using the following formula:
   = Line item/Total revenue
C. **Basis Point Change:** Calculates the difference in basis points (bps) of each line item. Basis points are often used in finance to analyze the change in the common size income statement. 100 basis points are equal to 1%. For example, if the net profit margin of the firm was 7.08% in the prior year and 7.78% in the current year, the basis point change is (7.78 – 7.08) * 100 or 70 bps.
   = (CY% – PY%) * 100

Once complete, Alana steps back from her analysis and takes a walk around the building, as she knows it is always best to clear your head after you finish typing and "crunching" a bunch of numbers. When she returns, she begins to study the numbers and understand what it all means. She remembers that year-over-year increases in Revenue and Profit are considered favorable while increases in Expense are considered unfavorable, as they reduce profitability. Mechanically, she puts a minus in excel in front of the formula (A) to adjust for this on the expense side.

She then asks herself the following questions:

1. Which product line is growing the most? Which is suffering from a decline in sales?
2. Which product contributes the most to total revenue? Which product contributes the least?
3. How is the contribution to total revenue changing each year? Which product is increasing its contribution to total revenue?
4. Which expense is growing the most? Which is declining?
5. Which expense is the greatest as a percent of revenue?
6. Which expense is growing as a percent of revenue?

Alana knows that crunching the numbers is the easy part and is curious as to reasons for the historical financial performance of Celgene. She also knows that in general, sales growth is driven by increases in volume and quantity. In the pharmaceutical sector, she also appreciates the more specific drivers to changes in sales.

- *Population growth* — When there are more people taking the drug, it increases the overall quantity of products needed, and therefore is a key indicator that sales will increase (volume)
- *Earlier diagnosis* — Advances in medicine accelerate the timeline in which a patient would need the drug, which would lead to earlier treatments and increased usage (volume)
- *Duration* — Effective medications keep patients alive longer, which increases the patients' use for a longer period of time (volume)
- *Timing of patent removal* — When a patent expires, generic alternatives can enter the market, which creates pricing pressure on the branded product (price)
- *Innovation pipeline* — While there are a lot of phases in this process, it is dependent on the use case, clinical trial, and regulatory/approval process. The timeline and probability of success are assigned at each step of the process and differ with each product (volume and price)
- *In-line products* — These include the potential ancillary uses or other markets for existing products, possibly in combination with other treatment regimes to increase efficacy (volume)

In addition, she rereads Celgene's 10-Ks, 10-Qs, Annual Reports, Press Releases, and Conference Call Transcripts and Presentations, and finds the following explanations:

REVLIMID® — Recent growth is due to the increase in volume (quantity) globally resulting from people taking for longer periods of time (duration), gains in market share versus its competitors and the combined use of the drug in conjunction with other.

POMALYST® — Recent growth is due to increases in both volume and price in the US, increases in volume in Europe due to people taking for longer periods of time (duration), partially offset by decreases in price in Europe, as well as gains in market share versus its competitors.

OTEZLA® — Recent growth is due to increases in international sales as a result of adoption in key non-US markets, an increase in leadership position in the US market and new patients (patient acquisition). Otezla now leads Japan in market share of new patients after being in market only 1 year, as well as realizing additional market share gains in France.

ABRAXANE® — Market share is remaining stable.

In addition, the Company generates other revenue from other products that are currently in its portfolio and licensing arrangements. Cost of goods sold as a percentage of sales has decreased in the recent two years as the company's sales mix trended to lower-cost products. Research and development total dollar expenses have increased due to increased spending related to clinical trials and other activity. Selling, general and administrative expense, although increasing in total dollars, is leveraging as a percentage of sales.

Forecasting for Next Year

Now that Alana better understands Celgene's historical financial performance, she can use that information to form assumptions of future performance. As she begins to update her model and reforecast the 2018 & 2019 Income Statement, she reviews the guidance for 2018 that Celgene disclosed in its 3Q earnings press release (Appendix B). Alana knows that management provides more specific guidance for 2018, being that three quarters have already been completed, but 2019 is less clear, since management will not officially release guidance until they report year-end numbers in another three months.

When Alana first started at Capital Partners, she remembers how frustrated and unsure of herself she was. In school, there always seemed to be one "right" answer to the problems in class. As an analyst, she had to quickly get comfortable with ambiguity, as the companies she analyzes merely provide a range of possible values for the next year's profit, and even less guidance for the year that follows. Having been in the role for over a year, she is much more comfortable with using her best-educated case to update these models. With that confidence, she sets in to methodically update 2018 as she works her way down the P&L, line by line.

As she reviews the guidance provided by Celgene, she realizes that the guidance associated with the Revenue line items is using % change as a driver. She can type the assumption in the 2018 column for % change and use this to calculate 2018 as follows: 2017 $ × (1 + % change). She also noticed that there is no guidance for a couple of the line items and she will just have to look at historical trends to make an estimate.

Alana then reviews the additional information related to expenses and realizes that there is no specific guidance related to each of the individual expenses. She sees that there is an assumption for operating margin and determines that she is going to estimate each line of operating expense using % of Total Revenue as a driver. She can type the assumption in the 2018 % of Revenue column and use this to calculate 2018 as follows: 2018 % of Revenue × 2018 Total Revenue.

Finally, she notes that the tax rate given is not really as a % of Total Revenue but as a % of Income Before Taxes, so while she enters the assumption in the 2018 % of Total Revenue column, she calculates the 2018 Income Tax Provision as 2018 % × 2018 Income Before Income Taxes.

As she completes the remainder of the income statement to arrive at an estimated Adjusted Net Income and EPS, she double-checks that her results are consistent with the final assumptions given in Appendix B. If they are not, she knows she has to modify one of the drivers above. Alana also reassures herself that she does not have to be "exactly" right because there is no "exact answer," and she just needs to fit in the range of Adjusted Net Income and EPS given.

The Assignment

Alana now needs to project 2019 and the guidance is less specific (Appendix C). She must again study the historical trends. In addition, she looks at Celgene's discussion of future growth drivers (Appendix D), as well as her own view related to expectations regarding future performance.

1. Project 2019 Revenue ($17.1 billion total)
   - Project based on year-over-year increase in 2018 revenue for each major product line. Review year-over-year trends in growth and check by reviewing contribution to total revenue. Take into account industry and product-specific drivers for top 4 products.
   - Use % change as the driver. Write brief (1 line) rationale to support the assumption.
2. Project 2019 Expenses
   - Project based on common size income statement and basis point (bps) trends for each expense category.
   - Use % of Total Revenue as the driver. Review by checking bps trend. Write brief (1 line) rationale to support the assumption.
3. Sanity check the adjusted net income and EPS.
   - Adj Net Income should increase 14–16% and EPS is approximately $10.30.

Make sure to also calculate the year-over-year percent growth, the common size income statement, and the basis point change in each line item for 2018 and 2019, as these will help ensure the 2019 forecast makes sense. *Note: While the forecast does not need to exactly equal the revenue and EPS projections, it does need to be within $0.1 billion of Total Revenue and $.01 of Adjusted Net Income.*

Appendices

Appendix A. Celgene Adjusted Income Statements (Fiscal Years 2015–2017)

Celgene Corporation and Subsidiaries Income Statement ($ million)

	Adj. GAAP Income Statement			% Change		% of Revenue			bps Δ	
	2015	**2016**	**2017**	**2016**	**2017**	**2015**	**2016**	**2017**	**2016**	**2017**
REVLIMID®	$5,801	$6,974	$8,187							
POMALYST®/ IMNOVID®	984	1,311	1,614							
OTEZLA®	472	1,017	1,279							
ABRAXANE®	967	973	992							
Other	937	910	901							
Net Product Sales	9,161	11,185	12,973							
Other Revenue	95	44	30							
Total Revenue	9,256	11,229	13,003							
Expenses										
Cost of Goods Sold (Excl Amortization of Acquired Intangible Assets)	388	405	432							
Research and Development	2,044	2,508	2,749							
Selling, General and Administrative	2,011	2,139	2,279							
Total Costs and Expenses	4,443	5,052	5,460							
Operating Income	4,813	6,177	7,543							
Other Income and (Expense)										
Interest and Investment Income, Net	31	30	105							
Interest (Expense)	(311)	(500)	(522)							
Other Income (Expense), Net	48	(52)	24							
Income Before Income Taxes	4,581	5,655	7,150							
Income Tax Provision	698	885	1,134							
Adjusted Net Income	$3,883	$4,770	$6,016							
Fully Diluted Weighted Ave. Shares Out	*824.9*	*803.3*	*808.7*							
EPS	*$4.71*	*$5.94*	*$7.44*							

Source: SEC filings, company press releases, conference calls and investor slide presentations as of 3Q 2018.

Appendix B. Celgene Management Projections for 2018

Revenue	
REVLIMID Net Sales	18.48% increase vs 2017
POMALYST/IMNOVID Net Sales	23.92% increase vs 2017
OTEZLA Net Sales	25.10% increase vs 2017
ABRAXANE Net Sales	0.81% increase vs 2017
Total Revenue	17.10% increase vs 2017
Adjusted Operating Margin	~55.5%
Adjusted Tax Rate	~17.0%
Adjusted Net Income	~$6.431–$6.468 billion
Adjusted EPS	~$8.75–$8.80 per share
Weighted Average Diluted Shares	~735 million

Source: 3Q 2018 10-Q filing.

Other guidance from the Company relating to expenses:

- CoGS as % revenue — CoGs increase as launch new products.
- R&D as % revenue — Likely to increase based on increased regulatory work and milestone payments.
- SG&A as % revenue — Due to acquisitions and replacement of senior executives, will likely have increased overhead costs going forward.
- Interest & Investment income — Calculated based on average cash balance * assumed interest rate. Assume $2.5 billion of excess cash earning 1% interest.
- Interest expense — Calculated based on average debt balance * interest rate on debt. Debt is estimated to be $20 billion and carries an estimated 3.5% interest rate.[1]
- Income tax — based on estimated tax rate.

Appendix C. Celgene Projections for 2019[2]

Total Revenue	$17.1 billion
Adjusted Net Income Growth	14–16% increase vs 2018
Adjusted EPS	$10.30 per share

[1]Estimated rate based on 2017 10-k debt outstanding.

[2]Author estimate based on Sell-Side Analyst consensus.

Appendix D. Additional Company Commentary on 2019 Product Sales

REVLIMID® — Celgene indicates that future growth is going to be driven by additional uses as determined in clinical trials, the expectation that patients will use Revlimid for longer (duration). Alana also notes that Revlimid will come off patent in early 2022 and full generics will come online in 2026. While this will not really impact 2018 and 2019 financial performance, it is important to note from a strategic standpoint that Celgene will need to focus on other products in its portfolio as the pricing for Revlimid will significantly decrease when the generic brand is introduced to the marketplace.

POMALYST® — Celgene indicates that future growth is going to be driven by increased share and duration when used in combination with other drugs as well as positive results from its Phase III clinical trial.

OTEZLA® — Celgene indicates that future growth is going to be driven by development of new uses in addition to a once-a-day formula (decision on 1× formula expected by year-end 2017) which will also increase usage. Positive results are also expected for multiple Phase III trials, but will be partially offset by increased competition in existing markets. That said, there is expected growth from new programs, which could eventually be as much at $500 million at maturity.

ABRAXANE® — Celgene indicates that future growth is going to be driven by the combined use in multiple clinical trials with the potential to be the preferred chemo partner drug for breast and non-small cell lung cancers. There is also the potential for use to treat pancreatic cancer, which is still in the early trial phase.

Other Products — Celgene indicates that two of its current products, Vidaza and Thalmoid, are projected to decrease as they approach patent expiration. While there are five new late-stage products expected to launch through 2020, they will likely not contribute to revenues in 2018 and 2019. At the same time, there will be expenses associated with their development, some of which may be capitalized, and others that will be expensed throughout the year.

Part V

Long-Term Financing

https://doi.org/10.1142/9789811216749_0015

Case 15

Johnson & Johnson Capital Structure and Funding Decisions

Harvey A. Poniachek

Rutgers Business School, USA

Introduction

The financial policy of US nonfinancial publicly traded firms and their capitalization structure[1] changed drastically over the last century.[2] The leverage ratios, defined in terms of debt/(debt + equity), were between 10% and 15% from 1920 to 1945, 45% by 1970, and peaked at 47% in 1992.[3] By comparison, the leverage ratios of regulated public companies remained stable between 40% and 50%. The sharp expansion of leverage of unregulated US firms can be explained by changes in the macroeconomic environment, increased corporate tax rates, growth in financial intermediation, and the implications of substantial government borrowing.[4]

---

[1] Francis A. Longstaff and Ilya A. Strebulaev, "Corporate Taxes and Capital Structure: A Long-Term Historical Perspective," NBER Working Paper 20372, August 2014.

[2] A firm's capital structure is defined in terms of its debt leverage debt/equity, or the ratio of a firm's debt/(debt + equity) or debt/assets or debt/equity.

[3] John R. Graham, Mark T. Leary, and Micheal R. Roberts, "A Century of Capital Structure: The Leveraging of Corporate America," NBER Working Paper 19910, February 2014 (Graham).

[4] *Ibid.*

The Trade-off Theory of Capital Structure

Taxes in the US create an incentive for firms to employ debt because interest expense on debt is a taxable expense that shields taxable income from corporate taxes. For instance, at a corporate tax rate of 21%, each dollar in interest expense reduces taxes by $0.21. According to Modigliani–Miller ("MM"), in a world with corporate taxes and tax shielding benefits the value of the firm increases with leverage. However, as more debt is added the value of the firm declines due to financial distress or bankruptcy cost that offset the tax advantage of leverage. That is, a firm's capital structure decision involves a trade-off between the tax benefits of debt and the costs of financial distress or bankruptcy, and there is an optimal amount of debt, which is the firm's target debt level. A firm with low anticipated profits will likely take on a low level of debt, while a more successful firm would probably take on more debt.

The **trade-off theory** maintains that a firm chooses its capitalization structure by balancing the financial distress or bankruptcy costs of debt and tax shield benefits. The capital structure is optimized where the marginal benefit of debt equals the marginal cost of financial distress or bankruptcy. The firm value rises with the incremental expansion of debt, it reaches a maximum and thereafter, as additional debt is added, the firm's value diminishes and the weighted average cost of capital ("WACC") goes up, as illustrated in Exhibit 1.

The trade-off theory is the longest-standing theory of capital structure. It contains a large body of empirical work on capital structure[5] that provides the following observations:

- Firms establish their optimal capital structure by selecting the debt ratio that maximizes their value;
- Profitable firms with high taxable income should borrow more than unprofitable firms because they are more likely to benefit from tax shielding of debt and thus should have higher leverage ratios. However, empirical findings show that more profitable firms tend to have lower leverage ratios, which negates the trade-off theory;

[5] Andrew B. Abel, "Optimal Debt and Profitability in the Trade-Off Theory," *The Journal of Finance* 73, no. 1 (February 2018): 95–143.

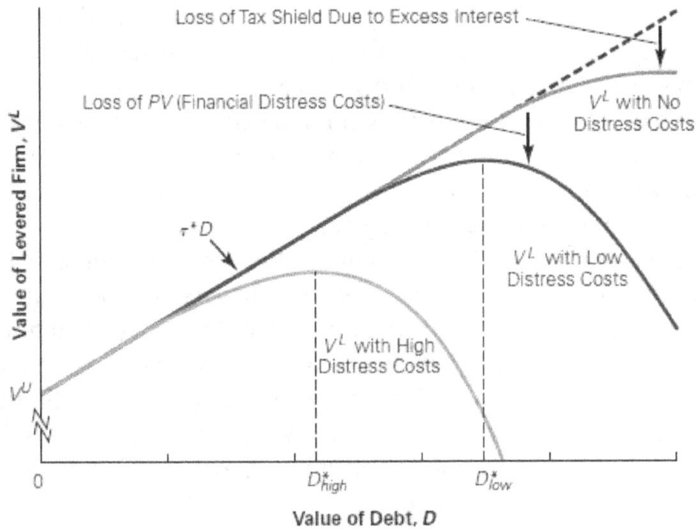

Exhibit 1. Optimal Leverage with Taxes and Financial Distress Costs

Source: Berek and DeMarzo, *Corporate Finance*, 3rd ed. (Pearson).

- Firms with substantial tangible assets should borrow more than firms with mainly intangible assets because tangible assets can be liquidated and reduce the cost of bankruptcy;
- Less risky firms should borrow more than riskier firms, and firms with volatile operating income rely mainly mostly on equity;
- Companies should have target capital structures.

The firm value, Vl, equals the value of the unlevered firm, Vu, plus the present value of the tax shield, PV tax shield, minus the present value of the bankruptcy cost, PV Bankruptcy cost, as follows:

$$Vl = Vu + PV\ Tax\ Shield - PV\ Distress\ or\ Bankruptcy\ cost$$

Alternative Theories

The **agency cost theory** maintains that in a leveraged firm conflicts of interest could arise between managers, stockholders, and bondholders. The agency cost theory of financial structure maintains the debt could reduce the agency cost in two ways. In fact, the cost per dollar of non-necessary perquisite consumption is equal to the manager's percentage ownership of the firm. If the firm finances its expansion with debt, the manager's ownership of the firm will not decline and with a stock repurchase it might actually increase. However, issuing debt might decrease the non-necessary perquisition consumption of the manager due to debt service obligation that enhances management discipline.

On the other hand, when financial distress is imminent stockholders are likely to choose investment strategies that reduce the value of the bonds, whereas bondholders protect themselves by raising the interest rate that they require on the bonds. Financial distress may provide mangers with incentives to apply several strategies, including asset substitution and under investment. Asset substitution involves promising investors' investment in safe assets but instead substituting risky investments. If the investment is successful, shareholders earn the benefit, otherwise bondholders and creditors experience losses. Underinvestment occurs when debt is risky and the gain from the investment will accrue to debt holders rather than shareholders.

The **pecking-order theory** asserts that each firm chooses its leverage ratio based on financing needs by adhering to a hierarchy of financing sources that prefer internal financing when available, and debt is preferred over equity if external financing is required. That is, firms first fund investment projects out of retained earnings, and additional projects are funded with debt and to some extent by equity. Hence, the amount of leverage is determined by investment needs rather than by a target debt-to-equity ratio. Thus, firms have no target capital structure and the leverage ratios observed in the marketplace fluctuate randomly. The pecking-order theory is consistent with the fact that the vast majority (90%) of corporate investments in the US is funded internally through retained earnings, and why profitable firm borrows less than unprofitable firms.

The pecking-order theory is at odds with the trade-off theory on some issues that are addressed below.

- The pecking-order theory does not imply a target amount of leverage.
- Profitable firms need less external financing and rely less on debt.
- Firms may accumulate slack to avoid external funding.

Exhibit 2 provides data on the capitalization structure of several sectors and companies at the end of 2018. The $D/(D + E)$ averages indicate a

Exhibit 2. Capital Structure in Select Sectors and Companies

Sector	Ticker	Date	*D/A*	*E/A*	*D/D + E*	*E/D + E*
Technology	MSFT	20180630	0.3165	0.3196	0.4976	0.5024
	GOOGL	20181231	0.0172	0.7630	0.0221	0.9779
	FB	20181231	0.0000	0.8643	0.0000	1.0000
	INTC	20181231	0.1961	0.5860	0.2508	0.7492
	CSCO	20180731	0.1869	0.3972	0.3200	0.6800
	VZ	20181231	0.3998	0.2066	0.6593	0.3407
	AVERAGE		0.1861	0.5228	0.2916 0.34996	0.7086
Consumer Goods	AAPL	20180930	0.2563	0.2930	0.4666	0.5334
	BA	20181231	0.0908	0.0035	0.9630	0.0370
	NKE	20180531	0.1539	0.4354	0.2611	0.7389
	PG	20180630	0.1763	0.4470	0.2829	0.7171
	PM	20181231	0.6777	−0.2698	1.6614	−0.6614
	AVERAGE		0.1693	0.1818	0.7270	0.2730
Food Companies	KO	20181231	0.3048	0.2290	0.5710	0.4290
	KHC	20181231	0.2979	0.5009	0.3730	0.6270
	PEP	20181231	0.3644	0.1881	0.6596	0.3404
	SBUX	20180930	0.3763	0.0487	0.8855	0.1145
	YUM	20181231	2.3610	−1.9191	5.3430	−4.3430
	AVERAGE		0.3359	0.2417	0.6223	0.3777
Healthcare	ABT	20181231	0.28820	0.45736	0.38655	0.61345
	JNJ	20181231	0.18100	0.39065	0.31662	0.68338
	MRK	20181231	0.23967	0.32530	0.42422	0.57578
	PFE	20181231	0.20643	0.39993	0.34044	0.65956
	UNH	20181231	0.22718	0.35684	0.38899	0.61101
	AVERAGE		0.2183	0.4040	0.3501	0.6499

Note: YUM was excluded from the average.
Source: S&P Compustat.

substantial variability among the various sector, with the average being 29.1% for technology, 72.7% for consumer goods, 62.3% for food, and 35.0% for healthcare. Firms base their capital structure decisions on their industry averages and the need for a certain amount of financial slack.

Data shows debt ratios are low in high-growth industries and where the managers have a high-equity ownership and/or there is significantly greater family involvement are funded by all-equity firms than in levered firms.

Furthermore, data shows that

- *Most nonfinancial corporations have relatively low debt–asset ratios.*
- *Some firms use no debt.*
- *Most corporations employ target debt–equity ratios.* [Graham and Harvey asked 392 chief financial officers (CFOs) whether their firms use target debt–equity ratios.[6] Their study indicates that the great majority of the firms use targets, though the strictness of the targets varies across companies. They find some support for both the pecking-order and trade-off capital structure hypotheses.]

It is very difficult to establish the optimal capital structure ratio. Generally, as Graham and Harvey suggest, firms use the financial ratios of the industry as a guide. This means the CFO should know how his firm's financial decision compares to that of the firm's competitors. If the firm's financial ratios are different from those of its competitors, then the question must be asked as to why. If the deviation from the industry norm can be explained, then it is not a problem, but if not, then you must be able to explain the deviation. Here are some questions:

Does your firm have a different tax rate than your competitors? If your tax rate is higher, then that fact might explain why your firm has a higher degree of leverage. If not, perhaps you need to reduce your leverage exposure.

Is the operating or business risk of your firm different from the competitors? If your firm is riskier it should carry less debt on its balance sheet. If you have less fixed costs and are less risky, then your firm might be able to carry more debt than its competitors.

How dependent is your future profitability upon continuing the planned investment strategy? The more dependent the firm is upon discretionary investment, the more risky is the firm. When a firm becomes

[6] John R. Graham and Campbell R. Harvey, "The Theory and Practice of Corporate Finance: Evidence from the Field," *Journal of Financial Economics* 60, no. 2–3 (2001): 187–243.

financially strapped, it can easily cut down its R&D or maintenance program, but doing might hurt the future profitability of the firm and value of existing assets that may have been used for collateral. If so, the firm should reduce its level of debt compared to its competitors.

Leverage and the Cost of Capital

Assuming a constant level of debt, according to Modigliani and Miller, the relationship between leverage and the after-tax weighted average cost of capital, ATWACC, is given by:

$$\text{ATWACC} = R_{\text{EU}}(1 - TL)$$

where R_{EU} is the cost of equity of an unlevered firm, T is the corporate tax rate, and L is the leverage ratio defined as the ratio of the market value of debt to total value of the firm. The relationship between the cost of equity and leverage is given by:

$$R_{\text{EL}} = R_{\text{EU}} + (1 - T)(R_{\text{EU}} - R)D/S$$

where R_{EL} = cost of equity of levered firm
R_{EU} = cost of equity to unlevered firm
R = pre-tax cost of debt
D = Market value of debt
S = Market value of equity

The above equation assumes that the cost of debt does not increase with leverage. But in reality cost of debt should increase with debt. An ad hoc solution to solve the new ATWACC is to adjust the above relationship by the change of the cost of debt. That is, the new cost of equity is

$$R_{\text{EL}} = R_{\text{EU}} + (1 - t)(R_{\text{EU}} - R)D/S + \Delta R.$$

To find the new ATWACC, we use the definition

$$\text{ATWACC} = \text{LR}(1 - T) + (1 - L)R_{\text{E}}$$

where L is the percentage of financing done through debt, R is the new cost of debt, T is the tax rate, and R_{EL} is the new cost of equity. This approach will allow the ATWACC to rise if the change in the cost of debt is significant enough.

Johnson & Johnson Business[7]

Johnson & Johnson and its subsidiaries ("the Company" or "JNJ") had $82.6 billion in sales in 2020 and approximately 134,500 employees worldwide engaged in the research and development, manufacture, and sale of a broad range of health care products. JNJ is organized into three business segments: Consumer Health, Pharmaceutical, and Medical Devices. Johnson & Johnson is a holding company incorporated in the State of New Jersey in 1887, with operating companies conducting business in virtually all countries of the world.

The Executive Committee of Johnson & Johnson is the principal management group responsible for the strategic operations and allocation of the resources of the Company. This Committee oversees and coordinates the activities of the Company's three business segments. Senior management groups at US and international operating companies are each responsible for their own strategic plans and the day-to-day operations of those companies. Each subsidiary within the business segments is, with limited exceptions, managed by residents of the country where located.

Investments and activities in some countries outside the US are subject to higher risks than comparable US activities because the investment and commercial climate may be influenced by financial instability in international economies, restrictive economic policies, and political and legal system uncertainties. Raw materials essential to the Company's business are generally readily available from multiple sources. The temporary unavailability of those raw materials would not likely have a material adverse effect on the financial results of the Company.

In all their product lines, the Company's subsidiaries compete with companies both locally and globally. The competitive environment requires substantial investments in continuing research. In addition, the development and maintenance of customer demand for the Company's consumer products involve significant expenditures for advertising and promotion. The Company's subsidiaries obtain patent protection on their products and processes where possible. They own, or are licensed under, a significant number of patents in the US and other countries relating to their products, product uses, formulations, and manufacturing processes, which in the aggregate are believed to be of material importance to the Company in the operation of its businesses. The Company's subsidiaries face patent challenges from third parties, including challenges seeking

[7]Form 10K.

to manufacture and market generic and biosimilar versions of the Company's key pharmaceutical products prior to expiration of the applicable patents covering those products.

The Company's businesses are subject to varying degrees of governmental regulation in the countries in which operations are conducted, and the general trend is toward increasingly stringent regulation and enforcement. In the US, the drug, device, and cosmetic industries have long been subject to regulation by various federal and state agencies, primarily as to product safety, efficacy, manufacturing, advertising, labeling, and safety reporting. The exercise of broad regulatory powers by the US Food and Drug Administration (the US FDA) that result in increases in the amounts of testing and documentation required for US FDA approval of new drugs and devices and a corresponding increase in the expense of product introduction. Similar trends are also evident in major markets outside of the US. The global regulatory landscape changed as the COVID-19 pandemic continues to affect the US and global economies. The US FDA and other health authorities have shifted resources and priorities to meet the many challenges presented by the pandemic. Pandemic-related disruptions could negatively impact the processing of regulatory submissions and slow agency review times necessary for the approval or clearance of new drugs and devices.

The Company's businesses operate in highly competitive product markets and competitive pressures could adversely affect the Company's earnings. Interruptions and delays in manufacturing operations could adversely affect the Company's business, sales, and reputation. The Company relies on third parties to manufacture certain of its products. Any failure by or loss of a third-party manufacturer could result in delays and increased costs, which may adversely affect the business.

The Company faces a variety of risks associated with conducting business internationally, including foreign *currency exchange*: In fiscal 2020, approximately 48% of the Company's sales occurred outside of the US, with approximately 23% in Europe, 7% in the Western Hemisphere, excluding the US, and 18% in the Asia-Pacific and Africa region. Changes in currency rates impact the Company's revenues and expenses. While the Company uses financial instruments to mitigate the impact of fluctuations in currency exchange rates on its cash flows, unhedged exposures continue to be subject to currency fluctuations.

The Company faces challenges in maintaining profitability of operations in economies experiencing high inflation rates. The Company has accounted for operations in Argentina (beginning in the fiscal third quarter of 2018) and Venezuela as highly inflationary, as the prior 3-year cumulative inflation rate surpassed 100%. While the Company strives to maintain profit margins in these areas through cost reduction programs, productivity improvements, and periodic price increases, it might experience operating losses because of continued inflation. In addition, the impact of currency devaluations in countries experiencing high inflation rates or significant currency exchange fluctuations could negatively impact the Company's operating results.

JNJ currently maintains investment-grade credit ratings with Moody's Investors Service and Standard & Poor's Ratings Services. Any downgrade of its credit ratings by a credit rating agency, whether because of its actions or factors which are beyond its control, can increase the cost of borrowing under any indebtedness it may incur, reduce market capacity for its commercial paper or require the posting of additional collateral under its derivative contracts. There can be no assurance that JNJ will be able to maintain its credit ratings, and any additional actual or anticipated changes or downgrades in the credit ratings, including any announcement that the ratings are under review for a downgrade, may have a negative impact on liquidity, capital position and access to capital markets.

Dividends. The Company increased its dividend in 2020 for the 58th consecutive year. Cash dividends paid were $3.98 per share in 2020 and $3.75 per share in 2019.

Johnson & Johnson and Subsidiaries
Consolidated Balance Sheets

On January 3, 2021 and December 29, 2019
(Dollars in Millions except Share and Per Share Amounts) (Note 1)

	2020	2019
Assets		
Current Assets		
Cash and Cash Equivalents (Notes 1 and 2)	$13,985	17,305
Marketable Securities (Notes 1 and 2)	11,200	1,982
Accounts Receivable Trade, Less Allowances for Doubtful Accounts $293 (2019, $226)	13,576	14,481
Inventories (Notes 1 and 3)	9,344	9,020

(Continued)

	2020	2019
Assets		
Current Assets		
Prepaid Expenses and Other Receivables	3,132	2,392
Assets Held for Sale (Note 18)	—	94
Total Current Assets	**51,237**	**45,274**
Property, Plant and Equipment, Net (Notes 1 and 4)	18,766	17,658
Intangible Assets, Net (Notes 1 and 5)	53,402	47,643
Goodwill (Notes 1 and 5)	36,393	33,639
Deferred Taxes on Income (Note 8)	8,534	7,819
Other Assets	6,562	5,695
Total Assets	**$174,894**	**157,728**
Liabilities and Shareholders' Equity		
Current Liabilities		
Loans and Notes Payable (Note 7)	$2,631	1,202
Accounts Payable	9,505	8,544
Accrued Liabilities	13,968	9,715
Accrued Rebates, Returns, and Promotions	11,513	10,883
Accrued Compensation and Employee-Related Obligations	3,484	3,354
Accrued Taxes on Income (Note 8)	1,392	2,266
Total Current Liabilities	**42,493**	**35,964**
Long-Term Debt (Note 7)	32,635	26,494
Deferred Taxes on Income (Note 8)	7,214	5,958
Employee Related Obligations (Notes 9 and 10)	10,771	10,663
Long-Term Taxes Payable (Note 1)	6,559	7,444
Other Liabilities	11,944	11,734
Total Liabilities	**111,616**	**98,257**
Commitments and Contingencies (Note 19)		
Shareholders' Equity		
Preferred Stock — Without Par Value (Authorized and Unissued 2,000,000 Shares)	—	—
Common Stock — Par Value $1.00 per Share (Note 12) (Authorized 4,320,000,000 Shares; Issued 3,119,843,000 Shares)	3,120	3,120

(Continued)

(Continued)

	2020	2019
Assets		
Shareholders' Equity		
Accumulated other Comprehensive Income (Loss) (Note 13)	(15,242)	(15,891)
Retained Earnings	113,890	110,659
	101,768	97,888
Less: Common Stock Held in Treasury, at Cost (Note 12) (487,331,000 Shares and 487,336,000 Shares)	38,490	38,417
Total Shareholders' Equity	**63,278**	**59,471**
Total Liabilities and Shareholders' Equity	**$174,894**	**157,728**

Note: See Notes to Consolidated Financial Statements.

Johnson & Johnson and Subsidiaries

Consolidated Statements of Earnings

(Dollars and Shares in Millions except Per Share Amounts) (Note 1)

	2020	2019	2018
Sales to Customers	$82,584	82,059	81,581
Cost of Products Sold	28,427	27,556	27,091
Gross Profit	54,157	54,503	54,490
Selling, Marketing, and Administrative Expenses	22,084	22,178	22,540
Research and Development Expense	12,159	11,355	10,775
In-process Research and Development (Note 5)	181	890	1,126
Interest Income	(111)	(357)	(611)
Interest Expense, Net of Portion Capitalized (Note 4)	201	318	1,005
Other (Income) Expense, Net	2,899	2,525	1,405
Restructuring (Note 20)	247	266	251
Earnings Before Provision for Taxes on Income	16,497	17,328	17,999
Provision for Taxes on Income (Note 8)	1,783	2,209	2,702
Net Earnings	**$14,714**	**15,119**	**15,297**

(Continued)

	2020	2019	2018
Net Earnings per Share (Notes 1 and 15)			
Basic	**$5.59**	**5.72**	**5.70**
Diluted	**$5.51**	**5.63**	**5.61**
Average Shares Outstanding (Notes 1 and 15)			
Basic	**2,632.8**	**2,645.1**	**2,681.5**
Diluted	**2,670.7**	**2,684.3**	**2,728.7**

Johnson & Johnson and Subsidiaries

Consolidated Statements of Comprehensive Income

(Dollars in Millions) (Note 1)

	2020	2019	2018
Net Earnings	$14,714	15,119	15,297
Other Comprehensive Income (Loss), Net of Tax			
Foreign Currency Translation	(233)	164	(1,518)
Securities			
Unrealized Holding Gain (Loss) Arising During Period	1	—	(1)
Reclassifications to Earnings	—	—	1
Net Change	1	—	—
Employee Benefit Plans			
Prior Service Credit (Cost), Net of Amortization	1,298	(18)	(44)
Gain (Loss), Net of Amortization	(1,135)	(714)	(56)
Effect of Exchange Rates	(229)	(1)	92
Net Change	(66)	(733)	(8)
Derivatives & Hedges			
Unrealized Gain (Loss) Arising During Period	1,000	(107)	(73)
Reclassifications to Earnings	(53)	7	(192)
Net Change	947	(100)	(265)
Other Comprehensive Income (Loss)	649	(669)	(1,791)
Comprehensive Income	$15,363	14,450	13,506

Note: The tax effects in other comprehensive income for the fiscal years 2020, 2019, and 2018 respectively: Foreign Currency Translation; $536 million, $19 Million, and $236 million; Employee Benefit Plans: $21 million, $222 million, and $4 million; Derivatives & Hedges: $252 million, $27 million, and $70 million.

Johnson & Johnson and Subsidiaries

Consolidated Statements of Equity
(Dollars in Millions) (Note 1)

	Total	Retained Earnings	Accumulated Other Comprehensive Income (Loss)	Common Stock Issued Amount	Treasury Stock Amount
Balance, December 31, 2017	**$60,160**	**101,793**	**(13,199)**	**3,120**	**(31,554)**
Cumulative Adjustment [(1)]	(486)	(254)	(232)		
Net Earnings	15,297	15,297			
Cash Dividends Paid ($3.54 per Share)	(9,494)	(9,494)			
Employee Compensation and Stock Option Plans	1,949	(1,111)			3,060
Repurchase of Common Stock	(5,868)				(5,868)
Other	(15)	(15)			
Other Comprehensive Income (Loss), Net of Tax	(1,791)		(1,791)		
Balance, December 30, 2018	**59,752**	**106,216**	**(15,222)**	**3,120**	**(34,362)**
Net Earnings	15,119	15,119			
Cash Dividends Paid ($3.75 per Share)	(9,917)	(9,917)			
Employee Compensation and Stock Option Plans	1,933	(758)			2,691
Repurchase of Common Stock	(6,746)				(6,746)
Other	(1)	(1)			
Other Comprehensive Income (Loss), Net of Tax	(669)		(669)		
Balance, December 29, 2019	**59,471**	**110,659**	**(15,891)**	**3,120**	**(38,417)**
Net Earnings	14,714	14,714			

(Continued)

(Continued)

	Total	Retained Earnings	Accumulated Other Comprehensive Income (Loss)	Common Stock Issued Amount	Treasury Stock Amount
Balance, December 29, 2019	**59,471**	**110,659**	**(15,891)**	**3,120**	**(38,417)**
Cash Dividends Paid ($3.98 per share)	2,217	(931)			3,148
Employee Compensation and Stock Option Plans	(10,481)	(10,481)			
Repurchase of Common Stock	(3,221)				(3,221)
Other	(71)	(71)			
Other Comprehensive Income (Loss), Net of Tax	649		649		
Balance, January 3, 2021	**$63,278**	**113,890**	**(15,242)**	**3,120**	**(38,490)**

Johnson & Johnson and Subsidiaries

Consolidated Statements of Cash Flows

(Dollars in Millions)

Cash Flows from Operating Activities	2020	2019	2018
Net Earnings	$14,714	15,119	15,297
Adjustments to Reconcile Net Earnings to Cash Flows from Operating Activities			
Depreciation and Amortization of Property and Intangibles	7,231	7,009	6,929
Stock-Based Compensation	1,005	977	978
Asset Write-Downs	233	1,096	1,258
Contingent Consideration Reversal	(1,148)	—	—
Net Gain on Sale of Assets/Businesses	(111)	(2,154)	(1,217)
Deferred Tax Provision	(1,141)	(2,476)	(1,016)
Credit Losses and Accounts Receivable Allowances	63	(20)	(31)

(Continued)

(*Continued*)

Cash Flows from Operating Activities	2020	2019	2018
Changes in Assets and Liabilities, Net of Effects From Acquisitions and Divestitures			
Decrease/(Increase) in Accounts Receivable	774	(289)	(1,185)
Increase in Inventories	(265)	(277)	(644)
Increase in Accounts Payable and Accrued Liabilities	5,141	4,060	3,951
Increase in Other Current and Non-Current Assets	(3,704)	(1,054)	(275)
Increase/(Decrease) in Other Current and Non-Current Liabilities	744	1,425	(1,844)
Net Cash Flows from Operating Activities	**23,536**	**23,416**	**22,201**
Cash Flows from Investing Activities			
Additions to Property, Plant, and Equipment	(3,347)	(3,498)	(3,670)
Proceeds from the Disposal of Assets/Businesses, Net	305	3,265	3,203
Acquisitions, Net of Cash Acquired	(7,323)	(5,810)	(899)
Purchases of Investments	(21,089)	(3,920)	(5,626)
Sales of Investments	12,137	3,387	4,289
Credit Support Agreements Activity, Net	(987)	338	—
Other (Primarily Licenses and Milestones)	(521)	44	(464)
Net Cash Used by Investing Activities	**(20,825)**	**(6,194)**	**(3,167)**
Dividends to Shareholders	(10,481)	(9,917)	(9,494)
Repurchase of Common Stock	(3,221)	(6,746)	(5,868)
Proceeds from Short-Term Debt	3,391	39	80
Repayment of Short-Term Debt	(2,663)	(100)	(2,479)
Proceeds from Long-Term Debt, Net of Issuance Costs	7,431	3	5
Repayment of Long-Term Debt	(1,064)	(2,823)	(1,555)
Proceeds from the Exercise of Stock Options/ Employee Withholding Tax on Stock Awards, Net	1,114	954	949
Credit Support Agreements Activity, Net	(333)	100	25
Other	(294)	475	(173)
Net Cash used by Financing Activities	**(6,120)**	**(18,015)**	**(18,510)**
Effect of Exchange Rate Changes on Cash and Cash Equivalents	89	(9)	(241)

(*Continued*)

(Continued)

Cash Flows from Financing Activities	**2020**	**2019**	**2018**
Net Cash used by Financing Activities	**(6,120)**	**(18,015)**	**(18,510)**
(Decrease)/Increase in Cash and Cash Equivalents	(3,320)	(802)	283
Cash and Cash Equivalents, Beginning of year	17,305	18,107	17,824
Cash and Cash Equivalents, End of Year	**$13,985**	**17,305**	**18,107**
Supplemental Cash Flow Data			
Cash Paid during the Year for:			
Interest	$904	995	1,049
Interest, Net of Amount Capitalized	841	925	963
Income Taxes	4,619	4,191	4,570
Supplemental Schedule of Non-cash Investing and Financing Activities			
Treasury Stock Issued for Employee Compensation and Stock Option Plans, Net of Cash Proceeds/Employee Withholding Tax on Stock Awards	$1,937	1,736	2,095
Conversion of Debt	27	1	6
Acquisitions			
Fair Value of Assets Acquired	$7,755	7,228	1,047
Fair Value of Liabilities Assumed and Noncontrolling Interests	(432)	(1,418)	(148)
Net Cash Paid for Acquisitions	**$7,323**	**5,810**	**899**

Johnson & Johnson (JNJ)

Valuation Measures

	Current	**12/31/2020**	**9/30/2020**	**6/30/2020**	**3/31/2020**	**12/31/2019**
Market Cap (Intraday)	418.01B	414.31B	391.88B	370.19B	345.19B	384.00B
Enterprise Value	428.09B	421.29B	403.14B	379.75B	353.59B	395.28B
Trailing P/E	28.86	24.75	26.17	21.94	23.29	27.78
Forward P/E	16.75	17.42	16.42	18.15	14.64	16.05
PEG Ratio (5 yr expected)	2.33	2.93	3.22	4.11	2.88	3.43
Price/Sales (ttm)	5.14	5.20	4.94	4.55	4.29	4.82
Price/Book (mrq)	6.61	6.43	6.22	6.04	5.80	6.60
Enterprise Value/Revenue	5.18	18.74	19.12	20.71	17.09	19.05
Enterprise Value/EBITDA	17.89	114.67	64.37	66.49	42.70	64.60

Note: https://finance.yahoo.com/quote/JNJ/key-statistics?p=JNJ.

The Assignment

Mr. Robert McGraw, MBA, CPA is Vice President in the CFO's office of Johnson and Johnson ("JNJ") pharmaceuticals in New Jersey, where he has been responsible for issues relating to funding and capitalization for the past 6 years. He was previously a partner at a Big Four accounting firm for a decade and was part-time lecturer at Rutgers Business School, Finance and Economics Department.

The issue before JNJ was how to fund their expected capital expansion related to Covid-19 R&D and vaccine manufacturing expansion in the next 3 to 5 years. Robert noted that sales are expected to expand annually at 2.5% to 5% and sales to fixed assets to be approximately 4.40. The company considered the likelihood of issuing new equity, expanding borrowing through bond issuing and/or bank loans, and reducing dividends. These funding options were discussed extensively by the Board of Directors, who asked the CFO to prepare a position paper and recommendations on funding strategies for the next meeting in 4 weeks.

Robert was asked by the CFO to address the funding issue and submit recommendations within 3 weeks. He summoned his senior staff and outlined the JNJ's need to raise the necessary capital while maintaining the company's credit rating and adhere to the general practices in the pharmaceutical industry in terms of the capitalization structure.

Robert and team began their task by reviewing JNJ's annual and quarterly reports, including Form 10K, 10Q, and some dozen brokerage reports on pharmaceutical companies. Following the review, Robert was ready to address the following issues.

1. Determine whether JNJ capital structure on 12/31/2020 was within the pharmaceuticals industry and its major companies' averages.
2. Assess the implications of raising 5–20% additional debt on the cost of debt and credit rating.
3. Estimate the implications of raising additional equity on the cost of equity and dilution.
4. Simulate what funding JNJ should pursue and its implications on WACC, cost of debt, cost of equity, dilution implication of issuing new equity, S&P and Moody's financial ratings. You could apply the Monte Carlo Simulation Solver by Excel or by Palisade (www.palisade.com). To find the new WACC, use the methodology of relevering beta that was introduced in Chapters 13 and 14. Use the CAPM to calculate the

new cost of equity as leverage increases. However, this model assumes that the cost of debt does not change. If you assume that additional leverage increases the cost of debt, add that premium to the cost of equity you calculated using new leverage beta. Then use the definition of WACC to find the new discount rate.

5. Provide a summary recommendation to JNJ BOD.

https://doi.org/10.1142/9789811216749_0016

Case 16

Starbucks Coffee Company: A Comprehensive Financial Analysis*

Armand Gilinsky, Jr.† and Raymond H. Lopez‡

†Sonoma State University, USA

‡Pace University, USA

Introduction

Starbucks Coffee has been growing rapidly and expanding its market share in the specialty coffee segment of the industry. Its global initiation has taken it outside of North America to Europe and Asia. During this time period, the firm has financed its expansion primarily through the use of internally generated cash flow and currently has a capital account composed of $7.1 million in long-term debt and $1.7 billion in equity at book value (with a market value of $9.3 billion). The case addresses this capital structure and proposes three recapitalization plans, adding debt and repurchasing common stock. Starbucks explores the impact of these plans on the firm's beta (B) coefficient, cost of equity, weighted average cost of capital (WACC), projected earnings per share, and the final valuation of the firm's share, with projections over the next 4 years.

---

*This case is adapted from the published case of the same title at the *Journal of Finance Case Research* 11 (2009): 29–70. If you are faculty teaching this case, you can contact Professor Lopez for a copy of the Instructor's Manual. His email address is rlopez@pace.edu.

> "I've been in the finance business my entire career and I have studied finance history," said Michael Casey, Starbucks' chief financial officer. "However, yields on most corporate bonds are at 40-year lows and investors are very receptive to quality corporate debt instruments. This is a great time to take on debt, funds that will surely be needed to support our growth strategies."

Could Mr. Casey convince Howard Schultz, chairman and chief global strategist of Starbucks? He had just returned to Seattle from an investment banking conference in NYC and was sharing some of his findings with Mr. Schultz. "Mike, you know how successful we have been at developing and expanding the "Starbucks Experience" on a global basis. We have accomplished these goals with primarily a debt-free capital structure, which has eliminated the financial risks of paying interest on bonds. Sure, we sold some convertible debt years ago, but we converted it quickly to add to our equity. I'm just not sure this is the time to change our capital structure."

In addition to meeting the financial needs of global business expansion, Starbucks recently announced an extension and expansion of its stock buyback activities.[1] Ten million shares had just been added to the program with 3.6 million shares already purchased under the June 2002 plan. The primary purpose of this plan was to offset dilution from the firm's long-standing employee compensation program.

Mr. Casey's proposal could radically alter the capital structure of the firm. Based on presentations at the conference and discussions with other CFOs, he was preparing three scenarios for evaluation by Mr. Schultz and the board, moving from a no-debt structure to either 20%, 35%, or 50% debt based on book values for debt and equity. Introducing low-cost debt into the capital structure would reduce the firm's weighted average cost of capital (WACC) contributing to growth and enhancing profit margins.

"Mike," questioned Howard, "while our WACC will decline, what about the additional financial risks of debt? How will equity investors who have owned the shares of a growing debt-free company react to such a change? And our business risks are growing as we expand

[1]Press Release, Starbucks Corporation, March 31, 2003.

internationally. Maybe an all-equity capital structure will be optimum over the next 5 to 10 years. Although I'm not convinced, I think your proposals are worth bringing to the board. Put some details together for the May meeting."

Middle East, Latin America, and the Pacific Rim. Worldwide, more than 22 million customers visited Starbucks coffeehouses weekly in early 2003, up from 20 million in 2002[2] and 9 million in 1999.[3]

The Starbucks Story[4]

The firm began operations in 1971 by opening its first retail store in Seattle's Pike Place Market. Starbucks was named after the first mate in Herman Melville's *Moby Dick* and by 2003 had grown to its position as the world's leading retailer, roaster, and brand of specialty coffee. The company operated coffeehouses in North America and Europe. Howard Schultz joined the company in the early 1980s. Starbucks had already become a highly respected roaster and retailer of whole bean and ground coffees in the local Seattle area. A business trip to Italy opened Schultz's eyes to the rich traditions of the espresso beverage. Upon his return to Seattle, Schultz introduced espresso drinks into the retail stores, and they became an essential element of the firm's vision. In addition to its well-situated coffeehouses, Starbucks sold coffee and tea products through its specialty operations including starbucks.com.

Coffee aficionados could also find Starbucks in a variety of carefully chosen venues including United Airlines, Horizon Air, Seattle's Key Arena, Chicago's Wrigley Field, University of Washington athletic facilities, Experience Music Project interactive museum, Hyatt Hotels, Barnes & Noble bookstores throughout North America, and Chapters, Inc. bookstores in Canada. Since 1991, Starbucks coffee had been available at licensed airport locations and travel plazas operated by HMS Host in the

---

[2]Interview with Howard Schultz by Nick Cottam, "Starbucks drinks to success," NASDAQ (September–October 2002): 18–21.

[3]Nelson D. Schwartz, "Still Perking After All These Years," *Fortune* (May 24, 1999): 203–210.

[4]Company Profile, Starbucks Corporation, April 2003.

US licensed locations were also found on college campuses through a licensing with ARAMACK Corp., SYSCO, and Sodexho. The firm also licensed locations in select supermarkets across the US.

Howard Schultz established what came to be known as the "Starbucks Experience..." "You get more than the finest coffee when you visit a Starbucks — you get great people, first-rate music, and a comfortable and upbeat meeting place," said Schultz. "We establish the value of buying a product at Starbucks by our uncompromising quality and by building a personal relationship with each of our customers. Starbucks is rekindling America's love affair with coffee, bringing romance and fresh flavor back to the brew."

Mr. Schultz had instituted a "passion for quality" into every aspect of company operations. Starbucks offered coffee lovers a selection of coffees from around the world. Company coffee buyers personally traveled to the coffee-growing regions of Central America, Africa, and Indonesia in order to select the finest Arabic beans. After these quality beans arrive at one of the firm's three roasting facilities, Starbucks professional roasters pursue the art of creating the rich signature Starbucks Roast®. This dark roast was not just a color — it was the cumulative result of expert roasters knowing coffee and bringing balance to all of its flavor attributes.

In addition to quality coffee, Starbucks featured a variety of hand-crafted beverages, Tazo® teas, freshly baked pastries, and in some markets a selection of high-quality sandwiches and salads. Starbucks merchandise included exclusive espresso machines and coffee brewers, unique confections, and other coffee and tea-related items.

Music had been important to Starbucks since the company was founded. In 1995, the firm began selling compilations covering a wide range of tastes including jazz, blues, folk, and world music. Since 1999, Hear Music had been the voice of music at Starbucks, increasing the complexity of Starbucks' musical selections.

In the spring of 1995, the Frappuccino® blended beverage, a low-fat creamy iced coffee drink, was introduced to the Starbucks line of beverages. The next year (1996) a joint venture between the company and the Pepsi-Cola Company, the North American Coffee Partnership, began selling Frappuccino® as a bottled coffee drink. Five flavors were available in grocery channels nationwide by 2003, as well as in select Starbucks coffeehouses. In 2002, Starbucks Double Shot™ joined the ready-to-drink product lineup as part of the joint venture.

Another product extension initiative commenced in October 1995 between the company and Dreyers' Grand Ice Cream. This joint venture was formed to supply a premium line of coffee ice creams to both the grocery channel and the coffeehouses. By July 1996, Starbucks had become the number one brand of coffee ice cream in the United States. In 2003, consumers could enjoy seven delectable flavors including Java Chip and Coffee Almond Fudge.

Starbucks' early success in grocery channels led to the test sale of coffee in supermarkets in Portland, Oregon in 1996 and Chicago in 1997. In 1998, the company and Kraft Foods entered into a licensing agreement to accelerate the growth of Starbucks products in grocery channels nationwide. This deal blended Kraft's' extensive knowledge of selling, marketing, and distributing packaged foods directly to grocery customers with Starbucks' premium product line.

In 1996, the first overseas location for a Starbucks coffeehouse was opened in Tokyo, Japan. By early 2003, there were more than 400 retail outlets in Japan. We need to establish strong alliances with local companies if we are to be successful. "It will continue to be imperative for us to build roots in local communities and international market," said Peter Maslen, President of Starbucks Coffee International. "Therefore, we will seek opportunities with companies that have expertise in the marketplace and, more importantly, share similar values, vision, and business philosophy."

In addition to Japan, Starbucks opened coffeehouses in the following locations: Hawaii and Singapore in 1996; the Philippines in 1997; the UK, Taiwan, Thailand, New Zealand, and Malaysia in 1998; Beijing, Kuwait, South Korea, and Lebanon in 1999; United Arab Emirates, Hong Kong, Shanghai, Australia, Qatar, Saudi Arabia, and Bahrain in 2000; Switzerland and Austria in 2001; and Oman, Germany, Spain, Mexico, Puerto Rico, Southern China — Macau and Shenzhen, Greece, and Indonesia in 2002.

In 2003, Starbucks Coffee International, a wholly owned subsidiary of the company, announced plans to acquire its licensed operations in Switzerland and Austria from its partner, Bon Appetit Group. "As Starbucks continues to expand its presence worldwide, one of our key long-term global strategies is to establish a larger equity position in our international business," said Howard Schultz. "The opportunity to convert the Swiss and Austrian operations to company-operated markets is consistent with this strategy. In the past few years, we have pursued similar opportunities by acquiring our licensed operations in Thailand and Australia as well as increasing our equity position in our South Korean business."

While details of the transaction were not made public, it would be treated as a cash purchase. The first Starbucks locations opened in Zurich, Switzerland on March 7, 2001, and Vienna, Austria on December 7, 2001. Upon completion of this acquisition, Starbucks will company-operate 14 stores in Switzerland and 7 stores in Austria, and will continue to expand the business in both markets.

Another recent initiative in the Starbucks story was the introduction of in-store wireless hot spots, allowing customers to browse the Internet while sipping their Cappuccino. The first such Wi-Fi "hot spot" was installed in the fall of 2001 on a trial basis. The company integrated this hot spot with its corporate VPN on the network to access applications and databases that streamline such functions as hiring, sales, inventory, and a host of other business tasks. According to James Shook, Starbucks Vice President of Information Technology, this double-duty network served more than 2,000 stores in North America, with a goal of 2,500 stores by year-end 2003. By adding this technology to its stores, the company expected to attract more customers and keep them in the store longer, thus increasing purchases of coffee and other beverages.[5]

In November 2001, the company launched its original re-loadable stored value Starbucks Card which allowed customers to purchase company beverages and other merchandise. Like a prepaid debit card, it provided frequent customers with a convenient and secure payment method. It also provided the company with the benefits of float, since the card is purchased for cash and then used at a future time (perhaps days or weeks later). In February of 2003, Starbucks, in conjunction with Bank One and Visa U.S.A., announced a strategic relationship to develop innovative new consumer payment products that would enable Starbucks to enhance consumer convenience and reward customer loyalty. The first payment product to be launched later in the year would combine the benefits and convenience of a re-loadable stored value Starbucks Card and a VISA credit card all in one. With more than 11 million original Starbucks Cards activated to date, these new features were expected to be embraced enthusiastically by Starbucks customers.

> "The Starbucks Card has redefined the stored value card market by becoming the ideal payment solution for a high-volume, low-ticket retail environment," said Howard Schultz. "By partnering with Bank One and

[5]Tim Greene, "Starbucks gets win-win from Wi-Fi," *Network World* (July 14, 2003).

VISA to offer a dual function card, we can provide customers with a choice of convenient payment products that both enhances and rewards the 'Starbucks Experience' they enjoy."

Starbucks Business[6]

Starbucks Corporation, together with its subsidiaries, purchased and roasted high-quality whole bean coffees and sold them along with fresh, rich brewed coffees, Italian-style espresso beverages, cold blended beverages, a variety of pastries and confections, coffee related accessories and equipment, a selection of premium teas and a line of compact discs primarily through company-operated retail stores. The company also sold coffee and tea products through other channels of distribution. Starbucks also sold these items through certain of its equity investees, as well as bottled Frappuccino® and Starbucks Doubleshot™ coffee drinks and a line of premium ice creams. These non-retail channels were collectively categorized as "Specialty Operations" within the Starbucks organization.

The firm's objective was to establish Starbucks as the most recognized and respected brand in the world. In order to achieve this goal, the company planned to continue rapid expansion of its retail operations within as well as outside North America. In addition, plans called for expansion of Specialty Operations as well as selective pursuit of other opportunities to leverage the Starbucks brand though introduction of new products and the development of new distribution channels.

Company-Operated Retail Stores

The core of Starbucks' business and its largest operating division in terms of net revenues was the company-operated retail stores. Starbucks' strategy for expanding its retail business was to increase market share in existing markets and open stores in new markets where opportunities existed to become the leading specialty coffee retailer. In 1992 and 1993, the firm developed a 3-year geographic expansion plan that targeted areas that had favorable demographic profiles for a Starbucks "customer," as well as being able to be serviced and supported by the company's operations infrastructure. Within each target region, a large city was selected to serve

[6]Annual Report 2002, Starbucks Corporation, Form 10K.

as a "hub," with a goal of opening at least 20 stores in that hub within 2 years. Teams of Starbucks' managers and other personnel would be located in the hub city to support the growth institutions. Once the stores in the hub city were operating efficiently, additional stores would be opened in smaller, surrounding "spoke" areas within the region. Management believed that its "Starbucks everywhere" approach would ultimately benefit the firm. Delivery and management costs would be reduced, customer lines would be shorter at each store and increased foot traffic at all stores would enhance the firm's competitive position.[7]

As a firm with global ambitions, Starbucks had a two-pronged approach to store expansion outside of the United States. They would either open company-owned and company-operated stores or license a reputable and capable local firm with retailing expertise in the target host country to develop and operate new retail outlets. In most countries, Starbucks chose a local partner/licensee to assist in recruiting individuals, setting up supplier relationships, locating suitable store sites, and catering to local market conditions. These partners/licensees should have strong retail/restaurant experience, share values and a corporate culture comparable with Starbucks, and be committed to good customer service. In addition, they had to possess talented management and strong financial resources and have demonstrated brand-building skills. To efficiently manage and coordinate these growing activities, the firm created a new subsidiary, Starbucks Coffee International, to orchestrate overseas expansion and build the Starbucks brand globally via licensees.

In support of these strategies, the firm opened 614 new company-operated stores during fiscal year 2002, net of store closures. At year-end, Starbucks had 3,496 company operated stores in 43 states, the District of Columbia, and five Canadian provinces (these stores comprised the firm's North American retail operating segment). Under the company's International Retail business unit, there were 322 stores in the United Kingdom, 33 stores in Australia, and 29 stores in Thailand. Company-operated retail stores accounted for approximately 85% of net revenues during fiscal 2002, up slightly from 84% during fiscal 200.

The firm's overall growth rate in net revenues generally declined from 1995 through 2001, before rising in 2002. Exhibit 1 shows the components of growth between comparable (same-store) sales and growth from

[7]Cora Daniels, "Mr. Coffee," *Fortune* (April 14, 2003): 139–140.

Exhibit 1. Starbucks Coffee Company Revenue Growth Breakdown 1995–2002

Year	Comparable Store Sales Growth (%)	Store Growth (%)	Total Net Revenue Growth (%)
2002	6	18.2	24.2
2001	5	16.6	21.6
2000	9	20.1	29.1
1999	6	22.9	28.9
1998	5	29.2	34.2
1997	5	34.8	39.8
1996	7	43.0	50.0
1995	9	54.3	63.3

Note: Fiscal year ends September. Comparable store sales growth includes only company-operated stores open 13 months or longer.
Source: Starbucks Coffee Company, Annual Reports and 10Ks.

net new store outlets. While store growth has trended downward from levels above 50% in 1995, same-store sales have generally been between 5 and 9% per year. Both growth avenues are expected to continue expanding in the next few years.

Specialty Operations

This division of the company was structured to develop the Starbucks brand outside of the company-owned retail store environment through a multitude of channels. Starbucks' strategy was to reach customers where they work, travel, shop, and dine by establishing relationships with prominent third parties that shared the company's values and commitment to quality. These relationships could take a variety of forms, some of which were arrangements through business alliances, international retail store licensing agreements, grocery channel licensing agreements warehouse club accounts, interactive operations, equity investors, and other initiatives related to the firm's core business. In certain situations, Starbucks had an equity ownership interest in license operations. During fiscal 2002, specialty operations revenues (which included royalties and fees from licenses as well as product sales) accounted for 15% of company net revenues compared with 16% of net revenues in fiscal 2001. These net revenues reached $2.79 billion in fiscal 2002, up 25.3% from $2.23 billion in fiscal 2001.

Business Alliances

This operating segment included two divisions that together accounted for 45% of specialty revenues in fiscal 2002, down slightly from 46% in fiscal 2001. The largest was the North American Food Service Accounts while the other was the North American Retail Store Licensing group. The Foodservice Accounts division sold whole bean and ground coffees to office coffee distributors, hotels, airlines, retailers, and restaurants as well as institutional foodservice companies that supplied business, industry, education, and healthcare accounts. In fiscal 2002, the company had approximately 5,600 foodservice accounts, up from approximately 5,500 accounts in fiscal 2002. Net revenues grew to $133.9 million in fiscal 2002, up 3% from the $130.0 million in fiscal 2001.

The Retail Store Licensing group complimented the firm's company-owned retail store operation. Although the company did not generally relinquish operational control of its stores in North America, in situations in which a master concessionaire or other company controlled or could provide improved access to desirable retail space, the company would license its operations. As part of these arrangements, Starbucks received license fees and royalties and sold coffee and related products for resale in the licensed locations. Employees working in these licensed locations had to follow Starbucks' detailed store-operating procedures and attend training sessions similar to those given to Starbucks store managers and employees. As of fiscal year-end 2002, the company had 1,078 licensed stores in continental North America, up from 809 stores at the end of fiscal 2001. Revenues from these stores were $89.3 million in fiscal 2002, up 42% from the $62.9 million generated in fiscal 2001. Since the number of stores grew by 33.3%, average store revenues collected by Starbucks grew from $77,750 to $82,839.

Another segment of Specialty Operations was the International Retail Store Licensing group. Retail stores located outside of North America, the United Kingdom, Thailand, and Australia were operated through a number of licensing arrangements with prominent retailers. During fiscal 2002, the firm opened 294 new international licensed stores, up from 282 stores opened in fiscal 2001. At fiscal year-end 2002, the company operated 928 licensed international retail stores, up from 634 stores at year-end 2001. Net revenues to Starbucks from these business units grew by 54.7% in fiscal 2002 and accounted for 17% of division net revenues, up from 13% in fiscal 2001.

Grocery channel licensing with Kraft Foods, Inc. had net revenues of $64.5 million in fiscal 2002, up 9.9% from the $58.7 million in fiscal 2001. Pursuant to the agreement with Kraft, that firm managed all distribution, marketing, advertising, and promotions for Starbucks' whole bean and ground coffee in grocery and mass merchandise stores. Starbucks earned royalties based on a percentage of total net sales. At the end of fiscal 2002, the firm's whole bean and ground coffees were available throughout the United States in approximately 18,000 supermarkets.

Another outlet for Starbucks products was the Warehouse Club. These accounts purchased whole bean and ground coffees in North America. As part of its agreement with Kraft, they also distributed Starbucks products to warehouse club stores; a distribution fee was paid to Kraft for these services. Net revenues from this business unit were $64.5 million in fiscal 2002, up 18.3% from the $54.5 million generated in fiscal 2001.

Starbucks coffee and coffee-related products were also conveniently available via mail order and online. The company maintained a website, www.starbucks.com, since 1998 where an online store allowed customers to purchase coffee, gifts, and other items via the Internet. The company also published and distributed a catalog of business gifts that offered coffees, certain food items, and select coffee-making equipment and accessories. At fiscal year-end 2002, approximately 1,650 company-operated retail stores offered customers high-speed wireless Internet access.

Management believed that its interactive operations supported its retail store expansion into new markets and reinforced brand recognition and the "Starbucks Experience" for customers in existing markets. Growth in the last few years certainly supported these beliefs. In fiscal 2002, this division produced $34.7 million in net revenues, up 65.2% from the $21 million in fiscal 2001.

The company had two non-retail domestic 50–50 joint ventures which produced and distributed Starbucks branded products. The North American Coffee Partnership, a joint venture with the Pepsi-Cola Company, a division of PepsiCo, Inc., developed and distributed ready-to-drink coffee-based products such as Frappuccino and Starbucks Double Shot coffee drinks. These products were available in approximately 200,000 supermarkets, convenience and drug stores, and other locations throughout the United States and Canada.

The Starbucks Ice Cream Partnership with Dreyers Grand Ice Cream, Inc. developed and distributed premium ice creams through over 20,000 supermarkets throughout the United States. Starbucks sold

Exhibit 2. United States Beverage Consumption Volume (Millions of Gallons)

Beverage Category	2002P	2001	2000	1999	1998	1997	1996
Soft Drinks	15,153	15 ,023	14,925	14,895	14,820	14,385	13,940
Coffee	**7,770**	**7,710**	**7,700**	**7,750**	**7,800**	**7,854**	**7,901**
Milk	6,950	6,910	6,885	6,918	6,880	6,890	6,924
Beer	6,353	6,241	6,202	6.136	6,002	5,922	5,898
Bottled Water	6,000	5,400	4,950	4,570	4,070	3,730	3,100
Tea	1,940	1,910	1,870	1,850	1,825	1,788	1,744
Juices	1,830	1,790	1,750	1,720	1,710	1,702	1,692
Powdered Drinks	1,320	1,340	1,350	1,370	1,360	1,365	1,358
Wine	586	557	552	538	519	512	497
Distilled Spirits	365	357	354	343	334	320	329
Cider (Beverage Alcohol)	10	11	10	10	9	7	6
Totals	48,277	47,249	46,548	46,101	45,329	44,485	43,389

Note: P = Preliminary.
Source: Adams Wine Handbook 1999, 2003.

roasted coffee for use by both of these partnerships with net revenues of $8.4 million in fiscal 2001 and $9.9 million in fiscal 2002.

Product Supply

Starbucks was committed to selling only the finest whole bean coffees and coffee beverages. To ensure compliance with its rigorous coffee standards, the firm controlled its coffee purchasing, roasting, and packaging as well as distribution of coffee to its retail stores. Starbucks purchased green coffee beans from coffee-producing regions around the world and custom roasted them to its exacting standards for its many blends and single-origin coffees.

The supply and price of coffee were subject to significant volatility. While most coffee trades in the commodity market, coffee of the quality sought by Starbucks tended to trade on a negotiated basis at a substantial premium above commodity coffee prices. Supply of and demand for high-quality beans determined its final price. Many factors influenced supply and price including weather, political, and economic conditions in growing areas. In addition, green coffee prices had been affected and could continue to be affected by certain organizations and associations that had historically attempted to influence prices through agreements establishing export quotas or restricting coffee supplies. To secure adequate supplies, Starbucks routinely entered into fixed-price purchase commitments for future delivery of coffee. While the prices paid might be higher, secure supplies of quality beans were of prime concern. The company believed that its policies would continue to be successful and that premium coffee beans would be available to meet anticipated needs.

Starbucks also purchased significant quantities of fluid milk from multiple suppliers whose processing facilities were concentrated near company retail stores. They also purchased large quantities of paper and plastic products from several companies to supply retail stores as well as manufacturing and distribution operations.

Beverage Consumption in the United States

The volume of alcoholic and non-alcoholic beverages consumed by Americans had been growing modestly over the last 7 years. By far, the largest category was soft drinks which in 2002 was almost double the next largest category — coffee (Exhibit 2). It may be observed that coffee volumes have actually been declining in this period from 7.9 billion gallons in 1996 to 7.7 billion gallons in 2002. Almost all other beverage categories experienced some growth in this period, with bottled water growing at a remarkable 10.8% per year.

Although coffee consumption has declined modestly in recent years, the US market accounts for 20% of the world's coffee, solidly in first place. The market is actually composed of three segments, each of which has experienced its own unique characteristics and growth record. The largest segment was coffee packaged for brewing or mixing by the consumer usually in the home. Most of the decline in total industry volume has been in this market. Ready-to-drink packaged coffee beverages have performed in a stable fashion over the last few years. These products are consumed in the home as well as at the workplace. The category of freshly brewed coffee for immediate consumption has been the growth engine of the industry. While still small in terms of volume, its revenue share is considerably higher due to the trend towards specialty coffees served in restaurants as well as in coffee houses.

On a per capita basis, coffee consumption has lagged behind most of the beverage industry categories, although still remaining in second place behind soft drinks. Bottled water once again has exhibited the most rapid growth record, almost doubling its per capita consumption in just 7 years. With coffee's declining trend, it could be expected to lose its second-place position to bottled water in the next few years.

Coffee tends to be one of the cheapest categories, while the alcoholic beverages (beer, distilled spirits, and wine) are generally more expensive. The result is that, based on retail sales data, coffee is in seventh place, with sales of soft drinks greater than coffee by more than nine times! However, the trend in retail sales of coffee has been up if only modestly over this period. So, higher prices have more than made up for the declining trend in volume. Based on retail sales, on a percent of market basis, coffee has experienced an even greater decline over the last few years. From 3.8% of the beverage marketplace in 1996, coffee's percentage has declined steadily to only 3.1% in 2002. Even with the trend towards specialty coffee consumption at higher price points, the overall position of the industry continued to decline. The National Coffee Association of USA, Inc. surveys consumers on an annual basis to identify trends in consumption patterns. Most coffee categories are experiencing declining consumption (regular, soluble [instant], and decaffeinated) while the only growing component of the market is gourmet.

Competition

Its prime competitors for coffee beverage sales were coffee shops, restaurants, and street carts. Tangentially, the company's coffee products also competed with the traditional commercial-grade coffee industry, where demand, sales, and consumption had been relatively stable for at least two decades. In contrast, the specialty coffee industry segment had expanded exponentially, with strong growth supported by the ready-to-drink market. This increase was attributed to growing consumer awareness of and appreciation for fine coffee. Other factors were the emergence of coffee bars, featuring on expanding array of premium coffee beverages, as well as the adoption of a healthier lifestyle that prompted some consumers to substitute coffee for alcoholic beverages. The image of coffee consumption had evolved from a breakfast or after-dinner beverage to a drink that could be enjoyed at any time of the day. Coffee bars fostered the idea that a high-quality coffee beverage could be enjoyed with family and friends or business associates, creating a relaxing yet productive experience.

Retail Coffee Houses

In this segment of the specialty coffee marketplace none of its competitors had achieved the national and international exposure and scope of Starbucks. Firms such as Diedrich's Coffee, Peet's Coffee & Tea, Inc., Tully's Coffee Corporation, Caribou Coffee, Green Mountain Coffee, Barnie's Coffee and Tea, Coffee Beanery, Cafe Appassionato, and Second Cup Coffee were regional in scope, while growing sales at very different rates with a wide variety of corporate strategies. Currently, Starbucks US specialty coffee house sales were greater than all the others, combined!

Other companies selling specialty coffee were primarily small local or regional chains that may have aspired to compete against Starbucks but were finding it quite difficult and challenging. A few of the names include New World Coffee (30 outlets), Brew Hatta (15 outlets in Delaware and Pennsylvania), Caribon Coffee (241 locations in 9 states), Second Cup Coffee (the largest chain based in Canada), and Bad Ass Coffee (30 outlets in 10 states and Canada). From this brief summary of the history of some Starbucks competitors, and their strategies and performance, one may conclude that it has been increasingly difficult to compete with Starbucks successfully. Many have tried, while few have succeeded. "Going up against Starbucks is just not a wise strategy," opined an unnamed former rival. "Everybody who tried it is in trouble."[8]

Donut Shops. A more rapidly growing group of competitors that could provide increased competition in the next few years were the donut shops that also sold coffee, some of it of the specialty variety. Dunkin Donuts was the largest firm, with approximately 5,000 worldwide retail outlets, second to the Starbucks' total of 5,886. As the number one donut marketer, it was interesting that donuts were not the largest revenue generator for the firm. This Randolph, Massachusetts Company, a wholly owned subsidiary of Allied Domecq PLC generated more revenue from selling coffee than donuts! In fact, the firm was the world's largest coffee and baked goods chain, selling approximately 4.4 million donuts and 2.5 million cups of coffee every day. They were also the largest retailer of coffee-by-the-cup. More than 40% of the company's sales come from coffee, with some individual stores actually exceeding 50% level.

[8]"The U.S. Coffee & Tea Market," *Packaged Facts* (September 1999 and September 2002).

Two other rapidly growing brands were also expanding store locations rapidly in major US markets. Krispy Kreme and Tim Horton's, each with less than 200 outlets currently, had their sites on continued rapid expansion, especially in their coffee sales categories. The ready-to-drink market continued to increase market share both domestically and in international locations. Starbuck's management believed it had been quite successful in this market segment.[9]

Whole Bean Coffee — Retail. The second and much smaller market segment for the company was whole bean coffees sold at retail through supermarkets, specialty retailers, and a growing number of specialty coffeehouses. Starbucks' whole bean coffees and its coffee beverages competed indirectly against all other coffees on the market. The company believed that its customers choose among retail products primarily on the basis of quality, service, and convenience and, to a lesser extent, on price.

The supermarket segment of the marketplace was believed to be the most competitive distribution channel for specialty whole bean coffee, in part because supermarkets offered customers a broad variety of choices without having to make a separate trip to a specialty coffee store. A number of nationwide coffee manufacturers as well as regional specialty coffee companies sold whole bean coffees in supermarkets. Kraft General Foods (the parent of Maxwell House), Procter & Gamble (the marketer of Folgers and Millstone brands), and Nestle, all distribute their coffee products through supermarkets.

Regional specialty coffee companies selling whole-bean coffees in supermarkets include brands such as Green Mountain, Allegro, Brothers, and Peaberry. With such a broad variety of brands literally at their fingertips, consumers in supermarkets could easily substitute one of them for Starbucks, especially if they were a few dollars per pound less than Starbucks.

To put the growth of specialty coffee into perspective, data from the National Coffee Association showed that regular coffee still accounted for 87% of all coffee conserved in the United States in 2002. While average consumption of regular coffee per day has declined in recent years, the specialty coffee market segment has been strengthening. It would seem that gourmet coffee sales still have room for rapid growth in the foreseeable future.

[9]Press Release, Starbucks Corporation, October 24, 2002.

Financial History

The company has been "public" since 1992 when it sold shares in an IPO. Upon completion of that sale, the firm's market cap reached $273 million. The stock, listed on the NASDAQ, has now been trading for just over a decade. In 1993, a convertible debenture was sold, bringing the company $80.5 million at an interest rate of 4.5%. In 1995, another convertible debenture was sold with a coupon rate of 4.25%, netting the company $165 million. Both offerings served as deferred equity issues rather than more permanent debt offerings. Consequently, the 4.5% debentures were converted to common stock in 1996, while the 4.25% issue was converted in 1997. Since that time the firm has financed its longer-term asset needs with internally generated cash flow. The number of common shares outstanding has grown nominally each year due to the issuance of options.

Since the public offering in 1992, there have been four 2-for-1 stock splits, the latest one occurring in April 2001. The resulting capital account of the firm shows literally no long-term debt and equity at market value of approximately $9.4 billion in April 2003. See Exhibit 3 for the performance of Starbucks' common stock since its IPO in 1992.

Financial Performance

Within the perspective of the overall performance of the coffee industry over the last decade, management strategies and execution of Starbucks Company had been quite remarkable. Its growth by almost any measure of operating and financial performance has resulted in excellent returns for all company stakeholders and especially their shareholders. Balance sheets for the last 4 years (presented in Exhibit 4) show a decidedly conservative organization with almost no long-term debt and the book value of stockholder's equity exceeding $1.7 billion, supporting assets of $2.3 billion at year-end 2002. Income statements for the last 5 years show significant yet balanced growth with exceptional control of expenses (Exhibit 5). Statements of cash flows (Exhibit 6) clarify details of operations, investing, and financing activities.

Although the firm was expanding its outlets through wholly owned stores as well as joint ventures, asset growth had been in line with sales. Yet there were financial commitments that do not necessarily show up on a firm's balance sheet. Leasehold improvements (Exhibit 7) and future

Exhibit 3. Starbucks Coffee Company Stock Prices and Earnings 1992–2002

	Stock Prices		EPS	*P/E* Ratio	
Year	High	Low	(Fiscal Year)	High	Low
2002	25.7	18.4	.60	42.8	30.7
2001	25¾	13.5	.46	60.0	29.3
2000	25.4	11.6	.36	70.6	32.2
1999	20½	6.9	.27	75.9	25.6
1998	15	7.2	.22	68.2	32.7
1997	11.2	6.5	.165	67.9	39.4
1996	10.1	3.6	.12	84.2	30.0
1995	5.6	2,8	.95	58.9	29.5
1994	4.1	2.4	.055	74.5	43.6
1993	3.5	2.0	.035	100.0	57.1
1992	2.4	1.3	.02	120.0	65.0

Notes: Fiscal year ends September.
Stock Price Range for calendar year.
Prices and EPS adjusted for four 2-for-1 stock splits:
Sept. 1993, Dec. 1995, March 1999, April 2001.
Source: Standard & Poor's.

rentals under non-callable lease obligations (Exhibits 8 and 9) represent financial commitments that contribute to business risk. These data must be incorporated into any evaluation of a firm's debt capacity.

Starbucks Management Expectations[10]

In October 2002, the company hosted its fourth biennial Analyst Conference at its worldwide headquarters in Seattle. Feature presentations were made by the management team responsible for leading Starbucks' global growth strategy. The North American leadership team highlighted Starbucks' strengths in extending the brand into complementary channels

[10] *Ibid.*

Exhibit 4. Starbucks Coffee Company Balance Sheet (Fiscal Year Ends September) (in Millions)

	Sept. 29, 2002	Sept. 30, 2001	Oct. 1, 2000	Oct. 3, 1999
Assets				
Current Assets				
Cash and Cash Equivalents	$174.6	$113.2	$70.8	$66.4
Short-Term Investments — Available-for-Sale Securities	217.3	101.4	57.6	51.4
Short-Term Investments — Trading Securities	10.4	5.9	3.8	—
Accounts Receivable, Net	97.6	90.4	76.4	47.6
Inventories	263.2	221.3	201.7	180.9
Prepaid Expenses and Other Current Assets	42.4	29 .8	18.7	19.0
Deferred Income Taxes, Net	42.2	31.9	29.3	21.1
Total Current Assets	$847.5	$593.9	$458.2	$386.5
Equity and Other Investments	106.0	63.1	55.8	68.1
Property, Plant and Equipment, Net	1,265.8	1,135.8	930.8	760.3
Other Assets	53.6	31.9	25.4	23.5
Goodwill, Net	19.9	21.8	21.3	14.2
Total Assets	$2,292.7	$1,846.5	$1,491.5	$1,252.5
Liabilities and Stockholders Equity				
Current Liabilities				
Accounts Payable	$136.0	$127.1	73.7	$56.1
Checks Drawn in Excess of Bank Balances	74.9	62.0	56.3	63.8
Accrued Compensation and Related Costs	105.9	81.5	69.7	43.9
Accrued Occupancy Costs	51.2	35.8	29.1	23.0
Accrued Taxes	54.1	70.3	35.8	30.8
Other Accrued Expenses	72.3	40.1	39.0	32.5
Deferred Revenue	42.3	26.9	7.3	.5
Current Portion of Long-Term Debt	.7	.7	.7	.7
Total Current Liabilities	$537.5	$445.3	$311.7	$251.2
Deferred Income Taxes, Net	22.5	19.1	21.4	32.9
Long-Term Debt	5.1	5.8	6.5	7.0
Other Long-Term Liabilities	1.0	.4	3.6	.4
Shareholders Equity				
Common Stock and Additional Paid-in Capital	891.0	791.6	750.9	651.0
Other Additional Paid-in Capital	39.4	—	—	—

(*Continued*)

Exhibit 4. (*Continued*)

	Sept. 29, 2002	Sept. 30, 2001	Oct. 1, 2000	Oct. 3, 1999
Retained Earnings	804.8	589.7	408.5	313.9
Accumulated Other Comprehensive Loss	(8.6)	(5.4)	(11.0)	(3.9)
Total Shareholders Equity	$1,726.6	$1,375.9	$1,148.4	$961.0
Total Liabilities and Shareholders Equity	$2,292.7	$1,846.5	$1,491.5	$1,252.5

Note: Totals may not add up due to rounding.
Source: Company 10K and Annual Reports.

and products outside the retail store business as well as continued focus on the core retail business. Key drivers of the company's retail business include continuous product innovation, speed of service initiatives, and leading-edge store development. Mark Wesley, Senior Vice President, Store Development and Asset Management, reiterated the firm's long-term global store target of more than 25,000 stores. "We believe that North America alone can support at least 10,000 company-owned and licensed Starbucks locations," stated Mr. Wesley. "We are experiencing tremendous early success with the opening of stores in non-traditional locations, such as off-highway and other unique real estate sites, with innovative and flexible new store designs."

Starbucks Coffee International managers identified an even larger target for stores outside of North America. They expect to be able to operate more than 15,000 locations as a long-term goal. "We are in the very early stages of development in international markets," stated Peter Maslen, President, Starbucks Coffee International. "With a presence now in 30 countries across the globe, we have been able to demonstrate that the Starbucks business model can be extremely successful in many diverse communities around the world. In addition to retail stores, we look forward to launching our consumer products business internationally with the introduction of a ready-to-drink coffee-based beverage in one international market in the next 18 months. We are building infrastructure to ultimately support the potential for at least 6,000 stores in Asia-Pacific, 7,500 stores in Europe, the Middle East, and Africa, 1,500 stores in Latin America, and a robust consumer products business in each region."

Company representatives also highlighted financial goals for the next 3 to 5 years that would be the result of global retail store expansion and

Exhibit 5. Starbucks Coffee Company Income Statements (in Millions) (Fiscal Year Ends September)

	2002	2001	2000	1999	1998
Net Revenue					
Retail	$2,793	$2,230	$1,824	$1,423	$1,103
Specialty	496	419	354	263	206
Total Net Revenue	$3,289	$2,649	$2,178	$1,686	$1,309
Cost of Sales and Related					
Occupancy Costs	1,350	1,113	962	748	579
Store Operating Expenses	1,121	876	705	544	419
Other Operating Expenses	127	93	78	55	45
Depreciation and Amortization					
Expenses	206	164	130	98	73
General and Administrative Expenses	202	151	110	90	78
Income from Equity Investees	36	29	20	3	1
Merger Expenses					8.9
Operating Income					
Interest and Other Income, Net	9	11	7	7	7
Interest-Related Investment Losses		3	59		
Gain on Sale of Investment	13				
Earnings Before Income Taxes	$341.4	$288.9	$160.6	$164.0	$116.4
Income Taxes	126.3	107.7	66	62.3	48
Net Earnings	$215.1	$181.2	$94.6	$101.7	$68.4
Net Earnings per Share — Basic	0.56	0.48	0.25	0.28	0.19
Net Earnings per Share — Diluted	0.54	0.46	0.24	0.27	0.18
Weighted Average Shares Outstanding (in Millions)					
Basis	385.6	380.6	371.2	363.7	352.2
Diluted	397.5	394.4	386	377.1	367.5

Note: Totals may not add up due to rounding.
Source: Company 10K and Annual Reports.

growing specialty businesses. They projected revenue growth of approximately 20% per year with earnings per share growth of approximately 20–25% per year. By the end of fiscal 2005 (September), they expected to be operating 10,000 stores worldwide in 60 countries. More specifically, for

Exhibit 6. Starbucks Coffee Company Consolidated Statement of Cash Flows (Fiscal Year Ends September) (in Millions)

	Sept. 29, 2002	Sept. 30, 2001	Oct. 1, 2000	Oct. 3, 1999	Sept. 27, 1998
Operating Activities					
Net Earnings	$215.1	$181.2	$94.6	$101.7	$68.4
Adjustments to Reconcile Net Earnings to Net Cash Provided by Operating Activities					
Depreciation and Amortization	221. 1	177.1	142.2	107.5	80.9
Gain on Sale of Investment	(13.4)	—	—	—	—
Interest-Related Investment Losses	—	2.9	58.8	—	—
Provision for Impairment and Asset Disposals	26.9	11.0	5.8	2.5	7.2
Deferred Income Taxes, Net	(6.1)	(6.1)	(18.3)	.8	2.1
Equity in Income of Investors	(22.0)	(15.7)	(15.1)	(2.3)	0
Tax Benefit from Exercise of Non-Qualified Stock Options	44.2	30.9	31.1	18.6	9.3
Cash Provided (Used) by Changes in Operating Assets and Liabilities:					
Net Purchases of Trading Securities	(5.7)	(4.0)	(1.4)	—	—
Accounts Receivable	(6.7)	(20.4)	(25.0)	3.8	(19.8)
Inventories	(41.4)	(19.7)	(19.5)	(36.4)	(23.5)
Prepaid Expenses and Other Current Assets	(12.5)	(10.9)	.9	(7.6)	(2.5)
Accounts Payable	5.5	54.1	15.6	4.7	4.6
Accrued Compensation and Related Costs	24.1	12.1	25.4	7.6	9.9
Accrued Occupancy Costs	15.3	6.8	6.0	5.5	5.3
Accrued Taxes	(16.2)	34.5	5.0	12.4	7.2
Deferred Revenue	15.3	19.6	6.8	(.5)	.2
Other Accrued Expenses	34.0	2.8	5.7	10.8	1.6
Net Cash Provided by Operating Activities	$477.7	$456.3	$318.6	$229.6	$152.2
Investing Activities					
Purchase of Available-for-Sale-Securities	(340.0)	(184.2)	(118.5)	(122.8)	(51.4)
Maturity of Available-for-Sale-Securities	78.3	93.5	58.8	85.1	112.1
Sale of Available-for-Sale-Securities	144.8	46.9	49.2	3.6	5.1
Purchase of Businesses, Net of Cash Acquired	—	—	(13.5)	(15.7)	—
Additions to Equity and Other Investments	(6.1)	(12.9)	(43.9)	(30.8)	(12.4)

(*Continued*)

Exhibit 6. *(Continued)*

	Sept. 29, 2002	Sept. 30, 2001	Oct. 1, 2000	Oct. 3, 1999	Sept. 27, 1998
Proceeds From Sale of Equity Investment	14.8	—	—	—	—
Distributions from Equity Investors	22.8	16.9	14.3	9.0	2.8
Additions to Property, Plant, and Equipment	(375.5)	(384.2)	(316.5)	(257.9)	(201.9)
Additions to Other Assets	(24 .5)	(4.6)	(3.1)	(6.9)	(3.2)
Net Cash Used by Investing Activities	(485.3)	(428.5)	(373.2)	(336.3)	(148.8)
Financial Activities					
Increase/(Decrease) in Case Provided by Checks Drawn in Excess of Bank Balances	12.9	5.7	(7.5)	29.5	4.8
Proceeds from Sale of Common Stock Under Employee Stock Purchase Plan	16.2	13.0	10.3	9.4	4.6
Proceeds from Exercise of Stock Options	91.3	46.7	58.5	33.8	20.8
Principal Payments on Long-Term Debt	(.7)	(.7)	(1.9)	(1.2)	(2.0)
Repurchase of Common Stock	(52.2)	(49.8)	—	—	—
Net Cash Provided by Financing Activities	67.4	14.8	59.4	71.5	28.3
Effect of Exchange Rate Charges on Cash and Cash Equivalents	1.6	(174)	(297)	—	—
Net Increase in Cash and Cash Equivalents	61.3	42.4	4.4	(35.2)	31.5
Cash and Cash Equivalents:					
Beginning of the Year	113.2	70.8	66.4	101.7	70.1
End of Year	174.6	113.2	70.8	66.4	101.7
Investing Activities					
Purchase of Available-for-Sale-Securities	(340.0)	(184.2)	(118.5)	(122.8)	(51.4)
Maturity of Available-for-Sale-Securities	78.3	93.5	58.8	85.1	112.1
Sale of Available-for-Sale-Securities	144.8	46.9	49.2	3.6	5.1
Purchase of Businesses, Net of Cash Acquired	—	—	(13.5)	(15.7)	—
Additions to Equity and Other Investments	(6.1)	(12.9)	(43.9)	(30.8)	(12.4)
Proceeds from Sale of Equity Investment	14.8	—	—	—	—
Distributions from Equity Investors	22.8	16.9	14.3	9.0	2.8
Additions to Property, Plant, and Equipment	(375.5)	(384.2)	(316.5)	(257.9)	(201.9)

(Continued)

Exhibit 6. (*Continued*)

	Sept. 29, 2002	Sept. 30, 2001	Oct. 1, 2000	Oct. 3, 1999	Sept. 27, 1998
Additions to Other Assets	(24.5)	(4.5)	(3.1)	—	—
Net Cash Used by Investing Activities	(485.3)	(428.5)	(373.2)	(336.3)	(148.8)
Financial Activities					
Increase/(Decrease) in Case Provided by Checks Drawn in Excess of Bank Balances	12.9	5.7	(7.5)	29.5	4.8
Proceeds from Sale of Common Stock Under Employee Stock Purchase Plan	16.2	13.0	10.3	9.4	4.6
Proceeds from Exercise of Stock Options	91.3	46.7	58.5	33.8	20.8
Principal Payments on Long-Term Debt	(.7)	(.7)	(1.9)_	(1.2)	(2.0)
Repurchase of Common Stock	(52.2)	(49.8)	—	—	—
Net Cash Provided by Financing Activities	67.4	14.8	59.4	71.5	28.3
Effect of Exchange Rate Charges on Cash and Cash Equivalents	1.6	*(.2)*	*(.3)*	*(.1)*	*(.1)*
Net Increase in Cash and Cash Equivalents	61.3	42.4	4.4	(35.2)	31.5
Cash and Cash Equivalents					
Beginning of the Year	113.2	70.8	66.4	101.7	70.1
End of Year	174.6	113.2	70.8	66.4	101.7

Source: Starbucks Coffee Company, Annual Reports and 10Ks.

fiscal 2003 they expected to open at least 1,200 stores worldwide and achieve comparable store sales growth of 3–7% with monthly anomalies.

The Final Challenge

In preparing for his board presentation, Mike Casey contacted a few of the investment bankers he had met at the conference. The results were three specific scenarios for moving Starbucks to a more balanced capital structure either immediately with three different sized debt issues or a phase-in to the target debt levels over a 5-year time frame. He also prepared financial statements to show how the company could maintain its agreed-upon debt level. With growing cash flows, the firm would need to be much more active in the bond markets than it had been in recent years. Without

Exhibit 7. Starbucks Coffee Company Property, Plant, and Equipment (in Thousands)

Item	Sept. 29, 2002	Sept. 30, 2001	Oct. 1, 2000	Oct. 3, 1999
Land	$11,310	$6,023	$5,084	$5,084
Buildings	30,961	19,795	19,795	19,795
Leasehold Improvements	1,131,382	960,732	754,132	591,640
Roasting and Store Equipment	516,129	421,150	354,806	273,612
Furniture, Fixtures & Other	282,068	239,900	181,702	130,223
Total	$1,971,850	$1,647,600	$1,315,519	$1,020,354
Less: Accumulated Depreciation and Amortization	(814,427)	(605,247)	(446,403)	(320,982)
	$1,157,423	$1,042,353	$869,116	$699,372
Work in Progress	108,333	93,431	61,643	60,917
Property, Plant, and Equipment, Net	$1,265,756	$1,135,784	$930,759	$760,289

Source: Starbucks Coffee Company, Annual Reports, 1999–2002.

Exhibit 8. Starbucks Coffee Company Rental Expenses Under Operating Lease Agreements (in Thousands)

<table>
<tr><th>Fiscal Year Ended</th><th>Sept. 29, 2002</th><th>Sept. 30, 2001</th><th>Oct. 1, 2000</th><th>Oct. 3, 1999</th><th>Sept. 27, 1998</th></tr>
<tr><td>Minimum Rentals — Retail</td><td>$200,827</td><td>$150,510</td><td>$114,239</td><td rowspan="2">$95,613</td><td rowspan="2">$75,912</td></tr>
<tr><td>Minimum Rentals — Other</td><td>19,143</td><td>16,033</td><td>12,910</td></tr>
<tr><td>Contingent Rentals</td><td>5,415</td><td>4,018</td><td>3,743</td><td>1,581</td><td>1,406</td></tr>
<tr><td>Total Expenses</td><td>$225,385</td><td>$170,561</td><td>$130,892</td><td>$97,194</td><td>$77,318</td></tr>
</table>

Exhibit 9. Minimum Future Rentals Under Non-cancellable Lease Obligations as of September 29, 2002 (in Thousands)

Fiscal Year Ending	Amount ($)
2003	248,026
2004	243,519
2005	232,641
2006	219,384
2007	203,394
Thereafter	863,874
Total Minimum Lease Payments	2,101,829

Source: Starbucks Coffee Company, Annual Reports, 1999–2002.

continued bond sales, growing retained earnings and net worth would reduce the firm's debt ratio. By the end of April, Mr. Casey was ready with his ideas. He called Mr. Schultz to arrange a briefing before the board meeting. "Howard, I have the information we spoke about in March. Can we get together for a preview?" "Sure," said Mr. Schultz, "I'll see you tomorrow afternoon in my office."

https://doi.org/10.1142/9789811216749_0017

Case 17

Starbucks: Dividends, Repurchases, or Lattes?*

Susan White

University of Maryland, USA

Introduction

John Silverton had finally made it to the West coast after years of growing up and schooling on the East. Eight months ago, in May 2009, John graduated from the University of Maryland's Smith School with a degree in finance, and he was anxious to put all his years of study to work in his analyst position in the Chief Financial Officer's office at Starbucks in Seattle. Starbucks was considering initiating a dividend, and John had been tasked with researching both dividend initiations and the appropriateness of a dividend for Starbucks. His boss needed the research to determine his own recommendations to Starbucks' upper management and ultimately to the firm's board of directors. John knew from his course work that dividends and stock repurchases were linked and were just different ways of returning cash to investors. Starbucks had made semi-regular repurchases. Would continuing or even stepping up repurchases be

*This case was originally published as "Starbucks: Dividends, Repurchases or Lattes?", *Journal of Financial Education*, 42, no. 4 (Winter 2016): 358–379. The author and editors thank the journal publisher for allowing us to reprint the article in this book.

a better way of returning cash to shareholders than a dividend initiation? He was aware that the dividend/repurchase decision was also part of a firm's overall financing choice. Firms that paid dividends could potentially need more external financing to compensate for the funds distributed to shareholders.

Starbucks' Business

Starbucks was a roaster and retailer of specialty coffee. Formed in 1985, the firm sold roasted whole coffee beans, brewed coffees, espresso beverages and teas, and food items and beverage-related accessories and equipment. The firm's stated goal was "to maintain Starbucks standing as one of the most recognized and respected brands in the world. To achieve this goal, the Company plans to continue disciplined global expansion of its retail and licensed store base, to introduce relevant new products in all its channels, and to selectively develop new channels of distribution" (Starbucks 2009 10K report).

Starbucks was divided into three operating segments: United States (73% of revenues), International (19%), and Global Consumer Products ("GCP", 8%). The US and International segments owned and licensed retail stores across the US and in 40 countries. The largest international operations were in the United Kingdom, Japan, and Canada. The GCP segment included sales of packaged coffee, tea, and other branded products in grocery stores, warehouse clubs, convenience stores, and foodservice accounts. Starbucks had 11,128 US stores (6,764 company-owned and 4,364 licensed), and 5,507 international stores (2,068 owned and 3,439 licensed) for a total of 16,635 stores. Its stores provided 84% of its total revenues in 2009. Starbucks also partnered with other companies, for example, licensing Nestlé's Starbucks Ice Cream, Beam Global Spirits Starbucks Liqueur, and PepsiCo's bottled Frappuccino. Starbucks owned Seattle's Best Coffee and Torrefazione Italia.

Starbucks sold the "Starbucks experience" that was "built upon superior customer service as well as clean and well-maintained company-operated retail stores that reflect the personalities of the communities in which they operate, thereby building a high degree of customer loyalty" (Starbucks 2009 10K report). Starbucks' largest input expense was coffee beans which were grown in warm climates, sometimes in countries with unstable governments. Starbucks also pledged to buy ethically grown coffee and to not purchase coffee where the workers were poorly treated.

The firm employed 142,000 people worldwide, with about 110,000 in the US, of whom 105,000 were employed by retail stores and the remainder in firm administrative and regional offices.

Starbucks' Strategy

Starbucks had been criticized for overexpansion as it saw revenues fall during the recession following the 2007–2008 financial crisis. The company responded by closing 900 of its less profitable stores and laying off employees in 2008–2009. CEO Howard Schultz ran Starbucks from 1987 and made it into one of the world's most recognized brands. He stepped down as CEO in 2000, but remained chairman, and took over the company again in 2008. By year-end 2009, Starbucks' fortunes were improving under Schultz's leadership. Since then he cut $600 million in costs through store closings. In Starbucks' 2009 fourth quarter conference call, Schultz said:

> "A more disciplined focus on operations and the introduction of numerous initiatives to permanently improve our cost structure each contributed to the positive earnings momentum that we're seeing. In addition, and even more important, are the outstanding performance of our partners and the many innovations we introduced to improve our in-store customer experience in the US and abroad. All of these efforts have set the stage for what we believe will be long-term revenue and profit growth. That said, we know that we have more work to do."

Analysts were optimistic about Starbucks' newest product, Via instant coffee. A Morningstar analyst, for example, commenting on Starbucks' single-serve coffee and tea products, said, "Starbucks' evolution into a diversified retail and consumer goods platform remains on track, and opportunities in the $100 billion packaged coffee, tea, and ready-to-drink markets are undeniable."[1] Via was not only expected to do well, but it was expected to generate follow-on opportunities in this market.

---

[1] http://library.morningstar.com/stocknet/MorningstarAnalysis.aspx?Country=USA&Symbol=SBUX.

At the firm's 2010 annual meeting, Schultz said he expected to increase sales at existing U.S. stores, in particular through Via coffee, and expand internationally. As growth in domestic same-store sales and net new stores declined, Shultz recognized that much of the firm's future growth would occur internationally. In addition to heavy investment in China, Starbucks was looking to expand into other areas in Asia, including India and Vietnam. Starbucks was particularly proud of its Via instant coffee, which was considered a success in branding and marketing. After a successful introduction in Starbucks stores, Via was then sold in grocery stores domestically. The firm hoped to expand its Via success through international channels.

The first quarter of 2010 (October to December 2009) saw a 4% rise in same-store sales, the first quarterly gain in US stores in 2 years. According to Schultz, "Starbucks' strong performance in Q4 and fiscal 2009 overall is the result of our successful efforts to improve our customer and partner experiences, the initiatives and innovations we have introduced over the past 18 months and significant, permanent changes we have made to our cost structure. We are seeing broad-based improvement across our global business."[2]

Starbucks' Risks

Starbucks' 10K report listed the potential risk factors facing the firm:

- Decline in consumer demand and lower revenue per transaction, increased competition, lack of customer acceptance of new products or prices, commodity cost increases, labor cost increases, and higher construction costs associated with new stores.
- Lower success in implementing strategic initiatives, such as the "Starbuck experience" and new products like Via.
- Economic conditions. As a premium-priced coffee provider, Starbucks saw sales decline in economic recessions.
- Starbucks depended on US operations to provide the bulk of its revenues and net income, and international operations to provide future growth.

[2] Starbucks Press Release, "Starbucks Posts Strong Fourth Quarter and Fiscal 2009 Results," http://news.starbucks.com/archive.cfm?section_id=1&archiveYear=2009&start_row=11. Retrieved September 9, 2013.

The Industry

The beverage market was highly competitive, with many other quick-service restaurants and specialty coffee shops. In addition to its main coffee and pastries business, Starbucks was engaged in selling CDs, books, and other lifestyle products. Its secondary industries included coffee and tea, candy and confections, consumer electronics and appliances, music, video and book entertainment, and home furnishings and housewares. Starbucks was primarily part of the specialty eateries industry which was relatively new, highly competitive that experienced high growth in the 1990s and 2000s. While the products of various eateries were substitutable for each other, consumers often made purchases on the basis of brand and product mix. Starbucks' management believed that consumers chose their coffee based on quality, service, convenience, and price. This meant that significant factors included location, store atmosphere, and quality were important. Starbucks offered premium products and premium pricing and faced heavy competition from less expensive alternatives sold at Dunkin Donuts and from McDonald's McCafe. Entry barriers in the industry were low, with operating costs consisting of lease expense, labor, and cost of sales. Starbucks' growth was very dependent on consumer preferences and income.

The negative impact of Starbucks' premium pricing became apparent in the 2008–9 financial crisis and great recession. Sales were down and growth slowed significantly as many consumers turned to lower-cost coffee alternatives. Starbucks was also impacted by social trends, for example, a shift toward healthy, lower-calorie foods. The company adjusted its menu to include low-calorie alternatives and published the calorie content of its products.

Starbucks' Performance

As a premium coffee and beverage seller, Starbucks had a difficult time during the 2008 recession. (Note that Starbucks ended its fiscal year in September, so the 2009 10K report included the fourth quarter of 2008.) The last quarter of the calendar year was the first quarter of its fiscal year and was typically the quarter that provided the most profits. Because of the recession, the first quarter of the 2009 fiscal year was well below Starbucks' typical performance. Starbucks' overall stock performance is contained in Exhibit 1. Starbucks stock performed poorly relative to the

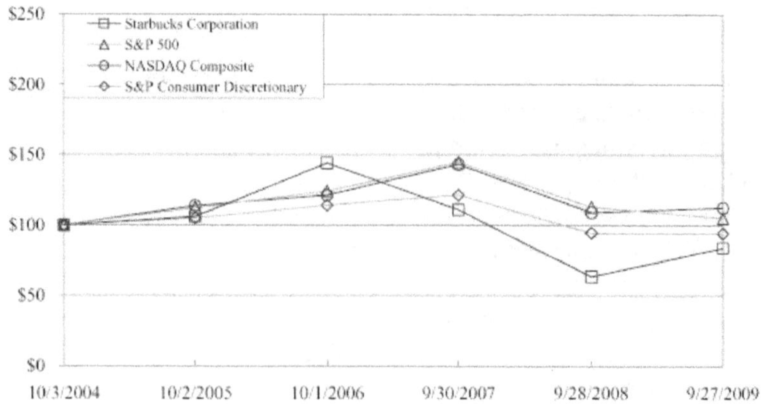

Exhibit 1. Starbucks Stock Performance (from 2009 10K Report)

S&P 500, the Nasdaq Composite, and the S&P Consumer Discretionary sector, a group that included Starbucks. A $100 investment in Starbucks in 2004 would only have been worth $8.99 at fiscal year-end 2009, while the same investment in the Nasdaq Composite Index would have been worth $112.55. Fiscal 2009 was a difficult year for the firm. With reduced consumer spending, Starbucks' profitability was adversely impacted. The year was marked with store closings, including 800 stores in the US, 61 in Australia, and 41 in other countries. Another 100 international stores were expected to close in 2010. Starbucks still ended the year with no outstanding short-term debt and $650 million in cash and short-term investments.

As fiscal 2009 progressed, Starbucks improved, as stated by Troy Alstead, Executive Vice President and Chief Financial Officer.[3] "Excellent execution throughout our organization contributed significantly to our performance this quarter. Our store partners have embraced the cost disciplines and efficiency initiatives that are enabling us to expand our operating margin. In doing this, they have also delivered increased service speed, measurably improved customer service, customer satisfaction, and an overall enhanced Starbucks Experience."

Starbucks expected low to mid-single-digit revenue growth in 2010. Analysts had estimated 2010 revenues of $9.9 to $10.5 billion,

[3]Starbucks Press Release, "Starbucks Posts Strong Third Quarter Results Fiscal 2009 Results," http://news.starbucks.com/article_display.cfm?article_id=249. Retrieved September 9, 2013.

and revenue growth rates from 1 to 5%. Starbucks also was expecting greater growth in the future than had been achieved in the immediate past. According to CFO Alstead, "Improving top-line trends, coupled with a disciplined operational focus in both our stores and our support organization, position us well for long-term, profitable growth. As a result, we are increasing our non-GAAP EPS outlook for fiscal year 2010 to a range of 15–20% growth over fiscal 2009."[4] After accounting for store closures, Starbucks expected to add 100 stores in the US and 200 internationally. It anticipated operating cash flow of $1.4 billion for 2010 and free cash flow of $900 million. The firm expected to continue to improve operational efficiency. It expected its operating margin to improve, following its 2009 improvement to 5.7% from 4.9% in 2008. Capital expenditures of $500–$550 million were predicted, with about half of this amount allocated to renovations and store equipment upgrades, about a quarter to systems upgrades, and a quarter to new stores and other capital investments. CEO Schultz said, "We are reinvigorating the physical environment of our stores through new store concepts and designs. All newly constructed company-operated stores worldwide will be LEED-certified[5] beginning this calendar year, with projection, construction, and cost parameters. This initiative, coupled with locally relevant store designs and renovations, is helping us form deeper connections to customers in their own neighborhoods." Schultz continued, "I would be remiss if I limited my comments on innovation to only the customer experience. Behind the scenes, we have continued to build on our work to drive efficiency through lean processes, optimal scheduling, and technology upgrades. These innovations, though not always visible, continue to help drive margin growth and customer and partner satisfaction." CFO Alstead echoed these sentiments in the fourth quarter conference call, stating, "We shifted our culture and business model from one dependent on high topline growth to one that is more disciplined and operationally efficient, laying the foundation for

---

[4] Starbucks Press Release, "Starbucks Posts Strong Fourth Quarter and Fiscal 2009 Results," http://news.starbucks.com/archive.cfm?section_id=1&archiveYear=2009&start_row=11. Retrieved September 9, 2013.

[5] LEED (Leadership in Energy & Environmental Design) was an internationally recognized green building certification system. Companies received points toward different levels of LEED certification based on the building's energy efficiency and impact on the environment.

profitable growth in the future. We have improved the Starbucks experience for our customers through a rededicated focus on in-store operational excellence. We have raised the bar on innovation, launching products and concepts that once again set the standard for the industry… We are confident that the best days for Starbucks still lie ahead as we look to capitalize on the strength of our global brand and the abundant opportunities that remain in markets and channels around the world."

As John considered his research task, he recognized that Starbucks' cash was paramount in making a determination about the firm's dividend policy, both cash on the balance sheet and free cash flow to equity holders. He remembered an investment banking guest speaker in one of his classes who said, "GAAP is crap and cash is king." In short, how Starbucks accounted for its earnings was less important than its cash holdings and free cash flow. Starbucks had cash and short-term investments of $666.1 million at fiscal year-end 2009, compared to $322.3 million in 2008. Cash was invested in investment grade debt, stock mutual funds, and stock exchange-traded funds, all of which were "available for sale," in other words, not needed for operations. John also considered CFO Alstead's comments in the fourth quarter 2009 conference call, "our top priority for cash of course is investing back in our existing business, making sure we're maintaining the excellence of the assets that we have in place. And next priority is to fund the growth opportunities that we have, VIA, new store growth around the world, and so on. And we see abundant opportunities there." Alstead believed that the year that had just passed amply demonstrated Starbucks' cash-generating power. Alstead said, "I do expect that as we move, again, into 2010, we will have excess cash above and beyond those critical business needs that I've described in the business." However, Alstead was concerned about the business environment and the fact that the firm was recovering from poor performance during the great recession. He said, "I also remain a bit cautious about this economic environment that we're in. We are on the front end here of the first holiday quarter, which is our strongest cash-producing quarter of the year. So we're not going to make any conclusions on how best to deploy that excess cash until we come through this quarter."[6]

[6]Fourth Quarter 2009 Conference Call.

Stock Repurchases and Dividends

Starbucks' stock repurchase history is in Exhibit 2. Until the 2009 recession, the firm had made regular stock repurchases. Share repurchases had been decreasing in number and total dollar value as Starbucks' price declined after the financial crisis. In 2005, for example, the firm repurchased 5.7% of its outstanding shares, and by 2008 that percentage had declined to 1.7% of shares. The average price paid compared to the average price of stock for the year increased, with Starbucks paying less per share for its repurchases than the average year's stock price in 2005 and 2006 as the stock price increased. Starbucks paid more per share repurchased than the average yearly price in 2007 and 2008 as the stock price declined.

Starbucks' competitors also made regular share repurchases. McDonald's repurchased 50.3 million shares in 2009 for $2,854 million. McDonald's highlighted the fact that the firm had raised its dividend every year since it initiated dividends in 1976. Yum! Brands' vision statement called for at least 10% EPS growth annually and it did not repurchase any shares in 2009, but repurchased $1,434 million in stock in 2008 and $1,154 million in 2007. Darden Restaurants also repurchased shares in addition to paying dividends. The firm repurchased $144.9 million and $159.4 million in common stock in 2009 and 2008, respectively. Wendy's repurchased 12.1 million shares in 2009 for $46.6 million. Brinker International was also conservative in its 2009 repurchases, buying one million shares for $20 million. Information about select competitors is in Exhibit 3.

Exhibit 2. Starbucks Stock Repurchases

Starbucks did not repurchase any of its shares during the fiscal year 2009. Numbers in Millions except "Average Price per Share of Shares Acquired."

	2009	2008	2007	2006	2005
Number of Shares Acquired	0	12.2	33.0	25.6	45.1
Average Price per Share of Shares Acquired (Average Stock Price for the Year is in Parentheses)	0	$24.12 ($13.99)	$30.72 ($27.33)	$32.34 ($33.11)	$25.26 ($28.12)
Total Accrual-Based Cost of Acquired Shares	0	$295.3	$1,012.7	$828.0	$1,139.226
Total Cash-Based Cost of Acquired Shares	0	$311.4	$996.8	$854.045	$1,113.647

Source: 2005–2009 Starbucks' 10K report.

Exhibit 3. Starbucks Competitors

Data from Thomson One Financial.

Brinker International: Ticker symbol EAT. Brinker-owned, operated, and franchised restaurants including Chili's and Maggiano's Little Italy. Its 1,000+ restaurants were located in the US and worldwide. Founded in 1977, the firm was headquartered in Dallas, Texas.

Brinker International	2009	2008	2007	2006	2005
Sales	3,276,362	3,860,921	4,007,771	3,785,406	3,749,539
Net Income	79,166	51,722	230,049	213,950	158,456
Depreciation	161,800	165,229	189,162	190,206	179,908
Capital Expenditures	–93,600	–270,400	–354,600	–430,500	–334900
Cash	94,156	54,714	84,823	55,615	41,859
Total Assets	1,948,947	2,193,122	2,318,021	2,221,779	2,156,124
Long-Term Debt	893,141	1,071,209	969,468	629,600	607,208
Return on Equity (in Percent)	12.75	7.39	24.46	19.52	14.56
Dividend (per share)	0.44	0.44	0.38	0.39	0.10
High Stock Price for the Year	21.62	30.35	35.74	28.77	28.37
Low Stock Price for the Year	3.88	14.65	20.99	23.4	19.28
Year-End Stock Price	15.88	19.62	29.29	35.41	39.82
Book Value per Share	4.72	4.76	4.25	5.01	4.28
P/E Ratio at Year End	20.36	39.24	15.19	22	33.22
Number of Shares	102,124.842	101,216.461	110,127.072	125,306.325	89,182.804
Beta	1.78				
2010 Analyst Estimated					
Dividend Growth Rate	23.40%				

Darden Restaurants: Ticker symbol DRI. Darden Restaurants include Red Lobster, Olive Garden, Longhorn Steakhouse, Bahama Breeze, Seasons 52, Capital Grille, Eddie V's, and Yard House. Founded in 1968, the firm had about 2,000 restaurants and 185,000 employees.

Darden Restaurants	2009	2008	2007	2006	2005
Sales	7,217.50	6,626.50	5,587.10	5,353.60	5,278.11
Net Income	372.20	377.20	201.40	338.20	290.61
Depreciation	283.10	245.70	200.40	197.00	213.22
Capital Expenditures	–535.54	–429.40	–346.40	–316.40	–329.35
Cash	62.90	43.20	30.20	42.30	42.80
Total Assets	5,025.20	4,730.60	2,880.80	3,010.20	2,938.45
Long-Term Debt	1,632.30	1,634.30	491.60	494.70	350.32
Return on Equity (in Percent)	24.69	30.13	17.33	27.01	23.72

(Continued)

Darden Restaurants	**2009**	**2008**	**2007**	**2006**	**2005**
Dividend	0.90	0.76	0.59	0.43	0.24
High Stock Price for the Year	40.26	47.08	45.88	42.75	39.06
Low Stock Price for the Year	13.54	20.99	33.29	28.8	29.3
Year-End Stock Price	36.17	31.74	45.32	36.51	32.80
Book Value per Share	12.27	10.13	8.61	8.81	8.52
P/E Ratio at Year End	12.75	10.88	20.38	17.7	19.74
Number of Shares	140.400	145.1	148.800	156.900	163.400
Beta	0.95				
2010 Analyst Estimated					
Dividend Growth Rate	30.8%				

McDonald's: Ticker symbol MCD. McDonald's operates and franchises restaurants in the US and worldwide. Founded in 1940 and headquartered in Oak Brook, Illinois, the firm has over 30,000 restaurants in more than 100 countries. McDonald's introduced McCafe, coffee drinks that compete directly with Starbucks.

McDonald's	**2009**	**2008**	**2007**	**2006**	**2005**
Sales	22,745	23,522	22,787	20,895	19,117
Net Income	4,551	4,313	2,395	3,544	2,602
Depreciation	1,216.20	1,207.80	1,192.80	1,190.00	1,249.50
Capital Expenditures	−1,952	−2,136	−1,947	−1,742	−1,607
Cash	1,796.00	2,063.40	1,981.30	2,128.10	4,260.40
Total Assets	30,225.00	28,462.00	29,392.00	28,974.00	29,989.00
Long-Term Debt	10,578.00	10,218.00	9,301.00	8,408.00	10,137.00
Return on Equity (in Percent)	34.00%	30.60%	15.10%	18.40%	17.60%
Dividend	2.05	1.63	1.50	1.00	0.67
High Stock Price for the Year	64.75	64.02	63.69	44.68	35.69
Low Stock Price for the Year	56.03	45.79	54.67	38.95	31.48
Year-End Stock Price	62.44	62.19	58.91	44.33	33.72
Book Value per Share	4.52	4.14	3.64	2.87	2.22
P/E Ratio at Year End	14.97	16.24	29.81	15.34	16.37
Number of Shares	1,077.000	1,115.000	1,165.000	1,204.000	1,263.000
Beta	0.47				
2010 Analyst Estimated					
Dividend Growth Rate	11.10%				

Wendy's: Ticker symbol WEN. Wendy's operates and franchises fast food restaurants. It owns more than 6,000 restaurants and 20+ foreign countries. Wendy's was founded in 1884 and headquartered in Dublin, Ohio. Note that in 2008, Wendy's merged with Arby's becoming Wendy's/Arby's Group, but retaining the WEN ticker symbol.

Wendy's	**2009**	**2008**	**2007**	**2006**	**2005**
Sales	3,580.80	1,822.80	1,263.70	1,243.30	727.30
Net Income	5.10	–479.70	16.10	94.00	224.00
Depreciation	190.30	88.30	66.20	123.70	129.00
Capital Expenditures	–108.30	–115.42	–130.10	–110.00	–181.00
Cash	591.72	90.09	211.20	457.61	230.56
Total Assets	4,975.40	4,645.60	1,454.60	1,560.40	2,809.50
Long-Term Debt	1,500.80	1,081.20	711.50	701.90	894.50
Return on Equity (in Percent)	0.22%	–20.13%	3.58%	9.29%	10.88%
Dividend	0.08	0.08	0.32	0.32	0.32
High Stock Price for the Year	5.80	9.82	42.22	67.19	56.40
Low Stock Price for the Year	3.55	2.63	25.94	31.75	36.73
Year-End Stock Price	4.69	4.75	8.76	21.74	16.74
Book Value per Share	6.02	15.08	3.27	12.73	5.97
P/E Ratio at Year End	465.00	–1.45	54.56	26.19	8.58
Number of Shares	466.20	185.70	92.30	86.60	70.00
Beta	0.47				
2010 Analyst Estimated Dividend Growth Rate	0%				

Yum! Brands. Ticker symbol YUM. Yum operates over 30,000 restaurants in 120 countries including Kentucky Fried Chicken, Pizza Hut, and Taco Bell. Founded in 1997, the company was headquartered in Louisville, Kentucky.

Yum! Brands	**2009**	**2008**	**2007**	**2006**	**2005**
Sales	10,836	11,304	10,435	9,561	9,349
Net Income	1,071	964	909	824	762
Depreciation	580.00	556.00	542.00	479.00	469.00
Capital Expenditures	–797	–935	–742	–614	–609
Cash	239.00	229.00	789.00	319.00	158.00
Total Assets	7,148.00	6,527.00	7,188.00	6,368.00	5,797.00
Long-Term Debt	3,207.00	3,564.00	2,924.00	2,045.00	1,649.00
Return on Equity (in Percent)	96.14%	Neg.	79.81%	56.75%	52.59%

(Continued)

Yum! Brands	2009	2008	2007	2006	2005
Dividend	0.78	0.68	0.75	0.53	0.43
High Stock Price for the Year	36.64	41.34	40.27	31.74	53.29
Low Stock Price for the Year	23.47	22.25	27.69	22.47	45.12
Year-End Stock Price	35.38	30.28	38.54	58.80	46.88
Book Value per Share	2.38	−0.20	2.28	2.74	2.61
P/E Ratio at Year End	15.52	14.92	22.15	19.47	17.62
Number of Shares	469.000	459.000	499.000	530.000	556.000
Beta	0.98				
2010 Analyst Estimated					
Dividend Growth Rate	13%				

Institutions owned about 72% of Starbucks' shares, and the top 10 institutional investors owned 38% of the firm. Many of its institutional owners were mutual funds and its top investors included Fidelity, Vanguard, Capital World Investors, T. Rowe Price, BlackRock Institutional Trust, and State Street Global Advisors. While it was impossible to tell how many shares were held in retirement accounts vs. taxable accounts, Starbucks had some prominent retirement account owners, including TIAA-CREF, which owned close to 6.9 million shares, about 1% of its total shares.

Starbucks' Financing Policy

Starbucks' debt and lease data is contained in Exhibit 4. Even though its total debt and debt as a percent of assets had been increasing over the past 5 years, the firm maintained a low, relative to its industry competitors, debt ratio of 10.2%, compared to the industry median of 25.8%. Over half of the firm's 2008 $1,263.3 million in debt was short-term debt was paid off in 2009, leaving the firm with $549.5 million in debt. Starbucks also had a significant operating lease obligation for store rentals, with an obligation of $714.7 million in 2010. John's immediate conclusion was that Starbucks was far from overburdened with debt, and if the firm instituted a dividend payment it would have adequate financial slack to handle additional debt if needed.

Starbucks' bonds maturing in 2017 were rated BBB by Standard & Poor's and Baa3 by Moody's. Both agencies rated Starbucks' outlook as

Exhibit 4. Starbucks' Debt and Lease Data

Debt Information	**Sept. 27, 2009**	**Sept. 28, 2008**
Commercial Paper (Weighted Average Interest Rate of 3.4%)	—	$414
Revolving Credit Facility (Weighted Average Interest Rate of 3.5%)	—	300
Current Portion of Long-Term Debt	0.2	0.7
Short-Term Debt	$0.2	$713.7
6.25% 10-Year Senior Notes, due August 2017	549.2	549.2
Other Long-Term Debt	0.1	0.4
Long-Term Debt	$549.3	$549.6
Total	$549.5	$1,263.3

Lease Information			
Fiscal Year Ended	9/27/09	9/28/08	9/30/07
Minimum Rentals	$690.0	$709.1	$609.9
Contingent Rentals	$24.7	$32.0	$28.2
Total	$714.7	$741.1	$638.1

Note: Minimum future rental payments under noncancellable operating leases as of September 27, 2009: (in millions)

Fiscal Year Ending:	
2010	$706.7
2011	669.0
2012	612.3
2013	551.0
2014	488.1
Thereafter	1,362.1
Total	$4,389.2

Note: Capital lease obligations, varying maturities, with the latest maturity in 2015; September 2009: $7.8 million and September 2008: $6.7 million.

Source: Starbucks 2009 10K report, numbers in millions.

negative, a rating that was changed to stable in August 2009. Starbucks' short-term credit rating was raised to A-2 from A-3 during 2009, but Moody's remained at P-3, keeping commercial paper more expensive for the firm. Consequently, Starbucks turned instead to a $1 billion revolving credit line for its short-term financing needs, which carried an interest rate of 0.21% to 0.67% over the LIBOR or the greater of the bank's prime rate or the greater of the Federal Funds Rate plus 0.5%. The firm's higher 2009 operating cash flow allowed it to reduce short-term borrowings from $713 million in 2008 to zero in 2009. Starbucks' financial statements are in Exhibits 5 through 7. See Exhibit 8 for information about interest rates. Starbucks' competitors had a history of paying regular dividends.

Exhibit 5. Starbucks Balance Sheet

In Millions	2009	2008	2007	2006	2005
Assets					
Cash And ST Investments	673.8	322.3	438.69	453.64	307.04
Cash	599.8	269.8	281.26	227.66	111.59
ST Investments	74	52.5	157.43	225.98	195.45
Receivables (Net)	271	329.5	287.93	224.27	190.76
Total Inventories	664.9	692.8	691.66	636.22	546.3
Other Current Assets	426.1	312.3	278.21	215.65	165.24
Current Assets — Total	2,035.80	1,748.00	1,696.49	1,529.79	1,209.33
Investment in Unconsol Subsidiaries	313.2	267.9	234.47	205	198.66
Other Investments	115.8	106.1	45.4	19.9	63.28
Property Plant and Equipment — Net	2,536.40	2,956.40	2,890.43	2,287.90	1,842.02
Property Plant Equip — Gross	5,700.90	5,717.30	5,306.58	4,257.70	3,467.58
Accumulated Depreciation	3,164.50	2,760.90	2,416.14	1,969.80	1,625.56
Other Assets	440.4	466.3	477.09	386.35	200.78
Tangible Other Assets	113.1	133.2	219.42	186.92	72.89
Intangible Other Assets	327.3	333.1	257.67	199.43	127.88
Total Assets	5,441.60	5,544.70	5,343.88	4,428.94	3,514.07
Liabilities & Shareholders' Equity					
Accounts Payable	267.1	324.9	390.84	340.94	220.98
Short Term Debt	0.2	713.7	712.22	702.46	277.75

(Continued)

Exhibit 5. (*Continued*)

In Millions	2009	2008	2007	2006	2005
Accrued Payroll	239.2	253.6	332.33	288.96	232.35
Income Taxes Payable	57.2	14.8	38.5	50.6	41.5
Other Current Liabilities	1,017.30	882.7	681.68	552.66	454.42
Current Liabilities — Total	1,581.00	2,189.70	2,155.57	1,935.62	1,227.00
Long Term Debt	557.1	556.3	552.02	4.36	2.87
LT Debt	549.3	549.6	550.12	1.96	2.87
Capitalized Lease Obligations	7.8	6.7	1.9	2.4	0
Provision for Risks and Charges	43.4	N/A	N/A	N/A	N/A
Deferred Income	266	303.9	271.74	203.9	166.18
Deferred Taxes	−135.2	−127.9	N/A	N/A	N/A
Other Liabilities	72.4	113.5	63.19	45.82	16.23
Total Liabilities	2,384.70	3,035.50	3,042.51	2,189.70	1,412.28
Minority Interest	11.2	18.3	17.25	10.74	11.15
Common Equity	3,045.70	2,490.90	2,284.12	2,228.51	2,090.63
Common Stock	0.7	0.7	0.74	0.76	90.97
Capital Surplus	186.4	39.4	39.39	39.39	39.39
Retained Earnings	2,793.20	2,402.40	2,189.37	2,151.08	1,939.36
Foreign Exchange Gain/Loss	66.2	52.5	54.62	43.94	21.57
Gain/Loss on Marketable Securities	−0.8	−4.1	0	−6.67	−0.65
Total Liabilities & Shareholders' Equity	5,441.60	5,544.70	5,343.88	4,428.94	3,514.07
Number of Shares (millions)	738.7	731.5	749.8	766.1	789.6

Exhibit 6. Starbucks Income Statement

In Millions	2009	2008	2007	2006	2005
Revenues	9,779.10	10,383.00	9,411.50	7,786.94	6,369.30
Cost of Goods Sold	4,301.30	4,590.10	3,975.05	3,153.38	2,578.17
Depreciation, Depletion & Amortization	563.3	604.5	491.24	412.63	367.21
Gross Income	4,914.50	5,188.40	4,945.21	4,220.94	3,423.92
Selling, General & Administrative Expenses	3,878.10	4,201.10	3,705.14	3,160.84	2,523.03

Exhibit 6. (*Continued*)

In Millions	2009	2008	2007	2006	2005
Other Operating Expenses	264.4	330.1	294.14	260.09	197.02
Operating Expenses — Total	9,007.10	9,725.80	8,465.56	6,986.93	5,665.43
Operating Income	772	657.2	945.94	800.02	703.87
Extraordinary Credit — Pretax	26.8	0	0	0	0
Extraordinary Charge — Pretax	337.9	266.9	N/A	N/A	21.2
Non-Operating Interest Income	15	9	40.62	20.69	17.13
Other Income/Expense — Net	–0.2	0	0	0	21.2
Earnings Before Interest and Taxes (EBIT)	475.7	399.3	986.56	820.71	721
Interest Expense on Debt	41.3	60.6	42.1	11.1	1.3
Interest Capitalized	2.9	7.2	3.9	2.7	N/A
Pretax Income	437.3	345.9	948.36	812.31	719.7
Income Taxes	168.4	144	383.73	324.77	301.98
Current Domestic Income Taxes	200.3	214.7	392.03	389.96	325.13
Current Foreign Income Taxes	26.3	40.4	31.18	12.4	14.11
Deferred Domestic Income Taxes	–58.2	–111.1	–39.49	–77.59	–37.26
Equity in Earnings	121.9	113.6	108.01	93.94	76.75
Net Income	390.8	315.5	672.64	581.47	494.47
Extraordinary Items	0	0	0	–17.21	0
Net Income Available to Common	390.8	315.5	672.64	581.47	494.47

Source: Thomson One.

Exhibit 7. Starbucks Cash Flow Statement

In Millions	2009	2008	2007	2006	2005
Net Income	390.80	315.50	672.64	581.47	494.47
Depreciation, Depletion & Amortization	563.30	604.50	491.24	412.63	367.21
Deferred Income Taxes & Investment Tax Credit	(69.60)	(117.10)	(37.33)	(84.32)	(31.25)
Other Cash Flow	273.70	380.30	45.38	(0.08)	121.52
Funds From Operations	1,158.20	1,183.20	1,171.93	909.69	951.94
Funds From Other Operating Activities	230.80	75.50	159.29	221.94	(28.33)
Decrease/Increase in Receivables	N/A	N/A	N/A	0.00	(49.31)
Decrease/Increase in Inventories	28.50	(0.60)	(48.58)	(85.53)	(121.62)
Increase/Decrease in Accounts Payable	(53.00)	(63.90)	36.07	104.97	9.72

(*Continued*)

Exhibit 7. (*Continued*)

In Millions	2009	2008	2007	2006	2005
Increase/Decrease in Income Taxes Payable	57.20	7.30	86.37	132.73	#N/A
Increase/Decrease in Other Accruals	N/A	N/A	38.63	54.42	22.71
Decrease/Increase in Other Assets/Liabilities	198.10	132.70	46.80	15.35	110.17
Net Cash Flow — Operating Activities	1,389.00	1,258.70	1,331.22	1,131.63	923.61
Capital Expenditures	445.60	984.50	1,080.35	771.23	643.99
Net Assets from Acquisitions	0.00	74.20	53.29	91.73	21.58
Increase in Investments	129.20	71.80	237.42	639.19	643.49
Decrease in Investments	116.00	95.90	225.66	700.32	1,095.67
Disposal of Fixed Assets	42.50	0.00	0.00	#N/A	0.00
Net Investing Activities	4.80	52.00	56.55	39.20	7.92
Net Cash Flow — Investing	421.10	1,086.60	1,201.95	841.04	221.31
Net Proceeds from Stock	57.30	112.30	176.94	159.25	163.56
Stock Repurchases and Redemptions	0.00	311.40	996.80	854.05	1,113.65
Long Term Borrowings	0.00	0.00	548.96	0.00	0.00
Change in Short Term Borrowings	(713.10)	2.20	10.25	423.00	277.00
Reduction in LT Debt	0.70	0.60	0.78	0.90	0.74
Net Financing Activities	14.30	13.00	89.55	117.37	0.00
Other Sources — Financing	15.90	14.70	93.06	117.37	0.00
Other Uses — Financing	1.60	1.70	3.51	0.00	0.00
Net Cash Flow — Financing	(642.20)	(184.50)	(171.89)	(155.33)	(673.83)
Effect Of Exchange Rate On Cash	4.30	0.90	11.27	3.53	0.28
Inc/Dec in Cash and Short Term Investments	330.00	(11.50)	(31.35)	138.80	28.76

Source: Thomson One.

Exhibit 8. Interest Rates

	1-Month	3-Month	6-Month	12-Month
LIBOR	0.2317	0.2501	0.3993	0.8979
Treasury Bills	0.05	0.08	0.18	0.42
	5-Year	**10-Year**	**20-Year**	**30-Year**
Treasury Bonds	2.65	3.85	4.6	4.65
	Daily	**Intraday**	**Intraday**	
		Low	High	
Federal Funds	0.12	0.05	0.375	
Prime Rate	3.25%			

Note: Rates as of January 2010.
Source: Federal Reserve Bank of New York and US Treasury Department.
LIBOR from: http://www.wsjprimerate.us/libor/libor_rates_history.htm.

Growth or Value? Future Yields?

John was aware that Starbucks' top management had talked, albeit obliquely, about future distributions. In the fourth quarter 2009 conference call, his boss, CFO Alstead, said, "We are evaluating how to distribute excess cash and what is the appropriate distribution strategy. We're having those discussions with our Board. And I would expect as we get somewhere to the latter half of our second quarter, then we will conclude that work and be ready to talk about what the next step is for us. So, more to come."

John knew that firms that paid dividends tended to be more mature firms, and that paying dividends could be interpreted as a signal that the firm's growth had slowed. Schultz made comments along these lines in the firm's most recent first quarter 2010 conference call in January 2010 stating that "For the first time, we were beginning to see traffic in our US stores slow; competitors were focusing their efforts on taking share from us; and like many fast-growing companies before us, we had allowed success to make us complacent. What we did not know 2 years ago was that we would have to undergo this top to bottom transformation against the backdrop of the worst global economic crisis of our generation."

Starbucks had been growing at a fast pace, but had been slowing down. With a beta of 0.75, IT was considerably less risky than the overall market. What dividend yield would be appropriate? Exhibit 9 contains

Exhibit 9. Dividend Paying Stocks

	Price May-10	Dividend	Dividend Yield (%)
AT&T	22.72	1.65	7.3
Kinder Morgan Energy Partners	60.98	4.2	6.9
Altria	19.74	1.34	6.8
Royal Dutch Shell	50.27	3.36	6.7
First Energy	37.6	2.2	5.9
American Electric Power	29.17	1.64	5.6
GlaxoSmithKline	34.7	1.871	5.4
Lockheed Martin	64.95	2.34	3.6
Johnson & Johnson	57	1.96	3.4
Caterpillar	52.4	1.68	3.2
Kellogg	47.67	1.5	2.80
Exxon Mobil	61.99	1.68	2.7

Source: Prices from Yahoo Finance; dividends from company websites.

some prices and yields for other major companies that pay dividends. Would the stock market place a negative interpretation on a decision to initiate a dividend and assume that the firm's high growth days were over? Would investors who expected Starbucks to deliver capital gains sell, potentially depressing the stock price, or would new shareholders want to purchase a newly dividend-paying stock? It was difficult to predict when the economy would recover and how Starbucks would react. Analyst year-end opinions about Starbucks' future were largely positive. For example, JP Morgan, Jefferies, and Piper Jaffray all listed Starbucks as a "buy" with the expectation of significant stock price growth over the next year, with target stock prices of $25, $25, and $26, respectively. The reports praised Starbucks' brand equity, margin recovery, and improved transactions and noted that the cost-cutting efforts of the previous year were bearing fruit. Morgan Stanley and Deutsche Bank were less optimistic, rating the company as "hold." Deutsche Bank's price target was only $19. Starbucks' price in December 2009, when the reports were written was $21, with 1-year growth rates predicted to be 19% to 24%. Morgan Stanley cited Starbucks' commitment to up to $1 billion in stock buybacks as a key value driver for the company. All of the analysts made note of Starbucks' successful cost-cutting efforts and expected them to continue to be a strong factor in the firm's future profitability. A summary of analyst expectations is contained in Exhibit 10.

John also remembered Alstead's statement that he considered dividend and share repurchase programs to be strong signals of a firm's financial health. He further stated that the firm had many profitable growth opportunities by evolving into a more diversified growth company and that shareholders would benefit both from returns on Starbucks' investments and from cash distributions.[7] John needed to take management's desires about the future direction of the firm into consideration in his report.

Starbucks' stock price had begun its recovery from the financial crisis. Was it likely to continue an upward trajectory? Was Starbucks a growth stock? A value stock? Starbucks stock split and stock price information is in Exhibits 11 and 12. As John drank his triple venti caramel macchiato, he pondered the complex recommendations his boss would need to make the final presentation about dividends, repurchases, and their impact on the firm.

[7]CFO Alstead remarks are adapted from Starbucks' second quarter 2010 conference call.

Exhibit 10. Analyst 2010 Estimates

Analyst Estimates 2010	Deutsche Bank	Piper Jaffray	J.P. Morgan	Morgan Stanley	Jeffries & Co.
P/E	21.7	23.0	17.7	20.0	19.8
EPS	$1.00	$1.00	$1.10	$1.18	$1.08
EPS Growth	24%	88%		15.6%	34.2%
PEG (Price/Earnings Growth)		1.3			
Revenue	$9.97 billion	$9.91 billion	$10.3 billion	$10.52 billion	$9.94 billion
Revenue Growth	2%	1.3%	2.5%	4.8%	1.7%
Domestic Same Store Revenue Growth	2.4%	0% (3% 2011)	3%	3%	2% (combination of domestic and international)
International Same Store Revenue Growth	0.3%	0% (3% 2011)	2%	3%	
EBIT	$1.14 billion	$1.11 billion	$1.22 billion	$1.45 billion	$1.2 billion
EBIT Growth	11.0%	3.6%	11.8%	9%	20.9%
EBIT Growth (Long Term)	8%				
EBIT Margin	11.4%	11.2–11.8%	11.9–13% in next 2 years	12.7% in base case; 14% in best case (with US store margins at 17%) and 10% in worst case	17–18% in next 5 years
Net Income	$750 million	$740.1 million			$821.3 million; profit margin of 8–8.6% in next 5 years
Risk Premium	6%				
Terminal Growth	3%				
Free Cash Flow (Cash Flow from Operations – Capital Exp.)			$813.5 million (Net income + Depreciation – Capital Expenditures)	$1.03 billion	
Cash from Operations				$1.58 billion	
Cash and Equivalents				$1.02 billion	

Exhibit 11. Starbucks' Stock Split History

September 29, 1993	Two for one
December 1, 1995	Two for one
March 19, 1999	Two for one
April 1, 2001	Two for one
October 21, 2005	Two for one

Source: Starbucks Investor Relation's website.

Exhibit 12. Starbucks' Stock Prices (Fiscal Year End)

October 1, 2005	$27.20
October 1, 2006	$36.30
October 1, 2007	$25.66
October 1, 2008	$12.63
October 1, 2009	$18.25
January 15, 2010	$22.06 (time of case)

Source: Yahoo Finance.

Analyst report highlights:

Deutsche Bank: "We note good traction around operational improvements domestically, which bodes well for further margin gains and improving comps. Importantly, the new concepts hone in on the company's strongest core equity: a great coffee experience. Regarding Via instant, CEO Howard Schultz is quite bullish given better taste and effective cost to consumer vs. competition, both at home and abroad. Finally, the international business appears to be re-staging with the ultimate goal of better profit growth, but the replacement of Martin Coles as international head suggests near-term results may be spotty."

Recommendation: Hold — 2010 Price Target: $19

Piper Jaffrey: "We believe the company warrants a 1.3′ PEG (Price/Earnings Growth) due to the company's continued dominant position in terms of brand equity, margin recovery, improved transaction trends, and continued benefits of FY09's cost-cutting initiatives."

Recommendation: Overweight — 2010 Price Target: $26

Jefferies & Co.: "Coming into 2010, we believe Starbucks has more top and bottom momentum than any other company in the restaurant sector. While admittedly late on the upgrade, we believe the likelihood of material EPS upside in 2010 leaves plenty of room for the shares to run."

Recommendation: Buy — 2010 Price Target: $25

Morgan Stanley: "With a rebounded top line, favorable comparisons, and cost cuts that should reach their full impact in December 2009, estimates could be understated for the current quarter, with cost savings and pricing benefits that will persist through the year. In FY2010, focus will move from cost-cutting to rekindling top-line growth through new platforms (Via, lower-cost store formats and international) and improving international margins. While management feels good about margin and top-line improvements, the greatest risk to shares remains that expectations get ahead of the company's ability to deliver." Morgan Stanley thought the firm would have increased capital expenditures to support its growth, estimating capital expenditures of $525 million, $550 million, and $575 million, respectively, in 2010, 2011, and 2012.

Recommendation: Equal Weight: Price Target: $22

J.P. Morgan: "Despite the stock's recent run-up, we continue to believe the company represents an excellent 'beat and raise' story with room for continued estimate upside relative to consensus as US comps continue to improve and the international margin story takes hold." J.P. Morgan also noted that Starbucks' cash position would increase, estimating a 2010 net debt to EBITDA ratio of –0.1 times and a net debt to free cash flow ratio of –0.2 times.[8] The J.P. Morgan report also noted that 2.52% of Starbucks' margin improvement is attributable to its cost savings campaign.

[8]Net debt is calculated as s firm's debt minus its cash. A negative net debt ratio means that Starbucks would have more cash than its debt. EBITDA is earnings before interest, taxes, depreciation and amortization.

Recommendation: Overweight — Price Target: $25

***Source*: Analyst reports.**

Deutsche Bank, "Starbucks Corporation: Not to Be 'out-coffeed'," December 9, 2009.
Jefferies & Company, "Starbucks Corp.," November 23, 2009.
J.P. Morgan, Starbucks: "US Momentum, International Opportunities in 2010," December 21, 2009.
Morgan Stanley, Starbucks Corp.: Notes from the Northeast," December 11, 2009.
Piper Jaffray, "Starbucks: Overweight," December 14, 2009.

https://doi.org/10.1142/9789811216749_0018

Case 18

Gateway Computers: Financing an Acquisition*

Susan White

University of Maryland, USA

Introduction

Gateway Computers just purchased eMachines and wanted to consolidate this purchase as well as finance its future growth. Gateway had success with convertible offerings in the past and wanted to choose among convertible debt, convertible preferred stock, and common equity. The firm needed to decide which financing option was the best fit for its current and future funds needs and to appropriately price the chosen financing vehicle.

It was almost Christmas Eve 2004 and Angela was not happy to be sitting at her desk instead of having dinner with her family. Her boss had asked her to finish up her report recommending which financing package Gateway Computers should choose to finance its expected 2005 growth. Gateway had drastically altered its operations during 2004, and after successful consolidation and restructuring, the company was looking at moving forward toward expansion in the coming year.

---

*The original version of this case was published by the author in the *Journal of Financial Education*, 36(3/4), Fall/Winter 2010, 143–154. The author and the editors thank the publisher of the journal for allowing us to incorporate the case in this book.

The Company

Gateway Computers sold desktop and notebook computers, servers, and personal computer-related products. In addition, Gateway offered customized websites (eSource) to facilitate order management requirements. For example, eMarketplace, part of its eSource service, was used to manage online purchases.

Gateway started its life in 1985 in an Iowa farmhouse, where Chairman Ted Waitt marketed personal computers. Its customer base soon expanded to include educational institutions, government, and businesses. Gateway went public in December 1993 with an initial public offering that raised $138.8 million with the sale of 8,720,000 shares at $15 a share. By 2004, Gateway was the third largest personal computer company in the US and was among the top ten worldwide. The firm had a market share of about 6.2% of the market, based on units shipped, according to International Data Corporation.

Gateway had four main business segments: direct, professional, retail, and international:

- The Direct division sold Gateway-branded products and services directly to customers, primarily through advertisements placed in traditional and electronic media through promotions at www.gateway.com and through its telephone call centers. Gateway used its trademarked black and white spot design on its product packaging in order to generate significant brand awareness and amass a loyal customer base.
- The Professional division focused on medium to large businesses, education and government. The firm had telephone-based and field sales teams, in addition to marketing through local, regional and national value-added resellers. In 2004, Gateway added customer sales options through internet-based tools. Gateway then set up customized websites, called eSource sites, to maintain its order management requirements. Gateway's eMarketplace facilitated online purchases of technology products that were designed to help businesses and other institutions operate efficiently.
- The Retail division sold Gateway and eMachines (which it acquired in early 2004) products directly through retailers, including consumer electronics stores, computer superstores, and warehouse clubs. Gateway products continued to be sold through television shopping retailers. Sales to Best Buy, for example, represented 23% of net sales for 2004, and the retail channel became Gateway's largest channel in 2004.

- Before 2004, the International Division sales were limited to Mexico and Canada. Gateway expanded its international markets to include those of eMachines in Japan and the United Kingdom. Gateway planned on further international expansion in Western Europe and Asia. About 5% of Gateway's 2004 revenues came from outside North America, compared to the negligible amounts in prior years.

Gateway Products

Gateway believed the future was in notebooks. Industry analysts predicted that notebook sales would exceed desktop sales in the US by 2007. Gateway wanted to capitalize on this trend by competing on quality, features, service and support, strong relationships with component suppliers, and competitive costs. Gateway's latest notebook line was built on thin-and-light platforms and featured extended battery life. Gateway professional desktops featured innovative designs, including the cool-and-quiet BTX architecture.

Gateway products and services included:

- *Desktop PCs*: Gateway offered a range of models for consumers under the Gateway and eMachines brand names, and for business customers under the Gateway brand. Certain models could be customized. Desktops represented about 54% of Gateway's total sales.
- *Notebook PCs*: Gateway notebooks were sold to consumer and professional customers. Gateway sold accompanying docking stations, wireless enablement, and various multimedia applications. The systems offered included ultraportable, convertible tablets and high-performance desktop replacement notebooks. Notebooks represented 22% of sales, and it is expected to increase in the future.
- *Monitors*: Gateway sold thin film transistor and cathode ray tube monitors under Gateway and eMachines brands, ranging in size from 15 to 19 inches.
- *Servers and Storage*: Gateway-branded servers and storage products were available to professional and small business customers. Each could be custom-built according to the customers' needs. Servers could be either tower-based or rack-mounted configurations with Windows operating software. Servers and storage products represented about 2% of revenues.
- *Convergence/Non-PC Products and Services*: This included peripherals, software, accessories, extended warranty services, training, internet access, TVs, digital music players, and enterprise system/networking

products and services. This segment represented about 22% of sales. Convergence products included plasma and LCD TVs and an MP3 Photo Jukebox, while peripherals comprised printers, scanners, PC accessories, CD and DVD burners, storage devices, surge protectors, and other accessories. Most items produced were made by other companies and simply marketed by Gateway, although a few had the Gateway brand. Over 6,000 products were sold through the Direct and Professional segments and through www.gateway.com. Fee-based service and support offerings included extended service plans, extended warranties, and accidental damage programs. Gateway's professional services support included technology planning services, implementation services such as custom installation and imaging, productivity services such as customized learning solutions, maintenance services, and end-of-life service such as data migration and asset recovery services.

Gateway partnered with financial institutions, which provided financing to purchase or lease Gateway products. About 26% of Gateway's Direct sales were financed by third parties.

Gateway expected to end 2004 with a backlog of unfilled orders of $78 million, compared to $80 million in the prior year. Normally, a backlog could be considered a good portent, but the company did not believe its backlog was a meaningful indicator of future sales, since customers could cancel or reschedule orders. Gateway's business was somewhat seasonal, with more retail sales in the second half of the year and more Professional sales in the second and third quarters.

Gateway Development and Intellectual Property

Gateway focused its product development on designing and developing competitively priced personal computer systems and non-PC products that met industry standards and incorporated features that Gateway believed its customers wanted. Gateway ended its desktop and server manufacturing operations in 2004, moving to third-party original design manufacturers. Gateway and its affiliates, Spotware Technologies, Inc. and Amiga Development LLC had about 400 US patents and a number of related foreign patents, most of which were issued in the 5 years prior. Gateway generally did not own the software in its machines, but instead licensed software from a number of developers, including Microsoft.

Industry Competition

The personal computer industry was highly competitive, with aggressive pricing, short life cycles, and customers who were very price sensitive. Gateway's primary competitors were Dell, Hewlett Packard, Apple Computer, IBM, and Toshiba, and in some regions, Acer and Fujitsu. Gateway expected continued pressure to lower its product prices, for the industry forecast for computer wholesaling and manufacturing was bleak. IBIS World Industry Report, for example, predicted real revenue growth of only 3% annually in the computer wholesaling industry and contraction of 4% a year in the computer manufacturing business.

Performance was highly dependent on the economic outlook — households and businesses both cut back on their technology purchases during economic downturns. The poor economic condition contributed to the expected decrease in selling prices. At the same time, competing imports were expected to increase, and both of these factors contributed to falling profitability in the industry. In addition, the computer wholesale business was in a mature life cycle stage, with falling profit margins and increasing technological innovation. The computer manufacturing business in the U.S. was in a declining life cycle stage, with new, enhanced products replacing existing ones, high technological change, and production capacity moving to low labor-cost countries.

eMachines Acquisition

Gateway acquired eMachines, Inc., a privately held personal computer company, on March 11, 2004. Gateway's professional and consumer businesses were expected to benefit from eMachines' low-cost structure, profitability, personal computer market strength, third-party retail network, and international presence. The purchase price of $262 million included $41 million in cash, $215 million in common stock, and direct transaction costs of $6 million. The common stock issued included 5.3 million shares of restricted common stock issued to eMachines management and contingent upon their continued employment with Gateway through 2005 and 2006. The common stock was valued as the average price over the 2-day period before and 2-day period after January 30, 2004, when the acquisition was announced. The restricted shares were valued at $27 million.

After the merger, Gateway completely overhauled the distribution of its products, closing 188 company-owned Gateway stores and launching

Gateway products in more than 3,000 retail locations, including Best Buy, Circuit City, CompUSA, Costco, Micro Center, and Office Depot. Gateway and eMachines products were sold in over 6,300 retail locations in North America alone. Gateway began its international expansion by entering the Japanese market with the Gateway brand and introducing eMachines in the Mexican retail market. Total employment in 2004 fell from 7,400 employees at the start of the year to only 1,900 expected employees by the end of 2004. The Gateway management team was headquartered in Irvine, California, and the company maintained product development and sales operations centers in North Sioux City, South Dakota, and Kansas City, Missouri.

Gateway's Operations and Financial Results

The year 2004 was a big turnaround year for the firm. Unit sales increased significantly; unit sales in the fourth quarter of 2004 alone were 128% above sales in the same period in 2003. The company posted two consecutive quarters of operating profits in quarters 3 and 4 of 2004, after 10 straight quarterly losses. Gateway also had the largest U.S. sequential personal computer growth of the major PC companies in the fourth quarter. Gateway's income statement and balance sheet are provided in Exhibits 1 and 2.

In addition, Gateway experienced a major shift in its distribution channels as it moved more heavily into retail sales. The firm intended to increase its professional and international sales as well. The professional market, which included business, government, and education, comprised about two-thirds of the PC market, but only a third of Gateway's sales. Gateway planned on investing in additional direct sales resources in education and government and in its online information technology infrastructure. Gateway also wanted to increase indirect channels, such as value-added resellers, solution providers, direct marketers, and business retail.

Gateway's Past Financing

In 1999, Gateway entered into a strategic relationship with America Online, Inc. (AOL) to increase its sales and distribution channels and capabilities. As part of the agreement, AOL agreed to invest $800 million — which was

Exhibit 1. Gateway Income Statements

Gateway Inc	Annual Balance Sheet (in Millions)											
	Dec-04	Dec-03	Dec-02	Dec-01	Dec-00	Dec-99	Dec-98	Dec-97	Dec-96	Dec-95	Dec-94	Dec-93
Assets												
Cash & Equivalents	343.509	1,089.037	1,066.721	1,166.054	614.070	1,336.371	1,328.467	632.249	516.360	169.429	243.889	132.242
Net Receivables	420.799	210.151	502.410	501.445	544.755	646.339	558.851	510.679	449.723	405.283	252.910	170.207
Inventories	196.324	114.136	88.761	120.270	315.069	191.870	167.924	249.224	278.043	224.916	120.229	177.529
Prepaid Expenses	58.270	49.549	99.783	0.000	0.000	0.000	0.000	0.000	0.000	0.000	0.000	0.000
Other Current Assets	80.715	200.604	197.697	335.155	793.166	522.225	172.944	152.531	74.216	66.561	37.132	20.542
Total Current Assets	1,399.617	1,663.477	1,955.372	2,122.924	2,267.060	2,696.805	2,228.186	1,544.683	1,318.342	866.189	654.160	500.520
Gross Plant, Property & Equipment	493.856	923.499	1,033.559	1,048.420	1,308.696	1,092.004	765.578	453.304	324.479	218.968	113.799	80.485
Accumulated Depreciation	391.199	592.586	552.548	439.991	411.282	346.344	234.590	116.835	82.114	48.705	24.489	16.864
Net Plant, Property & Equipment	102.657	330.913	481.011	608.429	897.414	745.660	530.988	336.469	242.365	170.263	89.310	63.621
Other Investments	3.792	14.642	43.678	88.170	0.000	0.000	0.000	0.000	0.000	0.000	0.000	0.000
Intangibles	251.011	13.983	23.292	36.304	165.914	52.302	65.944	82.590	0.000	0.000	0.000	0.000
Deferred Charges	9.559	0.000	0.000	0.000	0.000	0.000	0.000	0.000	0.000	0.000	0.000	0.000
Other Assets	5.151	5.423	6.054	131.030	822.156	459.921	65.262	75.529	112.704	87.559	27.110	0.140
Total Assets	1,771.787	2,028.438	2,509.407	2,986.857	4,152.544	3,954.688	2,890.380	2,039.271	1,673.411	1,124.011	770.580	564.281
Liabilities												
Long Term Debt Due In One Year	0.000	0.000	0.000	0.000	0.000	5.490	11.415	13.969	15.041	13.564	3.767	4.446
Notes Payable	50.000	0.000	0.000	0.000	0.000	0.000	0.000	0.000	0.000	0.000	0.000	0.000
Accounts Payable	532.329	415.971	278.609	341.122	785.345	898.436	718.071	488.717	411.788	235.064	183.299	126.328
Taxes Payable	114.090	0.000	0.000	0.000	0.000	0.000	0.000	26.510	40.334	27.905	0.200	2.800
Accrued Expenses	313.708	325.943	421.425	604.307	694.769	762.972	583.138	430.668	316.032	232.361	143.613	76.676

(Continued)

Exhibit 1. *(Continued)*

	Annual Balance Sheet (in Millions)											
Gateway Inc	**Dec-04**	**Dec-03**	**Dec-02**	**Dec-01**	**Dec-00**	**Dec-99**	**Dec-98**	**Dec-97**	**Dec-96**	**Dec-95**	**Dec-94**	**Dec-93**
Other Current Liabilities	112.525	257.090	240.315	200.599	150.920	142.812	117.050	44.042	16.574	16.397	17.996	44.594
Total Current Liabilities	1,122.652	999.004	940.349	1,146.028	1,631.034	1,809.710	1,429.674	1,003.906	799.769	525.291	348.875	254.844
Long Term Debt	0.000	0.000	0.000	0.000	0.000	2.998	3.360	7.240	7.244	10.805	27.131	29.145
Deferred Taxes	19.840	0.000	0.000	0.000	0.000	0.000	0.000	0.000	0.000	6.744	6.990	0.000
Investment Tax Credit	0.000	0.000	0.000	0.000	0.000	0.000	0.000	0.000	0.000	0.000	0.000	0.000
Other Liabilities	84.258	109.696	127.118	82.636	141.171	124.862	112.971	98.081	50.857	25.652	11.549	0.000
Total Liabilities	1,226.750	1,108.700	1,067.467	1,228.664	1,772.205	1,937.570	1,546.005	1,109.227	857.870	568.492	394.545	283.989
Equity												
Preferred Stock — Redeemable	0.000	197.720	195.422	193.109	0.000	0.000	0.000	0.000	0.000	0.000	0.000	0.000
Preferred Stock — Nonredeemable	0.000	200.000	200.000	200.000	0.000	0.000	0.000	0.000	0.000	0.000	0.000	0.000
Total Preferred Stock	0.000	397.720	395.422	393.109	0.000	0.000	0.000	0.000	0.000	0.000	0.000	0.000
Common Stock	3.749	3.244	3.240	3.239	3.239	3.200	1.566	1.541	0.768	0.746	0.724	0.724
Capital Surplus	950.675	734.550	732.760	731.623	741.646	656.870	365.986	299.483	289.512	280.447	274.400	274.352
Retained Earnings	(693.623)	(215.776)	310.518	630.222	1,657.402	1,408.844	976.823	629.020	525.261	274.326	100.911	5.216
Less: Treasury Stock	15.764	0.000	0.000	0.000	21.948	51.796	0.000	0.000	0.000	0.000	0.000	0.000
Common Equity	245.037	522.018	1,046.518	1,365.084	2,380.339	2,017.118	1,344.375	930.044	815.541	555.519	376.035	280.292
Total Equity	245.037	919.738	1,441.940	1,758.193	2,380.339	2,017.118	1,344.375	930.044	815.541	555.519	376.035	280.292
Total Liabilities & Equity	1,471.787	2,028.438	2,509.407	2,986.857	4,152.544	3,954.688	2,890.380	2,039.271	1,673.411	1,124.011	770.580	564.281
Common Shares Outstanding	372.216	324.392	324.072	323.973	323.403	319.286	313.138	308.256	307.024	298.212	289.584	289.536

Note: Note that the 2004 balance sheet does not include the $200 million that Gateway intends to issue. If issued by December 31, 2004, $300 million would be added to cash On the liabilities side of the balance sheet, $300 million would be added to the appropriate account, depending on the type of financing issued.

Source: Gateway 10K report, 2004

Exhibit 2. Gateway Income Statements

	Annual Income Statement											
Gateway Inc	4-Dec	3-Dec	2-Dec	1-Dec	Dec-00	Dec-99	Dec-98	Dec-97	Dec-96	Dec-95	Dec-94	Dec-93
Sales	3,649.73	3,402.36	4,171.33	5,937.90	9,600.60	8,645.56	7,467.93	6,293.68	5,035.23	3,676.33	2,701.20	1,731.66
Cost of Goods Sold	3,144.45	2,711.58	3,430.06	4,683.40	7,352.52	6,611.64	5,816.13	5,130.47	4,009.84	3,022.45	2,325.66	1,452.88
Gross Profit	505.283	690.788	741.267	1,254.50	2,248.08	2,033.92	1,651.80	1,163.22	1,025.39	653.881	375.536	278.785
Selling, General, & Administrative Expense	517.346	845.645	994.404	1,262.95	1,528.60	1,304.15	1,052.05	786.168	607.533	366.787	216.505	121.682
Operating Income Before Deprec.	−12.063	−154.857	−253.137	−8.457	719.477	729.775	599.751	377.047	417.857	287.094	159.031	157.103
Depreciation, Depletion, & Amortization	112.225	163.973	159.458	199.976	189.084	134.105	105.524	86.774	61.763	38.086	18.034	7.963
Operating Profit	−124.288	−318.83	−412.595	−208.433	530.393	595.67	494.227	290.273	356.094	249.008	140.997	149.14
Interest Expense	0.8	0	0	0	0	0	0	0	0	0	0	0
Non-Operating Income/ Expense	21.047	19.328	35.496	47.86	−102.693	67.809	47.021	27.189	26.622	13.085	5.106	4.848
Pretax Income	−104.041	−299.502	−377.099	−160.573	427.7	663.479	541.248	317.462	382.716	262.093	146.103	153.988
Total Income Taxes	−35.37	−101.83	−128.21	−54.59	145.42	225.58	184.02	107.94	130.12	89.11	49.68	52.36
Income Before Extraordinary Items & Discontinued Operations	−68.67	−197.67	−248.89	−105.98	282.28	437.90	357.22	209.52	252.59	172.98	96.43	101.63
Preferred Dividends	7.991	11.138	11.323	0	0	0	0	0	0	0	0	0
Available for Common	−76.66	−208.81	−260.21	−105.98	282.28	437.90	357.22	209.52	252.59	172.98	96.43	101.63
Earnings per Share	−0.206	−0.561	−0.699	−0.285	0.758	1.176	0.960	0.563	0.679	0.465	0.259	0.273

Note: Numbers in millions, except for per share information.

Source: Gateway 10K report, 2004

later reduced to $600 million — in Gateway over a 3-year period. In December 1999, Gateway sold $200 million of common stock to AOL for cash and shares of AOL, its first funding from AOL.

In 2001, Gateway received $200 million in exchange for a convertible note due on December 22, 2030, in connection with its agreement with AOL. This was Gateway's second funding from AOL. This note was retired in December 2001 when Gateway issued 50,000 non-voting Series C Redeemable Convertible Preferred Stock. The Series C preferred stock had a fair value of $193 million when it was issued. The preferred stock paid semi-annual 1.5% dividends. The preferred stock contained a put option. The holder could put the preferred stock to Gateway in December 2004, 2009, and 2014 at face value plus accrued and unpaid dividends. Gateway could satisfy the put option with cash or common stock, or some combination. The preferred stock was also convertible into 5,938,948 shares of common stock at any time prior to December 2020, provided Gateway's common stock traded over $33.68 for five consecutive days. Gateway was also allowed to redeem the preferred stock for cash at any time after December 22, 2004, for face value plus accrued and unpaid dividends.

Gateway also issued 50,000 shares of non-voting Series A Convertible Preferred Stock to AOL in exchange for $200 million in December 2001, its third and final funding from AOL. The Series A preferred stock provided dividends at an annual rate of 2.92%, payable quarterly. This preferred stock was scheduled to convert into 22,238,283 shares of Gateway common stock on December 24, 2004, based on a conversion rate of $8.99, as specified in the agreement with AOL.

On December 22, 2004, Gateway repurchased from AOL all the outstanding Series A and Series C preferred stock, along with 2.7 million shares of common stock, for $315.6 million. This payment included $280 million in cash and the application of a $35.6 million credit towards amounts due to Gateway from AOL. The 2.7 million shares were placed into Gateway's Treasury stock.

Gateway also issued warrants[1] to purchase 850,191 shares of common stock at $5.97 per share in exchange for consulting services during 2002.

---

[1]Warrents, issued by corporations, are the right to buy shares of stock at a specified price within a specified time period.

The warrants would expire on April 5, 2006. Prior to 2002, Gateway had issued warrants to purchase 624,750 shares of common stock at $8.92 per share. These warrants would expire on September 4, 2005.

Gateway's common stock information is in Exhibit 3. Information about Gateway's future obligations and cash flows from investing activities is detailed in Exhibit 4.

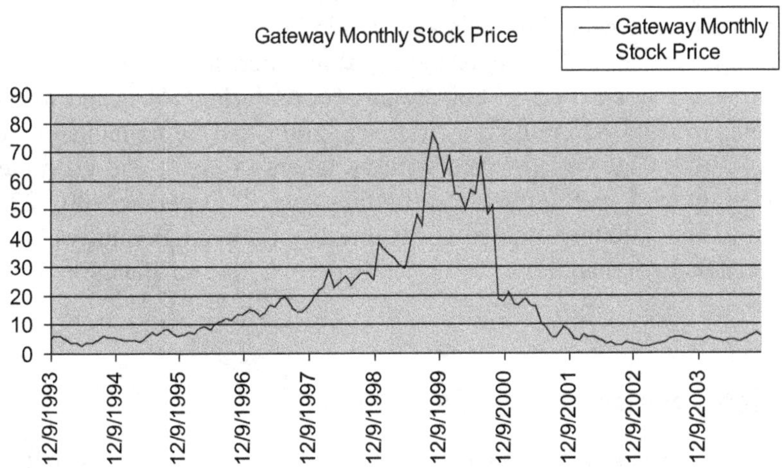

Exhibit 3. Stock Prices

Note: Standard deviation of monthly returns: 0.185.
Source: Yahoo Finance historical prices.

Exhibit 4. Gateway's Future Obligations

Payments Due by Period in Thousands					
	Total	**<1 Year**	**2–3 Years**	**4–5 Years**	**>5 Years**
Operating Leases	115,811	27,533	46,750	29,394	12,134
Royalty/Licensing Agreements	42,495	34,179	5,758	758	1,800
Debt, Including Estimated Interest Obligations	391,216	7,105	14,210	213,901	156,000
Estimated Purchase Obligations	101,278	101,278	—	—	—
Total	650,800	170,095	66,718	244,053	169,934

Source: Gateway 10K report, 2004.

Gateway's Current Financing

As of mid-December, Gateway had no debt, other than revolving credit facilities, allowing the company to borrow up to $200 million. Interest on borrowings was based on the LIBOR rate and was secured by the firm's accounts receivable and inventory. The credit facility covenants required Gateway to always maintain $150 million in unrestricted cash and marketable securities. The agreement would expire on October 31, 2009, at which time all outstanding balances would be due. As of December 30, Gateway had $50 million outstanding at an interest rate of 3.71%. The company did not expect to borrow any more during 2004, and in fact, expected to repay $25 million by March 1, 2005, and the remainder by the end of 2005. Gateway also had standby letters of credit and guarantees amounting to $36.9 million outstanding as of December 30, 2004. Gateway had 5,000,000 shares of preferred stock, at a par value of $0.01, authorized for issuance. As of December 30, 2004, no shares had been issued.

Which Financing and How Much?

Angela's boss suggested an analysis assuming a $300 million near-future need for funds. This would cover a number of contingencies, including buying back stock issued for the eMachines purchase if management decided the new stock was too dilutive, and could cover future expansion needs. Gateway believed the purchase of eMachines was just the first of its growth opportunities. The firm wanted a continuing source of funds both to incorporate its purchases into the firm and make future purchases. No dollar figure had been determined as needed over the next few years, but $300 million was reasonable for future acquisitions, given the size of the eMachines purchase.

Gateway was considering the sale of senior convertible notes in a private placement to institutional investors. Gateway's cost of debt for its existing credit was 3.71%, which would be the interest rate the firm would expect to pay on non-convertible debt. It expected that the rate on convertible debt would be considerably lower, because of the value of the conversion feature. It estimated that it could borrow at a rate of 1.5 to 2% and that at this interest rate, the convertible securities would have a conversion premium of about 40% above the current stock price. Gateway's bonds

Exhibit 5. Interest Rate Information

1-Year Treasury	2.67%
5-Year Treasury	3.6%
10-Year Treasury	4.23%

Source: Yahoo Finance.

were all callable, and they expected that the firm would call the convertibles when the stock price was 15% above the conversion price. Gateway's stock price as of year-end 2004 was $6.02. Gateway's current stock price information is contained in Exhibit 3. Exhibit 4 contains information about Gateway's future obligations and Exhibit 5 has risk-free interest rates.

Another option for Gateway was the issuance of convertible preferred stock. Up to 5,000,000 shares of $100 par value convertible preferred stock were authorized, although Gateway did not believe it would need, or want, to issue the full authorized amount. The preferred stock would carry a dividend of 1.5 to 2%, as would the convertible debt. The preferred stock conversion value would also be about 40% above the current stock price. The preferred stock would be callable, but again, Gateway expected it would not call the stock at the exact moment that the stock traded for 40% above its current price. More likely, Gateway would call the preferred when the common stock price was 15% above the conversion price.

The final option was the issuance of common shares. The stock price had been climbing upward reasonably steadily, and the stock price reached $6.02 on December 30, 2004. While this was slightly below the 2004 high of $6.92 reached on December 1, it was considerably higher than the low for the year on June 14 of $3.67. With transaction costs, Gateway thought it could issue common shares at $5.25 a share.

Of the options, what should Angela recommend? Are these options sufficient? What about considering straight debt or nonconvertible preferred stock? What financing vehicle would best suit Gateway's needs with financing obligations that Gateway could handle without difficulty?

https://doi.org/10.1142/9789811216749_0019

Case 19

JetBlue Airways Corporation Aircraft Leasing versus Buying

Ivan E. Brick and Harvey A. Poniachek

Rutgers Business School, USA

Part I. Leasing Versus Borrowing

A lease is a contractual agreement between a lessor who owns an asset and lessee who obtains the right to use the asset in exchange for periodic payments to the lessor.[1] Leasing could be deemed as an alternative to purchasing assets where the lessor, the owner, retains title to the assets and the lessee pays for its use.[2] Leasing is popular and accounts for 1/3 of the capital investment of US companies. There are several types of leases, including:

1. Traditional leases,[3]
2. Sale-and-leaseback transactions,

---

[1] Stephen A. Ross, Randolph W. Westerfield, Jeffrey F. Jaffe, and Bradford D. Jordan, *Corporate Finance*, 11th ed. (McGraw Hill Education, 2019), Chapter 21, Leasing (RWJ).

[2] Jonathan Berk and Peter DeMarzo, *Corporate Finance*, 4th ed. (Pearson, 2017), Chapter 25, Leasing (BD).

[3] Prior to 2019, accounting standards required for the lessee to distinguish between long-term (known as financial or capital leases) and short-term leases (operating leases). However, the passage of Accounting Standard Codification (ASC) 842, which requires a financial lessee to recognize assets and liabilities on the balance sheet for leases with terms of more than 12 months, that distinction is no longer valid.

3. Combination leases, and
4. Synthetic leases.

Sales-and-leaseback arrangements occur when a firm sells its property to another firm and simultaneously leases the property back. That is, the seller receives the purchase price from the buyer and retains the use of the property. Leases offered under a variety of terms are called combination leases. They contain cancellation clauses and prepayment provisions. Synthetic leases are utilized in real estate where a firm seeking to acquire real estate establishes a special purpose entity (SPE) that obtains the funding constituting 97% debt and 3% equity. The SPE would then acquire the asset and lease the property to the firm for 3 to 5 years with an option to extend the lease.

Financial Theory of Leasing

In a perfect market, the cost of leasing is equivalent to the cost of purchasing and reselling the (residual) asset, according to the following equation.[4]

$$\text{PV(Leasing payments)} = \text{Purchase price} - \text{PV(Residual value)}$$

Instead of leasing, you could obtain a loan for the purchase of the asset,[5] where

$$\text{PV(Loan payments)} = \text{Purchase price}$$

$$\text{PV(Leasing payments)} - \text{PV(Residual value)} = \text{PV(Loan payments)}$$

How should a firm decide whether to buy or lease an asset? In a perfect market, the decision is irrelevant, but in a market with various frictions, such as taxes, the benefit and cost need to be considered.

Leasing for Corporations

Leasing is a form of financing. The choice that the firm makes is either to purchase the asset and finance it through normal means (e.g., debt, retained earnings, and new equity financing) or by leasing. Intuitively,

[4] Jonathan Berk and Peter DeMarzo, *Corporate Finance*, 4th ed. (Pearson, 2017), Ch. 25, Leasing, 891 pp.

[5] *Ibid.*

you choose to lease the asset instead of purchasing if and only if the cost of leasing is lower than the cost of buying.

To evaluate the lease, one must understand the tax implications of the lease. There are two types of lease arrangements as far as the IRS is concerned. The lease is classified as a **true lease** if (1) the life of the lease is less than 80% of the life of the asset and (2) that the user (lessee) does not have the right to purchase the asset at the end of the life of the lease at significantly lower price than the prevailing market price. Otherwise the lease is classified as an **installment sale**. If the lease is a true lease then the lease payment is tax deductible to the lessee and the lessor receives the tax benefits of depreciation.

In this chapter, we will evaluate the benefits of leasing by taking the present value of the incremental cash flows of leasing compared to buying. That is, we want to know how much better off is the firm to lease the asset instead of buying it. To determine whether leasing is beneficial, we want to determine the difference in the cash flows if the firm leases the assets as opposed to buying them.

The main benefit of leasing is that the firm does not have to pay the purchase price for the asset. Let us denote the purchase price of the asset as I. The firm pays the lessor lease payments (which we will assume for now are constant through the life of the asset). However, if the lease is a true lease, the lease payments are tax deductible. Let Lease represent the periodic lease payment and T denote the tax rate, then the periodic incremental after-tax cash flow is Lease $(1 - T)$. Furthermore, the lessee no longer can claim as a tax deduction the depreciation expense of the asset. Again, assuming straight-line depreciation, the incremental cost of the lease of losing the tax benefits of depreciation is T * Dep, where Dep is the annual depreciation expense. In addition, the lessee does not have rights to the salvage value of the asset as it belongs to the lessor. We, thus compare the present value of the initial payment saved to the incremental cash flows the lessee loses to the lessor. As is usually done in capital budgeting, we use an after-tax discount rate.

Assume that Company A enters into a lease agreement for a highly automated packing machinery valued at $100,000 for 5 years at the cost of $20,000 each year payable at the beginning of each year. The after-tax interest rate is the appropriate discount rate for the lease. Assuming that the company's cost of borrowing is 7%, the statutory tax rate is 21% and the after-tax interest rate is 5.53% (7% × (1 – 0.21)). In this example, we will assume the lease is a true lease despite the lease term equals the length of the life of the asset.

Exhibit 1. Cash Flow of a True Lease ($, 000)

	0	1	2	3	4	5
Avoiding the Purchase Price on New Machine	100					
Lost Depreciation Tax Shield		–4.2	–4.2	–4.2	–4.2	–4.2
Lease Payments	–20	–20	–20	–20	–20	
Tax Shield on Lease Payment	4.2	4.2	4.2	4.2	4.2	
Cash Flow on Lease	84.2	–20	–20	–20	–20	–4.2

$$\text{NPV lease} = 84.2 - 20/(1.0553) - 20/(1.0553)^2 - 20/(1.0553)^3 - 20/(1+0.0553)^4 + 4.2/(1.0553)^5 = 11.08928.$$

The lease payments are contractual obligations like the principal and interest payments on secured debt and could be deemed as debt service payments. The tax benefits of depreciation that are lost should be the same risk as debt since generally depreciation benefits are in jeopardy only if the firm is in financial distress. Let T denote the tax rate, R denote the cost of debt and WACC denote the after-tax weighted average cost of capital. A formula that one can use to analyze the lease versus purchase decision is given below:

Incremental benefit of leasing =

$$I - \sum_{t=1}^{n} (\text{Lease payment}(1-T) + T * \text{ Depreciation})(1+R(1-T))^t$$

$$- \text{ After-tax salvage value} / (1+\text{WACC})^n.$$

This leaves us with the question as to why we have two different discount rates? Note that the cash flows discounted by *R*, the cost of debt, are generally lot less risky than the typical cash flows of a project. For example, once you sign the lease contract, you must pay the lease payment. It is like debt! You also know that the tax laws require you to lose the tax benefits of depreciation which are valuable only as long as you are solvent. The life of the lease is denoted as *n*. Also, we snuck in the WACC as our discount rate for salvage value. This is not necessarily correct. The point that is being made is that generally the estimate of the salvage value is far less certain than the lease payment or the depreciation benefit. We need another discount rate for that part of the formula. Instead of making one up, we are using the weighted average cost of capital, which is certainly greater than the after-tax cost of debt. Naturally, the more confident you are about the estimate of the salvage value, the closer the second discount rate should be to the after-tax cost of debt.

Example of Leasing in a Perfect World Without Taxes

The purchase price of a machine is \$100,000, its expected residual value after 5 years is \$30,000, the APR is 6% with monthly payments at the end of the month (or a periodic rate of .5% per month) and compounding. The monthly lease payments in a perfect capital market without taxes is found as follows:

$$\text{PV(Lease payments)} = 100{,}000 - 30{,}000/(1 + 0.005)^{60} = \$77{,}758.83$$

$$\$77{,}758.83 = L + L \times [1 - 1/(1 + 0.005)^{60}]/(0.005)$$

$$L = \$1{,}503.30 \text{ per month}$$

Alternatively, you purchase a \$100,000 machine by borrowing the funds for 5 years at 6% APR and subject to monthly debt payments due at the end of each month with a balloon payment of \$30,000 at the end of the fifth year. Applying the present value of an annuity formula, the loan's monthly debt service payments are as follows:

$$M \times [1 - 1/(1 + 0.06/12)^{60}]/0.005 + 30{,}000/(1.005)^{60} = 100{,}000$$

$$M = \$1{,}503.30 \text{ monthly payments}$$

As shown above, in a perfect market the cost of leasing and purchasing assets is equivalent to the cost of borrowing to purchase the asset.

Example: True Lease

As the CFO of Mantle Inc., you are considering whether or not you should purchase or lease an asset that will increase your firm's sales. Assume that the WACC of your firm is 12% and your cost of borrowing is 8%. You are considering purchasing an asset for \$1 million. The asset has a 5-year life and the depreciation expense is \$200,000 per year. The expected incremental annual sales are \$1.15 million per annum and the incremental costs are 74% of sales. There is no working capital associated with the project. Assume that the salvage value of the asset is zero at the end of the fifth year. Alternative to purchasing the asset, you may lease the asset for

\$230,000 per year for 5 years. Let the tax rate equal 34%. Assume that the IRS is generous and it allows us to treat the lease as a true lease so that the lease payments are tax deductible to your firm. This means that should you lease the asset, you will not be able to take tax deductions for the depreciation expense. (In reality, this lease should be treated as an installment sale which has different tax implications. But the true lease assumption is a useful pedagogical framework that will enhance, hopefully, your understanding of the lease versus buy decision. Later on in the case you will learn more about the cash flow implications of an installment sale.) Should you lease, buy or reject the project?

We begin the solution by first finding the NPV of the project without the lease option. Why do we do that? Let's leave that question open for now and we will answer that question fairly soon. Exhibit 2 summarizes the cash flows for the project.

The NPV of the project is given by $-\$1{,}000{,}000 + \$265{,}340 * A_{5,12\%} = -\$42{,}508.68$. Instead of writing the annuity formula, we use the notation $\$265{,}340 * A_{5,12\%}$ which is equivalent to using your financial calculator by using the following inputs: $N = 5$, $i = 12\%$, and PMT = 265,340. If there were no leasing option, then you would reject the project. However, you have the option to lease the asset for \$230,000 per annum. Recall that the incremental benefit of the lease is given by:

$$I - \sum_{t=1}^{n} (\text{Lease payment}(1-T) + T * \text{ Depreciation}) / (1 + R(1-T))^t$$
$$- \text{ After-tax salvage value} / (1 + \text{WACC})^n.$$

We can plug into the above formula, noting that I = \$1 million, lease payment = \$230,000, depreciation = \$200,000, T = .34 and R = 8%. In other words, the incremental value of this lease is given by:

$$\$1{,}000{,}000 - [\$230{,}000(.66) + .34(\$200{,}000)]A_{5,5.28\%} = \$55{,}702.$$

Exhibit 2. The cash flow of the project without the lease option

	$t = 0$	$t = 1–5$
Sales		\$1,150,000
– Costs		–\$851,000
– Long-Term Investment	–\$1,000,000	
– T(Sales – Costs – Dep)		–\$33,360
= Total Cash Flow	–\$1,000,000	\$265,340

This means that leasing is better than buying by \$55,702. Hence, if we were to lease the asset, the true NPV is –\$42,508.68 + \$55,702 = \$12,193.32. In other words, the lease terms were so generous, it made an unprofitable project profitable.

One question that remains is why we exclude the benefits of the assets that are being leased. The reason is that these benefits are not incremental since those benefits exist whether the firm leases or purchases the assets. For example, assume that a company considers buying or leasing a machine that costs \$100,000 and could save it \$60,000 annually for 5 years. Assume a tax rate of 21%. The issue before the company is whether to lease or buy? The analysis is shown in Exhibit 3 in the same way we showed the analysis in Exhibit 1.

Depreciation and its tax shield effects are derived as follows: (\$100,000/5) × 0.21).

1. As shown above, the company has an after-tax operating savings of \$47,400 from the use of a machine regardless of whether it buys or leases.

Exhibit 3. Cash Flows of Purchasing and Leasing

	0	**1**	**2**	**3**	**4**	**5**	**PV**
Buy	(100,000)						
After-Tax Operating Savings		47,400	47,400	47,400	47,400	47,400	
Depreciation Tax Benefit		4,200	4,200	4,200	4,200	4,200	
Total	(100,000)	51,600	51,600	51,600	51,600	51,600	
Lease							
Lease Payments		(20,000)	(20,000)	(20,000)	(20,000)	(20,000)	
Tax Benefit of Lease		4,200	4,200	4,200	4,200	4,200	
After-Tax Operating Savings		47,400	47,400	47,400	47,400	47,400	
Total		31,600	31,600	31,600	31,600	31,600	
Lease Minus Buy	100,000	(20,000)	(20,000)	(20,000)	(20,000)	(20,000)	
Present Value at 8% * (1 – 0.21)	100,000	(18,811)	(17,693)	(16,641)	(15,652)	(14,722)	**16,481**

2. If the company leases, it could save $100,000 in the initial cash *flow* in Year 0.
3. In leasing the machine, the company gives up the depreciation tax benefits.
4. If the company leases the machine, it must pay **$20,000** rent per year for 5 years, which is due at the end of the first year.

Please note that the operating savings are listed both in the purchase and lease options of the table. When we take the difference between purchasing versus leasing, operating savings are netted out. Hence, our formula above denotes the incremental value of the lease. It only tells you how much better of you are leasing versus buying. Hence, if purchasing the asset with no lease option had an NPV of –$30,000, then the incremental value of the lease of $16,481 would still make purchasing the asset not profitable.

Example: Installment Sale

To value an installment sale lease, we first construct a cash flow analysis for the leased assets and then apply the NPV in the manner described below. Consider the following example. Assume that Company A enters into a lease agreement for a highly automated packing machinery valued at $100,000 for 5 years at the cost of $21,500 each year payable at the beginning of each year. Assume that the life of the asset is also 5 years, and therefore the lease is considered to be an installment sale. Assuming that the company's cost of borrowing is 7% then with a statutory tax rate of 21% the after-tax interest rate is 5.53 (7 × (1 – 0.21)). Recall that our lease formula is given by:

$$I - \sum_{t=1}^{n} (\text{Lease payment}(1-T) + T * \text{ Depreciation}) / (1 + R(1-T))^t$$
$$- \text{ After-tax salvage value} / (1 + \text{WACC})^n.$$

However, since lessor is able to deduct the depreciation, expense is no longer an incremental cash flow loss to the lessor. Moreover, since only the implicit interest portion of the lease is tax deductible, the term lease payment (1 – *T*) should be replaced by [Interest portion of the lease

(1 – *T*) + Principal portion of the lease]. Accordingly, the incremental cash flows are given below:

	0	1	2	3	4
Lease Payment	21.5	21.5	21.5	21.5	21.5
Implicit Interest Rate	3.75%				
Principal Balance	$78.50	$59.95	$40.70	$20.72	$0.00
Implicit Interest Payment		$2.95	$2.25	$1.53	$0.78
Principal Payment		$18.55	$19.25	$19.97	$20.72
After-Tax Lease Payment		$20.88	$21.03	$21.18	$21.34
Value of Lease Payments	$4.61				

We are assuming the initial investment is 100 and the annual lease payment is 21.5, payable at the beginning of the year. The IRS would calculate the implicit interest rate of the loan, using the excel function =rate(4,21.5,–78.5,0,0). Since you are making the first payment at time zero, then the amount borrowed is only 78.5. The implicit interest rate is therefore 3.75%. We then figure out the principal balance for each subsequent year using the following steps based upon loan amortization. Note that the interest portion and the principal portion of the lease payment must equal to the total annual lease payment. The after-tax lease payment as (1 – *T*) implicit interest payment + the implicit principal payment. We then discount the yearly total after-tax lease payment by 5.53% and subtract that out from 78.5 which yields a profit of $4.61. Note that we do not include the depreciation expense since that is not an incremental cash flow that is lost since with a financial lease or borrowing the lessee is able to deduct the depreciation expense.

Lease Accounting Guidelines

The Financial Accounting Standard Board (FASB) issued Statement of Financial Accounting Standards (FAS) No. 13, Accounting for Leases, in November 1976, which was years later codified as Accounting Standard Codification (ASC) 840. FAS No. 13 classified leases from the standpoint of the lessee in terms of *Capital leases and Operating leases*. If at its inception a lease met one or more of the following four criteria, the lease was classified as a capital lease by the lessee. Otherwise, it was classified as an operating lease.

1. The lease transfers ownership of the property to the lessee by the end of the lease term.
2. The lease contains a bargain purchase option for the lessee at the end of lease contract.
3. The lease term is equal to 75% or more of the estimated economic life of the leased property.
4. The present value at the beginning of the lease payments equals or exceeds 90% of the fair value of the leased property.

Under FAS No. 13, financial leases were present value of their lease payments and appeared on the balance sheet, whereas all other leases were classified as operating leases and were reported off-balance sheet. Firms often preferred to categorize leases as operating leases to keep them off the balance sheet. Due to such widespread abuse, FASB issued in 2016 new rules that went into effect in early 2019.

On February 25, 2016, The Financial Accounting Standards Board issued an Accounting Standards Update 2016-02, also known as Accounting Standard Codification (ASC) 842, that requires a lessee to recognize assets and liabilities on the balance sheet for leases with terms of more than 12 months. The ASU went into effect for public companies for fiscal years beginning after December 15, 2018, while private companies have to follow the new accounting requirements from December 15, 2019 onward. ASC 842 represents a significant overhaul of the accounting treatment for operating leases that ends one of the largest forms of off-balance sheet accounting phenomenon. Moreover, the company would generally have to restate its balance sheet for prior leases that were categorized as operating leases. Under the new financial reporting requirements for lessees, companies will no longer be able to structure lease agreements to achieve off-balance-sheet reporting and will, in many cases, have to monitor the effect of this change on their debt-to-capital ratio and related debt covenants, among other things. ASC 842 defines a lease as the right to control the use of identified property for a period of time in exchange for consideration. Since December 15, 2018, lessees of financial leases who are public companies must follow several significant requirements:

- Recognize a right-of-use asset and a lease liability on the balance sheet, initially measured at the present value of the lease payment, on the balance sheet.
- Recognize interest on the lease liability on the income statement.
- Classify repayments of the principal portion of the lease liability and payments of interest on the lease liability in the statement of cash flows.

The treatment of operating and finance leases will differ on the income statement under the new ASC 842 standard. For finance leases, the interest and amortization of the lease are presented separately on the income statement. However, for operating leases, the two are combined into a single line item.

Part II. JetBlue Airways Corporation[6]

Overview of the Company

JetBlue Airways Corporation (JetBlue or JB) is New York's Hometown Airline. In 2018, JetBlue carried over 42 million Customers with an average of 1,000 daily flights and served 105 destinations in the United States, the Caribbean, and Latin America. JB was incorporated in Delaware in August 1998 and commenced service on February 11, 2000. As of the end of 2018, it is the sixth largest passenger carrier in the US based on available seat miles (ASMs). JB believes its differentiated product and culture combined with its competitive cost structure enables it to compete effectively in the high-value geographies it serves. Looking to the future, JB plans to continue to grow in its high-value geographies, invest in industry-leading products, and provide award-winning service by its more than 22,000 dedicated employees. Going forward, JB believes that it will continue to differentiate itself from other airlines, enabling it to continue to attract a greater mix of customers and to drive further profitable growth.

[6]Based on the Annual Report and 10K.

JB is focused on delivering solid results for its shareholders, customers, and crewmembers.

The US airline industry is extremely competitive, challenging and results are often volatile. It is uniquely susceptible to external factors such as fuel costs, downturns in domestic and international economic conditions, weather-related disruptions, the spread of infectious diseases, the impact of airline restructurings or consolidations, and military actions or acts of terrorism. JB operates in a capital and energy-intensive industry that has high fixed costs, as well as heavy taxation and fees. Airline returns are sensitive to slight changes in fuel prices, average fare levels, and passenger demand.

The industry's principal competitive factors include fares, brand and customer service, route networks, flight schedules, aircraft types, safety records, code-sharing and interline relationships, in-flight entertainment and connectivity systems, and frequent flyer programs. Price competition is intense in airline industry. JB's ability to operate successfully and grow in this environment depends on, among other things, its ability to operate at costs equal to or lower than our competitors.

Aircrafts

As of December 31, 2018, JB operated a fleet consisting of 63 Airbus A321 aircraft, 130 Airbus A320 aircraft and 60 Embraer E190 aircraft as summarized below[1]:

Aircraft	Owned	Capital Leased	Operating Leased	Total
Airbus A320	115	4	11	130
Airbus A321	60	2	1	63
Embraer E190	30		30	60
Total	205	6	42	253

As of December 31, 2018, their aircraft leases had an average remaining term of approximately 5 years, with expiration dates between 2019 and 2028. They have the option to extend most of these leases for additional periods or to purchase the aircraft at the end of the related lease term.

Ground Facilities

Airports

All of their facilities at the airports are under leases or other occupancy agreements. Space is leased directly or indirectly from the local airport authority on varying terms dependent on prevailing practices at each airport. The passenger terminal service facilities consisting of ticket counters, gate space, operations support area, and baggage service offices generally have agreement terms ranging from less than 1 year to 5 years. They can contain provisions for periodic adjustments of rental rates, landing fees, and other charges applicable under the type of lease. Under some of these agreements, they are responsible for the maintenance, insurance, utilities, and certain other facility-related expenses and services.

Others (Hangars, Warehouses, Corporate Offices)

JB leases the following hangars and airport support facilities at its focus cities:

- New York — At John F. Kennedy International Airport, they have a ground lease agreement which expires in 2030 for an aircraft maintenance hangar, an adjacent office, and warehouse facility, including a storage facility for aircraft parts. These facilities accommodate our technical support and catering operations. They also lease a building from the Port Authority of New York and New Jersey which is mainly used for ground equipment maintenance work.
- Boston — A ground lease agreement which expires in 2022 for a building which includes an aircraft maintenance hangar and support space. They also have leases for facilities to accommodate our ground support equipment maintenance and catering operations.
- Orlando — A ground lease agreement for a hangar which expires in 2035. We also occupy a training center, JetBlue University, with a lease agreement expiring in 2035 which we use for the initial and recurrent training of our pilots and inflight crewmembers, as well as support training for our technical operations and airport crewmembers.

JB's primary corporate offices are located in Long Island City, New York, with its lease expiring in 2023. For offices in Salt Lake City, the lease expires in 2022.

Contractual Obligations

(in Billions)	Total	2019	2020	2021	2022	2023	Hereafter
Debt and Capital Lease Obligations	1.9	0.4	0.3	0.3	0.3	0.2	0.4
Lease Commitments	1	0.2	0.1	0.1	0.1	0.1	0.4
Other	11.5	1.5	1.7	1.7	1.6	1.9	3.1
Total	14.4	2.1	2.1	2.1	2	2.2	3.9

Off-Balance Sheet Arrangements

Prior to 2019, none of JB's operating lease obligations are reflected on its consolidated balance sheets. Although some aircraft lease arrangements are with variable interest entities, as defined by the Consolidations topic of the Codification, none of them require consolidation in the financial statements. The decision to finance these aircraft through operating leases rather than through debt was based on an analysis of the cash flows and tax consequences of each financing alternative and a consideration of liquidity implications. JB is responsible for all maintenance, insurance, and other costs associated with operating these aircraft. However, the company is not obligated to provide any residual value or other guarantees to our lessors.

Current maturities of long-term debt and capital leases: $309 million (2018) and $196 million (2017).
Long-term debt and capital lease obligations: $1,361 million (2018) and $1,003 million (2017).

Part III. The Assignment

Linda Spencer, a Rutgers Business School graduate, class of 2010, with an MBA in Finance and Supply Chain, is Managing Director in a prestigious North East consulting firm. She oversees a staff of a dozen professionals that specialized in investment and capital budgeting. On May 2, 2019, she attended a fundraising event in New York where she met several executives from JetBlue. The brief discussion related to their interest in leasing or purchasing several aircrafts from Airbus and possibly from Boeing and the merit of leasing versus borrowing and purchasing.

Ms. Spencer was invited to JetBlue for a discussion of the company's leasing versus buying concerns and asked to make a presentation on the above issues that could possibly yield to a lucrative engagement for her firm. Upon returning to her office she assigned her staff the following task:

1. Provide a general comparison between leasing and purchasing; determine the benefit and cost of leasing versus buying a 777-300ER for $361.5 million. The life of the aircraft is 30 years. Boeing is providing two options for the lease. One is a 30-year lease whereby JetBlue pays an annual lease payment equal to 4.2% of the total price of the aircraft. Assume a straight-line depreciation with no salvage value at the end of 30 years. The second option is a 12-year lease where the annual lease payment is 4% of the total payment. Boeing is willing to let you purchase the plane at the end of the lease term at its stated book value. Which is the better option? Assume a 30-year bond YTM of 3.70%, cost of equity of 12%, and statutory tax rate of 21%.
2. What are the cash flows and accounting implications of leasing versus borrowing under the new accounting regulations?
3. What are your recommendations for JetBlue in light of their 2018 financial conditions as reflected by their Annual Report and 10K?

https://doi.org/10.1142/9789811216749_0020

Case 20

Warrants and Convertibles

Elizabeth Chorvat[*] and Terrence Chorvat[†]

[*]*University of Notre Dame, USA*

[†]*George Mason University, USA*

This case addresses securities that allow the holders to acquire stock directly from the issuing corporation either by purchase (warrants) or by exchanging convertible debt of the corporation for its stock. One can deem warrants and convertible debt as two different types of the same category of securities. That is, convertible notes can be thought of as debt with an embedded warrant allowing one to view both of them as securities that allow the holder to purchase stock directly from the issuer. The case discusses when a corporation might want to issue these types of securities and examines in particular the issuances of convertible debt by Amazon and Tesla. These two examples illustrate different strategies for the use of these securities.

The Problem

You are a financial consultant to two relatively young companies, Amazon and Tesla, wishing to raise capital. The technology on which these businesses are based has only recently emerged and the profit potential, while quite large, is essentially unproven. Your projections for future cash flow indicate that the company is not likely to generate positive cash for a few years.

1. How might the projections of the future cash flow influence your decision of whether to use convertible debt?
2. How might it influence the decisions regarding the structure of this debt? For example, how might it affect the preferred maturity of the debt?
3. Does it make a difference if the proceeds of the debt offering will be used to expand the business into a new area or to fund continuing capital needs of an existing business?
4. What characteristics of the business plan would incline you to issue convertible notes?
5. What factors would influence the optimal mix of equity, convertible notes, and straight debt in raising new capital for the business.

Introduction

Warrants are a form of call option. That is, they give the holder the right, but not the obligation, to purchase a particular number of shares of the stock of the issuer at a particular price (the strike price). The shares acquired via a warrant are not currently traded but are purchased from the issuing company with the exercise price going to the company as a contribution to capital rather than to an outside holder. As a result, the exercise of a warrant adds to the paid-in capital of the corporation and increases the number of outstanding shares.

Convertible securities are debt issued by a corporation that can be converted into equity of that corporation, and one can think of these securities as debt with an embedded warrant. This embedded warrant has a strike price based on a conversion ratio which is specified at the time of the issuance. The conversion ratio determines the strike price of this embedded warrant. Typically, the ability of the holders to convert their debt into shares of the corporation is conditioned on the occurrence of a number of events. For example, the agreement may require that the stock price of the corporation rises above a certain level before the debt becomes convertible into stock, or conversely that it becomes callable as debt when the stock rises above a certain level. Another common requirement is that a certain amount of time passes before the debt becomes convertible, which might be the term of the debt itself. In addition, the conversion ratio may vary depending on the occurrence of events specified at the time of the issuance of the note.

The purpose of the issuance of either of these types of securities is to raise capital for business operations of the firm. In general, convertible notes immediately raise an amount of capital equal to the principal amount of the debt.[1] However, if the warrants are compensatory then they will generally not immediately increase the capital of the corporation.[2] If warrants are issued in exchange for cash, then the amount paid to purchase the warrant immediately increases the capital of the firm. The primary way in which warrants generate capital for the firm is if they are exercised, in which case the strike price of the warrant is paid directly to the firm, thus increasing its capital.

One of the benefits of convertible bonds to the issuer is that commonly the interest rate on convertible debt is lower than it would be for straight debt, and the holders of convertible debt can often share in the potential growth in the value of the company. The holders' convertible debt can share in the increase in the value of the company if the debt is converted into equity. Because of the embedded option in these securities, the interest rate can be less than that of traditional debt. The lower interest rate reduces the liquidity needs of the corporation as compared to straight debt.

In addition to lower cost, convertibles involve several additional expenses. An issuer of convertible debt needs to make all of the decisions that would be associated with debt and equity combined. For example, the issuer needs to decide the principal amount of the bonds, the interest rate, the conversion rate, the terms that allow the debt to be called by the issuer as well as any prerequisites to conversion. In addition, the issuer will also need to decide whether and when to redeem the notes or allow their conversion into stock or on the other hand whether to let the holders decide what occurs with these notes. In sum, convertible securities are significantly more complicated than straight debt or straight equity that could increase the transaction costs of obtaining capital (Exhibit 1).

As of March 31, 2018, there were 452 convertible debt issuances with a market capitalization of the US market for convertible securities was

---

[1] If the notes are sold at a discount to the principal then the amount raised will only be the issue price rather than the principal amount.

[2] Except to the extent that they substitute for cash compensation, in which case they indirectly increase the capital of the corporation by preventing an outflow of capital.

Exhibit 1. Terminology

Call Option: A security which gives the holder the right, but not the obligation, to buy an agreed quantity of a particular commodity or financial instrument (the underlying) from the seller of the option at a certain time (the expiration date) for a certain price (the strike price). Exchange-traded options are generally settled at exercise for an amount of cash equal to difference between the strike price and the value of the stock at that time. Non-exchange traded options can be either cash-settled or physically settled (i.e., they result in an actual transfer of the underlying).

Convertible Debt: A type of debt security that can be converted into a predetermined amount of the underlying company's equity at certain times during the bond's life, usually at the discretion of the bondholder.

Conversion Premium: This is the increase in the value of shares that would be necessary for the use of the conversion option to make sense. The is equal to $1 - \frac{\text{Conversion price}}{\text{Current price of the stock}}$.

Conversion Price: The strike price of the option embedded in a convertible note. This is calculated as $\frac{\text{Principal amount of the bond}}{\text{Number of shares per bond}} = \text{Conversion price}$.

Conversion Ratio: The number of common shares received at the time of conversion for each convertible security.

Conversion Value: The value of the stock that would be received if a convertible note were converted into shares today, or Number of shares per bond × Current price of the stock. This is generally compared to the value of the bond to determine if the debt or the equity value of the note has influence on the price.

Dilution: An increase in the total number of shares that divides a fixed amount of earnings.

Diluted Earnings per Share (EPS): The earnings per share a company would have if the total number of shares is calculated assuming that the outstanding warrants have been exercised and that the convertible debt has been converted into equity.

Warrants: A security that entitles the holder to buy the underlying stock of the issuing company at an agreed-upon strike price until the expiry date. These are generally physically settled options.

Subordinated Debt: A loan or security that ranks below other loans or securities with regard to claims on assets or earnings.

Source: Stephen A. Ross, Randolph W. Westerfield, Jeffrey F. Jaffe, and Bradford D. Jordan, *Corporate Finance*, 11th ed. (McGraw Hill Education, New York, 2019); Jonathan Berk and Peter DeMarzo, *Corporate Finance*, 4th ed. (Pearson, IL, 2017).

$218 billion.[3] By October 9, 2018, there had been over $40 billion in new issuances of convertible notes in 2018 by US issuers alone.[4]

[3] *Barclays Convertible Market Watch*, December 2016.

[4] Brian Chappatta, "The Best 2018 Bond Strategy Has a Stock-Market Problem," *Bloomberg Opinion*, October 9, 2018.

Amazon.com's Convertible Debt Strategy

We first examine the use of convertible notes by Amazon.com ("Amazon"). To date, there have been two issuances of convertible debt by Amazon[5]: On February 3, 1999, Amazon completed an issuance of convertible notes to institutional investors and on February 16, 2000, Amazon completed an issuance of convertible notes which were denominated in euros to the public market. The following section discusses both sets of notes.

Company Background

At the time of its convertible debt offerings, Amazon was already the leading online retailer of books. Amazon's high inventory turnover, lack of investment in expensive retail real estate, and reduced personnel requirements gave it meaningful structural economic advantages relative to traditional booksellers. By the end of 1998 (a little before the first convertible notes were issued), Amazon had had net sales of over $774 million since it had started its business in 1995.[6]

Specifics of the Convertible Notes Issued by Amazon and Use of the Funds from Their Issuances

On February 3, 1999, Amazon completed a $1.25 billion issuance of convertible subordinated notes ("CSN") to institutional investors. The notes had a 10-year term. At maturity and at other specified times, the holders of these notes could convert them into Amazon stock at a price of $156.05 per share. Amazon had the right to redeem the debt at par if the value of the stock ever traded above $234. The notes were callable at any time after 3 years. The notes had a stated rate of interest of 4.75%, paid semi-annually. These notes were subordinated to all of the prior debt issued by Amazon. Because they were issued to institutional investors, they did not need to be registered with the Securities and Exchange Commission (SEC).[7] Morgan Stanley was the lead underwriter.

---

[5]Prior to its IPO, Amazon had issued preferred stock which was convertible into common stock. Right before the IPO, all of these shares were converted into common shares.

[6]Amazon's 1998 Annual Report.

[7]Rule 144A of the Securities Act of 1933 allows the issuance of securities to so-called "qualified investors" without registration with the SEC.

The intention to issue these notes was announced by Amazon on January 28, 1999. Initially, Amazon's managers had intended to issue $500 million in principal of these bonds. However, because the demand for the notes was strong, they decided to increase the amount of the debt offering to $1.25 billion.[8] This was the largest issuance of convertible debt up until that time.[9] On January 28, 1999, the day in which the terms of the debt offering were fixed both in principal amount and interest rate, Amazon shares closed down 2.2%.[10] The broader market was higher that day.

On February 16, 2000, Amazon completed the issuance of a group of 10-year notes called Premium Adjustable Convertible Securities ("PEACS"), which was another subordinated convertible security, but denominated in euros. The lead underwriter for this issuance was Donaldson, Lufkin, and Jenrette. These notes paid a stated rate of interest of 6.875% payable annually in arrears in February of each year. These notes were subordinated to all outstanding debt of the company, except the convertible notes issued the previous year which were equal in priority. The principal amount of this debt as well as the amount of capital raised by this offering was €690 million.

Amazon had first announced that it would offer these notes on February 7, 2000. The notes were sold and the interest rate was set as of February 11, 2000. On the date of the announcement, Amazon shares lost 4.5% of their value while the broader market was essentially unchanged. The price of Amazon stock was unchanged on February 11, the day the issuance was priced (the S&P 500 lost 2% that day). Amazon's share price dropped 4.2% on February 16, the day the issuance closed (the S&P lost 1% that day).

---

[8]Gregory Zuckerman and George Anders, "Amazon.com Launches Convertible Debt Issue," *Wall Street Journal*, January 29, 1999.

[9]This is measured by proceeds raised at issuance. There had been prior issuances of convertible debt that had a larger principal amount, for example, Kodak had issued convertible notes with a principal amount of $3.2 billion in 1992 (Zuckerman and Anders 1999). Since that time there have been issuances of convertible securities debt were larger. For example, as discussed in the next section one of Tesla issuances of convertible debt was larger.

[10]The adjusted close the day before was 62.8125 while the close on January 28, 1999 was 61.4375 which is a loss of 2.189% while the S&P 500 that day was up 1.79%, indicating that it was likely some negative event which impacted Amazon that day.

The PEACS notes were initially convertible into Amazon stock at a rate of €104.97 per share. Under the terms of the issuance, the conversion price could be reset on February 16 of 2001 and 2002, but the price per share could never go below €84.883. On February 16, 2002, the conversion price was reset to the minimum. Under the terms of the offering, these notes could be redeemed after February 13, 2003, at a price of €1,000 per note, the issue price.

Moody's had assigned a rating of Caa3 to both of these notes at the time of their issuance while Standard and Poor's had given them a CCC rating. Part of the reason the rating agencies gave these notes these low ratings was that at the time of the issuance of both the CSN and PEACS debt they did not expect Amazon to generate positive cash flow for the next 2 years as it would be investing heavily in intangibles, fixed assets, and other working capital during that period.[11]

At the time of the issuances of both sets of convertible notes, Amazon was seeking capital infusions in connection with a plan by the management to become the predominant e-commerce company in as many markets as reasonably possible. Before either of these sets of notes were issued, Amazon had already established itself as the predominant bookseller on the internet and wished to utilize the goodwill that it had built up with consumers to enter other markets. It also wished to expand its operations outside of the United States.

With regards to the capital raised from the CSN notes, the balance sheets indicate that total of cash and marketable securities of Amazon rose from $373.445 million at the end of 1998 to $706.188 million at the end of 1999 and total assets rose from $648.460 million at the end of 1998 to $2,471.551 million at the end of 1999. The increase in the total assets of the company during 1999 was $1.783 billion while the cash raised from the issuance of this debt was $1.25 billion or about 70% of this increase. Because cash is fungible, we cannot directly trace the use of the funds raised by the issuances of these notes, however, we can note that after this offering Amazon acquired significant additional distribution facilities as well as acquiring a number of on-line companies. Amazon also developed partnerships with a number of other internet companies soon after this capital was raised. It seems therefore that the capital raised by this debt offering was used to expand Amazon's business. In its annual report for

[11]At the same time, Moody's upgraded the other outstanding long-term debt of the company to Caa1.

the activities that occurred in 1999, Amazon stated that it used $178.4 million of the cash raised by the CSN debt offering to retire its Senior Discount Notes that had been issued in May 1998 which paid interest at a 10% rate. Under the view adopted by Amazon, this convertible debt offering raised a net of $1.104 billion in new capital for the company.

Between the end of 1998 and the end of 1999, the company's net annual sales grew from $610 million to $1.64 billion. In 1997, the sales of books constituted all of Amazon's sales. By the end of 1999, non-book items constituted more than half of its sales. Amazon's distribution capacity grew from 300,000 square feet to over 5 million square feet during 1999. Total assets grew from 648 million before the issuance of these notes to 2,471 million in 2002 after the issuance of both sets of notes. One can reasonably argue that Amazon used the proceeds from the CSN debt offering to invest in new businesses, plant, and equipment.

In contrast to what occurred after the issuance of the CSN notes, the capital raised by the PEACS offering appears to have been used to protect the company from the market conditions that caused many of Amazon's fellow internet-based companies to go bankrupt. The balance sheets in the annual reports for 2000 and the following years show how the capital raised by PEACS offering was used. During the year in which the PEACS notes were issued, the total assets of Amazon actually dropped from $2.471 billion at the end of 1999 to $2.135 billion at the end of 2000 while long-term debt increased from $1.466 billion to $2.127 billion. Furthermore, the shareholder's equity was actually negative at the end of 2000. The increase of $661 million in long-term debt is approximately equal to the amount of debt incurred from the issuance of PEACS.

In order to understand the differences in the use of the capital from these two issuances, one should recall that the PEACS notes were issued at a time that was challenging for many companies whose business was based on the internet. During 2000 and 2001 the stock market, particularly stocks of internet-based companies, suffered a major downturn. For example, the NASDAQ 100 index, which was heavily weighted towards internet-based companies at the time, declined over 40% during 2000 and dropped another 26% in 2001. In total, the NASDAQ 100 lost about 60% of its value from the beginning of 2000 until the end of 2001. Moreover, even the broader S&P 500 index dropped a little over 9.2% during 2000 and it lost a further 10.5% in 2001. Many internet-based companies did not survive this downturn. Some commentators have argued that part of the reason Amazon survived was because of the capital it raised from the convertible debt offerings.[12] One might note that the cash-on-hand at the end of 2000 was $822,435,000 versus $133,309,000 at the end of 1999. This is an increase of about $690 million, an amount which is almost exactly equal to the amount of capital raised by the PEACS issuance, net of financing costs.[13] That is, this debt offering allowed Amazon to have significantly higher cash reserves. This increase in cash on hand allowed it to pay interest on its outstanding debt, thus preventing an involuntary bankruptcy filing.

One of the aspirations of the management of Amazon with respect to the PEACS was fulfilled: the international expansion of the business. In 2000, the international segment of the business accounted for $381 million in sales. By 2002, the international segment accounted for $1.17 billion in sales, approximately a threefold increase in 2 years.

Note the difference in the interest rates offered on these notes. The CSN paid 4.75% interest, while the PEACS paid over 6.8%, or more than 2% higher. This difference in the interest rates is not entirely explained by the difference between prevailing dollar interest rates and euro interest rates. At the time of the issuance of the PEACS, the 12-month Euro LIBOR (the longest LIBOR maturity) was about 4.08% while the 12-month US Dollar LIBOR was 6.8%. The 12-month US Dollar LIBOR at the time of issuance of the CSN notes was 5.1%. So at the time of their issuance, the CSN notes paid interest which was 43 basis points below the then-current 12-month Dollar LIBOR rate, while the PEACS paid almost 3% above the 12-month Euro LIBOR rate, although it was approximately at the 12-month US LIBOR rate. Based on this evidence, one can argue that the PEACS were paying a higher rate of interest than the CSN notes paid if you take into account the prevailing interest rates for the relevant currencies at the time of issue.

If we continue to focus on the interest rates, we can see one of the key benefits of issuing convertible debt as opposed to straight debt: the lower interest rate that can be paid on convertible debt as opposed to straight debt. Less than a year before the CSN notes were issued, Amazon has issued straight debt (referred to in the Amazon corporate filings as "Senior Discount Notes"), on which an interest rate of 10% was paid, while the

[12]For example, see Justin Fox, "How Amazon Trained Its Investors to Behave," *Harvard Business Review,* January 30, 2013.

[13]The 2001 10-K for Amazon states that the issuance of the PEACS raised $693 million net of financing costs of $16 million.

CSN debt, which was junior to the early notes, only paid a 4.75% rate of interest for debt of similar maturity. Another way to see the value of the convertible feature is to observe that the interest rates on both sets of convertible notes were at or slightly below the prevailing 12-month US LIBOR rates for their respective currencies at the time they were issued, even though they had a 10-year maturity. This means that even though the convertible notes had terms significantly longer than 12 months and were based on the credit of a risky company, the conversion feature had enough value to reduce the interest rate to lower than that charged by banks to other prominent banks for only a 12-month term. Thus, we see that convertible notes can significantly reduce the amount of interest paid to raise capital, although at the price of potential dilution of existing shareholders.

One of the key features in considering the ability of a company to service debt, and consequently in determining the credit rating of the debt, is the cash flow of the operations. As noted above, Moody's gave the convertible debt offerings a Caa3 rating and Standard and Poor's gave them a CCC rating in large measure because they did not believe that Amazon would generate positive cash flow for a few years after the issuance of these notes. One might argue that the rating agencies were correct in their cash flow projections for Amazon in that it wasn't until 2002 that Amazon had positive cash flow from operations.[14]

As noted above, a number of commentators suggested that it was the cash reserves provided by these convertible note issuances that allowed Amazon to survive the dot-com bubble. That is, while most of the companies whose primary business was based on internet sales faced significant challenges in 2000 and 2001, Amazon not only survived this period but it grew very quickly once it came out of the downturn.

As time went on, Amazon's business became more and more successful. Exhibit 2 shows that beginning with 2002, Amazon generated significant positive cash flows from its operations. The positive cash flows of the various business in which Amazon engaged were sufficient so that on November 24, 2003, Amazon redeemed $200 million of the outstanding CSN notes. During 2004, Amazon redeemed an additional $150 million of these notes. Finally, in February 2008, the Amazon board of directors

[14]Often accounting entries for a particular year change in later reports as better information about the "true" value of the entry comes to light. The numbers given in the charts in this case study reflect the final reported numbers, as these are arguably the most accurate because they involve the use of the most information.

Exhibit 2. Annual Amazon Cash Flow From Operations

Year	Cash Flow from Operations (in Millions of $)
1999	–90
2000	–130
2001	–120
2002	174
2003	392
2004	566
2005	733
2006	702
2007	1,405
2008	1,697
2009	3,293

Source: Amazon's Annual 10-K Filings.

authorized a debt repurchase program to redeem all of its outstanding convertible debt. Under this plan, holders of $605 million in principal amount of the CSN notes, elected to convert their notes into stock. As a result, Amazon converted this debt into 7.8 million shares of common stock. During the same year, the company redeemed the remaining $294 million of the principal amount of the CSN notes for cash. By the end of 2008, all the notes of the CSN issuance of convertible debt had either been redeemed or converted to equity so that the debt balance of these notes was zero.

As for the PEACS, €200 million of this debt was redeemed in 2005 and a further €250 million of this debt was redeemed in 2006 at cost of $265 million and $300 million, respectively. In 2009, Amazon redeemed the remaining outstanding principal balance of €240 million of the PEACS at a cost of $319 million, so that by the end of 2009 none of these notes were outstanding. None of the PEACS notes had been converted into shares of Amazon.

The reported fair value of these convertible notes given in Exhibit 3 indicates the market beliefs about the likely success of Amazon as a business. Of course, these values reflect the operation of at least three forces: The beliefs about the likely survival of Amazon,

Exhibit 3. Reported Principal and Value of the Convertible Notes as of the End of Each Year

		1999	2000	2001	2002	2003	2004	2005	2006	2007	2008
CSN	Value	1,416,750	471,000	625,000	925,000	1,060,000	907,000	868,000	883,000	1,100,000	N/A
	Principal	1,249,807	1,249,807	1,249,807	1,249,807	1,050,000	899,760	899,760	899,760	899,760	N/A
PEACS	Value $	N/A	248,000	310,000	531,000	869,717	935,086	586,000	320,000	350,000	335,000
	Prin. $	N/A	608,787	650,463	724,500	869,711	935,000	580,000	317,000	350,000	335,000
	Prin. €	N/A	690,000	690,000	690,000	690,000	690,000	490,000	240,000	240,000	240,000

Source: Amazon's Annual 10-K Filings.

prevailing interest rates, and fluctuations in the euro-dollar exchange rate (this can be seen by the difference in the value of the principal in dollars versus that in euros).

The issuance of PEACS notes was the subject of litigation by a group of investors led by Sagamore Capital Management. The plaintiffs argued that Amazon had made materially false statements in its promotional material for these notes concerning the future revenues of the company due to the arrangements between Amazon and a variety of other companies engaged in e-commerce such as Drugstore.com, Audible.com, etc. The plaintiffs also alleged that Amazon had also overstated the size of its customer base and the value of the companies that it had acquired. As part of the settlement, Amazon paid $20 million into a fund to compensate investors and also paid about $6.3 million in attorney's fees of the plaintiffs. The settlement was finalized on October 20, 2005.

Tax Treatment

At the time of issuance, convertible debt is treated the same as any other debt. That is, the issuance of the debt is not a taxable event but is treated in the same way that a loan is treated. When interest is paid on the note, this is taxable income to the holder. Furthermore, the conversion of the note into stock is treated as if a warrant were exercised for a strike price equal to the conversion price. That is, the stock is purchased for the exercise price with the bond. This may result in some accrued, but unpaid interest being included in the income of the holder at that time, but in general it is treated the same as a purchase of stock directly from the company which is not a taxable event for the company and it is treated as a purchase by the holder. The holder will obtain a basis in the stock equal to amount paid for the stock (i.e., the principal amount of the debt). The conversion of the bond into stock will also not result in any cancellation of indebtedness income.

For tax purposes, all the interest expense of both issues was treated as deductible interest expense. For most of the years under discussion, Amazon did not generate large profits. Indeed, it was not until 2003 that Amazon generated an annual profit and it wasn't until 2009 that it had made a net profit as measured from the time when it was incorporated. As a consequence, the interest deductions did not seem to have a significant impact on the income tax position of Amazon until 2006 when it had used up its net operating losses. It was around this time that Amazon began redeeming these notes.

Accounting Treatment

One of the key issues with convertible notes is how they affect the accounting entries for the capital of the corporation. From a theoretical perspective is not clear if they should be considered as long-term debt of the company or should they be treated as equity, or perhaps as something else. This arises because the conversion feature of the notes plays an important role in how both investors and managers treat them and so needs to be valued taking into account the hybrid feature of these securities.

Under GAAP accounting, convertible notes can be treated as debt in some circumstances while in others they are properly treated as equity. In the accounting statements issued by Amazon, the company treated the convertible notes as exclusively debt (while discussing the convertible features of the debt). For example, Amazon did not include them as equity on the balance sheets, nor did they consider the potential shares that would be issued if these notes were converted into equity in the calculation of earnings per share.[15] In its accounting reports issued during the relevant years, Amazon's reporting of earnings per share did not include the potentially dilutive effects of the convertible notes. While there was a disclosure of the potential number of shares that might be issued if the conversion rights of the notes were exercised, this was generally not directly valued.[16]

One further accounting issue that arose specifically in connection with the PEACS was that since these notes were denominated in euros, the outstanding principal amounts had to be converted to dollars for inclusion on the balance sheets reported in their required filings and reports to shareholders. That is, since the primary accounting reports issued by Amazon are denominated in dollars, the effect of the conversion rate between euros and dollars would need to be taken into account. Of course, since part of the ostensible purpose of the issuance of these notes was to

[15]See Notes 9 and 10 of the Notes on the Consolidated Financial Statements, 10-K for 1999.

[16]As discussed in connection with the convertible debt issued by Tesla, the GAAP accounting rules concerning convertible changed a few years after the Amazon notes were issued.

assist in the expansion of Amazon's business in Europe the currency risks due to the collection of revenue in euros or currencies with high correlations to the euro were partly offset by the fact that Amazon paid interest on these bonds in euros.

Tesla's Convertible Debt Strategy

Next we examine the strategy that Tesla, Inc. ("Tesla") followed in its use of convertible notes.[17] Tesla's use of convertible debt has been both more aggressive as well as somewhat idiosyncratic as compared to Amazon's strategy. Tesla has adopted an innovative approach to convertible debt as a tool to raise capital to fund significant expansion in its production.

Company Background

Tesla was founded in 2003 by a group of engineers who believed that electric cars could be superior to traditional gasoline-powered cars. Tesla has to date produced two models of car: The Tesla Roadster intended to compete in the high-performance automobile market and the Model S which is cheaper and intended to compete in the general automobile market. In producing these cars, Tesla has faced a number of technological challenges, particularly with regard to the batteries necessary to store the electricity used for propulsion. Over time, Tesla has expanded beyond building all-electric vehicles to also become involved in developing highly scalable clean energy generation and as well as products to store electric power.

Specifics of the Notes Issued by Tesla and Use of the Funds Generated by Their Issuance

Tesla's strategy has been to use the issuance of convertible debt as a significant part of its capital structure. In its financial statements, Tesla explicitly mentions that because convertible debt can share in the upside potential of the company, the interest rate that these notes pay can be lower than would be the case for traditional debt. The annual interest rates

[17] When these notes were issued, the name of the company was Tesla Motors, Inc. The name of the company was changed in February 2017 to Tesla, Inc.

on the convertible note offerings run from essentially zero to a maximum of 2.375%, with the other notes having interest rates of 1.25% and 1.5%. Given the rather risky nature of the company, it is fair to say that these interest rates are substantially below the rates the company would have to pay for subordinated debt without a conversion feature. These lower interest rates reduce the cash flow expense of issuing debt, and also it can help to control the dilution events of attempting to raise direct equity financing. We will focus on the issuance of convertible debt which occurred after the initial public offering of Tesla stock on June 29, 2010. This is in part because better information is available about these issuances as well as the company's behavior after the additional capital generated by these issuances. There have been as of this writing four issuances of convertible debt by Tesla since its initial public offering of equity.[18]

Tesla Convertible Note Issuances

The first of these notes was issued on May 22, 2013 (Exhibit 4).[19] On that day, Tesla issued $660 million in principal amount of convertible notes, which paid a stated rate of interest of 1.5%. The embedded warrant

Exhibit 4. Dates and Interest Rates of the Four Tesla Convertible Note Offerings in Connection with the Issuance of Convertible Securities

Issuance	May, 2013	Feb., 2014	Feb., 2014	Mar., 2017
Maturity	June, 2018	Mar., 2019	Mar., 2021	Mar., 2022
Interest Rate	1.5%	0.25%	1.25%	2.38%

Source: Tesla's Annual 10-K Filings.

[18] There are other notes that are convertible into Tesla stock that were issued by an acquired subsidiary, Solar City. These notes when issued were convertible into Solar City stock. However, after the acquisition of Solar City by Tesla, these notes became convertible into Tesla stock. Because these notes were not initially issued by Tesla, they are not considered in this case study.

[19] In connection with this offering of convertible notes Tesla granted a number of warrants to Morgan Stanley, the lead underwriter. On November 14, 2017, Tesla agreed with Morgan Stanley to partially terminate such warrants, and in connection with such partial termination, Tesla issued 16,960 shares of common stock to Morgan Stanley.

allowed for shares to be purchased at $124.52 per share.[20] These notes were scheduled to be due on June 1, 2018. Then on March 5, 2014, there were two concurrent issues of convertible debt. One of these had a maturity of 2019 and the other a maturity of 2021. The interest rates were 0.25% and 1.25%, respectively. The embedded warrants for these issues have a strike price of $359.87 per share. These issuances raised $800 million from the 2019 notes and $1.2 billion from the issuance of the 2021 notes. In April of 2014, there were additional issuances of these same notes (i.e., notes with the same maturity and strike price as those issued in March 2014), which raised $120 million and $180 million in principal amounts, respectively. Finally, on March 15, 2017, Tesla announced it would issue additional convertible debt as well as common stock. The pricing date for both of these issuances was on March 16, 2017. Tesla issued $977.5 million of principal of convertible notes that pay a stated interest of 2.375%. These notes will be convertible to Tesla common stock at a price of $327.50 per share. These notes are due in 2022. Concurrently with this last issuance of convertible debt, Tesla also issued common stock of 1.539 million shares at a price of $262 a share. For this issuance of both convertible notes and common shares, Goldman Sachs was the lead underwriter.

To see the effect of these issuances on value of the equity in Tesla, Tesla stock was up 8% on May 16, 2013, the date of the announcement of the first set of notes and down 0.4% on May 22, 2013, the date of the issuance. The S&P 500 was down 0.5% of the date of announcement and down 0.8% on the date of issuance. On February 26, 2014, the date of the announcement of the notes issued in 2014, the stock was up 2% while on March 5, the date of the issuance of two different sets of convertible notes, Tesla stock was down about 0.9%. The broader market was essentially unchanged on both days. On March 15, 2017, the date of the announcement of the 2017 issuance, Tesla shares were up approximately 0.9%, while they were up 2.5% on March 16th, the day the notes were priced. The S&P 500 was up a little over 0.8% on the 15th and essentially unchanged the next day. One might note that the closing price of Tesla shares on March 15, 2017, the day before the issuance of convertible debt and common stock, was actually lower than the price of the secondary equity offering ($255.73 versus $262).

---

[20]The closing price on May 22, 2013 for Tesla stock was 87.24, so the embedded warrants were out of the money at the time of issuance.

The Tesla notes due in 2018 were convertible into Tesla stock for most of the period in which they were been outstanding (except for 2013 and one quarter of 2014). It was not until 2016 that any significant number were converted and by the end of 2017 the overwhelming majority had been converted into Tesla stock. During 2016, Tesla exchanged $454.7 million in principal amount of the notes due in 2018 for 3.65 million common shares. During 2017, Tesla exchanged approximately $199.52 million in aggregate principal amount from the 2018 maturity notes for 1.51 million shares of common stock. At the end of 2017, at least one of the conditions permitting the holders of the 2018 Notes to convert the notes to equity before the maturity of the notes had been met. Thus, the 2018 Notes were classified as current liabilities. In 2018, Tesla redeemed the remaining notes from this issuance (a little over $5 million in principal amount) for cash. The notes from the other issuances have not been either redeemed or converted at the time of the writing of this chapter.

To get a feel for how the funds generated by the issuance of these convertibles were used, we can examine a few particularly relevant entries from Tesla's balance sheets. The entries for current assets, property, total assets, and liabilities are given in Exhibit 5 (amounts are as of the year-end and are in thousands of dollars).

The first thing that one notices from these numbers is the growth in the size of the company in these 5 years. Total assets have increased to 25 times what they were, with similar growth in the size of the total liabilities. Plant and equipment has increased by 18-fold. We see that the convertible debt issuance of 2013 represented the lion's share of the increase in liabilities for 2013 ($660 million out of an increase of $760 million). Similarly, the convertible notes issued in 2014 represented the majority of increase in total liabilities for that year as well. This was not true for

Exhibit 5. Illustrative Balance Entries for the Relevant Years

	Current Assets	Plant and Equip., etc.	Total Assets	Total Liabilities
2012	527,768	552,229	1,114,190	989,490
2013	1,265,939	738,494	2,416,930	1,749,810
2014	3,198,657	1,829,267	5,849,251	4,879,345
2015	2,791,568	3,403,334	8,092,460	6,961,471
2016	6,259,796	5,982,957	22,664,076	16,750,167
2017	6,579,520	10,027,522	28,655,372	23,022,980

Source: Tesla's Annual 10-K Filings.

2017 issuance of convertible debt, as the increase in total liabilities in 2017 was over $6 billion dollars.

As with Amazon, we can get a feel for the perceived success of the corporation by looking at the changes in the value of the convertible notes. Exhibit 6 gives market value of the notes at the end of each year. The prices given in the table are based on a principal amount of $100. When the value of the note is above $100, then the note is selling above its par value. This means that the value of the conversion feature is significantly greater than both the discount for the time value of money until the maturity of the bonds as well as any discount due to default risk. We can see the market perceived a decrease in the fortunes of Tesla between the end of 2015 and 2016. One can also see that the market believed that the prospects of the company significantly improved in 2017.

Again, as with Amazon, we can also understand Tesla's ability to service its debt by looking at the cash flow operations during the period in which the notes have been outstanding. Tesla has largely had negative cash flow from operations (which is related to capital expenditures on plant, equipment, and research) (Exhibit 7).

Exhibit 6. Time Series of the Value of Tesla Convertible Debt

Note Maturity	2013	2014	2015	2016	2017
2018	139.59	187.75	195.57	179.24	N/A
2019	N/A	93.00	94.46	92.50	106.13
2021	N/A	90.92	92.50	86.40	108.38
2022	N/A	N/A	N/A	N/A	117.20

Source: Tesla's Annual 10-K Filings.

Exhibit 7. Tesla's Cash Flow from Operations

Year	Cash Flow from Operations (in Thousands of Dollars)
2012	–263,815
2013	264,804
2014	–57,337
2015	–524,499
2016	–123,829
2017	–60,654

Source: Tesla's Annual 10-K Filings.

Tax Treatment

As was the case with the Amazon convertible notes discussed above at the time of issuance, the Tesla convertible debt is treated the same as any other debt. When interest is paid on the note, this is taxable income to the holder. Furthermore, the conversion of the note into stock is treated as if a warrant were exercised for a strike price equal to the conversion price. That is, the stock is purchased for the exercise price with the bond. This may result in some accrued, but unpaid interest being included in income at that time, but in general it is treated the same as a purchase of stock directly from the company which is not a taxable event for the company and it is treated as a purchase by the holder. The holder will obtain a basis in the stock equal to amount paid for the stock. The conversion of the bond into stock will also not result in any cancellation of indebtedness income.

Tesla has treated the interest payments on these notes as tax-deductible interest. However, the tax benefit of these deductions is not a current benefit because the company has not made a profit so there is no taxable income from which these deductions can be used to reduce taxes owed. However, should the company turn a profit, the net operating loss carry-forwards generated by these deductions might be able to reduce taxes.[21]

Accounting Treatment

In May 2008, the FASB issued *FASB Staff Position APB 14-1*. This pronouncement requires issuers of convertible debt to separately account for the debt and equity features of the convertible debt which can be settled partly or entirely for cash. That is, unless the instrument is straight debt or is to be paid in stock at maturity, the issuer must determine the separate values of the warrants embedded in the notes and then by subtraction determine the value of the debt portion of the notes.

In accordance with this requirement, the accounting statements for Tesla show the calculations of the value of the conversion feature of this

[21]Under the tax law, particularly the Tax Cuts and Jobs Act of 2017 there are substantial limits on the deductibility of interest as well as the use of net operating loss carryforwards. While this case will not discuss these rules in detail, the effect the potential effect they may have on the positive tax attributes of issuing debt capital is considered in analyzing the business strategy of Tesla.

debt and bifurcated the treatment of the debt between debt and equity based on this calculation. Tesla reported that the conversion feature connected with the notes due in 2018 was $82.8 million, for the notes due in 2019 it was $188.1 million, and for those due in 2021, $369.4 million. This resulted in these amounts being subtracted from the liabilities of the company and added to the shareholders' equity. This resulted in increasing the effective interest rate paid on the debt to 4.29%, 4.89%, and 5.96% respectively. For the convertible notes issued in 2017 and maturing in 2022, $145.6 million of the principal of these notes was treated as shareholder's equity, which then created an effective interest rate on these notes of 6%.

Hedging Strategy of Tesla

One of the most interesting features of Tesla's strategy with regard to convertible debt is that the company has engaged in hedging transactions to mitigate the potentially dilutive effects on historic shareholders of holders of these notes electing to convert them into equity. To see why current shareholders might be worried about the dilutive effects of the conversion feature of these notes, we can first consider how warrants can dilute the equity interests in the firm. If a corporation issues a warrant that has a strike price of $100 at a time when the value of the stock is $90, then the warrant will not be exercised at that time. However, if the price of the stock rises to $130 per share, then the holder might very well exercise the warrant and purchase shares that are worth $130/share for $100/share. This can dilute the value of the shares of the company because less capital is flowing into the corporation that the current market value of the shares that are being purchased. To see this more concretely, if there are 10 million shares outstanding before the exercise of the warrants, then the price of $130 per share tells us that the market value of the equity of the firm is $1.3 billion. If 1 million new shares are issued as a result of the exercise of warrants which have a strike price of $100, then a total of $100 million of new equity capital will be brought into the firm from this share issuance. As a result of this, the value of the historic shares may be diluted. This occurs because the total equity capital of the firm will now be $1.4 billion ($1.3 billion + $100 million) which is spread over 11 million shares instead of 10 million. The equity value per share drops from $130 per share ($1.3 billion/10 million) to $127.27 per share ($1.4 billion/11 million).

Thus, the stock issuance as a result of the exercise of the warrants would here dilute the value of the historic shares.

We can see then that outstanding warrants represent a potential opportunity for dilution. Because warrants give the holders of these instruments the right, but not the obligation to purchase stock at a given price, these instruments will only be exercised when the value of the stock exceeds that of the conversion price. That is, they will only be exercised when there will be a dilutive effect.

We can see how this would apply to convertible debt by focusing on the warrant feature of a convertible note, recalling that the conversion feature is essentially the same as granting a warrant to the holder of the convertible bond. In this case, the exercise price of the embedded warrant is the conversion price (that is, the principal amount of the bond divided by the conversion ratio). If at the time of the exercise of the conversion feature, the value of the stock is significantly higher than the conversion price this could result in dilution in the same way that it could with a warrant. That is, if the notes had a conversion price of $100 per share, when the current market price of the stock is $130 per share, one might view this as having the same type of dilutive effect as a similarly structured warrant.

To see the dilution from an accounting perspective, first note that the amount of capital represented by the convertible debt is essentially the principal amount of the note (in general, this is the original issue price). Upon conversion, this capital is transferred from debt capital to equity capital. Thus, the amount of the equity inflow from the conversion of the bond will be the principal amount of the debt. The current market price of the convertible does not represent the amount of the equity inflow, as this is not the amount by which the equity of the firm increases from the conversion. The equity of the firm increases by the principal amount of the debt, which is used to calculate the conversion price.

Of course, if all of the convertible bonds are converted to common stock as soon as the value of the stock rises even slightly above the conversion price, then the level of dilution would be rather limited. It is unclear if this will happen though because once the notes are converted into common stock, the holders will lose the protection from a drop in the value of the equity that a bond would afford. That is, the value of the equity will fluctuate with the market, which will almost certainly be more volatile than the bond itself. Thus, some bondholders may refrain from exercising the conversion feature until the difference between the stock price and the conversion price is substantial.

One might also note that one could view this transaction differently. A key difference between a standard warrant and a convertible bond is that the corporation already has the capital invested in its business at the time of the conversion of the bond to stock, while with a warrant the share issuance brings in new capital. Because the company already receives the capital from the issuance of the bond at the time of issuance, one might wish to view the convertible notes as equity from the time of this initial offering. From this perspective, then the amount of capital that flowed into the business of the corporation at the time of the bond issuance was actually greater than the value of the shares represented by the conversion ratio at that time (the conversion price for these notes is almost always higher than the stock price at the time of issuance). Thus, one could argue that the situation of the convertible debt is not really like that of the holding of a warrant. This view results from viewing the holders of convertible notes as already holding the stock into which the note can be converted, but also holding the right to put the stock to the company for the principal amount.

There are generally problems with trying to fit this latter view to the actual legal rights of the holders of convertible debt prior to conversion. The bondholders do not have the right to collect any dividends that might be paid during the time of before the conversion of the note into stock, nor do they have any voting rights that might normally accompany the ownership of common shares. In addition, if they convert the bonds, they will have the right to the return of their principal amount, which an equity would not have. Thus, because the initial capital infusion is not equity capital at the time it enters the corporation it is not the same as the capital infusions from the exercise of warrants. In sum, while there are differences between the exercise of a conversion feature of a bond and the exercise of warrants, the two are more similar than they are different.

In connection with the notes issued in 2018, Tesla entered into transactions where it purchased call options on 5.3 million shares of its own stock with an exercise price of $124.52 and also sold warrants on 5.3 million shares of its stock with an exercise price of $184.48. The purchased options have the effect of increasing the amount of paid-in capital equal to the difference between the then-current value of the shares and the amount paid for the shares. This follows because the purchased options will increase in value by almost exactly the same amount that the newly issued shares due to the conversion of the debt are worth more than the strike price. The net cost of the hedges entered into in connection with the notes due in 2018 was $57.2 million.

In connection with the notes issued in March of 2014, Tesla purchased options to buy stock at a price of $359.87 a share (the strike price of the embedded warrants) and then sold warrants with a strike price of $512.66 to match the shares for the notes due in 2019 and $560.64 for the notes due in 2021. This effectively increased the strike price on the embedded warrants in the convertible notes for purposes of dilution of existing shareholders to $512.66 and $560.64, respectively. These hedges cost a net amount of $186.3 million, while the additional hedges for the notes issued in April 2014 were $27.9 million. In connection with the 2017 issuance of convertible debt, Tesla purchased calls for 3.0 million of its own shares with a strike price of $327.50 and sold calls with a strike price of $655.00. The net cost of the hedging transactions entered into in 2017 was $151.2 million.

Questions

1. In what ways were the situations facing the management of Amazon similar to those facing Tesla during the periods in which each of them issued convertible securities?
2. What differences in the business needs for capital affected the different strategies for the use of convertible notes?
3. How were the liquidity needs of the Amazon and Tesla businesses different? Were the strategies different? How did these differences affect the terms (interest rates, terms of conversion, etc.) of the notes?
4. Why did Moody's upgrade the previously outstanding debt, the so-called Senior Discount Notes, of Amazon in 1999, when the company issued the subordinated convertible notes? That is, why would the issuance of additional debt improve the likelihood of payment of pre-existing debt?
5. When might it make sense to issue securities denominated in a currency other than the primary currency in which the business operates.
6. In general, the stock price of Tesla has risen on the announcement of new issuances of convertible debt. Why might the price of stock rise on the announcement of such potentially dilutive securities?
7. Why might the issuance of convertible debt be a better idea for companies that are new or whose stock price is more volatile?
8. What is the theory behind Tesla's hedging strategy? What about feature of option prices does it appear the company is trying to exploit?

Appendix A. Consolidated Balance Sheets

This Appendix gives the balance sheets for the years around the time that these two companies issued convertible debt. Because not all items are reported for all years the balance sheets have been grouped into years for which similar items have been reported. Reported numbers are in thousands. The source for all of the data is the balance sheets reported annually in Form 10-K for each of the respective years.

Amazon

Assets
1998 & 1999
(in thousands, except per share data)

	December 31	
	1999	**1998**
Current Assets		
Cash and Cash Equivalents	$133,309	$71,583
Marketable Securities	572,879	301,862
Inventories	220,646	29,501
Prepaid Expenses and Other Current Assets	85,344	21,308
Total Current Assets	1,012,178	424,254
Fixed Assets, Net	317,613	29,791
Goodwill, Net	534,699	174,052
Other Purchased Intangibles, Net	195,445	4,586
Investments in Equity-Method Investees	226,727	7,740
Other Investments	144,735	—
Deferred Charges and Other	40,154	8,037
Total Assets	$2,471,551	$648,460
Liabilities and Stockholders' Equity		
Current Liabilities		
Accounts Payable	$463,026	$113,273
Accrued Expenses and Other Current Liabilities	126,017	34,413
Accrued Advertising	55,892	13,071
Deferred Revenue	54,790	—
Interest Payable	24,888	10
Current Portion of Long-Term Debt and Other	14,322	808
Total Current Liabilities	738,935	161,575
Long-Term Debt and Other	1,466,338	348,140

(*Continued*)

(Continued)

	December 31	
	1999	1998
Commitments and Contingencies Stockholders' Equity		
Preferred Stock, $0.01 par Value:		
Authorized Shares — 150,000		
Issued and Outstanding Shares — None	—	—
Common Stock, $0.01 par Value:		
Authorized Shares — 1,500,000		
Issued and Outstanding Shares — 345,155 and 318,534		
Shares at December 31, 1999 and 1998, Respectively	3,452	3,186
Additional Paid-in Capital	1,195,540	298,537
Note Receivable for Common Stock	(1,171)	(1,099)
Stock-Based Compensation	(47,806)	(1,625)
Accumulated Other Comprehensive Income (Loss)	(1,709)	1,806
Accumulated Deficit	(882,028)	(162,060)
Total Stockholders' Equity	266,278	138,745
Total Liabilities and Stockholders' Equity	$2,471,551	$648,460

Amazon

2000 & 2001

(in thousands, except per share data)

Assets

	December 31	
	2001	2000
Current Assets		
Cash and Cash Equivalents	$540,282	$822,435
Marketable Securities	456,303	278,087
Inventories	143,722	174,563
Prepaid Expenses and Other Current Assets	67,613	86,044
Total Current Assets	1,207,920	1,361,129
Fixed Assets, Net	271,751	366,416
Goodwill, Net	45,367	158,990
Other Purchased Intangibles, Net	34,382	96,335
Investments in Equity-Method Investees	10,387	52,073
Other Investments	17,972	40,177
Deferred Charges and Other	49,768	60,049
Total Assets	$1,637,547	$2,135,169

(Continued)

	December 31	
	2001	**2000**
Liabilities and Stockholders' Equity		
Current Liabilities		
Accounts Payable	$444,748	$485,383
Accrued Expenses and Other Current Liabilities	305,064	272,683
Unearned Revenue	87,978	131,117
Interest Payable	68,632	69,196
Current Portion of Long-Term Debt and Other	14,992	16,577
Total Current Liabilities	921,414	974,956
Long-Term Debt and Other	2,156,133	2,127,464
Commitments and Contingencies Stockholders' Equity		
Preferred Stock, $0.01 par Value:		
Authorized Shares — 500,000		
Issued and Outstanding Shares — None	—	—
Common Stock, $0.01 par Value:		
Authorized Shares — 5,000,000		
Issued and Outstanding Shares — 373,218 and 357,140		
Shares at December 31, 2001 and 2000, Respectively	3,732	3,571
Additional Paid-in Capital	1,462,769	1,338,303
Deferred Stock-Based Compensation	(9,853)	(13,448)
Accumulated Other Comprehensive Loss	(36,070)	(2,376)
Accumulated Deficit	(2,860,578)	(2,293,301)
Total Liabilities and Stockholders' Deficit	$1,637,547	$2,135,169

Tesla

2012 & 2013

(in thousands, except per share data)

	December 31	
	2013	**2012**
Assets		
Current Assets		
Cash and Cash Equivalents	$845,889	$201,890
Restricted Cash	3,012	19,094
Accounts Receivable	49,109	26,842

(Continued)

(*Continued*)

	December 31	
	2013	**2012**
Assets		
Inventory	340,355	268,504
Prepaid Expenses and Other Current Assets	27,574	8,438
Total Current Assets	1,265,939	524,768
Operating Lease Vehicles, Net	382,425	10,071
Property, Plant and Equipment, Net	738,494	552,229
Restricted Cash	6,435	5,159
Other Assets	23,637	21,963
Total Assets	$2,416,930	$1,114,190
Liabilities and Stockholders' Equity		
Current Liabilities		
Accounts Payable	$303,969	$303,382
Accrued Liabilities	108,252	39,798
Deferred Revenue	91,882	1,905
Capital Lease Obligations, Current Portion	7,722	4,365
Customer Deposits	163,153	138,817
Convertible Debt, Current Portion	182	—
Long-Term Debt, Current Portion	—	50,841
Total Current Liabilities	675,160	539,108
Common Stock Warrant Liability	—	10,692
Capital Lease Obligations, Less Current Portion	12,855	9,965
Deferred Revenue, Less Current Portion	181,180	3,060
Convertible Debt, Less Current Portion	586,119	—
Resale Value Guarantee	236,299	—
Long-Term Debt, Less Current Portion	—	401,495
Other Long-Term Liabilities	58,197	25,170
Total Liabilities	1,749,810	989,490
Stockholders' Equity		
Preferred Stock; $0.001 par Value; 100,000,000 Shares Authorized; No Shares Issued and Outstanding	—	—
Common Stock; $0.001 par Value;		

(Continued)

	December 31	
	2013	**2012**
2,000,000,000 Shares Authorized as of December 31, 2013 and 2012, Respectively;		
123,090,990 and 114,214,274 Shares Issued and Outstanding as of December 31, 2013 and 2012, respectively	123	115
Additional Paid-In Capital	1,806,617	1,190,191
Accumulated Deficit	(1,139,620)	(1,065,606)
Total Stockholders' Equity	667,120	124,700
Total Liabilities and Stockholders' Equity	$2,416,930	$1,114,190

Tesla

2014 & 2015

(in thousands, except per share data)

Consolidated Balance Sheets 2014 & 2015
(in Thousands)

	December 31	
	2015	**2014**
Assets		
Current Assets		
Cash and Cash Equivalents	$1,196,908	$1,905,713
Restricted Cash and Marketable Securities	22,628	17,947
Accounts Receivable	168,965	226,604
Inventory	1,277,838	953,675
Prepaid Expenses and Other Current Assets	125,229	76,134
Total Current Assets	2,791,568	3,180,073
Operating Lease Vehicles, Net	1,791,403	766,744
Property, Plant and Equipment, Net	3,403,334	1,829,267
Restricted Cash	31,522	11,374
Other Assets	74,633	43,209
Total Assets	$8,092,460	$5,830,667

(Continued)

(*Continued*)

	December 31	
	2015	**2014**
Liabilities and Stockholders' Equity		
Current Liabilities		
Accounts Payable	$916,148	$777,946
Accrued Liabilities	422,798	268,883
Deferred Revenue	423,961	191,651
Resale Value Guarantees	136,831	—
Customer Deposits	283,370	257,587
Long-Term Debt and Capital Leases	633,166	611,099
Total Current Liabilities	2,816,274	2,107,166
Deferred Revenue	446,105	292,271
Long-Term Debt and Capital Leases	2,040,375	1,818,785
Resale Value Guarantee	1,293,741	487,879
Other Long-Term Liabilities	364,976	154,660
Total Liabilities	6,961,471	4,860,761
Convertible Senior Notes (Notes 8)	42,045	58,196
Stockholders' Equity:		
Preferred Stock; $0.001 par Value; 100,000 Shares Authorized; No Shares Issued and Outstanding	—	—
Common Stock; $0.001 par Value; 2,000,000 Shares Authorized as of December 31, 2015 and 2014, Respectively; 131,425 and 125,688 Shares Issued and Outstanding as of December 31, 2015 and 2014, Respectively	131	126
Additional Paid-in Capital	3,414,692	2,345,266
Accumulated Other Comprehensive Loss	(3,556)	(22)
Accumulated Deficit	(2,322,323)	(1,433,660)
Total Stockholders' Equity	1,088,944	911,710
Total Liabilities and Stockholders' Equity	$8,092,460	$5,830,667

Tesla

2012 & 2013

(in thousands, except per share data)

Consolidated Balance Sheets

	December 31	
	2017	**2016**
Assets		
Current Assets		
Cash and Cash Equivalents	$3,367,914	$3,393,216
Restricted Cash	155,323	105,519
Accounts Receivable, Net	515,381	499,142
Inventory	2,263,537	2,067,454
Prepaid Expenses and Other Current Assets	268,365	194,465
Total Current Assets	6,570,520	6,259,796
Operating Lease Vehicles, Net	4,116,604	3,134,080
Solar Energy Systems, Leased and to be Leased, Net	6,347,490	5,919,880
Property, Plant and Equipment, Net	10,027,522	5,982,957
Intangible Assets, Net	361,502	376,145
Goodwill	60,237	—
MyPower Customer Notes Receivable, Net of Current Portion	456,652	506,302
Restricted Cash, Net of Current Portion	441,722	268,165
Other Assets	273,123	216,751
Total Assets	$28,655,372	$22,664,076
Liabilities		
Current Liabilities		
Accounts Payable	$2,390,250	$1,860,341
Accrued Liabilities and Other	1,731,366	1,210,028
Deferred Revenue	1,015,253	763,126
Resale Value Guarantees	787,333	179,504
Customer Deposits	853,919	663,859
Current Portion of Long-Term Debt and Capital Leases	796,549	984,211
Current Portion of Solar Bonds and Promissory Notes Issued to Related Parties	100,000	165,936
Total Current Liabilities	7,674,670	5,827,005

(Continued)

(*Continued*)

	December 31	
	2017	**2016**
Long-Term Debt and Capital Leases, Net of Current Portion	9,415,700	5,860,049
Solar Bonds Issued to Related Parties, Net of Current Portion	100	99,164
Convertible Senior Notes Issued to Related Parties	2,519	10,287
Deferred Revenue, Net of Current Portion	1,177,799	851,790
Resale Value Guarantees, Net of Current Portion	2,309,222	2,210,423
Other Long-Term Liabilities	2,442,970	1,891,449
Total Liabilities	23,022,980	16,750,167
Commitments and Contingencies (Note 17)		
Redeemable Noncontrolling Interests in Subsidiaries	397,734	367,039
Convertible Senior Notes (Note 13)	70	8,784
Equity		
Stockholders' Equity		
Preferred Stock; $0.001 par Value; 100,000 Shares Authorized; No Shares Issued and Outstanding	—	—
Common Stock; $0.001 par Value; 2,000,000 Shares Authorized; 168,797 and 161,561 Shares Issued and Outstanding as of December 31, 2017 and December 31, 2016, Respectively	169	161
Additional Paid-In Capital	9,178,024	7,773,727
Accumulated Other Comprehensive Gain (loss)	33,348	(23,740)
Accumulated Deficit	(4,974,299)	(2,997,237)
Total Stockholders' Equity	4,237,242	4,752,911
Noncontrolling Interests in Subsidiaries	997,346	785,175
Total Liabilities and Equity	$28,655,372	$22,664,076

Part VI

Short-Term Finance

https://doi.org/10.1142/9789811216749_0021

Case 21

Gemini Electronics Company: Principles of Working Capital Management

Ronald Richter and Arthur S. Guarino

Rutgers Business School, USA

Introduction

Gemini Electronics Company (Gemini) manufactures electronic components for large computer manufacturers in the United States and abroad that range from firms producing retail products to those making custom computers for corporations and US government. Gemini has grown in the last decade organically and through acquisitions that were generally very successful.

Overall, Gemini has been profitable and growing at a steady rate. However, a large acquisition in 2013 increased sales but diminished profits in that year that has yet to recover. Following the acquisition, Gemini's short-term debt leverage expanded, and a liquidity crunch was looming. Recent downgrades of Gemini's credit rating resulted in higher borrowing costs and difficulty in raising capital. Cash balances expanded disproportionately to short-term debt and an increase in the cash conversion cycle with accounts receivables and inventory balances increasing at a faster rate. The increase in cash balances was another example of inefficient use of working capital.

Company History

Gemini Electronics Company was established in 1952 by three engineers who graduated from the California Institute of Technology (CalTech). Frank Wagner held graduate degrees in physics and electrical engineering from CalTech, where he met Albert Rothman who was completing his Ph.D. in electrical engineering. Joseph Card was attending CalTech for his graduate degrees in chemical and electrical engineering. They all liked working with computers and shared a dream of running their own companies. They shared many hours discussing the advantages that computers could have for society and industry and the potential to start a company that made electronic components. They were natural-born problem solvers and loved working on electronic machines that others would not go near. Their lives revolved around school and solving difficult problems of electronic devices that had broken down. They completed their graduate studies and while Albert obtained a teaching position at Stanford, Frank and Joseph went into industry at defense firms in California. They stayed in touch and met weekly fixing electronic devices, talking about computers and about jointly owning a company.

After several years, Frank heard about an electronics firm called Gemini Electronics Company near San Francisco that was desperately seeking a buyer due to financial difficulties. Frank contacted Albert and Joseph about making a bid for the company. Frank had saved some money since graduate school and he knew he could get a sizeable loan from his father who was an accomplished attorney in New York City. Joseph knew he could borrow some money from his in-laws and parents, while Albert was able to scrap a few dollars together from his own savings. They were able to get the necessary funds to purchase the company after making a deal with the owners who were looking to get out as soon as possible. Frank, Joseph, and Albert had to make deals with their suppliers and creditors since the company owed a substantial amount of money to them. It boiled down to the suppliers still selling parts and materials to the company by extending longer payment terms. The creditors were convinced to wait longer for their money.

Frank, Joseph, and Albert were both excited about going into their own business but also scared out of their wits at the possibility of failure. They took over the manufacturing facilities and by working with the employees were able to streamline the assembly process, cut costs, and start looking for new vendors who could give them better terms. It was not easy, and at times they were cutting it too close. In little over a year, through hard work and determination, using their intelligence, common sense, and plenty of chutzpah, they were able to break even, and their cash flow was starting to turn positive. They realized they were not out of the woods yet, but things were starting to look better. They started to obtain new customers for their electronic components, both in the United States and overseas. Sometimes they had to borrow more money from Frank's father and Joseph's in-laws, but they were able to pay it back sooner than anticipated.

Gemini diversified its product lines by making components for companies manufacturing computers for other firms and for the US government. This led the company into more research and development which meant hiring freshly minted engineers from CalTech and other schools across the United States and Canada. Albert was the head of the research and development department and started with a bare-bones budget. His crew of bright, eager, and resourceful engineers was able to come up with some new ideas dealing with electronic components and computers that were noticed by the rest of their industry. This eventually led to a multi-million-dollar contract from a large East Coast company. While the sale was substantial, it meant a significant upfront investment and drain on cash resources. From then on, Gemini turned a profit each year, saw sales increase steadily, their cash flow grew at a reliable rate, and they were then able to increase their operations by fivefold.

Financially, they were able to obtain more capital from East Coast investors who were always looking for new opportunities. When Frank, Albert, and Joseph made their pitch for $10 million in new capital towards the end of 1961, they were delighted when investors offered $20 million, which involved revising Gemini's long-term growth plans and expanding operations beyond their wildest dreams. The company eventually went public and was listed on NASDAQ. Frank, Albert, and Joseph were still running the company, but they had to hire a new set of managers to help grow the company and deal with the competition that was coming from nearby Silicon Valley.

Current Condition

Julia Na became CFO of Gemini Electronics Company 7 years ago and has been with the firm over 20 years. She started as a clerk in the finance department and worked her way up to CFO. She went back to school on a part-time basis to earn her MBA in finance and a law degree, studying nights and weekends while still a full-time employee of Gemini. It has been a career with more ups than downs, but she managed to raise a family, obtain her graduate degrees and become a key manager at the only company she has ever worked for.

The firm encountered several problems due to a large acquisition it made in 2013 which made the management team wonder whether it was a good deal. First, the cash conversion cycle (CCC) was taking longer because the company's days sales outstanding (DSO) deteriorated from 59.5 days prior to the acquisition to 76.2 days in post-acquisition. To offset the lengthening CCC, the company's knee-jerk reaction was to increase it Days Payable Outstanding (DPO) which had a positive effect on the cash conversion cycle, but it put immense pressure on the company's suppliers. By increasing the DPO from 55 days to over 80 days, the suppliers were very concerned about their cash flow and how would they continue to operate with Gemini, but they felt that they had no leg to stand on when negotiating with Gemini. While increasing the DPO was a quick fix for Gemini, it could have led suppliers into insolvency or to cease selling to Gemini. Julie was able to break down its working capital issues into four groups: Cash, Accounts Receivable, Inventory, and Accounts Payable.

Cash

Currently, the company maintains over ten banking relationships with over 100 bank accounts. This banking structure has led to inefficient cash management and loss of opportunity by not maximizing cash balance visibility. These bank relationships assist the company with its cash management needs, short-term debt, and short-term investment needs. Because the focus of the company's growth has been on product market issues, the management of the cash has been neglected, leading to cash management inefficiencies. Exhibit 1 lists the major cash balances held by the various operating locations as of December 31, 2015. The company is concerned about the inefficient use of the cash and Julie has been charged with trying

Exhibit 1. Cash Balances and Debt Balance by Subsidiary

Country Operating Company	Cash Balances (in Millions of $)	Borrowing Amount (in Millions of $)
United States	$50	$20
Canada	$15	$5
United Kingdom	$45	$20
Germany	$20	$0
Japan	$35	$10
China	$65	$0
Brazil	$0	$25
France	$0	$30
Italy	$10	$20
Mexico	$20	$20
Total Balances	$260	$150

to utilize cash more cost-effectively. The borrowing amount states the current loan balance that each subsidiary has, and it appears that pooling positive cash balances against these loan balances would result in a more efficient cash management structure.

The following are current market interest rates as of December 31, 2015:

US Treasury Rates (also the investment rate for Gemini): 0.14% annually

Borrowing Rates: A rated companies: 3.49% annually
Baa rated companies: 4.51% annually
BB rated companies: 5.93% annually
B rated companies: 8.30% annually

Accounts Receivable

Gemini has seen an increase in its DSO after the acquisition, adversely affecting its cash flow. DSO increased from 59 days to 76 days, impacting the firm's liquidity. With the liquidity crunch, there has been a downgrading of Gemini's credit rating causing concern in renegotiating the line of credit used to support its working capital investment. The firm has been downgraded to "junk" status and had seen an increase in borrowing cost of approximately 200 basis points with concern about supporting its higher investment in accounts receivable. Customers were asked to pay sooner, but they declined to pay any sooner than what they have become accustomed to over the past few years.

The credit rating of the majority of the firm's customers is still at investment grade, and they range from A to AA. Because of the competitor's credit status, there may be an opportunity to utilize supply chain finance to assist in accessing capital. While the DSO prior to the major acquisition was 59 days, the actual payment terms to all customers were net 45 days. Gemini would like to collect within the terms and receive their cash in 45 days.

Another opportunity with the firm's accounts receivable is to offer better terms to its customers. The firm is considering offering better terms to its customers to attract sales and secure current sales. If the firm adopts discounted terms, management feels that the firm can positively impact its DSO and assist in bringing in cash sooner. However, there is concern that the discounted terms will be too costly. The table below shows the various credit terms the firm's competitors offer:

Competitor	Credit Terms
A	2/10, net 30
B	1/10, net 30
C	2/10, net 45
D	1/10, net 45
E	.5/5, net 60

Inventory

The firm saw an increase in Days Inventory Outstanding (DIO) after the acquisition by a little more than 20%, going from 47.2 days to 58.2 days from 2013 to 2014. This is also a concern for the firm managing its working capital since this use of cash reduced liquidity for the firm. When benchmarking DIO against its competitors, the firm is definitely running at a higher inventory investment. The average DIO of its competitors ranges from 40 to 45 days. The firm believes it can better manage its DIO through the implementation of a new Enterprise Resource Planning (ERP) system that will better connect the firm to its customer's demand, resulting in a more efficient supply chain. The question the firm is asking itself is what would be the cash benefit of lowering its DIO versus the cost to implement an ERP system. The ERP implementation will cost approximately $50 million company-wide. In evaluating whether the investment in the ERP system makes sense it was determined that the risk of the ERP system implementation is comparable to the general risk of Gemini and its Weighted Average Cost of Capital (WACC) for Gemini is 8.5%.

Accounts Payable

To offset the increased DSO and DIO, the firm took the short-term policy of delaying paying its bills and increasing its DPO from 25 days in 2012 to 90 days in 2014. While this was a policy to offset the runaway investments in accounts receivable and Inventory, many of the suppliers for Gemini are struggling. Approximately 50% of the suppliers have fallen well below investment grade and are hovering around the "B" status. These suppliers are finding it harder and harder to obtain liquidity funding and even one key supplier recently declared bankruptcy due to not being able to renew a line of credit with its banks. The firm is very reliant on materials from its suppliers in order to manufacture its product. Utilizing the short-term strategy of simply increasing DPO to obtain a better cash position may backfire on the firm, and management is looking to change the firm's payment strategy. The firm cannot afford to have another key supplier go bankrupt due to the domino effect on its own business. Gemini should consider introducing supply chain financing to its vendors to help support their business and build a stronger relationship with Gemini.

Financial Statements

According to the most recent 10-K filings, Exhibits 2–4 provide the income statement, balance sheet, and working capital metrics of the company.

Exhibit 2. Income Statement

Gemini Electronics					
Income Statement (All Numbers in Millions)					
	2011	**2012**	**2013**	**2014**	**2015**
Revenues	$883.4	$983.2	$1,553.4	$1,667.2	$1,596.8
Cost of Goods Sold	$513.5	$594.3	$1,034.7	$1,078.0	$1,026.4
Gross Profit	**$369.9**	**$388.9**	**$518.7**	**$589.2**	**$570.4**
as a Percent of Sales	*41.9%*	*39.6%*	*33.4%*	*35.3%*	*35.7%*
Operating Expenses	$211.3	$240.1	$400.6	$414.7	$376.4
Operating Income (EBIT)	**$158.6**	**$148.8**	**$118.1**	**$174.5**	**$194.0**
as a Percent of Sales	*18.0%*	*15.1%*	*7.6%*	*10.5%*	*12.1%*
Interest Expenses	$0.8	$13.9	$23.6	$14.6	$15.9
Profit Before Taxes (EBT)	**$157.8**	**$134.9**	**$94.5**	**$159.9**	**$178.1**
as a Percent of Sales	*17.9%*	*13.7%*	*6.1%*	*9.6%*	*11.2%*
Taxes	$51.7	$30.1	$28.3	$48.7	$49.1
Net Income	**$106.1**	**$104.8**	**$66.2**	**$111.2**	**$129.0**
as a Percent of Sales	*12.0%*	*10.7%*	*4.3%*	*6.7%*	*8.1%*

Exhibit 3. Balance Sheet

Gemini Electronics						
Balance Sheet (All Numbers in Thousands)						
	2010	**2011**	**2012**	**2013**	**2014**	**2015**
Assets						
Cash and Cash Equivalents	$98.4	$115.5	$20.2	$107.7	$121.0	$112.3
Net Receivables	$109.0	$131.7	$150.7	$355.5	$340.3	$332.8
Inventory	$64.9	$83.7	$90.0	$177.5	$168.5	$153.6
Other Current Assets	$52.1	$49.2	$44.4	$63.7	$71.0	$69.4
Total Current Assets	**$324.4**	**$380.1**	**$305.3**	**$704.4**	**$700.8**	**$668.1**
Net Property, Plant, and Equipment	$109.6	$120.6	$117.9	$171.9	$159.5	$158.3
Goodwill	$191.6	$300.0	$303.7	$555.8	$540.7	$514.0
Intangible Assets	$226.6	$332.8	$313.9	$523.6	$477.5	$425.6
Other Long-Term Assets	$196.7	$47.2	$46.7	$47.5	$40.0	$42.1
Total Long-Term Assets	$724.5	$800.6	$782.2	$1,298.8	$1,217.7	$1,140.0
Total Assets	**$1,048.9**	**$1,180.7**	**$1,087.5**	**$2,003.2**	**$1,918.5**	**$1,808.1**

Exhibit 3. (*Continued*)

Gemini Electronics						
Balance Sheet (All Numbers in Thousands)						
	2010	**2011**	**2012**	**2013**	**2014**	**2015**
Liabilities						
Accounts Payable	$26.9	$30.5	$51.2	$262.3	$268.7	$184.0
Short-Term Debt	$50.0	$53.0	$49.0	$285.0	$300.0	$289.0
Other Current Liabilities	$91.1	$105.7	$100.6	$193.2	$207.4	$210.8
Total Current Liabilities	**$168.0**	**$189.2**	**$200.8**	**$740.5**	**$776.1**	**$683.8**
Long-Term Debt	$353.4	$378.5	$222.6	$379.3	$258.5	$239.1
Other Long-Term Liabilities	$155.6	$169.9	$157.8	$307.1	$290.1	$279.4
Total Long-Term Liabilities	$509.0	$548.4	$380.4	$686.4	$548.6	$518.5
Total Liabilities	**$677.0**	**$737.6**	**$581.2**	**$1,426.9**	**$1,324.7**	**$1,202.3**
Stockholders' Equity						
Common Stock at Par Value						
Paid-in Capital	$304.9	$317.0	$321.9	$321.7	$342.1	$350.9
Retained Earnings	$124.8	$182.7	$238.3	$252.2	$311.7	$372.1
Treasury Stock	($14.8)	($17.1)	($11.5)	($4.2)	($18.3)	($21.0)
Accumulated Other Loss	($43.0)	($39.5)	($42.4)	$6.6	($41.7)	($96.2)
Total Stockholders' Equity	$371.9	$443.1	$506.3	$576.3	$593.8	$605.8
Total Liabilities and Stockholders' Equity	**$1,049**	**$1,181**	**$1,088**	**$2,003**	**$1,918.5**	**$1,808.1**

Exhibit 4. Working Capital Metrics

Gemini Electronics					
Financial Statement Analysis (Working Capital Metrics)					
	2011	**2012**	**2013**	**2014**	**2015**
Working Capital Ratio	**2.0**	**1.5**	**1.0**	**0.9**	**1.0**
Cash Conversion Cycle					
Days Sales Outstanding	49.7	52.4	59.5	76.2	76.9
Days Inventory Outstanding	52.8	53.3	47.2	58.6	57.3
Days Payables Outstanding	(20.4)	(25.1)	(55.3)	(89.9)	(80.5)
Total Conversion Cycle in Days	**82.1**	**80.7**	**51.4**	**44.8**	**53.7**

The Assignment

Gemini Electronics Company

To**:** Financial Analyst
From**:** Julia Na — CFO
Date**:** July 27, 2019
Re**:** Working Capital Management Recommendations

Our current conditions of working capital management are experiencing significant challenges. We need to improve our cash conversion, inefficient use of cash, accounts receivable, inventory, and accounts payable. More specifically:

1. How can we manage our cash in a more efficient manner given the many bank accounts that we have with our relationship banks? What is the effect of pooling our cash globally and potentially reducing interest expense or increasing our interest income?
2. The company's DSO has increased from 59.5 days pre-acquisition to 76.2 post-acquisition which affects our accounts receivables. What can be done to revert to our pre-acquisition position? How much cash can be freed up with a reduction in DSOs and is there a cost of doing so?
3. Regarding inventory, Gemini has experienced an increase in DIO after the acquisition by slightly more than 20%, increasing from 47.2 days in 2013 to 58.2 days in 2014. The average DIO for our competitors ranges from 40 to 45 days. How can we improve the DIO using the proposed ERP system implementation? Does the ERP system have an acceptable financial payoff using the metrics of NPV, IRR, and payback period?

4. The age of accounts payable has lengthened to the point that suppliers may either not want to do business with us anymore or that they will want only cash on delivery. What should Gemini do to supporting its suppliers but still maintain longer DPOs than the suppliers wish to offer?
5. ***Given the company's financial statements and your knowledge of finance, what do you propose we do to improve Gemini's working capital management? I need this analysis with your recommendations in one week.***

Thank you,
Julia Na
Chief Financial Officer

Principles of Working Capital Management

***Keywords*:** Working capital management, Accounts receivable, Inventory, Accounts payable, Balance sheet, Income statement, Subsidiary, Sales, Net property, Plant and equipment, Goodwill, Intangible assets, Acquisition, Net income, Cash flows, Liquidity, Cash, Current assets, Current liabilities, Cash conversion cycle, Days sales outstanding, Days inventory outstanding, Days payable outstanding, Discounted terms, Liquidity crunch, Supply chain finance, Cash pooling, Credit spread, Enterprise Resource Planning system, Weighted average cost of capital, Net present value, Internal rate of return, Payback period

Appendix. Terms for the Case Study

Working Capital Management[1]

Working capital management refers to a company's managerial accounting strategy designed to monitor and utilize the two components of working capital, current assets, and current liabilities, in order to ensure the most financially efficient operation of the company. The primary purpose of working capital management is to make sure the company always maintains sufficient cash flow to meet its short-term operating costs and short-term debt obligations.

[1]https://www.investopedia.com/terms/w/workingcapitalmanagement.asp.

Current Assets[2]

Current assets represent all the assets of a company that are expected to be conveniently sold, consumed, utilized, or exhausted through the standard business operations, which can lead to their conversion to a cash value over the next 1-year period. Since current assets is a standard item appearing in the balance sheet, the time horizon represents 1 year from the date shown in the heading of the company's balance sheet. Current assets include cash, cash equivalents, accounts receivable, stock inventory, marketable securities, pre-paid liabilities, and other liquid assets. In a few jurisdictions, the term is also known as ***current accounts***.

Current Liabilities[3]

Current liabilities are a company's debts or obligations that are due within 1 year or within a normal operating cycle. Furthermore, current liabilities are settled by the use of a current asset, such as cash, or by creating a new current liability. Current liabilities appear on a company's balance sheet and include short-term debt, accounts payable, accrued liabilities, and other similar debts.

Cash Conversion Cycle

The Cash Conversion Cycle (CCC) relates to three accounts in the Working Capital and determines how long it takes a business operating cycle to turn into cash. The three accounts are accounts receivables, inventory, and accounts payable. The formula for the CCC is Days sales outstanding + Days inventory outstanding − Days payables outstanding. The goal of an organization is to maintain the shortest CCC in relation to their business in order to generate cash quickly.

Days Sales Outstanding

Days sales outstanding (DSO) is a measure of the average number of days it takes a company to collect payment after a sale has been made. DSO is

[2] https://www.investopedia.com/terms/c/currentassets.asp.

[3] https://www.investopedia.com/terms/c/currentliabilities.asp.

often determined on a monthly, quarterly or annual basis, and can be calculated by dividing the amount of accounts receivable during a given period by the total value of credit sales during the same period and multiplying the result by the number of days in the period measured.[4]

The formula for DSO is:

$$\frac{\text{Average accounts receivable}}{\text{Annual revenues}} \times 365$$

Days Inventory Outstanding

The days sales of inventory (DSI) is a financial ratio that indicates the average time in days that a company takes to turn its inventory, including goods that are a work in progress, into sales.[5]

$$\text{The formula for DIO is: } \frac{\text{Average inventory}}{\text{Annual cost of goods sold}} \times 365$$

Days Payable Outstanding

Days payable outstanding (DPO) is a financial ratio that indicates the average time (in days) a company takes to pay its bills and invoices to its trade creditors, which includes suppliers, vendors, or other companies. The ratio is calculated on a quarterly or annual basis and indicates how well the company's cash outflows are being managed.

A company with a higher amount of DPO takes longer to pay its bills, which means that it retains the available funds for a longer duration. It may allow the company an opportunity to utilize the available cash in a better way to maximize the benefits.[6]

$$\text{The formula for DPO is: } \frac{\text{Average accounts payable}}{\text{Annual cost of goods sold}} \times 365$$

---

[4] https://www.investopedia.com/terms/d/dso.asp.

[5] https://www.investopedia.com/terms/d/days-sales-inventory-dsi.asp.

[6] https://www.investopedia.com/terms/d/dpo.asp

Discounted Terms

What is an early payment discount? ***An early payment discount is a reduction in the amount on a supplier's invoice if the customer pays the supplier promptly.*** The early payment discount is also known as a cash discount. (The seller may refer to the early payment discount as a sales discount. The buyer may refer to the early payment discount as a purchase discount.) Not all companies offer early payment discounts. If the discount is allowed it will appear on the sales invoice.

***Examples of Early Payment Discounts*:** Assume that a company sells goods on credit and offers an early payment discount expressed as *1/10, net 30*. This means that a customer is allowed to deduct 1% of the invoice amount if payment is made within 10 days (instead of paying the full amount in 30 days). In other words, the customer saves 1% for paying 20 days early. Therefore, an invoice of $1,000 with terms of *1/10, net 30* means that the $1,000 obligation will be settled in full for $990 if it is paid within 10 days.[7]

Calculating the Implicit Interest Rate on Discounted Terms

When granting discount terms, there is an implicit interest rate that needs to be compared to a company's opportunity cost in order to evaluate the cost/benefit analysis of granting or accepting the discounted terms. If the discounted terms' implicit interest rate is higher than a firm's opportunity cost, the buyer should take the discounted terms.

The formula for the buyer is the following:

$$\frac{\text{Discount}}{\text{Discounted payment}} \times \frac{365}{\text{Days difference between discount and full payment}} =$$

Using the example above of 1/10, net 30 yields an implicit interest rate of:

$$\frac{1}{99} \times \frac{365}{(30-10)} = .0101 \times 18.25 = .1843 = 18.43\%$$

[7]https://www.accountingcoach.com/blog/what-is-an-early-payment-discount.

Liquidity Crunch

A time when cash resources are in short supply and demand is high. During a ***liquidity crunch***, businesses and consumers are charged high interest rates on loans which are more difficult to obtain. Also known as ***liquidity crisis*** and ***credit crunch***.[8] A liquidity crunch can also relate to one firm if they have trouble obtaining capital at a point in time.

Supply Chain Finance

Supply chain finance (SCF) is a set of technology-based business and financing processes that link the various parties in a transaction — buyer, seller, and financing institution — in order to lower financing costs and improve business efficiency. SCF provides short-term credit that optimizes working capital for both the buyer and the seller.

SCF utilizes business solutions that optimize working capital and provide liquidity to businesses. Under SCF, suppliers sell their invoices or receivables at a discount to banks or other financial service providers, often called factors. In return, the suppliers get faster access to the money they are owed, enabling them to use it for working capital, while buyers generally get more time to pay. Instead of relying on the creditworthiness of the supplier, the bank deals with the buyer.

How Supply Chain Finance Works

There are a number of SCF transactions, including an extension of buyer's accounts payable terms, inventory finance, and payables discounting. SCF solutions differ from traditional supply chain programs to enhance working capital, such as factoring and payment discounts, in two ways:

- SCF connects financial transactions to value as it moves through the supply chain.
- SCF encourages collaboration between the buyer and seller, rather than the competition that often pits buyer against the seller and vice versa.

For example, the buyer will attempt to delay payment as long as possible, while the seller seeks to be paid as soon as possible. SCF works

[8] http://www.businessdictionary.com/definition/liquidity-crunch.html.

especially well when the buyer has a better credit rating than the seller and can thus access capital at a lower cost. The buyer can leverage this advantage to negotiate better terms from the seller, such as an extension of payment terms, which enables the buyer to conserve cash or use it for other purposes. The seller benefits by accessing cheaper capital, while having the option to sell its receivables to receive immediate payment.[9]

Cash Pooling

Cash pooling is a financial management strategy that allows companies to maximize both their current credit and debit positions so that the corporation receives the most benefit from those positions. In addition, it can help the company to avoid a number of costly bank fees, as well as help reduce the opportunity of damaging the reputation of the corporation because of negative balances on a bank account. In effect, this strategy helps make the most of the resources that are available.[10]

Credit Spread

A credit spread is the difference in yield between a US Treasury bond and another debt security of the same maturity but different credit quality. Credit spreads between US Treasuries and other bond issuances are measured in basis points, with a 1% difference in yield equal to a spread of 100 basis points.[11]

---

[9] https://www.investopedia.com/terms/s/supply-chain-finance.asp.

[10] https://www.wisegeek.com/what-is-cash-pooling.htm.

[11] https://www.investopedia.com/terms/c/creditspread.asp.

https://doi.org/10.1142/9789811216749_0022

Case 22

Gadgets Co: Trade Finance Case Study

Alisa Rusanoff

Crescendo Asset Management, USA

Business Description

Company "Gadgets Co" founded in 2007 is an importer, distributor, and wholesaler of computer and electronic accessories to specialty TV and big box retailers. It has ~ $200.0M+ of revenues and its largest customers are QVC, Rodgers, and Home Shopping. Together, these three clients account for 95% of total sales. Gadgets Co's core business is bundling electronic devices like Apple (Beats) Headphones and Samsung products together with accessories that are mostly imported from China (cases, chargers, sleeves, cords, stands, speakers, keyboards). Gadgets Co has distribution rights from these suppliers and has access to various discounts and special promotions.

Gadgets Co has a long-term relationship with QVC, its largest "bundle program" customer. QVC sells most of its inventory online as well as has several TV shows where they also sell Gadgets Co's products live — TSV (Today's Special Value) and daily sales vary from $8M to $10M.

Historically, QVC purchased the bundled kits, paid Gadgets Co upfront, and kept the inventory at a QVC warehouse. In 2014, QVC had $80M+ in leftover inventory that they had acquired from Gadgets Co over the prior 5 years. QVC exercised leverage in their business relationship and requested Gadgets Co repurchase this inventory at cost. Although Gadgets Co had no contractual obligation to buy back the inventory from QVC, it wanted to maintain a positive relationship with its largest customer. Gadgets Co was able to concurrently negotiate a new/expanded business relationship with QVC as a result of this repurchase accommodation. Gadgets Co took a significant one-time hit to its Income Statement and Balance sheet because of the repurchase.

Since then, however, the financials of the company have been improving: revenue has been increasing with margins remaining stable (there is an exception in 2016, largely driven by capital constraints and the resulting inventory shortages, see exhibit below). After 2015, Gadgets Co improved its business model and nurtured better relationships with its customers. Together with QVC senior management, Gadgets Co reinvented their operational model and now employs a "drop-ship" model, where the company is responsible for all fulfillment and logistics, including managing the inventory and the real-time offers for the various bundles. Instead of being paid upfront and shipping containers to QVC distribution centers, once a customer order is received at QVC, Home Shopping, or Rodgers, an invoice, pick-up ticket, and shipping label are automatically generated at Gadgets Co's own warehouse. Gadgets Co then picks and packs the orders and UPS picks up and ships the orders to the end customers every day. Payment terms with its major customer vary from 30 to 45 days.

QVC no longer carries inventory risk, and was willing, as a result, to expand Gadgets Co's distribution and product lines. Gadgets Co made investments in new systems and opened a new large warehouse to accommodate the "drop-ship" model and the expanded business relationship. Gadgets Co's pivot to this model is part of its long-term plan to achieve better annual sales growth, while relieving their customer's inventory risk and optimizing their own stock balances and inventory returns. The model has since been successfully implemented by other customers as well.

As a result of this pivot in strategy, the company has $10.0M worth of inventory in its warehouse that they can use as collateral in order to secure additional financing. 80% of this inventory comprises of Apple and Samsung products (with the rest being accessories, like headphones, cases, holders, wireless chargers, cables, adapters, etc.).

Current Situation

The Company's existing creditors have decided to not extend the bank credit line due to balance sheet concerns. Meanwhile, the business needs additional capital to support its revenue growth and demand from its long-term customers.

Gadgets Co hired a new CFO in 2019 to explore new financing opportunities, supply chain financing and factoring (accounts receivable financing). The new CFO identified the following weaknesses and strengths of the Company.

Company Weaknesses

- Negative equity caused by the 2014 hit;
- Negative working capital (current liabilities exceed current assets);
- Seasonality, as about 45% of sales occur in Q4 holiday season;
- Low margins, due to competitive nature of the business;
- Product returns average 16–17% annually (Gadgets Co provides 30 days of free returns, which is 75% of the returns and 15% are physical damages; returns are usually higher after holidays sales);
- Client concentration (three major clients account for 95% of total sales);
- Aged Accounts Payable (due to cash flow constraints, Gadgets Co delays payments to its suppliers, which hurts the company's relationships with its long-term suppliers);
- Inventory shortages, due to general cash flow constraints.

Company's Strengths

- 10+ years track record of successful business relationships;
- Strong customer base — QVC, Rogers, HSN, and others that have great financials, always pay on time and are receptive to Gadgets Co's sales initiatives;
- Strong supplier relationships — long and stable relationships with a diversified pool of suppliers in the US and China and exclusive contracts with Apple, Samsung, and others;
- TV shows, such as TSV (Today's Special Value) on QVC channel, and other unique sales opportunities usually lead to higher margins and

quick inventory turnover. QVC usually issues a purchase order ("PO") to the company outlining the expected volume and specifying the products requested for sale;

- Continuously updated products (iPhone, headphones, cases, etc.) on a yearly basis, that generate constant demand;
- Drop-ship business model;
- Good collateral: Inventory worth $10M.

The CFO Outlines the Following Difficulties That Gadgets Co Is Currently Facing

1. Expiring bank line which wouldn't be renewed due to the Company's distressed balance sheet. Negative working capital issue means they cannot organically fund inventory purchases;
2. Maintaining monthly operating expenses of ~$900K (comprise mostly of salaries, rent, shipping, and freight charges);
3. Capital required for purchasing inventory for an upcoming Christmas season;
4. Meeting demand from opportunistic TSV shows that happen 3–4 times a year and require short-term inventory financing. Purchase orders are available from the buyers (purchase order, or PO, is an official document issued by a buyer committing to pay the seller for the sale of specific products to be delivered in the future. In practice, some POs can be cancellable for various reasons);
5. Sustaining its overall sales growth which requires additional working capital and adjustable revolving credit facility to address seasonality; and
6. Being able to work with distributors offering opportunistic sales but unattractive payment terms as well as taking advantage of prepayment discounts offered by some suppliers.

Exhibit 1. Historical Financial Statements

Balance Sheet	**2014**	**2015**	**2016**	**2017**	**2018**
Current Assets					
Cash & Restricted Cash	644	21,563	556	(22,638)	1,014,832
Accounts Receivable	23,302,171	43,157,196	19,741,958	21,015,058	19,483,563
Inventory	6,024,613	8,002,496	10,282,879	26,796,551	23,033,335
Inventory vs Reverse Provision	6,774,562	4,975,965	2,146,990	2,860,000	4,862,623
Prepaids and Other Current Assets	3,217,658	3,835,697	4,113,141	977,048	542,649
	39,319,648	59,992,917	36,285,524	51,626,019	48,937,002
Other Assets	144,617	73,586	33,073	33,073	—
Total Assets	**$39,464,265**	**$60,066,503**	**$36,318,597**	**$51,659,092**	**$48,937,002**
Current Liabilities					
Accounts Payable & Accrued Expenses	10,292,411	18,221,490	21,997,257	27,624,469	40,140,917
Senior Loan Payable	28,209,678	46,097,767	28,685,429	32,778,287	19,484,062
Reserve Provision	9,590,259	9,636,700	7,039,113	9,892,347	8,468,114
	48,092,348	73,955,957	57,721,799	70,295,103	68,093,093
Other Long Term Liabilities	7,224,829	6,979,128	6,823,977	6,656,186	—
Members Deficit	(15,852,913)	(20,868,582)	(28,227,218)	(25,292,197)	(19,156,091)
Total Liabilities and Members Deficit	**$39,464,265**	**$60,066,503**	**$36,318,597**	**$51,659,092**	**$48,937,002**

Income Statement	**2014**	**2015**	**2016**	**2017**	**2018**
Gross Sales	**101,296,320**	**129,734,046**	**101,990,302**	**161,805,234**	**219,193,296**
Sales Returns and Allowances	43,280,287	21,226,558	20,084,828	24,052,925	34,128,161
Net Sales	58,016,033	108,507,488	81,905,474	137,752,309	185,065,135
Cost fo Goods Sold	52,011,329	97,041,673	75,110,629	117,677,066	169,118,224
Gross Profit	**$6,004,704**	**$11,465,815**	**$6,794,845**	**$20,075,243**	**$15,946,911**
	10.4%	*10.6%*	*8.3%*	*14.6%*	*8.6%*
Operating Expenses	5,495,534	8,437,009	8,826,027	10,983,002	11,066,137
Income from Operations	509,171	3,028,806	(2,031,182)	9,092,241	4,880,773
Interest, factor commissions & Other Income Taxes	1,552,284	6,777,680	3,743,629	4,523,938	1,176,660
Income before Taxes	**$(1,043,114)**	**$(3,748,874)**	**$(5,774,811)**	**$4,568,303**	**$3,704,114**

Exhibit 2. Q3–Q4 Sales Forecast/Seasonality

	June	July	August	September	October	November	December
Right Side Up	1,610,000	1,897,500	1,380,000	1,150,000	1,412,500	1,675,000	1,100,000
QVC	5,902,073	8,326,021	6,788,674	6,269,012	9,430,851	17,086,617	25,186,488
HSN	2,897,381	4,087,319	3,332,622	3,077,515	4,629,691	8,387,976	12,364,276
Rogers	1,931,588	2,724,879	2,221,748	2,051,677	3,086,460	5,591,984	8,242,851
Other Customers	447,603	617,876	497,727	455,116	673,143	1,187,518	1,700,805
TOTAL AR	**$12,788,645**	**$17,653,595**	**$14,220,771**	**$13,003,320**	**$19,232,645**	**$33,929,095**	**$48,594,420**
Sales Plan Gross	**$14,689,500**	**$20,493,250**	**$15,476,750**	**$15,242,000**	**$23,370,500**	**$40,703,750**	**$56,862,500**

Exhibit 3. Current Receivable Report

Customer Name	Outstanding Amount	Concentration
QVC, Inc	9,662,272	67.8%
Rogers Media, Inc	1,774,858	12.5%
HSN	2,193,586	15.4%
Walmart Merchant	58,135	0.4%
Zulily LLC	33,029	0.2%
Walmart Merchant	22,297	0.2%
Groupon LLC	6,118	0.0%
AMAZON	459,014	3.2%
Dover Street Market	12,146	0.1%
Sacai Asoc Co. Ltd	8,556	0.1%
Amazon.com	5,458	0.0%
Maxfield Enterprises	4,049	0.0%
Groupon DC	3,979	0.0%
	$14,243,496	**100.0%**

Assignment

- What alternative methods could the Company use to finance its inventory purchases and operating expenses?
- How can the company leverage its long relationship and excellent payment history with its strong clients as well as its inventory valued at $10M and early payment discounts offered by their suppliers?
- Build a simple cash flow forecast (provided $5M inventory facility and a factoring facility at 75% advance rate).

- Make gross and net income projections for the company if the revenue in 2019 is expected to be $250M, indicate how the margins change with additional cost of capital under various facilities.

Appendix

Informational Section

Alternative methods of financing started to develop in the wake of the Global Financial Crisis of 2008 and have been growing rapidly since then. It has effectively leveraged technological advances and adopted automated tools in order to disintermediate traditional lenders such as banks and other legacy financial institutions. Despite a low interest rate environment and burgeoning demand, banks permanently decreased lending activities to the SME (Small and Medium-sized Enterprise) market post 2008, citing capital requirements and risk tolerances. The growing volume needs in the SME market and international supply chain opened an opportunity for trade finance as one of the instruments to provide liquidity. According to the World Trade Organization, some 80–90% of the world trade relies on trade finance, which makes international supply chains and, thus, economic growth highly dependable on this type of financing.

One of the main advantages trade finance offers is consistent long-term debt ratios — trade finance is considered to be an off-balance sheet transaction and is represented in current Accounts Payable, which means businesses don't need to give up on equity either. These are usually flexible true-sale financing structures with less covenants and could be either recourse or non-recourse. The working capital freed up in these transactions helps improve DSO (days of sales outstanding) and DPO (days payables outstanding), fulfill more orders, keep a necessary level of inventory, increase trade, onboard new customers, and enter new markets. Below are some of the most typical trade finance products that support both domestic and international trade:

1. Supply Chain Financing ("SCF"): SCF, sometimes called reverse factoring[1], is a trade finance mechanism which allows a supplier to receive an early payment on their invoice. The trade finance company

[1] Botta, Alessio, Reinrad Höll, Reema Jain, Nikki Shah, and Lit Hau Tan. 2020. "Supply-Chain Finance: A Case of Convergent Evolution?" The 2020 McKinsey Global Payments Report, 19–26.

steps in and pays the supplier early, and the supplier takes a discount on their invoice for the privilege of early payment (but it could also be structured with a fee paid by the buyer). It helps provide liquidity to both parties, optimize working capital, negotiate better terms, and grow sales volume. Supply Chain finance usually represents a higher cost of capital for the SME as it has a much higher concentration risk due to its structure and is often unsecured.
2. Factoring: Factoring, or accounts receivable financing[2], is one of the oldest finance tools by which a company brings cash flow forward — By selling its accounts receivable at a discount it uses the cash to grow sales, pay operating expense, and take vendor discounts. This ultimately results in a better bottom line and a healthier financial outlook. The cost to the company is a small percentage of sales. For example, if a company wants to factor $100,000.00 worth of their invoices, a factoring company ("Factor") could advance 80%, or $80,000.00 cash will be provided to the company on day 1. Factor gets paid directly by the end debtor (client's customer) on the due date on the invoice — if entire $100,000.00 payment comes in, Factor depending on the agreed rate can charge $2,000.00, and send the remaining $8,000.00 ("reserves") back to the client.

Factoring usually provides the lowest cost of capital solution for SMEs among other Trade Finance mechanisms due to risk diversification — the more diverse the end debtor list is, the lower the concentration risk is. Also, the end debtor list could vary from smaller distributors and retailers to public companies, the latter bearing minimum credit risk for the Factor.

In addition to regular credit and operational risk, there are several risks to be considered for a financier in factoring — Potential Accounts Receivable dilution caused by discounts, disputes of invoices, damaged and spoiled products, end customer returns, etc. The financier must perform historical AR dilution analysis to underwrite the transaction and assign an appropriate advance rate for the client to mitigate these types of risks. For instance, if historical dilution is 10% on average, the advance rate on a factored invoice shall not exceed 90% of its face value. To mitigate other potential risks as well as a discount fee, a typical factor would advance close to 80% of the face value.

---

[2]Jones, Stephen A. 2018. Credit Risk, *Trade and Receivables Finance. A Practical Guide to Risk Evaluation and Structuring*, 87–98. Palgrave Macmillan, UK.

3. Purchase Order Financing ("PO Finance"): PO Financing goes a step before a trade invoice is issued and could be factored. A purchase order is a commercial paper outlining details such as description of goods, quantities, agreed-upon prices, etc. Purchase Order financing is typically riskier than factoring and thus requires higher cost of capital and lower advance rate to account for any business, operational, credit, and product quality risks. Once the purchase order is fulfilled by a seller, an invoice is issued and can be factored. Typically PO and AR Financing companies work together and specify their financing structures by means of an intercreditor agreement.

   Other alternative trade finance solutions include:

4. Letters of Credit ("LC"): Letters of credit are another method of providing secure financing used in international trade. A buyer makes an arrangement with an issuing bank to offer a payment term contingent on presentation of stipulated documents — with shipping and insurance paperwork, commercial invoices describing the specifics of the goods, etc. one can make possible a title transfer of the goods. The issuing bank is then responsible for a payment to an exporter upon satisfactory submission of the proper documentation[3].
5. Inventory Financing: Inventory financing is a form of credit used to pay for inventory that may not be intended for immediate sale or use. The main risk here is inventory depreciation, write-downs, obsolescence, and shelf life depending on the type of product and industry. The advance rate on inventory financing is usually the lowest among all the other Trade Finance types.

Trade Finance has several specific risks worth mentioning (apart from the potentially higher cost of capital). Among major risks are:

- Credit Risk: Credit risk measures the probability of default resulting from a seller not being able to recover a payment from an end customer (debtor). Identifying, quantifying, and continuously monitoring this risk is crucial in managing a sustainable and balanced portfolio. In many cases, to mitigate counterparty risk, exporters and financiers obtain

[3]Cenzon, Bernadette. 2015. *Guidebook on Trade and Supply Chain Finance*, 44. APEC Policy Support Unit.

trading credit insurance to insure up to 90–100% of the face value of the invoice at risk.

- Political and Country Risk: International trade involves various geopolitical tensions such as trade quotas, import duties, political instabilities, and sanctions that have direct impact on businesses. It is important for all parties to monitor the news and regional trends in real time, as well as pursue diversification across customers and countries.
- Foreign Exchange Risk: Exchange rate volatility could be caused by various factors like economic conditions, monetary policy, and foreign affairs. Hedging techniques like forward contracts and options, diversification, and other instruments help mitigate this risk.
- Fraud Risk: Trade finance involves a lot of paperwork supporting the sale — shipment, freight insurance, warehouse receipts, quality check reports, etc. Therefore exporters, importers, brokers, and capital providers should have robust internal controls to prevent fraud as there is no guaranteed protection against this type of risk. Among the most common fraud cases are "double billing" or duplicate invoice financing, forged documents, and collateral fraud.

Part VII

Mergers and Acquisitions

https://doi.org/10.1142/9789811216749_0023

Case 23

The Takeover of Sterling Drug Company*

Ingo Walter

New York University, Stern School of Business, USA

The Companies

The Hoffmann-La Roche (Roche or the Company) group of firms posted $6 billion sales and employed over 45,000 workers worldwide in 1987, with 10,000 people employed at its $1.5 billion US operations. Sterling Drug employed 21,000 worldwide. Its US sales of pharmaceutical specialties totaled $360 million in 1987. The acquisition would make the combined group the 5th largest drug firm in the world as regards pharmaceutical sales. The company produced Valium and a broad range of other drugs and healthcare products. Sterling made Bayer aspirin, Phillips Milk of Magnesia, Mop & Glo, and Lysol disinfectant, among other over-the-counter (OTC) products, as well as a range of proprietary drugs and diagnostics such as Omnipaque non-radioactive imaging dye.

---

*Prepared entirely from published materials by Prof. Ingo Walter, New York University, August 1990 (for classroom use only).

On January 5, 1988, F. Hoffmann-La Roche & Co. of Basel, Switzerland launched an unsolicited offer to acquire the Sterling Drug Company of New York.

The company indicated that it wanted to reenter the US consumer products and OTC drug businesses by acquiring Sterling, according to an open letter from CEO Fritz Gerber. Roche had written off the US consumer products business 5 years earlier by selling its Pantene shampoo operation to Richardson-Vicks, which also acquired the right to develop certain Roche products for US OTC sale. Meanwhile, Roche's major Swiss competitors, Sandoz and Ciba-Geigy, were strengthening their OTC operations worldwide. Over-the-counter products made up less than 20% of Sterling's total sales of over $2 billion/year in 1987. Internal development of an OTC business was very costly and buying a critical mass of existing OTC products was very attractive. Sterling had Bayer aspirin, sales of which grew 25% in January–September 1987. Its total proprietary drug sales rose 10% during the same period.

Besides the OTC business, Roche was interested in Sterling's proprietary preparations activities, which would allow it to enter this part of the US market — especially analgesics. World proprietary sales totaled $23 billion/year in 1987, of which the US accounted for $10 billion/year. The acquisition would also strengthen Roche's own activities in the diagnostics sector, which accounted for 11% of 1987 sales. Indeed, Roche management suggested that the two firms' overall activities, including their R&D efforts, would strongly complement each other.

Pharmaceutical companies were considered to be more vulnerable to takeovers in the wake of the October 1987 stock market crash and the decline in the value of the dollar during 1985–88. The industry was being reevaluated in light of a number of takeover bids. Prospective buyers were most likely to come from abroad because assets in the US were considered less expensive for foreign firms, which did not have to write off goodwill expenses and consequently did not suffer the resulting decrease in the net earnings. Hoffmann's bid for Sterling was being closely monitored by analysts since its outcome could influence other foreign companies seeking US acquisitions. If Hoffmann's attempt succeeded, other foreign concerns might be encouraged to make their own, while a loss could deter takeover activity in this sector. Indeed, the Roche offer marked at the end of a long-standing but unspoken "gentlemen's agreement" among major world drug companies that had all but prevented hostile takeovers in the industry.

The Bid

The Roche tender offer was for $72/share, or a total of $4.14 billion. The offer represented a 27% premium over recent prices of Sterling's stock.

Roche indicated that the entire purchase price would come from its own resources, and that the offer was not contingent on financing or further evaluation of Sterling. The company confirmed that a bank syndicate had formally committed to provide all of the financing — a $1 billion loan commitment from Swiss Bank Corporation in addition to $3.2 billion from Union Bank of Switzerland, Credit Suisse, Morgan Guaranty, Banque Nationale de Paris, and Deutsche Bank. Under the Roche offer, Sterling's management would remain largely unchanged.

Buy-Side Advisory

Wall Street's takeover community was reportedly stunned by disclosure that a commercial bank, Morgan Guaranty Trust Co., was selected to advise Roche in its unsolicited tender offer. Morgan Guaranty was chosen over First Boston Corp., which had previously handled much of Roche's business. Morgan's fees were reportedly well below conventional investment banking levels for comparable advisory services.

The Response (Defenses)

Following an emergency meeting of the Sterling board, the Roche offer was termed "grossly inadequate" and rejected as not being in the fundamental interest of shareholders. In its defense, Sterling undertook the following actions in rapid succession:

1. It established a $2 billion revolving line of credit to facilitate a possible recapitalization and payment of a special dividend to shareholders.
2. It set up severance agreements (golden parachutes) with major executives in case of a takeover.
3. It considered a variety of other defensive options such as asset sales and even possible liquidation of the company.
4. Although the company preferred to remain independent, it began seeking a second buyer to serve as a 'white knight'. The company's management, who did not hold a large amount of Sterling stock, focused on a potential buyer not in the drug business, which would be likely to rely on current management's expertise to run the company. Firms such as Eastman Kodak, General Electric, and Procter & Gamble were said to have expressed interest in acquiring Sterling.

5. The company noted that Roche's bid could well be affected by possible passage of legislation in Delaware that would limit hostile takeovers of firms incorporated in that state.
6. It filed suit against Hoffmann-La Roche, charging US income tax evasion through transfer pricing, as well as filing false and misleading financial statements. Sterling charged that Roche was buying its stock through a non-transparent offer that did not disclose the most basic information required by the Securities Exchange Act of 1934. Sterling claimed that Roche did not provide the required information about the Swiss family that controlled the company and HLR Acquisition Inc., a subsidiary formed to bid for Sterling.
7. Its suit to block the takeover included the charge that two Bermuda-based affiliates of Hoffmann-La Roche, Atlantis Finance and Canadian Pharmholding, had traded in Sterling's stock and options before the offer was announced. This triggered an SEC investigation, wherein the Commission asked Switzerland to waive its banking secrecy laws to help its review of the allegation. After the bid was launched, Roche had indeed sold 90,000 shares of Sterling for $75/share. Although a Swiss analyst speculated that the shares were sold to push the price down, US traders did not think this was the case. The company subsequently turned over to the SEC the required information, while the Swiss Bankers Association assembled the information from member institutions. No evidence of insider trading was found.

Defense Advisory (Compensation)

Sterling retained Morgan Stanley to serve as financial adviser in its defense against the hostile Roche bid. A fee schedule was established that would make it more profitable for Morgan Stanley to either arrange a bid of over $80/share for Sterling or keep Sterling independent. Sterling would pay $10 million to Morgan Stanley if it was not acquired by Roche within 6 months following January 5, 1988, and its independence was not immediately threatened. Morgan Stanley would receive an additional $15.2 million plus $1.4 million for each $1/share offer above $80/share if Roche or any other bidder succeeded in a takeover.

Ensuing Events

Four days after the initial bid, on January 11, 1988, Sterling received an improved takeover bid of $4.4 billion from Hoffmann-La Roche, or $76/share — higher than the original $72/share bid, but still lower than Sterling's closing stock price on the New York Stock Exchange (NYSE), which had already risen because of arbitrage activity. A drug industry analyst at Prudential-Bache suggested that Sterling would not be able to remain independent, and that the higher Hoffmann-La Roche bid would complicate Sterling's search for a white knight.

Ten days later, on January 21, 1988, Roche raised its bid to $4.62 billion or $81/share. The Swiss company was, according to traders, attempting a classic "bear hug" — rapidly raising the price to pressure the target to accept the bid while scaring off potential friendly buyers. While Sterling had still not identified any friendly suitors, Johnson & Johnson, Nestle, Pfizer, and Yamanouchi Pharmaceutical were mentioned by analysts. The chance of a US company buying Sterling dropped as the price rose because any such acquirer would have to amortize Sterling's goodwill on its income statements over 30–40 years without tax deductibility.

The Outcome

A few days later, the Eastman Kodak Company of Rochester, N.Y. launched a tender offer of $89.50/share for Sterling's 7 million shares — an offer that would expire at midnight on February 22, 1988. Hoffmann-La Roche immediately withdrew its bid. Sterling Drug was thus acquired by Kodak for $5.1 billion, and the two firms signed a definitive merger agreement. The Kodak bid was financed in large part by a 3-year, $5 billion syndicated revolving credit from about 30 US and foreign banks, led by Bankers Trust Company in return for a $2.5 million fee. Bankers Trust had bested several other major banks in competing for the transaction. The acquisition of Sterling would make Kodak a $1 billion/year drug company, and also give it a $1 billion/year household product business. It would provide the company's pharmaceuticals division, formed in 1986, with a worldwide infrastructure for drug registration and marketing. In turn, Sterling could eventually market Kodak's biotech-based pharmaceuticals. It would operate as a separate subsidiary in Kodak's operations, giving it a measure of operational independence that its management feared it might lose.

The transaction was explained by Kodak management as a key step toward its goal of becoming one of the world's top 10 drug companies in 10–12 years. The acquisition was six times larger than any previous Kodak acquisition. The company's position in the drug industry was enhanced by its collection of some 500,000 chemical compounds, as well as high degree of biotechnology expertise in research and drug production. Kodak's fledgling pharmaceutical business had achieved most of its successes in the laboratory, not in the marketplace. The acquisition of Sterling would give Kodak a well-established position in the pharmaceutical market worldwide and provide it with valuable experience in how to channel new drugs through the US federal regulatory process.

Kodak indicated that it wanted to achieve 10% return on investment from the Sterling acquisition which meant that Sterling would have to post an annual profit of $510 million, as compared with its record profit of $297 million in 1987. The acquisition raised the company's debt to 50% of total capital, but management expected to drop it back to 35% by 1993. Analysts postulated that Kodak's income might lose 45–60 cents/share because of the interest costs on the $5 billion loan, while Kodak itself projected a 15–25 cents/share decline for 1988. Kodak also paid for goodwill in the deal — the difference between Sterling's book value and the purchase price — of $4.1 billion. Kodak's dividends would not be affected by the purchase, according to the firm.

Outside observers regarded the transaction as either helping or hindering the interests of Kodak shareholders. Some saw it as a tool that would let Kodak exploit Sterling Drug's vast resources, while others viewed it as a poison pill that could weigh the company down to the point of appearing unattractive to buyers. Many analysts thought that Kodak paid too high a price. Standard & Poor's subsequently lowered its rating on Kodak's senior debt, commercial paper, and subordinated debt.

Hoffmann-La Roche announced that it still planned to make acquisitions despite the Sterling setback.

The Controversy

During the 3-week battle in January 1988, Sterling blasted its longtime banker, Morgan Guaranty, for providing investment banking services to Roche. In a letter to Morgan's chairman Lewis T. Preston, Sterling chairman John M. Pietruski said he was shocked and dismayed by what he considered to be Morgan's unethical conduct in aiding and abetting a surprise raid on one of its longtime clients.

In his letter, Pietruski said Morgan was "privy to our most confidential financial information," including shareholder lists, and asked Preston, "How many relationships of trust and confidence do you have to have with a client before you consider not embarking on a course of action that could be detrimental to [its] best interest?" The Sterling chairman said his company was reviewing "all our dealings" with Morgan and intended to "bring the matter to the attention" of other Morgan clients.

A spokesman for Morgan Guaranty said, "Although Mr. Preston intends to respond to Mr. Pietruski directly, I can say that we are acting properly in this transaction." However, the charges seem particularly embarrassing to Morgan, which has traditionally emphasized strong client relationships as a way of differentiating itself from other corporate finance competitions.

Sterling's criticism highlights the hazards for big banks as they elbow their way into the takeover arena. Firms such as Bankers Trust New York Corp., Citibank, and Manufacturers Hanover had been increasing their presence in takeovers, both as a source of takeover financing and as investment bankers, sometimes to the distress of their traditional banking clients. Gillette Co., for instance, severed its longtime banking relationship with Citibank in 1987, after the bank agreed to help Revlon Group Inc. pursue a hostile bid for the company.

Others criticized Sterling's defense as being particularly onerous, especially the insider trading and other charges aimed at Roche. They suggested that Sterling management was more interested in its own future than that of the firm or its shareholders and was abetted in this by the advice it received from Morgan Stanley.

The Assignment

1. Did Morgan Guaranty act properly? What consequences, if any, do you see resulting from this case for the bank?
2. Assuming the defensive strategy was the product of Morgan Stanley's advice, did the firm violate any standards of proper conduct?
3. Assess the conduct of Sterling's management and its board in how the battle was conducted in terms of their respective interests.

https://doi.org/10.1142/9789811216749_0024

Case 24

The Acquisition of Bioverativ, Inc. by Sanofi, S.A.*

Harvey A. Poniachek

Rutgers Business School, USA

Assignment Questions and Required Analysis

Samuel Weinberg is the Managing Director of business development at North East Venture Capital, Inc. (NVC). He graduated in 2009 from Rutgers Business School with a degree in finance, and previously earned a BA in accounting and economics from the State University of New York Albany. Following his graduation from Rutgers, he was hired by J.P. Morgan capital markets, and after a couple of years he was lured away by Morgan Stanley.

NVC has $50 billion under management and is predominantly engaged in mergers and acquisitions, funding of early startups in the medical field, and speculation in biomedical securities. The company's performance has beaten the S&P 500 for the past five years. In past years, NVC made substantial investments in Biogen and it spun off the entity Bioverativ, Inc.

Following the tender offer by Sanofi, S.A. to Bioverativ, Inc., Samuel Weinberg requested his staff to perform the following analysis and provide him with a written report by the end of the week.

---

* Prepared from a tender offer made by Sanofi, S.A. and affiliate to Bioverativ, Inc. on February 9, 2018, and filed with the SEC on Schedule TO.

1. What type of proposed merger is it: Horizontal, vertical, or conglomerate, friendly or hostile?
2. Did the Board of Bioverativ, Inc. obtain the best price in accordance with the Revlon Duties? Did the Board of the target company follow the Trans Union Case of Smith v. van Gorkum? (The Revlon and Smith v. van Gorkum court cases are available on the Web).[1]
3. Apply the 10-K data and use the discount cash flow valuation approach to determine whether the price offered for the target is consistent with your findings?
4. Based on the application of the Market Approach by utilizing the enclosed comparable data, determine whether the proposed prices are approximately consistent with your analysis?
5. Based on the facts and your analysis, would you recommend that Bioverativ, Inc.'s shareholders vote to accept the tender offer?

The Tender Offer and Merger Agreement

The tender offer by Blink Acquisition Corp. ("*Merger Sub*"), a Delaware corporation ("*Purchaser*") and an indirect wholly owned subsidiary of Sanofi, a French *société anonyme* ("*Sanofi*" or "*Parent*") offered to

[1]Revlon, Inc. v. MacAndrews & Forbes Holdings, Inc., 506 A.2d 173, 1986 Del. LEXIS 1053, 66 A.L.R.4th 157, Fed. Sec. L. Rep. (CCH) P92,525 (Del. March 13, 1986), see https://www.casebriefs.com/blog/law/corporations/corporations-keyed-to-klein/mergers-acquisitions-and-takeovers/revlon-inc-v-macandrews-forbes-holdings-inc/.
Revlon, Inc. v. MacAndrews & Forbes Holdings, see https://law.justia.com/cases/delaware/supreme-court/1986/506-a-2d-173-1.html.
Revlon, Inc. v. MacAndrews & Forbes Holdings, Inc., Delaware Supreme Court 506 A.2d 173 (1986), see https://www.quimbee.com/cases/revlon-inc-v-macandrews-forbes-holdings-inc.
Smith v. Van Gorkom, 488 A.2d 858, 1985 Del. LEXIS 421, 46 A.L.R.4th 821, Fed. Sec. L. Rep. (CCH) P91,921 (Del. January 29, 1985), see https://www.casebriefs.com/blog/law/corporations/corporations-keyed-to-hamilton/duty-of-care-and-the-business-judgment-rule/smith-v-van-gorkom-2/.
Thomas C. Wagner, Smith v. van Gorkom, 488 A.2d 858 (Del. 1985), *Florida State University Law Review* 14, no. 1 (Winter 1985), Article 4.
Bernard S. Sharfman, "The Enduring Legacy of Smith v. Van Gorkom," *Delaware Journal of Corporate Law* 33 (2008), see https://www.djcl.org/wp-content/uploads/2014/08/The-enduring-legacy-of-smith-v.-van-gorkom.pdf.

purchase any and all of the outstanding shares of Bioverativ, Inc. ("The Company") at $105.00 per Share in cash, net of applicable withholding taxes and without interest (the "*Offer Price*"). The Offer will expire 1 minute after 11:59 p.m. (12:00 midnight), New York City time, on March 7, 2018 (the "*Expiration Time*"), unless Purchaser has extended or earlier terminated the period during which the Offer is open in accordance with the Merger Agreement.

The Offer is being made pursuant to an Agreement and Plan of Merger, dated January 21, 2018 (as it may be amended or supplemented from time to time, the "*Merger Agreement*"), between Bioverativ, Sanofi, and Purchaser. The Offer is conditioned upon, among other things, the satisfaction or waiver of the following conditions:

(i) the number of Shares validly tendered in the Offer and not withdrawn as of the Expiration Time, together with any Shares (if any) owned by Parent and its affiliates and excluding any Shares tendered pursuant to guaranteed delivery procedures that have not yet been "received" (as such term is defined in Section 251(h)(6)(f) of the Delaware General Corporation Law, as amended (the "*DGCL*")), represents at least a majority of the then outstanding Shares (the "*Minimum Tender Condition*");

(ii) the expiration or termination of the waiting period under the Hart-Scott-Rodino Antitrust Improvements Act of 1976, as amended, and the rules and regulations promulgated thereunder (the "*HSR Act*") and that all consents of, and/or filings with, any governmental authority of competent jurisdiction or pursuant to any antitrust laws have been obtained and are in full force and effect and any applicable waiting period with respect thereto has expired;

(iii) the absence of any law or order that would make the Offer or the Merger illegal or otherwise preventing or prohibiting the consummation of the Offer or the Merger;

(iv) the accuracy of the Company's representations and warranties under the Merger Agreement (subject to customary materiality qualifiers);

(v) the absence, since the date of the Merger Agreement, of any fact, circumstance, condition, event, change, development, occurrence, result, or event which, individually or in the aggregate, has had, or would reasonably be expected to have, a Company Material Adverse Effect (as defined in the Merger Agreement);

(vi) the Merger Agreement has not been terminated;

(vii) the Merger Agreement provides, among other things, that following (but on the same day as) the consummation of the Offer and subject to the satisfaction or waiver of certain conditions set forth in the Merger Agreement, Purchaser will be merged with and into the Company (the "*Merger*"), with the Company surviving the Merger as an indirect wholly owned subsidiary of Parent (the "*Surviving Corporation*"). Upon the consummation of the Merger (the "*Effective Time*"), the Company will cease to be a publicly traded company. A copy of the Merger Agreement is filed as Exhibit (e)(1) to this Schedule 14D-9 and is incorporated herein by reference;

(viii) the Merger will be governed by Section 251(h) of the DGCL and effected without a vote of the Company stockholders. The Offer is made only for Shares and is not made for any Options or RSUs. The Merger Agreement provides that each Option and RSU (collectively, the "Company Equity Awards") that is outstanding as of immediately prior to the consummation of the Offer will become fully vested as of immediately prior to, and contingent upon, the consummation of the Offer and will be canceled and converted into the right to receive the Offer Price (less the applicable exercise price in the case of Options) in cash.

The Merger Agreement requires the Surviving Corporation to fulfill and honor in all respects the obligations of the Company and its subsidiaries pursuant to (i) any indemnification agreement in effect between the Company or any of its subsidiaries and any individual who, at the Effective Time is, or at any time prior to such time was, a director or officer of the Company or of a subsidiary (each, an "*Indemnified Party*") that was made publicly available on the EDGAR website or made available to Parent prior to the execution of the Merger Agreement, and (ii) any indemnification or exculpation provision set forth in the certificate of incorporation or bylaws of the Company, in each case as in effect on the date of the Merger Agreement.

The Merger Agreement

On January 21, 2018, Biogen, Parent, and the Company entered into a letter agreement (the "*Letter Agreement*") in connection with the Merger, which, among other things, addresses aspects of that certain Tax Matters Agreement, dated as of January 31, 2017, by and between Biogen and the Company (the "*Tax Matters Agreement*"). The Agreement may be terminated (i) by mutual written consent of the parties, subject to the terms of the Letter Agreement.

Recommendation of the Board of Directors

On January 21, 2018, Bioverativ Board of Directors unanimously (i) declared that the Merger Agreement, the Merger and the other Transactions, including the Offer, are advisable, fair to, and in the best interests of, the Company and its stockholders, (ii) adopted and approved the Merger Agreement, the entry by Bioverativ into the Merger Agreement, and the consummation of the Transactions, including the Offer and the Merger, on the terms and subject to the conditions set forth therein, (iii) determined to recommend that the Company's stockholders (other than Parent and its subsidiaries) accept the Offer and tender their Shares to Purchaser pursuant to the Offer, (iv) resolved to take all actions necessary so that the restrictions on business combinations and stockholder vote requirements contained in Section 203 of the DGCL and any other applicable law and authorized that the Merger be governed by Section 251(h) of the DGCL and consummated as soon as practicable following the consummation of the Offer. Accordingly, our Board of Directors unanimously recommends that stockholders tender their Shares to Purchaser pursuant to the Offer.

Background of the Offer and Merger Discussion

The Company became an independent, publicly traded firm on February 1, 2017, when it was spun off from Biogen. The Company has regularly evaluated different strategies for improving its competitive position and enhancing stockholder value, including acquisitions, joint ventures, collaborations, and other potential business opportunities.

In May 2017, a representative of Lazard Fréres & Co. LLC ("*Lazard*"), contacting on behalf of Sanofi, Dr. Alexander Denner, Chief Investment Officer of Sarissa Capital and a member of our Board of Directors, and stated that Sanofi would be interested in having a discussion with the Company. Following this contact, on May 12, 2017, Serge Weinberg, the Chairman of Sanofi, contacted Brian Posner, Chairman of our Board of Directors, to request an opportunity to meet to discuss Sanofi's interest in acquiring the Company. Mr. Posner stated that the Company was not for sale. Following this discussion, the Company contacted a representative of Paul, Weiss to provide legal advice in connection therewith.

On May 15, 2017, Mr. Weinberg and Mr. Posner had a follow-up call, during the course of which a meeting was scheduled for May 19, 2017. A meeting was held on May 19, 2017, in Greenwich, CT, with Dr. Olivier Brandicourt, Chief Executive Officer of Sanofi, Mr. Weinberg, Dr. Denner, and Mr. Posner in attendance. During the course of this meeting, Mr. Weinberg discussed Sanofi's interest in acquiring the Company. Mr. Weinberg stated that Sanofi was only interested in pursuing a **friendly transaction**. At the conclusion of this meeting, Mr. Posner stated that the Company was focused on executing its current business plan and growing its operations as a standalone business but that he would convey Mr. Weinberg's interest to our Board of Directors. Following the meeting, Mr. Posner updated each member of our Board of Directors regarding the substance of the May 19, 2017 meeting. On May 23, 2017, Mr. Posner called Mr. Weinberg, confirming that the Company was focused on executing its current business objectives and growing its operations as a standalone business and was not for sale. During that call, Mr. Weinberg acknowledged that he understood and, that from Sanofi's perspective, the matter was now closed. Following the May 23, 2017 call, Mr. Posner sent an email to each member of our Board of Directors with an update on the substance of the May 23, 2017 call and confirming that Mr. Weinberg informed him that the matter was now closed.

On September 12, 2017, Mr. Posner received a message from Mr. Weinberg requesting a telephonic conversation. On September 13, 2017, Mr. Posner reported the outreach from Sanofi to the directors at a regularly scheduled meeting of the Board of Directors. During the course of this meeting, the Board of Directors discussed the fact that the Company was not for sale and was focused on executing its current business plan and growing its operations as a standalone business. However, the Board of Directors authorized Mr. Posner to schedule a telephonic discussion with Mr. Weinberg and to report back to the Board of Directors.

Following the September 13, 2017 meeting of the Board of Directors, Mr. Posner and Mr. Weinberg spoke by telephone on September 15, 2017. In the course of this discussion, Mr. Weinberg expressed Sanofi's interest in pursuing an acquisition of the Company and Mr. Posner stated that the

Board of Directors remained confident in the future of the Company as a standalone business and was not interested in pursuing such a transaction at that time. Following the phone call with Mr. Weinberg, Mr. Posner provided a further update to the Board of Directors regarding the substance of the conversation.

In late October 2017, Dr. Denner was contacted by a representative of Lazard inquiring as to the Company's interest in engaging in discussions about a potential transaction with Sanofi. The representatives of Lazard conveyed to Dr. Denner the possibility of Sanofi submitting a private proposal letter with respect to a potential acquisition. Dr. Denner indicated that in order for our Board of Directors to consider entering into discussions with Sanofi regarding a potential transaction, Sanofi must offer a "preemptive" price; that is, a price that is sufficiently high that it would obviate the need for a pre-signing market check. Dr. Denner reported Lazard's outreach to Mr. Posner. This outreach was then conveyed to the members of the Board of Directors.

On November 3, 2017, Mr. Posner and Mr. Weinberg spoke by telephone. Mr. Weinberg conveyed details of Sanofi's non-binding acquisition proposal, which included a proposed price of $98.50 per share, payable in cash. During the course of this discussion, Mr. Posner indicated that the Company was not for sale, but that he would present the Sanofi proposal to our Board of Directors. Following this discussion, Mr. Weinberg delivered an email to Mr. Posner attaching the Sanofi proposal letter (the "*November 3 Proposal*"). The November 3 Proposal noted that the price represented an 84% premium to the closing price of the Shares of $53.65 on November 2, 2017, and a premium of 73% to the 60 trading day volume weighted average closing price of $56.92.

On November 7, 2017, the Board of Directors held a special telephonic meeting with certain members of senior management and representatives from Paul, Weiss in attendance. At the meeting, our Board of Directors reviewed the non-binding November 3 Proposal submitted by Sanofi and discussed next steps with respect to its response to Sanofi. During the course of this meeting, the Board of Directors requested that the Company's management team prepare an overview of the Company's long-range plan as a standalone business. A representative of Paul, Weiss then reviewed certain legal matters for our Board of Directors' consideration in connection with its evaluation of the non-binding November 3 Proposal from Sanofi and reviewed the fiduciary obligations of the Board of Directors. In addition, the Board of Directors discussed the potential engagement of J.P. Morgan Securities LLC ("*J.P. Morgan*") and Guggenheim Securities, LLC ("*Guggenheim Securities*") as outside financial advisors to the Company, based on, among other things, J.P. Morgan's and Guggenheim Securities' respective credentials as sophisticated investment banks with substantial knowledge and experience in the biopharmaceutical industry and mergers and acquisitions generally, as well as each firm's familiarity with the Company.

Following this meeting, the Board of Directors voted by written consent to approve the engagement of each of J.P. Morgan, Guggenheim Securities, and Paul, Weiss by the Company, subject to finalization of the terms of each such engagement and management initiated negotiation of such engagement letters.

On November 16, 2017, Mr. Weinberg contacted Mr. Posner requesting an update on when Sanofi could expect a response from the Company regarding Sanofi's non-binding November 3 Proposal. Mr. Posner responded that the Company was reviewing the November 3 Proposal with management and the Company's legal and financial advisors and that the Company would respond to Sanofi as soon as it could. On November 21, 2017, a meeting of our Board of Directors was convened to discuss the Company's preliminary long-range plan as a standalone business and the Company's response to Sanofi's non-binding November 3 Proposal. Representatives from J.P. Morgan, Guggenheim Securities, and Paul, Weiss were in attendance as well as members of senior management. At the meeting, certain members of senior management presented the Company's long-range plan as a standalone business, which had been developed to reflect management's views on each of the Company's products and product candidates. The Board of Directors discussed in detail the financial model, and members of management responded to questions from the Board of Directors in relation to management's projections. The members of senior management, representatives of J.P. Morgan and Guggenheim Securities, and the Board of Directors also discussed the Company's performance and its portfolio and product pipeline, as well as assumptions used in preparing the management projections.

During this meeting, representatives of J.P. Morgan and Guggenheim Securities made a joint presentation with respect to Sanofi's non-binding November 3 Proposal and discussed with the Board of Directors certain financial and market information, including a preliminary illustrative valuation analysis regarding the Company. During the course of this meeting, representatives of Paul, Weiss reviewed certain legal matters for the consideration of the Board of Directors in connection with its evaluation of the non-binding offer from Sanofi, including certain tax considerations. Our Board of Directors also discussed the benefits to the Company of avoiding a protracted sales process that could potentially distract the management team at a critical time for the Company. The Board of Directors weighed the potential benefits and risks, including the potential risk of leaks and the impact that a leak could have on the Company as well as the risk that Sanofi might withdraw its offer if a leak were to occur, of reaching out to a broader or narrower group of other industry participants in order to gauge their interest in submitting a proposal to acquire the Company. The Board of Directors then determined to reconvene thereafter to continue its deliberations regarding the November 3 Proposal.

On November 25, 2017, a meeting of the Board of Directors was convened by teleconference to discuss the Company's potential response to the November 3 Proposal. Representatives of J.P. Morgan, Guggenheim Securities, and Paul, Weiss were in attendance, as were certain members of senior management. During the course of this meeting, the Board of Directors authorized the Company to negotiate and enter into a confidentiality agreement with Sanofi that would include customary standstill provisions with a customary "fall away" provision providing that the standstill obligations[2] would terminate in certain circumstances, including upon the Company entering into a binding agreement related to a change of control of the Company, in order to facilitate discussions between the parties. At the conclusion of this meeting, our Board of Directors based on

[2]In connection with proposed mergers and acquisitions of public companies, the target company often requests that the potential acquiror enter into a **standstill agreement** providing protection of the public target from unwanted takeover attempts by the potential acquiror. Standstill agreements provide various levels of protection and stability to the target company and its board of directors to conduct an orderly sale process. The rationale for the target company's request for a standstill agreement is simple — the target wants the process to be consensual and the terms mutually agreed upon. So, before providing confidential information about its business and operations and before the potential acquiror has committed to enter into a definitive acquisition agreement, the target company wants to ensure that the potential acquiror does not use the confidential information to launch a hostile bid of the target if the parties cannot reach a mutual agreement on the terms of the sale. Breaching a Standstill Agreement Can Result in Substantial Liability. See K. L. Gates, "Standstill Considerations in an M&A Context: Recent Developments and Some Practice Pointers," March 2011, https://www.jdsupra.com/legalnews/standstill-considerations-in-an-ma-cont-21364/.

the foregoing directed Mr. Posner to communicate to Sanofi that the offer price of $98.50 per share did not reflect the full value of the Company, but that the Company was willing to have members of the Company's senior management meet with Sanofi to discuss the Company's long-range plan as a standalone business and other sources of value with a view toward Sanofi submitting a revised proposal if it wished to do so.

On November 27, 2017, Mr. Posner had a telephonic discussion with Mr. Weinberg, during which Mr. Posner communicated the message that had been authorized by the Board of Directors regarding the insufficiency of the November 3 Proposal and an offer for a management presentation. On the call, Mr. Weinberg stated that he would need to confer with others at Sanofi prior to agreeing to a management presentation. On November 29, 2017, Mr. Weinberg called Mr. Posner and accepted the Company's offer to participate in a management presentation, which was subsequently arranged to be held on December 18, 2017.

On December 1, 2017, Paul, Weiss delivered a draft confidentiality agreement to Weil, Gotshal & Manges LLP ("*Weil*"), counsel to Sanofi, which contained customary standstill provisions with a customary "fall away" provision[3] providing that the standstill obligations would terminate in certain circumstances, including upon the Company entering into a binding agreement related to a change of control of the Company. On December 5, 2017, the Company and Sanofi entered into the Confidentiality Agreement (which was effective as of December 4, 2017, and included customary standstill provisions for a period of one year with a customary "fall away" provision providing that the standstill obligations would terminate in certain circumstances) in connection with the sharing of certain confidential information of the Company with Sanofi.

On December 14, 2017, the Board of Directors convened a meeting with certain members of senior management by teleconference to discuss the upcoming management meeting with Sanofi to be held on December 18, 2017. This meeting was attended by J.P. Morgan, Guggenheim Securities, and Paul, Weiss. Certain members of senior management provided the Board of Directors with an overview of the management presentation that would be presented on December 18, 2017. On December 15, 2017, a meeting of the independent directors of our Board of Directors was convened to discuss the Company's upcoming management meeting

[3]Fall away provisions in legal agreements ensure that stipulated restrictive covenants no longer apply if certain conditions are satisfied.

with Sanofi to be held on December 18, 2017. This meeting was attended by representatives of Paul, Weiss. During the course of this meeting, the Board of Directors discussed the Company's long-range plan as a stand-alone business, the assumptions underlying the management projections, the benefits of a cash payment to the Company's stockholders as compared to the risk of achieving the goals of the Company's long-range plan and the Company's strategy for engaging in discussions with Sanofi.

On December 17, 2017, the Board of Directors convened a meeting to discuss the Company's upcoming management presentation to Sanofi. This meeting was attended by representatives of Paul, Weiss. During the course of this meeting, the Board of Directors discussed the Company's long-range plan as a standalone business, the assumptions underlying the management projections, and the Company's strategy for engaging in discussions with Sanofi.

On December 18, 2017, the management presentation meeting was held in person at the offices of Paul, Weiss in New York City. During this meeting, representatives of J.P. Morgan and Guggenheim Securities met with senior representatives of Sanofi and representatives of Lazard and Weil to discuss management's projections and assumptions supporting management's projections, the Company's product pipeline and next generation products, various therapeutic approaches, as well as general trends in the hemophilia marketplace. At the conclusion of the meeting, Mr. Cox, Dr. Denner, and Mr. Posner on behalf of the Company, and Dr. Brandicourt and Mr. Weinberg on behalf of Sanofi, met in a private session to discuss Sanofi's non-binding November 3 Proposal. During this meeting, the Company's representatives stated that they believed the management presentation highlighted the Company's value above and beyond the value presented in the November 3 Proposal and Sanofi's representatives indicated an intent to consider what the Company had presented during the management presentation and to determine what impact, if any, such presentation would have on Sanofi's views regarding the Company's value.

On December 18 and 19, 2017, Bioverativ's Board of Directors held its regularly scheduled meeting at the offices of Paul, Weiss in New York City. In addition to addressing the regular business of the Company, our Board of Directors deliberated on the discussions with Sanofi, and portions of the meetings were attended by representatives of J.P. Morgan, Guggenheim Securities, and Paul, Weiss.

On December 20, 2017, representatives from Lazard provided J.P. Morgan and Guggenheim Securities with a list of additional questions from Sanofi, as follow-up to the December 18 management presentation. On December 21, 2017, representatives from J.P. Morgan and Guggenheim Securities had discussions with representatives from Lazard regarding the work plan for responding to Sanofi's additional questions.

On December 23, 2017, Bioverativ's Board of Directors convened a telephonic meeting to discuss the Company's response to Sanofi's follow-up requests and questions. During the course of this meeting, our Board of Directors instructed Mr. Cox to call Dr. Brandicourt directly to discuss the most efficient process for responding to the information requests. Our Board of Directors further discussed that while the Company was willing to provide further information to Sanofi, the Company was not engaging in negotiations with Sanofi regarding a potential transaction at such time. Between December 24, 2017 and January 3, 2018, representatives of Sanofi and the Company and, in certain instances, their respective financial advisors held a series of telephone calls with respect to Sanofi's follow-up requests arising out of the December 18, 2017 management presentation.

On December 27, 2017, Bioverativ's Board of Directors convened a special telephonic meeting with certain members of senior management and a representative from Paul, Weiss joining a portion of the call. Mr. Cox provided an update on the Company's responses to Sanofi's ongoing diligence. Mr. Posner provided an update on discussions with Sanofi and its representatives that he had received from the Company's financial advisors. The Board of Directors also discussed Sanofi's request for a meeting between the parties on January 3, 2018. During the course of this meeting, our Board of Directors asked numerous questions of the Company's senior management team relating to the assumptions underlying, and potential adjustments to the management projections and the expected risks to the Company's long-range plan as a standalone business. Our Board of Directors also discussed certain tax considerations relevant to any transaction involving the Company in light of the restrictions and obligations under the Tax Matters Agreement, including the requirement to provide Biogen with a copy of an "unqualified tax opinion" reasonably satisfactory to Biogen with respect to any transaction resulting in a change of control of the Company.

On December 30, 2017, the company's Board of Directors convened a special telephonic meeting with certain members of senior management and a representative of Paul, Weiss in attendance. During the meeting, our Board of Directors continued its discussion from its prior meeting and discussed the further request from the representative of Lazard for a meeting between the two companies. Following these discussions, the Board of Directors discussed that it would be willing to proceed with negotiations with Sanofi regarding a potential sale of the Company if Sanofi were prepared to make a sufficiently compelling offer, and authorized Mr. Cox, Dr. Denner, and Mr. Posner to meet with Sanofi on January 3, 2018. On January 3, 2018, an in-person meeting was held in New York City at the offices of Weil, with Dr. Brandicourt and Mr. Weinberg (participating by videoconference) representing Sanofi, and Mr. Cox, Dr. Denner, and Mr. Posner (participating by videoconference) representing the Company. In the course of this meeting, Sanofi verbally conveyed a revised offer price of $101.50 per share in cash and emphasized that Sanofi believed this price represented a full valuation of the Company. Mr. Posner expressed his disappointment to Mr. Weinberg at the level of the offer. Mr. Weinberg indicated to Mr. Posner, Mr. Cox, and Dr. Denner that he was disappointed in the Company's response and that he was going to find it very difficult to go back to the board of directors of Sanofi and request a higher price.

On the evening of January 3, 2018, the company's Board of Directors held a special telephonic meeting, with representatives of J.P. Morgan, Guggenheim Securities, Paul, Weiss, and certain members of senior management in attendance for part of the meeting. The directors who were in attendance at the meeting with Sanofi provided an update to our Board of Directors of that meeting and discussion ensued between our Board of Directors and its outside legal and financial advisors. During the course of this meeting, the Chairman of our Board of Directors asked each member of our Board of Directors whether he or she would consider a sale of the Company at this time. Our Board of Directors also discussed the benefits to the Company of avoiding a protracted sale process that could potentially distract the management team at a critical time for the Company. Our Board of Directors also discussed the assumptions underlying, and potential adjustments to, the management projections as well as the risks associated with their achievement, including new competitive entrants, such as Hemlibra, and probabilities of pipeline successes. Representatives of J.P. Morgan and Guggenheim Securities reviewed a list of potential alternative acquirors and our Board of Directors discussed their belief that Sanofi was financially prepared given its cash on hand and its significant interest in developing the hemophilia business and its desire to expeditiously complete its diligence and execute a transaction. No decision was taken at this meeting and our Board of Directors agreed to reconvene the following day.

On January 4, 2018, a special telephonic meeting of Bioverativ's Board of Directors was held with certain members of senior management and representatives of J.P. Morgan, Guggenheim Securities, and Paul, Weiss also in attendance to continue the discussion from the January 3 meeting of our Board of Directors. During the course of this discussion, our Board of Directors concluded that it would be willing to proceed with negotiations for a sale of the Company at a price of $105.00 per share in cash and that Dr. Denner was authorized to negotiate with representatives of Lazard, acting on behalf of Sanofi, to determine whether Sanofi was prepared to proceed on this basis.

During the course of the January 4, 2018 meeting of Bioverativ's Board of Directors, Dr. Denner received a call from a representative of Lazard. In the course of this phone call, and consistent with instruction from our Board of Directors, Dr. Denner informed the representative of Lazard that the Company was prepared to move forward with discussions if Sanofi committed to a price of $105.00 per Share in cash. After checking with certain representatives from Sanofi, the representative from Lazard called Dr. Denner back and conveyed that Sanofi was prepared to move forward on that basis, but that Sanofi would require the Company to agree to a period of exclusivity through January 26, 2018, during which, among other things, the Company would be prohibited from soliciting alternative proposals from other parties.

Immediately following his discussion with the representative of Lazard, the Board of Directors then discussed the terms of Sanofi's latest non-binding offer with representatives of J.P. Morgan, Guggenheim Securities, and Paul, Weiss, as well as certain members of senior management. At the conclusion of the meeting, the Board gave careful consideration the factors deemed relevant to its determination, including (i) the significant premium offered by Sanofi (and the fact that Sanofi's latest offer price was conditioned upon, among other things, an exclusivity period through January 26, 2018), (ii) the level of interest and engagement demonstrated by Sanofi to date, (iii) the proposed accelerated timeline to announce the transaction, (iv) the risk that Sanofi might decide not to proceed with a transaction if the Company did not commit to move forward on the terms proposed in Sanofi's January 4, 2018 offer, (v) the risk of a leak, particularly given the upcoming J.P. Morgan Healthcare Conference, and (vi) the fact that the anticipated terms of the proposed transaction would not make it difficult for other potential interested parties to submit a superior proposal during the pendency of the transaction, the Board of Directors resolved by vote to authorize the grant of exclusivity to Sanofi until January 26, 2018 and to authorize certain members of the Company's senior management and the Company's outside legal and financial advisors to proceed with negotiations with Sanofi regarding the proposed transaction.

Following the meeting of Bioverativ's Board of Directors on January 4, 2018, representatives of the Company advised representatives of Sanofi that the Company was prepared to proceed with Sanofi on the basis of Sanofi's January 4, 2018 offer to acquire the Company at a price of $105.00 per Share payable in cash. Later on January 4, 2018, representatives of Weil circulated to representatives of Paul, Weiss a draft exclusivity agreement to be entered into by the Company. Paul, Weiss subsequently sent Weil its proposed revisions to such exclusivity agreement.

Confidentiality Exclusivity Agreement

On December 5, 2017, the Company and Parent entered into a customary Confidentiality Agreement (which was effective as of December 4, 2017) (the "*Confidentiality Agreement*") in connection with a possible transaction involving Bioverativ.

On January 6, 2018, the Company and Sanofi entered into the Exclusivity Agreement (which was dated as of January 5, 2018), whereby the Company granted Sanofi a period of exclusivity until January 26, 2018, a copy of which is filed as Exhibit (e)(3) hereto and incorporated herein by reference. The Company and Parent entered into an exclusivity agreement on January 6, 2018 (which was dated as of January 5, 2018) (the "*Exclusivity Agreement*"), whereby, in connection with Parent's consideration of a possible transaction between the Company and Parent and the requirement that Parent expends a substantial amount of time and resources to evaluate such a transaction, the Company and Parent agreed that, from January 5, 2018 through 11:59 p.m. EST on January 26, 2018 (or the earlier execution and delivery of a definitive written agreement providing for a transaction between Parent and the Company), the Company and its representatives would not, directly or indirectly, solicit, initiate, pursue, knowingly facilitate, knowingly encourage, engage in or otherwise enter into any discussions, negotiations, agreements, or arrangements (including by providing any non-public information) with any person or entity (other than Parent or its representatives) concerning an Alternative Transaction (as defined in the Exclusivity Agreement). The obligations under the Exclusivity Agreement terminated upon the execution of the Merger Agreement.

On January 8, 2018, the Company provided representatives of Sanofi with access to an electronic data room in connection with Sanofi's confirmatory due diligence review of the Company. Sanofi continued to perform due diligence through the data room and in meetings with certain Company representatives through the execution of the Merger Agreement.

On January 11, 2018, Weil delivered an initial draft of the proposed Merger Agreement to Paul, Weiss. Over the next 10 days, the Company, Sanofi, Paul, Weiss, and Weil discussed the terms of the Transactions, including the size of the termination fee, the circumstances under which the Company could negotiate alternative proposals and accept superior offers, the steps necessary to ensure compliance with the terms of the Tax Matters Agreement, Sanofi's obligations to obtain required regulatory approvals, the representations and warranties and the interim operating restrictions.

During the period beginning January 12, 2018, and through the execution of the Merger Agreement, the Company held a number of diligence calls with Sanofi and its representatives on a variety of confirmatory matters, including the Company's human resources, manufacturing, research and development plans, medical and regulatory matters, tax compliance, operations and supply chain, finance, compliance, intellectual property, and general legal matters.

On January 15, 2018, the Board of Directors convened a meeting with certain members of senior management. Representatives of J.P. Morgan, Guggenheim Securities, and Paul, Weiss were also in attendance. A representative of Paul, Weiss provided our Board of Directors with an update on the discussions with Sanofi, including the terms of the draft merger agreement. Our Board of Directors also discussed with members of senior management and the Company's legal and financial advisors a plan for contacting Biogen, which included a discussion of the Letter Agreement that would be sought to be entered into with Biogen and Sanofi relating to certain restrictions and obligations under the Tax Matters Agreement.

On January 16, 2018, Paul, Weiss delivered comments on the draft Merger Agreement to Weil, and delivered to Weil a draft Letter Agreement addressing the Company's obligations under the Tax Matters Agreement to (i) provide Biogen with a copy of an "unqualified tax opinion" reasonably satisfactory to Biogen with respect to any transaction resulting in a change of control of the Company and (ii) indemnify Biogen in the event the proposed transaction caused the Spin-Off to fail to qualify as tax-free and Sanofi's agreement to guarantee the performance of such indemnity from and after the closing of the proposed transaction. During the course of the day of January 16, 2018 and into January 17, 2018, representatives from Paul, Weiss and Weil discussed and implemented changes to the initial draft Letter Agreement.

On January 17, 2018, the Company provided a draft of a Letter Agreement to Biogen, reflecting comments previously discussed between representatives from Paul, Weiss and Weil. The initial draft of the proposed Letter Agreement addressed the Company's obligations under the Tax Matters Agreement to provide Biogen with a copy of an "unqualified tax opinion" reasonably satisfactory to Biogen with respect to any transaction resulting in a change of control of the Company and to indemnify Biogen in the event the transaction caused the spinoff to not qualify as tax-free and a proposed guarantee of such indemnity by Sanofi from and after the closing of the proposed transaction.

On January 19, 2018, the Board of Directors reviewed the terms of the Merger Agreement and the Letter Agreement and focused in particular on provisions related to the termination fee, requesting that the Company attempt to lower the fee previously proposed by Sanofi. During the course of this meeting, a representative of Paul, Weiss reviewed with our Board of Directors their fiduciary duties under applicable law and representatives from J.P. Morgan, Guggenheim Securities, and Paul, Weiss discussed the financial and legal terms of the current draft of the Merger Agreement.

During the period from January 19, 2018 to January 21, 2018, the parties and their respective representatives continued to negotiate the terms of the draft agreements and exchanged several drafts of the Merger Agreement. In this same period, the Company and Sanofi exchanged drafts of the Letter Agreement with Biogen.

On January 20, 2018, the Company entered into an engagement letter with Guggenheim Securities, and on January 21, 2018, the Company entered into an engagement letter with J.P. Morgan, effective as of November 15, 2017, pursuant to which each of J.P. Morgan and Guggenheim Securities, respectively, would be formally engaged as outside financial advisor in connection with the proposed transaction.

On January 21, 2018, a special telephonic meeting of our Board of Directors was held, which was also attended by representatives of senior management and representatives of J.P. Morgan, Guggenheim Securities, and Paul, Weiss. At this meeting, a representative from Paul, Weiss reminded our Board of Directors of their fiduciary duties under applicable law and reviewed with our Board of Directors the terms of the Merger Agreement, focusing on certain changes to the terms discussed at the meeting of the Board of Directors on January 19, 2018.

Each of J.P. Morgan and Guggenheim Securities then reviewed with our Board of Directors their respective financial analysis of the $105.00 per Share cash consideration to be paid in the Transactions to the holders of Shares pursuant to the Merger Agreement, which was consistent with the financial analysis that each of J.P. Morgan and Guggenheim Securities, respectively, had delivered to our Board of Directors at the meeting on January 19, 2018.

After further discussing potential reasons for and against the proposed transaction including the Board of Directors' analysis of the possible alternatives to the proposed transactions, the Board of Directors unanimously adopted resolutions (i) declaring that the Merger Agreement, the Merger and the other Transactions, including the Offer, are advisable, fair to, and in the best interests of, the Company and its stockholders, (ii) adopting and approving the Merger Agreement, the entry by the Company into the Merger Agreement, and the consummation of the Transactions, including the Offer and the Merger, (iii) recommending that the Company's stockholders (other than Parent and its Subsidiaries) accept the Offer and tender their Shares to Purchaser pursuant to the Offer, (iv) resolving to take all actions necessary so that the restrictions on business combinations and stockholder vote requirements contained in Section 203 of the DGCL and any other applicable law, and (v) agreeing and authorizing that the Merger be governed by Section 251(h) of the DGCL and consummated as soon as practicable following the consummation of the Offer.

Following the meeting of our Board of Directors on January 21, 2018, the Company, Sanofi, Paul, Weiss, and Weil finalized the terms of the Merger Agreement. On the morning of January 22, 2018, prior to the opening of trading of the Shares on the NASDAQ, Sanofi and the Company issued a joint press release announcing the execution of the Merger Agreement and the forthcoming commencement of the Offer to acquire all of the outstanding Shares at a price of $105.00 per Share in cash. The joint press release is included as Exhibit (a)(7) hereto and is incorporated herein by reference. On February 7, 2018, Merger Sub commenced the Offer and the Company filed this Schedule 14D-9.

Reasons for Recommendation by Bioverativ Board

The Board of Directors of Bioverativ consulted with senior management of the Company regarding, among other things, the Company's industry, and its business and prospects as an independent company. The Board of Directors consulted with its financial advisors regarding the financial aspects of the Transactions, as well as the fairness, from a financial point of view, to the Company's stockholders of the consideration to be received by such stockholders pursuant to the Transactions. The Board of Directors also consulted with its legal counsel regarding the Board of Directors' legal duties, the terms of the Merger Agreement, and related issues. In the course of reaching its unanimous determination, our Board of Directors carefully considered numerous factors, including the following non-exhaustive list of material factors and benefits that weighed positively in favor of its unanimous decision, among others and not necessarily in order of relative importance:

- *Premium to Market Price.* The Board of Directors considered:
  - the current and historical market prices of the Shares, including the market performance of the Shares relative to those of other participants in the Company's industry and general market indices, and the fact that the Offer Price represents a compelling premium to historical market prices of the Shares, including (1) a 63.8% premium to the closing price of the Shares on January 19, 2018, the last full trading day prior to the public announcement of the transaction; (2) a 79.0% premium to the 30-day volume weighted average price ("*VWAP*") for the Shares; (3) a 92.7% premium to the 60-day VWAP for the Shares; (4) a 83.6% premium to the closing price of the Shares on November 2, 2017, the last full trading day prior to Parent's initial offer of $98.50 per Share; and (5) a 89.6% premium to the closing price of the Shares on January 3, 2018, the last full trading day prior to the parties' agreement on the Offer Price of $105.00 per Share;
  - the fact that the Company negotiated an increase in the consideration payable in the Offer to $105.00 per Share from Sanofi's initial proposal of $98.50 per Share on November 3, 2017; and
  - the fact that since the Company's initial separation from Biogen on February 1, 2017, the per-share trading price of the Shares has never exceeded the level of the Offer Price.

- *Cash Tender Offer; Certainty of Value.* The Board of Directors considered that the Offer Price is all cash and that under the DGCL the second-step merger can be completed immediately following the consummation of the Offer, without a vote of the Company's stockholders, so that the Transactions provide certainty, immediate value and liquidity to our stockholders for their Shares, especially when viewed against any internal or external risks and uncertainties associated with the Company's standalone strategy.

  The Company's Operating and Financial Condition; Prospects of the Company. Bioverativ's Board of Directors considered the Company's business, financial condition, and results of operations and concluded that the Offer Price is more favorable to the Company's stockholders in the short term than the potential value that could be expected to be generated were the Company to remain independent and execute on its current business and financial plans. The Board of Directors considered, among other factors, that its stockholders would continue to be subject to the risks and uncertainties of the Company if it remained independent. These execution risks and uncertainties included risks relating to revenue concentration and dependency on the Company's products, ELOCTATE and ALPROLIX; potential failure to compete effectively with other hemophilia treatments; potential difficulties and delays in clinical trials of product candidates; regulatory developments involving current and future products and product candidates; and other risks and uncertainties, including the risk factors set forth in the Company's Annual Report on Form 10-K for the fiscal year ended December 31, 2016, and subsequent quarterly reports on Form 10-Q.

- *Potentially Interested Counterparties.* The Board of Directors considered, after discussions with J.P. Morgan and Guggenheim Securities and senior management, that (i) a broader outreach to potential acquirors could delay a potential transaction and cause significant disruption at a critical stage of the Company's development, putting at risk a transaction with Sanofi at the price negotiated, (ii) other potential partners had not approached the Company to inquire about a strategic transaction with the Company, and (iii) should any such potential counterparty be interested in pursuing a transaction on terms more favorable to the Company and its stockholders than those contemplated by the Merger Agreement, such counterparty would be able to pursue such an offer for the Company despite Sanofi and the Company having entered into the Merger Agreement.

- *Fairness Opinions.* The opinions, dated January 21, 2018, of each of J.P. Morgan and Guggenheim Securities to the Board of Directors as to the fairness, from a financial point of view and as of the date of the opinion, of the Offer Price to be paid to the Company's stockholders (in their capacity as such and other than Sanofi and Merger Sub), which opinion was based on and subject to the matters considered, the procedures followed, the assumptions made and various limitations of and qualifications to the review undertaken as more fully described under the section entitled "*Opinions of Bioverativ's Financial Advisors*" below. The full text of the written opinions of J.P. Morgan and Guggenheim Securities have been included as Annex I and Annex II, respectively, to this Schedule 14D-9 and are incorporated herein by reference.
- *Likelihood and Speed of Consummation.* The company's Board of Directors considered the likelihood of completion of the Transactions to be high, particularly in light of the terms of the Merger Agreement and the closing conditions to the Offer and the Merger, including:
  - the conditions to the Offer and the Merger being specific and limited;
  - the size and financial strength of Parent;
  - the likelihood of obtaining required regulatory approvals, and the commitments Sanofi agreed to in the Merger Agreement regarding regulatory approvals;
  - the remedy of specific performance available to the Company under the Merger Agreement in the event of breaches by Parent and Purchaser;
  - the fact that the Offer and the Merger are not subject to the conditionality and execution risk of any required approval by Parent's stockholders; and
  - the structure of the transaction as a cash tender offer for all outstanding Shares, with the expected result that a relatively short period will elapse before our stockholders receive the Offer Price, followed by the Merger under Section 251(h) of the DGCL, which would not require Company stockholder approval, and in which stockholders who do not validly exercise appraisal rights will receive the same consideration received by those stockholders who tender their Shares in the Offer. Our Board of Directors considered that the

potential for closing in a relatively short time frame could also reduce the amount of time during which the Company's business would be subject to the potential uncertainty of closing and related disruption.

- *Product Development and Regulatory Risks.* The Board of Directors considered that clinical trials can take years to complete, and the outcomes are uncertain. In addition to the risks inherent in the development and eventual commercialization of the Company's product candidates, the Board of Directors also considered the risks related to market acceptance of product candidates, if approved, and other factors affecting the revenues and profitability of biopharmaceutical product candidates generally.
- *Product Launch and Commercialization Risks and Costs.* The Board of Directors assessed the significant risks and considerable costs associated with a successful launch and commercialization by the Company of its product candidates that would impact the Company's prospects for substantially increasing stockholder value as a standalone company in excess of the Offer Price, given the risks and uncertainties in its business, including, among other things, the costs and risks associated with continuing the development of other pipeline drug candidates or acquisition of other commercial or pipeline assets; risks relating to competition from existing drugs and drugs under development; and risks relating to commercial drug sales.
- *Expansion Risk.* The Company plans to expand the marketing of its two products into additional geographies. Regulators of other jurisdictions have their own procedures for approval of product candidates. The Board of Directors considered that even if a product is approved, regulators may limit the indications for which the product may be marketed, require extensive warnings on the product labeling, or require expensive and time-consuming clinical trials or reporting as conditions of approval. The Board of Directors considered the risks inherent in obtaining regulatory approvals from regulatory authorities in additional jurisdictions to be able to sell the Company's products in such jurisdictions, which can take years to complete and the receipt of which are not guaranteed; the capital required to complete the regulatory approval processes; the timing and cost of product commercialization activities, including marketing and distribution arrangements, should the regulatory approvals be received; and the potential for revenue generation and profitability of the two products if sold in additional jurisdictions.

- *Best Strategic Alternative for Maximizing Stockholder Value.* The Board of Directors determined, after a thorough review of strategic alternatives and discussions with our management and its financial and legal advisors, that the Offer Price is more favorable to the Company's stockholders in the short term than the potential value that might have resulted from other strategic options available, including, but not limited to, remaining a standalone public company.
- *Negotiation Process.* The Board of Directors considered the enhancements that the Company and its advisors were able to obtain as a result of robust arm's-length negotiations with Parent, including the increase in the Offer Price proposed by Parent from the time of its initial indication of interest to the end of the negotiations, and the inclusion of provisions in the Merger Agreement that increase the likelihood of completing the Offer and consummating the Merger.
- *No Financing Condition.* The Board considered the fact that Parent and Purchaser would have sufficient cash resources to pay the amounts required to be paid under the Merger Agreement without obtaining third-party financing and that the Transaction is not subject to a financing condition.
- *Industry and Economy.* The Board of Directors considered the current state of the economy and assessed the stage of the pharmaceutical industry cycle, financing markets, uncertainty in drug pricing, and uncertainty surrounding forecasted economic conditions both in the near term and the long term, generally and within the Company's industry in particular, in addition to other geopolitical risk considerations.
- *Certain Management Projections.* The Board of Directors considered certain forecasts for the Company prepared by senior management of the Company, which reflected certain assumptions of the Company's senior management, including product revenue growth and future economic, competitive, and regulatory conditions. For further discussion, see "Certain Unaudited Prospective Financial Information."
- *Opportunity to Receive Unsolicited Proposals, Change Recommendation, or Terminate the Transactions in Order to Accept a Superior Proposal.* The Board of Directors considered the terms of the Merger Agreement permitting the Company to receive unsolicited proposals, and the other terms and conditions of the Merger Agreement, including:
    - that the Company may, subject to certain conditions, furnish, pursuant to entry into an acceptable confidentiality agreement, confidential

information with respect to the Company and its subsidiaries and access thereto to third parties making such an unsolicited proposal and participate or engage in negotiations or discussions with such third parties regarding unsolicited proposals that are made prior to the time that the Offer is consummated;

  - the provisions of the Merger Agreement allowing the Board of Directors in certain circumstances to terminate the Merger Agreement in order to enter into a definitive agreement with respect to an unsolicited superior proposal, subject to payment of a termination fee of $326 million, which amount the directors believed to be reasonable under the circumstances and taking into account the range of such termination fees in similar transactions, and the unlikelihood that a fee of such size would be a meaningful deterrent to other acquisition proposals. The Board of Directors also recognized that the provisions in the Merger Agreement relating to this fee were insisted on by Sanofi as a condition to entering into the Merger Agreement; and
  - its ability under the Merger Agreement to withdraw or modify its recommendation that the Company's stockholders tender their Shares to Purchaser pursuant to the Offer in certain circumstances, including in connection with a superior proposal or an event, occurrence or fact occurring or arising after the date of the Merger Agreement that was not known to our Board of Directors as of the date of the Merger Agreement.

- *Other Terms of the Merger Agreement.* The Board of Directors considered other terms of the Merger Agreement, as more fully described in Section 11, "The Merger Agreement; Other Agreements" of the Offer to Purchase. Certain provisions of the Merger Agreement that the Board of Directors considered important included:
  - *Termination Date.* The termination date under the Merger Agreement on which either Parent or the Company, subject to certain exceptions, can terminate the Merger Agreement, which is anticipated to allow for sufficient time to obtain required regulatory approvals and to consummate the Offer and the Merger while minimizing the length of time during which the Company would be required to operate subject to the restrictions on interim operations set forth in the Merger Agreement.
  - *Cooperation.* The Merger Agreement requires Parent and Purchaser to use their reasonable best efforts to consummate the Offer and the Merger.

- *Extension of the Offer*. Merger Sub's obligation to accept and pay for all Shares that have been validly tendered into the Offer and not validly withdrawn is subject to the satisfaction or waiver of a number of conditions. However, Sanofi and Merger Sub are required to extend the Offer beyond the initial Expiration Time if, at any otherwise scheduled Expiration Time (as such terms are defined in Section 11 — "Purpose of the Offer and Plans for Bioverativ; Summary of the Merger Agreement and Certain Other Agreements" in the Offer to Purchase), any condition has not been satisfied or waived, for up to 10 business days per extension [but not beyond the earlier to occur of (i) the valid termination of the Merger Agreement and (ii) the End Date (as such term is defined in Section 11 — "Purpose of the Offer and Plans for Bioverativ; Summary of the Merger Agreement and Certain Other Agreements" in the Offer to Purchase)]. (iii) *Company Material Adverse Effect.* The Board of Directors considered the provisions in the Merger Agreement that, among other things, specify that, subject to the terms of the Merger Agreement, any state of facts, circumstance, condition, event, change, development, occurrence, result, or effect resulting from (i) the public announcement or pendency of the Transactions, including, in each case, the impact thereof on relationships, contractual or otherwise, with customers, suppliers, vendors, lenders, investors, licensors, licensees, venture partners, or employees, (ii) changes in conditions generally affecting the industry in which the Company and the Company Subsidiaries operate (unless such changes have a disproportionate adverse impact on the Company and its subsidiaries as compared to any other participants in the industries in which the Company and its subsidiaries operate), (iii) the failure by the Company or any of the Company Subsidiaries to meet any internal or external projections or forecasts or any decline in the price of Shares are excluded from the determination of whether a Company Material Adverse Effect (as defined and more fully described in Section 11 — "Purpose of the Offer and Plans for Bioverativ; Summary of the Merger Agreement and Certain Other Agreements" in the Offer to Purchase) has occurred that would permit Sanofi to elect not to consummate the Offer.

- *Appraisal Rights.* The company's Board of Directors considered the availability of statutory appraisal rights to the Company's stockholders who do not tender their Shares in the Offer and otherwise comply with all required procedures for demanding appraisal under the DGCL.

Bioverativ Board of Directors also considered a variety of risks and other potentially adverse factors in determining whether to approve the Merger Agreement and the Transactions and recommend that stockholders tender their Shares pursuant to the Offer, including the following, which are not necessarily listed in order of relative importance:

- the fact that the Company would no longer exist as an independent, publicly traded company, and the Company's stockholders would no longer have the opportunity to participate in any potential future earnings or growth of the Company or benefit from the successful execution of the Company's current strategy as a public company;
- the fact that the Merger Agreement precludes the Company from actively soliciting alternative transaction proposals and restricts the Company's ability to engage in discussions regarding unsolicited alternative transaction proposals unless, subject to certain terms and conditions in the Merger Agreement, the Board of Directors determines, in good faith, a proposal constitutes or would be reasonably likely to constitute a superior proposal to the Transactions;
- the possibility that under certain circumstances, the Company may be required to pay Parent a termination fee of $326 million, including if the Company terminates the Merger Agreement to accept a superior proposal or the Board of Directors changes its recommendation;
- the potential risk of diverting management attention and resources from the operation of the Company's business and towards completion of the Offer and the Merger;
- the risk of incurring substantial expenses related to the Offer and the Merger;
- the risk that all conditions to the parties' obligations to complete the Offer and the Merger are not satisfied, and as a result, the Merger is not completed;
- the risks and costs to the Company if the Transactions do not close, including uncertainty about the effect of the proposed Offer and Merger on the Company's employees, customers, and key relationships, which may impair the Company's ability to attract, retain and motivate key personnel, and could cause customers, suppliers and others to seek to change existing business relationships with the Company;

- the possibility that another party might have been willing to pay a higher purchase price for the Company than the Offer Price;
- the possibility that, although the Offer and the Merger provide the Company's stockholders the opportunity to realize a premium to the price at which the Shares traded prior to the public announcement of the proposed transaction, the price of the Shares might have increased in the future to a price greater than the Offer Price;
- the potential conflict of interest created by the fact that the Company's executive officers and directors have financial interests in the Offer and the Merger that may be different from, or in addition to, those of other stockholders, as more fully described in "Item 3. Past Contacts, Transactions, Negotiations and Agreements — Arrangements between the Company and its Executive Officers, Directors and Affiliates."
- the fact that the gain realized by the Company's stockholders as a result of the Offer and the Merger generally will be taxable to the stockholders for US federal income tax purposes;
- the restrictions in the Merger Agreement on the conduct of the Company's business prior to the consummation of the Merger, which may delay or prevent the Company from undertaking business or other opportunities that may arise prior to the consummation of the Offer or the Merger;
- the potential effect of the public announcement of the Merger Agreement, including effects on the Company's revenues, customers, operating results and share price, and the Company's ability to attract and retain key management and personnel; and
- the risk of litigation in connection with the execution of the Merger Agreement, the completion of the Offer, and the consummation of the Merger.

Bioverativ's Board of Directors concluded that the risks, uncertainties, restrictions, and potentially negative reasons associated with the Offer and Merger were outweighed by the potential benefits of the Offer and Merger. The Board of Directors collectively reached the unanimous conclusion to approve the Merger Agreement and the Transactions in light of these various factors.

The foregoing discussion of the Board of Directors' reasons for its recommendation to accept the Offer is not meant to be exhaustive but addresses the material information and factors considered by our Board of Directors in connection with its recommendation. In view of the wide variety of reasons considered by the Board of Directors in connection with the evaluation of the Offer and the complexity of these matters, the Board of Directors did not find it practicable to, and did not, quantify or otherwise assign relative weights to the specific reasons considered in reaching its determination and recommendation. Rather, the directors made their determinations and recommendations based on the totality of the information presented to them, and the judgments of individual members of the Board of Directors may have been influenced to a greater or lesser degree by different reasons.

The foregoing description of the consideration by the Board of Directors of the reasons supporting the Merger Agreement, the Offer, the Merger, and the other Transactions contemplated by the Merger Agreement and its recommendation that stockholders tender their Shares pursuant to the Offer is forward-looking in nature. This information should be read in light of the factors discussed in the section entitled "*Cautionary Note Regarding Forward-Looking Statements*."

Bioverativ Management Projections

In connection with the merger transaction, senior management prepared certain internal financial analyses and forecasts relating to the long-term plan as a standalone company (the "*Management Projections*"). The Management Projections were provided to J.P. Morgan and Guggenheim Securities solely in connection with the rendering of their fairness opinions to the company's Board of Directors and performing their related financial analysis, as described stated below.

The Management Projections are probability-adjusted and took into account certain financial, operating, and commercial assumptions developed solely using the information available to our management at the time the Management Projections were created. Senior management assumed probabilities of success of products currently under development, considering certain assumptions that senior management believed to be common in the industry for assessing risks associated with development and commercialization.

A summary of the Management Projections:

	2018	2019	2020	2021	2022	2023	2024	2025	2026	2027	2028	2029	2030	2031	2032	2033	2034	2035
	($ in Millions)																	
Revenue	1,417	1,842	1,872	1,947	2,049	2,184	2,429	2,693	2,983	3,310	3,557	3,633	3,545	3,380	3,256	3,196	3,175	3,180
Operating income	586	836	902	971	1,027	1,039	1,061	1,125	1,119	1,120	1,388	1,445	1,463	1,476	1,488	1,540	1,552	1,569
Adjusted EBITDA[a]	$648	$997	$984	$1,075	$1,106	$1,110	$1,140	$1,193	$1,188	$1,191	$1,463	$1,522	$1,539	$1,551	$1,562	$1,614	$1,624	$1,640
Adjusted EPS[b]	$4.61	$7.04	$6.93	$7.56	$7.75	$7.76	$7.93	$8.28	$8.22	$8.23	$10.09	$10.50	$10.66	$10.79	$10.91	$11.29	$11.38	$11.50

Notes: [a]Adjusted EBITDA consists of earnings before interest income/expense, taxes, depreciation, and amortization, excluding the effect of stock-based compensation expense and certain non-recurring expenses primarily related to business combinations and one-time separation costs. Adjusted EBITDA is a non-GAAP financial measure and is not intended to represent, or to be used, as a substitute for operating income and net income as a measure of operating performance or for cash flows from operations as a measure of liquidity.
[b]Adjusted EPS, a non-GAAP measure, consists of net income, excluding the effect of stock-based compensation expense and certain non-recurring expenses primarily related to business combinations and one-time separation costs, divided by fully diluted shares outstanding.

At the direction of senior management, J.P. Morgan and Guggenheim Securities calculated from the Management Projections unlevered free cash flows as set forth below for use in their Whole Discounted Cash Flow Analysis and Going-Concern Discounted Cash Flow Analysis, respectively.

	2018	2019	2020	2021	2022	2023	2024	2025	2026	2027
	($ in Millions)									
Unlevered Free Cash Flow[a]	397	368	641	785	764	841	776	824	805	799

Note: [a]Unlevered Free Cash Flow consists of unlevered earnings after tax (including stock-based compensation expenses), adjusted for depreciation and amortization, capital expenditures, and changes in net working capital. Unlevered Free Cash Flow is a non-GAAP financial measure and is not intended to represent, or to be used, as a substitute for operating income and net income as a measure of operating performance or for cash flows from operations as a measure of liquidity.

In addition, at the direction of senior management, J.P. Morgan and Guggenheim Securities calculated from the Management Projections (excluding certain unidentified expenses, including selling, general and administrative, and research and development expenses) unlevered free cash flows as set forth below for use in their respective Sum-of-the-Parts Discounted Cash Flow Analyses.

Fairness Opinions of Financial Advisors[4]

Opinion by J.P. Morgan

January 21, 2018
The Board of Directors Bioverativ Inc.
225 Second Avenue
Waltham, MA 02451
Members of the Board of Directors:

You have requested our opinion as to the fairness, from a financial point of view, to the holders (in their capacity as such) of common stock, par

[4]United States Securities And Exchange Commission, Washington, D.C. 20549, Schedule 14D-9 (Rule 14d-101), Solicitation/Recommendation Statement Under Section 14(d)(4) of the Securities Exchange Act of 1934, Bioverativ Inc.

value $0.001 per Share (the "Company Common Stock"), of Bioverativ Inc., a Delaware corporation (the "Company"), of the consideration to be paid to such holders in the proposed Tender Offer and Merger (each as defined below) pursuant to the Agreement and Plan of Merger, dated as of January 21, 2018 (the "Agreement"), among the Company, Sanofi, a French *société anonyme* (the "Acquiror"), and its indirect, wholly owned subsidiary, Blink Acquisition Corp., a Delaware corporation ("Acquisition Sub"). Pursuant to the Agreement, the Acquiror will cause Acquisition Sub or another direct or indirect wholly owned subsidiary of the Acquiror to commence a tender offer for all the shares of the Company Common Stock (the "Tender Offer") at a price for each share equal to $105.00 (the "Consideration") payable in cash. The Agreement further provides that, following completion of the Tender Offer, Acquisition Sub will be merged with and into the Company (the "Merger") and each outstanding share of Company Common Stock, other than shares validly tendered and irrevocably accepted for purchase pursuant to the Tender Offer, that constitute Dissenting Shares (as defined in the Agreement) or are to be canceled pursuant to Section 2.05(b) and Section 2.05(c) of the Agreement, will be converted into the right to receive an amount equal to the Consideration in cash. The Tender Offer and Merger, together and not separately, are referred to herein as the "Transaction."

In connection with preparing our opinion, we have (i) reviewed the Agreement; (ii) reviewed certain publicly available business and financial information concerning the Company and the industries in which it operates; (iii) compared the proposed financial terms of the Transaction with the publicly available financial terms of certain transactions involving companies we deemed relevant and the consideration paid for such companies; (iv) compared the financial and operating performance of the Company with publicly available information concerning certain other companies we deemed relevant and reviewed the current and historical market prices of the Company Common Stock and certain publicly traded securities of such other companies; (v) reviewed certain internal financial analyses and forecasts prepared by the management of the Company relating to its business; and (vi) performed such other financial studies and analyses and considered such other information as we deemed appropriate for the purposes of this opinion.

In addition, we have held discussions with certain members of the management of the Company with respect to certain aspects of the Transaction, and the past and current business operations of the Company, the financial condition and future prospects and operations of the Company, and certain other matters we believed necessary or appropriate to our inquiry.

In giving our opinion, we have relied upon and assumed the accuracy and completeness of all information that was publicly available or was furnished to or discussed with us by the Company or otherwise reviewed by or for us. We have not independently verified any such information or its accuracy or completeness and, pursuant to our engagement letter with the Company, we did not assume any obligation to undertake any such independent verification. We have not conducted or been provided with any valuation or appraisal of any assets or liabilities, nor have we evaluated the solvency of the Company or the Acquiror under any state or federal laws relating to bankruptcy, insolvency, or similar matters. In relying on financial analyses and forecasts provided to us or derived therefrom, we have assumed that they have been reasonably prepared based on assumptions reflecting the best currently available estimates and judgments by management as to the expected future results of operations and financial condition of the Company to which such analyses or forecasts relate. We express no view as to such analyses or forecasts or the assumptions on which they were based. We have also assumed that the Transaction and the other transactions contemplated by the Agreement will be consummated as described in the Agreement. We have also assumed that the representations and warranties made by the Company and the Acquiror and Acquisition Sub in the Agreement and the related agreements are and will be true and correct in all respects material to our analysis. We are not legal, regulatory, or tax experts and have relied on the assessments made by advisors to the Company with respect to such issues. We are not expressing any view or rendering any opinion regarding the tax consequences of the Transaction to the Company or to the holders of Company Common Stock. We have further assumed that all material governmental, regulatory, or other consents and approvals necessary for the consummation of the Transaction will be obtained without any adverse effect on the Company or on the contemplated benefits of the Transaction.

Our opinion is necessarily based on economic, market, and other conditions as in effect on, and the information made available to us as of, the date hereof. It should be understood that subsequent developments may affect this opinion and that we do not have any obligation to update, revise, or reaffirm this opinion. Our opinion is limited to the fairness, from a financial point of view, of the Consideration to be paid to the holders of the Company Common Stock (in their capacity as such) in the proposed Transaction and we express no opinion as to the fairness of any consideration paid in connection with the Transaction to the holders of any other class of securities, creditors or other constituencies of the Company or as to the underlying decision by the Company to engage in the Transaction. Furthermore, we express no opinion with respect to the amount or nature of any compensation to any officers, directors, or employees of any party to the Transaction, or any class of such persons relative to the Consideration to be paid to the holders of the Company Common Stock in the Transaction or with respect to the fairness of any such compensation.

We note that we were not authorized to and did not solicit any expressions of interest from any other parties with respect to the sale of all or any part of the Company or any other alternative transaction.

We have acted as financial advisor to the Company with respect to the proposed Transaction and will receive a fee from the Company for our services, a substantial portion of which will become payable only if the proposed Transaction is consummated. In addition, the Company has agreed to indemnify us for certain liabilities arising out of our engagement. Please be advised that during the two years preceding the date of this letter, neither we nor our affiliates have had any other material financial advisory or other material commercial or investment banking relationships with the Company. In addition, during the two years preceding the date of this letter, neither we nor our affiliates have had any material financial advisory or other material commercial or investment banking relationships with the Acquiror. In addition, we and our affiliates hold, on a proprietary basis, less than 1% of the outstanding common stock of each of the Company and the Acquiror. In the ordinary course of our businesses, we and our affiliates may actively trade the debt and equity securities or financial instruments (including derivatives, bank loans, or other obligations) of the Company or the Acquiror for our own account or for the accounts of customers and, accordingly, we may at any time hold long or short positions in such securities or other financial instruments.

On the basis of and subject to the foregoing, it is our opinion as of the date hereof that the consideration to be paid to the holders of the Company Common Stock in the proposed Transaction is fair, from a financial point of view, to such holders (in their capacity as such).

The issuance of this opinion has been approved by a fairness opinion committee of J.P. Morgan Securities LLC. This letter is provided to the Board of Directors of the Company (in its capacity as such) in connection with and for the purposes of its evaluation of the Transaction. This opinion does not constitute a recommendation to any shareholder of the Company as to whether such shareholder should tender its shares into the Tender Offer or how such shareholder should vote with respect to the Transaction or any other matter. This opinion may not be disclosed, referred to, or communicated (in whole or in part) to any third party for any purpose whatsoever except with our prior written approval. This opinion may be reproduced in full in any proxy or information statement mailed to shareholders of the Company but may not otherwise be disclosed publicly in any manner without our prior written approval.

Very truly yours,
J.P. Morgan Securities LLC

Detailed Discussion by Opinion of J.P. Morgan Securities LLC

Pursuant to an engagement letter dated January 21, 2018, the Company retained J.P. Morgan as its financial advisor in connection with the proposed Offer and Merger.

In arriving at its opinion, J.P. Morgan, among other things:

- reviewed the Merger Agreement;
- reviewed certain publicly available business and financial information concerning the Company and the industries in which it operates;
- compared the proposed financial terms of the Offer and Merger with the publicly available financial terms of certain transactions involving companies J.P. Morgan deemed relevant and the consideration received for such companies;
- compared the financial and operating performance of the Company with publicly available information concerning certain other companies J.P. Morgan deemed relevant and reviewed the current and historical market prices of the Shares and certain publicly traded securities of such other companies;
- reviewed the Management Projections prepared by the management of the Company relating to its business and which are summarized above under “Certain Unaudited Prospective Financial Information”; and
- performed such other financial studies and analyses and considered such other information as J.P. Morgan deemed appropriate for the purposes of its opinion.

In addition, J.P. Morgan held discussions with certain members of the management of the Company with respect to certain aspects of the Offer and Merger, and the past and current business operations of the Company, the financial condition and future prospects and operations of the Company, and certain other matters J.P. Morgan believed necessary or appropriate to its inquiry.

J.P. Morgan's opinion was based on economic, market, and other conditions as in effect on, and the information made available to J.P. Morgan as of, the date of such opinion. J.P. Morgan's opinion noted that subsequent developments may affect J.P. Morgan's opinion, and that J.P. Morgan does not have any obligation to update, revise, or reaffirm such opinion. J.P. Morgan's opinion is limited to the fairness, from a financial point of view, of the Offer Price to be paid to the Company's stockholders (in their capacity as such) in the proposed Offer and Merger, and J.P. Morgan has expressed no opinion as to the fairness of any consideration to the holders of any other class of securities, creditors or other constituencies of the Company or the underlying decision by the Company to engage in the Offer and Merger.

Summary of Financial Analyses

Public Trading Multiples. Using publicly available information, J.P. Morgan compared selected financial data of the Company with similar data for selected publicly traded companies engaged in businesses which J.P. Morgan judged to be analogous to the Company or aspects thereof. However, none of the selected companies reviewed is identical to the Company, and certain of these companies may have characteristics that are materially different from those of the Company. The analyses necessarily involve complex considerations and judgments concerning differences in financial and operations characteristics of the companies involved and other factors that could affect the companies differently than they would affect the Company. The companies selected by J.P. Morgan were as follows:

- Shire plc.
- Vertex Pharmaceuticals Inc.
- Alexion Pharmaceuticals Inc.
- Incyte Corporation
- BioMarin Pharmaceutical Inc.
- UCB S.A.

- Jazz Pharmaceuticals plc.
- United Therapeutics Corporation.
- Swedish Orphan Biovitrum AB.

With respect to the selected companies, the information J.P. Morgan presented included the multiple of enterprise value, referred to in this section as "*EV*" (calculated as net equity value plus (i) the principal or face amount of total debt and non-convertible preferred stock plus (ii) the book value of any non-controlling/minority interests plus (iii) the book value of any contingent consideration less (iv) cash, cash equivalents, and short- and long-term marketable investments, and (v) the book value of any non-consolidated investments), to estimated 2018 Adjusted EBITDA [calculated as net income plus net interest income (expense), provision for income taxes, depreciation, amortization plus stock-based compensation], referred to in this section as "Adjusted EBITDA," and the multiple of price to estimated 2018 earnings per Share, referred to in this section as "EPS," as of January 19, 2018.

Estimated financial data for the selected companies, including the estimated EV and EPS of the companies, was based on the selected companies' filings with the SEC and publicly available analyst consensus estimates for the calendar year ended 2018 that J.P. Morgan obtained from FactSet Research Systems as of January 19, 2018. Results of these analyses were presented for the selected companies, as indicated in the following table:

	EV/Adjusted EBITDA Price/EPS 2018E	
Selected Company	**2018E Multiple**	**Multiple**
Shire plc	9.1×	8.4×
Vertex Pharmaceuticals Inc	NM*	NM*
Alexion Pharmaceuticals Inc	14.3×	17.4×
Incyte Corporation	NM*	NM*
BioMarin Pharmaceutical Inc	NM*	NM*
UCB S.A.	10.9×	15.2×
Jazz Pharmaceuticals plc	10.1×	11.5×
United Therapeutics Corporation	6.7×	11.9×
Swedish Orphan Biovitrum AB	10.5×	16.7×

*EV/Adjusted EBITDA multiples above 25.0× and price/EPS multiples above 35.0× listed as not meaningful ("NM").

Based on the above analysis, J.P. Morgan then selected an EV/Adjusted EBITDA 2018E reference range for the Company of 10.0× to 14.0× and a price/EPS 2018E reference range for the Company of 11.5× to 17.0×. These EV/Adjusted EBITDA 2018E multiples were then applied to the Company's estimated Adjusted EBITDA for the calendar year ended 2018, as set forth in the Management Projections (see "Certain Unaudited Prospective Financial Information"), yielding implied trading values for the Shares of approximately \$59.00 to \$82.25 (rounded to the nearest \$0.25) per Share, and these price/EPS 2018E multiples were then applied to the Company's estimated EPS for the calendar year ended 2018, as set forth in the Management Projections (see "Certain Unaudited Prospective Financial Information"), yielding implied trading values for the Shares of approximately \$53.00 to \$78.50 (rounded to the nearest \$0.25) per Share, which J.P. Morgan compared to the value of the Offer Price of \$105.00 per Share.

Selected Transaction Analysis. Using publicly available information, J.P. Morgan examined selected transactions with respect to businesses which J.P. Morgan judged to be analogous to the Company's business or aspects thereof. Using publicly available information, J.P. Morgan calculated, for each selected transaction, the multiple of the target company's (i) EV implied in the relevant transaction (calculated on the basis of the upfront consideration payable in the selected transaction and excluding any potential earn-outs) to the target company's estimated Adjusted EBITDA at the time of such relevant transaction and (ii) the price in the relevant transaction to the target company's EPS for the next twelve-month period for 2018, referred to in this section as "NTM." Estimated financial data for the selected transactions, including the EV and EPS of the companies involved in the analysis, was based on the selected companies' filings with the SEC and publicly available equity research estimates. Results of this analysis were presented for the selected transactions, as indicated in the following table:

			EV/NTM Adjusted		
				EBITDA Price/ NTM	
Announcement Date	**Target**	**Acquiror**	**EV (\$bn)**	**Multiple**	**EPS Multiple**
01/26/17	Actelion Ltd.	Johnson & Johnson	\$29.6	NM*	NM*
01/11/16	Baxalta Incorporated	Shire plc	36.8	16.4×	21.5×

(Continued)

(*Continued*)

03/16/15	Salix Pharmaceuticals, Inc.	Valeant International Inc.	15.8	NM*	NM*
11/17/14	Allergan, Inc.**	Actavis plc	66.0	18.2×	26.3×
07/18/14	Shire plc**	AbbVie Inc.	57.2	20.7×	26.6×
04/07/14	Questcor Pharmaceuticals, Inc.**	Mallinckrodt plc	5.5	8.7×	12.2×
02/16/11	Genzyme Corporation	Sanofi	22.7***	13.2×	19.0×
06/07/10	Talecris Biotherapeutics Holdings Corp.	Grifols, S.A.	4.0	10.3×	16.3×
05/16/10	OSI Pharmaceuticals, Inc.	Astellas Pharma Inc.	3.6	15.7×	18.0×

Notes: *EV/Adjusted EBITDA multiples above 25.0× and price/EPS multiples above 35.0× listed as "*NM*."
**Selected transaction includes redomicile/tax synergy component.
***Selected transaction includes $5.58 per Share intrinsic value of contingent value right per proxy filed on 03/07/11.

Based on the above analysis and other factors that J.P. Morgan considered appropriate, J.P. Morgan then selected an EV/NTM Adjusted EBITDA multiple reference range for the Company of 13.0× to 18.0×. These multiples were then applied to the Company's estimated Adjusted EBITDA for calendar year 2018, as set forth in the Management Projections (see "Certain Unaudited Prospective Financial Information"), yielding implied trading values for the Shares of approximately $76.50 to $105.50 (rounded to the nearest $0.25) per Share, which J.P. Morgan compared to the value of the Offer Price of $105.00 per Share. J.P. Morgan also selected a price/NTM EPS multiple reference range for the Company of 18.0× to 23.0×. These multiples were then applied to the Company's estimated EPS for calendar year 2018, as set forth in the Management Projections (see "Certain Unaudited Prospective Financial Information"), yielding implied trading values for the Shares of approximately $83.00 to $106.25 (rounded to the nearest $0.25) per Share, which J.P. Morgan compared to the value of the Offer Price of $105.00 per Share.

Sum-of-the-Parts Discounted Cash Flow Analysis. J.P. Morgan conducted a sum-of-the-parts discounted cash flow analysis for the purpose of determining an implied fully diluted equity value per Share. In arriving at the implied fully diluted equity value per Share, J.P. Morgan calculated a range of terminal asset values for the Company by applying a terminal asset value growth rate of (10.0%) to the unlevered free cash flows for certain revenue-producing parts of the Company (excluding certain unidentified expenses, including selling, general and administrative and research and development expenses), which growth rate was chosen based upon the Company management's expected future growth rates for revenue and free cash flows from calendar year 2018 to calendar year 2035. The unlevered free cash flows and the range of terminal asset values were then discounted by J.P. Morgan using discount rates ranging from 8.25% to 10.25%, which range of discount rates (the "J.P. Morgan Discount Rates") were derived utilizing the capital asset pricing model to derive the cost of equity, and based upon an analysis of the Company's weighted average cost of capital and inputs that J.P. Morgan determined were relevant based on publicly available data, taking into account macroeconomic assumptions, estimates of risk, the Company's capital structure and other appropriate factors. This analysis indicated a range of estimated present values per Share of $90.50 to $109.50 (rounded to the nearest $0.25), which J.P. Morgan compared to the value of the Offer Price of $105.00 per Share.

WholeCo Discounted Cash Flow Analysis. J.P. Morgan calculated the unlevered free cash flows that the Company is expected to generate from calendar year 2018 through calendar year 2027 based on the Management Projections. J.P. Morgan also calculated a range of terminal asset values for the Company at the end of this period by applying terminal asset value growth rates ranging from 1.50% to 3.00% to the unlevered free cash flows for the Company during the final year of the 10-year period, which range of growth rates was chosen based upon the Company management's expected future growth rates for revenue and free cash flows. The unlevered free cash flows and the range of terminal asset values were then discounted by J.P. Morgan to present value as of December 31, 2017 using the J.P. Morgan Discount Rates. This analysis indicated a range of estimated present values per Share of $77.75 to $117.25 (rounded to the nearest $0.25), which J.P. Morgan compared to the value of the Offer Price of $105.00 per Share.

Other Information

J.P. Morgan observed certain additional information that did not provide the basis for the rendering of J.P. Morgan's opinion, but was used for informational purposes, including the following:

Transaction Premia. For reference purposes only and not as a component of its fairness analysis, J.P. Morgan applied the closing price per Share of $64.11 on January 19, 2018 (the last trading day prior to the execution of the Merger Agreement) to transaction premia ranging from 50.00% to 60.00%, which resulted in a range of estimated values per Share of $96.25 to $102.50, which J.P. Morgan compared to the value of the Offer Price of $105.00 per Share.

Historical Trading Range for the Company. For reference purposes only and not as a component of its fairness analysis, J.P. Morgan reviewed the historical trading prices of the Shares since the completion of the Spin-Off, noting that the low and high intraday prices during such period ranged from $41.88 to $65.09 per Share, as compared to the value of the Offer Price of $105.00 per Share.

Analyst Price Targets for the Company. For reference purposes only and not as a component of its fairness analysis, J.P. Morgan reviewed certain publicly available equity research analyst share price targets for the Shares obtained from FactSet Research Systems as of January 19, 2018, noting that the low and high share price targets ranged from $43.00 to $100.00 per Share, as compared to the value of the Offer Price of $105.00 per Share.

Analyses based upon forecasts of future results are inherently uncertain, as they are subject to numerous factors or events beyond the control of the parties and their advisors. Accordingly, forecasts and analyses used or made by J.P. Morgan are not necessarily indicative of actual future results, which may be significantly more or less favorable than suggested by those analyses. Moreover, J.P. Morgan's analyses are not and do not purport to be appraisals or otherwise reflective of the prices at which businesses actually could be acquired or sold. None of the selected companies reviewed as described in the above summary is identical to the Company, and none of the selected transactions reviewed was identical to the Offer and Merger. However, the companies selected were chosen because they are publicly traded companies with operations and businesses that, for purposes of J.P. Morgan's analysis, may be considered similar to those of the Company. The transactions selected were similarly chosen because their participants, size, and other factors, for purposes of J.P. Morgan's analysis, may be considered similar to the Offer and Merger. The analyses necessarily involve complex considerations and judgments concerning differences in financial and operational characteristics of the companies involved and other factors that could affect the companies compared to the Company and the transactions compared to the Offer and Merger.

J.P. Morgan received a fee from the Company of $3 million, which was payable upon the delivery by J.P. Morgan of its opinion, which will be credited against the total fee payable to J.P. Morgan upon the consummation of the Offer and Merger equal to 0.275% of the total consideration payable in the Offer and Merger. In addition, the Company has agreed to reimburse J.P. Morgan for its costs and expenses incurred in connection with its services, including the fees and disbursements of counsel, and will indemnify J.P. Morgan against certain liabilities arising out of J.P. Morgan's engagement.

Opinion by Guggenheim

January 21, 2018
The Board of Directors Bioverativ Inc.
225 Second Avenue
Waltham, MA 02451 Members of the Board:

We understand that Bioverativ Inc. ("Bioverativ") and Sanofi S.A. ("Sanofi") intend to enter into an Agreement and Plan of Merger to be dated as of January 21, 2018 (the "Agreement"), pursuant to which (i) an indirect, wholly owned subsidiary of Sanofi ("Merger Sub") will commence a tender offer to purchase any and all of the issued and outstanding common shares, par value $0.001 per Share, of Bioverativ (the "Shares" and, such tender offer, the "Offer") at a price of $105.00 per Share in cash (the "Offer Price") and (ii) following consummation of the Offer, Merger Sub will be merged with and into Bioverativ, with Bioverativ continuing as the surviving corporation and as a wholly owned subsidiary of Sanofi (the "Merger" and, taken together with the Offer as an integrated transaction, the "Transaction"), pursuant to which each Share (other than Shares validly tendered and irrevocably accepted for purchase pursuant to the Offer, that constitute Dissenting Shares (as defined in the Agreement), are held in treasury or are owned by Sanofi or its subsidiaries immediately prior to the Merger) will be converted into the right to receive the Offer Price. The terms and conditions of the Transaction are more fully set forth in the Agreement.

You have asked us to render our opinion as to whether the Offer Price is fair, from a financial point of view, to the holders of the Shares (in their capacity as such and other than Sanofi and Merger Sub).

In the course of performing our reviews and analyses for rendering our opinion, we have:

- Reviewed a draft of the Agreement dated as of January 20, 2018;
- Reviewed certain publicly available business and financial information regarding Bioverativ;
- Reviewed certain non-public business and financial information regarding Bioverativ's business and prospects (including certain financial projections for the years ending December 31, 2017 through December 31, 2035), all as prepared and provided to us by Bioverativ's senior management;
- Discussed with Bioverativ's senior management their strategic and financial rationale for the Transaction as well as their views of Bioverativ's business, operations, historical and projected financial results and future prospects, and the commercial, competitive and regulatory dynamics in the pharmaceutical sector;
- Reviewed the historical prices, trading multiples, and trading activity of the Shares;
- Compared the financial performance of Bioverativ and the trading multiples and trading activity of the Shares with corresponding data for certain other publicly traded companies that we deemed relevant in evaluating Bioverativ;
- Reviewed the valuation and financial metrics of certain mergers and acquisitions that we deemed relevant in evaluating the Transaction;
- Performed discounted cash flow analyses based on the probability-adjusted financial projections for Bioverativ as furnished to us by Bioverativ; and
- Conducted such other studies, analyses, inquiries, and investigations as we deemed appropriate. With respect to the information used in arriving at our opinion.
- We have relied upon and assumed the accuracy, completeness, and reasonableness of all industry, business, financial, legal, regulatory, tax, accounting, actuarial, and other information (including, without limitation, any financial projections, other estimates, and other forward-looking information) furnished by or discussed with Bioverativ or obtained from public sources, data suppliers and other third parties.

- We (i) do not assume any responsibility, obligation, or liability for the accuracy, completeness, reasonableness, achievability, or independent verification of, and we have not independently verified, any such information (including, without limitation, any financial projections, other estimates, and other forward-looking information), (ii) express no view, opinion, representation, guaranty, or warranty (in each case, express or implied) regarding the (a) reasonableness or achievability of any financial projections, other estimates, and other forward-looking information or the assumptions upon which they are based or (b) probability adjustments included in such financial projections and (iii) have relied upon the assurances of Bioverativ's senior management that they are unaware of any facts or circumstances that would make such information (including, without limitation, any financial projections, other estimates, and other forward-looking information) incomplete, inaccurate, or misleading.
- Specifically, with respect to any (i) financial projections, other estimates, and other forward-looking information furnished by or discussed with Bioverativ, (a) we have been advised by Bioverativ's senior management, and we have assumed, that such financial projections (including the probability adjustments reflected therein), other estimates, and other forward-looking information utilized in our analyses have been reasonably prepared on bases reflecting the best currently available estimates and judgments of Bioverativ's senior management as to the expected future performance of Bioverativ and (b) we have assumed that such financial projections, other estimates and other forward-looking information have been reviewed by Bioverativ's Board of Directors with the understanding that such information will be used and relied upon by us in connection with rendering our opinion and (ii) financial projections, other estimates, and/or other forward-looking information obtained by us from public sources, data suppliers and other third parties, we have assumed that such information is reasonable and reliable.

During the course of our engagement, we were not asked by Bioverativ's Board of Directors to, and we did not solicit indications of interest from any third parties regarding a potential transaction with Bioverativ.

In arriving at our opinion, we have not performed or obtained any independent appraisal of the assets or liabilities (including any contingent, derivative, or off-balance sheet assets and liabilities) of Bioverativ or any other entity or the solvency or fair value of Bioverativ or any other entity, nor have we been furnished with any such appraisals. We are not legal, regulatory, tax, consulting, accounting, appraisal, or actuarial experts and nothing in our opinion should be construed as constituting advice with respect to such matters; accordingly, we have relied on the assessments of Bioverativ's senior management and Bioverativ's other professional advisors with respect to such matters. We are not expressing any view or rendering any opinion regarding the tax consequences of the Transaction to Bioverativ or its securityholders [including with regard to the spin-off of Bioverativ from Biogen Inc. ("Biogen") in February 2017 (the "Spin-Off")].

In rendering our opinion, we have assumed that, in all respects meaningful to our analyses, (i) the final executed form of the Agreement will not differ from the drafts that we have reviewed, (ii) Bioverativ, Sanofi, and Merger Sub will comply with all terms and provisions of the Agreement, and (iii) the representations and warranties of Bioverativ, Sanofi, and Merger Sub contained in the Agreement are true and correct and all conditions to the obligations of each party to the Agreement to consummate the Transaction (including the Offer) will be satisfied without any waiver, amendment, or modification thereof. We also have assumed that the Transaction will be consummated in a timely manner in accordance with the terms of the Agreement and in compliance with all applicable laws, documents, and other requirements, without any delays, limitations, restrictions, conditions, waivers, amendments, or modifications (regulatory, tax-related, or otherwise) that would have an effect on Bioverativ or the Transaction in any way meaningful to our analyses or opinion.

In rendering our opinion, we do not express any view or opinion as to the price or range of prices at which the Shares or other securities or financial instruments of or relating to Bioverativ may trade or otherwise be transferable at any time, including subsequent to the announcement of the Transaction.

We have acted as a financial advisor to Bioverativ in connection with the Transaction and will receive a customary fee for such services, a substantial portion of which is contingent on successful consummation of the Transaction. A portion of our compensation is payable upon delivery of our opinion and will be credited against the fee payable upon consummation of the Transaction. In addition, Bioverativ has agreed to reimburse us for certain expenses and to indemnify us against certain liabilities arising out of our engagement.

Aside from our current engagement by Bioverativ, Guggenheim Securities, LLC ("Guggenheim Securities") has not been previously engaged during the past two years by Bioverativ, nor has Guggenheim Securities been previously engaged during the past two years by Sanofi, to provide financial advisory or investment banking services for which we received fees. As Bioverativ is aware, Guggenheim Securities acted as a financial advisor to Biogen in connection with the Spin-Off, for which we received agreed-upon compensation. Guggenheim Securities may seek to provide Bioverativ, Sanofi, Biogen, and their respective affiliates with certain financial advisory and investment banking services unrelated to the Transaction in the future, for which services Guggenheim Securities would expect to receive compensation.

Guggenheim Securities and its affiliates and related entities engage in a wide range of financial services activities for our and their own accounts and the accounts of customers, including but not limited to: asset, investment, and wealth management; insurance services; investment banking, corporate finance, mergers and acquisitions, and restructuring; merchant banking; fixed income and equity sales, trading and research; and derivatives, foreign exchange, and futures. In the ordinary course of these activities, Guggenheim Securities and its affiliates and related entities may (i) provide such financial services to Bioverativ, Sanofi, other participants in the Transaction and their respective affiliates, for which services Guggenheim Securities and its affiliates and related entities may have received, and may in the future receive, compensation and (ii) directly and indirectly hold long and short positions, trade and otherwise conduct such activities in or with respect to loans, debt and equity securities, and derivative products of or relating to Bioverativ, Sanofi, other participants in the Transaction and their respective affiliates. Furthermore, Guggenheim Securities and its affiliates and related entities and our or their respective directors, officers, employees, consultants, and agents may have investments in Bioverativ, Sanofi, and other participants in the Transaction and their respective affiliates.

Consistent with applicable legal and regulatory guidelines, Guggenheim Securities has adopted certain policies and procedures to establish and maintain the independence of its research departments and personnel. As a result, Guggenheim Securities' research analysts may hold views, make statements or investment recommendations and publish research reports with respect to Bioverativ, Sanofi, Merger Sub, other participants in the Transaction and their respective affiliates, and the Transaction that differ from the views of Guggenheim Securities' investment banking personnel.

Our opinion has been provided to Bioverativ's Board of Directors (in its capacity as such) for its information and assistance in connection with its evaluation of the Offer Price. Our opinion is not intended to be used or relied upon for any other purpose or by any other person or entity and may not be disclosed publicly, made available to third parties, or reproduced, disseminated, quoted from, or referred to at any time, in whole or in part, without our prior written consent; *provided, however*, that this letter may be included in its entirety in any Solicitation/Recommendation Statement on Schedule 14D-9.

Our opinion and any materials provided in connection therewith do not constitute a recommendation to Bioverativ's Board of Directors with respect to the Transaction, nor does our opinion constitute advice or a recommendation to any holder of Shares as to whether to tender any Shares pursuant to the Offer or how to act in connection with the Merger or otherwise. Our opinion does not address Bioverativ's underlying business or financial decision to pursue the Transaction, the relative merits of the Transaction as compared to any alternative business or financial strategies that might exist for Bioverativ or the effects of any other transaction in which Bioverativ might engage. Our opinion addresses only the fairness, from a financial point of view and as of the date hereof, of the Offer Price to the holders of the Shares (in their capacity as such and other than Sanofi and Merger Sub). We do not express any view or opinion as to (i) any other term, aspect, or implication of (a) the Transaction (including, without limitation, the form or structure of the Transaction) or the Agreement or (b) any other agreement, transaction document, or instrument contemplated by the Agreement or to be entered into or amended in connection with the Transaction or (ii) the fairness, financial, or otherwise, of the Transaction to, or of any consideration to be paid to or received by, the holders of any class of securities (other than as expressly specified herein), creditors, or other constituencies of Bioverativ or Sanofi. Furthermore, we do not express any view or opinion as to the fairness, financial, or otherwise, of the amount or nature of any compensation payable to or to be received by any of Bioverativ's or Sanofi's directors, officers or employees, or any class of such persons, in connection with the Transaction relative to the Offer Price or otherwise.

Our opinion has been authorized for issuance by the Fairness Opinion and Valuation Committee of Guggenheim Securities. Our opinion is subject to the assumptions, limitations, qualifications, and other conditions contained herein and is necessarily based on economic, capital markets and other conditions, and the information made available to us, as of the date hereof. We assume no responsibility for updating or revising our opinion based on facts, circumstances, or events occurring after the date hereof.

Based on and subject to the foregoing, it is our opinion that, as of the date hereof, the Offer Price is fair, from a financial point of view, to the holders of the Shares (in their capacity as such and other than Sanofi and Merger Sub).

Very truly yours,

Guggenheim Securities, LLC

GUGGENHEIM SECURITIES
Guggenheim Securities, LLC 330 Madison Avenue
New York, New York 10017 GuggenheimPartners.com

Detailed Discussion

At the January 21, 2018 meeting of the Board of Directors, Guggenheim Securities rendered an oral opinion, which was confirmed by delivery of a written opinion, to the Board of Directors on whether the Offer Price was fair, from a financial point of view, to the Company's stockholders (in their capacity as such and other than Sanofi and Merger Sub).

Summary of Financial Analyses

Overview of Financial Analyses

This "Summary of Financial Analyses" presents a summary of the principal financial analyses performed by Guggenheim Securities and presented to the Board of Directors in connection with Guggenheim Securities' rendering of its opinion. Such presentation to the Board of Directors was supplemented by Guggenheim Securities' oral discussion with the Board of Directors, the nature and substance of which may not be fully described herein.

Some of the financial analyses summarized below include summary data and information presented in tabular format. In order to fully understand such financial analyses, the summary data and tables must be read together with the full text of the summary. Considering the summary data and tables alone could create a misleading or incomplete view of Guggenheim Securities' financial analyses.

The preparation of a fairness opinion is a complex process and involves various judgments and determinations as to the most appropriate and relevant financial analyses and the application of those methods to the particular circumstances involved. A fairness opinion therefore is not readily susceptible to partial analysis or summary description, and taking portions of the financial analyses set forth below, without considering such analyses as a whole, would in Guggenheim Securities' view create an incomplete and misleading picture of the processes underlying the financial analyses considered in rendering Guggenheim Securities' opinion.

In arriving at its opinion, Guggenheim Securities:

- based its financial analyses on various assumptions, including assumptions concerning general business, economic and capital markets conditions, and industry-specific and company-specific factors, all of which are beyond the control of the Company and Guggenheim Securities;
- did not form a view or opinion as to whether any individual analysis or factor, whether positive or negative, considered in isolation, supported or failed to support its opinion;
- considered the results of all of its financial analyses and did not attribute any particular weight to any one analysis or factor; and
- ultimately arrived at its opinion based on the results of all of its financial analyses assessed as a whole and believes that the totality of the factors considered and the various financial analyses performed by Guggenheim Securities in connection with its opinion operated collectively to support its determination as to the fairness, from a financial point of view and as of the date of such opinion, of the Offer Price to be received by the Company's stockholders (in their capacity as such and other than Sanofi and Merger Sub) pursuant to the Offer and Merger to the extent expressly specified in such opinion.

Transaction Premia and Implied Transaction Multiples

Offer Price per Share		**$105.00**
	Bioverativ Stock Price	
Acquisition Premium/(Discount) Relative to Bioverativ's:		
Closing Stock Price at 01/19/18	$64.11	63.8%
VWAP:		
30-Day	58.67	79.0
60-Day	54.47	92.7
Transaction Enterprise Value/Estimated Revenue for Bioverativ:		
2017E — Bioverativ Management Estimates		9.7×
Wall Street Consensus Estimates		9.8
2018E — Bioverativ Management Estimates		8.1
Wall Street Consensus Estimates		8.2
2019E — Bioverativ Management Estimates		6.8
Wall Street Consensus Estimates		7.6
Transaction Enterprise Value/Estimated Adjusted EBITDA for Bioverativ:		
2017E — Bioverativ Management Estimates		21.0×
Wall Street Consensus Estimates		20.7
2018E — Bioverativ Management Estimates		17.6
Wall Street Consensus Estimates		18.3
2019E — Bioverativ Management Estimates		13.8
Wall Street Consensus Estimates		16.7
Offer Price/Estimated EPS for Bioverativ:		
2017E — Bioverativ Management Estimates		31.8×
Wall Street Consensus Estimates		32.5
2018E — Bioverativ Management Estimates		22.8
Wall Street Consensus Estimates		24.1
2019E — Bioverativ Management Estimates		17.9
Wall Street Consensus Estimates		21.3

Change-of-Control Financial Analyses. In evaluating the Company in connection with rendering its opinion, Guggenheim Securities performed various financial analyses which are summarized in the table below and described in more detail elsewhere herein, including certain discounted cash flow analyses, selected precedent merger and acquisition transactions analysis, and publicly traded companies analysis. Solely for informational reference purposes, Guggenheim Securities also reviewed the premiums paid in selected merger and acquisition transactions, the historical trading price range for the Shares and Wall Street equity research analysts' price targets for the Shares.

Summary of Change-of-Control Financial Analyses

Offer Price per Share		**$105.00**
	Reference Range for Bioverativ on a Change-of-Control Basis	
	Low	**High**
Financial Analyses		
Discounted Cash Flow Analyses		
Bioverativ Stand-Alone Sum-of-the-Parts DCF Valuation	$88.50	$106.75
Bioverativ Stand-Alone Going-Concern DCF Valuation	75.75	112.00
Selected Precedent M&A Transactions Analysis	$76.50	$106.25
Selected Publicly Traded Companies Analysis	$53.00	$ 82.25
For Informational Reference Purposes		
Premiums Paid in Selected Merger and Acquisition Transactions	$96.25	$102.50
Bioverativ's Stock Price Range Since the Spin-Off	41.88	65.09
Wall Street Equity Research Price Targets	43.00	100.00

Discounted Cash Flow Analyses. Guggenheim Securities performed two illustrative stand-alone discounted cash flow analyses including (i) a discounted cash flow analysis based on projected, risk-adjusted, after-tax unlevered free cash flows (after deduction of stock-based compensation) for each of the Company's existing and pipeline products and an estimate of its terminal/continuing value at the end of the projection period (a "*Sum-of-the-Parts DCF*") and (ii) a discounted cash flow analysis based on projected, risk-adjusted, after-tax unlevered free cash flows (after deduction of stock-based compensation) for the Company and an estimate of its terminal/continuing value at the end of 2027 (a "*Going-Concern DCF*"). In performing its illustrative discounted cash flow analyses:

- Guggenheim Securities based its (i) Sum-of-the-Parts DCF on the Management Projections (excluding certain unidentified expenses, including selling, general and administrative and research and development expenses) for each of the Company's existing and pipeline products prepared by the Company's senior management through 2035 and (ii) Going-Concern DCF on the Management Projections for the Company prepared by the Company's senior management through 2027.
- Guggenheim Securities used a discount rate range of 8.5%–10.5% based on its estimate of the Company's weighted average cost of capital, which Guggenheim Securities estimated based on, among other factors, (i) Guggenheim Securities' then-current estimate of the prospective US equity risk premium range, (ii) the then-prevailing yield on the 20-year US Treasury bond as a proxy for the risk-free rate, and (iii) Guggenheim Securities' investment banking and capital markets judgment and experience in valuing companies similar to the Company.
- In calculating the Company's terminal/continuing value for purposes of its discounted cash flow analyses, Guggenheim Securities used (i) for its Sum-of-the-Parts DCF, an illustrative perpetual growth rate of the Company's terminal year normalized after-tax unlevered free cash flow of negative 10% and (ii) for its Going-Concern DCF, an illustrative reference range of perpetual growth rates of the Company's terminal year normalized after-tax unlevered free cash flow of 1.5%–3.0%. The illustrative terminal/continuing values implied by the foregoing perpetual growth rate references, in the case of the Sum-of-the-Parts DCF, were determined based on future competitive and patent considerations, and in the case of the Going-Concern DCF, were cross-checked for reasonableness by reference to the Company's implied terminal year Adjusted EBITDA multiples.
- Guggenheim Securities' illustrative discounted cash flow analyses resulted in an overall reference range for (i) the Sum-of-the-Parts DCF analysis of $88.50–$106.75 per Share (rounded to the nearest $0.25) and (ii) the Going-Concern DCF analysis of $75.75–$112.00 per Share (rounded to the nearest $0.25), each for purposes of evaluating the Shares on a stand-alone intrinsic-value basis.

- It was noted that the Offer Price of $105.00 per Share was at the top of the foregoing DCF-based reference range based on the illustrative discounted cash flow analyses, which in Guggenheim Securities' view supported its assessment of the financial fairness of the Offer Price.

Selected Precedent Merger and Acquisition Transactions Analysis. Guggenheim Securities reviewed and analyzed certain financial metrics associated with certain selected precedent merger and acquisition transactions during the past several years involving companies in the pharmaceutical sector that Guggenheim Securities deemed relevant for purposes of this analysis. The following nine precedent merger and acquisition transactions were selected by Guggenheim Securities for purposes of this analysis:

Selected Precedent Merger and Acquisition (M&A) Transactions

Date Announced	Acquiror	Target Company
01/26/17	Johnson & Johnson	Actelion Ltd.
01/11/16	Shire plc	Baxalta Incorporated
03/16/15	Valeant Pharmaceuticals International Inc.	Salix Pharmaceuticals, Inc.
11/17/14	Actavis plc	Allergan, Inc.
07/18/14	AbbVie Inc.	Shire plc
04/07/14	Mallinckrodt plc	Questcor Pharmaceuticals, Inc.
02/16/11	Sanofi	Genzyme Corporation
06/07/10	Grifols, S.A.	Talecris Biotherapeutics Holdings Corp.
05/16/10	Astellas Pharma Inc.	OSI Pharmaceuticals, Inc.

Guggenheim Securities calculated, among other things and to the extent publicly available, certain implied change-of-control transaction multiples for the selected precedent merger and acquisition transactions (based on then-available Wall Street equity research consensus estimates, each company's most recent publicly available financial filings and certain other publicly available information, in each case as of January 19, 2018), which are summarized in the following table:

Selected Precedent M&A Transaction Multiples

	Transaction Enterprise	
	Value/NTM Adjusted EBITDA	**Transaction Stock Price/ NTM EPS**
Mean	14.7×	20.0×
Median	15.7	19.0
High	20.7	26.6
Low	8.7	12.2
Bioverativ Transaction		
Based on Wall Street Consensus Estimates	**18.3×**	**24.1×**
Based on Bioverativ Management Estimates	**17.6**	**22.8**

In performing its selected precedent merger and acquisition transactions analysis:

- Guggenheim Securities selected a reference range of transaction multiples for purposes of evaluating the Company on a change-of-control basis as follows: (i) transaction enterprise value (calculated on the basis of the upfront consideration payable in the selected transaction and excluding any potential earn-outs)/forward Adjusted EBITDA multiple range of 13.0×–18.0× based on the Management Projections (see "Certain Unaudited Prospective Financial Information"); and (ii) transaction stock price/forward EPS multiple range of 18.0×–23.0× based on the Management Projections (see "Certain Unaudited Prospective Financial Information").
- Guggenheim Securities' analysis of the selected precedent merger and acquisition transactions resulted in an overall reference range of \$76.50–\$106.25 per Share (rounded to the closest \$0.25) for purposes of evaluating the Shares on a change-of-control basis.
- It was noted that the Offer Price of \$105.00 per Share was at the top of the foregoing change-of-control transaction reference range based on the selected precedent merger and acquisition transactions analysis, which in Guggenheim Securities' view supported its assessment of the financial fairness of the Offer Price.

Selected Publicly Traded Companies Analysis. Guggenheim Securities reviewed and analyzed the historical price performance of the Shares, trading metrics, and historical and projected/forecasted financial performance compared to corresponding data for certain publicly traded companies that Guggenheim Securities deemed relevant for purposes of this analysis. The following nine publicly traded companies were selected by Guggenheim Securities for purposes of this analysis:

Selected Publicly Traded Companies

- Shire plc
- Vertex Pharmaceuticals Incorporated
- Alexion Pharmaceuticals, Inc.
- Incyte Corporation
- Swedish Orphan Biovitrum AB
- BioMarin Pharmaceutical Inc.
- UCB S.A.
- Jazz Pharmaceuticals plc
- United Therapeutics Corporation

Guggenheim Securities calculated, among other things, various public market trading multiples for the Company and the selected publicly traded companies (in the case of the selected publicly traded companies, based on then-available Wall Street equity research consensus estimates and each company's most recent publicly available financial filings), which are summarized in the table below:

Selected Publicly Traded Company Multiples

	Enterprise Value/ 2018E Adjusted EBITDA	Stock Price at 01/19/18/ 2018E EPS
Mean	10.3×	13.5×
Median	10.3	13.6
High	14.3	17.4
Low	6.7	8.4

(*Continued*)

Bioverativ: Trading Basis		
Based on Wall Street Consensus Estimates	**11.2×**	**14.7×**
Based on Bioverativ Management Estimates	**10.8**	**13.9**
Acquisition Basis		
Based on Wall Street Consensus Estimates	**18.3×**	**24.1×**
Based on Bioverativ Management Estimates	**17.6**	**22.8**

In performing its selected publicly traded companies analysis:

- Guggenheim Securities selected reference ranges of trading multiples for purposes of evaluating the Company on a stand-alone public market trading basis as follows: (i) trading enterprise value/forward Adjusted EBITDA multiple range of 10.0×–14.0× based on the Management Projections (see "Certain Unaudited Prospective Financial Information"); and (ii) trading price/forward EPS multiple range of 11.5×–17.0× based on the Management Projections (see "Certain Unaudited Prospective Financial Information").
- Guggenheim Securities' analysis of the selected publicly traded companies resulted in an overall reference range of $53.00–$82.25 per Share (rounded to closest $0.25) for purposes of evaluating the Shares on a stand-alone public market trading basis.
- It was noted that the Offer Price of $105.00 per Share was above the foregoing public market trading reference range based on the selected publicly traded companies analysis, which in Guggenheim Securities' view supported its assessment of the financial fairness of the Offer Price.

Other Financial Reviews and Analyses Solely for Informational Reference Purposes

In order to provide certain context for the financial analyses in connection with its opinion as described above, Guggenheim Securities undertook various additional financial reviews and analyses as summarized below solely for informational reference purposes. As a general matter, Guggenheim Securities did not consider such additional financial reviews and analyses to be determinative methodologies for purposes of its opinion.

Premiums Paid in Selected Merger and Acquisition Transactions. Guggenheim Securities reviewed, based on publicly available information, the implied premiums paid or proposed to be paid in connection with certain selected precedent merger and acquisition transactions during the past several years involving companies in the pharmaceutical sector that Guggenheim Securities deemed relevant for purposes of this analysis. These transactions included the nine above-referenced precedent transactions used in the *Selected Precedent Merger and Acquisition Transactions Analysis*, as well as seven other precedent transactions deemed relevant for purposes of this analysis. Based on this analysis, Guggenheim Securities selected an illustrative reference range of 50%–60% premia, which resulted in an illustrative range of \$96.25–\$102.50 per Share (rounded to closest \$0.25).

Share Price Trading History. Guggenheim Securities reviewed the Shares trading history since the Spin-Off through January 19, 2018, the Shares traded in a range of approximately \$42.00–\$65.00 per Share. Among other things, it was noted that the Offer Price of \$105.00 exceeded the all-time high trading price for the Shares of \$65.09 and the closing price of \$64.11 on January 19, 2018, the day prior to the planned announcement of the Transactions.

Wall Street Equity Research Analyst Stock Price Targets. Guggenheim Securities reviewed selected Wall Street equity research analyst stock price targets for the Company as published prior to January 19, 2018 (the last practicable trading day prior to the Company's board meeting to consider and approve the Transactions). It was noted that such Wall Street equity research analyst stock price targets for the Shares were \$43.00–\$100.00 per Share.

https://doi.org/10.1142/9789811216749_0025

Case 25

Green Landscape Inc., Leveraged Buyout (LBO)

Chris Droussiotis

Columbia University, USA
formerly Sumitomo Mitsui Banking Corporation

Company Background

Green Landscape Inc. (GLI) is a leading provider of landscape maintenance and snow removal services in the US. The company provides these recurring services to a diversified base of over 15,000 enterprise clients including fortune 500 companies.

GLI's landscape services represent approximately 82% of its revenue for the 12-month period ended 2000. These services primarily include lawn care, flower planting and care, and tree and shrub pruning. These services are through annual maintenance contracts. In addition to the maintenance contracts, GLI provides additional non-contractual supplemental enhancements (*not included in the projections*).

GLI's snow removal services represent approximately 18% of its revenue for the 12-month period ended 2000. The snow removal services to the same clients provide a counter-seasonal revenue stream for GLI in key seasonal markets.

The 5-year historical Income Statements and last year's Balance Sheets were as follows:

INCOME STATEMENT					
($ 000's)	HISTORICAL				
	1996	1997	1998	1999	2000
Landscape Business	93,935	103,226	109,814	118,080	123,000
Snow Removal Business	19,327	21,474	23,342	25,650	27,000
REVENUE	113,262	124,700	133,156	143,730	150,000
Sales Growth		10.1%	6.8%	7.9%	4.4%
COST OF SALES (excl. Deprec.)	58,896	62,350	67,910	70,428	75,000
Gross Profit	54,366	62,350	65,246	73,302	75,000
Gross Margin	48.0%	50.0%	49.0%	51.0%	50.0%
Selling, General & Administrative Expenses	17,669	19,079	19,574	22,146	22,500
EBITDA	**36,697**	**43,271**	**45,672**	**51,156**	**52,500**
% Sales	32.4%	34.7%	34.3%	35.6%	35.0%

BALANCE SHEET	2000		2000
Current Assets		**Current Liabilities**	
Cash	10,000	Accounts Payable	6,000
Accounts Receivable	15,000	Other Current Liabilities	7,000
Inventory	-	**Total Current Liabilities**	13,000
Other Current Assets	5,000		
Total Current Assets	30,000	Total Long Term Debt	100,000
Goodwill		Deferred Taxes	1,000
Capitalized Fees		**Total Liabilities**	114,000
Net PP&E	240,000		
Investment in JV	30,000	**Shareholder's Equity**	
		Common Stock	135,000
		Retained Earnings	51,000
		Total Shareholder's Equity	186,000
Total Assets	**300,000**	**Total Liabilities & Equity**	**300,000**

Last Year's Operation Assumptions (2000)

- Average Revenue per Landscape service (ARPS) per month: $820
- Average number of Landscape services per customer per year: 10 months

- Average Revenue per Snow removal service: $600 per month per customer
- Average number of Snow removal services: 3 months
- Number of total customers 2000 for both services: 15,000 corporate clients
- Cost of Revenue as 50% of Revenue
- Operating Expenses as 15% of Revenue

Projections' Assumptions (Years 2001–2010)

- Average Revenue per Landscape service per month increase: 6.0%
- Average Revenue per Snow removal service per month 6.0%
- Total customer annual growth rate increase: 2%
- Cost of Revenue: 50% of Revenues
- Operating Expense: 15% of Revenues
- Depreciation: 5% of Revenues
- Tax Rate at 34%
- Deferred Taxes as % of Tax Expense 5%
- Capex: 7% of Revenues per year
- Accounts Receivable days: 30
- No Inventory (service business)
- Other Current Assets as % of Revenues 1.0%
- Accounts Payable days: 20
- Other Current Liabilities as % of Revenue 1.5%
- No new Investments during the projected period

LBO Transaction Overview

Heinz Ward & Co (HW) is in the process of raising the necessary funds to cover the purchase price of the equity, refinance GLS's existing debt and pay $20 million in transaction fees. The proposed structure is as follows:

Debt Financing

After further credit review of the business plan, the maximum leverage that underwriters are willing to underwrite, based on debt capacity analysis, for both the bank loans and senior unsecured notes are maximum 3–4× bank debt/EBITDA and 5–6× total debt/EBITDA, respectively. These debt capacity multiples are what is recommended to be the advisable leverage, along with what the co-underwriters are comfortable underwriting given that GLI's business is seasonal.

Bank Debt: Spring Bank approved a loan based on the Company's last year's EBITDA. Spring Bank proposed three different floating rate tranches so it will be in a position to syndicate these tranches to potential loan buyers including other banks and Collateralized Loan Obligation (CLO) funds that prefer longer maturity tranches. The terms of the loan by tranches were as follows (money terms):

7-Year Revolving Credit Facility: $100 million at LIBOR + 3.5% on the funded portion and 0.50% on the unfunded portion. The revolver facility will be used for working capital purposes and is not anticipated to be used to fund the acquisition on day one (*use $0 to fund the acquisition*)

Term Loan A Facility (*this will be syndicated to traditional banks*)

Amount	1.5× 2000 EBITDA (approval based on Debt Capacity)
Interest	LIBOR + 3.5%
Term	7 years
Scheduled Payment	Year 2001: 5%, Year 2002: 5%, Year 2003: 8%, Year 2004: 10%, Year 2005: 12%, Year 2006: 15%, 2007: 45%

Term Loan B Facility (*this will be syndicated to CLO and private credit funds*)

Amount	2.0× 2000 EBITDA* (approval based on Debt Capacity)
Interest	LIBOR + 4.0%
Term	7 years
Scheduled Payment	Year 2001: 1%, Year 2002: 1%, Year 2003: 1%, Year 2004: 1%, 2005: 1%, Year 2006: 1%, Year 2007: 94%

LIBOR assumptions: Starting LIBOR at 0.60% and increase 0.5% in 2001, increase 0.5% in 2002, and increase 1.0% in 2003.

Senior Unsecured Notes: Morgan Stanley, an investment bank, managed to raise the Senior Unsecured Notes from various private bond investors. The terms of these notes (money terms) were as follows:

Amount	$100 million
Interest	7.5%
Term	8 years
Scheduled Payment	2001–2010: 0%, 2011: 100% (bullet payment)

Equity: The equity will be provided by the private equity firm HW. The equity amount will be the balance of the financing after the debt is calculated.

The Assignment

You are an officer at HW, a private equity firm that is looking to acquire Green Landscape Inc (GLI), a privately own company and a leading provider of landscape maintenance and snow removal services in the US. The asking price is $400 million, including the refinancing all the existing debt ($100 million on 2000). You were asked to evaluate the opportunity and report back if the asking price justifies HW's 25% equity return targets assuming that the transaction will be an LBO (using leverage to enhance the equity returns). You were also asked to determine if HW can afford to pay 20% higher price just in case that the transaction turns into an aggressive auction process.

To answer these questions, you need the following documents:

1. *Prepare the transaction sources and uses.*
2. *Prepare a full financial model based on the assumptions provided including the debt service.*
3. *Prepare the proforma balance sheet laying in the new capital (new debt and equity).*
4. *Prepare the debt schedules based on the approved terms.*
5. *Prepare an equity IRR and NPV analysis to determine if the HW can meet its targeted return of 25%.*
6. *Run a scenario in which HW is to pay 20% premium over the asking price and see if it meets the target.*

Part VIII

Corporate Risk Management

https://doi.org/10.1142/9789811216749_0026

Case 26

Bank of America: Financial Options and Corporate Finance

Harvey A. Poniachek

Rutgers Business School, USA

Introduction to Options

An option is a contract that provides the owner the right, but not the obligation, to buy or sell an asset on or before an agreed-upon date at a specific price that is called the exercise price or strike price. Options are available as calls and puts. A call option gives the owner the right to buy (and the seller the obligation to sell) an asset at a fixed exercise price during a particular time period. A put option provides the holder the right to sell, and the seller has the obligation to buy an asset for a fixed exercise price on or before maturity. An investor who sells a call option receives the option price, or premium, up front and is *obliged* to sell the asset at the exercise price if the option holder exercises the call options. An investor who *sells* a put option receives cash up front and is obligated to buy the asset at the exercise price if the option holder exercises the option.

An option contract is subject to the following features:

- A call or put provides the right to purchase or sell an asset at the exercise strike price.
- An American option could be exercised any time up to and including the expiration date (or maturity date), whereas a European option can only be exercised on the expiration date.

- The premium is the option price paid for the call or put or received for selling a call or put option.

An option contract value depends primarily on the relation between the spot price of the underlying assets and its strike price. For a European option, if, at the time of the option's maturity, its strike price exceeds the spot price, the option would then be worthless and not exercised. For a European put option, if the strike price is less than the stock price at the time of its maturity, the option will be valued at zero and expires worthless. Similarly, at the time of the option's maturity, an at-the-money[1] European option has zero payoff if exercised and therefore its value is zero. However, prior to the maturity, the value of these options can be positive. In particular, for the call option, it is possible that the underlying price of the asset can be greater than the exercise price, in which case, the holder of the call can profitably exercise the option. Similarly, for a put option, the underlying price can be lower than the exercise price in which case, the holder of the put option can profitably exercise the option.

Option prices are subject to upper and lower bounds. The lower bound of the European call option on non-dividend paying stock that is expiring at time T is maximum of zero and the stock price less the present value of the exercise price. That is the lower bound is given by $\text{Max}(0, S - Ee^{-rT})$. The lower bound for a dividend-paying stock is $\text{Max}(0, S - D - Ee^{-rT})$, where D is the level of dividends per share. The lower bound of the European Put option expiring in T is $\text{Max}(0, Ee^{-rT} - S + D)$. An American call option cannot be worth more than the assets (whether a stock, currency, etc.), so that $C < S$; and a put option cannot be worth more than the exercise or strike price, that is, $P < E$.

Options are a zero-sum game where one person's gain is another person's loss of the same amount. Call buyers expect the value of the underlying asset to rise before expiration and their potential gain is unlimited, while their loss is limited to the premium paid for the option contract. Call writers are sellers who expect the value of the underlying asset to fall, and their gain is limited to the premium received, while their potential loss is unlimited. Writers of covered calls own the underlying asset, and their cost of delivering the underlying asset is known. However, writers of naked calls do not own the underlying asset and must purchase it at the prevailing market price if the option is exercised, and they are thus subject to unknown and unlimited cost. Because American options can be

[1]That is, when the exercise price is equal to the spot price (whether a call or put).

Exhibit 1. Factors Affecting Option Prices

	European		American	
	Call	**Put**	**Call**	**Put**
Spot Price	+	–	+	–
Exercise/Strike Price	–	+	–	+
Maturity	?	?	+	+
Volatility	+	+	+	+
Interest Rate	+	–	+	–
Dividends	–	+	–	+

Note: Indicates the option price sensitivity to the factors affecting it.
Source: John C. Hull, *Fundamentals of Futures and Options Markets*, 9th ed. (Pearson, Hoboken, New Jersey, 2017), p. 228.

exercised even before the expiration date, the value of such options is at least as valuable as its European counterparts.

There are **six factors** that affect option prices, which include the price of the underlying assets; the exercise price or strike price; the maturity or expiration date; the volatility of the underlying asset; the interest rate on risk-free bonds, and the dividend — as shown in Exhibit 1. For instance, the call price (or premium) is directly related to the spot prices, that is, premium prices go up with the increase in spot price, with increase in volatility and interest rate. However, put prices (or premia) decline with higher spot prices and higher interest rates.

The Put-Call Parity

The Put-Call Parity[2] (PCP) states that you could construct a portfolio by **buying** a put option (Put) and the underlying stock (Stock), which should provide the same payoff as buying a call option (Call) and purchasing the present value of a risk-free zero-coupon bond, Ee^{-rT}, as follows[3]:

$$\text{Put} + \text{Stock} = \text{Call} + Ee^{-rT}$$

[2] John C. Hull, "Properties of Stock Options," in *Fundamentals of Futures and Options Markets*, 9th ed. (Pearson, Hoboken, New Jersey, 2017), Chapter 10, 235–239.
[3] Stephen A. Ross *et al.*, "Options and Corporate Finance," in *Corporate Finance*, 12th ed. (McGraw Hill, New York, 2019), Chapter 22, 681.

The put-call equation contains four variables, and it could be solved for each one at a time upon rearranging it. For instance, we can solve for the price of the stock as follows:

Price of stock = Price of Call – Price of Put + Present value of the exercise price

The above price of the stock formula states that you could replicate the purchase of a synthetic stock by buying a call, selling a put, and buying a present value of a zero-coupon bond.

The Black–Scholes Model

The Black–Scholes pricing formulas for European calls and puts of non-dividend paying stocks are as follows[4]:

$$C = So\mathrm{N}(\mathrm{d1}) - Ee^{-rT}\mathrm{N}(\mathrm{d2})$$

$$P = Ee^{-rT}\mathrm{N}(-\mathrm{d2}) - \mathrm{SoN}(-\mathrm{d1})$$

N(d1) and N(d2) are probabilities that we compute using the following formulas for d1 and d2 and then look the numbers up in the standard normal tables.

$$d_1 = \frac{\ln\left(\frac{S}{E}\right) + \left(R + \frac{\sigma^2}{2}\right)t}{\sigma\sqrt{t}}$$

$$d_2 = d_1 - \sigma\sqrt{t}$$

where σ is the standard deviation (or volatility) of the underlying asset returns.

Option Embedded Instruments and Financial Policies

Some corporate financial policies and financial instruments are embedded with implicit options features.[5] That is, options are embedded in corporate finance in the following areas:

[4] *Ibid.*, p. 304.

[5] Ross, *op. cit.*, p. 695.

1. Capital budgeting,
2. Valuation, and
3. Capital structure and funding decisions.[6]

Application of options in capital budgeting is referred to as real options and include the option to delay capital expenditures, to expand a project, or to abandon a project due to unexpected circumstances. The issue of capital budgeting is addressed in the case study relating to ConocoPhillips in this case book. Options could be embedded in equity and debt securities such as convertible and/or callable debt. Option pricing theory can explain the conflict between shareholders and bondholders;[7] the design and valuation of the securities, and the value of financial flexibility.

Bank of America Corporation[8]

Bank of America Corporation (BAC) is one of the world's largest financial institutions, with $2.8 trillion in assets and 208,000 employees. Its principal executive offices are located in Charlotte, North Carolina. BAC serves individual consumers, small- and middle-market businesses, institutional investors, large corporations, and governments, and has a large portfolio of financial instruments, including loans securities, and derivatives.

BAC is party to a large number of derivatives transactions that are subject to extensive regulations, including margin, reporting, registration, and position limits. The bank is a member of various central counterparties (CCPs) and is exposed to the risk of non-performance by clients for which they clear transactions, which may not be covered by available collateral. Liquidity is vital and is affected by interest and currency exchange rates, fluctuations in equity and futures prices, trading volumes and prices of securitized products, the implied volatility of interest rates

[6] Aswath Damodaran, "Options Application in Corporate Finance," in *Corporate Finance, Theory and Practice*, 2nd ed. (Wiley, Hoboken, New Jersey, 2001), Chapter 27, 81 pp. ("Damodaran").

[7] For example, option values increase with risk and one may view the equity of the firm as an option against the assets of the firm with an exercise price of the face value of debt outstanding. As leverage increases, the value of equity will decrease. But managers acting upon the interest of the shareholders would increase the risk of the underlying asset, thereby offsetting the decline in equity value.

[8] BAC 10-K 2020.

and credit spreads, and other economic and business factors. BAC funds its assets primarily with globally sourced deposits as well as secured and unsecured liabilities transacted in the capital markets, including the repo markets and asset securitization transactions, including with government-sponsored enterprises (GSEs).

There is a major transition in progress in global financial markets with respect to the replacement of the London Interbank Offered Rate (LIBOR), and certain other "benchmarks" that are used extensively across global financial markets and in business. In particular, LIBOR is used in many of products and contracts, including derivatives, loans, mortgages, floating-rate notes, and other adjustable-rate products and financial instruments. The aggregate notional amount of these products and contracts is material to BAC business, and there are significant risks and challenges associated with the transition that may result in significant uncertainty, or have other consequences that cannot be fully anticipated, which expose it to various financial, operational, supervisory, conduct and legal risks. Most Alternative Reference Rates (ARRs) are calculated on a compounded or weighted-average basis, and involve complex billing and reconciliation. Any mismatch between the adoption of ARRs in loans, securities, and derivatives markets may impact hedging or other financial arrangements that BAC implemented and may result in unanticipated market exposures. There can be no assurance that ARRs will be comparable or adequate alternatives to IBORs or perform in the same way.

Risk is inherent in all banking business activities and BAC takes a comprehensive approach to its management with a defined Risk Framework and an articulated Risk Appetite Statement, which are approved annually by the enterprise risk premium (ERC) and the Board. The seven key types of risk faced by BAC include the following:

1. Strategic risk is the risk to current or projected financial condition arising from incorrect assumptions about external or internal factors, inappropriate business plans, ineffective business strategy execution, or failure to respond in a timely manner to changes in the regulatory, macroeconomic, or competitive environments in the geographic locations in which we operate.
2. Credit risk is the risk of loss arising from the inability or failure of a borrower or counterparty to meet its obligations.
3. Market risk is the risk that changes in market conditions may adversely impact the value of assets or liabilities, or otherwise negatively

impact earnings. Market risk is composed of price risk and interest rate risk.

4. Liquidity risk is the inability to meet expected or unexpected cash flow and collateral needs while continuing to support the businesses and customers under a range of economic conditions.
5. Compliance risk is the risk of legal or regulatory sanctions, material financial loss, or damage to the reputation of the Corporation arising from the failure of the Corporation to comply with the requirements of applicable laws, rules and regulations, and the internal policies and procedures.
6. Operational risk is the risk of loss resulting from inadequate or failed processes, people, and systems, or from external events.
7. Reputational risk is the risk that negative perceptions of the Corporation's conduct or business practices may adversely impact its profitability or operations.

Credit Ratings

The borrowing costs and ability to raise funds are impacted by the credit ratings that is also important to customers or counterparties in certain markets and in certain transactions, including over-the-counter (OTC) derivatives. On April 22, 2020, Fitch Ratings (Fitch) upgraded its long-term and short-term senior debt ratings by one notch to AA-/F1+ and upgraded its preferred stock rating for the Corporation by one notch to BBB and downgraded its subordinated debt rating for the Corporation by one notch to A-. Moody's Investors Service (Moody's) affirmed its long-term and short-term debt ratings for the Corporation and all of its rated subsidiaries, which did not change during 2020, and Standard & Poor's Global Ratings also did not change during 2020.

Credit Risk Management

BAC manages credit risk based on the risk profile of the borrower or counterparty, repayment sources, the nature of underlying collateral, and other support given current events, conditions and expectations. It defines the credit exposure to a borrower or counterparty as the loss potential arising from all product classifications including loans and leases, deposit overdrafts, derivatives, assets held-for-sale, and unfunded lending

Exhibit 2. Financial Highlights (Obtained from 10-K Report)

(Dollars in Millions, Except per Share Information)	Summary Income Statement and Selected Financial Data 2020	2019
Income Statement		
Net Interest Income	**$43,360**	$48,891
Noninterest Income	**42,168**	42,353
Total Revenue, Net of Interest Expense	**85,528**	91,244
Provision for Credit Losses	**11,320**	3,590
Noninterest Expense	**55,213**	54,900
Income Before Income Taxes	**18,995**	32,754
Income Tax Expense	**1,101**	5,324
Net Income	**17,894**	27,430
Preferred Stock Dividends	**1,421**	1,432
Net Income Applicable to Common Shareholders	**$16,473**	$25,998
Per Common Share Information		
Earnings	**$1.88**	$2.77
Diluted Earnings	**1.87**	2.75
Dividends Paid	**0.72**	0.66
Performance Ratios		
Return on Average Assets	**0.67%**	1.14%
Return on Average Common Shareholders' Equity	**6.76**	10.62
Return on Average Tangible Common Shareholders' Equity	**9.48**	14.86
Efficiency Ratio	**64.55**	60.17
Balance Sheet at Year-End		
Total Loans and Leases	**$927,861**	$983,426
Total Assets	**2,819,627**	2,434,079
Total Deposits	**1,795,480**	1,434,803
Total Liabilities	**2,546,703**	2,169,269
Total Common Shareholders' Equity	**248,414**	241,409
Total Shareholders' Equity	**272,924**	264,810

commitments which include loan commitments, letters of credit, and financial guarantees.

Market Risk Management

Market risk is the risk that changes in market conditions may adversely impact the value of assets or liabilities, or otherwise negatively impact earnings. BAC traditional banking loan and deposit products are non-trading positions and are generally reported at amortized cost for assets or the amount owed for liabilities (historical cost). BAC trading positions are reported at fair value with changes reflected in income and are subject to various changes in market-based risk factors. The majority of this risk is generated by activities in the interest rate, foreign exchange, credit, equity, and commodities markets. In addition, the values of assets and liabilities could change due to market liquidity, correlations across markets, and expectations of market volatility. The corporation seeks to manage these risk exposures by using a variety of techniques that encompass a broad range of financial instruments.

Model risk is the potential for adverse consequences from decisions based on incorrect or misused model outputs and reports and it impacts all risk types including credit, market, and operational risks. The Enterprise Model Risk Policy defines model risk standards, consistent with risk framework and risk appetite, prevailing regulatory guidance, and industry best practice.

Interest Rate Risk

Interest rate risk represents exposures to instruments whose values vary with the level or volatility of interest rates. These instruments include loans, debt securities, certain trading-related assets and liabilities, deposits, borrowings, and derivatives. Hedging instruments used to mitigate these risks include options, futures, forwards, and swaps.

Foreign Exchange Risk and Trading Risk Management

Foreign exchange risk represents exposures to changes in the values of current holdings and future cash flows denominated in currencies other than the US dollar. Hedging instruments used to mitigate this risk include foreign exchange options, currency swaps, futures, forwards, and foreign currency-denominated debt and deposits.

To evaluate risks in trading activities, BAC focuses on the actual and potential volatility of revenues generated by individual positions. Quantitative measures of market risk are evaluated on a daily basis from a single position to the portfolio of the Corporation. These measures include sensitivities of positions to various market risk factors, such as the potential impact on revenue from a one basis point change in interest rates, and statistical measures utilizing both actual and hypothetical market moves, such as VaR and stress testing. Additionally, risk managers independently evaluate the risk of the portfolios under the current market environment and potential future environments. VaR is a common statistic used to measure market risk as it allows the aggregation of market risk factors, including the effects of portfolio diversification. A VaR model simulates the value of a portfolio under a range of scenarios in order to generate a distribution of potential gains and losses. VaR represents the loss that a portfolio is not expected to exceed more than a certain number of times per period, based on a specified holding period, confidence level, and window of historical data. BAC uses one VaR model consistently across the trading portfolios and it uses a historical simulation approach based on a 3-year historical data.

The primary VaR statistic is equivalent to a 99% confidence level, which means that for a VaR with a one-day holding period, there should not be losses in excess of VaR, on average, 99 out of 100 trading days. Within any VaR model, there are significant and numerous assumptions that will differ from company to company. The accuracy of a VaR model depends on the availability and quality of historical data for each of the risk factors in the portfolio. For positions with insufficient historical data for the VaR calculation, the process for establishing an appropriate proxy is based on fundamental and statistical analysis of the new product or less liquid position. This analysis identifies reasonable alternatives that replicate both the expected volatility and correlation to other market risk factors that the missing data would be expected to experience.

The total market-based portfolio VaR is the combination of the total covered positions portfolio and the fair value option portfolio. Covered positions are defined by regulatory standards as trading assets and liabilities, both on- and off-balance sheets, that meet a defined set of specifications. These specifications identify the most liquid trading positions which are intended to be held for a short-term horizon and where we are able to hedge the material risk elements in a two-way market. Foreign exchange and commodity positions are always considered covered positions, except for structural foreign currency positions that are excluded with prior regulatory approval.

Interest Rate Risk Management

Interest rate risk represents the most significant market risk exposure to BAC, and it is measured as the potential change in net interest income caused by movements in market interest rates. The bank prepares forward-looking forecasts of net interest income, and measures and evaluates the impact that alternative interest rate scenarios have on the baseline forecast to assess interest rate sensitivity under varied conditions. The overall goal is to manage interest rate risk so that movements in interest rates do not significantly adversely affect earnings and capital. Exhibit 3 presents the spot and 12-month forward rates used in the baseline forecasts on December 31, 2020 and 2019. During 2020, the asset sensitivity of the balance sheet increased in both up-rate and down-rate scenarios primarily due to continued deposit growth invested in long-term securities. BAC continues to be asset sensitive to a parallel upward move in interest rates with the majority of that impact coming from the short end of the yield curve.

The above sensitivity analysis assumes that BAC takes no action in response to these rate shocks and does not assume any change in other macroeconomic variables normally correlated with changes in interest rates.

Exhibit 3. Forward Rates

	December 31, 2020		
	Federal Funds	**3-Month LIBOR**	**10-Year Swap**
Spot Rates	**0.25%**	**0.24%**	**0.93%**
12-Month Forward Rates	**0.25**	**0.19**	**1.06**
	December 31, 2019		
Spot Rates	1.75%	1.91%	1.90%
12-Month Forward Rates	1.50	1.62	1.92

Exhibit 4. Estimated Net Interest Income Sensitivity to Curve Changes

(Dollars in Millions)	Short Rate (bps)	Long Rate (bps)	December 31 2020	December 31 2019
Parallel Shifts				
+100 bps Instantaneous Shift	+100	+100	**$10,468**	$4,190
–25 bps Instantaneous Shift	–25	–25	**(2,766)**	(1,500)
Flatteners				
Short-End Instantaneous Change	+100	—	**6,321**	2,641
Long-End Instantaneous Change	—	–25	**(1,686)**	(653)
Steepeners				
Short-End Instantaneous Change	–25	—	**(1,084)**	(844)
Long-End Instantaneous Change	—	+100	**4,333**	1,561

Interest Rate and Foreign Exchange Derivative Contracts

Interest rate and foreign exchange derivative contracts are utilized in asset and liability management (ALM) activities and serve as an efficient tool to manage interest rate and foreign exchange risk. BAC uses derivatives to hedge the variability in cash flows or changes in fair value on the balance sheet due to interest rate and foreign exchange components. Interest rate contracts are generally non-leveraged generic interest rate and foreign exchange basis swaps, options, futures, and forwards. In addition, the corporation uses foreign exchange contracts, including cross-currency interest rate swaps, foreign currency futures contracts, and foreign currency forward contracts and options to mitigate the foreign exchange risk associated with foreign currency-denominated assets and liabilities.

Changes to the composition of the derivatives portfolio during 2020 reflect actions taken for interest rate and foreign exchange rate risk management. The decisions to reposition the derivatives portfolio are based on the current assessment of economic and financial conditions including the interest rate and foreign currency environments, balance sheet composition and trends, and the relative mix of our cash and derivative positions. BAC uses interest rate derivative instruments to hedge the variability in the cash flows of the assets and liabilities and other forecasted transactions.

BAC hedges the net investment in non-US operations determined to have functional currencies other than the US dollar using forward foreign exchange contracts that typically settle in less than 180 days, cross-currency basis swaps, and foreign exchange options. The recorded net after-tax losses on derivatives were offset by gains on the net investments in consolidated non-US entities on December 31, 2020. Exhibit 4 presents derivatives utilized and shows the notional amount, fair value, weighted-average receive-fixed and pay-fixed rates, expected maturity, and average estimated durations of the open ALM derivatives on December 31, 2020 and 2019.

The Assignment

1. Valuing BAC's call and put options for 6 and 12 months under the following parameters by application of the Black–Scholes–Merton pricing formulas for European calls and puts with dividends:

Call	Puts
$S = 42.25$	$S = 42.25$
$K = 50.00$	$K = 38.00$
STDEV = 40%	STDEV = 40%
DIV = 0.72	DIV = 0.72
TIME = 6/12	TIME = 6/12
TIME – 1 YEAR	TIME – 1 YEAR
$I = 2.5\%$	$I = 2.5\%$

2. Valuing equity as an option BAC assets Values (*S*, spot rice) at \$2.9 trillion; the standard deviation of the assets is 40%. The debt (*K*, strike price) has a value of \$2.6 trillion, the US Treasury Bonds rate is 3.0%, and dividends are \$0.72. Value the firm's equity as a call option on the firm by application of the Black–Scholes–Merton model.
3. Value the bank's assets by application of the Black–Scholes–Merton model.
4. Estimate the call option 2 years hence under the assumption that $S =$ \$32 and all the other relevant inputs are as stated in question #2 above.
5. Describe how BAC protects itself against the various risks it faces as listed in the case.

Appendix. Introduction to Hedging Using Financial Instruments

Interest Rate Risk: Exhibit 4 demonstrates the impact of interest rate movement upon the portfolio assets should interest rates increase. One simple approach for the bank to hedge against interest rate movements is to ensure that the duration of the assets it purchases is funded by liabilities of equal duration. Recall from Case 12, the value sensitivity of an asset to changes in interest rate increases with its duration. Thus, if the bank matches the duration of its assets with that of its liabilities, then theoretically, if interest rates increase which reduces the value of the assets should also decrease the value of its liabilities.

The firm may also use financial instruments to hedge as well. One such instrument is a futures contract.

A futures contract is an agreement to buy or sell an underlying asset at a specified price sometime in the future. For example, assume today is November 2 and I am managing a portfolio of AAA corporate bonds for the corporation. If interest rates increase between now and the end of December when I plan to liquidate the portfolio to provide liquidity for the firm, the value of the bonds will decrease. Consider the following chart:

	Value Change of Corporate Bonds	Desired Change of Hedge Instrument
Interest Rates Increase	–	+
Interest Rates Decrease	+	–

Note that the chart indicates that if interest rates rise, the value of the corporate bonds will decrease. Accordingly, I want to use a financial instrument whose value will increase if interest rates increase. One such instrument is a futures contract on Treasury Bonds. Note that when I sell the futures contract, I am promising to sell a certain amount of Treasury securities for a given price. Should interest rates rise beyond what is expected, the price for which I can buy back these future contracts should be lower. In which case, I am making money on the future transactions which can be used to offset the potential loss of corporate bond securities. Please also note that should interest rate decrease, the corporate bond portfolio will increase in value, but then I will lose money with the hedging instruments. In other words, futures contracts hedge against increase and decrease in interest rates. But what if I only wanted to hedge against interest rate increases and not decreases in interest rates?

One way of solving that is to buy a put on the Treasury Bond futures contracts. For example, assume that I can buy a put with an exercise price equal to the futures contract price of November 2nd. If interest rates rise, the futures contract price should decline and I should be able to exercise the put and profit from the increase in interest rates. On the other hand, should interest rates decrease, the value of the put will fall and I have no incentive to exercise the put.

It is also important that when using future contracts, one must consider the duration of the underlying instrument. If the underlying asset that we wish to hedge has a maturity of 10 years, does it make sense to use a future contract of Treasury Bills or that of Treasury Bonds. The point of this appendix is only to introduce how firms can hedge, but it is beyond the scope of this chapter to explain the intricacies of hedging and some of the fallacies of the use of futures to perfectly hedge against interest rate risk.

For a more thorough introduction to hedging, please see Hull *et al.* (2013).[9]

[9]Hull, J., S. Treepongkaruna, D. Colwell, R. Heaney, and D. Pitt. *Fundamentals of Futures and Options Markets* (Pearson Higher Education AU, Hoboken, New Jersey, 2013).

https://doi.org/10.1142/9789811216749_0027

Case 27

Commodity Risk at Domino's

Susan Hume

The College of New Jersey, USA

Domino's and the Futures Markets: Less Talk, More Delivery?

> "Commodities tend to zig when the equity markets zag." — Jim Rodgers, Businessman, Investor

Since tossing and rebuilding its business model less than a decade ago, Domino's Pizza Inc. (DPZ) has delivered its business to become the world's largest international quick service pizza delivery business. "Without question, we are pleased with our … full-year 2017 performance — with results that continued to outpace the industry," said outgoing J. Patrick Doyle, President and Chief Executive Officer. "Our 2017 global retail sales growth and domestic comps outperformed the high-end of our stated 3 to 5-year outlook. This, along with tremendous net store growth and an incredibly low number of closures, helps validate that our long-term fundamental strength is well intact heading into 2018 … Every day you get better, or you get worse. You never stay the same."

The firm's domestic makeover strategy had two main ingredients: Ask the consumer what tastes the products should have and develop and use technology in all aspects of the product. Overall 95% of the company's sales are at franchises, where owners buy the products from Domino's supply chain. An important part of this change happened in its supply operations to insure high-quality food items from top suppliers. The key to the supply chain was to provide quality ingredients (cheeses, wheat, meats, and other toppings) at a favorable price in order to maintain selling a pizza with two toppings at a competitive $5.99 price. Customer satisfaction with the product increased substantially from Domino's supply chain modernization along with other product and technology innovations. The main ingredient to the success of Domino's business is the price of cheese, estimated to represent 30–40% of the firm's operating food cost and supplied by Leprino Foods which is estimated to control 85% of the pizza cheese market.[1] While the concept of supply chain is one important solution, incoming CFO Juliette LaRisk would like to review the entire process of Domino's program of monthly corporate commodity market meetings. The meetings forecast the expected market price of key commodities, relative to weather conditions, global supply and demand, and geopolitical conditions that impact market direction and volatility. She and her management team wonder if there is an opportunity to use commodity hedging techniques with exchange-traded futures and options contracts used by other food companies to further reduce costs. She notes DPZ's most recent Annual Report highlights the importance of "changes in operating expenses resulting from changes in prices of food (particularly cheese), fuel and other commodity costs" as a forward-looking business risk. Other companies in the food business manage price risk using financial futures so that there was a strategy of least regret when these prices rise. In addition to the food costs, some of these companies also hedge fuel costs. Reviewing the company's hedging policy is especially important as the price of milk (Class III) and manufactured cheese products has been low on a historical basis over the past 5 years (see Exhibits 1 and 2). Juliette LaRisk would like to strategically reevaluate DPZ's hedging policy using financial futures to hedge cheese price risk. Senior management could also a larger hedging program to protect margins to provide price stability for its: (1) truck and delivery car fuel needs, which are core to the company's supply chain and the franchisee's in-house delivery service, (2) wheat and box costs[2] and (3) manage other commodity food costs, especially wheat.

[1]See https://www.forbes.com/sites/chloesorvino/2017/05/23/james-leprino-exclusive-mozzarella-billionaire-cheese-pizza-hut-dominos-papa-johns/#26a4cd9b4958.

[2]When natural gas and oil prices as the feedstocks for resin plastics are high, companies such as Kraft may hedge its plastic containers and corrugated boxes while also using purchasing agreements with its suppliers. The lower prices for these feedstocks, which now

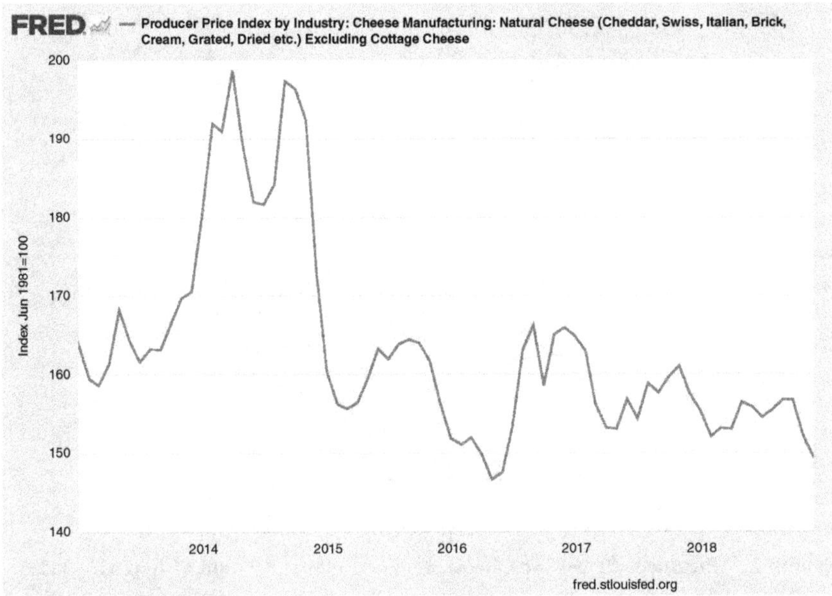

Exhibit 1. Producer Prices for Manufactured Cheese (2013–2018)

Source: U.S. Bureau of labor Statistics

Juliette understands the nature of market volatility, especially in commodities markets. She notes that the future is often surprisingly different than what we expect. She reflects on the market for wheat, where buyers at food manufacturers manage this uncertainty every day. For instance, over the course of last few years, flour prices have varied from $12.00 to $45.00 per cwt. Market fluctuations like this can impact the bottom line at Domino's and its franchisees and can leave business objectives unmet due to unplanned expenses.

Volatile conditions can happen in any market. Russia experienced an extreme drought in 2010 and banned grain exports starting on August 15, 2010. Compounding that issue were further weather challenges in the US, Australia, and Canada. Outside influences such as trade policies to redo tariffs, changes in the US Corporate Tax Rate, global and regional GDP growth, and political instability can contribute to volatile markets. For

include recycled plastic is a disincentive currently from using the futures markets (CME and LME) and forward purchase agreements with Koch Industries and Shell Petroleum. Currently these markets due to low prices and conservation efforts to go green are inactive. See https://www.ptonline.com/articles/four-ways-to-fight-sky-highresin-prices and https://informs-sim.org/wsc13papers/includes/files/012.pdf.

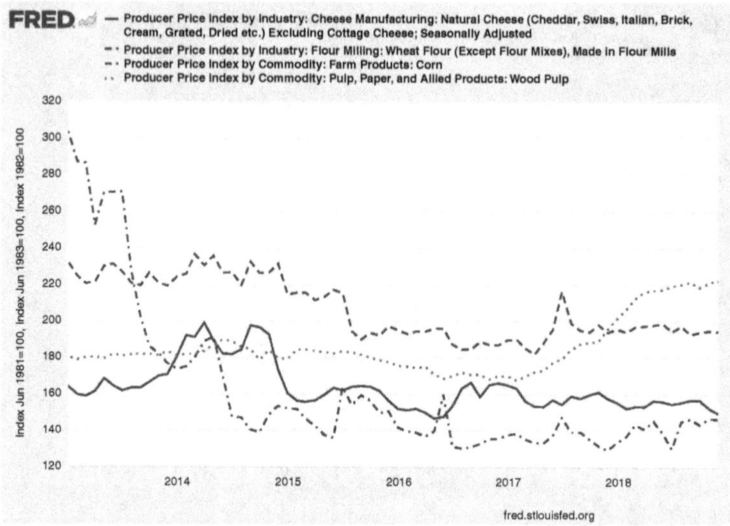

Exhibit 2. Producer Prices for Cheese, Flour, Corn, and Wood Pulp (2013–2018)

Source: U.S. Bureau of labor Statistics

instance, China's 2018 retaliation to limit agricultural imports to counter President Trump's tariff proposals have had large downward pressure on agricultural products paid to farmers.

Background

Business Description[3]

Domino's is a pizza restaurant chain headquartered in Ann Arbor, Michigan. Domino's operates under a franchise model that generates revenues and earnings primarily through royalties and selling necessary equipment and materials to its franchises. Founded in 1960, Domino's has developed into a brand known for selling handcrafted, quality food at competitive prices with easy and efficient ordering methods, enhanced by recent technological investments. Domino's operated as a private company until its IPO in 2004. Domino's has become the largest pizza chain in the world in 2017 selling more than 2 million pizzas each day through their global system, surpassing its long-time dominant competitor Pizza Hut.

[3]Information contained in background section is based upon research provided by TCNJ students Justin Fernandez, Todd Kutcher, Rishi Konkesa, and Matt Liebers. I am grateful for their contribution, comments, and suggestions.

Franchise Service Description

At year-end 2017, Domino's currently operates a network of over 14,000 franchises. Domestically Domino's has over 900 independent franchises — 90% of them being former Domino's employees. The domestic franchise model provides scale of operations for management, accounting, real estate for leases and locations, and a centralized supply chain for products used in restaurants. Internationally, Domino's operates using a master franchise model. This allows firms to buy the rights to Domino's brand, recipes, and marketing material to operate in a region of the world which is managed by four key firms. These agreements are with: Australian Domino's Pizza Enterprise; Domino's Pizza Group, which has the rights to most of Europe; Alsea SAB de CV, with the rights to Latin and South America; and Jubilant Foodworks, which owns the franchising rights in India. Additionally, Domino's trains new franchise owners and their staff with hands-on supervisory treatment and through a developmental program, franchise management school to ensure new franchisees are knowledgeable about Domino's history, its target market, and the day-to-day responsibilities of an owner. Many of the owners started working as a delivery driver or in other in-store operations and moved to ownership attracted by one of the highest franchise store earnings at $133,000. Franchise earnings are fueled by a commitment to same-store modernizations that is 85% completed which targets US store locations at a 6-mile radius.

At year-end 2017, there were 14,987 worldwide stores, with 37% of this share operating domestically either as company-owned or franchise establishments (see Exhibit 3). Domestic supply chain income from

Exhibit 3. Source Company Filings

franchisees was an important $1.7 billion of total sales, about 63% of total revenues, and over 67% of domestic revenues. Company-owned and franchise revenues are much smaller at $842 million. Domino's international master franchises have the right to operate a supply chain in their respective regions.

Domino's has a growth strategy that involves entering new foreign markets while enhancing current establishments with renovations and technology. The development of an effective business model structured around a reliable franchise system, supply chain revenue, and pizza theater store layout has enabled tremendous growth. Domino's Pizza has also effectively implemented the master franchise system; an independent franchise system that allows Domino's to more effectively penetrate a target market. By utilizing a master franchise system, the firm can establish international growth with market knowledge of the geographical area. This franchise system allows DPZ to navigate the local market and its associated laws, customs, culture, and consumer behavior to sustain growth. These master franchises currently account for 67% of international stores and have sufficient capital to grow and develop in local markets. There is potential for more than 5,300 more stores in the largest global markets, thus ensuring upside potential for the company's international operations. All franchisees are also able to effectively utilize the PULSE Franchise Office System, which provides key performance indicators that reduce food and labor costs while also reducing the time to process payroll by up to 80%.

Over the last 4 years, Domino's Pizza has attained a 40% increase in international sales including a reported 8.5% growth in domestic same-store sales growth (see Exhibit 4). Continued same-store sales growth demonstrates the effectiveness of Domino's management strategy and the ability to produce increased returns on existing assets. Further, Domino's strong same-store sales growth numbers indicate consumers are purchasing more goods at their local Domino's, which in turn has contributed to 18% YOY revenue growth as well as a 19% increase in YOY net income. Further, Domino's has been able to consistently outperform its competitors, outpacing industry revenue growth, sales growth, and EPS growth over the last 5 years. Evidenced by continued same-store sales growth and industry-leading financials, Domino's is positioned for continued success.

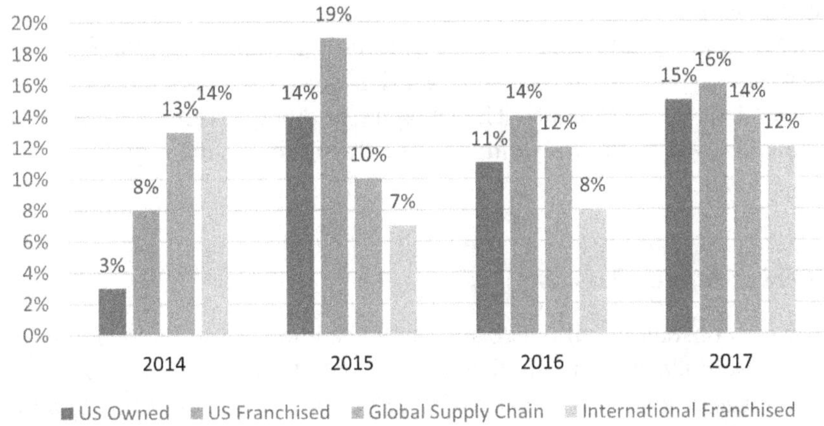

Exhibit 4. DPZ Revenue Growth by Segment

Source: Company Filings.

Geographical Location

Domino's operates in 85 different countries around the world with locations in over 5,700 cities. Within the United States, Domino's has over 5,500 stores; roughly 40% of its total stores are continuing to grow. The company is expanding into emerging markets, opening its first location in Thailand and Kenya over the past 4 years. Currently, Domino's largest international market resides in India where roughly 10%, or 1,123 of their stores are located. The diversification of Domino's global network as well as its overall business model helps the company reduce the risk of geographical economic conditions and potential geopolitical risk.

Industry Overview

The US Quick Service Retail (QSR) pizza segment is a \$35.8 billion category within the \$281.9 billion US QSR sector. The QSR pizza category is composed of three principal elements: delivery with \$10.0 billion or 28% of total sales, carryout with \$5.9 billion or 16.5% of total sales, and dine-in with 19.9 billion or 55.5% of total sales. The three industry leaders, including Domino's, account for 56% of US pizza delivery and the four industry leaders, including Domino's account for 47% of the carryout segment, with the remaining sales going to regional chains and independent establishments. The category is characterized by rapid international growth with heavy emphasis on the use of technology to increase convenience and efficiency.

Macroeconomic Trends

Growing consumer confidence and retail spending are still improving following the 2008 recession indicating a potential for growth in pizza sales. US Consumer comfort has grown by 56% since November 2012 and this has translated into a 23% growth in US Retail Trade Industries in real 2009 dollars. US real personal consumption expenditures in the food services and accommodations market have also grown $40.9 billion since 2015. The improvement of economic conditions compounded with the growth in food-related consumption indicates a strong and consistent growth in QSR pizza.

Demand Drivers

Consumer Preference for Delivery

The Millennial generation, which spends over 75% of total US restaurant dollars, has a strong preference for technology and delivery markets. Delivery currently accounts for 27% of all pizza sales and 6% of the total restaurant market, which is expected to grow to 11% by 2022. Orders placed through the Internet have annually grown by 3% since 2016 due to robust technological platforms, lower prices, new media programs, and loyalty programs that are attractive to the new consumer base. Online sales currently account for 32% of total delivery sales and a shift in preferences to delivery and online ordering will further increase the demand for pizza.

Improvement of International Economic Conditions

Continued international economic improvement along with changes in consumer income has led to increased international sales and will continue to grow pizza sales. Pizza markets in India, Saudi Arabia, the United Kingdom, and Germany all indicate optimistic consumer confidence as per the Nielsen Global Consumer Confidence Report. This optimistic consumer confidence will translate to increased personal spending and a growth in pizza sales.

Changes in Global Dietary Habits

Consumers now seek fresh, natural foods that have ingredients that help fight disease while also improving health. Consumers in emerging markets are also willing to pay a premium for foods with health benefits. In the Asia-Pacific region, a large growth market for pizza has a high demand for sustainably sourced ingredients. In Europe, genetically modified organism (GMO)-free products are more important. Currently, 47% of the surveyed populace desires GMO-free products compared to a 43% global average. The North American population also prefers the absence of high-fructose corn syrup (HFCS), with 32% of Americans avoiding HFCS for healthier alternatives. With the ability for pizza producers to create demographic-specific menus, there is potential for sustained growth in pizza in the global marketplace.

Cheddar Cheese Block Price

The largest food-related production cost for pizza retailers is the cost of cheese which is measured by the US Cheddar Cheese Block (CHECBLCK). CHECBLCK prices are expected to remain stable across all regions of the United States and are expected to decline globally. Cheese production in the United States has grown due to the 2% increase in milk production (USDA). There has also been a 6% increase in total natural cheese in storage between 2016 and 2017. Production stability has resulted in a 2017 average price of $1.64; while 5-year averages are steadily between $1.51 and $2.00. The weakening dollar has increased foreign demand for cheese and is expected to drive the price to a lower level across the globe, reducing costs for pizza manufacturing.

According to the latest USDA report, the all milk price forecast for 2018 is expected to rise to $16.20–$16.70 per cwt, which is at a higher range than last month's forecast of $15.60–$16.10. This increase reflects recent increases in dairy product prices, lower expected milk production, and higher expected exports. For 2019, milk production is expected at 1.3% which is below the 5-year average growth rate of 1.9%. Forecasts for 2019 are \$16.25–\$17.25 per cwt.[4]

President Trump's imposition of import international trade tariffs on steel, aluminum, and automobiles has possible retaliatory impact from China, Europe, and Japan, especially in agricultural goods. The US is 6th in global milk exports in 2017, accounting for 5.4% of the total export market. China has threatened to buy soybeans, corn, and dairy from countries other than the US.[5]

Domino's Supply Chain[6]

In the US, Domino's franchise owners depend on the company's integrated supply chain to purchase products for their stores. The types of products are wide ranging from ingredients for pizza, sandwiches, desserts, and all supplies, such as cardboard boxes. What are the supply chain operations for Dominos? According to the 2017 Annual Report, they are 18 US food supply and dough manufacturing centers, one vegetable processing center, one thin-crust manufacturing center, one equipment and supplies center, and more than 500 trailer drivers. In Canada, the company has five food supply and dough manufacturing centers. Over 523,000 US deliveries of 1.3 billion products were made last year. The average driver moves 2.5 million pounds of deliveries annually. These facilities supply fresh dough, equipment, and supplies to franchised and company-owned stores through the PULSE online system. Franchises have a direct connection electronically through the PULSE point of service terminals.

---

[4]USDA provides monthly estimates on animal production output and prices. See https://www.ers.usda.gov/topics/animal-products/dairy/market-outlook/.

[5]The short-term impact of retaliatory tariffs has been to greatly reduce the agricultural exports of US farmers requiring the US government to step in to provide support to farmers. See https://www.reuters.com/article/us-usa-trade-tariffs-factbox/tariff-wars-duties-imposed-by-trump-and-u-s-trading-partners-idUSKCN1UR5YD.

[6]To understand about the company's unique supply chain for dough manufacturing, see https://classic.qz.com/perfect-company-2/1148899/the-secret-behind-the-uss-most-successful-pizza-chain-is-a-hyper-efficient-dough-factory/.

How does this pizza franchising business model compare to the independent store owners? In the US today, consumers demand their food products be more natural, with a trend that helps those companies that understand this capture increased sales volume. The supply chain allows the power of bulk buying reducing costs and streamlining purchasing decisions. The small store owner pays market price for food and administrative costs.

During periods of rising price, the franchisee buys the ingredients from Domino's which means price increases are passed along directly to store owners. Recall from Exhibits 1 and 2, the price of mozzarella and cheddar cheese increased by 16% and 25%, respectively, in 2014 due to increased international demand for milk, and increased exporting from the US which reduced milk supply. Additional pressure on cheese prices was due to growth in domestic cheese consumption. A drought in the prior year put pressure on cattle feed and supply of cattle. This exacerbated cheese price pressure due to reduced milk supply.

Franchisees are required to pay a royalty fee of 5.5% of sales to the parent company, regardless if these franchisees make a profit or not. This means that it is up to the franchisee to manage the increasing costs of ingredients like cheese. If the franchisee increases menu prices to respond to the rising costs of ingredients, the parent company will continue to get its 5.5% royalty fee. Domino's has nationwide promotions to increase sales volumes which can be a pressure point on operating margins when commodity prices are rising. From Domino's perspective, it improves commodity cost increases with growth in volume. Patrick Doyle explains in the 2017 financial report that the growth of orders has allowed Domino's Pizza to offset the increase in food costs. Volume growth is also boosted by digital ordering incentives using data analytics via mobile apps, and advertising campaigns.

Logistics are at the heart of the company's supply chain. Domino's leverages its supply chain to maintain cost consistency for its franchisees. Domino's may hedge food costs operationally as well as financially using derivatives, but they have not done this for the last 10 years.

Over the past 5 years, Domino's has successfully controlled EBITDA relative to revenue, but this may become more challenging as the economic recovery pushes ingredient cost up. Exhibit 5 shows the improvement in EBITDA.

There are three primary ingredients used to make a Domino's pizza: cheese, premade dough, and tomato sauce. These ingredient suppliers are discussed below.

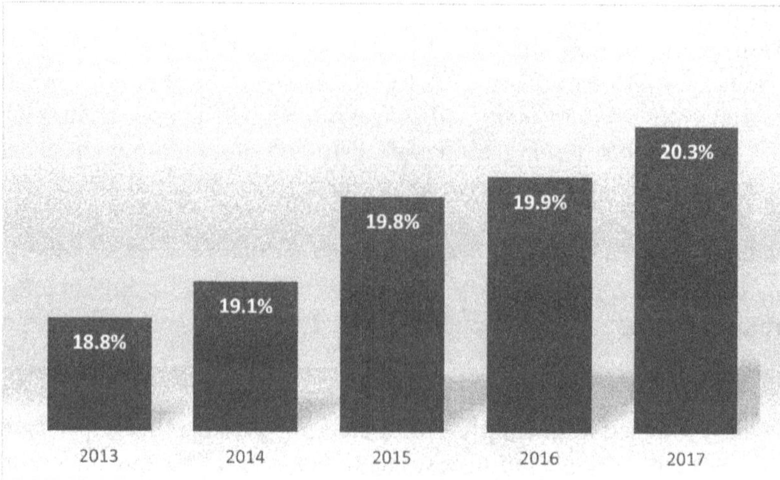

Exhibit 5. Dominos EBITDA — % Revenues

Source: Company Filings.

1. Domino's Cheese Supplier — Leprino Foods[7]
   Cheese is one of the most important ingredients of pizza accounting for 30 to 40% of the pizza price. Domino's stores consume over 3.5 million pounds of cheese per week (over 180 million pounds annually). Domino's purchases its shredded pizza cheese from a single private company, Leprino Food Company, headquartered in Denver. Leprino's is the world's largest mozzarella cheese producer with nine full-scale manufacturing supply locations throughout the US. Leprino's has estimated sales of $3 billion. Internationally, the company has joint production agreements in Brazil and the UK and sales offices in Asia. The company has total supply capacity of 6 million pounds of cheese per week as exclusive agent to meet Domino's and other large pizza makers' market demands. Given their scale, Leprino's can deliver quality cheese with impressive food safety procedures to meet Domino's 2 million pizzas a day worldwide needs, which means 3.5 million pounds of cheese per week. In the past, the average cost per unit of

[7]See https://www.forbes.com/sites/chloesorvino/2017/06/07/exclusive-leprino-foods-dairy-mozzarella-factory-colorado-innovation-billionaire/#2ea1a153a001 and leprino-foods.com and https://www3.gmu.edu/schools/vse/seor/studentprojects/graduate/2015 Fall/Dominos_Pizza_CaseStudy/Case%20Study%20Intro.html

cheese ranges from \$6.16 to \$7.96 (\$1.80 unit price difference) depending on manufacturing supply location.

2. Domino's Wheat Supplier — Ardent Mills[8]
Ardent Mills is one of the largest wheat suppliers in the US. It has 40 mill locations in the US, Canada, and Puerto Rico, three bakery mix facilities, and a specialty bakery. It is an independent joint venture of three large firms ConAgra Foods, Omaha, Cargill, Minneapolis, and CHS, St. Paul. The company provides a wide range of flours from traditional to ancient grains. It supplies to the largest food companies and commercial bakeries through distributors. It is estimated that Domino's buys 8 million pounds of flour a week from Ardent.

    Ardent has a risk management group for its customers that provides price limits embedded into the purchase contract and can provide futures contracts that the customer uses to mitigate risk through Cargill. Some of these company tools include (1) Trigger Cap™ to allow a maximum price during the flour shipment period while allowing prices to decline if the commodity price declines and zero fee cost to the customer, (2) Capped Average™ which sets maximum highest price with opportunity to benefit from declining prices if the average daily futures prices fall below the capped price level, and (3) Digital Range Accrual Contract™ that reduces weekly futures price levels and protects against market rallies when commodities markets are trading in ranges with zero cost structure.
3. Domino's Tomato Supplier — Paradise Tomato Kitchens, Inc.[9]
Paradise is the number one and only custom sauce pouch manufacturer in the US and uses only California-raised tomatoes. It has three manufacturing facilities and is headquartered in Louisville, KY. This product provides savings on delivery and labor costs over traditional canned product and provides a consistent, high-quality product. Domino's uses about 2.5 million pounds of pizza sauce per week in the US with sauce estimated to represent 12–16% of the pizza ingredient cost.

---

[8] Data on Ardent Mills is from website http://www.ardentmills.com/. Details of their hedging service are at http://www.ardentmills.ca/risk-management/customer.html and http://www.gmu.edu/schools/vse/seor/studentprojects/graduate/2015Fall/Dominos_Pizza_CaseStudy/Background.html.

[9] Information on Paradise Foods is based on information from the company's website. See http://www.paradisetomato.com/; http://www.gmu.edu/schools/vse/seor/studentprojects/graduate/2015Fall/Dominos_Pizza_CaseStudy/Background.html.

Technological Innovation

Domino's has been at the forefront of technological innovation utilizing Twitter feeds, Facebook Messenger, and Amazon's Echo unit to try to differentiate itself from competitors. Investment in technology has created a substantial digital demand for Domino's; over 60% of Domino's orders are now executed on digital platforms and over 50% of international sales come from digital channels. In stores, the PULSE point of sale ordering system is now used in most stores worldwide, connecting product supplies needs to automated purchasing. The company's investment in technology at the world headquarters in Michigan has led to market-leading customer engagement, evidenced in Applause's ARC Research Report which gave Domino's an industry-leading 85.3 consumer-engagement score on its app. Increasing customer engagement and the creation of a digital loyalty program have driven digital demand, helping boost sales over digital channels to $5.6 billion in 2016. The company's continued investment in technology will likely contribute to increase sales and reduce costs since DPZ has a head start in the industry begun over 10 years ago.

Hedging the Price of Cheese[10]

Understanding Domino's Pizza Operations

The franchisee perspective reflects the core of Domino's business model. If the franchisee grows revenues, contains costs, and maintains profits, Domino's is successful. Outlined below are the cost constraints that a franchisee faces.

Fixed Costs

- Equipment [oven, ingredient containers, specially designed and patented equipment, that is, pizza sauce ladle ("Spoodle"), continuous oven, counter prep station ("Make-line")]
- Lease and rental payments

[10]For an overview of understanding the commodity markets, see Mindy L. Mallory, *Price Analysis: A Fundamental Approach to the Study of Commodity Prices*, 11-13-2017, http://mindymallory.com/PriceAnalysis/.

Variable Costs

- Ingredients (cheese, dough, tomato sauce, toppings, other menu items). The dough is handmade in one of the 18 Domino's facilities, with six simple ingredients of flour, water, salt, sugar, yeast, and oil. Every 5 minutes 500 lb of dough is produced and supplied to stores twice a week. Flour is piped into the mixer from 70,000-pound silos above the mixing station. Each facility employs about 150 people.
- Labor: food preparers, drivers
- Energy for building
- Franchise royalty payments
- Advertising and marketing fees

Using Futures Hedging to Keep Cheese Costs Stable

While Domino's passes along ingredient costs to franchisees, maintaining price stability will improve each owner's success. The firm needs 3.5 million pounds of cheese weekly and has a contract with Leprino Foods exclusively. Using a futures contract on cheese is one solution and would protect supply chain costs.

Fluid cow's milk or "white gold" is perishable, unlike other commodity products, and is processed into various shelf-stable products. The largest trade in milk products is cheddar cheese, anhydrous milk (refined butter), whole milk powder, skim milk powder, and whey powder. In the US, fluid milk is collected by large cooperatives that process the milk into other products. The most widely active futures market for milk products is cheese futures (open interest 30,000–40,000) and III milk futures (open interest of 40,000).

As a percentage of supply chain revenues, the supply chain operating margin increased by 0.1% in 2017 due to procurement savings which were offset by labor and delivery costs. Domestic company store operating margin declined by 1.3% due to higher food, labor, and insurance costs, with the primary driver being labor costs. At a typical store, labor and food, including cheese account for 50–60% of the operating margin.

Strategies for Financial Derivatives Use

Domino's has buying power as a bulk purchaser from Leprino Foods that an independent pizza restaurant does not. However, hedging at the corporate level also provides price protection and can reduce supply chain costs, especially when prices are rising and volatile. Outlined below are four options for the company to consider.

Decision 1: Do Nothing and Buy from Leprino at the Spot Market Price (2018)

Domino's has long-term pricing contracts with Leprino Foods as the sole supplier. The company buys its cheese every week based on the current market price, purchasing 3.5 million pounds of cheese a year or about 290,000 pounds per month. This volume reflects annual domestic sales of $2 billion. Note that the cash market prices show an overall decreasing price of cheese, with a decreasing trend in the spring months when supply is high. However, the price average in 2017 is overall higher than 2016. Domino's can plan for its cheese needs as it models its sales based on seasonal demands and growth in sales in stores. What is difficult is that without price protection, it is subject to risk of high market prices when commodity feed costs for cows and milk production are increasing.

Decision 2: Lock in Forward Prices with Leprino

Leprino provides under its long-term agreement the ability for Domino's to lock in its cheese prices for extended time periods of up to 12 months. Assume that Domino's can receive a guaranteed price of $1.72/lb for all deliveries in 2017. Using this example, what is the cheese purchase cost for March 2018 for Domino's? What is the estimated food cost savings?

Decision 3: Lock in Cheese Prices Using Cheese Futures Market

The futures contract provides a guaranteed price for cheese. This is a benefit when prices are rising above the futures price. At the maturity date of the contract, there will be a gain on the contract to offset the rising price of buying cheese in the cash market. However, this is a dual-edged sword, since if cash prices decline, then Domino's will be locked into the higher price guaranteed by the future contract. Thus, the firm will see a loss on hedging with futures and a gain on closing out at the lower ending market price for cheese. Hedging with futures is a cost in a falling cash market.

Exhibit 6 shows the impact on Domino's from hedging purchase costs using CME cash-settled cheese futures contracts, which averages the

Exhibits 6. Futures Hedging Examples: Prices Rise (A) and Fall (B)

Using Futures Examples					
Date	**Action**	**Price**	**Volume**	**Price, $/lb**	**Cash Cost, $**
A. Rising Cheese Prices from $1.65 to $1.80					
Unhedged					
January 1	Domino's commits to buying 280,000 lb cheese in March	January USDA cash market price is $1.65/lb	280,000 lb	1.65	462,000
March 14	Cash cheese price settles at $1.80	March market price is $1.80/lb	280,000 lb	(1.80)	(504,000)
Unhedged Gain/(Loss)				(0.15)	(42,000)
Futures Hedge					
January 1	Buy 14 March CSC contracts from CME at $1.55/lb (where one futures contract provides 20,000 lb of cheese)	Buy Futures contract cost is $1.55/cwt	14 contracts	(1.55)	(434,000)
March 14	Close out futures contract	Sell Futures contract at $1.70/cwt	280,000 lb	1.70	476,000
Futures Gain/(Loss)				0.15	42,000
Net Hedging Gain/(Loss)				(0.00)	—
Net Price of Cheese		Ending Spot-Futures Gain	280,000 lb	1.65	462,000
B. Falling Cheese Prices from $1.65 to $1.40					
Unhedged					
January 1	Domino's commits to buying 280,000 lb cheese in March	January market price is $1.65/lb	280,000 lb	1.65	462,000
March 14	Cash cheese price settles at $1.40 (USDA)	March market price is $1.40/lb	280,000 lb	(1.40)	(392,000)
Unhedged Gain/(Loss)				0.25	70,000
Futures Hedge					
January 1	Buy 14 March CSC contracts from CME at $1.55/lb (where one futures contract provides 20,000 lb of cheese)	Futures contract cost is $1.55/cwt	14 contracts	(1.55)	(434,000)
March 14	Close out March futures contract (sell the contract)	$1.30	280,000 lb	1.30	364,000
Futures Gain/(Loss)				(0.25)	(70,000)
Net Hedging Gain/(Loss)				0	0
Net Price of Cheese		Ending Spot-Futures Gain	280,000 lb	1.65	(462,000)

block and brick prices reported by USDA. This example shows the impact when prices are rising from the date of the hedge.

This example shows how the company can lock in a fixed price without using a long-term purchase price contract from the supplier. How does the hedger know whether to buy or sell a futures contract? Companies construct a "long" futures hedge to secure a purchase price for a supply of cheese (or other commodities) that they require some time in the future. To implement the long hedge, the company buys enough cheese futures to cover the quantity of cheese required in the future. When you buy a futures contract you are "long" the derivative. If you agree to sell the contract, you are "short" the contract. Before hedging, Domino's does not own any cheese. The firm has a liability to pay for the product. To hedge Domino's would take an equal and opposite futures position. The firm buys ("goes long") the CME cheese futures that matures in March to hedge the cost for March. The futures contract allows the company to set the price at the beginning of January. At the maturity of the hedging period, Dominos would offset its hedge ("close its futures contract exposure") by selling 14 cheese futures contracts at the market price on the CME. On the cash side, prices were rising — the ending cheese price is \$1.80/lb. On the futures side, the gain is \$.15/lb as futures prices rose above initial purchase price. The net result is that Domino's net cheese cost is \$1.65/lb, which is cheaper by \$.15/lb than the ending market cash cost of \$1.80/lb.

Several points are worth noting when using a futures contract to hedge. First, market participants rarely take delivery of a futures contract. For this cheese contract, there is no product delivered; the ending cash market price fulfills the contract as this contract is cash settled. At the end of the hedge period, Domino's would close out its obligation by selling the futures contract. Since the firm started the hedge by buying cheese futures, then the firm sells the futures contract at the end of the hedge, closing out the futures obligation.

Second, and most important, companies hedge to reduce variability in costs. If cash costs increase during the hedge period, the firm uses the hedge to offset the cash costs with a futures gain. The downside to a long hedge is that the cheese hedger would have been better off without the hedge if the cheese price falls. There is a cost to hedging, in addition to trading costs, which can be seen when prices fall during the hedging period. If cash costs decrease, then since the firm has hedged it cannot take advantage of cheaper cheese costs. The firm will have a loss on the futures hedges to offset the cash gain. Rework this example when cash cheese prices fall to see what the net cost is when the ending March cash cost is \$1.40/lb (see Exhibit 6B).

Third, this example assumes the basis is constant and exchange costs are constant. Based on supply and demand the basis might increase or decrease. Recall that the basis is the difference between the cash market price and the futures contract. With rising prices (Exhibit 6A), the January basis is \$1.65 – 1.55 = +0.10, and unchanged for March (\$1.80 – 1.70 = +0.10). The buyer of physical cheese benefits when the basis weakens over time. In our example, this would be if the March basis got smaller to +0.05 from +0.10 in January. This example also assumes futures trading commissions are unchanged. The CME may change its trading cost to market participants. These include commission costs as well as margins required by the exchange for daily price changes ("variation margin") and the initial deposit ("initial margin").

To illustrate the potential benefit or cost of the basis, Exhibit 7 shows several different types of cheddar cheese markets over 2018. The CME future contract most widely used is the Cheddar Block futures. However, a purchaser may desire Cheddar Cheese Barrel futures. Note the variation in monthly basis is wide and this can cause improvement or worsen hedge results.

Finally, futures contracts are highly leveraged instruments as the buyer only pays 6.75% of cheese contract value. Based on a starting cheese price

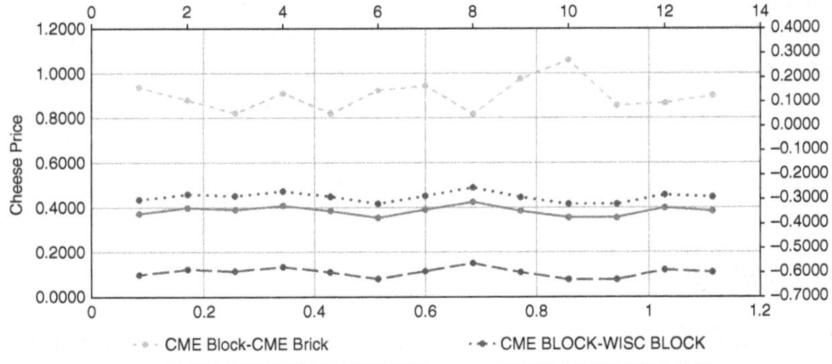

Exhibit 7. Cheese Prices and Basis Risk, Monthly Averages 2018

Source: USDA.

of $1.50/lb, 1 cheese futures contract requires an initial deposit of $2,025/ contract and with 14 contracts is a total initial deposit of $28,350. This compares to an outright cash purchase of $1.50 for 20,000 lb lots for a total cash payment of $420,000. If the price drops, the futures loss in percent terms is larger. If the price drops to $1.40/lb, the futures drop is $.10 times 20,000 lb totaling $2,000 loss/$2,025 for one contract or 98.8% loss in addition to margin required to maintain the account. For 14 contracts, this is loss $28,000/$28,350. The loss on the cash position for a $0.10/lb increase is less in percent terms: $39,200 loss/$420,000 or loss of 9.33% although overall more on an absolute dollar basis.

Decision 4: Use Futures Option Contracts

One alternative to the futures contract which in effect sets a forward guaranteed price for cheese purchases based on the futures price bought is an exchange-traded option on futures contract. Again, the CME offers cheese options contracts to protect the firm from price increases AND to benefit from price drops. An option contract provides the owner with the right to enter into a futures price commitment later at a set price today, but only if the price is in the option buyer's benefit. Options have a premium that the buyer pays at the outset for that right. Options have the same benefit as futures contracts as they are highly leveraged. The benefit is to limit losses but may also expire without value and lose the upfront premium. There are two types of options: call options and put options. Call options set a maximum price for cheese and put options establish a minimum price.

If Domino's forecasts that cheese prices will rise in 3 months, it can buy a March call option at $1.70/lb and pay a premium today of $.06/1 option contract. Since one contract is also for 20,000 lb cheese, this is $1,200 to insure payments if the price rises above $1.70. If the price is lower, Domino's forfeits the $.06 cost of the $1.70 call (call expires worthless) and buys cheaper cheese at the market price.

Conclusion

Domino's ability to manage its food ingredients costs through integrating financial derivatives into its supply chain operations at the headquarters level is a different way of doing business. The company already reviews and monitors the supply and demand for key commodities at the management level at its monthly Thursday meetings. Using financial derivatives represents a different way of doing business that can readily be integrated into the firm's knowledge of the markets. It has the technology basis, and research knowledge to strategically evaluate the benefits and costs to be ready to make this an integral part of its business. While it may not make sense to lock in hedging costs at the top of the pricing curve when prices for cheese, milk, wheat, corn, and fuel oil are at the highest levels, more research will provide further opportunities for the firm to maintain cost consistency. Juliette LaRisk pondered the introduction of financial derivatives as part of Domino's research on the question: To Hedge or Not to Hedge? She would like to recommend policy strategies to senior management.

https://doi.org/10.1142/9789811216749_0028

Case 28

Apple Takes a Bite Out of Financing Using Interest Rate Swaps

Susan Hume

The College of New Jersey, USA

Introduction

Santiago Garcia, a newly hired summer intern at Apple Inc's strategic finance group, is working in the managing director's team on its annual board presentation regarding capital finance. He is enthusiastic about putting his new finance knowledge into practice. His group is responsible for explaining the importance of using interest rate swaps to hedge debt expense. He would like to investigate and answer these questions:

1. What is an interest rate swap?
2. How is an interest rate swap an integral part of Apple's debt management and capital structure?
3. Under what circumstances does using an interest rate swap make sense?

Financing Background

Apple is one of the largest issuers of fixed-rate debt globally. This was not always the case. The company began its first corporate debt issuance program in 2013[1] in response to shareholders' pressure to improve stock price

[1] In 1996, Apple issued $661 million unsecured convertible 6% notes to provide important cash financing for restructuring needs during a period of weak sales.

performance. The firm's financial strategy is to innovate in intellectual property (phones, laptops, earbuds) and generate cash to shareholders. The debt strategy is used to arrange stock buybacks to retire equity and make dividend payments to shareholders. At year-end 2020, Apple had total long-term debt of \$98.667 billion and \$2.254 trillion market cap, making it the most valuable company in the world. Its total debt to equity ratio is 1.69 times on sales of \$274.515 billion. The firm's year-end P/E is 32 times, and its bond rating is AA+/Aa1 (S&P/Moody's).

This trend in debt issuance is representative of many US corporations where \$2.534 trillion of new corporate debt was issued in 2020, of which about 50% was investment grade. In essence, many American corporations are borrowing money to buy back their shares at historically low interest rates (1.8% yield to maturity). See Exhibit 1.

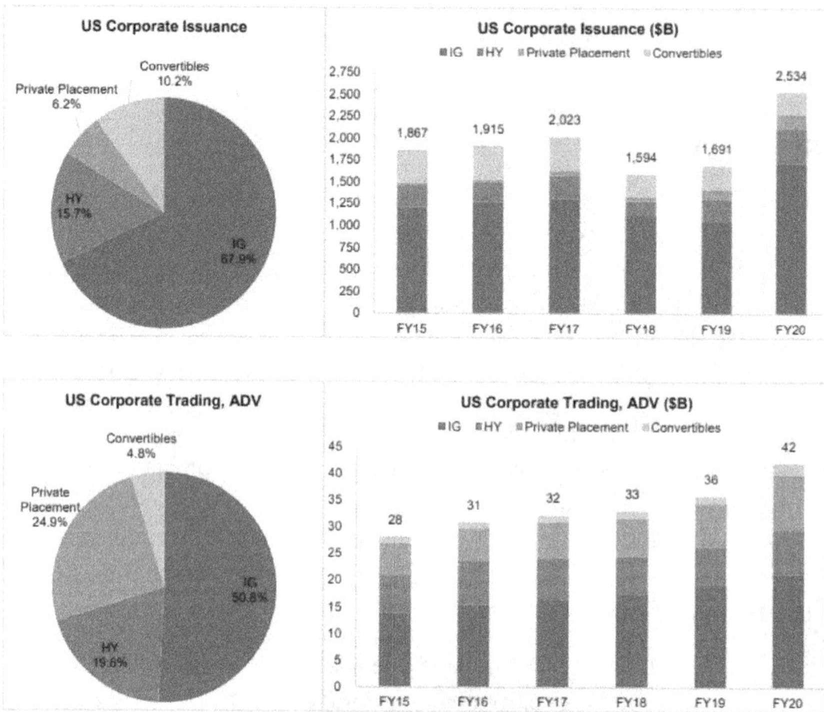

Exhibit 1. US Corporate Debt and Trading Issuance 2015–2020

Source: SIFMA Research Quarterly 4Q20 Report, US Fixed Income Markets-Issuance & Trading, p. 7. https://www.sifma.org/resources/research/fixed-income-chart/ for details. SIFMA data are updated regularly and now in an interactive format.

Santiago has collected data on Apple's financial statements, including debt details for selected years 2017 and 2020.

Interest Rate Swap — What Is It?

An interest rate swap (IRS) is a contract between two parties, where one party agrees to pay one stream of interest payments in exchange for receiving a different stream of interest payments from the other party, with a fixed maturity date. The most common type of interest rate swap is called a "plain vanilla" swap, with one party agreeing to make a fixed rate payment in return for a floating interest rate. There is usually a bank or broker to intermediate between the transacting parties and the swaps I cleared through a clearing house. Since the Global Financial Crisis and Dodd–Frank legislation, a clearinghouse mechanism was created to make the swaps market more visible, transparent and to reduce concentration risk from limited swaps providers. Swaps are available on organized exchanges and over-the-counter. Here is a sketch of a plain vanilla fixed vs. floating rate swap from Apple's perspective, typical for the firm during 2016 and 2017.

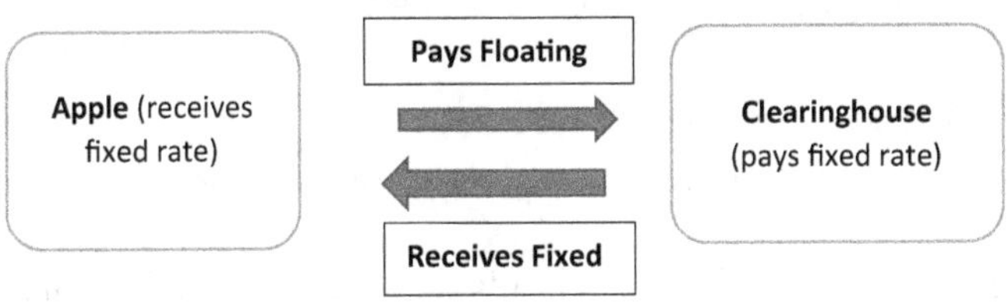

Interest rate swaps help a corporation manage bond expenses and yield curve risk. A corporation like Apple can change its interest expense sensitives by entering into a swap to match its expectations of interest rate changes. Further, when the yield curve across maturities is upward sloping as is usually the case, a corporation can substantially reduce its interest expense by moving to the shorter floating rate maturities. Santiago notes that the effective interest rates for debt issuance in 2017 on the company's 10-K reports lower rates than the coupon rates for several fixed rate notes, indicative of benefits of changing fixed debt expense to floating rate through interest rate swaps. Additionally, some floating rate notes have been converted to fixed effective rates using interest rate swaps.

Expected Interest Rate Change			
Rates Rising	Balance Sheet Debt		Interest Rate Swap Alternative
	Issue new fixed rate debt	or	Pay fixed rate on swap, if existing debt is floating rate
Rates Falling	Issue floating rate debt	and	Receive fixed rate on swap

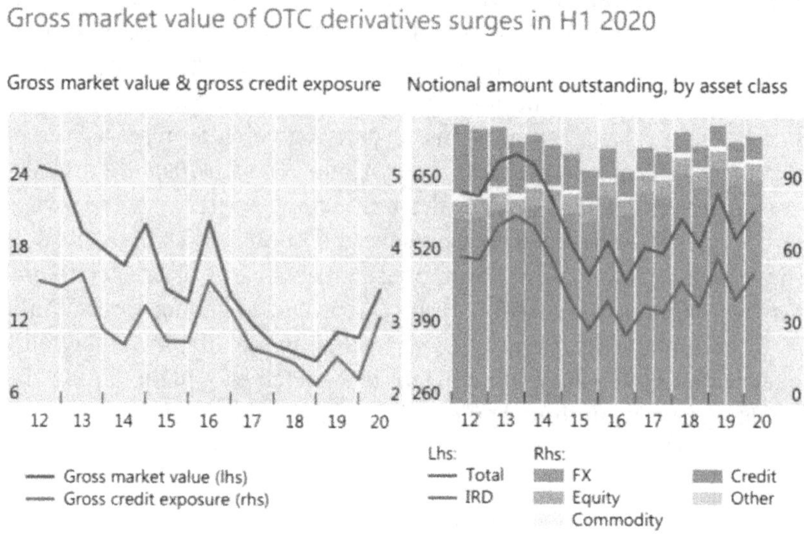

Exhibit 2. Derivatives Market Size 2012–2020

Source: BIS OTC derivatives statistics https://stats.bis.org/statx/srs/table/d5.2.

It is noteworthy that IRS is not only an essential tool for managing debt cost but is also used in many other ways from asset management, risk management, and, if approved by the Board, in speculation. For example, an IRS allows portfolio managers to change the duration of portfolio assets to match the duration of long-term liabilities. As shown in Exhibit 2, IRS notional principal outstanding represents a very large share of the derivatives market with diverse buyers, sellers, hedgers, market makers, and speculators.

The Swap Rate and Yield Curve — How Are They Determined? Why Are They Important?

In an IRS, the swap rate quote paid to Apple by the Clearinghouse is the fixed interest rate that equates the expected short-term floating rates over time. At the time an IRS is done, the total value of the fixed rate inflows on a present value basis will equal the present value of the floating rate payments. A plot of the swap rates over annual maturities reflects the supply and demand for bank credit and other factors including liquidity of money market deposits and bank credit quality. The USD swap curve while similar to riskless US Treasury yields tends to be positive over all maturities as banks have higher credit risk. There are times when USD swaps trade below US Treasuries at longer maturities. The pricing of the forward LIBOR curve is generally derived from the spot LIBOR rate and Eurodollar futures contracts traded on the CME.

Santiago has received the following indicative fixed rate USD interest rate swap quotes against 3-month LIBOR today.

An Example of a 5-Year Fixed Interest Rate Swap

Santiago examines Apple's new commitment in a fixed-for-floating interest rate swap that offsets fixed rate interest payments with a floating rate LIBOR index. The current 5-year fixed rate is 1.10% from Exhibit 3. Santiago notes that Apple is the buyer of the fixed interest rate when it agrees to pay the fixed swap rate. It is the corporation's obligation to pay the fixed rate for the life of the agreement. Santiago thinks of this fixed-rate payment like the coupon interest expense on a fixed-rate bond.[2]

Exhibit 3. Swap Yields Relative to US Treasury Yields

Tenor	USD Swap Fixed Rate (%)[a]	US Treasury Yield (%)	Swap Spread (T + bp)
1 year	0.21	0.06	+15
2 years	0.31	0.14	+17
3 years	0.55	0.32	+23
4 years	0.84	0.61	+23
5 years	1.10	0.89	+21

Note: [a]Fixed rate is calculated based on Actual Days/360 year. Indicative USD swap rates from Bloomberg, LLP, as provided by Tullett Prebon Financial Services.

[2]Obligations on a bond issue are legally different from a swap. A bond is an IOU governed by the terms of the indenture with the corporate issuer agreeing to make all interest and principal repayments. Swap contracts are financial contracts. To provide transparency, financial regulation was passed — The Dodd Frank Act 2010 which gave regulatory supervisory powers to the CFTC (for swap transactions) and SEC (for derivatives transactions related to swap on a security such as a bond, or stock).

The fixed payment of the swap is called being "long" the fixed rate or having "bought the fixed rate." The payor of the floating rate is "short" the swap. With a $100 million notional principal interest rate swap, Apple would make quarterly payments of $98,640 (or 0.011/4)($100,000,000) each period for the next 5 years. This is 0.21% above the 5-year US Treasury note. On the other side of the swap, Apple receives 3-month LIBOR which changes every 3 months. At the start of the swap, the floating LIBOR rate is 0.175%. Apple will receive a swap payment of $42,500, which is (0.00175/4)($100,000,000).

More About Swap Fixed Rates and the Forward Market

Santiago examined these annual swap fixed rates. He was noodling over the way that the swap fixed rates were constructed. He looked further at readings which explained that each fixed rate reflected the average of the compounded spot rate with successive 3-month forward rates. These are then discounted to today's value.

Where does the 1-year swap fixed rate quote come from? It is the geometric compounded average of the current spot rate and the successive quarterly forward rates. He found the following information with his research. Spot interest rate prices are the price of a deposit transaction today paid at the end of the period. This compares to the forward deposit rate, which is negotiated and priced today, but delivered at a future date. The forward deposit rates closely align with the Eurodollar futures contracts on the largest exchange-traded market at the CME (Chicago Mercantile Exchange). When we look at the Eurodollar futures contracts, we can find the forward rate by taking 100 minus futures price quote. For example, a 3-month futures price quote of 99.50 would be a forward 3-month LIBOR rate of 0.50% (this is 100 minus F, where F = futures price).[3] At origination, the swap fixed rate quote provided by market makers to Apple is established by solving for the swap fixed rate that makes the present value of all floating rate payments equal to the present value

[3] LIBOR floating rate is in transition to SOFR, the secured overnight financing rate. There are CME futures contracts to underly the transition to the new floating rate swap benchmarks.

Exhibit 4. Swaps — Compound and Discount Factors

Time (T)	Maturity	Futures Price (F) (CME) A	Rate (%) (R) (100 − F) B	Quarterly Forward Rate (%) R/4 = B/4 C	Implied Spot Rate (%) Geomean D	Discount Factor 1/(1+D) E
1	Spot Rate (0 × 3 Months)		0.175	0.0438	0.1750	0.9996
2	Forward (3 × 6 Months)	99.825	0.190	0.0475	0.1825	0.9991
3	Forward (6 × 9 Months)	99.74	0.260	0.0650	0.2083	0.9984
4	Forward (9 × 12 Months)	99.78	0.220	0.0550	0.2112	0.9979

of the fixed payments. The swap fixed rates for maturities of up to 3 years are priced by looking at the CME Eurodollar futures contract prices. On interest rate swap quotes from 3 to 10 years, the corporate bond rate is the underlying pricing structure.

Santiago was eager to test drive the math of these quotes. He found the following futures prices quotes for 1 year in Exhibit 4:

A spot interest rate is a compounded series of expectations of all interest periods. It can be generalized as a series of forward rates where:

$$(1 + S_t)^T = (1 + F_1) * (1 + F_2) * (1 + F_3) * (1 + F_4) * \cdots * (1 + F_t)$$

He practiced the calculations in the table. For example, he examined Column C, at time $T = 2$ which is the forward rate beginning in 3 months to 6 months. For each time T period, the implied spot rate is the geomean average of each quarterly rate. Since there are two time periods, this is $(1 + (R\ \text{spot}/4)) * (1 + (F6/4)) = 1.000438 * 1.000475 = 1.0009$. If there were $T = 3$ time periods, this expands to $(1 + (R\ \text{spot}/4)) * (1 + (F6/4)) * (1 + (F9/4)$. For each successive period, we are bootstrapping off the prior periods' average. Finally, in column D Santiago finds the "average" of the relevant segment of the LIBOR forward curve for 1 year. He practiced confirming the 1-year spot rate using the quotes in Exhibit 4. He noted that the rates for each period are adjusted for quarterly time periods. For example, the rate, R, of .175 is an annual rate and will be changed to a quarterly equivalent by dividing by 4.

Putting It All Together — Swap Fixed and Floating Rates

Santiago next collected information on the forward swap fixed rates to help him understand the pricing details that relate the swap fixed rate and floating rate better. Santiago is interested in the "plain vanilla" IRS with a benchmark variable rate of USD 3-month floating rate LIBOR.[4] At any time, an IRS is the PV of the fixed payments minus the floating payments. Santiago found this example for 1 year shown in Exhibit 5. First consider the fixed rate payments.

Santiago next examines the floating rate payments, finding the present value of each quarterly payment. This is his worksheet on the floating rate side in Exhibit 6 below.

Using the Excel spreadsheet, Santiago is asked to confirm that the PV of the fixed swap payments is equal to the forward LIBOR floating rate

Exhibit 5. Fixed Rate Payments

Period (A)	Days in Period (B)	Annual Forward Interest Rate (C)	Quarterly Forward Interest Rate (D) = C/4	Notional Swap Principal ($) (E)	Forward Discount Factor (F) = 1/(1+D) * Dt − 1	PV of Notional Principal ($) G = E X F X B/360	PV Total of Fixed Payments ($) (H) = Sum G1–G4
1	90	0.175%	0.04375%	100,000,000	0.9996	24,989,067	
2	90	0.190%	0.04750%	100,000,000	0.9991	24,977,203	
3	90	0.260%	0.06500%	100,000,000	0.9984	24,960,978	
4	90	0.220%	0.05500%	100,000,000	0.9979	24,947,257	99,874,506

Exhibit 6. Floating Rate Payments

Floating Rate Payments Discount Factor I	Floating Rate Payment Amounts J = G * 100,000	Present Value of Floating Rate Payments K	Total PV of Floating Rate Payments L = K1 + K2 + K3 + K4
0.9996	43,750	43,731	
0.9991	47,500	47,457	
0.9984	65,000	64,899	
0.9979	55,000	54,884	210,970

[4]The NYSE Group ICE is used as the reference bench market rate for swaps with major currency values. See IRS swap quotes: https://www.theice.com/marketdata/reports/.

Exhibit 7. At the Start: Fixed Payments Equal Floating Payments

Period (A)	Days in Period (B)	Present Value of Floating Rate Payment (L)	Present Value of Fixed Rate Payment (E) * Swap Fixed Rate * (B/360) * (I)	Difference
1	90	43,731	52,786	(9,055)
2	90	47,457	52,761	(5,304)
3	90	64,899	52,726	12,172
4	90	54,884	52,697	2,187
		210,970	210,970	—

payments. In short, is the pricing of the fixed swap rate such that the net present value is zero? Are the early expected profits Apple receives for the fixed payments equal to the losses later on during the ending periods of the swap? (Exhibit 7).

Complete the spreadsheet assignment by finding the missing cells highlighted in yellow. You can find the assignment by going to the link, https://www.business.rutgers.edu/faculty/ivan-brick.

Common Interest Rate Swap Lingo

Counterparty — the entity entering into the IRS, which could be a firm or government entity. When traded on an exchange, clearinghouse members are the entities and transactions trade through brokers or electronic networks.

Notional Principal — the amount of the contract that is used as the basis of agreement.

Fixed Rate Payments — the interest rate payments agreed to by the payor of the fixed rate, based on the fixed interest rate and the notional principal. Standard contracts use actual days with a 360-day year.

Floating Rate Payments — the variable interest rate agreed to by the payor of the floating rate. This rate is reset as agreed for a 1-, 3-, or 6-month period when the contract is started. It is reset as agreed during the swap contract. Historically the most widely used floating rate is LIBOR (London Interbank Offered Rate), a bank rate posted by large prime banks offered in USD as $1 million Eurodollar time deposits with maturities from overnight to 5 years. This rate for interest rate swaps is set to be replaced with an alternative reference rate SOFR (Secured Overnight Financing Rate) by year-end 2021. This reflects the lawsuits that brought the widely used quote of LIBOR as a pricing agreement for deposits and loans into question as a true cost of funds mechanism for pricing billions of dollars of loans and derivatives. The CME has added SOFRA alternative adjustment to 3-month LIBOR futures and options contracts as a fallback rate, where contracts will be converted to SOFRA price (LIBOR plus 26.161 bps). USD ICE quotes in LIBOR are expected to end in June 2023. According to the CME, over 1 million contracts are linked to SOFRA or SOFRA fallbacks.[5]

ISDA — International Swaps and Derivatives Association. A trade association of market participants that has created industry standards for standardized over-the-counter swap agreements since 1985. Check out their website which has many learning modules and important issues to discuss: https://www.isda.org/.

SOFR — **a true transaction-based short-term bank lending rate**. The New York Fed calculates SOFR by taking the volume-weighted median of transaction-level data from three sources: (1) tri-party repo data, (2) GCF Repo (General Collateral Finance repurchase agreements) transaction data, and (3) bilateral Treasury repo transactions cleared through FICC's DVP Service (Fixed Income Clearing Corporation's Delivery vs. Payment Service). In the US, SOFR is based on the overnight repo markets with about $1 trillion of daily transactions. Publication and trading of SOFR swaps began in May 2018.

[5]See July 2021 Rates Recap at https://www.cmegroup.com/newsletters/rates-recap/2021-07-rates-recap.html.

https://doi.org/10.1142/9789811216749_0029

Case 29

The Thor Corporation

Anoop Rai

Hofstra University, USA

Richard Mawby, Treasurer of the Thor Corporation, scheduled a meeting with his three junior associates to discuss the recent turbulence in the foreign exchange markets. In particular, he was worried about the exposure of the company's receivables and payables denominated in foreign currencies.

The company, a manufacturer of specialized speakers, had always purchased its raw materials and sold its products locally. This all changed recently when they received their first international order from Britain. As a test case, their new client ordered a total of 2,000 pieces of their high-end PC_2100 model to be delivered in two equal installments. The first batch of 1,000 pieces will be delivered on July 1, 2022, followed by a second batch 6 months later, on January 1, 2023. After several negotiations, the company agreed on a price of £200 each. All shipping charges will be borne by the British client. The terms of payment include a letter of credit that guarantees payment 90 days after shipment of the goods.

This year also saw the company import for the first time, hinges for mounting the speaker components. This component was previously purchased from a supplier in Iowa. Their new purchasing manager Brian Gomez, who had previously worked for a large electronic company, initiated this arrangement. The main consideration was price. He convinced Richard Mawby that the same hinges could be purchased at half the price with the same quality from a Brazilian manufacturer. After extensive negotiations, an initial contract was signed to import a total of 10,000 hinges at a price of BR16 (Brazilian Reals) each that included the cost of shipping. The terms of payment included a letter of credit that guaranteed payments 90 days after shipment of the goods. The shipment will also be delivered in two batches, 5,000 pieces on July 1, 2022, and the remaining 5,000 pieces on January 1, 2023.

Although Richard Mawby was aware of currency risk and hedging strategies, he was not concerned about them till today. This morning he read in the Financial Times that there was a strong probability that the dollar would appreciate in the near term. This got him thinking about his new overseas transactions, prompting him to schedule the meeting. He also called his bank manager, Stuart Elmer of State Bank, to obtain his opinion on this matter and to receive some preliminary quotes for foreign exchange hedging instruments.

At the meeting, he was surprised to find out that his junior associates were quite knowledgeable about foreign exchange volatility and its potential impact on their new overseas orders (he made a note to himself to ask them which business schools they attended). Although their current exposure may not affect their total cash flows significantly, they agreed to examine alternative hedging strategies in anticipation of growth in their foreign sales and purchases.

Richard Mawby distributed copies of the quotes faxed to him by his banker (see Exhibit 1) and informed them that the rates were effective as of today, February 15, 2022, and were valid till April 1, 2022. This should give them enough time to thoroughly study the issue. They next discussed the following hedging alternatives.

Forward Hedging

It would allow the company to purchase and sell foreign currencies forward and lock into a given rate. The bank manager said that transaction costs would run approximately 1/2% for both the 6-month and 1-year contracts.

Money Market Hedge

The banker told Richard that they could arrange money to be borrowed and invested in both countries. No collateral would be required for borrowing money overseas. The fees for spot currency transactions would be

1/2%. The fee for investing overseas would be 1/8%. The fees for borrowing both overseas and domestically would be approximately 3/4%. These rates are applicable for all countries.

Options Hedge

The banker also agreed to sell both call and put options on both currencies. The rates vary and are shown in Exhibit 1. There will be no additional fees for the purchase of options, as they would be covered in the premiums.

The discussion then turned to the forecasts of exchange rates. Everyone agreed that it was difficult to predict the rates that would prevail 6 to 12 months from today. Brian Gomez, one of the associates, agreed to look up several websites of federal agencies such as the Federal Reserve Bank and Small Business Administration, and financial institutions such as Merrill Lynch and Goldman Sachs, etc. and prepare a report that summarizes the market's expectation of the future spot rates for both currencies (see Exhibit 2).

At the end of the discussion, Richard Mawby asked the team to prepare a report on whether it is necessary to hedge their current exposures. If they recommend hedging their exposures, they should provide all necessary details. He requested that the report be prepared as quickly as possible so that he could inform the CEO of this latest development and seek permission in case a hedge is warranted.

Exhibit 1. Quotes Provided by State Bank

Date: January 12, 2022

Validity: These rates are guaranteed up to April 1, 2022

Please contact Stuart Elmer for any clarifications.

	British Pounds	Brazilian Reals
Spot Rates	\$1.56/£	\$0.30/BR
Six-Month Forward Rates	\$1.54/£	\$0.29/BR
One-Year Forward Rates	\$1.55/£	\$0.31/BR
Six-Month Borrowing Rates	8.00% per annum	12% per annum
One-Year Borrowing Rates	8.50% per annum	12.5% per annum
Six-Month Investing Rates	4.25% per annum	8% per annum
One-Year Investing Rates	4.75% per annum	8.5% per annum

(*Continued*)

Exhibit 1. (*Continued*)

Premiums for Calls and Puts

Type	Maturity	Exercise Price	Premium	Exercise Price	Premium
Call	6-month	$1.56/£	3.0%	$0.30/BR	1.75%
Call	6-month	$1.58/£	2.2%	$0.32/BR	0.50%
Call	6-month	$1.54/£	4.3%	$0.28/BR	4.00%
Call	12-month	$1.56/£	3.5%	$0.30/BR	2.25%
Call	12-month	$1.58/£	2.7%	$0.32/BR	1.50%
Call	12-month	$1.54/£	4.8%	$0.28/BR	4.75%
Put	6-month	$1.56/£	2.9%	$0.30/BR	1.75%
Put	6-month	$1.58/£	4.3%	$0.32/BR	4.00%
Put	6-month	$1.54/£	2.2%	$0.28/BR	1.25%
Put	12-month	$1.56/£	3.5%	$0.30/BR	2.25%
Put	12-month	$1.58/£	4.8%	$0.32/BR	4.75%
Put	12-month	$1.54/£	2.7%	$0.28/BR	1.75%

Note: Premiums are estimated on dollar notional values.

Transaction costs for borrowing locally and internationally are paid at the beginning of the contract.

Transaction costs for investing locally and internationally are paid at delivery or at the end of the contract.

Transaction costs for spot and forward contracts are paid at delivery or at the end of the contract.

Exhibit 2. Report by Brian Gomez

	First Shipment	Second Shipment
Shipment of speakers	July 1, 2022	Jan 1, 2023
Import of hinges	July 1, 2022	Jan 1, 2023

Expected Spot Rates (Quarterly)

	July 1, 2022	Oct 1, 2022	Jan 1, 2023	April 1, 2023
$/£	1.55/£	1.54/£	1.53/£	1.52/£
$/BR	$0.32/BR	$0.33/BR	$0.34/BR	$0.35/BR

After extensively researching several websites that provided forecasts on the future state of the economy, I have summarized what I believe is the market's expectations of the future foreign exchange rates. There are some wide variations in the forecasts, so I have taken the average of the rates which I thought were most credible. The selected rates coincide with the shipment dates for the export of speakers to Britain and the import of hinges from Brazil. Although the dollar is expected to get stronger against the pound, it appears that it is weakening against the Brazilian Real.

The margins of error for both estimates are quite high. For the July 1, 2022 rates, the estimates ranged from \$1.40/£ to \$1.70/£ and \$0.20/BR to \$0.40/BR. Consequently, I recommend that we consider ±0.15 cents to compensate for the uncertainty, perhaps even ±\$0.20 for additional safety. The company uses a cost of capital of 12% for evaluating projects of similar risk.

Income Statement and Balance Sheet for Thor Corporation December 31, 2021 (in US Dollars)

Income Statement	
Revenues	12,739,500
Cost of Good Sold	8,434,222
Overheads	1,200,234
Selling and Administrative Expenses	700,699
Miscellaneous Costs	452,344
Interest Expenses	672,333
Extraordinary Expenses	256,333
Earning before Taxes	1,023,335
Taxes (Adjusted for Loss Carryover)[a]	225,133.7
Net Income	798,201

Note: [a]Thor managed to save \$112,566 in taxes by applying loss carry-forwards for 2021.

Balance Sheet			
Cash	122,789	Accounts Payable	864,552
Marketable Securities (4%)[a]	242,673	Notes Payable (8%)[b]	1,400,893
Accounts Receivables	1,600,364	Accrued Taxes and Wages	700,527
Inventory	2,335,621	Long-Term Debt (12%)[c]	1,455,624
Net Plant and Equipment	3,897,777	Retained Earnings	2,577,628
	8,199,224	Common Stock	1,200,000
			8,199,224

Notes: [a]Marketable securities earn approximately 4% with average maturity being 3 months. Longer-term maturities earn ¼% more for every additional 3 months.

[b]Notes payable is generated through a $2,000,000 revolving line of credit. Current rate is 8%.

[c]Long-term debt has been obtained through a single creditor. Maturity is 10 years. Interest of 12% is payable annually.

Assignment

Please prepare a 4–5-page report for Richard Mawby with your recommendations on how the firm should hedge the above receivables and payables. Please provide an Excel sheet to show the expected payoffs. The report should explain your assumptions and the derived numbers reported in your exhibits. The report should end with a justification of your recommendations.

https://doi.org/10.1142/9789811216749_0030

Case 30

Colgate-Palmolive Company's Risk Management

Harvey A. Poniachek

Rutgers Business School, USA

Corporate Risk Management Approaches

In a perfect world described by Modigliani and Miller,[1] a firm's value does not depend upon hedging, but in the real marketplace with frictions and other market imperfections, firms' hedging could be quite beneficial. Risk is the possibility that the actual outcome is likely to deviate from the expected value, which is defined in terms of standard deviation or variance, whereas operational risks stem from operations that could generate a negative impact on the firm.

Corporate risk management is an integral part of operations strategy[2] and it utilizes hedging activity via derivatives or positions taking to offset

[1] F. Modigliani and M. Miller, "The Cost of Capital, Corporation Finance and the Theory of Investment," *American Economic Review* 48 (1958): 261–297.

[2] Jan A. Van Mieghem, "Risk Management and Operational Hedging: An Overview," in *Handbook of Integrated Risk Management in Global Supply Chains*, ed. Panos Kouvelis, Lingxiu Dong, Onur Boyabatli, and Rong Li. Operations Research and Management Science series (John Wiley & Sons, Inc., Hoboken, New Jersey, 2012), 13–49.

potential losses due to adverse movement in underlying assets.[3] Risk management requires the application of several steps, as follows[4]:

- Identify potential exposure to risk,
- Assess the risk, and
- Implement risk hedging programs.

Risk has always been present in business activities, but it increased with deregulation, sharp growth of derivative products, and globalization. Financial transactions have become more complex and regulatory requirements for risk management have broadened and universally adopted.[5] Risk management has become a critical corporate activity and an indispensable issue in corporate financial management.[6] Active risk management includes the board of directors (BOD) and chief risk officers (CRO) who are setting the risk "appetite" on the amount and type of risk that the corporation is willing to take in order to meet its strategic objectives. The BOD and CRO determine the risk exposure and identify the risk management policies, including allocation of capital against risks of each activity and business unit and price risk by ensuring that risk undertaken is correctly rewarded.[7]

The significance of risk management was highlighted during the global financial crisis of 2007 through 2009 that threaten the stability of the world economy. The financial crisis led to a wave of new legislation and regulatory requirements, including the Dodd–Frank Wall Street Reform and Consumer Protection Action (Dodd–Frank Act) in the United States, Basel 2.5 and III, the US Federal Reserve's Enhanced Prudential

---

[3]Pankaj Gupta, "A Review of Corporate Hedging Models and Their Relevance in Corporate Finance," *Theoretical Economics Letters* 7 (2017): 102–115.

[4]K. Froot, D. Scharfstein, and L. Stein, "Risk Management: Coordinating Corporate Investment and Financing Policies," *Journal of Finance* 48 (1993): 1629–1658.

[5]Deloitte's *Global Risk Management Survey*, 10th ed. was conducted in the second half of 2016.

[6]Satyajit Das, Risk Management, The Swaps & Financial Derivatives Library, 3rd ed. revised (John Wiley & Sons, Hoboken, New Jersey, 2006).

[7]Michel Crouhy, Dan Galai, and Robert Mark, "Corporate Risk Management: A Primer," *The Essential of Risk Management*, 2nd ed. (McGraw Hill Education, New York, 2016). Chapter 2, 46; Risk Management: A Helicopter View (Crouhy).

Standards (EPS), the European Market Infrastructure Regulation (EMIR), and Solvency II capital standards.

Firms are exposed to various risks that include[8]

- Market risk — refers to the risk of loss because of changes in the values of market prices/rates or factors that drive the value of financial instruments/transactions.[9]
- Credit risk — refers to the risk of loss arising from the default of the counterparties or their unwillingness or inability to fulfill their contractual obligations.
- Liquidity risk — refers to the risk of loss arising from the inability to sell securities at prevailing market prices without incurring a significant capital loss.
- Operational risk — arises from processing failure or from human or technical errors, systems failure; non-enforceability of contracts; and breach of regulatory requirements.
- Foreign exchange, interest rates, and commodity prices volatility created the need for risk management via hedging procedures for controlling financial risks

A survey of more than 1,100 risk managers from around the world shows that almost 90% of risk managers in nonfinancial firms hedge to increase expected cash flow, and 70% to 80% hedge to smooth earnings or to satisfy shareholders' expectations.[10] The survey addresses six areas of risk, including interest rate, foreign exchange, commodity, energy, credit, and geopolitical, and states that operational hedging is more common than financial hedging in all risk areas except foreign exchange. That is, for specific forms of financial risk, such as interest rate, foreign exchange, and commodity prices, firms generally use a mix of financial and operational methods to manage their risk. For example, 88% of firms use operational credit risk management relative to 40% using derivatives.

---

[8]Philippe Jorion, *Value at Risk, The New Benchmark for, Managing Financial Risk*, 2nd ed. (McGraw-Hill, New York, 2001) (Jorion).

[9]Crouhy, *op. cit.*, p. 33.

[10]Erasmo Giambona, John R. Graham, Campbell R. Harvey, and Gordon M. Bodnar, "The Theory and Practice of Corporate Risk Management: Evidence from the Field," *Financial Management* (Winter 2018): 783–832.

Most corporate risk management literature focuses on the use of derivatives like forwards, futures, swaps, and options in hedging corporate exposures to interest rates, foreign exchange rates, and commodity prices.[11] Yet, the scope of risk-management instruments is quite broader and it addresses financial instruments as well as real activities.[12] There is a trade-off between risk and return where the higher the risk the higher the return that can be realized. The trade-off between risk and expected return was first formulated by Markowitz, then Sharpe and Ross, respectively, developing the capital asset pricing model ("CAPM") and the arbitrage pricing theory.[13]

Most business decisions are made against the backdrop of an uncertain future, where some events could adversely affect business performance. Risk is commonly defined in terms, as follows:

1. The statistical dispersion of the rate of return around the mean, that is, by the standard deviation or variance, where the greater the dispersion the riskier the security.
2. Risk refers to how much the price of an asset or liability changes for a given change in some underlying factor.[14] For stocks, Beta measures the systematic risk and the sensitivity of the return from the investment to the return from the market portfolio in the context of the CAPM, with high-Beta stocks having more variable returns than low-Beta stock. The CAPM identifies two types of risks in the investment's return: The first component is systematic risk and the second component is non-systematic risk, which is diversifiable away and an investor should not expect to be compensated for bearing non-systematic risk.
3. For bonds, a most significant source of risk is changes in interest rates, and it's measured in terms of duration and convexity which reflect how bond prices change relative to a change in the interest rates. Higher duration means more price volatility for a given change in interest rates.

---

[11] Clifford W. Smith Jr., "Managing Corporate Risk."

[12] Jorion, *op. cit.*

[13] John C. Hull, *Risk Management and Financial Institutions* (Pearson, Hoboken, New Jersey, 2010) (Hull); John C. Hull, *Fundamental of Futures and Options Markets*, 9th ed. (Pearson, Hoboken, New Jersey, 2017), Chapter 3, Hedging Strategies Using Futures, 49; Chapter 7, Swaps, 161.

[14] Robert M. Conory, "Risk Management for Derivatives," UVA-F-1432, June 14, 2009.

4. Alternative measurements of market risk are reflected by the Greek alphabet that typically include delta (measured the price change in response to a change in an underlying variable), gamma (convexity), Vega (volatility), rho (interest rates), theta (time decay), rho (discount rate), and correlation/basis risk.

The risk assessment of an investment or trading portfolio via VaR (value at risk) analysis measures the potential loss using a probability approach based on an agreed confidence level (usually 2 or 3 standard deviations or 95% or 99% confidence levels) and time horizon (overnight to longer periods). VaR asks the question of "How bad can things get?" and compresses all the Greek letters for all the market variables underlying a portfolio into a single number.[15] VaR is used by financial institutions and their regulators to determine the amount of capital they should keep to cover anticipated market risk. Risk management supplements VaR analysis with sensitivity/stress testing and backtesting to analyze performance under extreme or stress conditions.

Deloitte's three-line of risk management model has been accepted by financial institutions as summarized by Deloitte and is composed of

- **First line:** Management (process owners) has the primary responsibility to own and manage risks associated with day-to-day operational activities. Other accountabilities assumed by the first line include design, operation, and implementation of controls.
- **Second line:** The second-line function enables the identification of emerging risks in daily operation of the business. It does this by providing compliance and oversight in the form of frameworks, policies, tools, and techniques to support risk and compliance management.
- **Third line:** The third-line function provides objective and independent assurance. While the third line's key responsibility is to assess whether the first- and second-line functions are operating effectively, it is charged with the duty of reporting to the board and audit committee, in addition to providing assurance to regulators and external auditors that the control culture across the organization is effective in its design and operation."[16]

---

[15] Hull, *op. cit.*

[16] Deloitte, https://www2.deloitte.com/us/en/pages/advisory/articles/modernizing-the-three-lines-of-defense-model.html.

Effective corporate risk management assumes that the future is uncertain and the financial risk that arises from uncertainty needs to be identified, measured, and mitigated.[17] Nonfinancial companies that are exposed to traditional business risks implement an effective risk-management strategy involving several steps.[18]

1. the identification, assessment, and quantification of risk exposures and risk tolerance;
2. the design of potential risk hedging instruments[19] and diversification for a wide spectrum of types of risk and hedging instruments; and
3. categorizing risk into silos help risk management, but recent trends tend to integrate measurement and management of various risks by applying enterprise-wide risk management or ERM.[20] Whether a corporation should hedge its risk has implications on its ability to compete in the marketplace. Hedging might affect the prices and number of products sold.[21]

Financial instruments for hedging risk have been developed over many decades, consisting of exchange-traded and over-the-counter instruments. Firms can reduce their exposure by hedging via financial contracts, including forwards, futures, options, and swaps, that generate cash flows that offset losses from price changes of the underlying exposure. Currency exposure could be hedged via forward contracts or by utilizing futures, options or futures options, or swaps. Interest rate risk could be hedged via futures, options, swaps, or forward rate agreements.

In hedging interest exposure, duration of the exposure and the hedge instrument need to be considered and accounted for by instituting a duration-based hedging.[22]

1. An assessment of the potential benefits and costs of risk management;
2. The selection and implementation of the strategy, risk diversification; and

---

[17] Crouhy, *op. cit.*

[18] Das, *op. cit.*; Jorion, *op. cit.*

[19] Jorion, *op. cit.*

[20] Crouhy, *op. cit.*, 15–16.

[21] *Ibid.*, 51.

[22] Jonathan Berk and Peter DeMarzo, in "Risk Management," *Corporate Finance*, 4th ed. (Pearson, Hoboken, New Jersey, 2017), Chapter 20 (Berk).

3. Stress testing and scenario analysis have become prominent features of risk management tools.

A corporation should engage in risk management after defining its objectives in terms of risk and return. It needs to determine the risk appetite of the firm in terms of the type of risk that the firm is willing to tolerate and the risk that should be hedged and which risk should the company assume as part of its strategy. The risk appetite might also include the maximum losses that the firm is willing to incur during a given time. Many firms use stress testing to articulate their risk appetite, that is, the firm analyzes the likely level of losses in a range of plausibility by several adverse scenarios.[23]

VaR applies to all financial instruments and types of financial risk, and it could be used to apprise senior management of the risks of trading and investment operations, set position limits for traders and business units, and assist in allocating capital across traders, business units, products, and even to the whole institution.[24]

Conclusion

The primary method of risk management is prevention, but some risks are too costly to prevent and are inevitable consequences of running a business.[25] Most of the risk is held by equity holders and some by debt holders. Insurance and financial markets afford firms to hedge some of their risks.

Colgate-Palmolive Company[26] and Risk Management

Colgate-Palmolive Company (the "Company" or "Colgate") is a leading consumer products company whose products are marketed in over 200 countries and territories throughout the world. Colgate was founded in 1806 and incorporated under the laws of the State of Delaware in 1923. The Company operates in several product segments: Oral, Personal and

---

[23] Crouhy, *op. cit.* pp. 55–56.

[24] Jorion, *op. cit.*

[25] Berk, *op. cit.*, Chapter 20.

[26] Colgate-Palmolive Company Annual Report for the Fiscal Year Ended December 31, 2017.

Home Care, and Pet Nutrition. Sales of Oral, Personal, and Home Care products accounted for 48%, 19%, and 18%, respectively, of the Company's total worldwide net sales in 2017. Colgate's Hill's Pet Nutrition segment ("Hill's" or "Pet Nutrition") is a world leader in specialty pet nutrition products for dogs and cats with products marketed in over 80 countries worldwide.

Types of Risk

Colgate does business in more than 200 countries and territories with approximately 70% of sales originating outside the US geographic diversity induced significant international risks relating to exposure to foreign currency, interest rate, commodity price, and credit. For hedging purposes, the company applies several approaches, including working capital management, selling price increases, selective borrowings in local currencies, and selective derivative instrument.

Foreign Exchange Risk

Unfavorable foreign exchange rates may reduce the dollar value of revenues, profits, and cash flows from foreign sources, or increase supply costs in dollars in those markets. To minimize the adverse impact of foreign currency movements, Colgate engages in hedging approaches through forwards currency contracts, currency options, and money market hedging, which is a substitute to forward currency hedging.[27] It is the Company's policy to enter into currency derivative contracts with terms and magnitudes that match the underlying exposure. The maturity of foreign currency contracts generally does not exceed 12 months and the contracts are valued using observable market rates.

Foreign assets and liabilities translated into US dollars follow the US GAAP and FASB regulations of the Current Rate Method or the Temporal

[27] Cheol Eun and Bruce Resnick, *International Financial Management*, 8th ed. (McGraw Hill Education, New York, 2018), Ch. 8, Managing Transaction Exposure, 198 pp. Ch. 14, Interest and Currency Swaps, 347.

Method.[28] The assets and liabilities of foreign subsidiaries, other than those operating in highly inflationary environments, are translated into US dollars at year-end exchange rates with resulting translation gains and losses accumulated in a separate component of shareholders' equity. Income and expense items are translated into US dollars at average rates of exchange prevailing during the year.

For subsidiaries operating in highly inflationary environments, local currency-denominated non-monetary assets, including inventories, goodwill and property, plant and equipment, are remeasured at their historical exchange rates, while local currency-denominated monetary assets and liabilities are remeasured at year-end exchange rates. Remeasurement adjustments for these operations are included in net income attributable to Colgate-Palmolive Company. Prior to the deconsolidation of the Company's Venezuelan operations in 2015, CP Venezuela was designated as hyper-inflationary and the functional currency for CP Venezuela was the US dollar. See Note 14, Venezuela for further information. Currently, none of the Company's subsidiaries operate in highly inflationary environments.

Interest Rate Exposure

The Company manages its fixed and floating interest rate through interest rate swaps in order to mitigate fluctuations in earnings and cash flows that may result from interest rate volatility. The notional amount and maturity date of the swaps generally match the exposed principal, and the swaps are valued using observable benchmark rates. Based on year-end 2020 variable rate debt levels, a 1% increase in interest rates would have increased Interest (income) expense by $15.

Exposure to Commodity Prices Fluctuation

The Company is exposed to price volatility related to raw materials that it uses in production, such as essential oils, resins, pulp, tropical oils, tallow,

[28] David K. Eiteman, Arthur I. Stonehill, and Michael H. Moffett, "Translation Exposures," *Multinational Business Finance*, 15th ed. (Pearson, Hoboken, New Jersey, 2019), Chapter 11, 328–330.

corn, poultry, and soybeans. Colgate manages its raw material exposures through a combination of cost containment measures, and commodity futures hedging contracts. Futures contracts are used primarily in the Hill's Pet Nutrition segment, to manage volatility related to raw material inventory purchases of certain traded commodities. The duration of the commodity contracts generally does not exceed 12 months. At the end of 2020, an unfavorable 10% change in commodity futures prices would have resulted in a net unrealized loss of $1.

Credit Risk

The Company is exposed to the risk of credit loss in the event of nonperformance by counterparties to financial contracts. However, Colgate's policy of contracting with diverse, creditworthy counterparties based upon their strong credit ratings diminishes credit risk.

Colgate-Palmolive Company

Consolidated Statements of Income for the Years Ended December 31

(Dollars in Millions except per Share Amounts)

	2017	2016	2015
Net Sales	**$15,454**	$15,195	$16,034
Cost of Sales	**6,174**	6,072	6,635
Gross Profit	**9,280**	9,123	9,399
Selling, General, and Administrative Expenses	**5,497**	5,249	5,464
Other (Income) Expense, Net	**194**	37	62
Charge for Venezuela Accounting Change	—	—	1,084
Operating Profit	**3,589**	3,837	2,789
Interest (Income) Expense, Net	**102**	99	26
Income before Income Taxes	**3,487**	3,738	2,763
Provision for Income Taxes	**1,313**	1,152	1,215
Net Income Including Noncontrolling Interests	**2,174**	2,586	1,548
Less: Net Income Attributable to Noncontrolling Interests	**150**	145	164
Net Income Attributable to Colgate-Palmolive Company	**$2,024**	$2,441	$1,384
Earnings per Common Share, Basic	**$2.30**	$2.74	$1.53
Earnings per Common Share, Diluted	**$2.28**	$2.72	$1.52

Colgate-Palmolive Company

Consolidated Balance Sheets as of December 31

(Dollars in Millions except Share and per Share Amounts)

	2017	2016
Assets		
Current Assets		
Cash and Cash Equivalents	**$1,535**	$1,315
Receivables (Net of Allowances of $77 and $73, Respectively)	**1,480**	1,411
Inventories	**1,221**	1,171
Other Current Assets	**403**	441
Total Current Assets	**4,639**	4,338
Property, Plant, and Equipment, Net	**4,072**	3,840
Goodwill	**2,218**	2,107
Other Intangible Assets, Net	**1,341**	1,313
Deferred Income Taxes	**188**	301
Other Assets	**218**	224
Total Assets	**$12,676**	$12,123
Liabilities and Shareholders' Equity		
Current Liabilities		
Notes and Loans Payable	**$11**	$13
Current Portion of Long-Term Debt	—	—
Accounts Payable	**1,212**	1,124
Accrued Income Taxes	**354**	441
Other Accruals	**1,831**	1,727
Total Current Liabilities	**3,408**	3,305
Long-Term Debt	**6,566**	6,520
Deferred Income Taxes	**204**	246
Other Liabilities	**2,255**	2,035
Total Liabilities	**12,433**	12,106
Commitments and Contingent Liabilities	—	—
Shareholders' Equity		
Common Stock, $1 Par Value (2,000,000,000 Shares Authorized, 1,465,706,360 Shares Issued)	**1,466**	1,466
Additional Paid-in Capital	**1,984**	1,691

(Continued)

(Continued)

	2017	2016
Retained Earnings	**20,531**	19,922
Accumulated Other Comprehensive Income (loss)	**(3,855)**	(4,180)
Unearned Compensation	**(5)**	(7)
Treasury Stock, at Cost	**(20,181)**	(19,135)
Total Colgate-Palmolive Company Shareholders' Equity	**(60)**	(243)
Noncontrolling Interests	**303**	260
Total Equity	**243**	17
Total Liabilities and Equity	**$12,676**	$12,123

The Assignment

Andrew Smith received his MBA in finance from New York University, Stern School of Business in 2010. He's currently a partner at a Big Four accounting firm in New York, where he renders risk management assessment and advice to major multinational clients of the firm. Colgate-Palmolive engaged his firm concerning its hedging and risk management policy in several areas specified below.

Andrew assembled his half dozen senior managers for a preliminary discussion and held a lengthy conference call with their office in London. Thereafter, he assigned the issues below to his staff and called a follow-up meeting within 1 week to review their finding and recommendations.

1. Assess Colgate's foreign exchange, interest, and commodity hedging policies.
2. Comment on whether a more passive approach by Colgate would have been more suitable.
3. Design a hedging strategy for Colgate's €100 million accounts payable due in 3 months.
4. What hedging strategy should Colgate pursue to address $100 million purchase of soybean in 6 months?

Part IX

Other Corporate Issues

https://doi.org/10.1142/9789811216749_0031

Case 31

Chapter 11 Case Study: Pacific Drilling, S.A.

Frank A. Oswald, Edward D. Wu, and Eitan E. Blander

Togut, Segal & Segal LLP, USA

Chapter 11 of the Bankruptcy Code is entitled *Reorganization* and provides a mechanism by which companies can reorganize their capital structure and make certain operational adjustments, all while under the protection of the automatic stay.[1] It is applicable in virtually all industries and has been used by corporations in a wide range of fields.

To demonstrate the concepts of bankruptcy and Chapter 11, we examine the Chapter 11 cases of Pacific Drilling, S.A. ("PacD") and its debtor affiliates (together with PacD, the "PacD Debtors"),[2] which were commenced on

[1] See 11 U.S.C. § 362(a).

[2] The debtors in the Chapter 11 cases were: Pacific Drilling S.A.; Pacific Drilling (Gibraltar) Limited; Pacific Drillship (Gibraltar) Limited; Pacific Drilling, Inc.; Pacific Drilling Finance S.à r.l.; Pacific Drillship S.à r.l.; Pacific Drilling Limited; Pacific Sharav S.à r.l.; Pacific Drilling VII Limited; Pacific Drilling V Limited; Pacific Drilling VIII Limited; Pacific Scirocco Ltd.; Pacific Bora Ltd.; Pacific Mistral Ltd.; Pacific Santa Ana (Gibraltar) Limited; Pacific Drilling Operations Limited; Pacific Drilling Operations, Inc.; Pacific Santa Ana S.à r.l.; Pacific Drilling, LLC; Pacific Drilling Services, Inc.; Pacific Drillship Nigeria Limited; and Pacific Sharav Korlátolt Felelősségű Társaság.

Although Pacific Drilling VIII Limited and Pacific Drilling Services, Inc. (collectively, the "Zonda Debtors") were debtors in these Chapter 11 cases, because of a pending arbitration dispute with a creditor, their Chapter 11 plan was confirmed well after the Chapter 11 plan

November 11, 2017, and were jointly administered under Case No. 17-13193 in the Bankruptcy Court for the Southern District of New York. The authors' firm was the lead bankruptcy counsel to the PacD Debtors.

Meet the Debtors

The PacD Debtors operate an international offshore drilling business that specializes in ultra-deepwater and complex well construction services. PacD is the ultimate parent company of the other individual PacD Debtors. The PacD Debtors own a fleet of drillships, comprised of seven high-specification floating rigs, delivered between 2010 and 2014, with a combined historical acquisition cost exceeding $5 billion. Their clients are large oil and gas companies that obtain the PacD Debtors' drilling services on a "day rate" contract basis and bear the economic risk and reward of the project.

When demand and rates are high, the PacD Debtors seek long-term contracts for their drillships with large exploration and production companies, and when demand and rates are low, the PacD Debtors keep their drillships active on short-term contracts or, if needed, utilize their internally developed process to maintain inactive drillships at the least possible cost while preserving the ability to redeploy the vessels in a timely and cost-effective manner.

Economic Context

The deepwater drilling market is highly cyclical. It is influenced by swings in oil price as well as the supply and demand for offshore drilling rigs. These cycles have typically lasted 5 to 10 years, with drillship utilization fluctuating from below 60% up to 99% and day rates fluctuating from breakeven costs of approximately $130,000–$180,000 up to $700,000 per day.

At the time of the bankruptcy filing in November 2017, the deepwater drilling market had been enmeshed in a significant decline since a drop in oil prices beginning in mid-2014. The significant and sustained decline in oil prices since mid-2014 led many of the PacD Debtors' existing and potential clients to delay or cancel various exploration and development

---

for each of the other debtors. In the interest of simplicity, this case study and the (valuation data presented in this case study) excludes the impact of the Zonda Debtors.

programs, which resulted in a reduction of drilling contracts awarded and day rates achieved across the sector. However, the demand for oil was projected to increase over the medium term, and the PacD Debtors expected a corresponding increase in demand for high-specification deep-water drilling services.

At the time of filing, the PacD Debtors had only one long-term contract for one ship, set to expire in August 2019, and were maintaining the bulk of their fleet in storage. For the year ending December 31, 2017, the PacD Debtors had total revenues of approximately $319,716,000 and a net loss of approximately $525,166,000. Below are select consolidated financial data from their filings with the Securities and Exchange Commission:

Select Income Statement Information for Years Ended December 31 (in Thousands)

	2017	2016	2015	2014	2013
Statement of Operations Data:					
Revenues					
Contract Drilling	$319,716	$769,472	$1,085,063	$1,085,794	$745,574
Costs and Expenses					
Operating Expenses	(244,089)	(290,038)	(431,261)	(459,617)	(337,277)
General and Administrative Expenses	(87,134)	(63,379)	(55,511)	(57,662)	(48,614)
Depreciation Expense	(278,949)	(275,901)	(243,457)	(199,337)	(149,465)
Loss from Construction Contract Rescission	—	—	(40,155)	—	—
Operating Income (Loss)	**(290,456)**	**140,154**	**314,679**	**369,178**	**210,218**
Other Income (Expense)					
Interest Expense	(178,983)	(189,044)	(156,361)	(130,130)	(132,211)
Write-off of Deferred Financing Costs	(30,846)	—	—	—	—
Gain (Loss) on Debt Extinguishment	—	36,233	—	—	(28,428)
Reorganization Items	(6,474)	—	—	—	—
Other Expense	(5,544)	(2,393)	(3,217)	(5,171)	(1,554)
Income (Loss) Before Income Taxes	**(512,303)**	**(15,050)**	**155,101**	**233,877**	**48,025**
Income Tax Expense	(12,863)	(22,107)	(28,871)	(45,620)	(22,523)
Net Income (Loss)	**$(525,166)**	**$(37,157)**	**$126,230**	**$188,257**	**$25,502**

Select Balance Sheet Information for Years Ended December 31 (in Thousands)

	2017	2016	2015	2014	2013
Cash, Cash Equivalents, and Restricted Cash	$317,448	$626,168	$116,033	$167,794	$204,123
Property and Equipment, Net	4,652,001	4,909,873	5,143,556	5,431,823	4,512,154
Total Assets	5,362,961	5,998,207	5,792,720	6,028,080	5,101,654
Long-Term Debt (Includes Current Maturities of Long-Term Debt, Net of Debt Issuance Costs)	3,043,967	3,145,449	2,845,670	3,101,021	2,368,451
Shareholders' Equity	2,151,801	2,666,200	2,692,055	2,578,872	2,399,924

Source: Pacific Drilling S.A., Annual and Transition Report (Form 20-F) (April 2, 2004).

Capital Structure

As of the petition date, the PacD Debtors' principal non-contingent liabilities consisted of outstanding funded secured debt against the assets of three separate groups of subsidiaries (Ship Groups A, B, and C) as follows:

Ship Group A[a]	
Revolving Credit Facility (the "RCF") • maturity date of June 2018	$475M
2020 Notes • maturity date of June 2020	$750M
Term Loan B • maturity date of June 2018	$718M
Ship Group B[b]	
Senior Secured Credit Facility (the "SSCF") • maturity dates of May 2019, May 2026, and November 2026 with respect to the three tranches	$661M
Ship Group C[c]	
2017 Notes • maturity date of December 2017	$439M

Note: [a]The Debtors as to Ship Group A include: Pacific Drilling, Inc.; Pacific Drilling Finance S.à r.l.; Pacific Drilling Limited; Pacific Drillship S.à r.l.; Pacific Scirocco Ltd.; Pacific Bora Ltd.; Pacific Mistral Ltd.; Pacific Santa Ana (Gibraltar) Limited; Pacific Santa Ana S.à r.l.; and Pacific Drillship Nigeria Limited.
[b]The Debtors as to Ship Group B include: Pacific Sharav S.à r.l.; Pacific Drilling VII Limited; and Pacific Drilling Operations, Inc.
[c]The Debtors as to Ship Group C include: Pacific Drillship (Gibraltar) Limited and Pacific Drilling V Limited.

Prior to the filing of the Chapter 11 cases, an "Ad Hoc Group" was formed to represent a majority of the holders of the 2017 Notes, the 2020 Notes, and the Term Loan B claims.[3] By the end of the Chapter 11 cases,

[3] In bankruptcy parlance, an ad hoc group is simply a coalition of holders of similar claims or interests whose members coalesce under their own volition for the purpose of having their collective interests represented. In contrast to ad hoc groups, the Bankruptcy Code expressly provides for the appointment of certain statutorily formed committees, such as the unsecured creditors' committee, whose expenses are paid for by the debtors' estates.

the Ad Hoc Group would represent, in terms of dollar amounts, approximately (i) 87.4% of the 2017 Notes, (ii) 74.9% of the 2020 Notes, and (iii) 79.2% of the Term Loan B claims.

As of the petition date, Quantum Pacific (Gibraltar) Limited and its affiliates (collectively, "QP") directly or indirectly owned about 70% of the equity interests in PacD. The common shares of PacD traded on the New York Stock Exchange and reached a peak market-implied value of approximately $2.7 billion in 2013. In September 2017, the shares were delisted for failure to meet capitalization requirements.

Reducing Expenditures

In response to deteriorating market conditions and in an effort to avoid bankruptcy, the PacD Debtors implemented various initiatives to reduce costs and increase efficiency. The PacD Debtors' total headcount decreased more than 50% from 1,606 employees and contractors as of December 31, 2014, to 773 employees and contractors as of December 31, 2017. The PacD Debtors also commenced reviews of rig maintenance costs, human resources and training costs, procurement and supply chain practices, and information technology contracts, among other expenditures. As a result, total operating expenses decreased by more than 52%, from $123.8 million in the fourth quarter of 2014 to $58.9 million in the third quarter of 2017. This was achieved by both reducing daily rig operating costs for active rigs by more than 40% and generating significant savings for idle rigs by storing them at less than $30,000 per day per rig. In addition, corporate overhead support was reduced by more than 25% over the same timeframe.

Out-of-Court Restructuring Attempts

For over a year prior to their bankruptcy filing, the PacD Debtors explored various restructuring alternatives with their stakeholders, including QP. Effective January 18, 2016, the PacD Debtors retained an investment bank to explore, together with their management team and outside legal counsel, out-of-court restructuring alternatives. These alternatives included the possibility of a variety of amend and extend ("A&E") and liability management transactions. The PacD Debtors' investment banker and outside counsel also assisted in the development of an A&E and liability management proposal, which, together with a financial forecast scenario prepared by the PacD Debtors, was presented to a group of lenders under the RCF (the "RCF Group") and the SSCF (the "SSCF Group," and together with the RCF Group, the "Bank Groups") between May 13 and May 23, 2016. The Bank Groups ultimately rejected the A&E and liability management proposal. Consequently, the PacD Debtors explored alternative strategies and transactions.

On October 5, 2016, the PacD Debtors successfully obtained consents to amend the debt incurrence covenant in the indenture for the 2017 Notes in order to enable them to fully utilize the availability under the RCF. Subsequently, the PacD Debtors presented an oil and offshore rig market outlook, two financial forecast scenarios for the debtors' business, and a revised A&E proposal to the Bank Groups on October 17, 2016, and to the Ad Hoc Group on November 15, 2016. In response to the A&E proposal, the Bank Groups presented their counterproposal on November 9, 2016, and the Ad Hoc Group presented its counterproposal on December 1, 2016.

In the first quarter of 2017, the PacD Debtors and the Bank Groups negotiated additional maintenance covenant headroom under the credit agreements for the RCF and the SSCF through mid-December 2017. During this time, the PacD Debtors also continued to explore potential out-of-court transaction alternatives. On February 14, 2017, the PacD Debtors provided the Ad Hoc Group with a preliminary preview of their performance for the fourth quarter of 2016, and presented the Ad Hoc Group with two alternative transaction proposals — a modified A&E proposal and a proposal to convert debt to equity. The PacD Debtors hoped that a consensus would form between the Ad Hoc Group and QP, and that this consensus could form the basis for the path towards a fully consensual restructuring.

Thereafter, the Ad Hoc Group rejected the PacD Debtors' A&E proposal and presented a counter-equitization proposal on March 3, 2017. In July 2017, prior to the impending December 1, 2017 maturity of the 2017 Notes, the PacD Debtors announced the launch of a private consent solicitation to extend the maturity date of the 2017 Notes to June 1, 2018. The PacD Debtors did not receive sufficient consents to approve the maturity extension, and the solicitation expired on August 2, 2017.

On September 6, 2017, the PacD Debtors presented two revised financial forecast scenarios and a revised equitization proposal to the Ad Hoc Group. The Ad Hoc Group submitted a counter-equitization proposal on

September 26, 2017, where the Group would equitize its debts for 97.5% of the company, and equity would retain 2.5% of the shares. The PacD Debtors presented a further revised equitization proposal to the Ad Hoc Group on October 13, 2017.

Facing the maturity on the 2017 Notes and the inability to reach consensus among its primary stakeholders, the PacD Debtors filed their Chapter 11 cases on November 12, 2017.

Chapter 11 and Reorganization

The *Pacific Drilling* Chapter 11 cases were precipitated by a decline in oil prices. When the PacD Debtors filed for Chapter 11, the general consensus was that they had an operationally sound business and that only a financial restructuring was required to emerge from bankruptcy. In other words, the PacD Debtors did not need to utilize bankruptcy to facilitate an operational restructuring, which debtors in other cases sometimes need to do, such as by closing unprofitable retail locations or unnecessary manufacturing plants. Rather, the PacD Debtors could emerge from Chapter 11 as a viable entity mainly by reducing their debt burden and building a stronger balance sheet with sufficient liquidity to withstand a prolonged downturn in energy prices.

As we will see, the PacD Debtors were able to accomplish these goals through Chapter 11, pursuant to which they (i) reduced their debt by approximately $2 billion by equitizing the 2017 Notes, the 2020 Notes, and the Term Loan B claims (who were collectively issued 32.6% of the common shares, exclusive of additional equity interests such holders would receive through the rights offering) and (ii) engaged in the following exit financing transactions:

- The PacD Debtors raised $1 billion in cash by issuing the following notes:
  - $750 million in first-lien notes maturing in October 2023 and
  - $250 million in second-lien notes maturing in April 2024, with interest payable in kind.
- They raised $500 million in cash through the following equity issuance:
  - A $460 million equity rights offering that provided holders of the 2017 Notes, the 2020 Notes, and the Terms Loan B claims with subscription rights to purchase up to 58.9% of the common shares of reorganized PacD at a price that represents a 46.9% discount to a

stipulated plan equity value of $1,472 million (based on a total enterprise value of $2,075 million).[4]

- o A $40 million private placement whereby QP purchased 5.1% of the equity of reorganized PacD.

The PacD Debtors used the amounts raised from the exit financing transactions to pay in full in cash the holders of the RCF claims (allowed at approximately $480.36 million) and the SSCF claims (allowed at approximately $661.5 million). The PacD Debtors' prepetition equity holders essentially received no distribution under the plan.[5] Ultimately, the plan and the foregoing exit financing transactions provided the reorganized PacD Debtors with approximately $400 million of cash upon emergence from Chapter 11. In order to understand what led to this outcome, it is important to understand the Chapter 11 plan process.

The Chapter 11 Plan Process

The Chapter 11 plan is akin to a blueprint that provides how creditors and interest holders will be treated and how a debtor will emerge from bankruptcy. A plan must classify creditors and interest holders into classes and specify the distribution, if any, that each such class will receive.[6] A Chapter 11 plan must be confirmed by the Bankruptcy Court and must satisfy the requirements of section 1129 of the Bankruptcy Code.[7] There are two alternative paths to confirmation. The first path is for the plan to be confirmed consensually, which is possible if all classes vote to accept (or are deemed to accept) the plan.[8] Alternatively, a plan that cannot be confirmed consensually can still be confirmed through a process called "cramdown."[9]

---

[4]The Ad Hoc Group also obtained a small percentage of shares in reorganized PacD in exchange for committing to backstop the equity issuance.

[5]However, as discussed, QP received equity interests pursuant to its participation in the private placement.

[6]See 11 U.S.C. § 1123(a).

[7]See 11 U.S.C. § 1129.

[8]See 11 U.S.C. § 1129(a).

[9]See 11 U.S.C. § 1129(b).

The Threat of Cramdown

Understanding cramdown is important because plan negotiations in a Chapter 11 case occur under the shadow of cramdown — meaning that a plan proponent will not provide the treatment requested by a creditor or interest holder that threatens to vote to reject the plan as long as the plan proponent can simply cramdown the plan over the rejecting class to achieve confirmation. Each class of claims or interests that votes to reject the plan must be crammed down in order for the plan to be confirmed.[10]

In turn, in order to understand cramdown, it is important to understand the "absolute priority rule" and the concept of valuation. As discussed more fully in the appendix below, the absolute priority rule, as codified by section 1129(b)(2) of the Bankruptcy Code, provides how claims and interests can be treated in order to satisfy the cramdown requirements. With respect to a class of secured claims, the Bankruptcy Code provides several alternative ways to achieve cramdown. For example, one way is to provide that secured creditors of that class will retain their liens and receive deferred cash payments equal to the present value of their allowed claims.[11] In *Pacific Drilling*, the plan was fully consensual, so there was no need to cram down any class of claims. However, to understand cramdown, imagine how it could have been used with respect to the RCF and SSCF claims. These claims were fully secured by their collateral. What actually happened in this case is that the PacD Debtors obtained exit financing to pay those claims in full in cash after the plan became effective. In fact, with that treatment set forth in the plan, holders of the RCF and SSCF claims did not actually vote on the plan because the Bankruptcy Code provides that classes that are "unimpaired" are deemed to accept the plan.[12] However, in another case where exit financing is harder to obtain, a debtor may consider cramming down the plan against an unwilling secured creditor, who may then be forced to accept deferred cash payments equal to the present value of its claim (at an interest rate that is likely to be heavily litigated) while retaining its lien.

---

[10]A class of creditors votes to accept the plan if (i) at least one-half of the creditors in that class votes to accept, and (ii) those creditors voting to accept represent at least two-thirds of the dollar amount of claims held by that class. Both of those criteria must be met in order for the class to accept the plan. 11 U.S.C. § 1126(c).

[11]See 11 U.S.C. § 1129(b)(2)(A)(i)(II).

[12]See 11 U.S.C. § 1126(f).

While the Bankruptcy Code provides several ways to cram down secured creditors, it is much more general in its treatment of unsecured claims. In order to comply with the absolute priority rule for unsecured claims, the Bankruptcy Code provides that the holders of such claims must receive property equal to the allowed amount of such claim (and such property may take many forms, such as equity in the reorganized debtor) or else those that are junior to such creditor (including equity holders) cannot receive any distribution under the plan.[13] A corollary to this rule is that a creditor cannot be paid more than in full.

Similarly, to cram down a class of equity interests, the Bankruptcy Code provides that each holder of equity interests must receive property equal to the value of such interest or else no junior interest holder may receive or retain any property under the plan on account of such junior interest.[14]

Negotiation Dynamics in Pacific Drilling

As in most Chapter 11 cases, the debtors in *Pacific Drilling* sought to negotiate with other parties in interest in the hopes of achieving a consensual confirmation. Such negotiations require the parties to have knowledge about the PacD Debtors' valuation and occur under the shadow of cramdown. Initially, the Ad Hoc Group demanded that they receive all of the equity of reorganized PacD. This was opposed by QP, who wanted to retain its equity interest in PacD. The Ad Hoc Group, however, asserted that the PacD Debtors' enterprise value was not sufficient to pay in full the holders of the 2017 Notes, the 2020 Notes, and the Term Loan B claim. Therefore, the Ad Hoc Group asserted that a plan that provided a distribution to equity holders could not be confirmed consensually because the holders of the debt claims would vote to reject such a plan and, further, such plan could not be confirmed through cramdown because the absolute priority rule prohibits equity holders from receiving a distribution when creditors will not be paid in full.

QP, however, was keen on remaining a stakeholder after the PacD Debtors emerged from Chapter 11. Where an equity holder is forbidden to

[13] See 11 U.S.C. § 1129(b)(2)(B).

[14] See 11 U.S.C. § 1129(b)(2)(C).

receive a distribution due to the absolute priority rule, it is still possible for such equity holder to receive new equity interests in the reorganized debtor through the so-called "new value exception." Under this exception, equity holders (or other parties-in-interest) can receive distributions "if they contribute new capital in money or money's worth . . . necessary for successful reorganization of the restructured enterprise."[15] In this manner, equity holders can argue that their treatment stems from the new money injected into the debtor, and not "on account of" their old interests, which would be prohibited by the absolute priority rule.[16]

Such an arrangement occurred here following mediated negotiations among QP, the Ad Hoc Group, and the PacD Debtors. As part of the consensual plan, QP would pay $40 million for 5.1% of the common shares of reorganized PacD. The plan also contemplated that QP would purchase $100 million of each of the new first and second lien notes being offered as part of the exit financing. Therefore, it could be argued that QP received these securities not on account of its prepetition equity interest, but due to its injection of new value by way of its purchase commitment.

Importance of Valuation

The concept of valuation is closely intertwined with many aspects of bankruptcy cases, including the Chapter 11 plan process. Among other reasons, valuation is important because it:

- Provides parties-in-interest with an understanding of how much the reorganized debtor is worth, which represents the value of the "pie" of which various stakeholders will then seek to recover as large of a slice as possible under bankruptcy law.

---

[15] See *Bank of America v. 203 North Lasalle St. Partnership*, 526 U.S. 434, 442 (1999) (citing *Case v. Los Angeles Lumber Prod. Co.*, 308 U.S. 106, 118, 60 S. Ct. 1, 9, 84 L. Ed. 110 (1939)).

[16] See 11 U.S.C. § 1129(b)(2) ("For the purpose of this subsection, the condition that a plan be fair and equitable with respect to a class includes the following requirements . . . the holder of any claim or interest that is junior to the claims of such class will not receive or retain under the plan on account of such junior claim or interest any property.")

- Provides secured creditors with an understanding of whether their claims are fully secured by their collateral. If the value of the collateral that secures a claim is worth less than the claim, the secured creditor is under-secured and, generally, the claim is bi-furcated into (i) a secured claim for the value of the collateral and, (ii) an unsecured claim for the deficiency.[17]
- Shows which creditors cannot be paid in full. The debt in the capital structure that can only receive a partial recovery is known as the "fulcrum security." How the holders of such claims vote in the plan process is critical. Creditors that are senior to the fulcrum security will be paid in full and will generally not be entitled to vote on the plan because they are "unimpaired."[18] Creditors that are junior to the fulcrum security will receive no distribution and are presumed to reject the plan as a result of being fully impaired.[19] For this reason, in *Pacific Drilling*, only the holders of the 2017 Notes, the 2020 Notes, and the Term Loan B claims were entitled to vote on the plan.
- Shows if creditors will be paid more than in full. Bankruptcy law does not permit creditors to be paid more than in full. For example, if the value of the new equity in the reorganized PacD to be distributed to the holders of the 2017 Notes, the 2020 Notes, and the Term Loan B claims were so valuable that the holders of such claims would be paid more than in full, QP could have argued that QP should receive a distribution on account of its old equity interest without contributing new value.
- Serves as the basis to determine the worth of new securities being issued under the plan for the purpose of determining how much a party in interest must pay to receive equity interests through a rights offering under the new value exception.

A valuation of the debtor will help creditors and interest holders decide how to vote on a Chapter 11 plan by allowing them to compare what they will actually receive under a plan against what they theoretically should receive under a proper valuation.

---

[17] See 11 U.S.C. § 506.

[18] See 11 U.S.C. § 1126(f).

[19] See 11 U.S.C. § 1126(g).

In order to provide creditors with adequate information to vote on a Chapter 11 plan, the Bankruptcy Code requires the distribution of a disclosure statement along with the plan.[20] In *Pacific Drilling*, the disclosure statement provided that holders of the 2017 Notes, the 2020 Notes, and the Term Loan B claims were estimated to receive a recovery of approximately 54.2%, 42.9%, and 42.9% on their claims, respectively.[21] These percentage recoveries were based on the distributions that these holders were to receive under the plan, which were equity interests in reorganized PacD and rights offering subscription rights to purchase further equity in reorganized PacD at a price that represented a discount to the stipulated plan value of the equity interests:

Treatment under the plan for the 2017 Notes
Each holder receives:
(A) its Pro Rata share of the 2017 Notes Claims
Allocation of 9.0% of the New Common Shares, subject to dilution by the Management Incentive Plan; and
(B) up to its Pro Rata share of the 2017 Notes Claims
Allocation of the Rights Offering Subscription Rights to purchase New Common Shares to be issued pursuant to the Rights Offering to the extent such Holder elects to exercise its Rights Offering Subscription Rights thereunder in accordance with the Rights Offering Procedures.

(Continued)

[20] See 11 U.S. Code § 1125. Section 1125(a)(1) defines "adequate information" as "information of a kind, and in sufficient detail, as far as is reasonably practicable in light of the nature and history of the debtor and the condition of the debtor's books and records, including a discussion of the potential material Federal tax consequences of the plan to the debtor, any successor to the debtor, and a hypothetical investor typical of the holders of claims or interests in the case, that would enable such a hypothetical investor of the relevant class to make an informed judgment about the plan…."

[21] See Docket No. 621 (*Modified Third Amended Disclosure Statement for the Modified Third Amended Joint Plan of Reorganization for Pacific Drilling S.A. and Certain of Its Affiliates Pursuant to Chapter 11 of the Bankruptcy Code*) (the "PacD Disclosure Statement") at 14.

(*Continued*)

Treatment under the plan for the 2020 Notes
Each holder receives: (A) its Pro Rata share of the 2020 Notes Claims Allocation of 12.1% of the New Common Shares, subject to dilution by the Management Incentive Plan; and (B) up to its Pro Rata share of the 2020 Notes Claims Allocation of the Rights Offering Subscription Rights to purchase New Common Shares to be issued pursuant to the Rights Offering to the extent such Holder elects to exercise its Rights Offering Subscription Rights thereunder in accordance with the Rights Offering Procedures.
Treatment under the plan for the Term Loan B Claims
Each holder receives: (A) its Pro Rata share of the Term Loan B Claims Allocation of 11.4% of the New Common Shares, subject to dilution by the Management Incentive Plan; and (B) up to its Pro Rata share of the Term Loan B Claims Allocation of the Rights Offering Subscription Rights to purchase New Common Shares to be issued pursuant to the Rights Offering to the extent such Holder elects to exercise its Rights Offering Subscription Rights thereunder in accordance with the Rights Offering Procedures.

The percentage recovery for the holders of the 2017 Notes, the 2020 Notes, and the Term Loan B claims was based on the value of the new equity interest they would receive under the plan, which required a valuation of the PacD Debtors. The disclosure statement included a valuation performed by the PacD Debtors' investment banker. As set forth in the disclosure statement, the total enterprise value of the reorganized PacD Debtors, estimated as of October 2018, was approximately $1,650 million to $2,500 million, with a mid-point of $2,075 million.[22] After deducting pro forma funded debt of $1,024 million and adding post-emergence cash of $421 million from the equity investment on account of the rights offering, the estimated total enterprise value implied a value for the common stock of reorganized PacD of approximately $1,047 million to $1,897 million, with a midpoint of $1,472 million.[23] In arriving at its valuation estimate, the investment banker applied discount cash flow analysis and a peer group trading analysis.

[22] See Appendix E (Valuation Analysis) to the PacD Disclosure Statement, at 4.

[23] *Id.*

In performing discount cash flow analysis, the investment banker discounted future cash flows from financial projections by a range of discount rates reflecting the weighted average cost of capital for the reorganized PacD Debtors. The present value of the PacD Debtors' unlevered after-tax free cash flows over the course of the period of the financial projections was then added to the value of the PacD Debtors beyond the projection period, known as the terminal value. The terminal value was calculated using a range of estimated multiples of EBITDA and a range of perpetuity growth rates. While the discount rates were not publicly disclosed during the Chapter 11 cases, the disclosure statement included the financial projections that were used in the discount cash flow analysis:

Income Statement ($ in Millions)	**4Q 2018**	**2019**	**2020**	**2021**	**2022**	**2023**	**2024**	**2025**
Total Revenues	**59**	**397**	**530**	**678**	**756**	**871**	**1,047**	**1,095**
Operating Expenses								
Drilling Cash Opex	–49	–262	–344	–410	–447	–447	–448	–447
Recognized Deferred Mobilization / Ramp-Up Cost	—	—	—	—	—	—	—	—
Recognized Deferred Project Costs (SPS, UWILD, Inspections, etc.)	0	–2	–6	–12	–15	–17	–18	–19
Integrated services	—	–24	–28	—	—	—	—	—
Shore-Based Support Costs	–6	–32	–36	–40	–41	–42	–44	–45
Total Opex	**–55**	**–320**	**–414**	**–462**	**–503**	**–506**	**–511**	**–511**
Corporate Overhead	–11	–42	–46	–50	–52	–53	–55	–56
Other G&A	–1	–5	–3	—	—	—	—	—
EBITDA	**–8**	**30**	**67**	**166**	**202**	**311**	**482**	**528**
Depreciation & Amortization	–64	–217	–133	–135	–137	–139	–140	–141
EBIT	**–72**	**–187**	**–65**	**31**	**65**	**173**	**342**	**387**
Net Interest Expense	–24	–99	–103	–108	–113	–119	–126	–134
Amortization of Deferred Financing Costs	–3	–11	–11	–11	–11	–9	–1	—
EBT	**–99**	**–296**	**–179**	**–87**	**–59**	**44**	**215**	**253**
Taxes	–1	–10	–16	–19	–21	–24	–29	–31
Net Income (Loss)	**–100**	**–306**	**–195**	**–106**	**–80**	**20**	**185**	**222**

(*Continued*)

(*Continued*)

Statement of Cash Flows (\$ in Millions)	**4Q 2018**	**2019**	**2020**	**2021**	**2022**	**2023**	**2024**	**2025**
Net Income	**–100**	**–306**	**–195**	**–106**	**–80**	**20**	**185**	**222**
Add-Back: Depreciation and Amortization	64	217	133	135	137	139	140	141
Add-Back: Capitalized PIK Interest	—	34	38	43	48	54	61	68
Net Change in Working Capital	25	1	–18	–28	17	–13	–29	–8
Cash from Operations	**–11**	**–54**	**–42**	**43**	**122**	**200**	**357**	**423**
Capital Expenditures	–45	–41	–22	–47	–22	–22	–22	–22
Free Cash Flow Before Financing Activities	**–56**	**–95**	**–63**	**–3**	**101**	**178**	**336**	**402**
Debt Repayments	—	—	—	—	—	—	—	—
Free Cash Flow After Debt Financing	**–56**	**–95**	**–63**	**–3**	**101**	**178**	**336**	**402**
Change in Restricted Cash	—	37	—	—	—	—	—	—
Net Change in Unrestricted Cash	**–56**	**–58**	**–63**	**–3**	**101**	**178**	**336**	**402**
Unrestricted Cash — Opening Balance	**384**	**328**	**270**	**207**	**203**	**304**	**482**	**818**
Net Change in Unrestricted Cash	–56	–58	–63	–3	101	178	336	402
Unrestricted Cash — Closing Balance	**328**	**270**	**207**	**203**	**304**	**482**	**818**	**1,219**

Balance Sheet Pro Forma December 31

(\$ in Millions)	**Q3 2018**	**2018**	**2019**	**2020**	**2021**	**2022**	**2023**	**2024**	**2025**
Current Assets									
Unrestricted Cash	384	328	270	207	203	304	482	818	1,219
Restricted Cash	37	37	—	—	—	—	—	—	—
Total Cash	**421**	**365**	**270**	**207**	**203**	**304**	**482**	**818**	**1,219**
Accounts Receivable	31	39	73	94	116	130	150	180	179
Materials and Supplies	84	83	83	83	83	83	83	83	83
Intangible Assets	118	86	—	—	—	—	—	—	—
Prepaid Expenses & Other Current Assets	11	11	11	11	11	11	11	11	11
Total Current Assets	**665**	**584**	**437**	**395**	**414**	**528**	**726**	**1,092**	**1,493**
Non-Current Assets	1,834	1,846	1,756	1,645	1,556	1,441	1,324	1,205	1,085
Net PP&E									
Other Assets	13	16	22	51	80	70	75	78	90
Long-Term Receivable	203	203	203	203	203	203	203	203	203
Total Non-Current Assets	**2,050**	**2,064**	**1,980**	**1,898**	**1,839**	**1,713**	**1,601**	**1,485**	**1,378**
Total Assets	**2,715**	**2,648**	**2,418**	**2,293**	**2,253**	**2,241**	**2,327**	**2,577**	**2,870**

(*Continued*)

	Balance Sheet Pro Forma December 31								
($ in Millions)	**Q3 2018**	**2018**	**2019**	**2020**	**2021**	**2022**	**2023**	**2024**	**2025**
Current Liabilities	36	43	73	94	105	114	115	116	116
Accounts Payables and Accrued Expenses									
Short-Term Debt	—	—	—	—	—	—	—	—	—
Other Current Liabilities	1	26	25	26	28	29	31	33	35
Total Current Liabilities	**38**	**68**	**99**	**120**	**133**	**143**	**146**	**148**	**151**
Non-Current Liabilities	969	971	1,016	1,065	1,118	1,177	1,240	1,302	1,370
Long-Term Debt									
Other Long-Term Liabilities	28	28	28	28	28	28	28	28	28
Total Non-Current Liabilities	**996**	**999**	**1,044**	**1,093**	**1,146**	**1,204**	**1,268**	**1,330**	**1,398**
Shareholders' Equity	**1,681**	**1,581**	**1,275**	**1,080**	**974**	**894**	**914**	**1,099**	**1,321**
Total Liabilities & Shareholders' Equity	**2,715**	**2,648**	**2,418**	**2,293**	**2,253**	**2,241**	**2,327**	**2,577**	**2,870**

Source: Appendix D (Financial Projections) to the PacD Disclosure Statement, at 3.

In addition to the DCF analysis, the PacD Debtors' investment banker utilized the peer group trading analysis to value the reorganized PacD Debtors through a comparison with other publicly traded entities with generally similar assets and characteristics. The total enterprise value for each peer company was determined by adding the company's market capitalization and its total net debt (using market prices, as available). The enterprise value of each peer company was then evaluated on a dollar value per drillship basis. As set forth in the PacD Debtors' disclosure statement:

> This [was] accomplished by segregating that portion of each selected public company's total enterprise value attributable to the present value of its respective contract backlog, discounted at its respective estimated weighted average cost of capital from that portion of its respective total enterprise value attributable to its respective rigs themselves. Rig value for each selected public company [was] then allocated by rig class and a value per drillship [was] calculated. The total enterprise value of the Reorganized Debtors [was] then calculated by applying the appropriate dollar value per drillship obtained from the selected public companies to each drillship in the Reorganized Debtors' fleet and adding to the sum of all such drillship values of the Reorganized Debtors the present value

of the Reorganized Debtors' contract backlog, discounted at its estimated weighted average cost of capital.[24]

As is often the case with valuation, the investment banker had to engage in complex considerations in both applying valuation methodologies and interpreting the results. For example, the investment bankers had to use their professional judgment in determining which public companies should be used in the peer group trading analysis. Ultimately, the PacD Debtors' plan was confirmed on a consensual basis. In other cases, disputes on valuation can be complex, prolonged, and costly.

Liquidation Analysis

A disclosure statement will also contain a liquidation analysis, which estimates the recovery that creditors would alternatively receive in the event that a debtor is liquidated under Chapter 7 of the Bankruptcy Code. Two purposes are served by the liquidation analysis. The first is to satisfy the "best interest of creditors" test, which is set forth in section 1129(a)(7) of the Bankruptcy Code.[25] Pursuant to this test, in order to confirm a Chapter 11 plan, every creditor that votes to reject a plan must receive at least as much as the creditor would receive in a hypothetical Chapter 7 liquidation.[26] The test differs from the cramdown requirements in that the test must be satisfied as to each and every creditor that votes to reject a plan, whereas, the cramdown requirements need only be satisfied as to entire classes that reject a plan.[27] As such, a class may accept a plan because the class has voted in favor of the plan by the requisite majorities, however, the best interest of creditors test must be satisfied as to each creditor in that class that votes to reject the plan.

A related purpose served by the liquidation analysis is to demonstrate to various stakeholders that they should vote in favor of the plan because

[24] *Id.* at 3.

[25] See 11 U.S.C. § 1129(a)(7).

[26] See 11 U.S.C. § 1129(a)(7)(A)(ii) ("The court shall confirm a plan only if all of the following requirements are met . . . [w]ith respect to each impaired class of claims or interests . . . each holder of a claim or interest of such class . . . will receive or retain under the plan on account of such claim or interest property of a value, as of the effective date of the plan, that is not less than the amount that such holder would so receive or retain if the debtor were liquidated under Chapter 7 of this title on such date.").

[27] See 11 U.S.C. § 1129(b).

the alternative may be liquidation under Chapter 7 of the Bankruptcy Code. Almost invariably, stakeholders stand to recover less in a liquidation under Chapter 7 than in a reorganization under Chapter 11. Liquidation values are inherently lower not only because they often entail the piecemeal liquidation of assets (as opposed to realizing the going-concern value of a business), but also because Chapter 7 requires the appointment of a trustee who, along with his professionals, must get up to speed and whose fees are entitled to priority.[28]

Below is the liquidation analysis that was annexed to the PacD Debtors' disclosure statement.[29] The analysis estimates the low-end and high-end range of liquidation values for the PacD Debtors' assets (which are estimated to be $1.46 billion and $1.84 billion, respectively) and then applies those values to determine the recovery available to creditors in a hypothetical Chapter 7 liquidation. The analysis satisfies the best interest of creditors test by demonstrating that creditors receive superior recoveries under the plan than under a Chapter 7 liquidation. For example, from the table below, it is apparent that the holders of the 2017 Notes are expected to obtain a recovery of 44.2% in a Chapter 7 liquidation, however, they are expected to recover 54.2% under the Chapter 11 plan. In the aggregate, creditors in *Pacific Drilling* are expected to receive approximately $500 million more under the Chapter 11 plan than in a Chapter 7 liquidation.

Consolidated Liquidation Analysis

	Recovery %			**Recovery $**		
($ Millions)	**Book Value**	**Low**	**High**	**Low**	**High**	**Mid**
Cash	$185.3	100.0%	100.0%	$185.3	$185.3	$185.3
Accounts Receivable	37.6	25.0%	40.0%	9.4	15.0	12.2
Inventory on Rigs	74.0	0.0%	0.0%	—	—	—
Inventory	11.3	40.0%	50.0%	4.5	5.7	5.1
Prepaid Assets	10.9	31.8%	49.5%	3.5	5.4	4.4
Other Current Assets	11.7	0.0%	0.0%	—	—	—
Fixed Assets	4,451.1	23.9%	32.2%	1,062.2	1,431.5	1,246.8
Other Long-Term Assets	26.7	4.1%	6.6%	1.1	1.7	1.4

(Continued)

[28] A chapter 7 trustee is entitled to a commission based upon a sliding scale statutory formula that is calculated on the amount the trustee distributes. 11 U.S.C. § 326.

[29] See Appendix C (Liquidation Analysis) to the PacD Disclosure Statement, at 4.

(Continued)

Consolidated Liquidation Analysis						
	Recovery %			Recovery $		
($ Millions)	Book Value	Low	High	Low	High	Mid
Intercompany Receivables from PDSI and PDVIII				198.8	199.4	199.1
Gross Proceeds from Liquidation	**$4,808.7**	**30.5%**	**38.3%**	**$1,464.8**	**$1,844.1**	**$1,654.4**
Wind Down Claims						
Wind Down Claims				62.6	74.0	68.3
Recovery $				62.6	74.0	68.3
Recovery %				100.0%	100.0%	100.0%
RCF Claim						
RCF Claim				475.0	475.0	475.0
Recovery $				475.0	475.0	475.0
Recovery %				100.0%	100.0%	100.0%
Term Loan B and 2020 Notes Claims						
Term Loan B and 2020 Notes Claims				1,493.1	1,493.1	1,493.1
Recovery from Secured Assets				9.8	204.7	107.2
Recovery from Deficiency Claim				213.6	227.1	220.4
Total Recovery $				223.4	431.8	327.6
Recovery %				15.0%	28.9%	21.9%
SSCF Claims						
SSCF Claims				661.5	661.5	661.5
Recovery from Secured Assets				437.4	541.1	489.2
Recovery from Deficiency Claim				71.6	77.3	74.4
Total Recovery $				509.0	618.4	563.7
Recovery %				76.9%	93.5%	85.2%
2017 Notes Claims						
2017 Notes Claims				453.7	453.7	453.7
Recovery from Secured Assets				144.3	187.1	165.7
Recovery from Deficiency Claim				31.3	38.5	34.9
Total Recovery $				175.6	225.6	200.6
Recovery %				38.7%	49.7%	44.2%

(Continued)

Consolidated Liquidation Analysis						
	Recovery %			Recovery $		
($ Millions)	Book Value	Low	High	Low	High	Mid
Post-Petition General Administrative Claims						
General Administrative Claims				20.3	20.3	20.3
Recovery $				18.0	18.1	18.1
Recovery %				88.7%	88.9%	88.8%
Pre-Petition General Unsecured Claims						
General Unsecured Claims				1.3	1.3	1.3
Recovery $				0.0	0.0	0.0
Recovery %				1.3%	1.4%	1.4%
Intercompany Payments to PDSI and PDVIII				1.2	1.3	1.2
Total Distributions				**$1,464.8**	**$1,844.1**	**$1,654.5**

Confirmation of the Plan and Emergence from Chapter 11

As referenced, the only parties entitled to vote on the PacD Debtors' plan were the holders of the 2017 Notes, the 2020 Notes, and the Term Loan B claims. Each of those classes voted to accept the plan, as set forth below:

Class	Class Description	Number Accepting	Number Rejecting	Amount Accepting	Amount Rejecting	Class Voting Result
6A(i)	6A(i) Term Loan B Claims	93 100%	0 0%	$690,666,045.11 100%	$0.00 0%	ACCEPT
6A(ii)	2020 Notes Claims	55 94.83%	3 5.17%	$706,391,742.59 98.29%	$12,273,625.59 1.71%	ACCEPT
6C	2017 Notes Claims	63 100%	0 0%	$439,029,182.69 100%	$0.00 0%	ACCEPT

On November 2, 2018, roughly one year after the bankruptcy cases were commenced, the plan was confirmed and became effective on November 19, 2018. Confirmation was the culmination and product of multi-party negotiations that occur in almost every Chapter 11 case. In these cases, the parties were able to negotiate an outcome that obviated the need for a contested confirmation hearing. In other cases, parties will litigate issues relating to valuation, the legal requirements for confirmation, and various other issues.

The *Pacific Drilling* case serves as an example of a successful reorganization — various parties entered with divergent goals and, over the course of multiple months of difficult negotiations, slowly moved towards a consensual resolution with the help of an experienced mediator. In the end, hundreds of jobs for employees and contractors were preserved, and the PacD Debtors were able to emerge from Chapter 11 with a far reduced debt burden and sufficient liquidity for a successful restructuring while it awaited the oil market to turn around.

Questions to Consider

1. Why was PacD a good candidate for reorganization under chapter 11? What distinguishes PacD from entities that should be liquidated?
2. Why was PacD in a better position to negotiate inside of bankruptcy? What chain of events would have otherwise occurred under non-bankruptcy law?
3. What leverage did QP have in negotiations on the Chapter 11 plan with the Ad Hoc Group and others?
4. Consider that equity holders are the most junior stakeholders in the capital structure, but at the same time may have rights to elect directors to the board of the debtor that will likely propose a plan. What stops the debtor's management from simply proposing a plan that provides for a distribution to equityholders even if the debtor is insolvent?
5. Why is valuation such a crucial aspect of reorganization? Which creditors benefit if a firm is undervalued? Which creditors benefit if it is overvalued?
6. Perform a valuation of PacD by application of the DCF approach utilizing a high and low scenario, and assess the implications of a financial recapitalization on existing shareholders.
7. What are the implications of the above valuation scenarios for bondholders' financial recapitalization under Chapter 11?

Appendix. Bankruptcy Overview

Article I of the US Constitution authorizes Congress to establish "uniform laws on the subject of bankruptcies throughout the United States."[30] The Bankruptcy Code was enacted in 1978 and has been amended several times.[31]

This appendix will discuss the overarching concepts of Chapter 11 of the Bankruptcy Code. In particular, Chapter 11 can be utilized for reorganization,[32] a process by which the debtor alleviates its financial difficulties by, among other actions, restructuring its debts, improving operational efficiency, and rejecting burdensome contracts. Separate chapters of the Bankruptcy Code mandate rules and procedures for liquidation cases, cross-border cases, cases for the adjustment of debts for individuals with regular income, family farmers and fishermen with a regular income, and municipalities.[33]

However, not every distressed firm will benefit equally from reorganization. Some debtors are unable to pay their debts as they become due simply because they cannot compete in the marketplace, regardless of the condition of their capital structure ("economic" issues), while others may generate positive value but are hamstrung by financial obligations that could be effectively remediated through reorganization ("financial" issues).[34] Debtors that file due to "economic" problems, whose operations cannot be addressed, should be liquidated for the benefit of creditors. In contrast, a "financially" distressed debtor may only need the "breathing

---

[30] US CONST. art. I, § 8, cl. 4.

[31] The Bankruptcy Code is codified in Title 11 of the United States Code. See 11 U.S.C. §§ 101-1532. The most recent significant amendment to the Bankruptcy Code was the Bankruptcy Abuse Prevention and Consumer Protection Act, or BAPCP, which was enacted in 2005.

[32] This is in contrast to a liquidating case under Chapter 7, see 11 U.S.C. §§ 701-784, pursuant to which a business (or individual) will liquidate its assets completely for the purpose of repaying creditors. Note that, technically, Chapter 11 can also be used to liquidate, rather than reorganize, businesses.

[33] See Chapters 7, 15, 13, 12, and 9, respectively.

[34] See Douglas G. Baird, *Bankruptcy's Uncontested Axioms*, 108 YALE L.J. 573, 580 (1998) for a discussion of the distinction between "financial" and "economic" distress. While an economically distressed firm would certainly run into financial distress as well, the two are not necessarily related.

room" of bankruptcy to regain its footing.[35] Chapter 11 reorganization is intended to rehabilitate these financially distressed companies that are victims of their circumstances and are likely to produce positive value once their debts are restructured.

The Chapter 11 Parties

Debtor in Possession

Unless cause exists, such as fraud or gross mismanagement, the current management of the debtor will retain control of the operating business.[36] Where current management retains control, the debtor is referred to as the "debtor in possession," or the "DIP," in effect making the debtor a fiduciary for creditors.[37] The DIP has the power to operate the business throughout the Chapter 11 case, and can generally continue operating its business in the ordinary course without seeking approval from the bankruptcy court.

Secured Creditors

Creditors who have valid prepetition liens against or security interests in assets of the debtor are well protected during a Chapter 11 case. If a debtor intends to use any assets encumbered by such liens or security interests during its Chapter 11 case, the debtor must provide "adequate protection" to the secured creditor to compensate against any potential diminution in

[35] See *id.* Baird gives the example of a toy company that borrowed a large amount of money to develop and market a toy tied to a movie that flopped as an instance of "financial" distress. Even if the firm hires new managers that are *guaranteed* to lead the firm to success, the firm may still be saddled with tremendous loan obligations based on the decisions of prior management. Such a firm is a good candidate for reorganization.

[36] The presumption that a debtor's management will continue to manage the debtor in Chapter 11 is contained in 11 U.S.C. §§ 1107 and 1108. 11 U.S.C. § 1104 provides the grounds and procedure for removing the current management and replacing it with a Chapter 11 trustee.

[37] See, for example, *In re Ngan Gung Rest.*, 254 B.R. 566, 570 (Bankr. S.D.N.Y. 2000) ("A [debtor in possession] owes a fiduciary duty to each creditor of the estate.") (citing *Commodity Futures Trading Commission v. Weintraub,* 471 U.S. 343, 355 (1985)).

the value of the security interest.[38] This is because the automatic stay prevents the secured creditor from exercising foreclosure remedies unless it obtains relief from the stay.

A secured creditor may have a security interest in more than just the hard assets of a debtor. For instance, a secured creditor may hold a security interest in "cash collateral" of the debtor, which refers to cash and cash equivalents in which a creditor has a secured interest.[39] It may also include intellectual property or other rights in contracts, leases, and the like. The debtor in possession may only use this cash collateral with the permission of the secured party or by an order of the court.

Unsecured Creditors Committee

A debtor's secured creditors are not the only party that will actively participate in and attempt to influence a debtor's restructuring process. Indeed, a committee of unsecured creditors (the "Creditors' Committee")[40] will often be the most vocal group during a Chapter 11 case, particularly if the debtor's assets are fully encumbered by secured claims which exceed the aggregate value of the debtor's assets. The Creditors' Committee is appointed by the local United States Trustee, who works under the umbrella of the US Department of Justice. The Creditors' Committee is typically composed of three to seven of the largest unsecured creditors that are willing to serve, although an effort will be made to ensure that the Creditors' Committee is made up of a diverse group of creditor interests.[41]

The Creditors' Committee is a fiduciary to the entire unsecured creditor body (not just to the creditors on the Creditors' Committee) and generally will monitor the debtor and the Chapter 11 case to ensure that

---

[38] See 11 U.S.C. § 361. Adequate protection may include "a cash payment or periodic cash payments," "an additional or replacement lien," or some other relief that results in the realization of the "the indubitable equivalent" of the secured creditor's interest in the collateral. See 11 U.S.C. §§ 361(a), (b), and (c), respectively.

[39] This may include, for example, accounts receivable in which a creditor has a secured interest. When the receivables are paid off, that cash payment becomes cash collateral.

[40] See 11 U.S.C. § 1102.

[41] Equity holders, tort victims, or other similar interests may also request that the court order the appointment of additional committees. See 11 U.S.C. § 1102(a)(2). Typically, such groups of creditors will have to demonstrate a reasonable likelihood of recovery in order to be recognized.

unsecured creditors are treated fairly and receive the maximum possible recovery during the reorganization.[42] A Creditors' Committee is useful because cases often involve large and diverse creditor pools made up of hundreds or thousands of claims. Each individual unsecured creditor is unlikely to have the means or incentive to actively participate in the bankruptcy process. The Committee is therefore appointed, in part, to ensure that the general unsecured creditor body has a voice and is adequately represented during the Chapter 11 case.

Key Provisions of the Bankruptcy Code

The Automatic Stay

As more fully discussed below, one of the most important protections offered to a debtor is the automatic stay (the "Automatic Stay") pursuant to section 362 of the Bankruptcy Code. The Automatic Stay comes into effect immediately upon the filing of a Chapter 11 petition or another petition for relief (hence, it is automatic) and, among other things, strictly prohibits the commencement or continuation of any collection activities, enforcements, litigations, or actions against a debtor on account of prepetition debts or obligations.[43]

The purpose of the Automatic Stay is to provide the debtor with a "breathing spell"[44] to allow the debtor to focus its attention on its restructuring free from creditor harassment and without the distraction of having to defend against multiple litigations in non-bankruptcy courts.[45] Section

---

[42] See 11 U.S.C. § 1103. Pursuant to 11 U.S.C. § 1103(c), a Creditors' Committee may: (1) consult with the debtor in possession concerning the administration of the estate; (2) investigate the acts, conduct, assets, liabilities, and financial condition of the debtor, the operation of the debtor's business and the desirability of the continuance of such business; (3) participate in the formulation of a plan; (4) request the appointment of a Chapter 11 trustee or examiner; and (5) perform such other services as are in the interest of those represented.

[43] See 11 U.S.C. § 362(a).

[44] See, for example, *E. Refactories Co. v. Forty Eight Insulations*, 157 F.3d 169 (2d Cir. 1998).

[45] *See CAE Indus. Ltd. v. Aerospace Holding Co.*, 116 B.R. 31, 32 (S.D.N.Y. 1990) ("The legislative history reveals that the section was intended 'to permit the debtor to organize his or her affairs without creditor harassment and to allow orderly resolution of all claims'").

362(a)(1) of the Bankruptcy Code provides a stay of all legal proceedings against the debtor that were or could have been commenced before the commencement of its Chapter 11 case.[46]

Under the Automatic Stay, once a debtor files for bankruptcy, any and all collection efforts by creditors must cease completely.[47] This includes liquidation of any collateral a secured creditor may have a right to and even requests for repayment by creditors.[48] In short, the Automatic Stay is the shield that protects a debtor during the pendency of its bankruptcy case.[49]

There are some exceptions, however. For example, a creditor can request that the court lift the automatic stay to allow repossession of collateral "for cause, including the lack of adequate protection" of the creditor's interest in the property.[50] Further, a creditor can also seek to lift the stay to continue a legal action involving the debtor if the creditor can demonstrate that that continuation of the action will not be unduly disruptive to the administration of the case.[51]

Selling Assets

Even while the Automatic Stay is in place, the debtor may continue to sell or encumber assets that it owns free and clear of any creditors' liens or encumbrances in the ordinary course of business. However, where such sales would not be in the debtor's ordinary course of business (i.e., where the debtor intends to sell non-productive assets, entire business units, or even substantially all of its assets), the debtor must first obtain court approval on notice to creditors. Section 363 of the Bankruptcy Code governs these sales and requires the debtor to comply with certain sale and notice procedures.[52]

---

[46] *In re Colin*, 35 B.R. 904, 907 (Bankr. S.D.N.Y. 1983).

[47] 11 U.S.C. § 362(a)(3).

[48] 11 U.S.C. § 362(a)(1) and (6), respectively.

[49] See, for example, *In re Deliland Foods Corp.*, 2005 WL 751929, at *1 (D. Del Mar. 31, 2005) (using the term "bankruptcy protection").

[50] See 11 U.S.C. § 362(d).

[51] *In re Sonnax Industries*, 907 F.2d 1280, 1285 (2d Cir. 1990), is frequently cited for articulating 12 factors to consider in the analysis.

[52] See 11 U.S.C. § 363.

Adequate Protection

Because the Automatic Stay prevents secured creditors from exercising remedies (e.g., foreclosing on the collateral securing their debts), there is a risk that their collateral will depreciate in value during the pendency of the bankruptcy case. Section 361 of the Bankruptcy Code therefore requires that the debtor provide secured creditors with "adequate protection" for the debtor's use of their collateral.[53] Where the bankruptcy court finds that collateral may decline in value, the debtor may be required to provide additional liens on other debtor property or it may have to make cash payments to offset such diminution in value.[54] The Bankruptcy Code further provides that bankruptcy courts can lift the Automatic Stay to permit repossession of collateral in instances where a bankruptcy court finds that the secured creditor's interest is not adequately protected.[55]

Financing

Even with the benefit of the Automatic Stay, Chapter 11 debtors often require financing during the pendency of their Chapter 11 case to ensure that they are able to continue to operate their business until a Chapter 11 plan, or some other resolution of the court, is reached and finalized. This is known as "DIP financing" or a "DIP loan." However, not surprisingly, a Chapter 11 debtor will often find that lenders are not willing to extend financing to a debtor without special protections.

To encourage lenders to provide financing to Chapter 11 debtors, the Bankruptcy Code therefore permits a debtor to provide a post-petition lender with what is known as a "priming lien," which is a secured claim that has "super-priority" over existing debt, equity and other claims. However, such priming liens come at the expense of other secured creditors, and a debtor will have to demonstrate that it was unable to obtain unsecured credit allowable as an administrative expense in order for the bankruptcy court to approve a priming lien.[56] The debtor will also be

---

[53] See 11 U.S.C. § 361.

[54] 11 U.S.C. § 361(1), (2).

[55] 11 U.S.C. § 362(d)(1)

[56] 11 U.S.C. § 364(c), (d).

required to demonstrate that other secured lenders that are "primed" by the priming lien are otherwise "adequately protected."[57]

In addition to favorable interest rates, a debtor may also entice lenders with security interests in unencumbered property, administrative claims with priority over other expenses, and/or subordinate liens.[58] As a general rule, DIP financing on a secured basis must be approved by the bankruptcy court, as such financing is not in the ordinary course of business.

Contracts

Section 365 of the Bankruptcy Code allows a debtor to "assume" or "reject" leases and certain types of contracts that have not been fully performed on both sides, known as "executory contracts." While the term "executory contract" is not defined in the Bankruptcy Code, the most widely accepted definition is "a contract under which the obligation of both the debtor and the counterparty to the contract are so far underperformed that the failure of either to complete performance would constitute a material breach excusing the performance of the other."[59]

A debtor can reject an executory contract, thereby terminating the debtor's obligation to perform and giving the counterparty a claim for breach of contract against the debtor's estate (and not against the reorganized debtor that emerges from Chapter 11) that is deemed to arise immediately before the date the case was commenced. In contrast, if a debtor assumes a contract or lease, the debtor must cure any pre-petition defaults and will become bound by the contract's prepetition obligations.[60] A debtor may also assume an executory contract and assign it to a third party.[61] Provisions that automatically cancel or terminate a contract or lease upon a bankruptcy filing are deemed void and unenforceable.[62]

---

[57] 11 U.S.C. § 364(d).

[58] 11 U.S.C. § 364(c).

[59] Vern Countryman, Executory Contracts in Bankruptcy (Part I), 57 Minn L. Rev. 439 (1973).

[60] 11 U.S.C. § 365(b)(1).

[61] With an exception for certain types of contracts, that is, intellectual property.

[62] See 11 U.S.C. § 365(e). Such provisions, which "modify the relationships of contracting parties due to the filing of a bankruptcy petition," see *In re Lehman Bros. Holdings Inc.*, 422 B.R. 407, 414 (Bankr. S.D.N.Y. 2010), are known as *ipso facto* clauses and are "generally unenforceable." *See In re AMR Corp.*, 730 F.3d 88 (2d Cir. 2013) (finding that there

The power under section 365 of the Bankruptcy Code to assume or reject unexpired leases and contracts allows a debtor to choose the contracts and leases it determines are most important to the reorganized debtor's future operations. Burdensome or unnecessary contracts can be shed. The Bankruptcy Code requires that contract counterparties continue to perform under a lease or contract until the debtor makes a determination as to whether it will assume or reject each contract. Section 365(d)(4) provides that a debtor must decide whether to assume or reject a nonresidential real estate lease within 120 days of the date the case was commenced.

The Absolute Priority Rule

Pursuant to the "absolute priority rule,"[63] senior tiers of creditors must be paid in full before any junior tier of creditors can receive any distribution. Creditors are entitled to the following priority: (1) secured creditors recover first to the extent of the value of their collateral, (2) unsecured creditors are paid *pro rata* any value remaining after secured creditors are paid in full, and (3) the remaining assets (if any exists after unsecured creditors are paid in full) goes to the debtor's equity holders.[64] The above, of course, is a simplified view of the absolute priority rule.

---

are three specific sections of the Bankruptcy Code which ban *ipso facto* clauses — § 365(e)(1) invalidating automatic acceleration or termination upon filing, § 541(c)(1)(B) invalidating clauses which terminate a debtor's interest in property upon filing, and § 363(l) which gives the trustee the right to use, sell, or lease property despite any *ipso facto* clauses). However, section 365(e) only prohibits *ipso facto* clauses in executory contracts. *Id.*

[63] The term "absolute priority rule," is a shorthand for the principle mandated by section 1129(b)(2) of the Bankruptcy Code that a liquidation plan must be "fair and equitable" to creditors.

[64] See *Bank of Am. Nat. Trust and Sav. Ass'n v 203 N. LaSalle St. Partnership*, 526 US 434 (1999) (Chapter 11 debtor's pre-bankruptcy equity holders could not, over objection of senior class of impaired creditors, contribute new capital and receive ownership interests in reorganized entity, when that opportunity was given exclusively to old equity holders under reorganization plan adopted without consideration of alternatives; plan violated absolute priority rule by its provision for vesting equity in reorganized business in the debtor's partners, without extending an opportunity to anyone else either to compete for that equity or to propose a competing reorganization plan).

https://doi.org/10.1142/9789811216749_0032

Case 32

The Essentials of Business Formation and Choice-of-Entity Issues

Jay Soled

Rutgers Business School, USA

Introduction

When taxpayers decide to form a business enterprise, the issue of choice of entity is always front and center. In the life cycle of a business enterprise, this is an important decision. Once the metaphoric die has been cast, it is nearly impossible to reroll. Thus, those contemplating commencing this choice-of-entity journey must pause and consider a plethora of factors.

This is not uncharted territory. Many of the nation's most famous companies and their founders have had to endure and resolve these issues as well. For example, Facebook, now a multibillion-dollar company, had its initial humble origins as a Florida limited liability company, and another well-known company, Micro-Soft (its original name), commenced its operations as a New Mexico general partnership. By way of contrast, Ford Motor Company began business operations over a century ago utilizing a Michigan corporate vehicle to get its operations off the ground. The question is why these different business enterprises and the extraordinarily talented entrepreneurs who launched them — Mark Zuckerberg, Bill Gates, and Henry Ford — each chose a different form of business entity to commence initial operations.

The following case study considers the choice of business entity issue and enumerates the factors that anyone starting a business enterprise should consider. Immediately after the case study is a series of heuristic questions for students to use to test themselves over the mastery of the material presented herein.

Background

Amy, Beth, and Cathy, three high school friends, have been contemplating establishing a new business that would protect the anonymity of their clientele's privacy on the internet. They want to know the available options for operating this business in a tax-efficient manner. In addition, they wish to learn about the legal governance and ethical issues that they may need to address.

In order to get this enterprise off the ground, each of the interested parties brings certain important items to the table. Amy, a recent MIT graduate, has the technical skill set to possibly make this dream a reality; Beth, a beneficiary of her father's estate, has a lot of cash to invest; and Cathy, who has been operating a computer-consulting business, owns the following assets (shown with their adjusted basis and fair market value), which she may wish to contribute:

Assets	Adjusted Tax Basis	Fair Market Value
Cash	$1,000,000	$1,000,000
Equipment	$100,000	$1,000,000
Inventory	$100,000	$1,000,000
Goodwill	$0	$1,000,000
	$1,200,000	$4,000,000

Note: A year earlier, when Cathy acquired the equipment, she took accelerated depreciation deductions that correspondingly reduced the adjusted tax basis of this purchased property.

In light of their different backgrounds, Amy, Beth, and Cathy had the following tentative thoughts: Amy would work full-time at this venture and commit herself to a four-year employment contract but would not receive any salary (all of them agree that Amy's skill set warrants $1 million annually of remuneration); Beth would contribute $4 million of her multimillion-dollar inheritance to the enterprise; and Cathy would assign the assets of her computer-consulting business to this initiative. At least to the three of them, this shared approach appears to be equitable and in line with achieving their primary objective of being equal co-owners.

The Assignment

The three high school friends harbor tremendous optimism that this enterprise will be a financial success. Notwithstanding their optimism, they readily concede that what they have in terms of skills, cash, and property, they lack in terms of fundamental accounting and legal knowledge. They have a plethora of questions on their minds that they trifurcate into the following three categories:

1. Tax Issues
   a. What legal structure should the prospective owners choose for the entity?
   b. What are the concomitant tax consequences associated with their choices?
   c. Can they take proactive measures to minimize their tax burdens?
   d. If the enterprise makes cash or property distributions, how will these distributions be treated at (i) the entity level and (ii) the owner level (i.e., by Amy, Beth, and Cathy)?
   e. If another high school friend, Diane, wishes to join the enterprise and contribute property with a tax basis in excess of fair market value (e.g., land with a \$4 million fair market value and a \$10 million adjusted tax basis), what tax and other considerations come into play?
2. Legal Issues
   a. What kind of legal documents should the parties put into place?
   b. What equity structure should the owners have in place?
3. Ethical Issues
   a. Should the owners and the business enterprise have the same accountant?
   b. Should the owners and the business enterprise have the same attorney?
   c. Do the parties have a fiduciary duty to each other and/or the enterprise?

The three of them decide that each should conduct research. Amy will learn more about tax, Beth will conduct due diligence on legal issues, and Cathy will investigate ethical concerns. Their general findings, set forth below, are broken down into three categories: (I) tax landscape, (II) legal concerns, and (III) ethical issues.

Tax Landscape

There is a long history of taxpayers bemoaning the Internal Revenue Code (Code) and its complexity. Amy recognizes that she doesn't have the time, energy, and resources to become a practicing accountant; but, by conducting numerous and exhaustive Internet searches and reading voraciously, she was able to assemble a number of important precepts about the Code's different tax treatments of (A) partnerships and (B) corporations. These differences and the salient features of each form of conducting business are set forth below.

Partnerships

In general, the Code treats partnerships as pass-through entities. While a partnership must annually file a Form 1065 (U.S. Return of Partnership Income), it pays no tax; however, each partner receives an information return (i.e., a Schedule K-1) and must report her distributive share of corresponding income and losses. The fact that there is only one layer of tax at the partner level makes partnerships an attractive entity through which to conduct business. In the case of a three-person equal partnership, for example, if the enterprise earns $3,000, at the end of the tax year, each partner must report $1,000 of earnings (this is true even if the partnership makes no distributions).

In several instances, however, the Code treats partnerships as standalone enterprises. For example, many tax elections are made at the partnership level rather than at the partner level (e.g., whether to have like-kind treatment apply to the sale of real estate). For this reason, partners must be circumspect and recognize that, with respect to certain decisions related to tax issues, the partnership speaks for all of them.

While delving into all of the attributes of partnership taxation would be beyond herculean, Amy learns the essential elements of partnership taxation, namely, those involving (1) formation, (2) operations, and (3) liquidation.

Formation

Congress wants to foster business growth and not impede start-up enterprises. Accordingly, the Code seeks to facilitate partnership formations and make them as inviting as possible. That being the case, when a partner contributes property to a partnership, this is generally not a taxable event to either the partners or the partnership. Three Code sections dictate this outcome:

- *Code section 721*: If certain conditions are met, partnership formations constitute nonrecognition events and, as such, are not taxable to either the partners or the partnership.
- *Code section 722*: A partner will have a carryover basis in her partnership interest equal to the amount of cash and the adjusted tax basis of any property that the partner contributed.
- *Code section 723*: The partnership will have a carryover basis in the property (if any) that the partners contributed to the partnership equal to the tax basis that the contributing partners had in such property.

However, if a partner contributes services, rather than property, to a partnership in return for a partnership interest, the receipt of such interest is not exempt from tax. Treas. Reg. Section 1.721-1.

In practical terms, if a prospective partner contributes appreciated real estate to the partnership with a \$100,000 adjusted basis and a \$1 million fair market value in return for a partnership interest (presumably worth \$1 million), the transfer will not be taxable to either the partnership or the partner. The partner will have a \$100,000 adjusted tax basis in the partnership interest that she receives, and the partnership will have a \$100,000 tax basis in the contributed real estate. Together, these three Code sections — 721, 722, and 723 — operate to defer tax but not to eliminate it.

Operations

As a partnership conducts business, it earns profits and sometimes suffers losses. In addition, in the ordinary course of business, it may make periodic distributions of cash and property to its members. In particular, there are four Code sections that address the tax consequences associated with partnership operations. They are as follows:

- *Code section 702*: This section requires that a partner's distributive share of income and losses be reported be broken down by income category (e.g., ordinary income versus capital gains) and reported on a Schedule K-1.

- *Code section 703*: This Code section instructs how a partnership should compute its overall taxable income.
- *Code section 705*: This Code section specifies when the tax basis of partnership interest should be increased (e.g., when the partnership earns income) and when the tax basis of a partnership should be decreased (e.g., when the partnership suffers losses or a distribution of cash/property is made).
- *Code section 731*: When a partnership distributes cash or other property to its partners, the partnership recognizes no gain or loss; and its partners, too, will not generally recognize gain or loss, unless the amount of cash distributed exceeds a partner's tax basis in the partnership (in which case the partner would recognize a gain).

Therefore, if a three-person equal partnership earns $900,000 ($300,000 related to the sale of a capital asset and $600,000 related to the sale of inventory), the tax consequences would be as follows: Each partner would report $100,000 of capital gains and $200,000 of ordinary income, and this would increase the tax basis of their partnership interest by $300,000 (i.e., $100,000 + $200,000). If the partnership subsequently made a $75,000 cash distribution to each partner, the recipient partner will not experience a gain or loss; instead, the tax basis that each partner had in her partnership interest would diminish by a corresponding dollar amount.

Liquidation

Once a partnership ceases doing business, the partners must wind up its operations. From a tax perspective, a liquidation largely proves to be a nonevent as the partnership terminates and its assets are distributed. The two major Code sections that come into play are the following:

- *Code section 731.* Once again, when a partnership distributes cash or other property to its partners, the partnership recognizes no gain or loss. However, while a partner generally will not recognize gain or loss, this is not true if (i) the amount of cash distributed exceeds the partner's tax basis in the partnership (in such a case, the recipient partner would recognize a gain); or (ii) the partnership distributes only cash, unrealized receivables, and/or inventory, and the basis of such distributed property does not exceed the partner's outside tax basis in the enterprise (in such a case, the recipient partner would then recognize a loss on the remaining tax basis).

- *Code section 732.* The tax basis of the property that a partner receives on a liquidating distribution will generally equal the property's tax basis in the hands of the partnership.

Returning a final time to our example of a three-person equal partnership, suppose it distributes the following assets to partners X (who receives cash), Y (who receives inventory), and Z (who receives accounts receivable):

Assets	Adjusted Tax Basis	Fair Market Value
Cash	$100,000	$100,000
Inventory	$0	$100,000
Accounts Receivable	$100,000	$100,000

Suppose the tax bases that X, Y, and Z have in the partnership are as follows:

Partner	Adjusted Tax Basis
X	$0
Y	$100,000
Z	$100,000

In this case, partner X would have to recognize a $100,000 capital gain because the $100,000 cash distribution exceeds her basis by an equivalent dollar amount; partner Y would have to recognize a $100,000 capital loss because her adjusted basis in the partnership (i.e., $100,000) exceeds the tax basis in the inventory (i.e., $0); and partner Z would receive the accounts receivable with a carryover basis of $100,000 and experience neither gain nor loss.

Corporations

As a preliminary matter, the Code treats corporations as independent taxpayers and taxes them in a like manner. Every year, every corporation must compute its taxable income, file a tax return (i.e., a Form 1120

(U.S. Corporation Income Tax Return)), and pay tax (currently, a flat 21% tax rate applies). When a corporation makes distributions to its shareholders, it does not get a deduction; however, the recipient shareholders must generally report the income that they receive as taxable dividends.

Akin to the partnership tax exercise, Amy learns the essential elements of corporate taxation, namely, those involving (1) formation, (2) operations, and (3) liquidation.

Formation

Consistent with its partnership-formation philosophy of spurring business and invigorating the economy, Congress rolls out the proverbial red carpet for corporate formations. In many instances, if properly handled, corporate formations can be orchestrated in a tax-free manner. Four Code sections frame this outcome:

- *Code section 351*: If one or more persons contribute property to a corporation that they control, no gain or loss will be recognized by the corporation or the shareholders.
- *Code section 368(c)*: This Code section defines *control* essentially to mean 80% or more of the corporate enterprise.
- *Code section 358*: A contributing shareholder will have a tax basis in the corporate shares that she receives equal to the contributed cash plus the adjusted tax basis of the contributed property.
- *Code section 362*: The recipient corporation will take a carryover tax basis in the contributed property that it receives equal to the tax basis in the hands of the contributing shareholder.

Under this framework, consider the implications if an entrepreneur has equipment with a $100,000 tax basis and a $1 million fair market value. He forms a corporation and contributes the equipment in return for 100 shares of stock. Because the contributing shareholder will control the corporation (i.e., own 80% or more of the outstanding shares of the new company), neither he nor the corporation will recognize a gain or loss upon formation. The shareholder will have a $100,000 tax basis in the 100 corporate shares that he receives, and the corporation will have a $100,000 tax basis in the contributed equipment.

Operations

As a corporation conducts business, it (like a partnership) earns profits and sometimes suffers losses. In addition, in the ordinary course of business, it (like a partnership) may make periodic distributions of cash and property to its shareholders. There are three Code sections that address the tax consequences associated with corporate operations. They are as follows:

- *Code section 11*: This Code section declares that all income that a corporation earns is taxed at a flat 21% rate.
- *Code section 301*: This Code section specifies that, in most circumstances, cash and property distributions that a corporation makes constitute dividends in the hands of its shareholders.
- *Code section 311*: If a corporation distributes property, gains associated with such property are recognized, but associated losses are disallowed.

Application of these three Code sections is relatively straightforward. If a corporation earns $1 million, it must pay $210,000 of corporate tax (i.e., 21% × $1,000,000). If the same corporation distributes the remaining $790,000 (i.e., $1,000,000 – $210,000), its shareholders report this amount as taxable dividends on their tax returns. Finally, if as part of the distribution the corporation distributes equipment with a $10,000 adjusted basis and a $100,000 fair market value, it must recognize a $90,000 gain (i.e., $100,000 – $10,000).

Liquidation

At some point in time, a corporation's life cycle will come to an end, and it will endure liquidation. In stark contrast to a partnership, in which the events surrounding a liquidation are largely tax free, the exact opposite is true for a corporate enterprise: in many instances, a corporate liquidation generates gain/losses at the corporate and shareholder levels. There are three Code sections that address the tax consequences associated with corporate liquidations. They are as follows:

- *Code section 331*: At the shareholder level, gains/losses are recognized on the difference between the cash and fair market value of the property that shareholders receive and the adjusted tax basis of their shares.
- *Code section 334*: Shareholders will have a fair market tax basis in the property that they receive from a corporate liquidation.

- *Code section 336*: At the corporate level, gains/losses are recognized on the property distributions that the corporation makes.

To illustrate, upon liquidation, suppose that a corporation has one shareholder who has a $200,000 tax basis in his shares and supposes further that the corporation owns one piece of real estate with a $1 million fair market value and a $400,000 tax basis. When the corporation distributes this property to the shareholder, it will recognize a $600,000 gain (i.e., $1,000,000 – $400,000). In addition, the shareholder will recognize an $800,000 gain (i.e., $1,000,000 – $200,000) and receive the distributed property with a $1 million adjusted tax basis.

Summary of Tax Landscape

As a general proposition, Amy's research revealed that partnerships enjoy more favorable tax treatment under the Code than corporations do. A final tidbit that Amy learned, though, is that to level the playing field for small-business enterprises, a corporation may make a so-called S corporation election and be treated essentially as a partnership for tax purposes (namely, as a pass-through entity, not subject to an independent layer of tax). She discovered that there are two major limitations associated with making this election, however: the number of shareholders that the corporation may have is limited to 100, and the corporation can only have one class of stock outstanding (although the company can issue both voting and nonvoting shares of the same class of stock).

Legal Concerns

With the tax issues apparently under control, Beth decided that it would be a good idea to get a handle on the business enterprise's legal issues. While Beth knew that law school wasn't in her future, she took a crack at reading a number of legal treatises on the subject of business formations and operations. Below are the results of her findings pertaining to (A) essential legal documents related to business formations and (B) essential legal documents related to business operations.

Essential Legal Documents Related to Business Formations

Business formations are in the province of state, rather than federal, law. Thus, those endeavoring to establish a business enterprise generally must secure state approval. How this approval is accomplished for partnerships and limited liability companies (LLCs) differs from the approval process for corporations. Subsection 1 explores the state approval process related to partnerships and LLCs, and Subsection 2 does the same for corporations.

Partnerships and Limited Liability Companies

As a preliminary matter, partnerships generally come in two forms: general partnerships and limited partnerships. A general partnership is usually an informal arrangement of two or more individuals or entities coming together and seeking to fulfill a common business objective; while simple in nature, from a legal liability standpoint, all of the partners in this arrangement have liability exposure. By way of contrast, a limited partnership consists of one or more general partners who work to achieve a business purpose and one or more limited partners who contribute funds or property to the enterprise but do not actively participate in the business; as part of this arrangement, the general partners remain legally liable for the partnership obligations, but the limited partners do not.

Because of potential liability exposure, approximately four decades ago states developed a platform for small businesses to follow that offered the dual virtues of being treated as a pass-through entity for tax purposes and, at the same time, receiving liability protection for all of its owners. These enterprises became known as limited liability companies and limited liability partnerships. A limited liability company allows its owners (known as members) to be shielded from the enterprise's liabilities; a limited liability partnership allows its owners (known as partners) to be shielded not only from the enterprise's liabilities but also from the liability of the other partners' actions (hence, the popularity of limited liability partnerships among professionals such as accountants, lawyers, and physicians).

To form these business enterprises, their owners must file documentation in the state in which they wish to operate. The following details each type of business enterprise and the typical formation documentation required:

- *General partnership*: A registration statement must be filed with the state's secretary of state.
- *Limited partnership*: A registration statement and a certificate of limited partnership must be filed with the state's secretary of state.

- *Limited liability company*: A registration statement and a certificate of formation must be filed with the state's secretary of state.
- *Limited liability partnership*: A registration statement and a certificate of formation must be filed with the state's secretary of state.

Once the owners form the business, the business should then utilize a Form SS-4 (Application for Employer Identification Number) to secure an employer identification number (EIN) from the Internal Revenue Service. With the EIN in hand, the business will be positioned to open up a bank account and commence operations.

Corporations

Many business entrepreneurs find the use of corporate entities attractive for two main reasons. First, corporations offer liability protection for all of their owners; more specifically, even if a corporation owes hundreds of thousands or perhaps even millions of dollars to creditors, its owners bear no responsibility for paying these obligations. Second, corporate ownership can be widespread; the number of investors who can own shares is unlimited, making this an attractive option for those enterprises that need to raise a lot of working capital.

Forming a corporate enterprise is a fairly straightforward endeavor. All that must be done is that its owners must file a certificate of incorporation in the state of incorporation. (Because the laws of Delaware are known to be favorable to management, this has become a preferred state of incorporation.) Once a certificate of incorporation has been filed, the corporation's owners are at liberty to secure a corporate EIN and commence business operations.

Essential Legal Documents Related to Business Operations

As businesses flourish, their owners often rely upon certain legal documents to ensure good governance and smooth operations. These legal documents often come in several forms, and, just as was the case regarding formations, their nature differs depending upon whether the enterprise of choice is a partnership/LLC or a corporation. Accordingly, Beth's legal landscape findings are categorized by partnerships and limited liability companies, Subsection 1; and corporations, Subsection 2.

Partnerships and Limited Liability Companies

When it comes to partnerships and limited liability companies, the most critical document that governs business affairs is the operating agreement (aka the partnership agreement). Most operating agreements fulfill four main objectives: (1) they limit the ability of its members to transfer ownership interests without entity approval; (2) they detail who controls business decisions or, alternatively, put a voting mechanism into place that governs how decisions are to be made; (3) they provide what is to happen to an owner's interest in the business enterprise upon certain events (generally, retirement, disability, and death) and, in addition, set forth a procedure to determine the fair market value of such interest; and (4) they detail a system to wind up the entity's affairs when the time of liquidation is at hand.

Absent an operating agreement, partners and members of partnerships and LLCs must rely upon state law to resolve their differences.

Corporations

When it comes to corporations, there are two critical documents: (a) the bylaws and (b) the shareholders' agreement.

a. *Bylaws*: A company's bylaws constitute its rule book. They describe the roles of its directors, officers, and employees and their respective responsibilities and how the company will select people to fulfill these roles. Furthermore, the bylaws often detail how often meetings should be held, how they should be conducted, their location, and the necessary quorum for votes to be taken. Finally, the bylaws systematize the manner in which the board of directors can offer amendments.
b. *Shareholders' agreement*: This critical document sets forth a framework for shareholders to interact between and among each other. Akin to operating agreements, there are four main objectives that these agreements are supposed to fulfill: (1) they limit the ability of a corporation's shareholders to transfer ownership interests without entity approval; (2) they detail who controls business decisions or, alternatively, put a voting mechanism in place that governs how decisions are to be made; (3) they provide what is to happen to an owner's interest in the business enterprise upon certain events (generally, retirement, disability, and death) and, in addition, provide a procedure

to determine the fair market value of such interest; and (4) they set forth a system to wind up the entity's affairs when the time of liquidation is at hand. Absent a shareholders' agreement, shareholders must rely upon state law to resolve their differences.

Summary of Legal Concerns

As a general proposition, Beth's research uncovered that the legal documents involving entity formation and governance for both partnerships and corporations share many of the same attributes. One important conclusion that Beth has drawn from her research is the importance of getting executed documentation into place before a business enterprise has a crisis rather than after the fact when it may be too late or when the vicissitudes of state law control.

Ethical Issues

Cathy's charge is to examine some of the ethical issues that may arise during the formation and operational phases of their proposed business enterprise. Yes, Cathy knows that she, Amy, and Beth intend to be "good citizens" and "do the right thing," but she wants to conduct research to learn if there are external rules that set forth governing codes of conduct and principles for themselves and the professionals whom that the business enterprise they establish retains. Over the course of Cathy's research, she discovers ethic rules that apply to (A) matters of business operations and (B) the accounting and legal professionals.

Ethical Rules Applicable to Business Operations

Whether Amy, Beth, and Cathy form a corporation or a partnership, they know that they must adhere to certain ethical standards (assuming that they wish to serve as corporate directors or officers).

In the case of corporations, the Model Business Corporation Act (which many state legislatures have adopted) declares that board directors and corporate officers must demonstrate a duty of loyalty and a duty of care to the corporate enterprise. These two standards applicable to directors and officers, respectively, are set forth below:

Section 8.30 Standards of Conduct for Directors

a. Each member of the board of directors, when discharging the duties of a director, shall act: (i) in good faith, and (ii) in a manner the director reasonably believes to be in the best interests of the corporation.
b. The members of the board of directors or a board committee, when becoming informed in connection with their decision-making function or devoting attention to their oversight function, shall discharge their duties with the care that a person in a like position would reasonably believe appropriate under similar circumstances.
c. In discharging board or board committee duties, a director shall disclose, or cause to be disclosed, to the other board or committee members information not already known by them but known by the director to be material to the discharge of their decision-making or oversight functions, except that disclosure is not required to the extent that the director reasonably believes that doing so would violate a duty imposed under law, a legally enforceable obligation of confidentiality, or a professional ethics rule.
d. In discharging board or board committee duties, a director who does not have knowledge that makes reliance unwarranted is entitled to rely on the performance by any of the persons specified in subsection (f)(1) or subsection (f)(3) to whom the board may have delegated, formally or informally by course of conduct, the authority or duty to perform one or more of the board's functions that are delegable under applicable law.
e. In discharging board or board committee duties, a director who does not have knowledge that makes reliance unwarranted is entitled to rely on information, opinions, reports, or statements, including financial statements and other financial data, prepared or presented by any of the persons specified in subsection (f).
f. A director is entitled to rely, in accordance with subsection (d) or (e), on:
    1. one or more officers or employees of the corporation whom the director reasonably believes to be reliable and competent in the functions performed or the information, opinions, reports or statements provided;
    2. legal counsel, public accountants, or other persons retained by the corporation as to matters involving skills or expertise the director

reasonably believes are matters (i) within the particular person's professional or expert competence, or (ii) as to which the particular person merits confidence; or
3. a board committee of which the director is not a member if the director reasonably believes the committee merits confidence.

Section 8.42 Standards of Conduct for Officers

a. An officer, when performing in such capacity, has the duty to act:
   1. in good faith;
   2. with the care that a person in a like position would reasonably exercise under similar circumstances; and
   3. in a manner the officer reasonably believes to be in the best interests of the corporation.
b. The duty of an officer includes the obligation:
   1. to inform the superior officer to whom, or the board of directors or the board committee to which, the officer reports of information about the affairs of the corporation known to the officer, within the scope of the officer's functions, and known to the officer to be material to such superior officer, board or committee; and
   2. to inform his or her superior officer, or another appropriate person within the corporation, or the board of directors, or a board committee, of any actual or probable material violation of law involving the corporation or material breach of duty to the corporation by an officer, employee, or agent of the corporation, that the officer believes has occurred or is likely to occur.
c. In discharging his or her duties, an officer who does not have knowledge that makes reliance unwarranted is entitled to rely on:
   1. the performance of properly delegated responsibilities by one or more employees of the corporation whom the officer reasonably believes to be reliable and competent in performing the responsibilities delegated; or
   2. information, opinions, reports or statements, including financial statements and other financial data, prepared or presented by one or more employees of the corporation whom the officer reasonably believes to be reliable and competent in the matters presented or by legal counsel, public accountants, or other persons retained by the corporation as to matters involving skills or expertise the officer reasonably believes are matters (i) within the particular person's

professional or expert competence or (ii) as to which the particular person merits confidence.

d. An officer shall not be liable to the corporation or its shareholders for any decision to take or not to take action, or any failure to take any action, as an officer, if the duties of the office are performed in compliance with this section. Whether an officer who does not comply with this section shall have liability will depend in such instance on applicable law, including those principles of Section 8.31 that have relevance.

In the case of partnerships, the Uniform Partnership Act (which many state legislatures have adopted) also provides a duty of loyalty and care. The applicable standard is set forth below:

Section 404 General Standards of Partner's Conduct

a. The only fiduciary duties a partner owes to the partnership and the other partners are the duty of loyalty and the duty of care set forth in subsections (b) and (c).
b. A partner's duty of loyalty to the partnership and the other partners is limited to the following:
    1. to account to the partnership and hold as trustee for it any property, profit, or benefit derived by the partner in the conduct and winding up of the partnership business or derived from a use by the partner of partnership property, including the appropriation of a partnership opportunity;
    2. to refrain from dealing with the partnership in the conduct or winding up of the partnership business as or on behalf of a party having an interest adverse to the partnership; and
    3. to refrain from competing with the partnership in the conduct of the partnership business before the dissolution of the partnership.
c. A partner's duty of care to the partnership and the other partners in the conduct and winding up of the partnership business is limited to refraining from engaging in grossly negligent or reckless conduct, intentional misconduct, or a knowing violation of law.
d. A partner shall discharge the duties to the partnership and the other partners under this [Act] or under the partnership agreement and exercise any rights consistently with the obligation of good faith and fair dealing.

e. A partner does not violate a duty or obligation under this [Act] or under the partnership agreement merely because the partner's conduct furthers the partner's own interest.
f. A partner may lend money to and transact other business with the partnership, and as to each loan or transaction the rights and obligations of the partner are the same as those of a person who is not a partner, subject to other applicable law.
g. This section applies to a person winding up the partnership business as the personal or legal representative of the last surviving partner as if the person were a partner.

Ethical Rules Applicable to Accounting and Legal Professionals

As professionals, accountants and lawyers are supposed to adhere to a code of ethics and self-police their members in order to protect the public. Cathy is convinced that working knowledge of these rules will give the upper hand to the business enterprise that she and her friends establish when working with these professionals if and when disputes arise with them.

While the source of these ethical codes varies — for accountants, they are largely found in the AICPA Code of Professional Conduct; and for lawyers, they are largely found in the *Model Rules of Professional Conduct* — they share many similarities:

- At all times, members should maintain their objectivity and integrity.
- They should avoid conflicts of interest.
- Their fees should be commensurate with the complexity of the work performed.
- Client information should always remain confidential.

Cathy learns that accountants and lawyers who fail to adhere to these ethical standards risk censure, suspension, monetary fines, and possible license forfeiture. With this information in hand, she plans to hold accountable for their actions any accountants and lawyers retained by the business enterprise. Simply put, Cathy knows that this knowledge will prove empowering.

Aside from the research that Amy, Beth, and Cathy conducted there are many other available research sources. Among the books that address business formations, five stand out. They are as follows:

1. ***The Founder's Dilemmas***: *Anticipating and Avoiding the Pitfalls that Can Sink a Startup*, by Noam Wasserman
2. ***The Lean Startup***: *How Today's Entrepreneurs Use Continuous Innovation to Create Radically Successful Businesses*, by Eric Ries
3. ***Profits First***: *Transform Your Business from a Cash-Eating Monster to a Money-Making Machine*, by Mike Michalowicz
4. ***Lucky or Smart?*** *Fifty Pages for the First-Time Entrepreneur*, by Bo Peabody
5. ***The $100 Startup***: *Reinvent the Way You Make a Living, Do What You Love, and Create a New Future*, by Chris Guillebeau.

Needless to say, the Internet is replete with timely and informative articles that you can read that offer sage advice on the elements to consider when forming your own business. Caveat emptor: Many of these articles will lead to websites (e.g., Legal Zoom and Bizfilings) designed to solicit your business. If, however, there is anything that Amy, Beth, and Cathy have learned, it is that cheap advice may prove very costly down the road.

https://doi.org/10.1142/9789811216749_0033

Case 33

Determining Transfer Pricing Profits and Losses

Robert A. Feinschreiber and Margaret Kent

Feinschreiber & Associates Law Firm, Key Biscayne, FL, USA

Introduction

Transfer pricing is a quantitative analytical methodology that enables multinational enterprises and their tax authorities to ascertain the applicable fair intercompany price of transactions among affiliated parties. This transfer pricing is designed to be an intercompany amount that results in a fair and equitable share that provides fair and just profits to each participating enterprise.[1]

Quite simply, the ideal transfer price determines the amount that both the related parties and tax authorities ascertain for ***related*** parties based on the pricing that is applicable to ***unrelated*** parties. Enterprises and governments have conflicting tax objectives impacting the tax base and revenue stream.

Transfer Pricing Methodologies

Transfer pricing is incredibly fact-specific where each enterprise within an industry, must have its own specific set of facts. Transfer pricing

[1] See, for instance, Robert Feinschreiber, *Transfer Pricing Methods: An Application Guide* (Wiley, 2004); Robert Feinschreiber and Margaret Kent, *Transfer Pricing Handbook: Guidance on OECD Regulations* (Wiley, Hoboken, New Jersey, 2012).

advisors on the corporate side and on the government side must develop the company's fact-specific transfer pricing analysis.[2]

At the first instance, the transfer pricing analyst preparers and other parties need to ascertain the magnitude and extent of a transfer pricing data inquiry. Do not be stymied by the large number of specialized areas you might need to undertake to consider this determination. Most often, you'll need the assistance of cost accountants, economists, contract lawyers, and knowledgeable transfer pricing experts. You might also need transfer pricing coordinators to complete this transfer pricing analysis.

Purposes of Ascertaining Transfer Pricing

We've selected a relatively common fact pattern for the transfer pricing example and when you understand the enterprise's fact pattern you can ascertain the best applicable transfer price. We examine the three facets of the enterprise's fact pattern:

1. Understanding the facts on the ground, similar to the banker's "know your customer".
2. Examining general tax and business issues.
3. After we've looked at the facts on the ground and the general tax and trade uses, we then turn our attention to transfer pricing.

The Rancher — Underling Fact Pattern

The enterprise in question is a US rancher who is involved in producing and selling cattle and pork products in the United States and abroad. The US rancher has various US and foreign subsidiaries of various types and locations. The purpose of these subsidiaries is to effectuate its cattle and pork sales activities. The rancher must undertake analysis of supply and demand separately for beef and pork, taking the gestation of animals into account.

[2]For further readings on transfer pricing regulations and methodologies, see OECD Transfer Pricing Guidelines for Multinational Enterprises and Tax Administrations 2017, https://www.oecd.org/tax/transfer-pricing/oecd-transfer-pricing-guidelines-for-multinational-enterprises-and-tax-administrations-20769717.htm; and 26 U.S. Code § 482 - Allocation of income and deductions among taxpayers, https://www.law.cornell.edu/uscode/text/26/482.

The rancher treats the cattle and pigs as two separate product areas. The reader of this piece, at the outset, needs to consider the extent of the production cost data that the rancher and the tax authorities might need. The answer to this question might change on the nature of these events that precipitated the inquiry.

Rancher's Land Utilization

Let's begin with the rancher's land utilization. The rancher acquires, uses, and disposes of land for various purposes. These land activities include cattle, pork, housing, farming, and for keeping the land fallow, for administration purposes, or for other purposes. The rancher might change its land allocation because of market conditions or for other purposes entirely. Do these issues matter for transfer pricing purposes? They might very well matter, depending on the facts.

All of the rancher's land is located within the United States. Does the presence of this locational fact alone mean that the rancher has no international tax issues? If your answer is "no," you've missed the point of this analysis, as least so far.

Let's shift our attention to the way in which the rancher utilizes animals for its production process. The rancher has both pigs and cattle. The rancher culls each herd. There are animal births and deaths during the year for both hogs and cattle. The rancher buys feed from outside sources and from its own rendering process. The rancher uses employees and independent contractors for its production facilities. The cost of feeding the animals is significant.

The Production Process

Now we need to understand the rancher's production process. The rancher might select among various options: The rancher might select cattle or hogs for breeding or might slaughter the animals and then sell them into the market. The rancher has options at the slaughterhouse to sell the beef or pork in the United States or sell the beef or pork to a foreign subsidiary for further foreign sales.

The rancher might treat certain animal parts as offal products in entering into a separate product stream. Offal products comprise animal parts such as hearts, lungs, livers, and so forth. These offal products have only limited value in the United States. Individuals in other countries favor offal products.

The rancher must decide the measures the slaughterhouse might take under the slaughtering process. Wastage from the slaughterhouse consists of various items, chief among them the animal's fat and bones. This rendering process produces tallow and meal.

The Rancher's Enterprises and Structure

The rancher designed its enterprises, subsidiaries, and other affiliates to enhance the rancher's cattle and pork sales activities. The rancher treats cattle and pork as being two separate product areas.

Slaughterhouses

The rancher has two slaughterhouses in the United States. The rancher uses one slaughterhouse for beef, designed in part to avoid beef-related activities that offend Hindus. The rancher uses one slaughterhouse for pork, designed in part to avoid pork-related activities that offend Muslims. The beef slaughterhouse sells its offal products to its subsidiary. The slaughterhouses sell fat and bones from the beef slaughterhouse to the rendering facility.

Slaughterhouse Foreign Distributors

The rancher sells its beef and pork products to the domestic US market, selling these products to US unrelated supermarket chains. The rancher has two foreign overseas distribution subsidiaries. The rancher has one subsidiary for pork products and another subsidiary for beef products.

Offal Products Distribution

Through its beef slaughterhouse subsidiary, the rancher sells offal products (hearts, lungs, kidneys, etc.) to a US offal products subsidiary. The offal products subsidiary then sells its offal products to its foreign subsidiary. The foreign subsidiary then sells the offal products to retail customers.

Offal Products — Foreign Distributor

The rancher's foreign subsidiary buys offal products from its US offal products company. The US offal products company sells its offal products to the related foreign distributor. The foreign distributor then sells the offal products to unrelated supermarkets in neighboring countries.

Rendering Facilities

The rancher has a US rendering facility. The rancher's slaughterhouses sell fat and bones from slaughterhouse process to the rendering facility. The rendering facility also acquires fat and bones from butcher shops. The rendering facility produces tallow and meal through a combined process.

US Tallow Facility

The rancher owns a US tallow company that produces a variety of soaps. The rancher's tallow company sells its tallow to its foreign distributor. This distributor sells its tallow to a soap company that brands the soap for sale into the market in which the soap company is located.

The Foreign Soap Company

The rancher's foreign soap company buys tallow from the rancher's tallow company. The related foreign soap company uses the tallow to produce soap. The soap products are sold everywhere.

The Meal Company

The rancher's rendering facility produces meal and well as producing tallow. The meal is a bone-based product that is heavy in weight compared with the tallow. The rancher sells the meal to unrelated parties in the US near the rendering facility, literally, for chicken feed.

Tax and Business Considerations

1. The rancher has both cattle and pig operations and incurs other operations as well. The rancher will change its land use policy over time for

these two principal operations as well as for other operations. How relevant are land use operations when we begin to examine the rancher's transfer pricing?
2. Argentina competes with the United States in the sale of meat. How do the Argentina's October economic troubles affect the marketing position of US meat purveyors?
3. How relevant is it that the rancher has more beef-oriented operations than it does for pork operations?
4. Some individuals prefer to eat non-meat products for health or environmental concerns. How would these issues impact transfer pricing structures?
5. Offal products are well-regarded operations overseas, but Americans for the most part do not favor offal products. How important is this fact?
6. How is the rancher to determine the allocated costs of the cow for the purposes of determining the cost of the offal products?
7. The rendering facility incurs chemical costs to produce tallow and meal. How do changes in production cost impact the profitability of both tallow and meal?
8. An issue exists as to whether tallow and meal are (a) byproducts from the slaughterhouse process? (b) Whether meal is a byproduct of the tallow process, or, alternatively, is a joint product of the tallow process?

The Assignment: Transfer Pricing Considerations

1. How does the rancher determine the cost of its offal products?
2. How should the rancher determine the revenues that it is to receive from the offal products?
3. How should the rancher determine the profitability of its offal products?
4. How does the rancher determine the profitability of its overseas sales operations?
5. Why is, or is not, the portion of the profit that the US enterprise receives from the offal products fair and equitable?
6. Why does the foreign tax authority care whether the rancher treats the US rendering costs as the byproduct or as a joint product when meal costs are unprofitable to the rancher?

https://doi.org/10.1142/9789811216749_0034

Case 34

FUJIFILM's Management of Research and Development Tax Credit

Peter F. De Nicola

FUJIFILM Holdings America Corporation, USA

Introduction

Internal Revenue Code ("IRC") Section 41, "Credit for Increasing Research Activities," was created in 1981 for the purpose of encouraging research and development ("R&D") within the US. The research tax credit has evolved over the years and allows more taxpayers and more activities to qualify for the tax credit. For most of its existence, the research tax credit was a temporary provision of the tax law that had to be renewed every few years, but in 2015, as part of the PATH Act, the credit was finally made permanent.

Research and development is beneficial to the US economy and, according to the Federal Reserve Bank of Philadelphia, has grown from 1.8% of US GDP in the 1970s to 2.9% in the 1990s.[1] The US became a global leader in R&D in the 20th century, funding as much as 69% of annual global R&D in the period following World War II. US R&D in 2018 was 112 times higher than it was in 1953 in current dollars, and more than 15 times higher in constant dollars. By sector, business-funded R&D

[1]Joseph R. Oliver, "Accounting and Tax Treatment of R&D: An Update," *The CPA Journal* (July 2003), http://archives.cpajournal.com/2003/0703/dept/d074603.htm.

grew the most during this period.[2] Business funding of R&D grew from $2.2 billion in 1953 to $404.2 billion in 2018, a compound annual growth rate (CAGR) of 8.3%. In constant dollars, business-funded R&D grew by a 5.0% CAGR during this period. In recent years, business-funded R&D has grown at a slower pace.

IRC Section 41(d) defines qualified research expenditure ("QRE") as research for which an expense may be claimed under Section 174. The expenses must meet a four-part test, as follows:

- First, they must create a new or improved business component. "Component" is defined broadly to include a product, process, computer software, technique, formula, or invention.
- Second, the taxpayer must demonstrate that it has attempted to eliminate uncertainty.
- Third, the taxpayer must demonstrate through modeling, simulation, or trial and error that it has evaluated one or more alternatives for achieving the desired result.
- Fourth, the experimentation must rely on the hard sciences, such as computer science, engineering, physics, or chemistry, for example.

Section 41 and Section 174 provide 20% R&D tax credit for increasing qualified research activities that exceed a base amount, or an *alternative simplified credit* (*ASC*) of 14% of the QREs that exceed a base amount. The research credit is computed as 20% of qualified research expenses for the current period over the base period. The base period is computed by applying the taxpayer's historic percentage of gross receipts spent on QREs to the four most recent years' average gross receipts.

The base amount may not be less than 50% of the qualified research expenses for the current year. For taxpayers that had QREs in calendar years 1984 through 1988, that period forms the basis for determining the fixed-base percentage. The base period must be adjusted when a portion of the business that incurred the expenses is either acquired or disposed. Taxpayers may elect an alternative simplified method for computing the research credit as equal to 14% of the qualified research expenses that

[2]US Research and Development Funding and Performance: Fact Sheet Updated January 24, 2020, Congressional Research Service: https://crsreports.congress.gov. R44307.

exceed fifty percent of the average qualified research expenses for the three preceding tax years. In cases where the taxpayer does not have a 3-year history of qualified research expenses, the credit is equal to 6% of the current year's research expenses.

Qualified research expenditures include the wages of employees directly engaging in, supervising, or supporting research activities, although the employees do not necessarily have to be degree-holding scientists or engineers to qualify. Experimentation performed by both employees and third-party contractors who engage in the improvement of projects and processes may be included in the computation. Supplies and charges for computer usage are also included in the research expenditures. In addition, 65% of amounts paid to third parties for qualified research are includible.

For periods prior to 2022, the taxpayer's deduction for research expenditures is reduced by the amount of the research credit, but alternatively a taxpayer can elect to claim a reduced credit in lieu of reducing the research expense deduction. Beginning with tax years after December 31, 2021, research expenses will be required to be capitalized and amortized over a period of 5 years. This change will constitute a change in the accounting method for purposes of IRC section 481. In addition, 36 states have enacted similar credit regulations to encourage companies to locate research facilities within their borders.

R&D costs are reported as a separate line item on certified audited financial statements, and have many similarities with those covered by IRC sections 41 and 174. Thus, the amount reported in the financial statements provides a starting point to identify R&D costs.[3]

In September 2017, the IRS issued guidance for Section 41 that provides a multistep approach for taxpayers to adjust the amount reported as R&D costs on their financial statements to the amount reported as QRE for income tax purposes.[4] The following five steps reconcile the amounts reported as R&D on the financial statements to the QRE amounts allowable under IRC sections 41 and 174. An additional (and optional) five steps provide guidance for separately identifying R&D expenses that exceed the adjusted ASC 730 R&D amount.

---

[3]Karen M. Cooley and Darlene Pulliance, "Computing Qualified Research Expenses," *The CPA Journal* (October 2019) ("Cooley").

[4]*Ibid.*

Step 1.
Determine the financial statement R&D expenses.

Step 2.
Foreign entities' R&D must be removed to determine amounts allowed for IRC section 41.

Step 3.
Remove costs that qualify as R&D for financial reporting purposes but do not meet the requirements of IRC sections 41 and 174.

Step 4.
Book wage and wage-related accounts, including stock options, must be adjusted to the amounts allowed under IRC sections 41 and 174. This is also a multistep process, described in Appendix D of the directive.

Step 5.
Identify the adjusted ASC 730 financial statement R&D expenses that are permissible under IRC sections 41 and 174 as wages, supplies, and computer rental or lease costs.

FUJIFILM's Section 41 Experience

FUJIFILM's management of Section 41 tax credit could provide a beneficial insight on how it handles this issue.

Company Background

Fuji Photo Film Co., Ltd. ("Fuji") was established in 1934 as a subsidiary of Daicel Corporation, a Japanese manufacturer of industrial chemicals. The company's first product was motion picture film. Over the next 10 years, the company's portfolio expanded to include photographic films and x-ray films. In the 1940s, Fuji began producing optical glasses, lenses, and photographic equipment for the Asian markets. After the Second World War, Fuji Photo diversified into medical diagnosis equipment, printing, electronic imaging, and magnetic materials fields.

In 1962, the company entered into a significant business alliance with UK-based Rank Xerox which created a joint venture, Fuji Xerox, that would endure for half a century. The joint venture resulted in Fuji's entry into the business products market. The company manufactured and distributed Xerox photocopiers throughout the Asia-Pacific region.

By 1965, the company set its sights on global expansion. It opened a sales and distribution company in the US with its first office in the Empire State Building. For the next 20 years, Fuji's US subsidiary functioned primarily as an importer and distributor of products manufactured in Japan. In the late 1980s, Fuji decided to expand its manufacturing capabilities to the US. As a result, it invested over a billion dollars on a new facility in Greenwood, South Carolina. Although the plant manufactured a wide range of products, most product development continued to be carried on in Japan.

The dawn of the 21st century brought many challenges for Fuji. Traditional analog film was on the decline with the advent of the new digital technology. Consumers were taking more pictures, but printing fewer. As cell phones developed, most included a camera which, for most consumers, was as good as the traditional cameras that they were accustomed to use. As a result of these changes, the consumer photography segment of the business took a substantial hit.

As if this were not enough of a blow, Fuji also saw a decline in their graphic arts and document products business as few documents were printed. This resulted in the company making a strategic decision to reinvent itself. Fuji decided to pursue a two-pronged approach. First, it would grab a larger share of the declining imaging markets. Second, it would pursue new ventures, particularly in the health care area.

With the decline of Fuji's chief rival in the photographic business, Eastman Kodak, the implementation of its first strategy to grab market share was quite successful. The second part of its strategy was more complex in that the company would need to seek out acquisitions in order to build a health care portfolio.

The company's expansion in the health care segment focused on several key areas: medical diagnostic imaging, regenerative medicine, stem cells, and pharmaceuticals. FUJIFILM already had a history in the area of diagnostic imaging. It had long been a manufacturer of x-ray film and equipment. It expanded its footprint in this area by developing digital radiography systems. FUJIFILM's medical imaging and information management systems were at the forefront of replacing traditional x-rays with systems that could digitally analyze and store vast amounts of patient information from across different modalities. In 2021, the company acquired Hitachi's medical imaging businesses.

In 2012, the company expanded further by acquiring Sonosite, a US manufacturer of portable ultrasound equipment. Continuing its expansion, FUJIFILM acquired Cellular Dynamics in 2015, a manufacturer of human cells, for use in basic research headquartered in Madison, Wisconsin. It also acquired Irvine Scientific in 2018, a California manufacturer of cell culture media, reagents, and devices for researchers and clinicians.

In the area of pharmaceuticals, FUJIFILM acquired Diosynth Biotechnologies, a North Carolina-based contract manufacturer of biopharmaceuticals. The company played a key role under the federal government's "Operation Warp Speed" project for the development and manufacture of COVID-19 vaccines.

The company's US acquisitions were not limited to the healthcare sector, however. The new millennium also saw the acquisition of Dimatix, a world leader in the manufacture of ink print heads for commercial and industrial printing. Complementing this business, FUJIFILM also acquired Imaging Colorants, a UK-based world leader in the development and manufacturer of inkjet inks and customized pigments for the inkjet industry.

The company has a significant research and manufacturing presence in the US. In the area of specialty chemicals, the company expanded into materials and chemicals used in the manufacture of semiconductors by establishing FUJIFILM Electronic Materials. The company also acquired Wako Chemicals, a Japanese manufacturer of pure chemicals and reagents with significant operations in the US.

Section 41 Experience

For most of its history, FUJIFILM in the US acted as an importer and distributor of products that were developed and manufactured in Japan. While the company began to manufacture some photographic products in the US in the late 1980s, most of the research associated with these products was still carried out in Japan. It wasn't until the 21st century that FUJIFILM acquired a portfolio of companies that conducted significant product research and development here in the US.

Because of this rapid change in the company's businesses, the FUJIFILM Tax Department was suddenly faced with the challenge of gathering the data for the computation of the research tax credit. The first challenge that the tax team faced was to obtain a clear understanding of each company's business. The businesses and products were diverse, and there was no standardized chart of accounts or general ledger system. Consequently, there was no universal solution for extracting the data for computing the credit.

Initially, the Tax Department hoped to collect the data by developing a standard questionnaire and workbook that could be sent to each company to collect the data. However, this idea was quickly abandoned since it was impossible to create a uniform workbook that would properly cover so many disparate businesses without being overly burdensome to the subsidiaries' staff who would have to fill them out.

The IRS Audit Techniques Guide for Research and Development Tax Credits instructs the examiner to engage in a detailed analysis of the taxpayer's research credit claims to insure that the taxpayer employs nexus between the taxpayer's records, the specific research projects, and the qualified research expenses. The IRS appears to suggest a preference for project accounting to support the tax credit. However, neither the statute nor the Treasury regulations have such a requirement. Moreover, the provisions in IRC Section 6001 and the regulations thereunder do not specifically address record-keeping requirements. Nevertheless, given the level of scrutiny that the research credit would receive on audit, the tax team decided that it would go to great lengths to document its research activities.

Given these parameters, the company decided to meet the "nexus" requirement on a business component basis. The tax team reached out to the controller of each company to insure that their accounting systems would be able to provide the data on a project basis. By establishing separate cost centers for each project, the companies were able to fulfill this requirement.

Since the IRS gives significant weight to contemporaneous documentation of research activities, it was important that each employee's time be tracked and documented. This was especially true for employees who split their time between research activities and other functions. While some of the newly acquired companies had time-tracking systems in place, others did not. The tax team assisted in implementing time-tracking systems for those companies that were lacking by adopting from those systems already in place at other subsidiaries that functioned well.

In addition to properly tracking employee engagement in the research and development process, the tax team sought to document the projects on which they were working. The IRC section 41 regulations recognize the breadth of activities and the objectives that form research and development. Consequently, taxpayers are given reasonable latitude in the manner in which they substantiate their research credits.

The courts have consistently supported this regulatory directive that the documentation for the research credit does not need to contain any particular documents or subscribe to any particular format. The evidence in support of the credit must only be in sufficiently usable form and detail to substantiate the expenditures (T.C. Memo 2009-50). With these parameters in mind, the tax team decided it would be more efficient and fruitful to personally interview the subject matter experts at each company, rather than relying on a single person (such as the controller) to gather the data.

The team reached out to the head of research and development as the first point of contact. The team gave each head a brief overview of the research and development credit and its importance to the company's bottom line. By providing this background information, the team was able to get a "buy in" from heads of research in the project.

In most cases, the department heads brought in their direct reports to assist in gathering the data. The team found that, in most cases, the individuals who were knowledgeable about the specific projects that were underway were also knowledgeable about the wage allocations for employees who were not on the time tracking systems. This was important because it captured additional wages that would otherwise have been missed if the team relied solely on the tracking systems

Since this was the first time that the tax team and the research groups worked together, it was important to develop a rapport that would serve the Tax Department well in the future. The team found that most of the R&D staff were excited to talk about the projects in which they were engaged. This set the stage for further discussions in future years as the tax team tracked the progress of the projects.

While the R&D staff was happy to talk about their work, they were not inclined to take time out from their normal duties to write up narratives for documenting the tax credit. For this reason, the interview approach worked well, because the tax team took notes and, in some cases, recorded their interviews for later transcription. The R&D staff shared with the tax team reports and information that they had created for other purposes. This provided additional background and support for the R&D credit files.

After an exhaustive data gathering process, the tax team then set about to organize the information they had collected. They put it into a standardized format with the expectation that someday their work would be reviewed by an IRS engineer. While going through the process, they noted any inconsistencies or gaps in data and arranged for follow-up calls with the subject matter experts.

The final documentation was broken down into two categories: product improvement and process improvement. Most of the R&D work fell into the product improvement category. That is, developing new products and updating existing ones. Most of the engineering staff were surprised to learn that developing or improving a manufacturing process could also qualify for the R&D credit. It is for this reason that a brief education in the R&D credit is important when starting the data gathering processes. In some cases, it was necessary to bring in another set of people into the discussion since the process improvement staff were often scattered in different departments.

The final end product was quite a collection of data: employee time reports, general ledger reports, account analyses, internal memoranda, feasibility studies, engineering test plans and results, process designs, patent disclosures, and Excel spreadsheets. The calculation of the R&D credit, however, was not the final step. It was important to go back to each subsidiary and tell them their contribution to the credit. The R&D teams then had a better understanding of their contribution to FUJIFILM's bottom line long before the products they were developing could be commercialized. This helped to establish a good working relationship between R&D and the Tax Department that has grown over the years.

The research and development activities should not be viewed solely from the position of generating a tax credit. Other taxes may be impacted as well. In the course of discussing the research process with the subject matter experts, it came to light that many of the supplies used in the process were removed from inventory. The tax team noted that this may create a use tax liability for the company and it worked with the accounting team to insure that these supplies were being captured and the appropriate use tax was being reported to the states and localities.

In addition, the tax team reviewed the fixed assets utilized in the research facilities and got a better understanding of how the equipment operated as well as its intended purpose. In many cases, the tax team was able to reduce the personal property taxes on this equipment by using shorter lives or excluding operating software which is intangible and exempt from taxation in most cases.

Overall, the end result was satisfactory on many levels and it underscored the importance of personal interaction with the research and development staff. It was much more productive and fruitful than sending out a questionnaire or workbook to be completed and returned to the Tax Department. In addition, it provided the tax team an opportunity to learn about FUJIFILM's portfolio of businesses.

The Assignment

1. Derive the R&D credit that Apple, Microsoft, and Oracle obtained for 2020 through qualified research in the US. Follow the IRS guidance of 2017 and utilize the firms' 10Ks and Annual Reports that were filed with www.sec.gov.
2. What was approximately the R&D credit that was obtained in 2020 by Disney, PepsiCo, and Moderna (following the same approach as in #1)?
3. Do the R&D credit to sales ratios reflect greater significance in some of the above companies?
4. Compare a high-tech company and a food company (from questions #1 and #2) with the experience of FUJIFILM.

https://doi.org/10.1142/9789811216749_bmatter

Index

E